Andrew Hudson
Paul Hudson
Matthew Helmke
Ryan Troy

Ubuntu

UNLEASHED

2010 Edition
Covering 9.10 and 10.4

SAMS | 800 East 96th Street, Indianapolis, Indiana 46240 USA

Ubuntu Unleashed 2010 Edition: Covering 9.10 and 10.4

ISBN-13: 978-0-67233-109-1

ISBN-10: 0-67233-109-8

Library of Congress Cataloging-in-Publication data is on file.

Printed in the United States of America

First Printing December 2009

Trademarks

All terms mentioned in this book that are known to be trademarks or service marks have been appropriately capitalized. Sams Publishing cannot attest to the accuracy of this information. Use of a term in this book should not be regarded as affecting the validity of any trademark or service mark.

Warning and Disclaimer

Bulk Sales

Sams Publishing offers excellent discounts on this book when ordered in quantity for bulk purchases or special sales. For more information, please contact:

U.S. Corporate and Government Sales
1-800-382-3419
corpsales@pearsontechgroup.com

For sales outside of the U.S., please contact:

International Sales
international@pearson.com

Acquisitions Editor
Debra Williams
Cauley

Development Editor
Michael Thurston

Managing Editor
Patrick Kanouse

Project Editor
Jennifer Gallant

Copy Editor
Paula Lowell

Indexer
Tim Wright

Proofreader
Leslie Joseph

Technical Editor
Dallas Releford

Publishing Coordinator
Kim Boedigheimer

Multimedia Developer
Dan Scherf

Cover and Interior Designer
Gary Adair

Composition
Mark Shirar

Contents at a Glance

Table of Contents

About the Authors

Andrew Hudson is a freelance journalist who specializes in writing about Linux. He has significant experience in Red Hat and Debian-based Linux distributions and deployments and can often be found sitting at his keyboard tweaking various settings and config files just for the hell of it. He lives in Wiltshire, which is a county of England, along with his wife, Bernice, and their son, John. Andrew does not like Emacs. He can be reached at andy.hudson@gmail.com.

Paul Hudson is a recognized expert in open-source technologies. He is also a professional developer and full-time journalist for Future Publishing. His articles have appeared in *Mac Format*, *PC Answers*, *PC Format*, *PC Plus*, and *Linux Format*. Paul is passionate about free software in all its forms and uses a mix of Linux and BSD to power his desktops and servers. Paul likes Emacs. Paul can be contacted through http://hudzilla.org.

Matthew Helmke has written articles for magazines such as Linux+ and Linux Identity. He cowrote Prentice Hall's The Official Ubuntu Book and O'Reilly's VMware Cookbook. He has also self published two books about Moroccan culture. Matthew is an active member of the Ubuntu Linux community as an administrator and Forum Council member for the Ubuntu Forums (http://ubuntuforums.org), and a member of the membership approval committee for Ubuntu in Europe, the Middle East, and Africa. He is currently a graduate student at the University of Arizona. You can find out more about Matthew at http://matthewhelmke.com.

Ryan Troy has more than 12 years of Unix/Linux system administration experience in industries ranging from web hosting to newspapers. He serves as technical administrator and chairman of the Ubuntu Forum Council and founded the Ubuntu Forums in 2004. He currently works for a Michigan based consulting company and specializes in Storage and Virtualization. You can find out more about Ryan at http://rtroy.com.

Dedication

To Bernice and John—the best supporters a man could ever wish for.

—Andrew Hudson

To World Peace—because this is about as close as I'm ever going to get to being in the Miss World competition.

—Paul Hudson

To Heather, Saralyn, Sedona and Philip—the most amazing family a guy could hope for.

—Matthew Helmke

To Holly, thanks for your continued support during projects I get involved with.

—Ryan Troy

Acknowledgments

Thanks to our colleagues at Sams Publishing, whose patience and persistence made this book possible.

Thanks also to my family who have supported me during the writing of this book. My son John now has his own keyboard and mouse—the computer will come in a few years!

My wife Bernice has the patience of a saint, allowing me to lock myself away when I needed to and being helpful when I've hit writer's block (and yes, it does happen!).

Finally, thanks to God who makes all things possible, including this book.

—Andrew Hudson

Thanks to Andrew, Shelley, Damon, Seth, Dallas, Mum and Dad, my wife, Ildiko; and, of course, God, who made all this possible. No book this big could be done without a lot of work from a dedicated team!

—Paul Hudson

Thanks to Andrew and Paul for trusting Ryan and I with this book and to Debra for connecting us with the opportunity. Thanks to Ryan for all his great work as well as all the staff at Sams. Continuing the tradition of this book's original authors, I also think God is pretty cool and that he deserves a shout out.

—Matthew Helmke

Thanks to Andrew and Paul for setting the foundation for this book, allowing Matthew and I the opportunity expand and update it. Thank you Matthew for asking me to collaborate with you on this project, you are a good friend. And finally, to the Ubuntu Forums community and staff, you guys rock!

—Ryan Troy

We Want to Hear from You!

As the reader of this book, *you* are our most important critic and commentator. We value your opinion and want to know what we're doing right, what we could do better, what areas you'd like to see us publish in, and any other words of wisdom you're willing to pass our way.

You can email directly to let us know what you did or didn't like about this book—as well as what we can do to make our books stronger.

Please note that we cannot help you with technical problems related to the topic of this book, and that due to the high volume of mail we received, we might not be able to reply to every message.

When you write, please be sure to include this book's title and author as well as your name and email address. We will carefully review your comments and share them with the author and editors who worked on the book.

Email: opensource@samspublishing.com

Mail: Debra Williams Cauley
Sams Publishing
800 East 96th Street
Indianapolis, IN 46240 USA

Reader Services

Visit our website and register this book at informit.com/register for convenient access to any updates, downloads, or errata that might be available for this book.

Introduction

Welcome to *Ubuntu Unleashed, 2010 Edition!* This book covers the free Linux distribution named Ubuntu and includes a fully functional and complete operating system produced by the Ubuntu Community, sponsored by Canonical Software. This book covers Ubuntu version 9.10.

Ubuntu directly descends from one of the oldest and most revered Linux distributions ever: Debian. Those of you who know nothing about Linux will likely not have heard of Debian; it is enough to know that it is considered to be one of the most stable and secure Linux distributions currently available. Ubuntu benefits directly from many contributions from free software developers across the world.

If you are new to Linux, you have made a great decision by choosing this book. Sams Publishing's *Unleashed* books offer an in-depth look at their subject, taking in both beginner and advanced users and moving them to a new level of knowledge and expertise. Ubuntu is a fast-changing distribution that can be updated at least twice a year. We have tracked the development of Ubuntu from early on to make sure that the information in this book mirrors closely the development of the distribution. A full copy of Ubuntu is included on the enclosed disc, making it possible for you to install Linux in less than an hour! No longer an upstart, Linux now has an enviable position in today's modern computing world. It can be found on machines as diverse as mobile phones and wristwatches, all the way up to super-computers—in fact, Linux currently runs on more than half of the world's top 500 supercomputers.

Do not let the reputation of Linux discourage you, however. Most people who have heard of Linux think that it is found only on servers, looking after websites and email. Nothing could be further from the truth because Linux is making huge inroads in to the desktop market, too. Corporations are realizing the benefits of running a stable and powerful operating system that is easy to maintain and easy to secure. Add to that the hundreds of improvements in usability, and Linux becomes an attractive proposition that tempts many CIOs. The best part is that as large Linux vendors improve Linux, the majority of those improvements make it into freely available distributions, allowing you to benefit from the additions and refinements made. You can put Ubuntu to work today and be assured of a great user experience.

This book provides all the information that you need to get up and running with Ubuntu. It even tells you how to keep Ubuntu running in top shape and how to adapt Ubuntu to changes in your own needs. You can use Ubuntu at home, in the workplace, or, with permission, at your school or college. In fact, you might want to poke around your school's computer rooms: You will probably find that someone has already beaten you to the punch—Linux is commonly found in academic institutions. Feel free to make as many copies of the software as you want; because Ubuntu is freely distributable all over the world, no copyright lawyers are going to pound on your door.

After an introduction to Linux and Ubuntu, you will find out how to get started with Ubuntu, including installation and initial configuration. We also take you through installing software, managing users, and other common administrative tasks. For the more technically minded, we also cover some starting steps in programming across several languages—why not pick one and try it out? Throughout this book, you will also find information about multimedia applications, digital graphics, and even gaming (for after-hours when you are finished tinkering). After you make it through this book, you will be well equipped with the knowledge needed to use Linux successfully. We do assume that you are at least familiar with an operating system already (even if it is not with Linux) and have some basic computer knowledge.

Licensing

Software licensing is an important issue for all computer users and can entail moral, legal, and financial considerations. Many consumers think that purchasing a copy of a commercial or proprietary operating system, productivity application, utility, or game conveys ownership, but this is not true. In the majority of cases, the *end user license agreement (EULA)* included with a commercial software package states that you have paid only for the right to use the software according to specific terms. This generally means you may not examine, make copies, share, resell, or transfer ownership of the software package. More onerous software licenses enforce terms that preclude you from distributing or publishing comparative performance reviews of the software. Even more insidious licensing schemes (and supporting legislation, especially in the United States) contain provisions allowing onsite auditing of the software's use!

This is not the case with the software included with this book. You are entirely free to make copies, share them with friends, and install the software on as many computers as you want—we encourage you to purchase additional copies of this book to give as gifts, however. Be sure to read the README file on the disc included with this book for important information regarding the included software and disk contents. After you install Ubuntu, go to http://www.gnu.org/licenses/gpl.html to find a copy of the GNU GPL. You will see that the GPL provides unrestricted freedom to use, duplicate, share, study, modify, improve, and even sell the software.

You can put your copy of Ubuntu to work right away in your home or at your place of business without worrying about software licensing, per-seat workstation or client licenses, software auditing, royalty payments, or any other type of payments to third parties. However, be aware that although much of the software included with Ubuntu is licensed under the GPL, some packages on this book's disc are licensed under other terms. There is a variety of related software licenses, and many software packages fall under a broad definition known as *open source*. Some of these include the Artistic License, the BSD License, the Mozilla Public License, and the Q Public License.

For additional information about the various GNU software licenses, browse to http://www. gnu.org/. For a definition of open-source and licensing guidelines, along with links to the terms of nearly three dozen open-source licenses, browse to http://www.opensource.org/.

Who This Book Is For

This book is for anyone searching for guidance on using Ubuntu and primarily focuses on Intel-based PC platforms. Although the contents are aimed at intermediate to advanced users, even new users with a bit of computer savvy will benefit from the advice, tips, tricks, traps, and techniques presented in each chapter. Pointers to more detailed or related information are also provided at the end of each chapter.

If you are new to Linux, you might need to learn some new computer skills, such as how to research your computer's hardware, how to partition a hard drive, and (occasionally) how to use a command line. This book helps you learn these skills and shows you how to learn more about your computer, Linux, and the software included with Ubuntu. System administrators with experience using other operating systems can use the information in this book to install, set up, and run common Linux software services, such as the *Network File System (NFS)*, a *File Transfer Protocol (FTP)* server, and a web server (using Apache, among others).

What This Book Contains

Ubuntu Unleashed is organized into seven parts, covering installation and configuration, Ubuntu on the desktop, system administration, programming and housekeeping, and a reference section. A disc containing the entire distribution is included so that you have everything you need to get started. This book starts by covering the initial and essential tasks required to get Ubuntu installed and running on a target system.

If you are new to Linux, and more specifically Ubuntu, first read the chapters in Part I, "Installation and Configuration." You will get valuable information on the following:

▶ Detailed steps that walk you through installation

▶ Critical advice on key configuration steps to fully install and configure Linux to work with your system's subsystems or peripherals, such as pointers, keyboards, modems, USB devices and power management

▶ Initial steps needed by new users transitioning from other computing environments

▶ Working with GNOME, the default desktop environment for Ubuntu

Part II, "Desktop Ubuntu," is aimed at users who want to get productive with Ubuntu and covers the following:

▶ Discovering the many productivity applications that come with Ubuntu

▶ Surfing the Internet and working with email and newsgroups

▶ Using Ubuntu to listen to music and watch video

▶ Using Ubuntu to download and manipulate images from digital cameras

▶ Setting up local printers for Ubuntu

▶ Understanding the current state of gaming for Linux

Moving beyond the productivity and desktop areas of Ubuntu, Part III, "System Administration," covers the following:

▶ Managing users and groups

▶ Automating tasks and using shell scripts

▶ Monitoring system resources and availability

▶ Backup strategies and software

▶ Network connectivity, including sharing folders and securing the network

▶ Internet connectivity via dial-up and broadband connections

Part IV, "Ubuntu as a Server" gives you the information you need to start building your own file, web and other servers for use in your home or office.

▶ Building and deploying web servers

▶ Database creation, management, and manipulation

▶ File and print servers

▶ Using FTP for serving files across the Internet and local networks

▶ Building and deploying email servers using Postfix and managing mailing lists

▶ Creating remote access gateways and services

- ▶ Configuring DNS for your network

- ▶ Using LDAP for storing information on users and security

Part V, "Programming Linux," provides a great introduction to how you can extend Ubuntu capabilities even further using the development tools supplied with it. This part covers the following:

- ▶ Programming in Perl, using variables and scripting

- ▶ An introduction to the Python language

- ▶ Writing PHP scripts and linking them to databases

- ▶ C and C++ programming tools available with Ubuntu and how to use the GNU C Compiler (gcc)

Part VI, "Ubuntu Housekeeping," looks at some of the more advanced skills you need to keep your system running in perfect condition, including the following:

- ▶ Securing your machine against attack from outsiders and viruses

- ▶ Performance tuning

- ▶ Command-line masterclass

- ▶ Advanced apt

- ▶ Kernel and module management and compilation

An extensive reference in Part VII, "Appendixes," gives you scope to explore in even more depth some of the topics covered in this book as well as providing historical context to Ubuntu and installation resources.

Conventions Used in This Book

A lot of documentation is included with every Linux distribution, and Ubuntu is certainly no exception. Although the intent of *Ubuntu Unleashed* is to be as complete as possible, it is impossible to cover every option of every command included in the distribution. However, this book offers numerous tables of various options, commands, and keystrokes to help condense, organize, and present information about a variety of subjects.

This edition is also packed full of screenshots to illustrate nearly all Ubuntu-specific graphical utilities—especially those related to system administration or the configuration and administration of various system and network services.

To help you better understand code listing examples and sample command lines, several formatting techniques are used to show input and ownership. For example, if the command or code listing example shows typed input, the input is formatted in boldface, as follows:

```
$ ls
```

If typed input is required, as in response to a prompt, the sample typed input also is in boldface, like so:

```
Delete files? [Y/n] y
```

All statements, variables, and text that should appear on your display use the same bold-face formatting. In addition, command lines that require root or super user access are prefaced with the sudo command, as follows:

```
$ sudo printtool &
```

Command-line examples that any user can run are prefaced with a dollar sign ($), like so:

```
$ ls
```

The following elements provide you with useful tidbits of information that relate to the discussion of the text:

NOTE

A note provides additional information you might want to make note of as you are working; augments a discussion with ancillary details; or points you to an article, a whitepaper, or another online reference for more information about a specific topic.

TIP

A tip can contain special insight or a timesaving technique, as well as information about items of particular interest to you that you might not find elsewhere.

CAUTION

A caution warns you about pitfalls or problems before you run a command, edit a configuration file, or choose a setting when administering your system.

Sidebars Can Be Goldmines

Just because it is in a sidebar does not mean that you will not find something new here. Be sure to watch for these elements that bring in outside content that is an aside to the discussion in the text. You will read about other technologies, Linux-based hardware, and special procedures to make your system more robust and efficient.

Other formatting techniques used to increase readability include the use of italics for placeholders in computer command syntax. Computer terms or concepts are also italicized upon first introduction in text.

Finally, you should know that all text, sample code, and screenshots in *Ubuntu Unleashed* were developed using Ubuntu and open-source tools.

Read on to start learning about and using the latest version of Ubuntu. Experienced users will want to consider the new information in this edition when planning or considering upgrades. There are many different Linux distributions from different vendors, but many derive from, or closely mimic, the Debian distribution.

PART I

Installation and Configuration

IN THIS PART

Installing Ubuntu

Not that long ago, the mere mention of installing Linux struck fear into the hearts of mortal men. Thanks to a campaign of fear, uncertainty, and doubt (commonly referred to as FUD), Linux garnered a reputation as something of an elitist operating system, only configurable by those in the know. Nowadays, it is a different story entirely, and Ubuntu is one of the easiest distros to install. In this chapter, we cover how to get started with the install disc, including booting into Ubuntu Live CD to test your system. Then we cover the actual installation of Ubuntu, looking at the various options available. The whole process is fairly pain-free under Ubuntu, as you are about to learn.

Before You Begin the Installation

Installing a new operating system is a major event, and you should make sure that you have properly thought through what is going to take place. The first thing to consider is how the hardware will be affected by the software that you propose to install. Although Ubuntu will run well on an extremely wide variety of hardware, it is worthwhile checking your hardware components out because there may be a banana skin waiting for you to slip up on. The following sections provide some areas for you to investigate and think about, and may even save you hours of frustration when something goes wrong. The sections are designed to complement the ideas and checklists presented in Appendix B, "Installation Resources."

You start by researching and documenting your hardware. This information will prove helpful later on during the installation.

Researching Your Hardware Specifications

At the absolute minimum, you should know the basics of your system, such as how much RAM you have installed, what type of mouse, keyboard, and (importantly) monitor you have. Knowing the storage capacity of your hard drive is also important because it will help you plan how you will divide it up for Ubuntu. It is also a good idea to find out whether you are using SATA drivers or the more traditional PATA drives. A small detail such as whether your mouse uses the USB or PS/2 interface will ensure proper pointer configuration—something that should happen without fail, but you will be glad you knew in case something goes wrong! The more information you have, the better prepared you will be for any problems.

Use the checklist shown in Table B.2 in Appendix B to inventory or at least record some basic features of your system. Items you need to know include the amount of installed memory, size of your hard drive, type of mouse, capabilities of the display monitor (such as maximum resolution), and number of installed network interfaces (if any).

Installation Options

Ubuntu is available in three forms: the Ubuntu distribution, the Ubuntu server distribution, and the Ubuntu alternative distribution. For most people, the main distribution should suffice; the alternate is mainly used for upgrading existing Ubuntu users to the latest version, as well as allowing installation on low-powered systems. As for the server installation, this gives you access to a LAMP server in about 20 minutes (Linux, Apache, MySQL, and PHP), but as you will learn in this book, all these components are available to the Ubuntu default distribution.

Planning Partition Strategies

Partitioning is a topic that can strike fear into the hearts of novice Linux users. Coming from a Microsoft world, where you might just be used to having one hard drive, it can seem a bit strange to use an operating system that makes partitioning important. Depending on your requirements, you may opt to have a single large partition to contain all your files or you may prefer to segment your installation across several partitions to match your individual needs. You also need to take into account such things as what you will use to back up your data. With the abundance of external hard drives and Flash-based memory sticks, you could use these; remember, however, to provision backup storage space equal to or in excess of your specific requirements. Thanks to the ever-decreasing prices of storage, you can buy a 500GB SATA drive for a little more than $100. You will thank yourself that you backed up your data when your primary hard drive goes down!

The needs of the business should be the primary concern when deciding to implement a Linux system. Be careful when specifying a system and ensure that you build in an adequate upgrade path that allows you to extend the life of the system and add any additional storage or memory.

Knowing how software is allocated on your hard drive for Linux involves knowing how Ubuntu organizes its file system, or layout of directories on storage media. This knowledge will help you make the most out of hard drive space; and in some instances, such as planning to have user directories mounted via NFS or other means, can help head off data loss, increase security, and accommodate future needs. Create a great system, and you'll be the hero of information services.

To plan the best partitioning scheme, research and know the answers to these questions:

- ▶ How much disk space does your system require?

- ▶ Do you expect your disk space needs to grow significantly in the future?

- ▶ Will the system boot just Ubuntu, or do you need a dual-boot system?

- ▶ How much data will require backup, and what backup system will work best? (See Chapter 13, "Backing Up" for more information on backing up your system.)

DVD Installation Jump-Start

To install Ubuntu from the disc included with this book, you must have at least a Pentium-class CPU, 3GB of hard drive space, and 256MB RAM. Most modern systems have significantly larger drives, and it is an idea to invest in more storage from your local computer store.

The Boot Loader

During installation, Ubuntu automatically installs GRUB (Grand Unified Boot Loader) to the Master Boot Record (MBR) of your hard drive. Handily enough, it also detects any other operating systems such as Windows and adds entries in GRUB as appropriate. If you have a specific requirement not to install GRUB to the MBR, you need to install using the Alternate disc, which will allow you to specify the install location for GRUB.

Installing from CD or DVD

Most PCs' BIOS support booting directly from a CD or DVD drive, and enable you to set a specific order of devices (such as floppy, hard drive, CD-ROM, or USB) to search for bootable software. Turn on your PC and set its BIOS if required (usually accessed by pressing a Function or Del key after powering on); then insert your Ubuntu disc and boot to install Ubuntu.

To use this installation method, your computer must support booting from your optical drive. You can verify this by checking your BIOS and then booting your PC.

Older PCs might prove problematic when you desire to boot to an install using optical media. The good news is that this should no longer be a problem with most post-1995 personal computers.

Step-by-Step Installation

This section provides a basic step-by-step installation of Ubuntu from the install disc. The install process itself is fairly straightforward, and you should not encounter any real problems.

It is useful to have your computer ready to connect to the Internet so that you can download updates as soon as you have finished the installation. Although typically you would be recommended to not have your computer connected up, Ubuntu's unique security configuration means that it effectively blocks all incoming network ports, so it is fairly secure until you start opening these ports.

Starting the Install

To get started, insert the DVD into your drive and reboot your computer. The initial screen offers a variety of languages for you to use during installation (see Figure 1.1) followed by a list of options for you to choose from (see Figure 1.2).

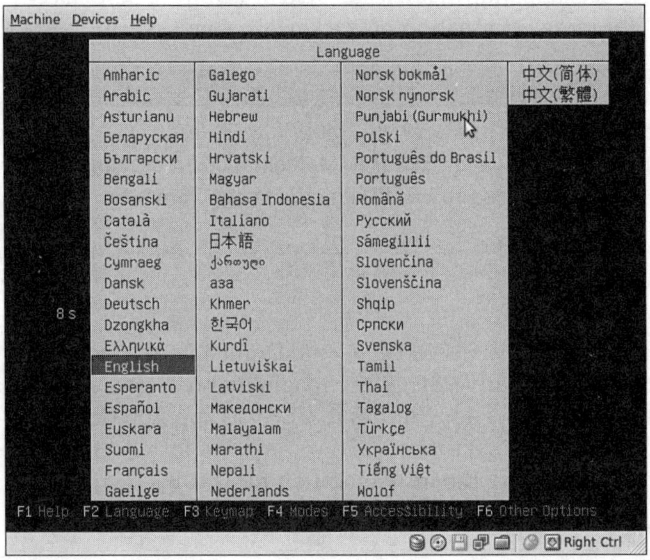

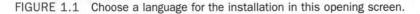

FIGURE 1.1   Choose a language for the installation in this opening screen.

However, four other options are on this screen that you need to be aware of. The second option is to Install Ubuntu, and this has the effect of running the installation program without booting into a live environment. If you select this option, you can pick up the walkthrough from Figure 1.4 later on in this section.

The next option, checking the CD for defects, can be a very useful step, especially if you've been having problems with installing Ubuntu. Should it detect any errors, you should consider downloading a fresh image from the Internet and burning a new CD. Next up is a memory checker, which can also aid troubleshooting; with the relative cheapness of RAM, it's a relatively small matter to replace any faulty memory that the checker finds.

Finally, you can elect to boot from the hard drive, something you might want to do if you've accidentally left the CD in after doing some work with it.

For any of the preceding options, use your cursor keys to move between them and press the Enter key to select one. Now back to the live CD installation!

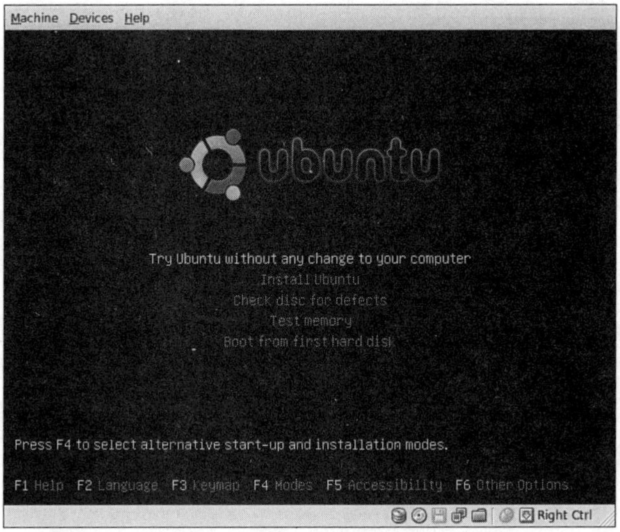

Machine Devices Help

Try Ubuntu without any change to your computer
Install Ubuntu
Check disc for defects
Test memory
Boot from first hard disk

Press F4 to select alternative start-up and installation modes.

F1 Help F2 Language F3 Keymap F4 Modes F5 Accessibility F6 Other Options

Right Ctrl

FIGURE 1.2   Ubuntu gives you five options to choose from when you're ready to proceed.

Ubuntu starts the process by loading components from the DVD into memory, and after about 30 seconds or so, you are presented with the GNOME desktop that you can use to start testing things out. Bear in mind that Ubuntu loads some parts of itself from memory and other parts from the DVD, so it will not be a true representation of the real performance of Ubuntu. Rather, it's designed to give you a taste of what to expect and allows you to test it with your hardware.

Thanks to the work that has gone into Ubuntu 9.10, the majority of your hardware should be fine, and you can proceed to install Ubuntu. You do this by double-clicking the Install icon helpfully located on your desktop (see Figure 1.3).

> **NOTE**
>
> If you find that some things don't work, don't panic. In these cases, Google is definitely your friend and you should do some research to see whether anyone else has had similar problems, or whether they've managed to install on similar hardware. Another great place to get help is the Ubuntu Forums at http://ubuntuforums.org, where you can interact with thousands of other Ubuntu fans.

After a couple of seconds, the Installation Welcome screen appears and prompts you to select a language (see Figure 1.4). As you can see, Ubuntu supports a wide range of languages, even native Welsh! Click forward when you have selected your language.

The next screen asks you to specify your location in the world. This is used for setting time and region options, so find the city closest to you on the map and select it. Figure 1.5 shows that we have selected London, but it could be another city that is closer to you. Ubuntu automatically chooses the time zone and detects the offset from Greenwich mean time (GMT) for you.

FIGURE 1.3   The standard Ubuntu desktop, complete with the helpful Install icon ready for you to make the switch to Ubuntu.

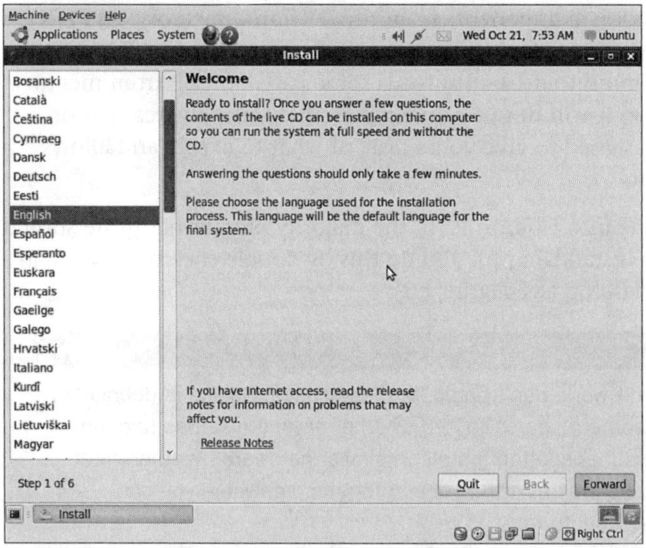

FIGURE 1.4   Select a language to use when installing Ubuntu.

Click Forward to continue to the next screen.

Following on from the Time and Region screen is the keyboard layout. Ubuntu will give a good guess at what type of keyboard is connected to your computer, but it allows you to change it in case it should differ. Make sure to find the correct layout for your keyboard (see Figure 1.6). If in doubt, use the text box at the bottom of the screen to try out all the keys.

When you are happy that the keyboard layout is correct, click Forward to move on to the partitioning.

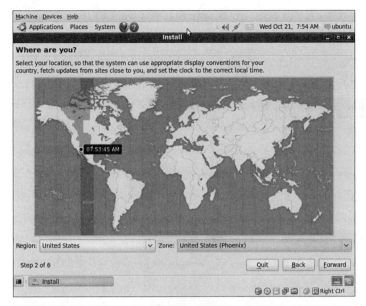

FIGURE 1.5   Choose the closest city to you in the world to allow Ubuntu to configure time and region settings correctly.

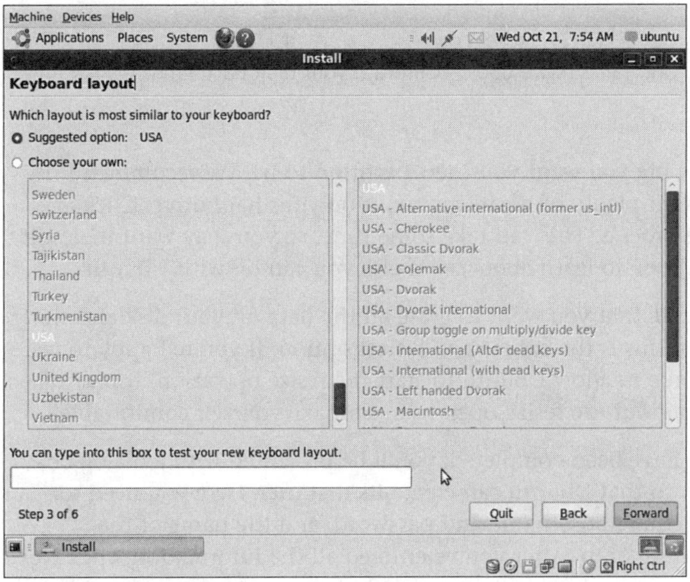

FIGURE 1.6   Choose the most appropriate keyboard layout for your computer, and then rigorously test it!

Partitioning under Linux used to be somewhat of a black art, but Ubuntu has made it easy. You have three main options (two of which are shown in Figure 1.7): resize the disk and use the freed-up space, erase and use the entire disc, or manually edit the partition table. Unless you have a requirement to do so, avoid the third option; it can seriously cause trouble with other operating systems. For now, we assume that you want to resize your partition.

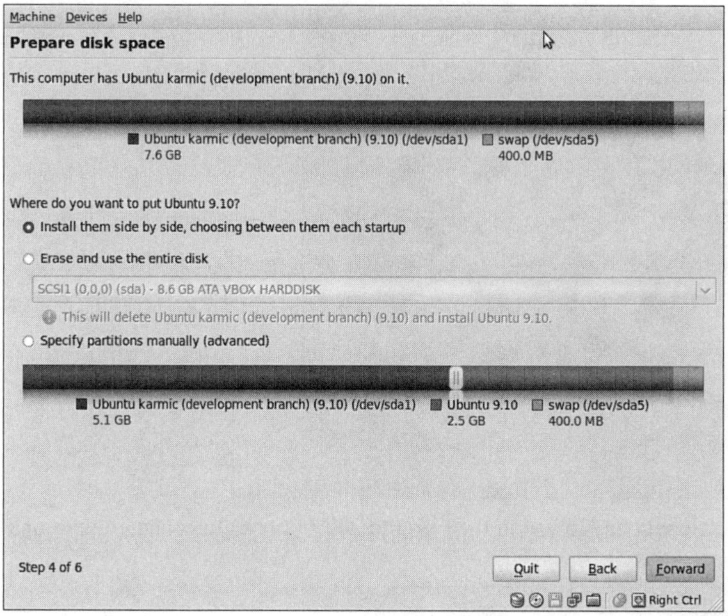

FIGURE 1.7   Tread carefully. One false move could obliterate your disk partitions. Wait, you wanted to do that?

Use the slider to choose how big you want your new partition to be. We recommend no less than 20GB, to give yourself plenty of breathing room on your hard drive. Click Forward to start the resizing process. This can take some time, so you may want to go off and read some more of this book to learn about what else you can do with Ubuntu.

Alternatively, you might decide that you want to erase all the data on your disk and start from scratch. In our opinion, this is the easiest and fastest option. If you're happy to resize your hard drive, click Continue to allow Ubuntu to start the resize operation. It may take some time for Ubuntu to carry out the resize operation, so make yourself comfortable!

After your partition settings have been completed, you'll be presented with a dialog box asking you for your identity, so that Ubuntu can create its first user. Here you need to input your full name, your required username and password, and the name of the computer that you are installing onto. After you've entered all the information, click Next to proceed to the migration screen where you can select to bring across information from a Windows partition or other Linux distribution. This screen (shown in Figure 1.9) is only available if you have elected to re-size your partitions.

CAUTION

When you set your password, be sure to remember what you entered! If you forget it, you will not be able to do much with your new system because you will not be able to log on to it.

When setting a password, make sure that it has a mixture of letters and numbers to make it more secure. For instance, a good example of a password is T1a5c0p. Although this may seem like garbage at first glance, the easy way to remember it is by remembering the phrase This Is A Good Choice Of Password, shortened to Tiagcop, and finally substituting some of the letters with similar-looking numbers. Experiment with some phrases to see what you can come up with.

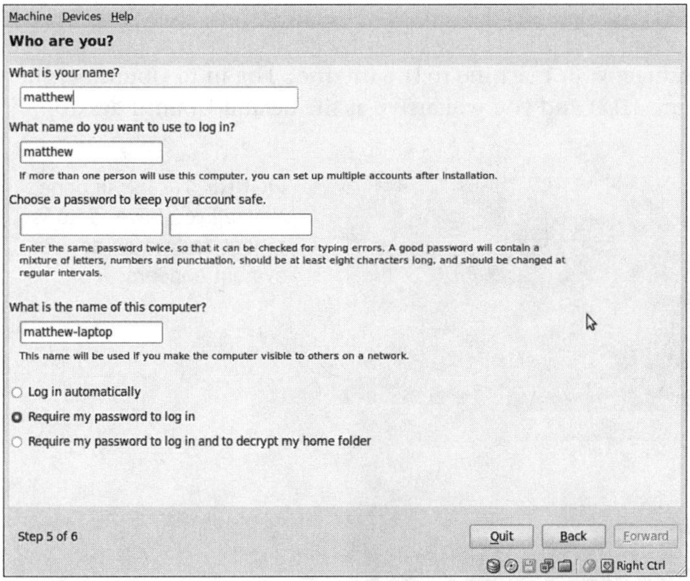

FIGURE 1.8   Fill out all the fields on this screen to give you and your computer an identity.

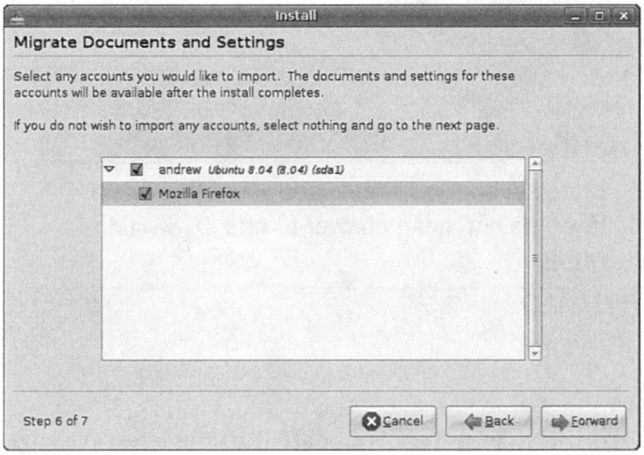

FIGURE 1.9   Want to move your documents and settings into Ubuntu? Just select the relevant boxes and it'll all come across.

The final screen summarizes what you've chosen to do, and you should go over the settings list to make sure there are no surprises. Click the Install button to begin the installation, and you can leave your computer alone for about ten minutes and make yourself a coffee.

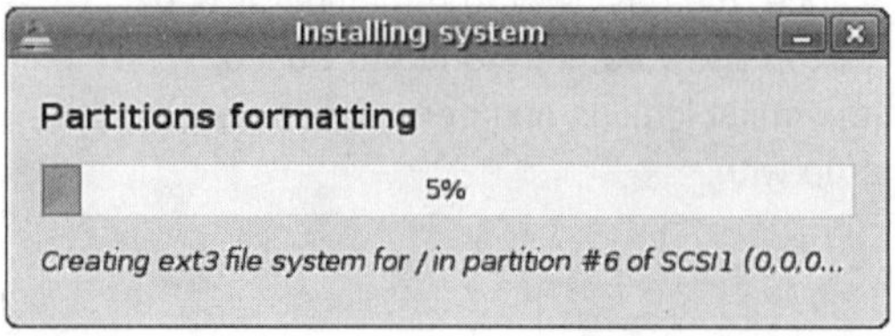

FIGURE 1.10   Sit back as Ubuntu takes over and installs itself to your hard drive.

At this point, get ready to connect your machine to the Internet. Log in to Ubuntu at the GDM welcome page (see Figure 1.12) and you will arrive at the default Ubuntu desktop (see Figure 1.13).

FIGURE 1.11   All done. Now all you have to do is reboot and watch as your system appears.

TIP

Ubuntu works well with other operating systems, and you should see your other operating system listed on the GRUB screen. If you do not, head on over to http://www.tldp.org to get a host of tips for configuring GRUB.

First Update

The first thing that you need to do with your new system is update it to the latest package versions. You do this mainly to ensure that you have the latest security updates available.

You can do this in a couple of ways in Ubuntu, but the easiest way to do it is to click the Updates icon in the panel to open the Update Manager. Your screen will darken, and you will be asked for a password. This password is the same as the one you used to log in to your system and is used in this case to authorize Ubuntu to make a systemwide change

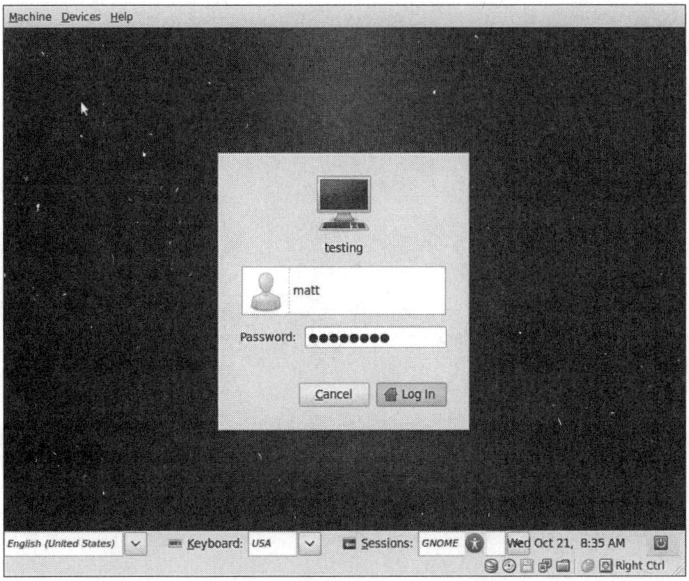

FIGURE 1.12   Enter your username and password to log on to your new system.

FIGURE 1.13   All ready for you to jump right in, the Ubuntu desktop welcomes you!

(install software, on this occasion). Another way to access the Update Manager is by going to System, Administration and choosing it from the menu.

Figure 1.14 shows the Update Manager in action.

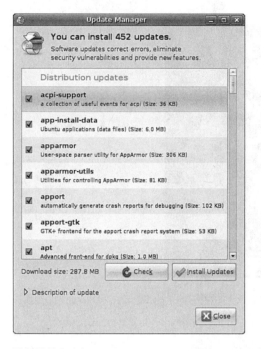

FIGURE 1.14   Get the latest security and bug-fix updates for your installed software by using Update Manager.

The application is easy to use because it automatically retrieves information on all the possible updates available to you. Just click Install Updates to start downloading and installing the necessary package updates.

If you want more information, just click the Show Details arrow, or if you want Ubuntu to check again, click the Check button to force Ubuntu to refresh the updates.

Wubi—The Easy Installer for Windows

One of the new additions to the Ubuntu CD is Wubi, which allows you to install an Ubuntu system within Windows. In effect, Wubi creates a large file to hold all the Ubuntu information and provides a way, using the Windows bootloader, to boot into Ubuntu without having to do any partitioning at all. What's more, it's almost as fast as the real thing and much faster than a Live CD. To get started with Wubi you need to simply insert the Ubuntu disc into your CD drive while Windows is booted. You'll see a screen similar to Figure 1.15.

Click the option to install inside Windows, to be taken to the next screen where you can choose some basic configuration options using the drop-down menus as shown in Figure 1.16.

Wubi creates an image file on your hard drive and modifies the Windows bootloader to allow you to boot into Ubuntu or Windows. Don't worry, though; your hard disk hasn't

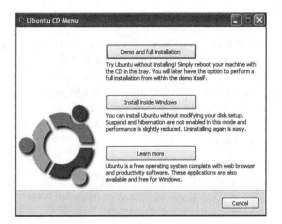

FIGURE 1.15   The auto-start menu gives you a gateway to Ubuntu. Click Install inside Windows to start the Wubi installation.

FIGURE 1.16   You can select some configuration options before you start the installation.

actually been modified, but a rather large file has been created to hold Ubuntu. When you restart your system you'll see the Ubuntu option, so press the down-arrow key and press Enter to begin booting into your new Ubuntu system.

The first time you start up a Wubi Ubuntu installation, it does some post-installation configuration before loading the GNOME desktop. You now have a fully functional Ubuntu system.

If you decide that you want to do a proper installation then you'll need to remove Ubuntu and Wubi. Fortunately, as part of the Wubi installation, an entry is added to the Add/Remove Programs tool in Windows allowing you to quickly and easily remove Wubi and the associated Ubuntu installation. Just remember to back up any files that you want to keep!

Shutting Down

At some point, you are going to want to shut your computer down. As with most things in Linux, there are different ways to do it. You can use the Quit icon located in the upper-right corner of your screen or use the same button located in the System menu. Either way, you can choose to shut down or restart your system. You can also choose to hibernate (saves a copy of the running state to disk and shutdowns) or suspend (saves the current running state to memory). We would recommend using either shutdown or reboot to ensure you get a clean system when it comes back up.

If you are working at the command line, you can immediately shut down your system by using the shutdown command like this:

```
$ sudo shutdown -h now
```

You can also use the shutdown command to restart your computer, as follows:

```
$ sudo shutdown -r now
```

For new users, installing Ubuntu is just the beginning of a new and highly rewarding journey on the path to learning Linux. For Ubuntu system administrators, the task ahead is to fine-tune the installation and to customize the server or user environment.

Reference

▶ http://www.ubuntu.com—The place to start when looking for news, information, and documentation about installing, configuring, and using Ubuntu.

▶ http://tinyurl.com/c2x5u—Symantec's PartitionMagic utility includes BootMagic, which can be used to support booting of Linux or, regrettably, other less-capable operating systems, such as Windows XP.

▶ http://www.v-com.com/product/System_Commander_Home.html—V Communications, Inc.'s System Commander, a commercial 4.2MB download that can be used to support booting of any operating system capable of running on today's PCs. An intelligent partitioning utility, Partition Commander, is included.

▶ http://www.nwc.com/columnists/1101colron.html—How to use Intel's Pre-execution Environment (PXE) protocol to remote boot workstations.

▶ http://www.gnu.org/software/grub/—Home page for the GRUB boot loader.

▶ http://www.ibiblio.org/pub/Linux/docs/HOWTO/other-formats/html_single/BootPrompt-HOWTO.html—The BootPrompt-HOWTO, a guide to using the boot prompt for passing kernel arguments.

▶ http://www.tldp.org/HOWTO/Installation-HOWTO/index.html—The Linux Installation-HOWTO, a guide to installing Linux, by Eric S. Raymond.

CHAPTER 2

Post-Installation Configuration

Now that the primary task has been completed (installing Ubuntu) you can begin to customize your new operating system. By default, Ubuntu presents you with a pretty blank canvas with which to personalize your experience. Some people choose to stick with the default look and feel, while others go for a full make over.

In this chapter, we'll take a look at getting up and running with Ubuntu, including a quick tour around the desktop. We will also take a look at some of the ways in which you can customize your Ubuntu installation, such as ensuring that date and time settings are correct, as well as show you how to do some basic administration tasks, such as identifying any problems with hardware. By the end of this chapter, you should feel comfortable enough to move on through the rest of the book.

> **NOTE**
>
> Throughout this chapter, we introduce you to several key applications relevant also to other chapters of this book. We include them here because they are essential to getting your system to work as you intend. You will find it worthwhile referring back to this chapter as you work your way through the book.

Troubleshooting Post-Installation Configuration Problems

A lot of work has gone into Ubuntu to make it as versatile as possible, but sometimes you may come across a piece of hardware that Ubuntu is not sure about. Knowing what to do in these situations is important, especially when you are working with Ubuntu for the first time.

Because Ubuntu (and Linux in general) is built on a resilient UNIX foundation, it is much more stable than other operating systems. You might find this surprising if you are used to the Blue Screens of Death found on a certain operating system from Redmond, Washington. However, even though things might seem to be working fine, Ubuntu could have a problem that might not affect the appearance of the system. Perhaps kernel modules for devices will not load, for example, or services cannot start for some reason. In this section, you learn how to examine some of Ubuntu's built-in error logs to help you diagnose any unseen faults. Ubuntu has a command that enables you to see detailed messages that are output directly by the operating system: the dmesg command, which is commonly used with the grep command to filter output. The dmesg command takes its output directly from the /var/log/messages file, so you can choose to either run dmesg directly or enter less /var/log/messages instead. The output is fairly detailed, so be prepared for an initial shock when you see how much information is generated. You might find it easier to generate a file with the dmesg output by using the following command:

```
$ dmesg > dmesg.txt
```

This takes the output from the dmesg command and stores it in a new text file called dmesg.txt. You can then browse it at your leisure using your choice of text editor such as vi or emacs. You can even use the less command, like so:

```
$ less dmesg.txt
```

The messages are generated by the kernel, other software run by /etc/init.d, and Ubuntu's runlevel scripts. You might find what appear to be errors at first glance, but some errors are not really problems (for example, if a piece of hardware is configured but not present on your system).

Thanks to Google, troubleshooting is no longer the slow process it used to be. You can simply copy and paste error messages into Google and click Find to bring up a whole selection of results similar to the problem you face. Remember, Google is your friend, especially http://www.google.com/linux, which provides a specialized search engine for Linux. You can also try http://marc.info, which browses newsgroup and mailing list archives. Either way, you are likely to come across people who have had the same problem as you.

It is important to only work on a solution to one problem at a time; otherwise, you may end up getting no work done whatsoever. You should also get into the habit of making backup copies of all files that you modify, just in case you make a bad situation worse. Use the copy command like this:

```
$ cp file file.backup
```

You should never use a .bak extension because this could get overwritten by another automatic process and will leave you frustrated when you try to restore the original file.

If something breaks as a result of you changing the original file, you can always copy the original back into place using the command like this:

```
$ cp file.backup file
```

(Something as simple as this can really save your bacon, especially when you are under pressure when you've changed something you shouldn't have on a production system. That is, if you are daft enough to make sweeping changes on a production system!)

The sudo command

If you have come across Linux, you are probably aware of the command line. As you will find as you work through this book, Ubuntu puts a lot of reliance upon the sudo command while working at the command line. This command is used in front of other commands to tell Ubuntu that you want to run the specified command with super user powers. This sounds really special, and it actually is. When you work using the sudo command, you can make wide-ranging changes to your system that impact the way it runs. Be extra careful when running any command prefixed with sudo, however; a wrong option or incorrect command can have devastating consequences.

The use of sudo is straightforward. All you have to do is enter it like this:

```
$ sudo command commandoptions
```

Just replace the word *command* with the command that you want to run, along with any options. For example, the following command opens your xorg.conf file in vi and enables you to make any changes as the super user before being able to save it:

```
$ sudo vi /etc/X11/xorg.conf
```

Whenever you execute a command using sudo, you are prompted for your password. This is the same password that you use to log in to Ubuntu, so it is important that you remember it.

Sometimes, however, you may want to work with a classic root prompt instead of having to type sudo in front of every command (perhaps if you have to work with lots of commands at the command line that require super-user access, for example). sudo enables you to do this by using the sudo -i command. Again, you are prompted for your password, which you should enter, after which Ubuntu gives you the standard root prompt, as follows:

```
#
```

From here, you can execute any command without having to keep entering sudo.

First Update

As discussed in Chapter 1, "Installing Ubuntu," you should update your software as soon as you log in to Ubuntu for the first time to benefit from any available security and bug fixes. In that example, we used the Update Manager, which is really a GUI wrapper for the command apt-get. In the background, Ubuntu automatically polls the software repositories configured as standard to determine whether any updates are available. When it detects that new versions of installed software are available, a pop-up message appears in the upper-right corner of your screen. By clicking the Updates icon in the panel, you automatically open Update Manager, but not before you are prompted for your password (because you are about to make a systemwide change).

Another way of updating your system, and one that can be quicker than Update Manager, is to use the command line. If you go to the Applications, Accessories menu and select the Terminal option, a blank screen displays. This is the command line (commonly referred to as the *terminal*) and is one of the most powerful features of Linux. It is covered in more detail in Chapter 30, "Command Line Masterclass," so we won't delve too deeply here.

You are greeted with a prompt similar to the one here:

```
andrew~$
```

A blinking cursor also displays. Ubuntu is awaiting your first command. Here we want to issue the following command:

```
$ sudo apt-get update
```

This command tells the package management utility apt-get to check in with the configured repositories and check for any updates for installed software. In a matter of seconds, Ubuntu completes all of this and your screen should look something like this:

```
$ sudo apt-get update
Password:
Get: 1 http://security.ubuntu.com hardy-security Release.gpg [189B]
Get: 2 http://security.ubuntu.com hardy-security Release [30.9kB]
Get: 3 http://gb.archive.ubuntu.com hardy Release.gpg [189B]
Get: 4 http://gb.archive.ubuntu.com hardy-updates Release.gpg [189B]
Get: 5 http://gb.archive.ubuntu.com hardy-backports Release.gpg [189B]
Hit http://gb.archive.ubuntu.com hardy Release
Get: 6 http://gb.archive.ubuntu.com hardy-updates Release [30.9kB]
Get: 7 http://security.ubuntu.com hardy-security/main Packages [25.1kB]
Get: 8 http://gb.archive.ubuntu.com hardy-backports Release [19.6kB]
Hit http://gb.archive.ubuntu.com hardy/main Packages
Get: 9 http://gb.archive.ubuntu.com hardy/restricted Packages [4571B]
Hit http://gb.archive.ubuntu.com hardy/universe Packages
Get: 10 http://gb.archive.ubuntu.com hardy/multiverse Packages [95.2kB]
Get: 11 http://security.ubuntu.com hardy-security/restricted Packages [4253B]
Get: 12 http://security.ubuntu.com hardy-security/universe Packages [5271B]
Get: 13 http://security.ubuntu.com hardy-security/multiverse Packages [1677B]
Get: 14 http://security.ubuntu.com hardy-security/main Sources [6227B]
Get: 15 http://security.ubuntu.com hardy-security/restricted Sources [974B]
Get: 16 http://security.ubuntu.com hardy-security/universe Sources [639B]
Get: 17 http://security.ubuntu.com hardy-security/multiverse Sources [533B]
Hit http://gb.archive.ubuntu.com hardy/main Sources
Get: 18 http://gb.archive.ubuntu.com hardy/restricted Sources [1478B]
Hit http://gb.archive.ubuntu.com hardy/universe Sources
Hit http://gb.archive.ubuntu.com hardy/multiverse Sources
Get: 19 http://gb.archive.ubuntu.com hardy-updates/main Packages [37.7kB]
Get: 20 http://gb.archive.ubuntu.com hardy-updates/restricted Packages [14B]
Get: 21 http://gb.archive.ubuntu.com hardy-updates/universe Packages [8363B]
Get: 22 http://gb.archive.ubuntu.com hardy-updates/multiverse Packages [866B]
Get: 23 http://gb.archive.ubuntu.com hardy-updates/main Sources [22.1kB]
Get: 24 http://gb.archive.ubuntu.com hardy-updates/restricted Sources [14B]
Get: 25 http://gb.archive.ubuntu.com hardy-updates/universe Sources [1823B]
Get: 26 http://gb.archive.ubuntu.com hardy-updates/multiverse Sources [427B]
Get: 27 http://gb.archive.ubuntu.com hardy-backports/main Packages [14B]
Get: 28 http://gb.archive.ubuntu.com hardy-backports/restricted Packages [14B]
Get: 29 http://gb.archive.ubuntu.com hardy-backports/universe Packages [14B]
Get: 30 http://gb.archive.ubuntu.com hardy-backports/multiverse Packages [14B]
Get: 31 http://gb.archive.ubuntu.com hardy-backports/main Sources [14B]
```

```
Get: 32 http://gb.archive.ubuntu.com hardy-backports/restricted Sources [14B]
Get: 33 http://gb.archive.ubuntu.com hardy-backports/universe Sources [14B]
Get: 34 http://gb.archive.ubuntu.com hardy-backports/multiverse Sources [14B]
Fetched 299kB in 2s (140kB/s)
Reading package lists... Done
```

Now you need to issue the command to upgrade your software by entering the following:

```
$ apt-get dist-upgrade
```

Because you have already checked for updates, Ubuntu automatically knows to download and install only the packages it needs. The dist-upgrade option intelligently works with newer packages to ensure that any dependencies that are needed can be satisfied. You can also use the option upgrade instead, but it isn't as smart as dist-upgrade.

---

apt-get **Alternatives**

Ubuntu has an alternative to apt-get called aptitude. It works in pretty much the same way as apt-get with the exception that aptitude also includes any recommended packages on top of the requested packages when installing or upgrading. You can use aptitude exactly as you would use apt-get, so for instance you could issue the command aptitude update and it would update the repository information. However, you can also issue just the command aptitude without any options, which brings up a text-based package manager that you can use to select packages.

Configuring Software Repositories

Ubuntu uses software repositories to get information about available software that can be installed onto your system. By default, it only allows access to a small portion of software (even though this software is officially supported by Ubuntu). However, Ubuntu is based on a much older Linux distribution called Debian. Debian has access to more than 17,000 different packages, which means that Ubuntu can have access to these packages, too.

To gain access to these additional packages, you need to make some changes to your repository configuration files by using the Software Sources GUI tool, found under the System, Administration menu and as shown in Figure 2.1. On the first tab (Ubuntu Software), you have five options to choose from, depending on your requirements. It is entirely up to you which options you check, but make sure that as a minimum the first check box is checked to allow you to select "official" software with Canonical support for Ubuntu. The more boxes you check, the wider your selection of software. It's also a good idea to make sure that the Proprietary Drivers box is checked in order to benefit from drivers that could enhance your system's performance.

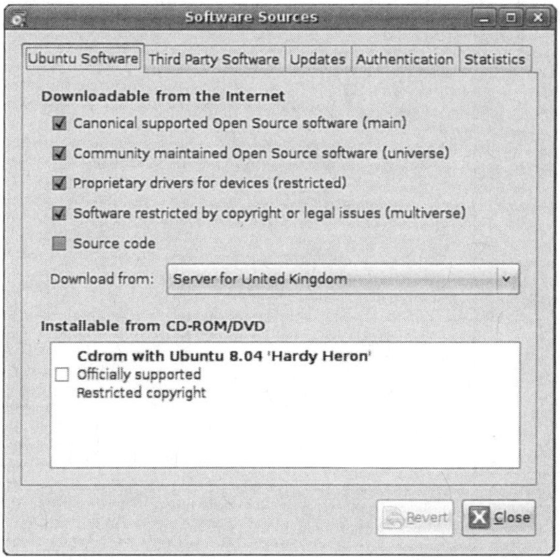

FIGURE 2.1   Enable both Universe and Multiverse repositories to allow access to a huge variety of software for Ubuntu.

Open Source Versus Proprietary

You will hear a lot of arguments about using Proprietary drivers within Ubuntu. Some people feel that it goes against what Open Source stands for, in that the underlying code that is used for the drivers cannot be viewed and modified by the wider community (as opposed to the actual driver developers). However, there is also a strong argument that says users should have to undergo the least amount of work for a fully functional system. This is certainly the case for graphics cards, although at the time of writing AMD has announced the open sourcing of the ATI graphics driver.

Ubuntu takes a middle of the road stance on this and leaves it up to the user to either enable or disable the repository that gives access to proprietary drivers. Why not give the open source drivers a chance before plumping for a proprietary one?

Once you are happy with your selections, switch to the Updates tab to configure Ubuntu's behavior when updates are available (see Figure 2.2). By default both the important security updates and recommended updates are checked to ensure that you have the latest bug fixes and patches. You can also choose to receive proposed updates and *back-ports* (software that is released for a newer version of Ubuntu but re-programmed to be compatible with 8.04), but we'd only recommend this if you are happy to carry out testing for the community as any updated software from these repositories can have an adverse effect on your system.

FIGURE 2.2   Configure which updates you want, and you want them to be handled in the Updates tab of Software Sources.

Ubuntu also allows you to configure how often it checks for updates, as well as how they are installed. By default Ubuntu checks daily for updates and, if there are any available, will notify you. However, you can change the frequency (something which is recommended if you want to have a structured update policy) and the actions Ubuntu carries out when it finds available updates. We recommend keeping the notification only option as this allows you to see what updates are available prior to them being installed. If you want to save time then choose Download All Updates in the Background to allow Ubuntu to silently download the updates prior to you choosing to install them.

CAUTION

We don't recommend selecting the option which automatically installs security updates. It's important that you have the option of choosing to install updates as there is always the chance that an update may cause problems. The last thing you want is for your system to suddenly stop working because an update was installed that has broken something without your knowledge.

Part of the magic of Ubuntu is the ease in which you can upgrade from major version to major version, such as moving from 9.04 to 9.10 for instance. Some Ubuntu releases are called LTS for Long Term Support and are intended for those who do not wish to upgrade their operating system as often. It is possible to do this. By ensuring that the release upgrade option is set to Long Term Supported releases only, you'll only be prompted to upgrade your version of Ubuntu to what will be the next Long Term Supported version, which, based on history, would be 10.04! After configuring your update options, click the Close button. Ubuntu prompts you with a message that the software information is out of date and needs to be refreshed; click Reload to retrieve the very latest update information. After a few seconds you are returned to your desktop and can carry on working.

Installing Graphics Drivers

Ubuntu is extremely good at detecting and configuring graphics cards. By default it ships with a number of proprietary drivers to allow graphics cards to work and will alert you to this by using the Hardware Drivers Manager. You can then choose to enable or disable the drivers as appropriate, depending on your personal preference. (See the "Open-Source Versus Proprietary" note earlier in this chapter.)

You can find the Hardware Drivers Manager under the System, Administration menu, and it is shown in Figure 2.3.

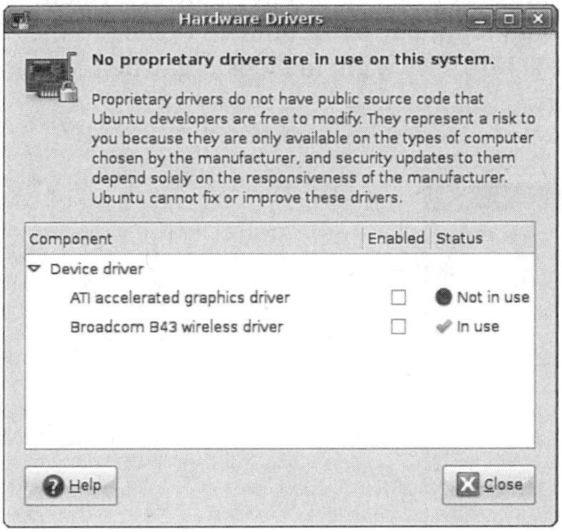

FIGURE 2.3   Toggle the usage of restricted drivers with a simple point-and-click interface. Here you can see that an Intel network driver has been enabled for use.

If you elect to use a listed proprietary driver, Ubuntu will first confirm that you are happy to proceed and then automatically download and install the driver. This may require you to log out and back in again in order for the driver to take effect.

For the most part, Ubuntu will detect and configure the majority of graphics cards from the start, and even if it has problems, it will attempt to give you a display of some sort. This feature is known as BulletProof X, and it allows you access to tools that may help you fix your problem by trying different combinations of graphics cards and monitors.

Changing Ubuntu's Look and Feel

GNOME, the default window manager for Ubuntu, has a number of options to change how it looks and feels. The default theme is Human; this takes a blend of the GNOME Clearlooks theme, mixes it with icons from the Tango Project, and adds a little spice direct from Ubuntu. However, it is not to everyone's taste, so in this section we look at changing the visual style of Ubuntu.

Changing the Desktop Background

Perhaps the easiest and most dramatic change you can make is to change the default desktop background. It is as simple as right-clicking on the desktop and selecting the option to Change Desktop Background to see the dialog box shown in Figure 2.4. Ubuntu comes with a small selection of wallpapers to start with, but we recommend going to the Web to find a great selection. Our favorite site is http://www.gnome-look.org, where you can find a great selection of desktop wallpapers.

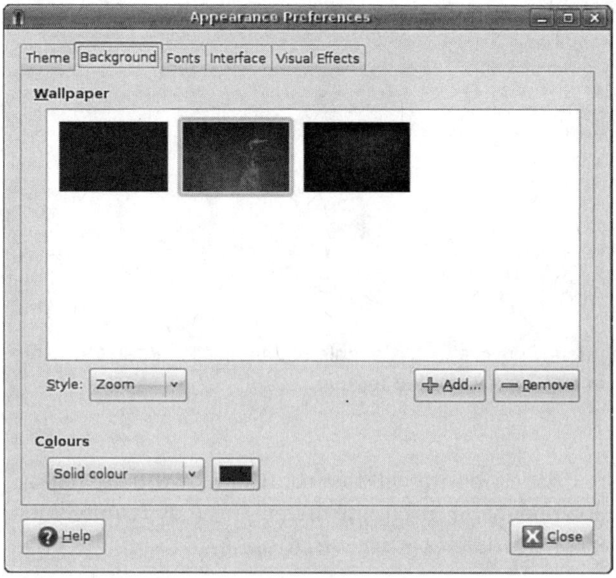

FIGURE 2.4   Choose one of the default wallpapers, or use the Add Wallpaper option to select your own image file.

As you click on a wallpaper, Ubuntu automatically applies it so that you can quickly see whether you like it. When you are happy with your selection, keep the dialog box open so we can change other aspects of the desktop.

Changing Colors

Next up is the colors that Ubuntu defaults to. When Ubuntu was originally launched in October 2004, it came with a predominantly brown theme, leading to some users questioning the style choices of the Ubuntu development team. Over time the brown has been replaced with a warm caramel color (which, to be honest, is only slightly better than the brown).

Thankfully, GNOME offers an array of tools to modify the defaults. Just head to the System, Preferences, Appearance option to quickly change the entire theme (see Figure 2.5). Or if you've kept the dialog box open as suggested earlier, click the Theme tab. You will see a list of predefined themes that you can choose from.

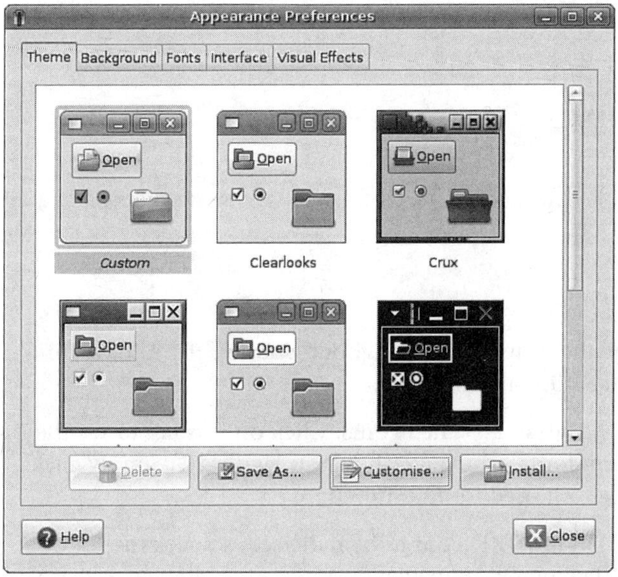

FIGURE 2.5   Either use the default themes or mix and match elements of them to match your specifications.

Alternatively, you can click the Customize button to mix up your own look and feel, as shown in Figure 2.6. You can choose to change the window decorations (title bar, minimize, maximize buttons, and so on), the general color scheme and the icon theme. As you

select an option, Ubuntu automatically applies it to the desktop so you can get an idea of
how it will look. When you're happy with your selections click Close to return to the
main Theme dialog box and move on to the next section.

FIGURE 2.6   Use any number of combinations of icons, colors, and window decorations to give
you a truly personalized look and feel.

Modifying System Fonts

GNOME also enables you to change the fonts used throughout Ubuntu. If you have difficulty reading one font, just exchange it for another.

In the Appearance dialog box you will see a tab called Fonts. Click on this tab to see the
options available for changing system fonts, which are shown in Figure 2.7. Simply click
on each font name to customize the font used for that function.

For instance, you may prefer your Window Title Font to be italicized, so click the font
name and select the Italic option. Clicking OK immediately applies the change, again
giving you a good idea of whether it works. Sometimes a font can look good within the
Font Preferences screen, but when it comes to using it you wonder why on earth you
chose it. Choose your fonts wisely!

Changing How Menus Look

You can also change the look of menus, including the location of text descriptions for
each icon, by selecting the Interface tab. To be honest, there's not much to look at here,
and you would only change any of these options if you had a burning desire to replace
your icons with text.

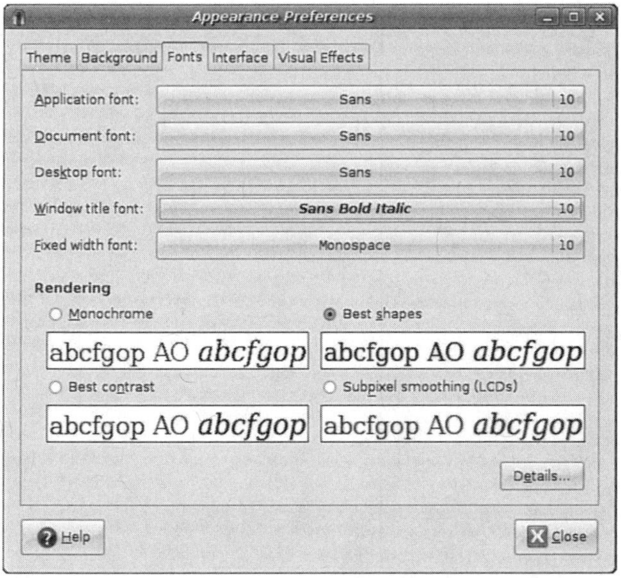

FIGURE 2.7 Keep your fonts relatively simple for ease of use, or if you prefer, indulge your love of calligraphic fonts!

Visual Effects

Perhaps the most exciting part of Ubuntu 9.10 is that by default it comes with some pretty snazzy visual effects to enhance the look and feel of your desktop. Click the Visual Effects tab to see the options available for configuring the level of effects, shown in Figure 2.9. In keeping with Ubuntu's philosophy of keeping things simple, there are three options to choose, from which you can elect to turn off all visual effects, use a basic set of effects, or use a lot of visual effects. If you choose this last option you will need to have a relatively fast computer (that is, purchased after 2004) with plenty of memory (at least 1GB) to ensure that the computer doesn't grind to a halt while rendering effects.

Preferred Behaviors

Ubuntu can detect and adapt to certain events that happen when you plug something into your computer or if you click on a link. Sometimes you may want Ubuntu to open one application rather than another, or sometimes to not do anything at all. This is called Ubuntu's behavior, and you can modify it to work as you want it to.

You can find the two main tools you need to do this under the System, Preferences menu, and you need use either Preferred Applications or Removable Drives and Media.

Preferred Applications

Preferred applications are the applications that Ubuntu calls upon when it wants to open an Internet site, an email, or a terminal (see Figure 2.9). Ubuntu makes it easy for you by automatically detecting the available options for you. Alternatively, if you want to specify

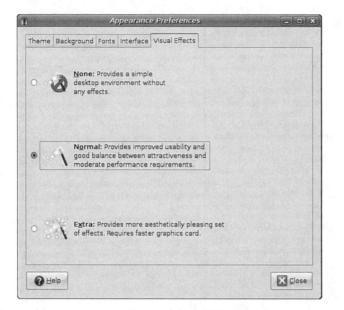

FIGURE 2.8   Wow your friends and colleagues by activating visual effects to enhance your user experience. Alternatively, switch them all off if you get a bit overwhelmed by windows flying everywhere!

your own particular application that may not appear in the list by default, select the Custom option within the application type and enter the command used to launch the application into the field along with any options, arguments, or switches that you want to use.

FIGURE 2.9   Setting preferred Internet applications.

Removable Drives and Media

In an increasingly connected world, you will find yourself plugging all sorts of devices and widgets into your computer. For the most part, it is usually multimedia files that you want to launch in a specific way. Ubuntu provides a great tool to configure the consequences of everything from plugging a digital camera into your computer, inserting a film DVD, and even plugging in a graphics tablet.

This handy tool goes by the catchy name of Removable Drives and Media, or to call it by its proper (package) name, gnome-volume-properties. With this tool, you can select the default command to run when Ubuntu detects the presence of a new drive or piece of hardware. Unlike the Preferred Applications tool, this tool does not detect the options for you, instead relying on you knowing the command needed to execute the correct application.

For example, in Figure 2.10, you can see the options for handling digital images in Ubuntu. When I connect my digital camera after a hard day's snapping, GNOME will detect its presence and launch F-Spot, ready for it to import my pictures directly into its library.

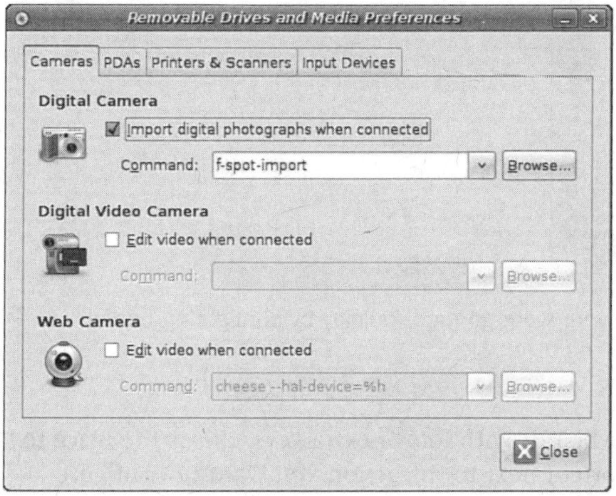

FIGURE 2.10   Take the hard work out of importing digital images by configuring gnome-volume-properties to work the way you want.

Other options include GNOME's behavior when removable drives (USB pen drives and the like) are connected, what to do in the event of a PDA or scanner being connected, and even more obscurely, what to do when a USB mouse is plugged in.

Input Devices

The primary interface between you and your computer is your keyboard and mouse. Both of these are essential to the correct usage of your computer, so it is important that they are configured correctly. Windows users will be familiar with the basic options available, so it could come as somewhat of a shock to learn that you can do a few more nifty things with a keyboard and mouse in Ubuntu.

Keyboard Shortcuts

If you have used a computer for more than a few years, you probably long for keyboard shortcuts for popular commands. Ubuntu allows you to set your own keyboard shortcuts for a wide variety of system commands. The easy-to-use Keyboard Shortcuts option under System, Preferences lists a lot of different actions that you can program shortcuts for (see Figure 2.11).

FIGURE 2.11   Make your life easier and your work go more quickly by configuring useful keyboard shortcuts.

If you have one of those multimedia keyboards with lots of extra keys, this is the place to configure their use. Just click on the shortcut next to the action you want to configure and press the key that you want to map to this action. Repeat this until you have exhausted all the combinations that you want to configure. Then click Close to finish.

Keyboard Layout

Getting the layout of your keyboard right can make a huge difference in how you work. When you installed Ubuntu (see Chapter 1), you would have specified the default keyboard layout to use. However, there may be times when you need to switch layouts, which you can do using the Keyboard tool in the System, Preferences menu (see Figure 2.12).

Certainly, I've had to configure this for my wife. You see, in the United Kingdom our @ key is located to the right of the colon/semicolon key, whereas in the United States it is located on the number 2 key. My wife spent quite a few years in the States and got used to the U.S. keyboard layout. So instead of her having to learn a new layout, I just configured

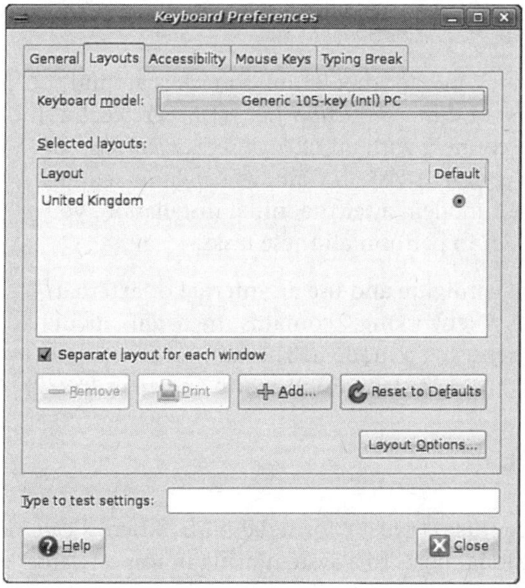

FIGURE 2.12   Use the Keyboard Layout tool to ensure that you have your keyboard settings configured correctly.

her login to use the U.S. layout and mine to use the U.K. layout, which has saved us from a number of arguments!

However, you can also use the Keyboard Layout tool to configure special key behaviors. For instance, some people prefer to swap the Caps-Lock and left Ctrl key around. You can set this option and others in the Layout Options tab. If you are not yet an l33t hacker, experiment with what's on offer; you may get some benefit from these customizations.

Finally, Ubuntu can also configure and enforce typing breaks, all in the name of good health. Simply set the length of working time, the duration of the break, and whether you want to be able to postpone. When this is activated at the end of the first length of working time, Ubuntu locks the computer and will not let you log back in until the break duration has passed. Of course, if you are in the middle of something important, setting the Postpone option may prove useful.

Mouse

There's not really much to configuring a mouse. Ubuntu does a great job of detecting most mice, except that it's not so good at configuring extra buttons over and above the left and right button and scroll wheel. The most useful option here is the Locate Pointer option, which highlights the mouse pointer when you press the Ctrl key. Of course, if you are left-handed, you can also swap the mouse buttons over, but this is a matter of personal preference.

Detecting and Configuring a Modem

More than 38 million users in the United States and another 85 million users around the world now connect to the Internet with cable or *digital subscriber line (DSL)* service, but for many users a modem is the standard way to connect with an *Internet service provider (ISP)* using the *Point-to-Point Protocol (PPP)*. Other common tasks for modems include sending and receiving faxes. If you add or change your modem after the initial installation, you must configure Ubuntu to use the new modem to perform all these tasks.

Ubuntu includes several tools you can use to configure and use an internal or external modem in your notebook or PC. Chapter 14, "Networking," contains the details about configuring Ubuntu to connect to the Internet using a modem. This section covers how to configure and use modems using serial ports (using a standard formerly known as RS232, but now called *EIA232*) or USB.

Configuring a Serial-Port Modem

Linux uses /dev/ttySX, /dev/ttyUSBX, or /dev/usb/ttyUSBX for serial ports, where X can range from 0 to 15. You can add many additional ports to a system using multiport cards or chained USB devices. A PC's integral serial ports are generally recognized at boot time. To see a list of recognized ports for your system, pipe the dmesg command output through the fgrep command, as follows:

```
$ sudo dmesg ¦ grep tty
ttyS00 at 0x03f8 (irq = 4) is a 16550A
ttyS01 at 0x02f8 (irq = 3) is a 16550A
```

In this example, the grep command reports that two serial ports have been recognized in the dmesg output. Note that the device matching ttyS00 is /dev/ttyS0, despite the kernel output. The PC's external modem can be attached (most likely using a male DB9 adapter) to either port. Under Linux, nearly all modem-dependent software clients look for a symbolic link named /dev/modem that points to the desired device. This link is not created by default; as root, however, you can create this device manually using the ln command like this:

```
$ sudo ln -s /dev/ttyS0 /dev/modem
```

In this example, /dev/modem will point to the first serial port.

Ubuntu's network-admin (shown in Figure 2.13 and found under System, Administration, Networking) will always detect the presence of a modem on the system. However, it does not activate the interface unless specifically told to do so. You can use the Auto-Detect button to find the correct modem port.

Configuring WinModems for Laptops

Other issues regarding modems focus on Linux notebook users with laptops using *controllerless* modems. These modems use proprietary software to emulate a hardware modem and are commonly referred to as *WinModems* due to the software being available

FIGURE 2.13   Ubuntu's network-admin will help you set up an appropriate modem.

only on Windows. Despite the release of binary-only drivers to enable use of some of these modems, these devices remain the bane of Linux notebook and some desktop users.

You might find some support for Lucent (but not Lucent AMR), Motorola SM56-type, the IBM Mwave, and Conexant HSF (not HCF) controllers. At the time of this writing, there was no support for any 3Com or U.S. Robotics controllerless modems. For links to drivers and more information, browse to the Linux WinModem web page at http://www. linmodems.org.

Configuring Power Management in Ubuntu

Advanced Configuration and Power Interface (ACPI) enables workstations and servers to automatically turn off when instructed to shut down. Most often used by Linux mobile users, ACPI can help extend battery sessions through the use of intelligent storage-cell circuitry, CPU throttling (similar to, but not the same as safety thermal throttling incorporated by Intel in Pentium III and IV CPUs), and control of displays and hard drives.

Most PCs support ACPI via the BIOS and hardware. ACPI support is configured, enabled, and incorporated in the Linux kernel.

ACPI information is constantly available through the `acpi` command, which looks like this:

```
$ acpi -V
    Battery 1: charged, 100%
    Thermal 1: ok, 47.0 degrees C
    AC Adapter  1: on-line
```

This example provides information such as battery charge status, percentage of charge, as well as current system temperature and status of the AC adapter.

Alternatively, you can use the GUI tool that Ubuntu provides, which can be found under the System, Preferences menu as the Power Management option (shown in Figure 2.14).

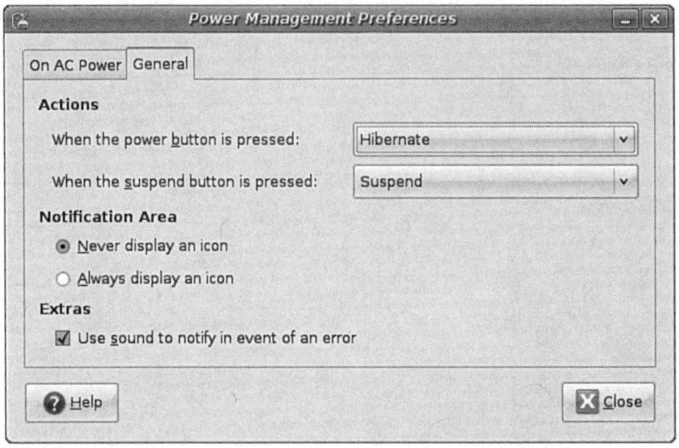

FIGURE 2.14   Gnome Power Management allows you to monitor battery status and configure specific power-related actions, such as closing the lid of your laptop or pressing the power button.

Fortunately, Ubuntu provides good support for suspend and hibernate. Suspend means that your computer writes its current state to memory and goes into a low power mode, while Hibernate writes the current state of the system to disk and powers off the computer. Either way, your computer will start much faster the next time you go to use it.

Setting the Date and Time

The Ubuntu installer queries during installation for default time zone settings, and whether your computer's hardware clock is set to *Greenwich mean time (GMT)*—more properly known as *UTC* or *coordinated universal time*.

Linux provides a system date and time; your computer hardware provides a hardware clock-based time. In many cases, it is possible for the two times to drift apart. Linux system time is based on the number of seconds elapsed since January 1, 1970. Your computer's hardware time depends on the type of clock chips installed on your PC's motherboard, and many motherboard chipsets are notoriously subject to drift.

Keeping accurate time is not only important on a single workstation, but also critically important in a network environment. Backups, scheduled downtimes, and other network-wide actions need to be accurately coordinated.

Ubuntu provides several date and time utilities you can use at the command line or during an X session, including these:

▶ date—Used to display, set, or adjust the system date and time from the command line

▶ hwclock—A root command to display, set, adjust, and synchronize hardware and system clocks

▶ time-admin—Ubuntu's graphical date, time, and network time configuration tool

Using the date Command

Use the date command to display or set your Linux system time. This command requires you to use a specific sequence of numbers to represent the desired date and time. To see your Linux system's idea of the current date and time, use the date command like this:

```
$ date
Tue Mar 18 20:01:43 GMT 2008
```

To adjust your system's time (say, to March 1927, 2008 at 8 a.m.), use a command line with the month, day, hour, minute, and year, like so:

```
$ sudo date 031908002008Wed Mar 19 08:00:00 GMT 2008
```

Using the hwclock Command

Use the hwclock command to display or set your Linux system time, display or set your PC's hardware clock, or to synchronize the system and hardware times. To see your hardware date and time, use hwclock with its --show option like so:

```
$ hwclock --show
Tue 18 Mar 2008 20:04:27 GMT  -0.034401 seconds
```

Use hwclock with its --set and --date options to manually set the hardware clock like so:

```
$ sudo hwclock --set --date "03/19/08 08:00:00"
$ hwclock --show
Wed 19 Mar 2008 08:00:08 AM GMT -0.151718 seconds
```

In these examples, the hardware clock has been set using hwclock, which is then used again to verify the new hardware date and time. You can also hwclock to set the Linux system date and time date using your hardware clock's values with the Linux system date and time.

For example, to set the system time from your PC's hardware clock, use the −hctosys option like so:

```
$ sudo hwclock --hctosys
```

To set your hardware clock using the system time, use the −systohc option like so:

```
$ sudo hwclock --systohc
```

Changing the Time and Date

Ubuntu's graphical X tool named time-admin can be used to set your system date and time. The client is found in System, Administration, Time & Date.

To make any changes to this tool you need to unlock it by clicking the Unlock button. You'll be asked to enter a password that corresponds with a user who has administrator privileges. Once you've done this, you are able to change any of the options.

Set the date and time by using the Calendar and Time fields. You can also have your workstation obtain updated date and time information via the Internet by choosing Remote Time Servers under the Select Servers button. To do this, you need to have ntpd time daemon support installed. If it is not present, Ubuntu asks whether you want to retrieve it, and then installs it so that you can proceed. After it has been installed, restart the time-admin client and you will now be able to select specific Internet time servers for you to synchronize with.

FIGURE 2.15   Use Ubuntu's time-admin client to set your system date and time.

Configuring and Using CD, DVD, and CD-RW Drives

Linux provides support for using a variety of CD and DVD devices and media. This section shows how to determine what device has been assigned to your CD drive and how to get additional drive information if the drive supports recording on optical media.

AT Attachment Packet Interface, or ATAPI, IDE-based CD drives are recognized during installation and work through the ide-cd kernel module. A symbolic link named /dev/cdrom is created and the device is mounted under /media/cdrom, both of which point to your CD's device (perhaps /dev/hdb or /dev/hdc). You can use many different types of CD drives with Linux, and you can easily replace, add, or upgrade your system to use a new drive. Part of a successful configuration involves the proper installation of the hardware and being able to determine the drive's device when using Linux.

Checking Drive Assignment

Linux recognizes CD and DVD drives upon booting if they are attached to your computer's motherboard with proper cabling and if they are assigned as either a master or slave on an IDE channel. Look through your kernel boot message for the drive device assignment, such as the following:

```
sr: DVDROM 10X, ATAPI CD/DVD-ROM drive
```

If you have a DVD-capable drive, you generally should also have a symbolic link named /dev/dvd and an entry under /media that point to your drive's device because many DVD clients, such as xine or vlc, look for /dev/dvd by default.

The first CD-RW drive is assigned to the device /dev/scd0 (although it might still be initially recognized while booting as an IDE device), with subsequent drives assigned to /dev/scd1, and so on. To initialize your drive for use, the following modules should be loaded:

```
Module        Size Used by  Not tainted
sg            30244  0 (autoclean)
sr_mod        15192  0 (autoclean)
cdrom         27872  0 (autoclean) [sr_mod]
ide-scsi       8128  0
scsi_mod      96572  2 [sr_mod ide-scsi]
```

Look for kernel message output regarding the device such as this:

```
Attached scsi CD-ROM sr0 at scsi0, channel 0, id 0, lun 0
sr0: scsi3-mmc drive: 0x/32x writer cd/rw xa/form2 cdda tray
Uniform CD-ROM driver Revision: 3.12
```

Your ATAPI-based CD-RW drive will then work as a SCSI device under emulation, and the symbolic link /dev/cdrom should point to /dev/scd0. You can also use the cdrecord command (included with Ubuntu's multimedia software packages) to acquire SCSI device information about your drive for later use during the burning operation, as follows:

```
# cdrecord -scanbus


scsibus1:
    1,0,0    0) 'HL-DT-ST' 'RW/DVD GCC-4120B' '2.01' Removable CD-ROM
    1,1,0    1) *
    1,2,0    2) *
    1,3,0    3) *
    1,4,0    4) *
    1,5,0    5) *
    1,6,0    6) *
    1,7,0    7) *
```

The pertinent information—1,0,0 in the example (SCSI bus, device ID, and logical unit number, or LUN)—can then be used during a burn operation like this:

```
# cdrecord -v speed=8 dev=1,0,0 -data -eject file_name.img
```

In this example, a CD-ROM data image named file_name.img is created on a CD-R or CD-RW media at a speed of 8, and the new disk will be ejected after the write operation has completed.

NOTE

Ubuntu also includes the dvdrecord, dvd+rw-format, and growisofs commands, which can be used with DVD-R and DVD-RW drives.

Configuring Wireless Networks

Wireless networking used to be a pig to configure for Linux, requiring a lot of complicated steps to connect to a wireless network. However, Ubuntu includes a great utility called Network Manager that makes connecting to and managing wireless networks extremely easy. Thanks to the inclusion of several wireless chipset drivers in the Ubuntu Linux kernel, it is now easy to connect to WEP and WPA encrypted wireless networks.

When you log in to Ubuntu, you should see the Network Manager applet appear in the top panel (see Figure 2.16). This is the applet that handles and monitors network connections.

FIGURE 2.16   The Network Manager notification applet, seen here already connected to a wireless network.

Click the applet icon in the toolbar to connect to a wireless network. If your wireless access point broadcasts its SSID, it should appear in the list under wireless networks (similar to Figure 2.16). Simply click on the required network and Network Manager will detect what encryption (if any) is in use and ask you for the passkey. Enter this and Network Manager will start the wireless connection. The passkey is then stored in the default keyring, a secure area that is unique to your login. From now on, whenever you log in to Ubuntu, the Network Manager connection will start automatically.

If for some reason your wireless network does not appear (you might have your SSID hidden), you must use the Connect to Other Wireless Network option, which brings up the screen shown in Figure 2.17.

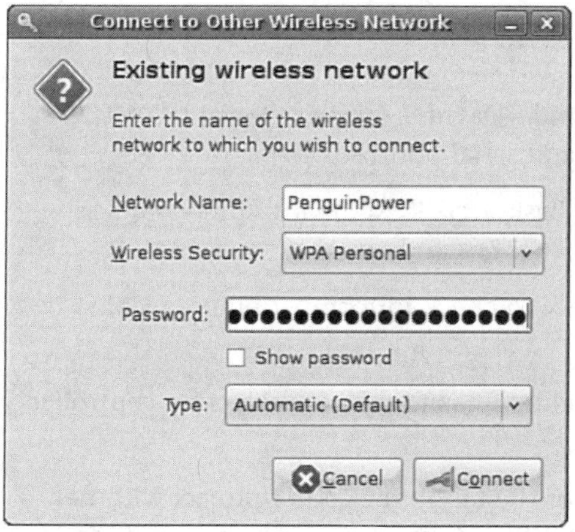

FIGURE 2.1   Configure your wireless network connection settings using Network Manager.

Network Manager can handle WEP and WPA Personal encryption. You are advised to use WPA encryption because it is the stronger of the two.

Network Manager can also connect to Cisco VPN connections, using the vpnc software. Install this using synaptic and you will be able to specify connection settings as appropriate, or if you have access to a predefined configuration (.pcf file) you can import it directly into Network Manager.

Related Ubuntu and Linux Commands

You will use these commands when performing post-installation configuration tasks:

▶ acpi—Views or uses power management settings and commands

▶ cdrecord—Gets SCSI device information and burns CD-ROMs

▶ dmesg—Views information reported by the Linux kernel

Reference

▶ The Linux Keyboard and Console HOWTO—Andries Brouwer's tome on keyboard and console issues; includes many troubleshooting tips.

▶ http://www.x.org/—The X.Org Foundation, home of X11R7.

▶ http://www.alsa-project.org—Home page for the Advanced Linux Sound Architecture project, an alternative set of sound drivers for Linux.

▶ http://www.opensound.com—Commercial sound drivers for Linux.

▶ /usr/src/linux-2.6/Documentation/power/pci.txt—Patrick Mochel's document regarding PCI power-management routes for Linux kernel and PCI hardware support programmers.

▶ http://tldp.org/HOWTO/Modem-HOWTO.html—One of the newest HOWTOs on using modems with Linux.

▶ http://tldp.org/HOWTO/Serial-HOWTO.html—David S. Lawyer's Serial HOWTO, with additional information about Linux and serial port use.

▶ http://www.camiresearch.com/Data_Com_Basics/RS232_standard.html—A description and tutorial on the EIA232 (formerly RS232) standard.

▶ http://www.qbik.ch/usb/devices/—The place to check for compatibility of USB devices for Linux.

▶ http://www.linmodems.org—This site provides links to several drivers for controller-less modem use under Linux.

▶ http://www.linux1394.org/—Home page for the Linux IEEE 1394 project with new information, links to updated drivers, and lists of compatible chipsets and devices.

▶ http://groups.google.com/—Search Usenet groups through Google; another alternative to http://marc.theaimsgroup.com/.

▶ http://www.linuxquestions.org/—The Linux Questions site, a useful set of community forums that can help you find answers to your more frustrating problems.

▶ http://cdrecord.berlios.de—Home page for the `cdrecord` command and related utilities.

CHAPTER 3

Working with GNOME

Imagine a world of black screens with white text, or for those of you who remember, green screens with green text. That used to be the primary interface for users to access computers with. Thankfully computing has moved on significantly and has adopted the graphical user interface or GUI as standard on most desktop and workstation platforms.

Ubuntu is no different and its primary window manager is called GNOME (the Gnu Network Object Model Environment). Based upon the ethos of simplicity by design, GNOME offers a rich and full interface that you can easily use to be productive. The principle design objectives include an intuitive system, meaning that it should be easy to pick up and use as well as good localization/internationalization support and accessibility.

GNOME is founded upon the X Window System, the graphical networking interface found on many Linux distributions which provides the basis for a wide range of graphical tools and window managers. More commonly known as just *X*, it can also be referred to as X11R7 and X11 (such as that found on Mac OS X). Coming from the world-renowned Massachusetts Institute of Technology, X has gone through several versions, each of which has extended and enhanced the technology. The open source implementation is managed by the X.Org foundation, the board of which is made up of several key figures from the open source world.

The best way to think about how X works is to see it as a client/server system. The X server provides services to programs that have been developed to make the most of the graphical and networking capabilities that are available under the server and in the supported libraries. X.Org provides versions for many different platforms, including Linux and Mac OS X. Originally implemented as XFree86, X.Org was forked when a row broke out over certain restrictions that were going to be included in the XFree86 license. Taking a snapshot of code that was licensed under the previous version of the license, X.Org drove forward with its own implementation based on the code. Almost in unison, most Linux distributions turned their back on XFree86 and switched their development and efforts to X.Org.

In this chapter you will learn how to work with GNOME and also the version of X that is included with Ubuntu. We will look at the fundamentals of X, as well as how to get X to work with any upgrades that might affect it, such as a new graphics card or that new flat panel display you just bought. We will also take a look at some of the other Window Managers that are included with Ubuntu, including KDE and Xfce.

The Ubuntu Family

When people talk about Ubuntu, they generally mean the original distribution launched in 2004 which uses the GNOME window manager. However, there are a number of derivatives of Ubuntu which use other window managers and they are freely available for you to download and use. For instance, Kubuntu uses the KDE window manager while Xubuntu uses Xfce instead. Despite their very visual differences, all three rely on the same core system, and it is also easy for you to add that window manager to your existing system by using one of the *-desktop meta-packages. These packages are designed to install all the base applications that are linked to that version of Ubuntu, so installing the kubuntu-desktop package would automatically install all the software needed for Kubuntu, while also retaining your existing desktop environment.

The GNOME Desktop Environment

A desktop environment for X provides one or more window managers and a suite of clients that conform to a standard graphical interface based on a common set of software libraries. When they are used to develop associated clients, these libraries provide graphical consistency for the client windows, menus, buttons, and other onscreen components, along with some common keyboard controls and client dialogs. The following sections discuss the primary desktop environment that is included with Ubuntu: GNOME.

GNOME: The GNU Network Object Model Environment

The GNOME project, which was started in 1997, is the brainchild of programmer whiz Miguel de Icaza. GNOME provides a complete set of software libraries and clients. GNOME depends on a window manager that is GNOME-aware. This means that to provide a graphical desktop with GNOME elements, the window manager must be written to recognize and use GNOME. Some compliant window managers that are GNOME-aware include Compiz (the default GNOME window manager in Ubuntu), Enlightenment, Metacity, Window Maker, IceWM, and beryl.

Ubuntu uses GNOME's user-friendly suite of clients to provide a consistent and user-friendly desktop. GNOME clients are found under the /usr/bin directory, and GNOME configuration files are stored under the /etc/gnome and /usr/share/gnome directories, with user settings stored in the home directory under .gnome and .gnome2.

A representative GNOME desktop, running the removable media preferences tool used for setting actions to events, is shown in Figure 3.1.

FIGURE 3.1   Ubuntu's GNOME desktop uses the Compiz window manager and offers a selection of GNOME themes.

You can configure your desktop in various ways and by using different menu items under the Preferences menu, which can be found as part of the main Desktop menu. The myriad of configurations options allow you to tailor every aspect of your system's look and feel. In Figure 3.2 you can see a selection of the preferences options available to you.

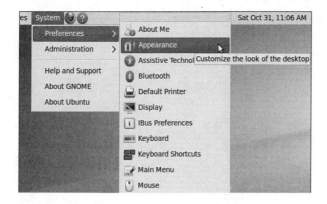

FIGURE 3.2   You can customize your Ubuntu desktop by using the Preference settings that are available in the System, Preferences menu.

Eye Candy for the Masses

Recent development work carried out on X has allowed the introduction of a number of hardware-accelerated effects within Ubuntu and its window managers. No longer do you have to drool at your Mac OS X-using colleagues when they work; now Ubuntu has a whole load of "wow" effects designed to add that professional touch to Linux.

Up until now, enabling these desktop effects has required a lot of work involving downloading specific packages and also configuring some of them using the console. However, with Ubuntu 8.04 this has been done away with and desktop effects are available out of the box, depending on whether your graphics card is powerful enough.

Ubuntu relies upon the Compiz window manager, which to most end users will not appear any differently to Metacity, the standard window manager in use by Ubuntu. You should already have the latest graphics card driver for your system as Ubuntu automatically gives you access to the proprietary driver through the Restricted Driver Manager. Check out Chapter 2, "Post-Installation Configuration," for more information on this tool.

Once you have verified your graphic driver situation, you will find a menu option under System, Preferences called Appearance (see Figure 3.3). Open it up and select the tab called Visual Effects. By default this is set to Normal, but try setting it to Extra and see what happens. After a couple of seconds you may see your window decorations (title bar, minimize and maximize buttons) disappear and then reappear. It may seem that nothing has happened but grab hold of the window title bar and move it around. If everything has gone according to plan then it should wobble! Click Close to save the settings and welcome to a world of fancy effects.

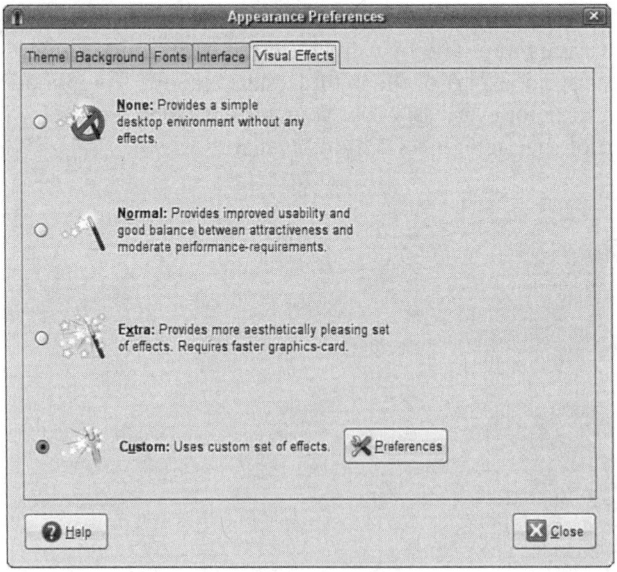

FIGURE 3.3   Use the Visual Effects tool to set the scene for some snazzy 3D effects.

The most obvious effect is that of "wobbly windows", which provide a fluid effect when you move your windows around the desktop area. Other effects include a smooth wipe from Desktop 1 to Desktop 2, activated by pressing Ctrl-Alt and either the left or right cursor key.

Basic X Concepts

The underlying engine of X11 is the X protocol, which provides a system of managing displays on local and remote desktops. The protocol uses a client/server model that allows an abstraction of the drawing of client windows and other decorations locally and over a network. An X server draws client windows, dialog boxes, and buttons that are specific to the local hardware and in response to client requests. The client, however, does not have to be specific to the local hardware. This means that system administrators can set up a network with a large server and clients and enable users to view and use those clients on workstations with totally different CPUs and graphics displays.

> **NOTE**
>
> What better way to demonstrate the capability of X to handle remote clients than by using its capabilities to produce this chapter. Although the OpenOffice.org file for this chapter resided on a Mac mini (running Ubuntu), the display and keyboard used were actually part of an Acer Ferrari notebook running Ubuntu 7.10, via an ethernet connection. Revisions were done using a Logitech keyboard and mouse of a desktop machine running Ubuntu 7.04, again connected to the Mac mini via X, but this time using a wireless connection.

Because X offers users a form of distributed processing, this means that Ubuntu can be used as a very cheap desktop platform for clients that connect to a powerful X server. The more powerful the X server, the larger the number of X-based clients that can be accommodated. This functionality can breathe new life into older hardware, pushing most of the graphical processing on to the server. A fast network is a must if you intend to run many X clients because X can become bandwidth-hungry.

X is hugely popular in the UNIX and Linux world for a variety of reasons. The fact that it supports nearly every hardware graphics system is a strong point, as well as strong multi-platform programming standards give it a solid foundation of developers committed to X. Another key benefit of X is its networking capability, which plays a central point in administration of many desktops and can also assist in the deployment of a thin-client computing environment. Being able to launch applications on remote desktops and also standardize installations serve to highlight the versatility of this powerful application.

More recent versions of X have also included support for shaped windows (that is, non-rectangular), graphical login managers (also known as *display managers*), and compressed fonts. Each release of X brings more features designed to enhance the user experience, including being able to customize how X client applications appear, right down to buttons and windows. Most office and home environments run Linux and X on their local machines. The more-enlightened companies and users harness the power of the networking features of X, enabling thin-client environments and allowing the use of customized desktops designed specifically for that company. Having applications launch from a single location makes the lives of system administrators a lot easier because they have to work on only one machine, rather than several.

Using X

X.Org 7.3 is the X server that is used with Ubuntu. The base Xorg distribution consists of 30 packages (almost 120MB), which contain the server, along with support and development libraries, fonts, various clients, and documentation. An additional 1,000 or more X clients, fonts, and documentation are also included with Ubuntu.

> **NOTE**
>
> A full installation of X and related X.Org 7.4 files can consume more—usually much more—than 170MB of hard drive space. This is because additional clients, configuration files, and graphics (such as icons) are under the /usr/bin and /usr/share directory trees. You can pare excessive disk requirements by judiciously choosing which X-related packages (such as games) to install on workstations. However, with the increased capacity of most desktop PC hard drives today, the size requirements are rarely a problem, except in configuring thin-client desktops or embedded systems.

The /usr directory and its subdirectories contain the majority of Xorg's software. Some important subdirectories are

- ▶ /usr/bin—This is the location of the X server and various X clients. (Note that not all X clients require active X sessions.)

- ▶ /usr/include—This is the path to the files necessary for developing X clients and graphics such as icons.

- ▶ /usr/lib—This directory contains required software libraries to support the X server and clients.

- ▶ /usr/lib/X11—This directory contains fonts, default client resources, system resources, documentation, and other files that are used during X sessions and for various X clients. You will also find a symbolic link to this directory, named X11, under the /usr/lib directory.

- ▶ /usr/lib/modules—This path to drivers and the X server modules used by the X server enables use of various graphics cards.

The main components required for an active local X session are installed on your system if you choose to use a graphical desktop. These components are the X server, miscellaneous fonts, a *terminal client* (that is, a program that provides access to a shell prompt), and a client known as a *window manager*. Window managers, which are discussed later in this chapter (see the section "Selecting and Using Window Managers"), administer onscreen displays, including overlapping and tiling windows, command buttons, title bars, and other onscreen decorations and features.

Elements of the `xorg.conf` File

The most important file for Xorg is the `xorg.conf` configuration file, which can be located in the `/etc/X11` directory. This file contains configuration information that is vital for X to function correctly, and is usually created during the installation of Ubuntu. Should you need to change anything post-install, you should use the `system-config-display` application, which we cover later in this chapter. Information relating to hardware, monitors, graphics cards, and input devices is stored in the `xorg.conf` file, so be careful if you decide to tinker with it in a text editor!

Bullet Proof X

Ubuntu 8.04 LTS comes with a rather useful feature called Bullet Proof X. In short, it is designed to work no matter what may happen, so in the event of some cataclysmic event which destroys your main X system you will still have some graphical way of getting yourself back into a fully functional X-based system. Thanks to Bullet Proof X you shouldn't need to edit your xorg.conf file, but it can be a good idea to understand what it is made up of, in case you ever need to troubleshoot an X problem.

Let's take a look at the contents of the file so that you can get an idea of what X is looking for. The components, or sections, of the `xorg.conf` file specify the X session or *server layout*, along with pathnames for files that are used by the server, any options relating directly to the server, any optional support modules needed, information relating to the mouse and keyboard attached to the system, the graphics card installed, the monitor in use, and of course the resolution and color depth that Ubuntu uses. Of the 12 sections of the file, these are the essential components:

- ▶ `ServerLayout`—Defines the display, defines one or more screen layouts, and names input devices.

- ▶ `Files`—Defines the location of colors, fonts, or port number of the font server.

- ▶ `Module`—Tells the X server what graphics display support code modules to load.

- ▶ `InputDevice`—Defines the input devices, such as the keyboard and mouse; multiple devices can be used.

- ▶ `Monitor`—Defines the capabilities of any attached display; multiple monitors can be used.

- ▶ `Device`—Defines one or more graphics cards and specifies what optional features (if any) to enable or disable.

- ▶ `Screen`—Defines one or more resolutions, color depths, perhaps a default color depth, and other settings.

The following sections provide short descriptions of these elements; the xorg.conf man page contains full documentation of all the options and other keywords you can use to customize your desktop settings.

The ServerLayout Section

As noted previously, the ServerLayout section of the xorg.conf file defines the display and screen layouts, and it names the input devices. A typical ServerLayout section from an automatically configured xorg.conf file might look like this:

```
Section "ServerLayout"
        Identifier      "single head configuration"
        Screen      0   "Screen0" 0 0
        InputDevice     "Mouse0" "CorePointer"
        InputDevice     "Keyboard0" "CoreKeyboard"
        InputDevice     "DevInputMice" "AlwaysCore"
EndSection
```

In this example, a single display is used (the numbers designate the position of a screen), and two default input devices, Mouse0 and Keyboard0, are used for the session.

The Files Section

The Files section of the xorg.conf file might look like this:

```
Section "Files"
    RgbPath      "/usr/lib/X11/rgb"
    FontPath    "unix/:7100"
EndSection
```

This section lists available session colors (by name, in the text file rgb.txt) and the port number to the X font server. The font server, xfs, is started at boot time and does not require an active X session. If a font server is not used, the FontPath entry could instead list each font directory under the /usr/lib/X11/fonts directory, as in this example:

```
FontPath "/usr/lib/X11/fonts/100dpi"
FontPath "/usr/lib/X11/fonts/misc"
FontPath "/usr/lib/X11/fonts/75dpi"
FontPath "/usr/lib/X11/fonts/type1"
FontPath "/usr/lib/X11/fonts/Speedo"
...
```

These directories contain the default compressed fonts that are available for use during the X session. The font server is configured by using the file named config under the /etc/X11/fs directory. This file contains a listing, or catalog, of fonts for use by the font server. By adding an alternate-server entry in this file and restarting the font server, you can specify remote font servers for use during X sessions. This can help centralize font support and reduce local storage requirements (even though only 25MB is required for the almost 5,000 fonts installed with Ubuntu and X) .

The Module Section

The Module section of the xorg.conf file specifies loadable modules or drivers to load for the X session. This section might look like this:

```
Section "Module"
        Load   "dbe"
        Load   "extmod"
        Load   "fbdevhw"
        Load "glx"
        Load "record"
        Load   "freetype"
        Load   "type1"
        Load   "dri"

EndSection
```

These modules can range from special video card support to font rasterizers. The modules are located in subdirectories under the /usr/lib/modules directory.

The InputDevice Section

The InputDevice section configures a specific device, such as a keyboard or mouse, as in this example:

```
Section "InputDevice"
        Identifier   "Keyboard0"
        Driver       "kbd"

        Option   "XkbModel"     "pc105"
        Option   "XkbLayout"    "us"
EndSection
Section "InputDevice"
        Identifier   "Mouse0"
        Driver       "mouse"
        Option       "Protocol" "IMPS/2"
        Option       "Device" "/dev/input/mice"
        Option       "ZAxisMapping" "4 5"
        Option       "Emulate3Buttons" "yes"
EndSection
```

You can configure multiple devices, and there might be multiple InputDevice sections. The preceding example specifies a basic keyboard and a two-button PS/2 mouse (actually, a Dell touchpad pointer). An InputDevice section that specifies use of a USB device could be used at the same time (to enable mousing with PS/2 and USB pointers) and might look like this:

```
Section "InputDevice"
        Identifier   "Mouse0"
```

```
        Driver      "mouse"
        Option      "Device" "/dev/input/mice"
        Option      "Protocol" "IMPS/2"
        Option      "Emulate3Buttons" "off"
        Option      "ZAxisMapping" "4 5"
EndSection
```

The Monitor Section

The Monitor section configures the designated display device as declared in the ServerLayout section, as shown in this example:

```
Section "Monitor"
        Identifier    "Monitor0"
        VendorName    "Monitor Vendor"
        ModelName     "Monitor Model"
        DisplaySize  300     220
        HorizSync    31.5-48.5
        VertRefresh  50-70
        Option "dpms"
EndSection
```

Note that the X server automatically determines the best video timings according to the horizontal and vertical sync and refresh values in this section. If required, old-style mode-line entries (used by distributions and servers prior to XFree86 4.0) might still be used. If the monitor is automatically detected when you configure X (see the "Configuring X" section, later in this chapter), its definition and capabilities are inserted in your xorg.conf file from the MonitorsDB database. This database contains more than 600 monitors and is located in the /usr/share/hwdata directory.

The Device Section

The Device section provides details about the video graphics chipset used by the computer, as in this example:

```
Section "Device"


        Identifier      "Intel Corporation Mobile 945GM/GMS,\
943/940GML Express Integrated Graphics Controller"


        Driver          "intel"


        BusID           "PCI:0:2:0"


EndSection
```

This example identifies an installed video card as using an integrated Intel 945 graphics chipset. The `Driver` entry tells the `Xorg` server to load the `intel` kernel module. Different chipsets have different options. For example, here's the entry for a NeoMagic video chipset:

```
Section "Device"
        Identifier    "NeoMagic (laptop/notebook)"
        Driver        "neomagic"
        VendorName    "NeoMagic (laptop/notebook)"
        BoardName     "NeoMagic (laptop/notebook)"
    Option      "externDisp"
    Option      "internDisp"
EndSection
```

In this example, the `Device` section specifies the driver for the graphics card (neomagic_drv.o) and enables two chipset options (`externDisp` and `internDisp`) to allow display on the laptop's LCD screen and an attached monitor.

The `Xorg` server supports hundreds of different video chipsets. If you configure X11 but subsequently change the installed video card, you need to edit the existing `Device` section or generate a new `xorg.conf` file, using one of the X configuration tools discussed in this chapter, to reflect the new card's capabilities. You can find details about options for some chipsets in a companion man page. You should look at these sources for hints about optimizations and troubleshooting.

The Screen Section

The `Screen` section ties together the information from the previous sections (using the `Screen0`, `Device`, and `Monitor Identifier` entries). It can also specify one or more color depths and resolutions for the session. Here's an example:

```
Section "Screen"
        Identifier "Screen0"
        Device     "Videocard0"
        Monitor    "Monitor0"
        DefaultDepth    24
        SubSection "Display"
                Viewport   0 0
                Depth    16
                Modes    "1024x768" "800x600" "640x480"
        EndSubSection
EndSection
```

In this example a color depth of thousands of colors and a resolution of 1024×768 is the default, with optional resolutions of 800×600 and 640×480. Multiple `Display` subsection entries with different color depths and resolutions (with settings such as `Depth 24` for millions of colors) can be used if supported by the graphics card and monitor combination. You can also use a `DefaultDepth` entry (which is 24, or thousands of colors, in the example), along with a specific color depth to standardize display depths in installations.

You can also specify a desktop resolution larger than that supported by the hardware in your monitor or notebook display. This setting is known as a *virtual* resolution in the `Display` subsection. This allows, for example, an 800×600 display to pan (that is, slide around inside) a virtual window of 1024×768.

> **NOTE**
>
> If your monitor and graphics card support multiple resolutions and the settings are properly configured, you can use the key combination of Ctrl+Alt+Keypad+ or Ctrl+Alt+Keypad- to change resolutions on the fly during your X session.

Configuring X

Ubuntu usually does a good job of detecting your graphics card and monitor, although sometimes problems can arise if the PC's video card is not recognized. If your display is not configured correctly then Ubuntu thankfully provides some tools to help you make changes to the way your display is set up.

You can use the following configuration tools, among others, to create a working `xorg.conf` file:

▶ `displayconfig-gtk`—This is Ubuntu's graphical configuration tool, which launches a handy GUI tool to help create an `xorg.conf` file.

▶ `Xorg`—The X server itself can create a skeletal working configuration.

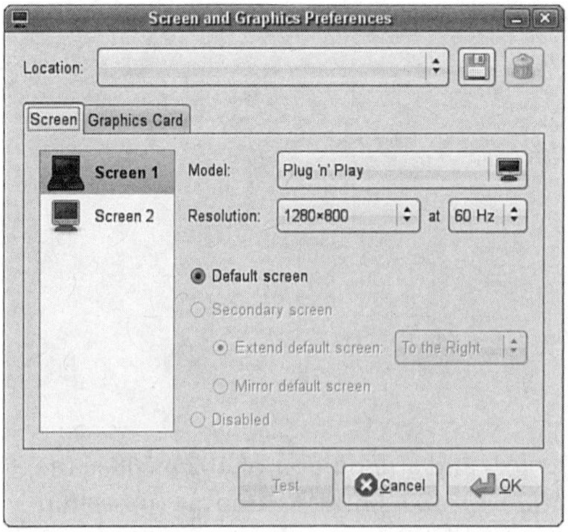

FIGURE 3.4 The *displayconfig-gtk* client provides a graphical configuration interface for creating or updating a system's *xorg.conf* file. Here you see the Screen Settings main screen, offering resolution and color-depth settings.

The following sections discuss how to use each of these software tools to create a working xorg.conf file.

Configuring X with the displayconfig-gtk Client

You can use the displayconfig-gtk client to create or update an xorg.conf file. You can start by clicking the Screens and Graphics menu item found under System, Administration

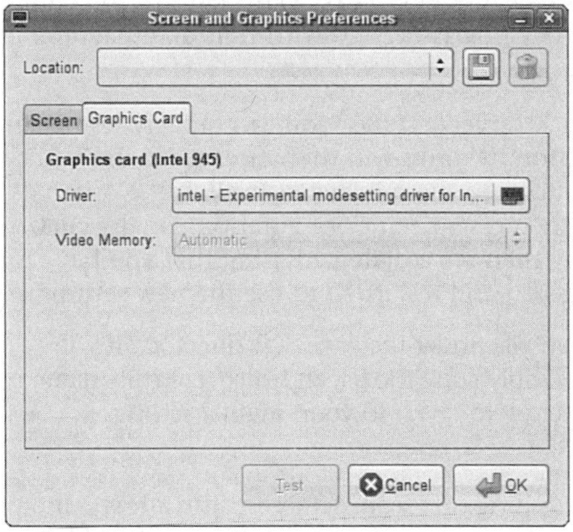

FIGURE 3.5 **displayconfig-gtk**'s hardware settings are used to configure a video card for X.

if you are already running X. You will be asked to enter your password in order to open the application; once you've done this you'll see a window similar to Figure 3.4.

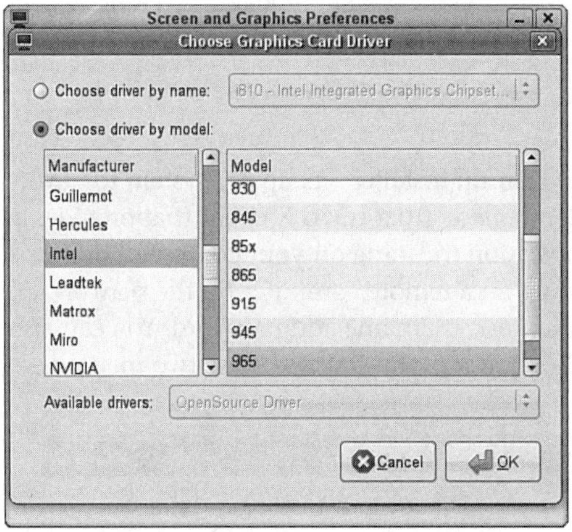

FIGURE 3.6   You can scroll to select the correct graphics card to use for your X sessions.

The Screen Settings window shows the current selected screen, along with details of the model, resolutions available, the refresh rate, and orientation. In the event that you are using two screens (dual- or multi-head displays) then you have the ability to select whether it is the primary or secondary screen, and the physical location of it.

If you click the Graphics Card tab, other configuration options become available, as shown in Figure 3.5.

Click the name of the graphics card to open up a list of alternative cards (shown in Figure 3.6). Simply select a manufacturer to see a list of cards associated with that manufacturer and to choose the correct one for your X sessions.

When you have finished your changes to your X server settings, you can quickly test them to see if they will work by clicking the Test button. Ubuntu will then attempt to use your chosen settings, allowing you to either choose to keep them or revert back to the original settings. If you are happy with the new mode then click Keep Configuration. Finally click the OK button to close the dialog box. You may then see a dialog advising that you have to log out and then log back in (or exit your X session and restart X) to use the new settings.

The new settings will be stored in a new xorg.conf file under the /etc/X11 directory. If you find that the new settings do not work, you can simply copy the backup xorg.conf file named xorg.conf.backup to xorg.conf in the same directory to revert to your original settings.

Using Xorg to Configure X

You can create the xorg.conf file manually by typing one from scratch using a text editor, but you can also create one automatically by using the Xorg server or configuration utilities (as discussed in the previous sections). As the root operator, you can use the following on the server to create a test configuration file:

```
# X -configure
```

After you press Enter, a file named xorg.conf.new is created in root's home directory, the /root directory. You can then use this file for a test session, like this:

```
# X –config /root/xorg.conf.new
```

Starting X

You can start X sessions in a variety of ways. The Ubuntu installer sets up the system to have Linux boot directly to an X session using a *display manager* (that is, an X client that provides a graphical login). After you log in, you use a local session (running on your computer) or, if the system is properly configured, an X session running on a remote computer on the network. Logging in via a display manager requires you to enter a username and password. You can also start X sessions from the command line. The following sections describe these two methods.

> **NOTE**
>
> If you have used the Server install then your system will boot to a text login—see "Command Line Quickstart" in Chapter 4 for more details on what to do here.

Using a Display Manager

An X display manager presents a graphical login that requires a username and password to be entered before access is granted to the X desktop. It also allows you to choose a different desktop for your X session. Whether or not an X display manager is presented after you boot Linux is controlled by a *runlevel*—a system state entry in /etc/event.d/. The following runlevels as handled by Ubuntu are as follows:

- ▶ 0 - halt (Do NOT set initdefault to this.)
- ▶ 1 - Multiuser text mode
- ▶ 2 - X - graphical multiuser mode
- ▶ 6 - reboot (Do NOT set initdefault to this.)

You may see mention of Runlevels 3 through 5; these can be ignored, as they are treated the same as Runlevel 2 in Ubuntu. Historically Ubuntu used the /etc/inittab file to handle runlevels, but with upstart this file no longer exists. Instead there are several files under the /etc/events.d/ directory, including an individual file for each of the virtual consoles (accessible by pressing Ctrl-Alt-F1 to F7). However, you are still able to create an inittab file, if you want to override any defaults held by Ubuntu. Make sure you create the inittab file as root and include at least one line similar to the following:

id:1:initdefault:

This will force your system to start up in text mode.

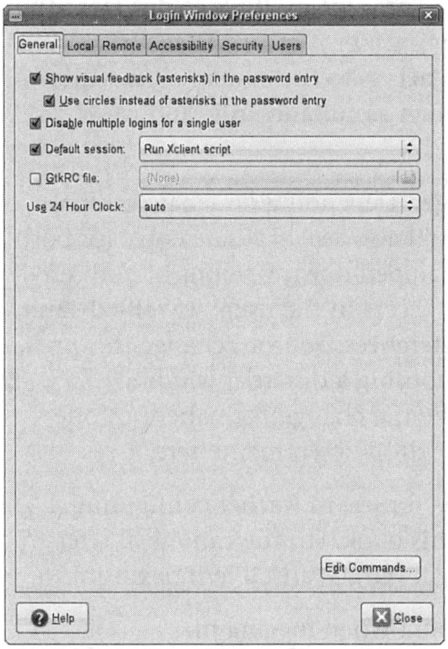

FIGURE 3.7   You use *gdmsetup* to configure the *gdmlogin* screen when using *gdm* as a display manager.

Configuring gdm

The gdm display manager is part of the GNOME library and client distribution included with Ubuntu and provides a graphical login when a system boots directly to X. Its login (which is actually displayed by the gdmlogin client) hosts pop-up menus of window managers, languages, and system options for shutting down (halting) or rebooting the workstation. Although you can edit (as root) gdm.conf under the /etc/gdm directory to configure gdm, a much better way to configure GNOME's display manager is to use the gdmsetup client.

You can use the gdmsetup client to configure many aspects of gdm. You launch this client from the System Menu, under Administration, Login Window. You will be prompted for your password and after you press Enter, you see the GDM Setup window, as shown in Figure 3.7.

You can specify settings for security, remote network logins, the X server, and session and session chooser setup by clicking on the tabs in the GDM Setup dialog.

On the General tab you'll see a handful of options, mostly to do with security. Showing visual feedback when entering passwords can be reassuring if you're not sure how many characters you've typed, although it can also pose a security risk if your password is a word closely associated with yourself. For instance, if your wife is named Bernice, and your password is seven characters long then it's a good bet that your password might be bernice. By default this setting is switched on, but it's more secure when it is turned off. Choosing circles rather than asterisks is a purely personal choice, and by default Ubuntu uses circles to show feedback when users enter passwords.

Another fairly important security feature is the ability to prevent multiple logins from the same user. This might sound innocuous at first, but if your user account details have been compromised then someone else might be able to gain access to the system even while you're using it. Ubuntu allows you to login multiple times simultaneously, and we strongly recommend that you disable it.

Next you are able to select your default window manager. Depending on what you have installed, you may see KDE and/or Xfce listed here. You'll also see a Failsafe entry for both GNOME and the terminal, which gives you access to stripped-down versions of both environments, in case anything prevents you from gaining access in the usual way. By default, Ubuntu uses the xclient script, which dictates your preferences. You can change this preference by pressing the F10 key when you log in and choosing a different window manager. You'll be prompted whether you want to make the change permanent or one-time only. It's simpler, however, to just change it in the drop-down menu here.

The option to use a gtkRC file should be ignored as it is for use in further configuring GNOME using GTK itself, and is outside the scope of this book. For the canonical reference to GTK, head on over to http://library.gnome.org/devel/gtk/unstable/index.html.

Finally you can force gdm to use the 24-hour clock format when logging in.

In Figure 3.8 you can see the Local tab, which we look at in more detail now.

The first option is to choose the style of greeter that will meet your users as they attempt to log on to the system. Ubuntu defaults to a graphical themed greeter, which is selected in the main selection area. You can change the selection by clicking one of the radio

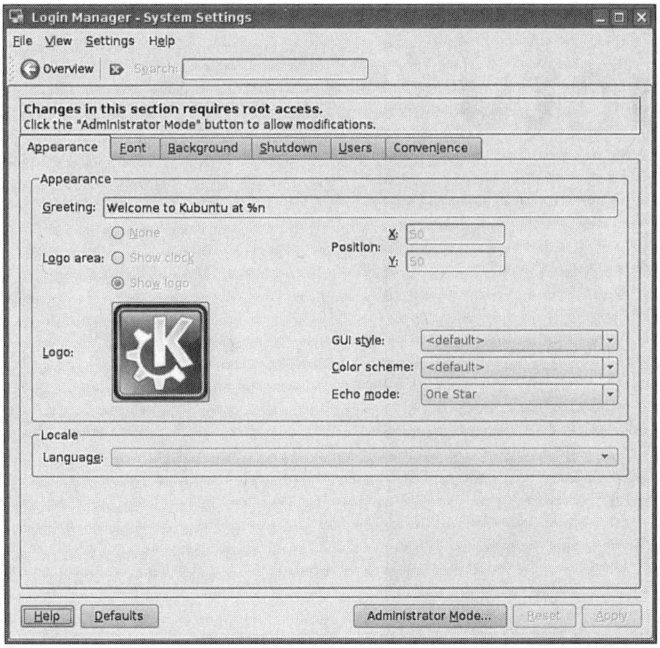

FIGURE 3.8   Customize how gdm will look to local users as they log on.

buttons to choose another theme, or, if you like randomness, you can select the Random from Selected option from the Theme drop-down menu and select multiple themes. That way, every time you boot up you'll see a different greeter depending on your selection.

If you choose to see a plain greeter, then the window will change to that shown in Figure 3.9 to allow you to define your options.

You can elect to use either a picture or a solid color to fill the screen, and by default Ubuntu selects a solid blue color in contrast with the usual brown coloring. You can play around with the settings, but we think you'll prefer the graphical greeter.

Moving on to the Remote tab, you can choose how people who log on remotely (that is, via the network) to your computer are greeted. You can choose to mirror the local greeter, or use a plain or themed greeter, depending on what you've selected for the local greeter. Whatever you select, it will provide a similar set of options as in the local tab, with the exception of the Configure XDMCP button in the bottom-right corner, shown in Figure 3.10.

FIGURE 3.9   Keeping it simple is the order of the day for using the Plain greeter.

What Is XDMCP?

XDMCP is a great way to show off the networking capabilities of X. It stands for the X Display Manager Control Protocol and it allows you to remotely access your computer using an X terminal. Remember earlier when you read that this book was put together using various displays and computers? The secret behind all of it is XDMCP.

Clicking the Configure XDMCP button takes you to another window that allows you to specify exactly how you want XDMCP to behave, as shown in Figure 3.11.

For the most part, the default options are sufficient.

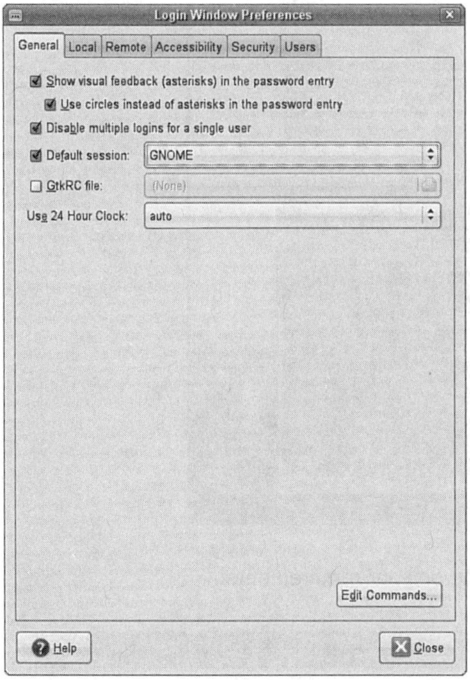

FIGURE 3.10 XDMCP—your route to remote logins, wherever you are on your network.

FIGURE 3.11 If you have very specific XDMCP needs then you can use these options to tailor it to your requirements.

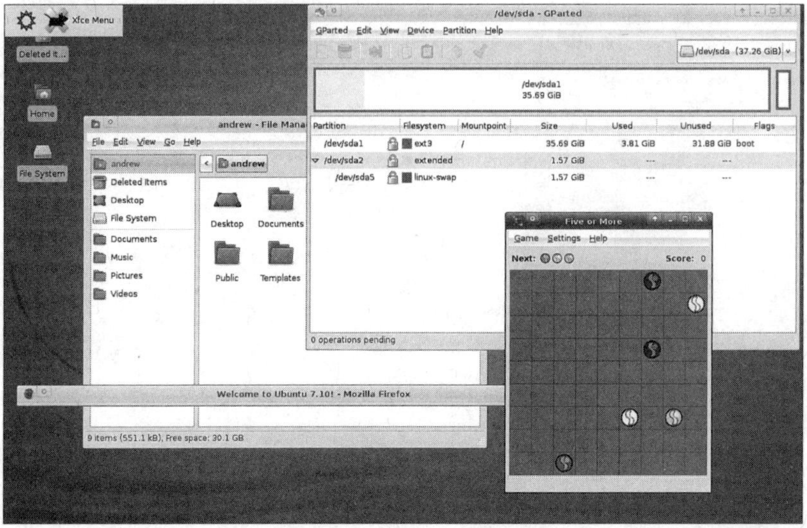

FIGURE 3.12   Lock down or loosen gdm depending on your requirements.

TIP

If you are not expecting many people to log on simultaneously via XDMCP, you may want to lower the Maximum remote sessions from its default of 16. That way you minimize the risk of unauthorized access to your system.

If you click the Close button on the dialog box, you will then be able to access your system from another Linux system by using XDMCP.

The next tab in the gdm setup dialog box deals with accessibility. Unless you have a specific need to, we suggest you leave this tab alone and move on to the more important Security tab, shown in Figure 3.12.

The first two options (Enable Automatic Login and Enable Timed Login) are pretty frightening in our opinion, and we're grateful that they're disabled by default. The first option, when activated, assumes that your system will always log in with the same user that you select in the drop-down menu. If you value your security at all, then you will never enable this on a computer that is actually used by end users, as it provides an open door to your system, inviting the would-be hacker to take a shot at wrecking your system. We'd also recommend never enabling the timed login feature, as this effectively does the same thing with the exception that you can set a time delay before Ubuntu logs in as the selected user.

CAUTION

We strongly recommend that you never set either of these two options. It's the equivalent of leaving your car unlocked, with the windows rolled down and signs up around it saying "Steal Me." Perhaps the only time you might consider selecting one or the other of these options is if you are creating a system that is designed to be used in a public access area, such as a kiosk or similar, where it would not be unusual for some dimwit to turn the computer off every so often! In this scenario, you may not be available to log on to the system and may prefer it to default to the locked-down account that you would have created.

Now that we have those two options out of the way, let's take a look at some of the others on this screen.

If you want to deter people from logging in, setting a login retry delay is one of the best ways of doing it. By setting this option, you force Ubuntu to wait the specified number of seconds before allowing the user to attempt logging in again, should he or she enter an incorrect password. Although not guaranteed to keep the determined hacker out of your system, it will nonetheless slow this person down, hopefully enough that you'll notice something or someone is attempting to gain access.

The Minimal UID option restricts logins to only those user accounts that have a UID of more than 1000. These are typically service accounts, but may include special accounts created by you that have a low UID. Make sure you don't set this number higher than any of your actual user account IDs; otherwise, you'll lock your users out of the system!

The next two options (Allow Local and Allow Remote System Administrator Login), which govern logins by system administrators, are both disabled by default in Ubuntu. This disabling has to do with the way that Ubuntu handles system administration rights in that there is no "root" account to speak of. Check out the sidebar "The Root User" in Chapter 10, "Managing Users," for more information on how Ubuntu handles the root user. If you enable the root account then you can enable these two check boxes to allow you to log in either locally or remotely (via XDMCP) as the root user.

If you are having problems with gdm or X, then you may want to enable the debug messages option as doing so may help you troubleshoot problems with your system. You'll commonly be asked to enable this option if you've made bug reports on Launchpad, the Ubuntu bug tracker.

By default, Ubuntu is set to deny any TCP connections to the X server, thus restricting the ability to use X forwarding. Unless you have a very specific need, you should leave this setting as is.

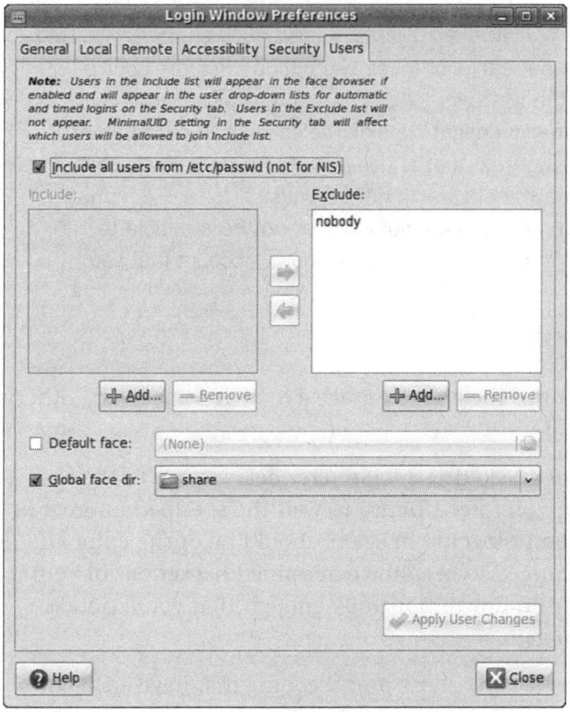

FIGURE 3.13   Include or exclude user accounts from appearing at login via the Users tab.

The final four options use permissions to ascertain whether users should be allowed to log in or not. The first option only allows the user to log in if she owns her home directory. By default, when creating new users, Ubuntu automatically assigns the new user as the owner of his or her home directory, so you should not need to change this option.

The other options on this tab allow you to restrict whether a user can log in based on the permissions applied to his or her home directory. By default, as long as your home directory has the correct group write permissions set on it, that user will be allowed to log in. For a more detailed discussion of permissions and user security, head on over to Chapter 10.

Finally, the Users tab (see Figure 3.13) enables you to specify which users are shown in the gdm login greeter that appears if you choose to use the face browser. By default, all regular users are shown in the greeter, but you can specifically hide different accounts according to your preferences by adding them to the exclude group.

All the changes that we've covered will take effect the next time you restart GNOME.

Configuring kdm

The kdm client, which is part of KDE (which we cover later), offers a graphical login similar to gdm. You configure kdm by running the System Settings option in the Kicker (K Menu).

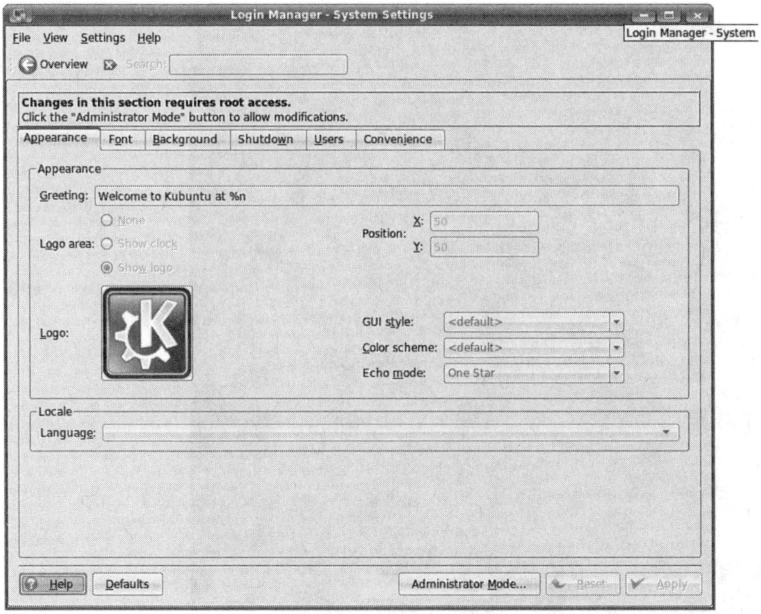

FIGURE 3.14   You configure **kdm** by choosing tabs and settings in the Login Manager dialog box.

When the System Settings window opens, click the Advanced tab and click on the Login Manager icon to see the window shown in Figure 3.14.

To make any changes to the KDE display manager while logged in as a regular user, you must first click the Administrator Mode button, and then enter your password. You can click on a tab in the Login Manager dialog to set configuration options. Options in these tabs allow you to control the login display, prompts, user icons, session management, and configuration of system options (for shutting down or rebooting). After you make your configuration choices in each tab, click the Apply button to apply the changes immediately; otherwise, the changes are applied when the X server restarts.

Using the xdm Display Manager

The xdm display manager is part of the Xorg distribution and offers a bare-bones login for using X. Although it is possible to configure xdm by editing various files under the /etc/X11/xdm directory, GNOME and KDE offer a greater variety of options in display manager settings. The default xdm login screen's display is handled by the xsetroot client, which is included with Xorg.

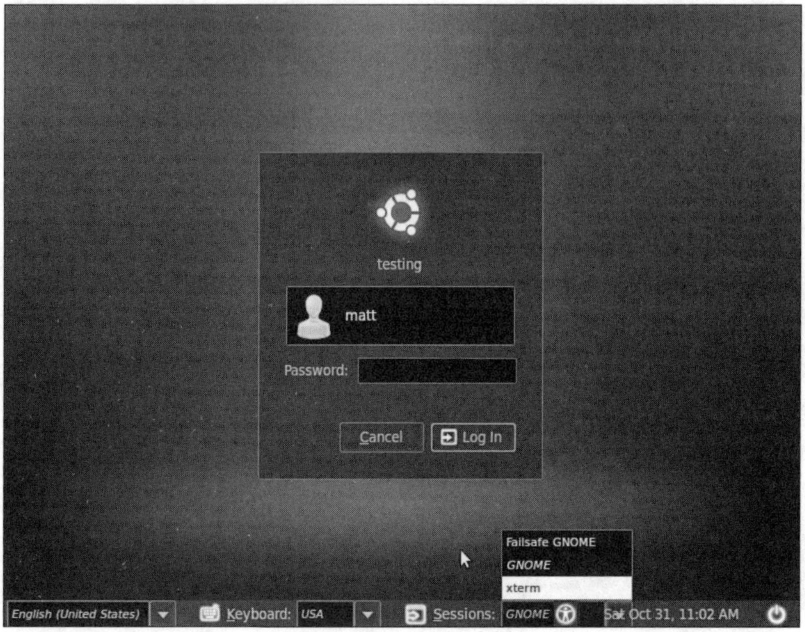

FIGURE 3.15   Use the Select Session option to select the desktop environment of your choice before you log in.

Changing Window Managers

Ubuntu makes it fairly painless to switch to another window manager or desktop environment. By *desktop environment*, we refer to not only the window manager but also the suite of related applications such as productivity or configuration tools.

First of all you need to ensure that you have the relevant desktop environment installed on your system and the easiest way to do this is by installing the relevant *-desktop package (as described earlier in the sidebar, "The Ubuntu Family". You can do this either at the command line with a simple `apt-get install kubuntu-desktop` (in the case of a KDE desktop) or you can use synaptic to install the relevant packages; just search for desktop and look for Xubuntu or Kubuntu. Once the download and installation has completed (you might want to grab a coffee while you wait) you are all set to change environment.

The first thing you need to do is to log out of Ubuntu by going to System, Quit. Then select the Log Out option. After a couple of seconds you will arrive at the graphical login prompt (as shown in Figure 3.15). At this point, press the F10 key to open the drop-down menu and click Select Session.

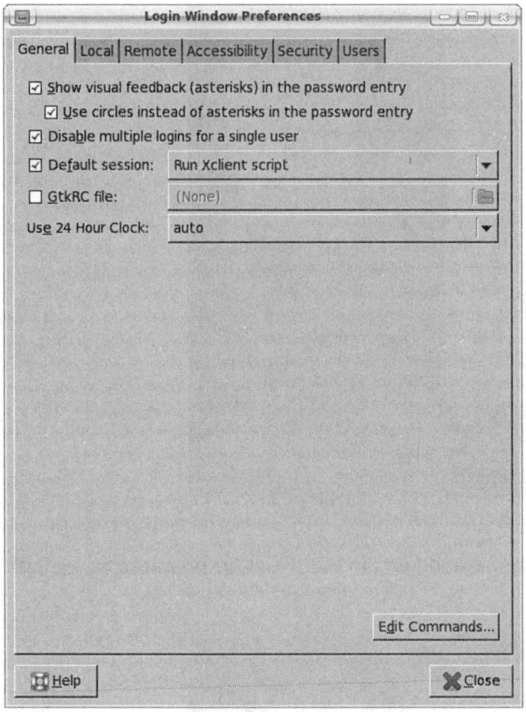

FIGURE 3.16 When you're ready to switch to another environment, use the Login Window to make the jump.

Here you can choose to switch your session to KDE (for example) and once you've clicked OK you'll be asked whether you want to make this a permanent change or just for one session (i.e., to try it out). At this point, it's probably better to choose 'For this session only'. Enter your user name and password to log in to your new desktop environment. Don't worry; because you selected For This Session Only you haven't yet committed yourself to switching permanently. Take the opportunity to try the new environment and make your mind up if you want to switch to it full time.

If you have made your mind up to switch to another environment full time then you can do it by taking one of two routes. The first one is to go to the Login Window (found under System, Administration, Login Window under GNOME and also found under the Kicker Menu, System, Login Window within KDE) and select the relevant window manager from the Default Session drop-down list, as shown in Figure 3.16.

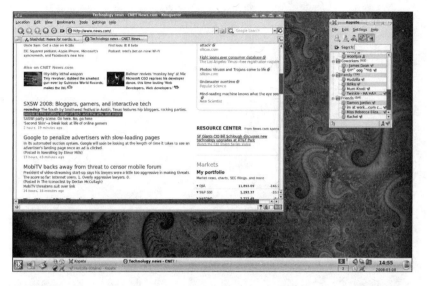

FIGURE 3.17   Unlimited customization options abound within KDE; just be prepared to switch!

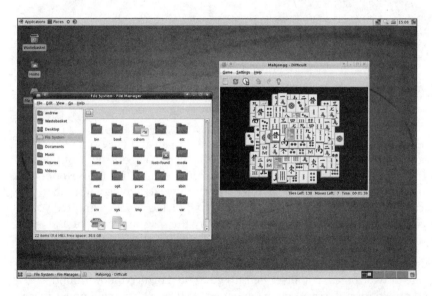

FIGURE 3.18   XFce—lightweight and simplicity, molded together in a great package.

Alternatively you can do it from the login window by pressing F10, clicking Select Session, choosing your desired window manager and selecting Make Default. This will set your default window manager to your specific choice.

Regardless of which route you take it's easy to change back should you not like your new environment.

The next section gives you a brief introduction to the two other main window managers other than GNOME that are available either in Kubuntu or Xubuntu.

KDE—The Other Environment

One of the great things about Ubuntu is the choice it allows you. When Ubuntu was originally released, it favored the GNOME desktop, but fairly early on the decision was made to create a KDE alternative named Kubuntu. If you install the `kubuntu-desktop` package (either using `apt-get` or `synaptic`) then you will have access to KDE and the associated Kubuntu applications.

3

KDE is somewhat different from GNOME in that it uses the QT libraries rather than GTK libraries, so the windows and other elements look different. Linus Torvalds himself has in the past expressed a distinct preference for KDE, and it also helps that KDE allows you to customize your working environment in pretty much any way imaginable.

A standard KDE desktop is shown in Figure 3.17.

XFce

XFce is another desktop environment, suitable for computers with not much memory or processing power. It's based upon the same GTK libraries that are in use by GNOME, so it shares some of the look and feel of the GNOME desktop. That said, it comes bundled with a number of Xfce-specific applications to replace GNOME tools such as nautilus.

Some people just prefer the simplicity of Xfce, so we will leave it up to you if you want to use it. You can get access to it by installing the xubuntu-desktop package (either with apt-get or synaptic) and a sample desktop is shown in Figure 3.18.

Reference

▶ http://www.x.org/—Curators of the X Window System.

▶ http://www.x.org/Downloads_mirror.html—Want to download the source to the latest revision of X? Start at this list of mirror sites.

▶ http://www.xfree86.org/—Home of The XFree86 Project, Inc., which provided a graphical interface for Linux for nearly 10 years.

▶ http://www.kde.org/—The place to get started when learning about KDE and the latest developments.

▶ http://www.gnome.org/—The launch point for more information about GNOME, links to new clients, and GNOME development projects.

▶ http://www.compiz.org/—The official page for the Compiz project, including Compiz Fusion, a set of plugins for the Compiz window manager.

▶ http://www.xfce.org/—The official home page for the XFce project.

# CHAPTER 4

Command Line Quickstart

The command line is one of the most powerful tools available for use with Ubuntu, and indeed Linux. Knowledge of the commands associated with it and also how to string them together will make your life with Ubuntu much easier.

This chapter looks at some of the basic commands that you need to know to be productive at the command line. You will find out how to get to the command line, and also get to grips with some of the commands used to navigate around the file system. Later on in this book is the Command Line Masterclass (Chapter 30), which explores the subject in more depth. The skills you learn in this chapter will give you confidence when you're called upon to work at the command line.

What Is the Command Line?

Hang around Linux users for any length of time and it will not be long before you hear them speak in hushed tones about the command line or the terminal. Quite rightly too, as the command line offers a unique and powerful way to interact with Linux. However, for the most part you may never need to access the command line because Ubuntu offers a slew of graphical tools that enable you to configure most things on your system.

But sometimes things go wrong and you may not have the luxury of a graphical interface to work with. It is in these situations that a fundamental understanding of the command line and its uses can be a real life saver.

> **NOTE**
>
> In Chapter 3, "Working with Gnome," you learned about BulletProofX, a project whose goal it is to always provide a fallback if your X server fails. Under Ubuntu 9.10, this has been further improved, although there will still be some instances where even BulletProofX won't save you.
>
> Don't be tempted to skip over this chapter as irrelevant; rather, work through the chapter and ensure that you are comfortable with the command line before moving on.

It is tempting to think of the command line as the product of some sort of black and arcane art, and in some ways it can appear to be extremely difficult and complicated to use. However, perseverance is key and by the end of this chapter you should at least be comfortable with using the command line and ready to move onto Chapter 30, "Command Line Masterclass."

More importantly, though, you will be able to make your way around a command line–based system, which you are likely to encounter if you work within a server environment.

This chapter introduces you to a number of commands, including commands that enable you to do the following tasks:

▶ **Perform routine tasks**—Logging in and out, using the text console, changing passwords, listing and navigating directories

▶ **Implement basic file management**—Creating files and folders, copying or moving them around the file system, renaming and ultimately deleting them (if necessary)

▶ **Execute basic system management**—Shutting down or rebooting, reading man pages, and using text-based tools to edit system configuration files

The information in this chapter is valuable for individual users or system administrators who are new to Linux and are learning to use the command line for the first time.

> **TIP**
>
> Those of you who have used a computer for many years will probably have come into contact with MS-DOS, in which case being presented with a black screen will fill you with a sense of nostalgia. Don't get too comfy; the command line in Linux is far superior to its distant MS-DOS cousin. Whereas MS-DOS skills are transferable only to other MS-DOS environments, the skills that you learn at the Linux command line can be transferred easily to other Unix-like operating systems, such as Solaris, OpenBSD, FreeBSD, and even Mac OS X, which allows you access to the terminal.

User Accounts

One concept you will have to get used to is that of user-based security. By and large, only two types of users will access the system as actual users. The first type is the regular user, of which you created one when you started Ubuntu for the first time (see Chapter 1, "Installing Ubuntu"). These users can change anything that is specific to them, such as the wallpaper on the desktop, their personal preferences, and so on. Note that the emphasis should be on anything that is specific to them, as it prevents regular users from making system-wide changes that could affect other users.

To make system-wide changes, you need to use super-user privileges which you should have if your account was the first one specified (i.e. when you specified a user during the installation). With super-user privileges you basically have access to the entire system and can carry out any task, even destructive ones! In order to use your super-user privileges you need to prefix the command you wish to execute with the command sudo. When you hit enter (after typing the remaining command) you will be prompted for your password, which you should type in followed by the Enter key. Ubuntu will then carry out the command, but with super-user privileges.

An example of the destructive nature of working as the super-user can be found in the age-old example of $sudo `rm` `-rf` `/`, which erases all the data on your hard drive. You need to be especially careful when using your super-user privileges, otherwise you may make irreparable damage to your system.

Don't let this worry you, though, as the ability to work as the super-user is fundamental to a healthy Linux system. Without it you would not be able to install new software, edit system configuration files, or do any number of administration tasks. By the end of this chapter you will feel comfortable working with your super-user privileges and be able to adequately administer your system.

Ubuntu works slightly differently to other Linux distributions by giving users super-user privileges by default. If you work with any other Linux distro you will quickly come across the `root` user, which is a super-user account. So rather than having to type in sudo before every command, the root account can simply issue the command and not have to worry about entering a password. You can tell when you are working at a root prompt because you will see the pound sign (#). Within Ubuntu the `root` account is disabled by default in preference to giving super-user privileges to users. If you wish to enable the root account then issue the command sudo `passwd`. When prompted, enter your user password. You will then be asked for a new UNIX password; this will be the password for the root account, so make sure and remember it. You will also be prompted to repeat the password, in case you've made any mistakes. Once you've typed it in and pressed Enter, the `root` account will now be active. You'll find out how to switch to `root` later on.

An alternative way of getting a root prompt, without having to enable the root account, is to issue the command sudo `-i`. After entering your password you will find yourself at a root prompt (#). Do what you need to do and when you are finished, type `exit` and press Enter to return to your usual prompt.

As with most things, Ubuntu offers you a number of ways to access the command line. You can use the Terminal entry in Applications, Accessories, but by far the simplest way is to press Ctrl + Alt + F1. Ubuntu switches to a black screen and a traditional login prompt that resembles the following:

```
Ubuntu 9.10 karmic karmic-dev tty1
karmic-dev login:
```

TIP

This is actually one of six virtual consoles that Ubuntu provides for your use. After you have accessed a virtual console, you can use the Alt key and F1 through F6 to switch to a different console. If you want to get back to the graphical interface, press Alt + F7. You can also switch between consoles by holding the Alt key and pressing either the left or the right cursor key to move down or up a console, such as tty1 to tty2.

Ubuntu is waiting for you to log in as a user, so go ahead and enter your username and press the return key. Ubuntu then prompts you for your password, which you should enter. Note that Ubuntu does not show any characters while you are typing your password in. This is a good thing because it prevents any shoulder surfers from seeing what you've typed or the length of the password.

Hitting the Return key drops you to a shell prompt, signified by the dollar sign:

```
andrew@karmic-dev ~]$
```

This particular prompt tells me that I am logged in as the user andrew on the system karmic-dev and I am currently in my home directory (Linux uses the tilde as shorthand for the home directory).

TIP

Navigating through the system at the command line can get confusing at times, especially when a directory name occurs in several different places. Fortunately, Linux includes a simple command that tells you exactly where you are in the file system. It's easy to remember because the command is just an abbreviation of present working directory, so type **pwd** at any point to get the full path of your location. For example, typing pwd after following these instructions shows /home/yourusername, meaning that you are currently in your home directory.

Using the pwd command can save you a lot of frustration when you have changed directory half a dozen times and have lost track.

Another way to quickly access the terminal is to go to Applications, Accessories and choose the Terminal entry. Ubuntu opens up gnome-terminal, which allows you to access the terminal while remaining in Gnome. This time, the terminal appears as black text on a white background. Accessing the terminal this way, or by using the Ctrl + Alt + F1 method makes no difference because you are interacting directly with the terminal itself.

Navigating Through the File System

Use the cd command to navigate through the Ubuntu file system. This command is generally used with a specific directory location or pathname, like this:

```
$ cd /etc/apt/
```

Under Ubuntu, the cd command can also be used with several shortcuts. For example, to quickly move up to the *parent* (higher-level) directory, use the cd command like this:

```
$ cd ..
```

To return to one's home directory from anywhere in the Linux file system, use the cd command like this:

```
$ cd
```

You can also use the $HOME shell environment variable to accomplish the same thing. Type this command and press Enter to return to your home directory:

```
$ cd $HOME
```

You can accomplish the same thing by using the tilde (~) like this:

```
$ cd ~
```

Don't forget the pwd command to remind you where you are within the file system!

Another important command to use is the ls command, which lists the contents of the current directory. It's commonly used by itself, but a number of options (or switches) available for ls give you more information. For instance, the following command returns a listing of all the files and directories within the current directory, including any hidden files (denoted by a . prefix) as well as a full listing, so it will include details such as the permissions, owner and group, size and last modified time and date:

```
$ ls -al
```

You can also issue the command

```
$ ls -R
```

which scans and lists all the contents of the sub-directories of the current directory. This might be a lot of information, so you may want to redirect the output to a text file so you can browse through it at your leisure by using the following:

```
$ ls -alR > listing.txt
```

TIP

The previous command sends the output of `ls -alR` to a file called listing.txt, and demonstrates part of the power of the Linux command line. At the command line you are able to use files as inputs to commands, or generate files as outputs as shown. For more information about combining commands, see Chapter 30.

We've included a table showing some of the top-level directories that are part of a standard Linux distro in Table 4.1.

TABLE 4.1   Basic Linux Directories

Name	Description
/	The root directory
/bin	Essential commands
/boot	Boot loader files, Linux kernel
/dev	Device files
/etc	System configuration files
/home	User home directories
/initrd	Initial RAM disk boot support (used during boot time)
/lib	Shared libraries, kernel modules
/lost+found	Directory for recovered files (if found after a file system check)
/media	Mount point for removable media, such as DVDs and floppy disks
/mnt	Usual mount point for local, remote file systems
/opt	Add-on software packages
/proc	Kernel information, process control
/root	Super-user (root) home
/sbin	System commands (mostly root only)
/srv	Holds information relating to services that run on your system
/sys	Real-time information on devices used by the kernel
/tmp	Temporary files
/usr	Secondary software file hierarchy
/var	Variable data (such as logs); spooled files

Knowing these directories can aid you in partitioning in any future systems, letting you choose to put certain directories on their own distinct partition.

Some of the important directories in Table 4.1, such as those containing user and root commands or system configuration files, are discussed in the following sections. You use and edit files under these directories when you use Ubuntu.

Linux also includes a number of GNU commands you can use to search the file system. These include the following:

▶ `whereis command`—Returns the location of the command and its man page.

▶ `whatis command`—Returns a one-line synopsis from the command's man page.

▶ `locate file`—Returns locations of all matching file(s); an extremely fast method of searching your system because `locate` searches a database containing an index of all files on your system. However, this database (about 4MB in size and named `slocate.db`, under the `/var/lib/slocate` directory) is built daily at 4:20 a.m. by default, and does not contain pathnames to files created during the workday or in the evening. If you do not keep your machine on constantly, you can run the `updatedb` command either using `sudo` or by using the `root` account to manually start the building of the database.

▶ `apropos subject`—Returns a list of commands related to subject.

Managing Files with the Shell

Managing files in your home directory involves using one or more easily remembered commands. If you have any familiarity with the now-ancient DOS, you recognize some of these commands (although their names are different from those you remember). Basic file management operations include paging (reading), moving, renaming, copying, searching, and deleting files and directories. These commands include the following:

▶ `cat filename`—Outputs contents of filename to display

▶ `less filename`—Allows scrolling while reading contents of filename

▶ `mv file1 file2`—Renames file1 to file2

▶ `mv file dir`—Moves file to specified directory

▶ `cp file1 file2`—Copies file1 and creates file2

▶ `rm file`—Deletes file

▶ `rmdir dir`—Deletes directory (if empty)

▶ `grep string file(s)`—Searches through files(s) and displays lines containing matching string

Note that each of these commands can be used with pattern-matching strings known as *wildcards* or *expressions*. For example, to delete all files in the current directory beginning with the letters abc, you can use an expression beginning with the first three letters of the desired filenames. An asterisk (*) is then appended to match all these files. Use a command line with the `rm` command like this:

```
$ rm abc*
```

Linux shells recognize many types of filenaming wildcards, but this is different from the capabilities of Linux commands supporting the use of more complex expressions. You learn more about using wildcards in Chapter 11, "Automating Tasks."

> **NOTE**
>
> Learn more about using expressions by reading the grep manual pages (man grep).

Working with Compressed Files

Another file management operation is compression and decompression of files, or the creation, listing, and expansion of file and directory archives. Linux distributions usually include several compression utilities you can use to create, compress, expand, or list the contents of compressed files and archives. These commands include

- ▶ bunzip2—Expands a compressed file

- ▶ bzip2—Compresses or expands files and directories

- ▶ gunzip—Expands a compressed file

- ▶ gzip—Compresses or expands files and directories

- ▶ tar—Creates, expands, or lists the contents of compressed or uncompressed file or directory archives known as *tape archives* or *tarballs*

Most of these commands are easy to use. The tar command, however, has a somewhat complex (although capable) set of command-line options and syntax. Even so, you can quickly learn to use tar by remembering a few simple invocations on the command line. For example, to create a compressed archive of a directory, use tar's czf options like this:

```
$ tar czf dirname.tgz dirname
```

The result is a compressed archive (a file ending in .tgz) of the specified directory (and all files and directories under it). Add the letter v to the preceding options to view the list of files added during compression and archiving. To list the contents of the compressed archive, substitute the c option with the letter t, like this:

```
$ tar tzf archive
```

Of course, if many files are in the archive, a better invocation (to easily read or scroll through the output) is

```
$ tar tzf archive ¦ less
```

> **TIP**
>
> In the previous code example, we used a pipe character (|). Each pipe sends the output of the first command to the next command. This is another of the benefits of the command line under Linux—you can string several commands together to get the desired results.

To expand the contents of a compressed archive, use tar's zxf options, like so:

```
$ tar zxf archive
```

The `tar` utility decompresses the specified archive and extracts the contents in the current directory.

Use Essential Commands from the `/bin` and `/sbin` Directories

The `/bin` directory (about 5MB if you do a full install) contains essential commands used by the system for running and booting Linux. In general, only the root operator uses the commands in the `/sbin` directory. Many (though not all) these commands are *statically* linked which means that such commands do not depend on software libraries residing under the `/lib` or `/usr/lib` directories. Nearly all the other applications on your system are *dynamically* linked—meaning that they require external software libraries (also known as *shared* libraries) to run.

Use and Edit Files in the `/etc` Directory

More than 10MB of system configuration files and directories reside under the `/etc` directory if you install all the software included with this book. Some major software packages, such as Apache, OpenSSH, and `xinetd`, have directories of configuration files under `/etc`. Other important system-related configuration files in `/etc` are

- ▶ `fstab`—The file system table is a text file listing each hard drive, CD-ROM, floppy, or other storage device attached to your PC. The table indexes each device's partition information with a place in your Linux file system (directory layout) and lists other options for each device when used with Linux (see Chapter 32, "Kernel and Module Management"). Nearly all entries in `fstab` can be manipulated by root using the `mount` command.

- ▶ `modprobe.d/`—This folder holds all the instructions to load kernel modules that are required as part of the system startup, and replaces the historic modprobe.conf file.

- ▶ `passwd`—The list of users for the system, along with user account information. The contents of this file can be changed by various programs, such as `useradd` or `chsh`.

- ▶ `shells`—A list of approved shells (command-line interfaces).

Protect the Contents of User Directories—`/home`

The most important data on a Linux system resides in the user's directories, found under the `/home` directory. Segregating the system and user data can be helpful in preventing data loss and making the process of backing up easier. For example, having user data reside on a separate file system or mounted from a remote computer on the network might help shield users from data loss in the event of a system hardware failure.

Use the Contents of the `/proc` Directory to Interact with the Kernel

The content of the `/proc` directory is created from memory and exists only while Linux is running. This directory contains special "files" that either extract information from or send information to the kernel. Many Linux utilities extract information from dynamically created directories and files under this directory, also known as a *virtual file system*. For example, the `free` command obtains its information from a file named `meminfo`:

```
$ free
             total       used       free     shared    buffers     cached
Mem:        1026320     822112     204208         0      41232     481412
-/+ buffers/cache:       299468     726852
Swap:       2031608          0    2031608
```

This information constantly changes as the system is used. You can get the same information by using the cat command to see the contents of the meminfo file:

```
$ cat /proc/meminfo
MemTotal:       1026320 kB
MemFree:         204200 kB
Buffers:          41252 kB
Cached:          481412 kB
SwapCached:           0 kB
Active:          307232 kB
Inactive:        418224 kB
HighTotal:       122692 kB
HighFree:           244 kB
LowTotal:        903628 kB
LowFree:         203956 kB
SwapTotal:      2031608 kB
SwapFree:       2031608 kB
Dirty:                0 kB
Writeback:            0 kB
AnonPages:       202804 kB
Mapped:           87864 kB
Slab:             21736 kB
SReclaimable:     12484 kB
SUnreclaim:        9252 kB
PageTables:        5060 kB
NFS_Unstable:         0 kB
Bounce:               0 kB
CommitLimit:    2544768 kB
Committed_AS:    712024 kB
VmallocTotal:    114680 kB
VmallocUsed:       6016 kB
VmallocChunk:    108148 kB
HugePages_Total:      0
HugePages_Free:       0
HugePages_Rsvd:       0
Hugepagesize:      4096 kB
```

The /proc directory can also be used to dynamically alter the behavior of a running Linux kernel by "echoing" numerical values to specific files under the /proc/sys directory. For example, to "turn on" kernel protection against one type of denial of service (DOS) attack known as *SYN flooding,* use the echo command to send the number 1 (one) to the following /proc path:

```
$ sudo echo 1 >/proc/sys/net/ipv4/tcp_syncookies
```

Other ways to use the /proc directory include

▶ Getting CPU information, such as the family, type, and speed from /proc/cpuinfo.

▶ Viewing important networking information under /proc/net, such as active interfaces information under /proc/net/dev, routing information in /proc/net/route, and network statistics in /proc/net/netstat.

▶ Retrieving file system information.

▶ Reporting media mount point information via USB; for example, the Linux kernel reports what device to use to access files (such as /dev/sda) if a USB camera or hard drive is detected on the system. You can use the dmesg command to see this information.

▶ Getting the kernel version in /proc/version, performance information such as uptime in /proc/uptime, or other statistics such as CPU load, swap file usage, and processes in /proc/stat.

Work with Shared Data in the /usr Directory

The /usr directory contains software applications, libraries, and other types of shared data for use by anyone on the system. Many Linux system administrators give /usr its own partition. A number of subdirectories under /usr contain manual pages (/usr/share/man), software package shared files (/usr/share/*name_of_package,* such as /usr/share/emacs), additional application or software package documentation (/usr/share/doc), and an entire subdirectory tree of locally built and installed software, /usr/local.

Temporary File Storage in the /tmp Directory

As its name implies, the /tmp directory is used for temporary file storage; as you use Linux, various programs create files in this directory.

Access Variable Data Files in the /var Directory

The /var directory contains subdirectories used by various system services for spooling and logging. Many of these variable data files, such as print spooler queues, are temporary, whereas others, such as system and kernel logs, are renamed and rotated in use. Incoming electronic mail is usually directed to files under /var/spool/mail.

Linux also uses /var for other important system services. These include the top-most File Transfer Protocol (FTP) directory under /var/ftp (see Chapter 18, "Remote File Serving with FTP"), and the Apache web server's initial home page directory for the system, /var/www/html. (See Chapter 17, "Apache Web Server Management," for more information on using Apache.)

Logging In to and Working with Linux

You can access and use a Linux system in a number of ways. One way is at the console with a monitor, keyboard, and mouse attached to the PC. Another way is via a serial console, either by dial-up via a modem or a PC running a terminal emulator and connected to the Linux PC via a null modem cable. You can also connect to your system through a wired or wireless network, using the telnet or ssh commands. The information in this section shows you how to access and use the Linux system, using physical and remote text-based logins.

> **NOTE**
>
> This chapter focuses on text-based logins and use of Linux. Graphical logins and using a graphical desktop are described in Chapter 3, "Working with Gnome."

Text-based Console Login

If you sit down at your PC and log in to a Linux system that has not been booted to a graphical login, you see a prompt similar to this one:

```
Ubuntu 9.10 karmic karmic-dev tty1
karmic-dev login:
```

Your prompt might vary, depending on the version of Ubuntu you are using. In any event, at this prompt, type in your username and press Enter. When you are prompted for your password, type it in and press Enter.

> **NOTE**
>
> Note that your password is not echoed back to you, which is a good idea. Why is it a good idea? Well, people are prevented from looking over your shoulder and seeing your screen input. It is not difficult to guess that a five-letter password might correspond to the user's spouse's first name!

Logging Out

Use the exit or logout commands to exit your session. Type the command and press Enter. You are then returned to the login prompt. If you use virtual consoles, remember to exit each console before leaving your PC. (Otherwise, someone could easily sit down and use your account.)

Logging In and Out from a Remote Computer

Although you can happily log in on your computer, an act known as a *local* login, you can also log in to your computer via a network connection from a remote computer. Linux-based operating systems provide a number of remote access commands you can use to log in to other computers on your local area network (LAN), wide area network (WAN), or the Internet. Note that not only must you have an account on the remote computer, but the remote computer must be configured to support remote logins—otherwise, you won't be able to log in.

NOTE

See Chapter 14, "Networking" to see how to set up network interfaces with Linux to support remote network logins and Chapter 11 to see how to start remote access services (such as sshd).

The best and most secure way (barring future exploits) to log in to a remote Linux computer is to use the ssh or Secure Shell client. Your login and session are encrypted while you work on the remote computer. The ssh client features many different command-line options, but can be simply used with the name or IP address of the remote computer, like this:

```
[andrew@karmic-dev ~]$ ssh 192.168.0.41
The authenticity of host '192.168.0.41 (192.168.0.41)' can't be established.
RSA key fingerprint is e1:db:6c:da:3f:fc:56:1b:52:f9:94:e0:d1:1d:31:50.
Are you sure you want to continue connecting (yes/no)?
```

yes

The first time you connect with a remote computer using ssh, Linux displays the remote computer's encrypted identity key and asks you to verify the connection. After you type **yes** and press Enter, you are warned that the remote computer's identity (key) has been entered in a file named known_hosts under the .ssh directory in your home directory. You are also prompted to enter your password:

```
Warning: Permanently added '192.168.0.41' (RSA) \
to the list of known hosts.
andrew@192.168.0.41's password:
andrew~$
```

After entering your password, you can then work on the remote computer. Again, everything you enter on the keyboard in communication with the remote computer is encrypted. Use the exit or logout commands to exit your session and return to the shell on your computer.

Using Environment Variables

A number of in-memory variables are assigned and loaded by default when the user logs in. These variables are known as shell *environment variables*, which can be used by various commands to get information about your environment, such as the type of system you are running, your home directory, and the shell in use. Environment variables are used by Linux operating systems to help tailor the computing environment of your system, and include helpful specifications and setup, such as default locations of executable files and software libraries. If you begin writing shell scripts, you might use environment variables in your scripts. Until then, you only need to be aware of what environment variables are and do.

The following list includes a number of environment variables, along with descriptions of how the shell uses them:

- ▶ PWD—To provide the name of the current working directory, used by the pwd command (such as /home/andrew/foo)

- ▶ USER—To declare the user's name, such as andrew

- ▶ LANG—To set language defaults, such as English

- ▶ SHELL—To declare the name and location of the current shell, such as /bin/bash

- ▶ PATH—To set the default location of executable files, such as /bin, /usr/bin, and so on

- ▶ TERM—To set the type of terminal in use, such as vt100, which can be important when using screen-oriented programs, such as text editors

- ▶ MACHINE—To declare system type, system architecture, and so on

---

NOTE

Each shell can have its own feature set and language syntax, as well as a unique set of default environment variables. See Chapter 15, "Remote Access for SSH and Telnet," for more information about using the different shells included with Ubuntu.

At the command line, you can use the env or printenv commands to display these environment variables, like so:

```
$ env
SSH_AGENT_PID=5761

SHELL=/bin/bash

DESKTOP_STARTUP_ID=

TERM=xterm
```

```
GTK_RC_FILES=/etc/gtk/gtkrc:/home/andrew/.gtkrc-1.2-gnome2

WINDOWID=56623199

USER=andrew

...
USERNAME=andrew

PATH=/usr/local/sbin:/usr/local/bin:/usr/sbin:/usr/bin:/sbin:/bin:/usr/games

DESKTOP_SESSION=default

GDM_XSERVER_LOCATION=local

PWD=/usr/local

LANG=en_GB.UTF-8

GNOME_KEYRING_PID=5714

GDM_LANG=en_GB.UTF-8

SHLVL=1

HOME=/home/andrew

LOGNAME=andrew

XDG_DATA_DIRS=/usr/local/share/:/usr/share/:/usr/share/gdm/

...
LESSOPEN=| /usr/bin/lesspipe %s

WINDOWPATH=7

DISPLAY=:0.0

LESSCLOSE=/usr/bin/lesspipe %s %s

COLORTERM=gnome-terminal

XAUTHORITY=/home/andrew/.Xauthority

_=/usr/bin/env
```

OLDPWD=/usr/share/locale

This abbreviated list shows a few common variables. These variables are set by configuration or *resource* files contained in the /etc, /etc/skel, or user /home directory. You can find default settings for bash, for example, in /etc/profile, /etc/bashrc, .bashrc, or .bash_profile files installed in your home directory. Read the man page for bash for details about using these configuration files.

One of the most important environment variables is $PATH, which defines the location of executable files. For example, if, as a regular user, you try to use a command that is not located in your $PATH (such as the imaginary command command), you will see something like this:

$ command
-bash: command: command not found

NOTE

If the command that you're trying to execute exists, but is not yet installed on your system, then Ubuntu will prompt you to install it, even giving you the correct command to do so.

However, you might know that command is definitely installed on your system, and you can verify this by using the whereis command, like so:

$ whereis command
command: /sbin/command

You can also run the command by typing its full pathname, or complete directory specification like this:

$ /sbin/command

As you can see in this example, the command command is indeed installed. What happened is that by default, the /sbin directory is not in your $PATH. One of the reasons for this is that commands under the /sbin directory are normally intended to be run only by root. You can add /sbin to your $PATH by editing the file .bash_profile in your home directory (if you use the bash shell by default, like most Linux users). Look for the following line:

PATH=$PATH:$HOME/bin

You can then edit this file, perhaps using the vi editor (discussed in this chapter), to add the /sbin directory like so:

PATH=$PATH:**/sbin:**$HOME/bin

Save the file. The next time you log in, the /sbin directory is in your $PATH. One way to use this change right away is to read in the new settings in .bash_profile by using the bash shell's source command like so:

```
$ source .bash_profile
```

You can now run commands located in the /sbin directory without the need to explicitly type the full pathname.

Some Linux commands also use environment variables, for example, to acquire configuration information (such as a communications program looking for a variable such as BAUD_RATE, which might denote a default modem speed).

To experiment with the environment variables, you can modify the PS1 variable to manipulate the appearance of your shell prompt. If you are working with bash, you can use its built-in export command to change the shell prompt. For example, if your default shell prompt looks like

```
[andrew@laptop ~]$
```

You can change its appearance by using the PS1 variable like this:

```
$ PS1='$OSTYPE r00lz ->'
```

After you press Enter, you see

```
linux-gnu r00lz ->
```

> **NOTE**
>
> See the bash man page for other variables you can use for prompt settings.

Using the Text Editors

Linux distributions include a number of applications known as *text editors* that you can use to create text files or edit system configuration files. Text editors are similar to word processing programs, but generally have fewer features, work only with text files, and might or might not support spell checking or formatting. The text editors range in features and ease of use, but are found on nearly every Linux distribution. The number of editors installed on your system depends on what software packages you've installed on the system.

Some of the console-based text editors are

▶ emacs—The comprehensive GNU emacs editing environment, which is much more than an editor; see the section "Working with emacs" later in this chapter

▶ joe—Joe's Own Editor, a text editor, which can be used to emulate other editors

▶ nano—A simple text editor similar to the pico text editor included with the pine email program

▶ vim—An improved, compatible version of the vi text editor (which we call vi in the rest of this chapter because it has a symbolic link named vi and a symbolically linked manual page)

Note that not all text editors described here are *screen oriented*. Some of the text editors for the X Window System, which provide a graphical interface, such as menu bars, buttons, scrollbars and so on, are

▶ gedit—A GUI text editor for GNOME

▶ kate—A simple KDE text editor

▶ kedit—Another simple KDE text editor

A good reason to learn how to use a text-based editor, such as vi, is that system maintenance and recovery operations generally never take place during X Window sessions (negating the use of a GUI editor). Many larger, more complex and capable editors do not work when Linux is booted to its single-user or maintenance mode. If anything does go wrong with your system, you probably won't be able to get into the X Window system, making knowledge and experience of using both the command line and text editors such as vi important. Make a point of opening some of the editors and playing around with them; you never know—you might just thank me someday!

Another reason to learn how to use a text-based editor under the Linux console mode is so that you can edit text files through dial-up or network shell sessions because many servers do not host graphical desktops.

Working with vi

The editor found on nearly every Unix and Linux system is, without a doubt, the vi editor, originally written by Bill Joy. This simple-to-use but incredibly capable editor features a somewhat cryptic command set, but you can put it to use with only a few commands. Although more experienced Unix and Linux users continue to use vi extensively during computing sessions, many newer users might prefer learning an easier-to-use text editor such as pico or GNU nano. Die-hard GNU fans and programmers definitely use emacs.

That said, learning how to use vi is a good idea. You might need to edit files on a Linux system with a minimal install, or a remote server without a more extensive offering of installed text editors. Chances are better than good that vi will be available.

You can start an editing session by using the vi command like this:

```
$ vi file.txt
```

The vi command works by using an insert (or editing) mode, and a viewing (or command) mode.

When you first start editing, you are in the viewing mode. You can use your cursor or other navigation keys (as shown later) to scroll through the text. To start editing, press the **i** key to insert text or the **a** key to append text. When finished, use the Esc key to toggle out of the insert or append modes and into the viewing (or command) mode. To enter a command, type a colon (**:**), followed by the command, such as **w** to write the file, and press Enter.

Although vi supports many complex editing operations and numerous commands, you can accomplish work by using a few basic commands. These basic vi commands are

- **Cursor movement**—h, j, k, l (left, down, up, and right)
- **Delete character**—x
- **Delete line**—dd
- **Mode toggle**—Esc, Insert (or i)
- **Quit**—:q
- **Quit without saving**—:q!
- **Run a shell command**—:sh (use 'exit' to return)
- **Save file**—:w
- **Text search**—/

NOTE

Use the vimtutor command to quickly learn how to use vi's keyboard commands. The tutorial takes less than 30 minutes, and it teaches new users how to start or stop the editor, navigate files, insert and delete text, and perform search, replace, and insert operations.

Working with emacs

Richard M. Stallman's GNU emacs editor, like vi, is included with Ubuntu and nearly every other Linux distribution. Unlike other Unix and Linux text editors, emacs is much more than a simple text editor—it is an editing environment and can be used to compile and build programs, act as an electronic diary, appointment book and calendar, compose and send electronic mail, read Usenet news, and even play games. The reason for this capability is that emacs contains a built-in language interpreter that uses the Elisp (emacs LISP) programming language. emacs is not installed in Ubuntu by default; instead you'll need to install it using apt-get or synaptic. The package you need is simply emacs.

You can start an emacs editing session like this_FIRST:

```
$ emacs file.txt
```

> **TIP**
>
> If you start emacs when using X11, the editor launches in its own floating window. To force emacs to display inside a terminal window instead of its own window (which can be useful if the window is a login at a remote computer), use the -nw command-line option like this: emacs -nw file.txt.

The emacs editor uses an extensive set of keystroke and named commands, but you can work with it by using a basic command subset. Many of these basic commands require you to hold down the Ctrl key, or to first press a *meta* key (generally mapped to the Alt key). The basic commands are listed in Table 4.2.

TABLE 4.2   Emacs Editing Commands

Action	Command
Abort	Ctrl+g
Cursor left	Ctrl+b
Cursor down	Ctrl+n
Cursor right	Ctrl+f
Cursor up	Ctrl+p
Delete character	Ctrl+d
Delete line	Ctrl+k
Go to start of line	Ctrl+a
Go to end of line	Ctrl+e
Help	Ctrl+h
Quit	Ctrl+x, Ctrl+c
Save As	Ctrl+x, Ctrl+w
Save file	Ctrl+x, Ctrl+s
Search backward	Ctrl+r
Search forward	Ctrl+s
Start tutorial	Ctrl+h, t
Undo	Ctrl+x, u

Working with Permissions

Under Linux (and Unix), everything in the file system, including directories and devices, is a file. And every file on your system has an accompanying set of permissions based on ownership. These permissions form the basis for security under Linux, and designate each file's read, write, and execute permission for you, members of your group, and all others on the system.

You can examine the default permissions for a file you create by using the umask command, or as a practical example, by using the touch command and then the ls command's long-format listing like this:

```
$ touch file
$ ls -l file
-rw-r—r— 1 andrew andrew 0 Feb 1 20:54 file
```

In this example, the touch command is used to quickly create a file. The ls command then reports on the file, displaying information (from left to right) in the first field of output (such as -rw-r—r— previously):

▶ **The type of file created**—Common indicators of the type of file are a leading letter in the output. A blank (which is represented by a dash in the preceding example) designates a plain file, d designates a directory, c designates a character device (such as /dev/ttyS0), and b is used for a block device (such as /dev/sda).

▶ **Permissions**—Read, write, and execute permissions for the owner, group, and all others on the system. (You learn more about these permissions later in this section.)

▶ **Number of links to the file**—The number one (1) designates that there is only one file, whereas any other number indicates that there might be one or more hard-linked files. Links are created with the ln command. A hard-linked file is an exact copy of the file, but it might be located elsewhere on the system. Symbolic links of directories can also be created, but only the root operator can create a hard link of a directory.

▶ **The owner**—The account that created or owns the file; you can change this designation by using the chown command.

▶ **The group**—The group of users allowed to access the file; you can change this designation by using the chgrp command.

▶ **File size and creation/modification date**—The last two elements indicate the size of the file in bytes and the date the file was created or last modified.

Assigning Permissions

Under Linux, permissions are grouped by owner, group, and others, with read, write, and execute permission assigned to each, like so:

```
Owner    Group    Others
rwx      rwx      rxw
```

Permissions can be indicated by mnemonic or octal characters. Mnemonic characters are

- ▶ r indicates permission for an owner, member of the owner's group, or others to open and read the file.

- ▶ w indicates permission for an owner, member of the owner's group, or others to open and write to the file.

- ▶ x indicates permission for an owner, member of the owner's group, or others to execute the file (or read a directory).

In the previous example for the file named file, the owner, andrew, has read and write permission, as does any member of the group named andrew. All other users may only read the file. Also note that default permissions for files created by the root operator will be different because of umask settings assigned by the shell.

Many users prefer to use numeric codes, based on octal (base 8) values, to represent permissions. Here's what these values mean:

- ▶ 4 indicates read permission.

- ▶ 2 indicates write permission.

- ▶ 1 indicates execute permission.

In octal notation, the previous example file has a permission setting of 664 (read + write or 4 + 2, read + write or 4 + 2, read-only or 4). Although you can use either form of permissions notation, octal is easy to use quickly after you visualize and understand how permissions are numbered.

NOTE

In Linux, you can create groups to assign a number of users access to common directories and files, based on permissions. You might assign everyone in accounting to a group named accounting, for example, and allow that group access to accounts payable files while disallowing access by other departments. Defined groups are maintained by the root operator, but you can use the newgrp command to temporarily join other groups to access files (as long as the root operator has added you to the other groups). You can also allow or deny other groups' access to your files by modifying the group permissions of your files.

Directory Permissions

Directories are also files under Linux. For example, again use the ls command to show permissions like this:

```
$ mkdir foo
$ ls -ld foo
drwxrwxr-x    2 andrew    andrew          4096 Jan 23 12:37 foo
```

In this example, the mkdir command is used to create a directory. The ls command and its -ld option is used to show the permissions and other information about the directory (not its contents). Here you can see that the directory has permission values of 775 (read + write + execute or 4 + 2 + 1, read + write + execute or 4 + 2 + 1, and read + execute or 4 + 1).

This shows that the owner and group members can read and write to the directory and, because of execute permission, also list the directory's contents. All other users can only list the directory contents. Note that directories require execute permission for anyone to be able to view their contents.

You should also notice that the ls command's output shows a leading d in the permissions field. This letter specifies that this file is a directory; normal files have a blank field in its place. Other files, such as those specifying a block or character device, have a different letter.

For example, if you examine the device file for a Linux serial port, you will see

```
$ ls -l /dev/ttyS0
crw-rw-- 1 root dialout 4, 64 Feb 1 19:49 /dev/ttyS0
```

Here, /dev/ttyS0 is a character device (such as a serial communications port and designated by a c) owned by root and available to anyone in the dialout group. The device has permissions of 660 (read + write, read + write, no permission).

On the other hand, if you examine the device file for an IDE hard drive, you see

```
$ ls -l /dev/sda
brw-rw-- 1 root disk 8, 0 Feb 1 19:49 /dev/sda
```

In this example, b designates a block device (a device that transfers and caches data in blocks) with similar permissions. Other device entries you will run across on your Linux system include symbolic links, designated by s.

You can use the chmod command to alter a file's permissions. This command uses various forms of command syntax, including octal or a mnemonic form (such as u, g, o, or a and rwx, and so on) to specify a desired change. The chmod command can be used to add, remove, or modify file or directory permissions to protect, hide, or open up access to a file by other users (except for root, which can access any file or directory on a Linux system).

The mnemonic forms of chmod's options (when used with a plus character, +, to add, or a minus sign, -, to take away) designate the following:

- ▶ u—Adds or removes user (owner) read, write, or execute permission

- ▶ g—Adds or removes group read, write, or execute permission

- ▶ o—Adds or removes read, write, or execute permission for others not in a file's group

- ▶ a—Adds or removes read, write, or execute permission for all users

- ▶ r—Adds or removes read permission

- ▶ w—Adds or removes write permission

- ▶ x—Adds or removes execution permission

For example, if you create a file, such as a readme.txt, the file will have default permissions (set by the umask setting in /etc/bashrc) of

```
-rw-rw-r--    1 andrew    andrew          12 Jan 2 16:48 readme.txt
```

As you can see, you and members of your group can read and write the file. Anyone else can only read the file (and only if it is outside your home directory, which will have read, write, and execute permission set only for you, the owner). You can remove all write permission for anyone by using chmod, the minus sign, and aw like so:

```
$ chmod -aw readme.txt
$ ls -l readme.txt
-r--r--r--    1 andrew    andrew          12 Jan 2 16:48 readme.txt
```

Now, no one can write to the file (except you, if the file is in your home or /tmp directory because of directory permissions). To restore read and write permission for only you as the owner, use the plus sign and the u and rw options like so:

```
$ chmod u+rw readme.txt
$ ls -l readme.txt
-rw-------    1 andrew    andrew          12 Jan 2 16:48 readme.txt
```

You can also use the octal form of the chmod command, for example, to modify a file's permissions so that only you, the owner, can read and write a file. Use the chmod command and a file permission of 600, like this:

```
$ chmod 600 readme.txt
```

If you take away execution permission for a directory, files might be hidden inside and may not be listed or accessed by anyone else (except the root operator, of course, who has access to any file on your system). By using various combinations of permission settings, you can quickly and easily set up a more secure environment, even as a normal user in your home directory.

Understanding Set User ID and Set Group ID Permissions

Another type of permission is "set user ID", known as *suid*, and "set group ID" (*sgid*) permissions. These settings, when used in a program, enable any user running that program to have program owner or group owner permissions for that program. These settings enable the program to be run effectively by anyone, without requiring that each user's permissions be altered to include specific permissions for that program.

One commonly used program with suid permissions is the `passwd` command:

```
$ ls -l /usr/bin/passwd
-rwsr-xr-x 1 root root 29104 Nov 6 19:16 /usr/bin/passwd
```

This setting allows normal users to execute the command (as root) to make changes to a root-only accessible file, /etc/passwd.

You also can assign similar permission with the chfn command. This command allows users to update or change finger information in /etc/passwd. You accomplish this permission modification by using a leading 4 (or the mnemonic s) in front of the three octal values.

> **NOTE**
>
> Other files that might have suid or guid permissions include at, rcp, rlogin, rsh, chage, chsh, ssh, crontab, sudo, sendmail, ping, mount, and several Unix-to-Unix Copy (UUCP) utilities. Many programs (such as games) might also have this type of permission to access a sound device.

Files or programs that have suid or guid permissions can sometimes present security holes because they bypass normal permissions. This problem is compounded if the permission extends to an executable binary (a command) with an inherent security flaw because it could lead to any system user or intruder gaining root access. In past exploits, this typically happened when a user fed a vulnerable command with unexpected input (such as a long pathname or option); the command would fail, and the user would be presented a root prompt. Although Linux developers are constantly on the lookout for poor programming practices, new exploits are found all the time, and can crop up unexpectedly, especially in newer software packages that haven't had the benefit of peer developer review.

Savvy Linux system administrators keep the number of suid or guid files present on a system to a minimum. The find command can be used to display all such files on your system:

```
# find / -type f -perm +6000 -exec ls -l {} \;
```

> **NOTE**
>
> The find command is quite helpful and can be used for many purposes, such as before or during backup operations. See the section "Using Backup Software" in Chapter 13, "Backing Up."

Note that the programs do not necessarily have to be removed from your system. If your users really do not need to use the program, you can remove the program's execute permission for anyone. You have to decide, as the root operator, whether your users are allowed to, for example, mount and unmount CD-ROMs or other media on your system. Although Linux-based operating systems can be set up to accommodate ease of use and convenience, allowing programs such as mount to be suid might not be the best security policy. Other candidates for suid permission change could include the chsh, at, or chage commands.

Working as Root

The root, or super-user account, is a special account and user on Unix and Linux systems. Super-user permissions are required in part because of the restrictive file permissions assigned to important system configuration files. You must have root permission to edit these files or to access or modify certain devices (such as hard drives). When logged in as root, you have total control over your system, which can be dangerous.

When you work in root, you can destroy a running system with a simple invocation of the rm command like this:

```
# rm -fr /
```

This command line not only deletes files and directories, but also could wipe out file systems on other partitions and even remote computers. This alone is reason enough to take precautions when using root access.

The only time you should run Linux as the super-user is when you are configuring the file system, for example, or to repair or maintain the system. Logging in and using Linux as the root operator isn't a good idea because it defeats the entire concept of file permissions.

> **NOTE**
>
> The next couple of paragraphs assume that you have enabled the root account, as described at the start of this chapter.

Knowing how to run commands as root without logging in as root can help avoid serious missteps when configuring your system. Linux comes with a command named su that enables you to run one or more commands as root and then quickly returns you to normal user status. For example, if you would like to edit your system's file system table (a simple text file that describes local or remote storage devices, their type, and location), you can use the su command like this:

```
$ su -c "nano -w /etc/fstab"
Password:
```

After you press Enter, you are prompted for a password that gives you access to root. This extra step can also help you "think before you leap" into the command. Enter the root password, and you are then editing /etc/fstab, using the nano editor with line wrapping disabled.

> **CAUTION**
>
> Before editing any important system or software service configuration file, make a backup copy. Then make sure to launch your text editor with line wrapping disabled. If you edit a configuration file without disabling line wrapping, you could insert spurious carriage returns and line feeds into its contents, causing the configured service to fail when restarting. By convention, nearly all configuration files are formatted for 80-character text width, but this is not always the case. By default, the vi and emacs editors don't use line wrap.

You can use sudo in the same way to allow you to execute one-off commands. The above example would look like this, using sudo:

```
$ sudo nano -w /etc/fstab
```

Creating Users

When a Linux system administrator creates a user, an entry in /etc/passwd for the user is created. The system also creates a directory, labeled with the user's username, in the /home directory. For example, if you create a user named bernice, the user's home directory is /home/bernice.

> **NOTE**
>
> In this chapter, you learn how to manage users from the command line. See Chapter 10, "Managing Users," for more information on user administration with Ubuntu using graphical administration utilities, such as the graphical users-admin client.

Use the useradd command, along with a user's name, to quickly create a user:

```
$ sudo useradd andrew
```

After creating the user, you must also create the user's initial password with the passwd command:

```
$ sudo passwd andrew
```

```
Changing password for user andrew.
New password:
Retype new password:
passwd: all authentication tokens updated successfully.
```

Enter the new password twice. If you do not create an initial password for a new user, the user cannot log in.

You can view useradd's default new user settings by using the command and its -D option, like this:

```
$ useradd -D
GROUP=100
HOME=/home
INACTIVE=-1
EXPIRE=
SHELL=/bin/bash
SKEL=/etc/skel
```

These options display the default group ID, home directory, account and password policy (active forever with no password expiration), the default shell, and the directory containing defaults for the shell.

The useradd command has many different command-line options. The command can be used to set policies and dates for the new user's password, assign a login shell, assign group membership, and other aspects of a user's account.

Deleting Users

Use the userdel command to delete users from your system. This command removes a user's entry in the system's /etc/passwd file. You should also use the command's -r option to remove all the user's files and directories (such as the user's mail spool file under /var/spool/mail):

```
$ sudo userdel -r andrew
```

If you do not use the -r option, you have to manually delete the user's directory under /home, along with the user's /var/spool/mail queue.

Shutting Down the System

Use the shutdown command to shut down your system. The shutdown command has a number of different command-line options (such as shutting down at a predetermined time), but the fastest way to cleanly shut down Linux is to use the -h or halt option, followed by the word now or the numeral zero (0), like this:

```
$ sudo shutdown -h now
```

or

```
$ sudo shutdown -h 0
```

To incorporate a timed shutdown and a pertinent message to all active users, use shutdown's time and message options, like so:

```
$ sudo shutdown -h 18:30 "System is going down for maintenance this evening"
```

This example shuts down your system and provides a warning to all active users 15 minutes before the shutdown (or reboot). Shutting down a running server can be considered drastic, especially if there are active users or exchanges of important data occurring (such as a backup in progress). One good approach is to warn users ahead of time. This can be done by editing the system Message of the Day (MOTD) motd file, which displays a message to users after login. To create your custom MOTD, use a text editor and change the contents of /etc/motd. You can also make downtimes part of a regular schedule, perhaps to coincide with security audits, software updates, or hardware maintenance.

You should shut down Ubuntu for only a few very specific reasons:

- ▶ You are not using the computer and want to conserve electrical power.

- ▶ You need to perform system maintenance that requires any or all system services to be stopped.

- ▶ You want to replace integral hardware.

TIP

Do not shut down your computer if you suspect that one or more intruders has infiltrated your system; instead, disconnect the machine from any or all networks and make a backup copy of your hard drives. You might want to also keep the machine running to examine the contents of memory and to examine system logs.

Rebooting the System

You should also use the shutdown command to reboot your system. The fastest way to cleanly reboot Linux is to use the -r option, and the word now or the numeral zero (0):

```
$ sudo shutdown -r now
```

or

```
$ sudo shutdown -r 0
```

Both rebooting and shutting down can have dire consequences if performed at the wrong time (such as during backups or critical file transfers, which arouses the ire of your system's users). However, Linux-based operating systems are designed to properly stop active system services in an orderly fashion. Other commands you can use to shut down and reboot Linux are the halt and reboot commands, but the shutdown command is more flexible.

Reading Documentation

Although you learn the basics of using Ubuntu in this book, you need time and practice to master and troubleshoot more complex aspects of the Linux operating system and your distribution. As with any operating system, you can expect to encounter some problems or perplexing questions as you continue to work with Linux. The first place to turn for help with these issues is the documentation included with your system; if you cannot find the information you need there, check Ubuntu's website.

Linux, like Unix, is a self-documenting system, with man pages accessible through the man command. Linux offers many other helpful commands for accessing its documentation. You can use the apropos command—for example, with a keyword such as partition—to find commands related to partitioning, like this:

```
$ apropos partition
diskdumpfmt          (8) - format a dump device or a partition
fdisk                (8) - Partition table manipulator for Linux
GNU Parted [parted]  (8) - a partition manipulation program
mpartition           (1) - partition an MSDOS hard disk
MPI_Cart_sub         (3) - Partitions a communicator into subgroups which form
                           lower-dimensional cartesian subgrids
partprobe            (8) - inform the OS of partition table changes
pvcreate             (8) - initialize a disk or partition for use by LVM
sfdisk               (8) - Partition table manipulator for Linux
```

To find a command and its documentation, you can use the whereis command. For example, if you are looking for the fdisk command, you can do this:

```
$ whereis fdisk
fdisk: /sbin/fdisk /usr/share/man/man8/fdisk.8.gz
```

Using Man Pages

To learn more about a command or program, use the man command, followed by the name of the command. Man pages for Linux and X Window commands are within the /usr/share/man, /usr/local/share/man, and /usr/X11R6/man directories; so, for example, to read the rm command's man page, use the man command like this:

```
$ man rm
```

After you press Enter, the less command (a Linux command known as a *pager*) displays the man page. The less command is a text browser you can use to scroll forward and backward (even sideways) through the document to learn more about the command. Type the letter **h** to get help, use the forward slash to enter a search string, or press **q** to quit.

NOTE

Although nearly all the hundreds of GNU commands included with Linux each have a man page, you must use the `info` command to read detailed information about using a GNU command. For example, to learn even more about `bash` (which has a rather extensive manual page), use the `info` command like this:

```
$ info bash
```

Press the **n** and **p** keys to navigate through the document, or scroll down to a menu item on the screen and press Enter to read about a specific feature. Press **q** to quit reading.

Related Ubuntu and Linux Commands

The following programs and built-in shell commands are commonly used when working at the command line. These commands are organized by category to help you understand the command's purpose. If you need to find full information for using the command, you can find that information under the command's man page.

- ▶ **Managing users and groups**—chage, chfn, chsh, edquota, gpasswd, groupadd, groupdel, groupmod, groups, mkpasswd, newgrp, newusers, passwd, umask, useradd, userdel, usermod

- ▶ **Managing files and file systems**—cat, cd, chattr, chmod, chown, compress, cp, dd, fdisk, find, gzip, ln, mkdir, mksfs, mount, mv, rm, rmdir, rpm, sort, swapon, swapoff, tar, touch, umount, uncompress, uniq, unzip, zip

- ▶ **Managing running programs**—bg, fg, kill, killall, nice, ps, pstree, renice, top, watch

- ▶ **Getting information**—apropos, cal, cat, cmp, date, diff, df, dir, dmesg, du, env, file, free, grep, head, info, last, less, locate, ls, lsattr, man, more, pinfo, ps, pwd, stat, strings, tac, tail, top, uname, uptime, vdir, vmstat, w, wc, whatis, whereis, which, who, whoami

- ▶ **Console text editors**—ed, jed, joe, mcedit, nano, red, sed, vim

- ▶ **Console Internet and network commands**—bing, elm, ftp, host, hostname, ifconfig, links, lynx, mail, mutt, ncftp, netconfig, netstat, pine, ping, pump, rdate, route, scp, sftp, ssh, tcpdump, traceroute, whois, wire-test

Reference

▶ http://www.winntmag.com/Articles/Index.cfm?ArticleID=7420—An article by a Windows NT user who, when experimenting with Linux, blithely confesses to rebooting the system after not knowing how to read a text file at the Linux console.

▶ http://standards.ieee.org/regauth/posix/—IEEE's POSIX information page.

▶ http://www.itworld.com/Comp/2362/lw-01-government/#sidebar—Discussion of Linux and POSIX compliance.

▶ http://www.pathname.com/fhs/—Home page for the Linux FHS, Linux Filesystem Hierarchy Standard.

▶ http://www.tldp.org/—Browse the HOWTO section to find and read The Linux Keyboard and Console HOWTO—Andries Brouwer's somewhat dated but eminently useful guide to using the Linux keyboard and console.

▶ http://www.gnu.org/software/emacs/emacs.html—Home page for the FSF's GNU emacs editing environment; you can find additional documentation and links to the source code for the latest version here.

▶ http://www.vim.org/—Home page for the vim (vi clone) editor included with Linux distributions. Check here for updates, bug fixes, and news about this editor.

▶ http://www.courtesan.com/sudo/—Home page for the sudo command. Check here for the latest updates, security features, and bug fixes.

PART II
Desktop Ubuntu

IN THIS PART

CHAPTER 5

On the Internet

In the modern world, the Internet is everywhere. From cell phones to offices, from games consoles to iPods, we are surrounded by multiple access routes to online information and communication. Ubuntu is no outsider when it comes to accessing information through the Internet and comes equipped with web browsers, email clients and other tools that you can use to connect to other people across the globe.

In this chapter we'll take a look at some of the popular Internet applications that are available with Ubuntu. You'll find out about Firefox, and its KDE alternative, Konqueror. We'll also investigate some of the email clients that you can install whilst using Ubuntu. Other topics include RSS feed readers, Instant Messaging (through IRC and other networks) and reading newsgroups. Finally we'll take a quick look at Ekiga, which is a videoconferencing program for Ubuntu.

A Brief Introduction to the Internet

The Internet itself was first brought to life by the U.S. Department of Defense in 1969. It was called ARPANet after the Department of Defense's Advanced Research Projects Agency. Designed to build a network that would withstand major catastrophe (this was the peak of the Cold War), it soon grew to encompass more and more networks to build the Internet. Then, in 1991, Tim Berners-Lee of CERN developed the idea of the World Wide Web, including Hypertext Transfer Protocol (HTTP) and Hypertext Markup Language (HTML). This gave us what we now know to be the Internet.

Getting Started with Firefox

One of the most popular web browsers, and in fact the default web browser in Ubuntu, is Mozilla Firefox (see Figure 5.1). Built on a solid code base that is derived from the Mozilla Suite, Firefox offers an alternative to surfing the Internet using Internet Explorer. There have been more than 265 million downloads of Firefox since its release in late 2004, and it has grabbed significant market share from Internet Explorer.

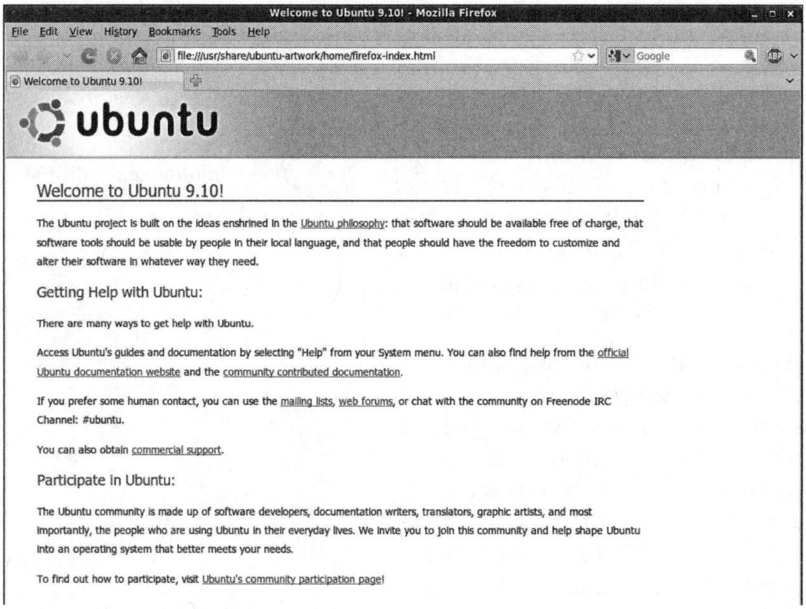

FIGURE 5.1   Mozilla Firefox—rediscover the Web. Firefox enables you to add on numerous upgrades, further enhancing your experience.

In Ubuntu you can find Firefox under the Applications, Internet menu at the top of your screen. An even simpler way to start Firefox is to click the small Firefox icon next to the System menu. Either way, Firefox opens.

Beyond the basic program is a wealth of plug-ins and extensions that can increase the capabilities of Firefox beyond simple web browsing. Plug-ins such as Shockwave Flash and Java are available instantly, as are multimedia codecs for viewing video content, whereas extensions provide useful additions to the browsing experience. For example, ForecastFox is an extension that gives you your local weather conditions, and Bandwidth Tester is a tool that calculates your current bandwidth. As Firefox grows, there will be more and more extensions and plug-ins that you can use to enhance your browsing pleasure.

Finding and obtaining these plugins and extensions is made very easy as Mozilla developers have helpfully created a site dedicated to helping you get more from Firefox. Particular favorites are the Adblock Plus and the StumbleUpon plugins. Adblock Plus allows you to nuke all those annoying banners and animations that take up so much bandwidth while you are browsing. StumbleUpon is a neat plugin that takes you to web pages based on your preferences. Be warned, though, that StumbleUpon can be quite addictive and you will end up wasting away many hours clicking the stumble button!

Flash

You can easily enable Flash in your browser by installing the `flashplugin-nonfree` package either by using `synaptic` or by using `apt-get`. Either way, Ubuntu will download this package, which will in turn retrieve the official package from Adobe and then install it on your system. A browser restart is required before you try to access any Flash-enabled content.

Another plugin that we make a lot of use of is Google BrowserSync. If, like us, you work across multiple computers then you will no doubt have had to re-create bookmarks at every different computer and try to keep them the same. Google makes this whole process much easier by allowing you to synchronize not only your bookmarks, but also your cookies, browser history and finally any saved passwords across multiple browsers. Bear in mind that you can choose what you want to synchronize, making it easy just to replicate your bookmarks.

Konqueror

KDE users have the option to use Konqueror, which is the default browser for KDE (see Figure 5.2). As well as handling file system navigation, Konqueror can also be used to surf the web. It, too, is based on the Gecko rendering engine as found in Firefox. It was decided that the newer Arora browser (version 0.10 and based on webkit), while good, wasn't as mature as would be preferred for use by default. However, you can download it from the repositories.

Choosing an Email Client

Back in the days of Unix, there were various text-based email clients such as `elm` and `pine` (Pine Is Not Elm). Although they looked basic, they allowed the average user to interact with his email, both for composing and reading correspondence. With the advent of mainstream computing and the realization that people needed friendly GUI interfaces to be productive came a plethora of email clients, with some of them being cross-platform and compatible among Linux, Windows, and Mac OS X, not to mention Unix.

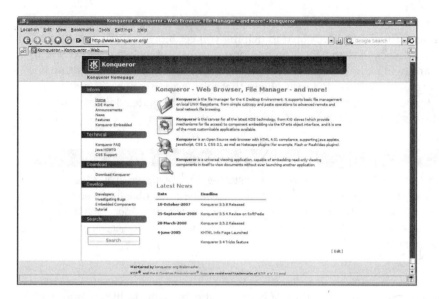

FIGURE 5.2   Konqueror, the standard KDE web browser.

Evolution

Evolution is the standard email client that comes with Ubuntu, and to call it an email client would be to sincerely underestimate its usefulness as an application. Not only does it handle email, but it can also look after contacts and calendaring, as well as managing your tasks (see Figure 5.3). The next section demonstrates how to configure Evolution to handle email.

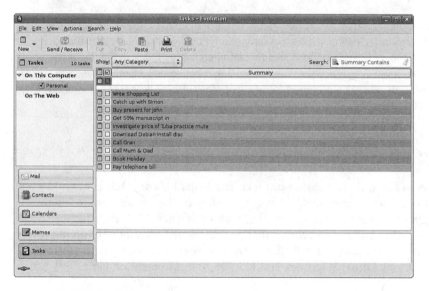

FIGURE 5.3   With Evolution you can handle all your email and contacts, as well as make appointments and track tasks.

You need to have the following information to successfully configure Evolution:

▶ Your email address

▶ Your incoming email server name and type (that is, pop.email.com, POP, and IMAP)

▶ Your username and password for the incoming server

▶ Your outgoing email server name (that is, smtp.email.com)

After you have all the information, you can start Evolution. The first screen you are presented with is the Account Setup Assistance screen, so click Next to get to the Identity screen (see Figure 5.4).

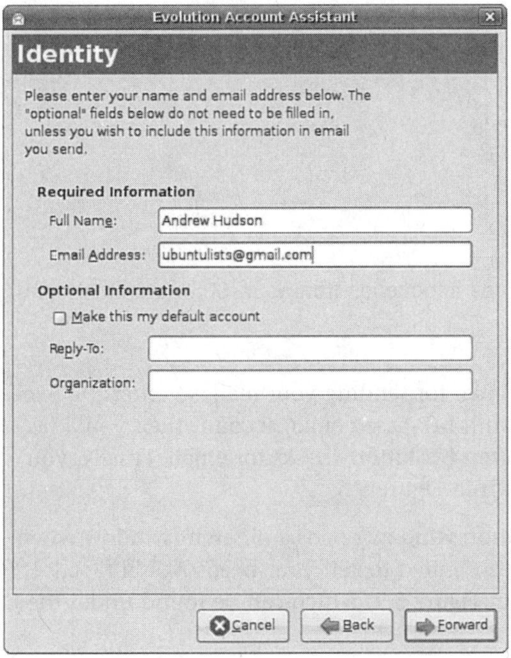

FIGURE 5.4   You can launch and configure Evolution with just a few simple commands. The Identity screen, the first of several screens, asks you to enter your information. Click Forward to proceed.

The next screen permits you to configure Evolution to use your Mail Transfer Agent. You can choose POP, IMAP, the local spools found in /var/mail in either mbox or maildir format, a local MTA, or None if you simply want to use the other features of Evolution. As shown in Figure 5.5, you can also set your password.

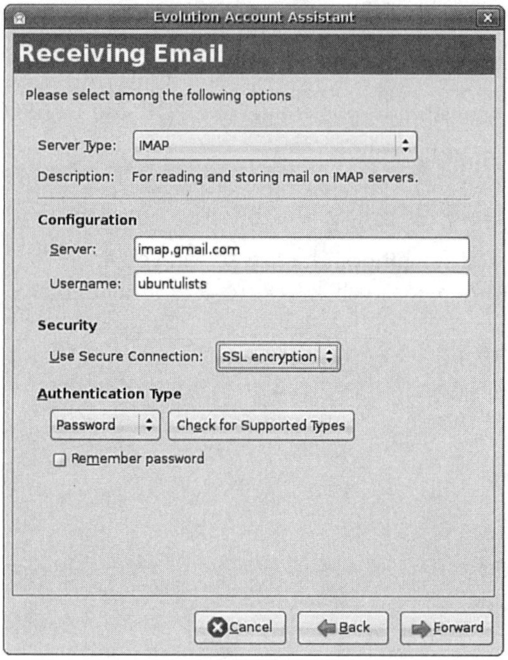

FIGURE 5.5   The Receiving Email screen requires information from your ISP or system administrator.

You must also choose between SMTP or Sendmail for sending your mail, so enter the relevant details as required. If you have chosen an IMAP-based email account then you'll be asked some more questions to govern how often Evolution checks for email. Finally, you will see the opening Evolution window, shown in Figure 5.6.

Each icon in the left pane of the main Evolution window opens a different window when selected. Each view has options that can be configured to suit your needs; you'll find access to the preferences dialog box (shown in Figure 5.7) which can be found under the Edit menu.

Mozilla Thunderbird

Mozilla Thunderbird (see Figure 5.8) is the sister program to Firefox. Whereas Firefox is designed to browse the web, Thunderbird's specialty is communication. It can handle email, network news (see later in this chapter), and RSS feeds.

Thunderbird is not installed by default with Ubuntu, so you will have to use either apt-get or synaptic to install it. As with Firefox, there are many plug-ins and extensions to enhance your email and newsreading.

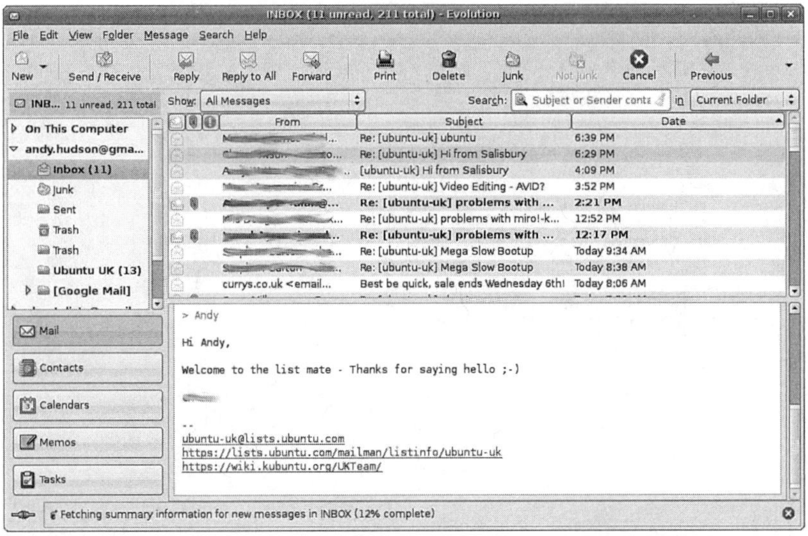

FIGURE 5.6 The standard Evolution display. On the left you can see buttons to choose Mail, Contacts, Calendars, Memos, and Tasks windows.

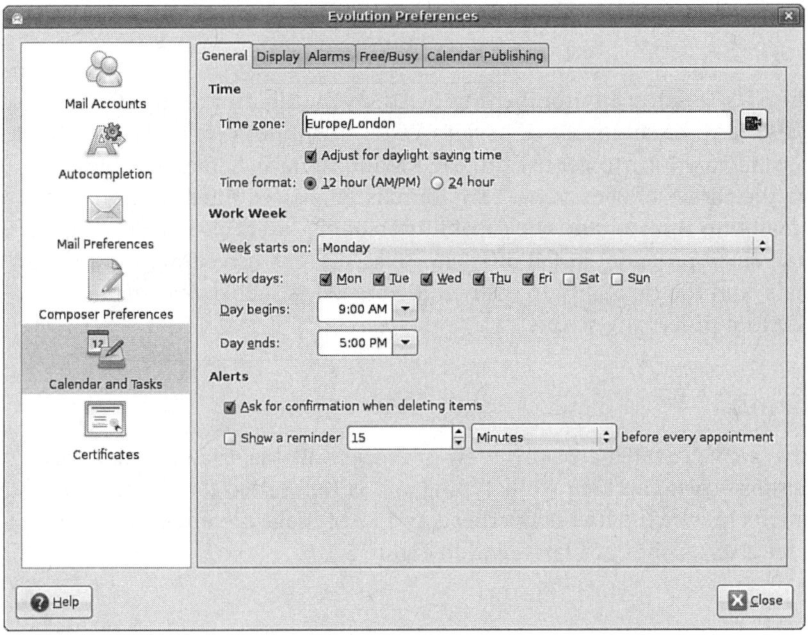

FIGURE 5.7 The calendar application Tools screen is where the information can be shared with others. Here, the times and dates can be configured.

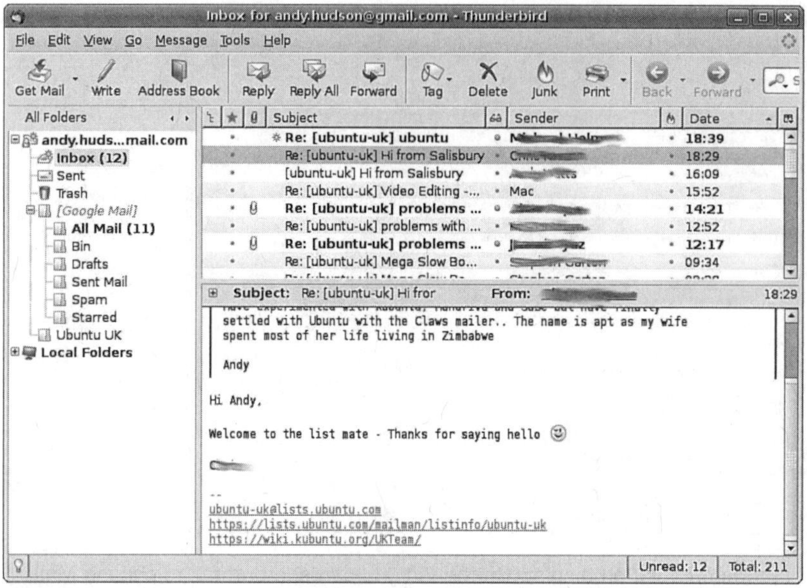

FIGURE 5.8   The natural companion to Firefox, Mozilla's lightweight email client, Thunderbird, can be found in use all over the world.

KMail

If you are using the KDE Desktop Environment rather than the Ubuntu default GNOME desktop, you will also have KMail installed. As with Balsa, it will not take users of Outlook Express or Mozilla Mail very long to get used to the KMail interface. Some useful features found in KMail are the choice of mbox or maildir formats, improved filter creation, the capability to sort mail into threads, and the capability to apply filters at the MTA. Figure 5.9 shows the KMail email program. KMail offers IMAP access, extensive filtering, mbox and maildir formats, and the capability to easily integrate MTAs such as Procmail, Spamassassin, or custom processing scripts.

Other Mail Clients

The mail clients that we've covered are only a few of those available. Claws Mail is very popular because it offers spell-checking while typing and is well suited for use in large network environments in which network overhead and RAM usage are important considerations. You can see a screenshot of Claws mail in Figure 5.10.

RSS Readers

RSS is one of the protocols of Web 2.0, the next generation of Internet content. Although RSS has been in use for a couple of years now, it has only recently started to really take off, thanks to adoption across a large number of websites and portals.

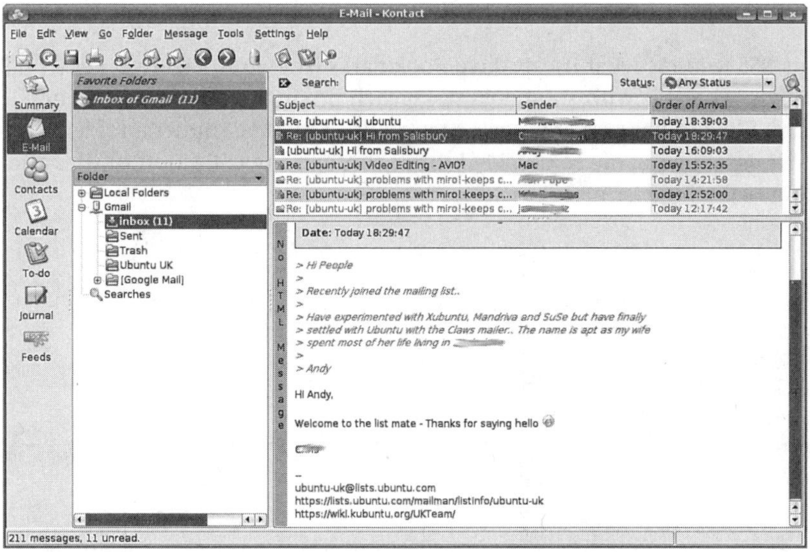

FIGURE 5.9   The KMail email client, part of the KDE Desktop Environment.

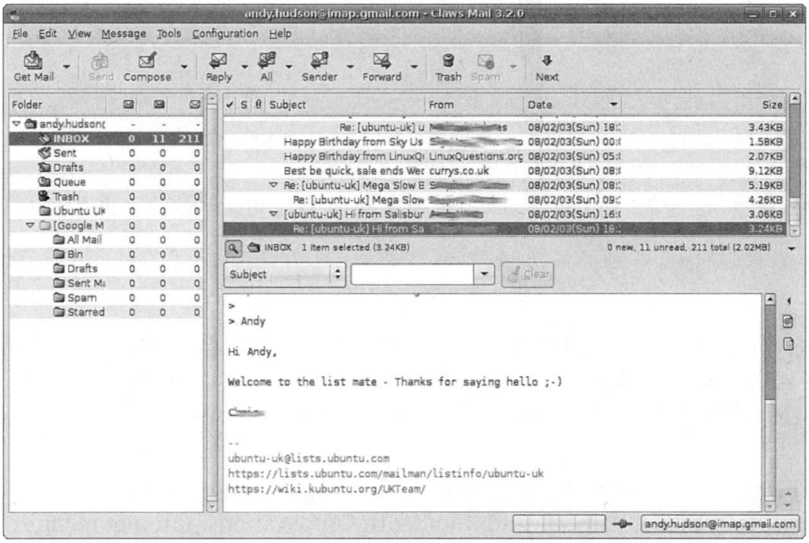

FIGURE 5.10   Claws Mail gives you a very resource-light, yet very powerful and fast mail client.

The key advantage of RSS is that you can quickly read news from your specific choice of websites at a time that suits you. Some services offer just the articles' headlines, whereas others offer full articles for you to view. RSS feeds can be accessed in various ways, even through your web browser!

Firefox

Firefox implements RSS feeds as what it calls Live Bookmarks (shown in Figure 5.11), which are essentially bookmarks with sub-bookmarks, each linking to a new page from your chosen website. I like to have several news sites grouped together under a folder on my toolbar called News, allowing me to quickly browse through my collection of sites and pick out articles that really interest me.

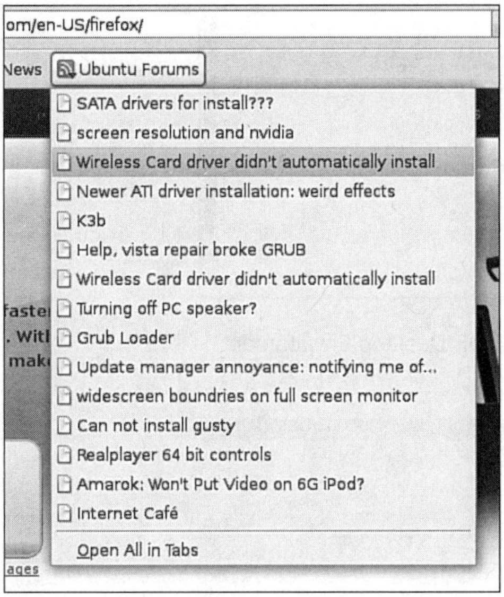

FIGURE 5.11   Live Bookmarks for Firefox, making all your news fixes just a mouse click away.

Liferea

Of course, not everyone wants to read RSS feeds with the browser. The main problem with reading RSS feeds with Firefox is that you get to see only the headline, rather than any actual text. This is where a dedicated RSS reader comes in handy, and Liferea (see Figure 5.12) is one of the best.

It is not installed by default, so you have to retrieve it by going to Applications, Add/Remove. After it is installed, you can find it under the Applications, Internet menu labeled simply Liferea.

By default, Liferea offers a number of RSS feeds, including Planet Debian, Groklaw, and Slashdot. Adding a new feed is very straightforward. All you need to do is select New Subscription under the Feeds menu and paste the URL of the RSS feed into the box. Liferea then retrieves all the current items available through that field, and displays the feed name on the left side for you to select and start reading.

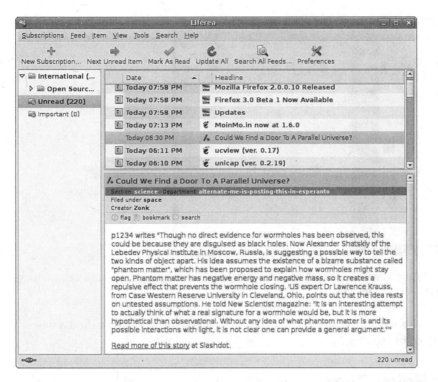

FIGURE 5.12   Read your daily news feeds with Liferea, a fantastic and easy-to-use RSS feed reader.

Instant Messaging with Pidgin

Instant Messaging is one of the biggest ways for people to interact over the web. AOL was the primary force behind this, especially in America, but other networks and systems soon came onto the market providing users with a wealth of choice.

No longer just a consumer tool, instant messaging is now a part of the corporate world, with many different companies deploying internal instant messaging software for collaboration.

Pidgin was created as a multi-protocol instant messaging client enabling you to connect to several different networks that use differing protocols, such as AIM, MSN, Jabber and others.

You can find Pidgin under Applications, Internet, listed as Pidgin Internet Messenger; it is shown in Figure 5.13.

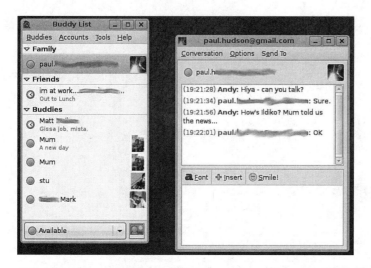

FIGURE 5.13   Pidgin is the Swiss army knife of instant messaging applications; it can work across many different IM networks.

Getting started with Pidgin is simple; when you start Pidgin you are asked to add a new account, as shown in Figure 5.14.

Internet Relay Chat

As documented in RFC 2812 and RFC 2813, the IRC protocol is used for text conferencing. Like mail and news, IRC uses a client/server model. Although it is rare for an individual to establish an IRC server, it can be done. Most people use public IRC servers and access them with IRC clients.

Ubuntu provides a number of graphical IRC clients, including X-Chat, licq, and Seamonkeychat, but there is no default chat client for Ubuntu. Ubuntu also provides the console clients epic and licq for those who eschew X. If you don't already have a favorite, you should try them all.

> **CAUTION**
>
> You should never use an IRC client while you are the root user. It is better to create a special user just for IRC because of potential security problems. To use X-Chat in this manner, you open a terminal window, use su to change to your IRC user, and start the xchat client.

X-Chat is a popular IRC client, and it is the client that is used in this chapter's example. The HTML documents for X-Chat are available in /usr/share/docs/xchat. It is a good idea to read them before you begin because they include an introduction to and cover some of the basics of IRC. You need to download and install X-Chat to launch the X-Chat

FIGURE 5.14   Pidgin makes light work of setting up your instant messenger accounts. You select the network protocol for the account (that is, AIM, MSN, and so on) and fill out your screen name and password, finally clicking Save to create the account within Pidgin and automatically log in. If any of your contacts are online, then they will appear in the buddy list window as shown earlier in Figure 5.13.

client, select the XChat IRC item from the Applications, Internet menu, or you can launch it from the command line, like this:

```
$ xchat &
```

The X-Chat application enables you to assign yourself up to three nicknames. You can also specify your real name and your username. Because many people choose not to use their real names in IRC chat, you are free to enter any names you desire in any of the spaces provided. You can select multiple nicknames; you might be banned from an IRC channel under one name, and you could then rejoin using another. If this seems slightly juvenile to you, you are beginning to get an idea of the type of behavior on many IRC channels.

When you open the main X-Chat screen, a list of IRC servers appears, as shown in Figure 5.15. After you choose a server by double-clicking it, you can view a list of channels available on that server by choosing Window, Channel List. The X-Chat Channel List window appears. In that window, you can choose to join channels featuring topics that interest you. To join a channel, you double-click it.

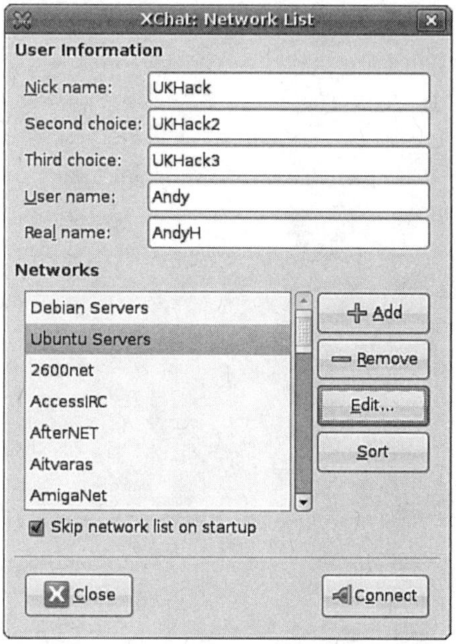

FIGURE 5.15   The main X-Chat screen presents a list of available public servers from which to select.

The Wild Side of IRC

Do not be surprised at the number of lewd topics and the use of crude language on public IRC servers. For a humorous look at the topic of IRC cursing, see http://www.irc.org/fun_docs/nocuss.html. This site also offers some tips for maintaining IRC etiquette, which is essential if you do not want to be the object of any of that profanity! Here are some of the most important IRC etiquette rules:

▶ Do not use colored text, all-capitalized text, blinking text, or "bells" (beeps caused by sending ^G to a terminal).

▶ Show respect for others.

▶ Ignore people who act inappropriately.

After you select a channel, you can join in the conversation, which appears as onscreen text. The messages scroll down the screen as new messages appear. For an example, see Figure 5.16.

TIP

You can establish your own IRC server even though Ubuntu does not provide one. Setting up a server is not a task for anyone who is not well versed in Linux or IRC.

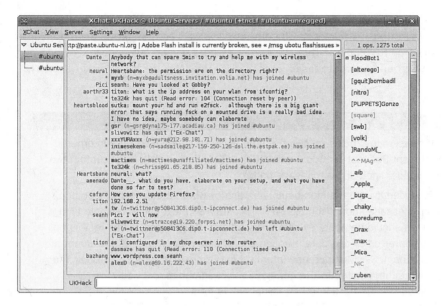

FIGURE 5.16   Join in an online chatroom about your favorite distro, with X-Chat.

A popular server is IRCd, which you can obtain from ftp://ftp.irc.org/irc/server/. Before you download IRCd, you should look at the README file to determine what files you need to download and read the information at http://www.irchelp.org/irchelp/ircd/.

Usenet Network Newsgroups

The concept of newsgroups revolutionized the way information was exchanged between people across a network. The Usenet network news system created a method for people to electronically communicate with large groups of people with similar interests. As you will see, many of the concepts of Usenet news are embodied in other forms of collaborative communication.

Usenet newsgroups act as a form of public bulletin board system. Any user can subscribe to individual newsgroups and send (or *post*) messages (called *articles*) to the newsgroup so that all the other subscribers of the newsgroup can read them. Some newsgroups include an administrator, who must approve each message before it is posted. These are called *moderated* newsgroups. Other newsgroups are *open*, allowing any subscribed member to post a message. When an article is posted to the newsgroup, it is transferred to all the other hosts in the news network.

Usenet newsgroups are divided into a hierarchy to make it easier to find individual newsgroups. The hierarchy levels are based on topics, such as computers, science, recreation, and social issues. Each newsgroup is named as a subset of the higher-level topic. For example, the newsgroup comp relates to all computer topics. The newsgroup comp.laptops relates to laptop computer issues. Often the hierarchy goes several layers deep. For example, the newsgroup comp.databases.oracle.server relates to Oracle server database issues.

> **NOTE**
>
> The format of newsgroup articles follows the strict guidelines defined in the Internet standards document Request for Comments (RFC) 1036. Each article must contain two distinct parts: header lines and a message body.
>
> The header lines identify information about when and by whom the article was posted. The body of the message should contain only standard ASCII text characters. No binary characters or files should be posted within news articles. To get around this restriction, binary files are converted to text data, through use of either the standard Unix uuencode program or the newer Multipurpose Internet Mail Extensions (MIME) protocol. The resulting text file is then posted to the newsgroup. Newsgroup readers can then decode the posted text file back into its original binary form.

A collection of articles posted in response to a common topic is called a *thread*. A thread can contain many articles as users post messages in response to other posted messages. Some newsreader programs allow the user to track articles based on the threads to which they belong. This helps simplify the organization of articles in the newsgroup.

> **TIP**
>
> The free news server news.gmane.org makes the Red Hat and Ubuntu mail lists available via newsgroups. The beta list is available as gmane.linux.redhat.rhl.beta. It is a handy way to read threaded discussions and easier than using the Ubuntu mail list archives.

The protocol used to transfer newsgroup articles from one host to another is Network News Transfer Protocol (NNTP), defined in RFC 975. (You can search RFCs at ftp://metalab.unc.edu/pub/docs/rfc/; look at the file rfc-index.txt.) NNTP was designed as a simple client/server protocol that enables two hosts to exchange newsgroup articles in an efficient manner.

The Pan News Client Newsreader

Whether or not your Ubuntu server is set up as a news server, you can use a newsreader program to read newsgroup articles. The newsreader programs require just a connection to a news server. It does not matter whether the news server is on the same machine or is a remote news server on the other side of the world.

Several programs are available for Unix systems to connect to news servers to read and post articles in newsgroups. Here we'll discuss the Pan news client.

Pan is a graphical newsreader client that works with GNOME and is the default newsreader for Ubuntu. If you have the GNOME libraries installed (and they usually are installed by default), you can also use Pan with the K Desktop Environment (KDE). Pan has the capability to download and display all the newsgroups and display posted news articles. You can launch it by using the GNOME or KDE desktop panel or from the command line of an X terminal window with the command pan &. Pan supports combining multipart messages and the yenc encoding/decoding protocol. Figure 5.17 shows a sample Pan display.

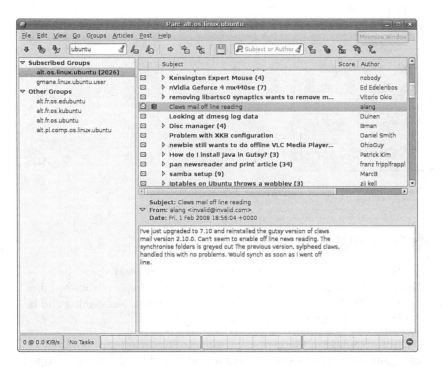

FIGURE 5.17   The Pan graphical newsreader is one of the nicest available for Linux, shown here displaying an image attached to a news article.

The first time you run Pan, a configuration wizard appears and prompts you for your news server name (also known as the NNTP name), connection port details, as well as optional username and password for that server. You are also able to set expiration options and prioritize a server over others. After the wizard is finished, you are prompted to download a list of the newsgroups the server provides; this might take a while. If you need to change the news server or add an additional server, you can access the Preferences item under the Edit menu to bring up the list of servers, which is shown in Figure 5.18. Then, you highlight the appropriate one and click Edit to change it or just click the New button to add a new news server.

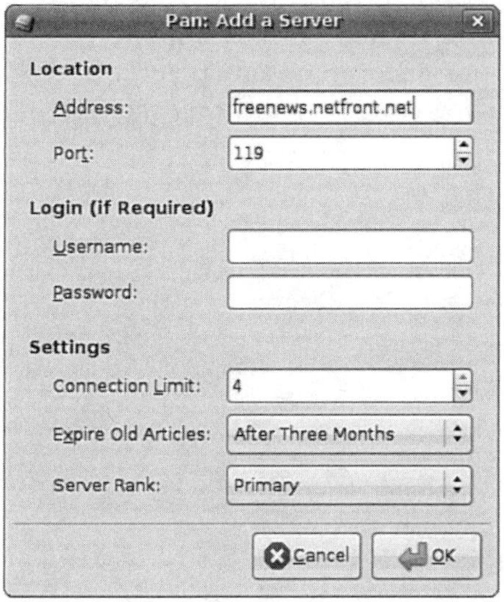

FIGURE 5.18   The Pan news server configuration window.

Videoconferencing with Ekiga

Ekiga is an Internet videoconferencing application that provides two-way voice and picture transmission over the Internet by using the H.323 protocol for IP telephony (also known as *Voice over IP* [VoIP]). It is an application similar to Microsoft NetMeeting and is provided with Ubuntu as the default videoconferencing client.

Before you can take full advantage of the phone and videoconferencing capabilities of Ekiga, you must configure a full-duplex–capable sound card and video device (see Chapter 7, "Multimedia Applications") as well as a camera.

Ekiga is found in the Internet menu as Videoconferencing; you click on the icon to launch it. When you start the Ekiga application for the first time, a configuration wizard runs and you are greeted by the first of four configuration screens. You simply enter your name, email address, and location and select your connection type. The settings for your audio and video devices are automatically detected; you can view them by selecting the Preferences item from the Edit menu. Figure 5.19 shows Ekiga in action, ready to dial another user.

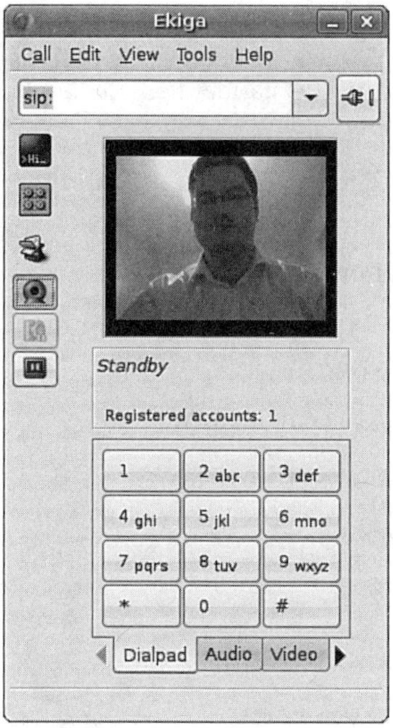

FIGURE 5.19   Ekiga is surprisingly simple to use. A video source is not necessary; a static picture can be used as well.

When you have Ekiga running, you must register (from within Ekiga) with the server at http://ekiga.net/ to enable conferencing; Ekiga does this automatically for you if you told it to do so during the initial configuration.

You can find an informative FAQ at the Ekiga home page at http://www.Ekiga.org/ that you should read in full before using Ekiga. Also, an excellent article about VoIP is at http://freshmeat.net/articles/view/430/.

NOTE

If you frequently use VoIP applications such as Ekiga, you will tire of repetitively typing in long IP addresses to make connections. To avoid this hassle, you can use a "gate-keeper"—similar in purpose to a DNS server—to translate names into IP addresses. OpenH323 Gatekeeper is one such popular gatekeeper application. It is not provided with Ubuntu, but you can obtain it from http://www.gnugk.org/.

Reference

▶ http://www.novell.com/—The home of Ximian Evolution, the standard email client for Ubuntu.

▶ http://www.mozilla.com/—The home page for Mozilla Firefox, Thunderbird, and the Mozilla Suite.

▶ http://www.spreadfirefox.com/—The Firefox advocacy home page is useful for converting those Internet Explorer types.

▶ http://www.konqueror.org/—The homepage for Konqueror.

▶ http://www.claws-mail.org/— The homepage for Claws, the email client.

▶ http://ekiga.net/—Sign up here for a free SIP account for use with Ekiga.

Productivity Applications

With the rapid growth of open source software, businesses have directly benefited from specific developments in office productivity suites. Many businesses already use OpenOffice.org and its commercial counterpart, StarOffice, and they are already enjoying the cost benefits of not having to pay license fees or support costs. Of course, more suites are available than just OpenOffice.org and in this chapter we will explore the options available to you as a user of Ubuntu.

NOTE

It's important to understand that OpenOffice.org is not 100% compatible with Microsoft Office. Why is this? Well, Microsoft is notoriously secretive about its proprietary file formats and the only way that OpenOffice.org could ensure compatibility would be to reverse-engineer each file format, an exercise akin to taking apart a telephone to see how it works. This reverse-engineering could be classed as illegal under U.S. law, which would make OpenOffice.org somewhat of a potential hot-potato if they chose this path. However, OpenOffice.org manages to maintain a very high standard of importing and exporting so you should not experience too many problems.

A productivity suite could be classed as containing two or more applications that could be used for creating documents, presentations, spreadsheets, and databases. Other applications could include email clients, calculators/formula editors, and even illustration packages. Commonly they are all tied together by a default look and feel, which makes sticking to one particular suite much easier. Because Ubuntu uses OpenOffice.org as its standard office suite, we will introduce you to Writer and Calc, the two most popular OpenOffice.org components. We will also take a brief look at some of the other Linux-based office suites that are available.

Working with OpenOffice.org

For the majority of users of productivity suites, OpenOffice.org should fulfill most, if not all, of your requirements. However, the first hurdle you need to get over is not whether it can do what you require of it, but rather whether it can successfully import and export to proprietary Microsoft formats at a standard that is acceptable to your needs. In the main, OpenOffice.org should import and export with minimal hassle, perhaps getting a bit stuck with some of the more esoteric Microsoft Office formatting. Given that most users do not go much beyond tabs, columns, and tables, this level of compatibility should suffice.

However, you are strongly advised to round up a selection of documents and spreadsheets that could potentially fall foul of the import/export filter and test them thoroughly (of course, keeping a backup of the originals!). There is nothing worse than for a system administrator who has deployed a new productivity suite than to suddenly get users complaining that they cannot read their files. This would quickly destroy any benefits felt from the other useful functions within OpenOffice.org, and could even spell the return of proprietary formats and expensive office suites. Many users do not mind switching to OpenOffice.org, largely because the user interface closely resembles that of similar Microsoft applications. This helps to settle users into their environment and should dispel any fears they have over switching. Such similarity makes the transition to OpenOffice.org a lot easier.

Of course, just looking similar to Microsoft applications is not the only direct benefit. OpenOffice.org supports a huge array of file formats, and is capable of exporting to nearly 70 different types of documents. Such a wide variety of file formats means that you should be able to successfully use OpenOffice.org in nearly any environment.

Introducing OpenOffice.org

OpenOffice.org contains a number of productivity applications for use in creating text documents, preparing spreadsheets, organizing presentations, managing projects, and more. The following components of the OpenOffice.org package are included with Ubuntu:

▶ **Writer**—This word processing program enables you to compose, format, and organize text documents. If you are accustomed to using Microsoft Word, the functionality of OpenOffice.org Writer will be familiar to you. You will learn how to get up and running with Writer later on in this chapter.

▶ **Calc**—This spreadsheet program enables you to manipulate numbers in a spreadsheet format. Support for all but the most esoteric Microsoft Excel functions means that trading spreadsheets with Excel users should be successful. Calc offers some limited compatibility with Excel macros, but those macros generally have to be rewritten. We walk through setting up a basic spreadsheet with some formulas as well as showing you how to build a basic Data Pilot later on in this chapter.

▶ **Impress**—This presentation program is similar to Microsoft PowerPoint and enables you to create slide show presentations that include graphs, diagrams, and other graphics. Impress also works well with PowerPoint files.

NOTE

The following five applications are not included by default with Ubuntu. You will need to use synaptic to retrieve them if required.

▶ **Math**—This math formula editor enables you to write mathematical formulas with a number of math fonts and symbols for inclusion in a word processing document. Such symbols are highly specialized and not easily included in the basic functionality of a word processor. This is of interest primarily to math and science writers, but Math can be useful to anyone who needs to include a complex formula in text.

▶ **Base**—This database was introduced with the OpenOffice.org 2.0 suite, which is provided with Ubuntu. It provides a fully functional database application.

▶ **Draw**—This graphics application allows you to create images for inclusion in the documents produced with OpenOffice.org. It saves files only in OpenOffice.org format, but it can import most common image formats.

▶ **Dia**—This technical drawing editor from the GNOME Office suite enables you to create measured drawings, such as those used by architects and engineers. Its functionality is similar to that of Microsoft Visio.

▶ **Planner**—You can use this project management application for project planning, scheduling, and tracking; this application is similar to, but not compatible with, Microsoft Project. It is found in the Office menu as the Project Planner item.

A Brief History of OpenOffice.org

The OpenOffice.org office suite is based on a commercial suite called StarOffice. Originally developed by a German company, StarOffice was purchased by Sun Microsystems in the United States. One of the biggest complaints about the old StarOffice was that all the component applications were integrated under a StarOffice "desktop" that looked very much like a Microsoft Windows desktop, including a Start button and menus. This meant that to edit a simple document, unneeded applications had to be loaded, making the office suite slow to load, slow to run, and quite demanding on system resources.

After the purchase of StarOffice, Sun Microsystems released a large part of the StarOffice code under the GNU Public License, and development began on what has become OpenOffice.org, which is freely available under the GPL. Sun continued development on StarOffice and released a commercial version as StarOffice 6.0. The significant differences between the free and commercial versions of the software are that StarOffice provides more fonts and even more import/export file filters than OpenOffice.org (these filters cannot be provided in the GPL version because of licensing restrictions) and StarOffice provides its own relational database, Software AG's Adabas D database. The StarOffice counterpart to OpenOffice.org 2.4 is StarOffice 8.

Configuring OpenOffice.org

The installation of OpenOffice.org is done on a systemwide basis, meaning that all users have access to it. However, individual users have to go into OpenOffice.org to configure it for their individual needs. This initial configuration happens transparently the first time you load any of the OpenOffice.org components, and might mean the application takes a little longer to load as a result. Be patient, and your desired application will appear.

TIP

OpenOffice.org is constantly improving its productivity applications. You can check the OpenOffice.org website (http://www.openoffice.org/) for the latest version. The website provides a link to download the source or a pre-compiled version of the most current working installation files. A more current version might offer file format support that you need. Should you need a Windows-compatible version, you will also find it at the website.

Shown in Figure 6.1 is the Office menu, which is found under Applications. You can see the entries for Database (Base), Presentation (Impress), Spreadsheet (Calc), and Word Processor (Writer).

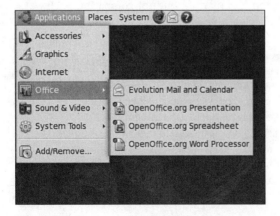

FIGURE 6.1   The OpenOffice.org suite provided by Ubuntu is simple to configure and use.

As is the case with many Linux applications, you may be somewhat overwhelmed by the sheer number of configuration options available to you in OpenOffice.org. Mercifully, a lot of thought has gone into organizing these options, which are available if you click the Tools menu and select Options. It does not matter which program you use to get to this dialog box; it appears the same if summoned from Writer, Impress, or Calc. It acts as a central configuration management tool for all OpenOffice.org applications. You can use it to set global options for all OpenOffice.org applications, or specific options for each individual component. For instance, in Figure 6.2, you can change the user details and information, and this is reflected across all OpenOffice.org applications.

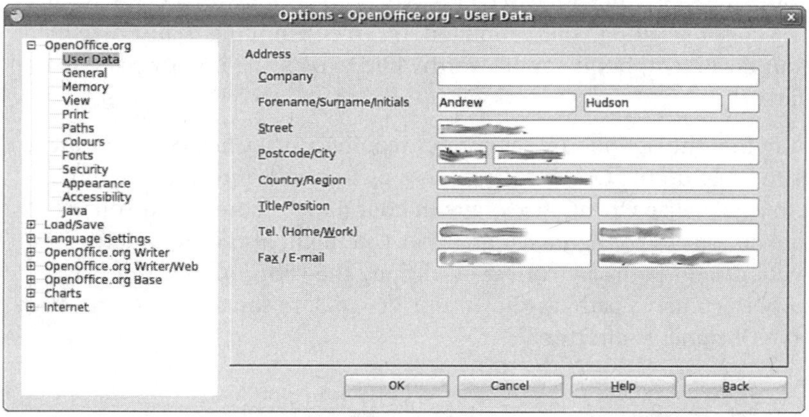

FIGURE 6.2   You can set user details for all OpenOffice.org applications from this dialog.

TIP

Two websites provide additional information on the functionality of OpenOffice.org:

http://lingucomponent.openoffice.org/download_dictionary.html—This site provides instructions and files for installing spelling and hyphenation dictionaries, which are not included with OpenOffice.org.

http://sourceforge.net/projects/ooextras/—This site provides templates, macros, and clip art, which are not provided with OpenOffice.org.

OpenOffice.org is a constant work in progress, but the current release is on par with the Sun version of StarOffice 8. You can browse to the OpenOffice.org website to get documentation and answers to frequently asked questions and to offer feedback.

Working with OpenOffice.org Writer

Out of all the applications that make up OpenOffice.org, the one that you are most likely to use on a regular basis is Writer, the OpenOffice.org word processor. With a visual style very similar to Microsoft's Word, Writer has a number of strengths over its commercial and vastly more expensive rival. In this section you will learn how to get started with Writer and make use of some of its powerful formatting and layout tools.

NOTE

You may be interested to know that Writer was the primary word processor chosen to write and edit this book.

Getting Started with Writer

You can access Writer by going to the Applications, Office menu and selecting OpenOffice.org Word Processor. After a few seconds Writer opens up with a blank document and a blinking cursor awaiting your command. It can be tempting to just dive in and start typing your document, but it can be worthwhile to do some initial configuration before you start work.

First of all, make sure that the options are set to your requirements. Click the Tools menu and select Options to bring up the Options dialog box, as seen in Figure 6.2. The initial screen allows you to personalize OpenOffice.org with your name, address, and contact details, but there are options to configure features that you might also want to alter. First of all, check that your default paths are correct by clicking the Paths option. You may prefer to alter the My Documents path, as shown in Figure 6.3, to something a little more specific than just the Documents directory.

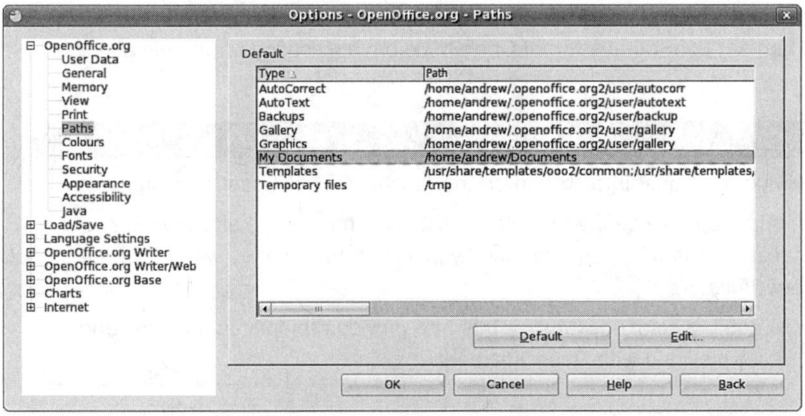

FIGURE 6.3   Click the Edit button to choose your default documents directory.

You might also want to change OpenOffice.org so that it saves in Microsoft Word format by default, should you so require. This can be done under the Load/Save General options shown in Figure 6.4, and it is a good idea if you value your work to change the Autorecovery settings so that it saves every couple of minutes.

Also shown in Figure 6.4 are a set of options that are specific to Writer. From top to bottom, they are

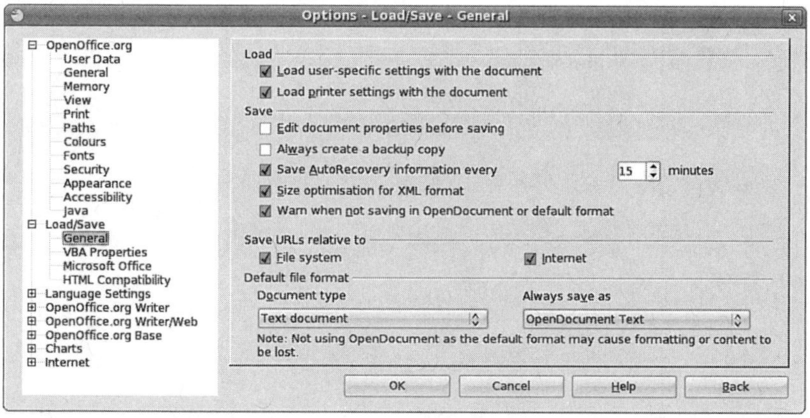

FIGURE 6.4   Make sure that you are working with most appropriate file formats for you.

▶ **General**—Specify options that affect the general use of Writer.

▶ **View**—Specify what you want Writer to display.

▶ **Formatting Aids**—Specify whether you want to see non-printing characters.

▶ **Grid**—Create a grid that you can use to snap frames and images in place.

▶ **Basic Fonts**—Select your default fonts for your document here.

▶ **Print**—Specify exactly what you want Writer to output when you print your document.

▶ **Table**—Set options for drawing tables within Writer.

▶ **Changes**—Define how Writer handles changes to documents.

▶ **Compatibility**—A set of rules that Writer uses to ensure close compatibility with earlier versions of Writer

▶ **AutoCaption**—Create automatic captions for images, charts, and other objects

A little bit of time working through these options can give you a highly personalized and extremely productive environment.

Working with Styles and Formatting

One of the significant benefits of using Writer is the ability you have to easily apply formatting and styles to extremely complex documents. Depending on the types of documents you work with, you might want to consider creating your own styles beyond the 20 included by default. You can access styles through either the Style drop-down box in the toolbar or the Styles and Formatting window shown in Figure 6.5. If you cannot see the window, press the F11 key to display it.

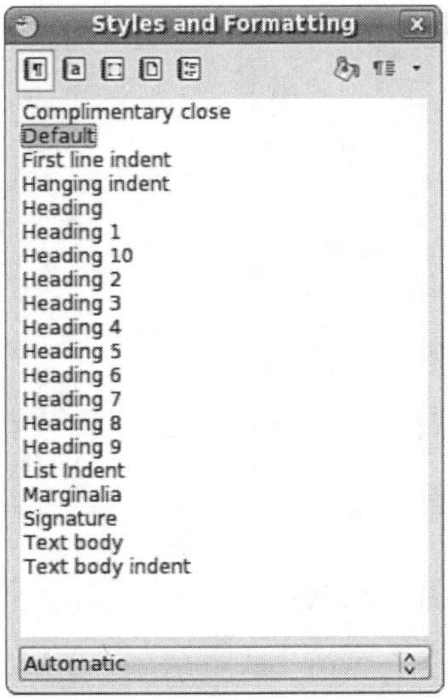

FIGURE 6.5   Writer's quick and easy-to-use Styles and Formatting tool.

The easiest way to work with the Styles and Formatting tool is to highlight the text you want to style and double-click the required style in the window. There are quite a few to choose from, but you might find them restrictive if you have more specialized needs. To start defining your own styles, press Ctrl+F11 to bring up the Style Catalogue, shown in Figure 6.6, where you add, modify and delete styles for pages, paragraphs, lists, characters and frames.

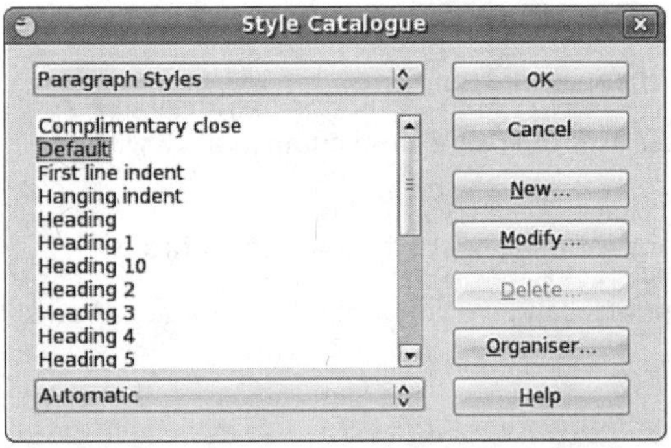

FIGURE 6.6   Writer's powerful Style Catalogue gives you control over every aspect of styling.

Working with OpenOffice.org Calc

The spreadsheet component of OpenOffice.org is named Calc, and is a very capable Excel alternative.

Calc is used for storing numerical information that you need to analyze in some way. So, for instance, you could use it to help you budget month by month. It can take care of the calculations for you, as long as you tell Calc what you want it to do. Anyone with experience in Excel will feel right at home with Calc.

In this section, we will show you how to get started with Calc, including entering formulas and formatting. We will also take a look at some of the more advanced features of Calc, including the Data Pilot feature, which allows you to easily summarize information.

Getting Started with Calc

You can either click the shortcut icon that is located on the top GNOME panel, or select Spreadsheet from the Office menu under the Applications main menu. Whichever route you take, the result is the same and Calc starts to load.

By default, Calc loads with a blank spreadsheet just waiting for you to enter information into it. In Figure 6.7, you can see that we have already started to enter some basic information into Calc.

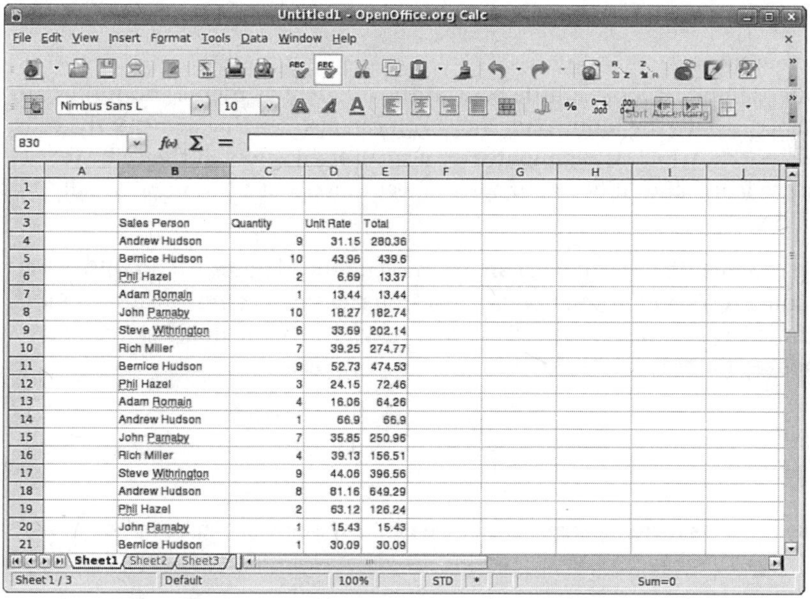

FIGURE 6.7   Use Calc to store numerical and statistical information.

Calc's layout makes it easy to organize information into rows and columns. As you can see in the example, we have sales people listed in the left column, customers in the second column, Invoice Date in the third column, and finally Revenue in the fourth column. At the moment, there are no formulas entered to help you interpret the data. Clicking the E30 cell selects it and enables you to enter in a formula in the top formula bar. If you enter in the equal sign, Calc knows that you are entering a formula and works accordingly.

In this example, we want to know the total revenue brought in up to now, so the formula to enter is =sum(E4:E29), followed by Return. Calc automatically enters the result into cell

E43 for you to see. Now you want to see what the average order value was. To do this, you have to obtain the number orders made. For this you can use the `counta` function to count the number of entries in a given list. This is usually used when you need to find out how many entries there are in a text list. So, in cell B30, enter **=counta(B4:B29)** and press Enter. Calc now counts the number of entries in the range and returns the total in B43. All that remains for you to do is divide the total revenue by the number of orders to find the average order value. So, in cell E31, enter the formula **=E30/B30** to get the average order value.

TIP

Calc offers some nifty little features that you can use quickly if you need to. The handiest one in our opinion is the capability to select multiple cells and see straight away the total and average of the range. You will find these figures in the bottom-right status bar. This has saved us numerous times when we have needed to get this information quickly!

Formatting Your Spreadsheets

Getting back to our example, it looks a little basic at the moment as there is no formatting involved. For instance, what's the billing currency? You can also see that some of the cells have text that does not fit, which is highlighted by a small right arrow in the cell. We should also add some labels and titles to our spreadsheet to make it a bit more visually appealing.

To start off, all the revenue figures can be changed into currency figures. To do this, select all the cells containing revenue information and click on the small coin icon shown in Figure 6.8. This immediately formats the cells so that they display the dollar sign and also puts in a thousands separator to make the numbers easier to read.

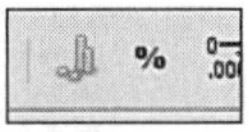

FIGURE 6.8   Make numbers more meaningful with the currency and percentage icons.

Now you need to space all the cells so that you can read all the information. A quick and easy way to do this is to click the area immediately to the left of column A and immediately above row 1 to select the entire spreadsheet. Now all you have to do is double-click the dividing lines and each column resizes according to its longest entry.

Next you can add a little color to the worksheet by using the paint can icon in the toolbar. Select the range B2 to E2 with the mouse cursor and click the background color icon to bring up the color window shown in Figure 6.9. Now select the color you want to use and Calc fills the cells with that color. You can also change the font color by using the icon immediately to the right in the same way.

Finally you need a couple more finishing touches. The first one is to enlarge the font for the column headers. Select the range B2 to E2 again and click the font size in the toolbar

FIGURE 6.9 Add a touch of color to an otherwise dull spreadsheet with the fill background icon.

to change it to something a little larger. You might also want to use the bold and italic options to emphasize the headers and also the totals some more.

If you have followed the steps as described, you should end up with a spreadsheet similar to the one in Figure 6.10.

	A	B	C	D	E	F
1						
2						
3		Sales Person	Quantity	Unit Rate	Total	
4		Andrew Hudson	9	$31.15	$280.36	
5		Bernice Hudson	10	$43.96	$439.60	
6		Phil Hazel	2	$6.69	$13.37	
7		Adam Romain	1	$13.44	$13.44	
8		John Parnaby	10	$18.27	$182.74	
9		Steve Withrington	6	$33.69	$202.14	
10		Rich Miller	7	$39.25	$274.77	
11		Bernice Hudson	9	$52.73	$474.53	
12		Phil Hazel	3	$24.15	$72.46	
13		Adam Romain	4	$16.06	$64.26	
14		Andrew Hudson	1	$66.90	$66.90	
15		John Parnaby	7	$35.85	$250.96	
16		Rich Miller	4	$39.13	$156.51	
17		Steve Withrington	9	$44.06	$396.56	
18		Andrew Hudson	8	$81.16	$649.29	
19		Phil Hazel	2	$63.12	$126.24	
20		John Parnaby	1	$15.43	$15.43	
21		Bernice Hudson	1	$30.09	$30.09	
22		Steve Withrington	2	$14.01	$28.02	

FIGURE 6.10 The finished spreadsheet, looking a lot better than before!

Summarizing Data with Calc

Calc includes a powerful tool that lets you summarize large groups of data to help you when you need to carry out any analysis. This tool is called a *data pilot*, and you can use it to quickly summarize data that might normally take a long time if you did the calculations manually. Using the sample spreadsheet from earlier, we will take you through how to build a simple data pilot, showing you how to analyze and manipulate long lists of data.

The previous section featured a spreadsheet that showed sales people, customers, date of invoice, and revenue. At the foot of the spreadsheet were a couple of formulas that enabled you to quickly see the total revenue earned and the average order value.

Now you want to find out how much sales people have earned individually. Of course you could add this up manually with a calculator, but that would defeat the point of using Calc. So, you need to create a data pilot to summarize the information.

First, you need to select all the cells from B2 to E42 as they contain the data you want to analyze. After these are selected, click on the Data menu and select Data Pilot, Start to open the Data Pilot Wizard. The first screen is shown in Figure 6.11 and is defaulted to Current Selection. Make sure that you choose this one to use the data in the selected range and click OK to continue.

FIGURE 6.11   Use either the current selection or an external data source to provide the data pilot with information.

The next screen enables you to lay out your data pilot as you want it. In this example you want to have Sales Person in the left column marked Row Fields, so click and drag the Sales Person option from the list on the right and drop it onto the Row Fields area. You're also interested in the average unit rate for each sales person, so drag Unit Rate into the Data Fields section and double-click it. In the window that comes up, select Average from the list and click the OK button. Finally, drag Revenue to the Data Field area so you can see how much revenue each sales person brought in. You should end up with something like Figure 6.12; you are almost ready to display your data pilot.

The final piece in the puzzle is to tell Calc where you want it to place the finished data pilot. To do this, click the More button to drop down some extra options and select the box Send Results To to choose a new sheet. When you click OK now, Calc builds the data pilot and displays it on a new sheet in your workbook. The new data pilot can be seen in Figure 6.13.

Office Suites for Ubuntu

As we have mentioned earlier, OpenOffice.org is the default application suite for Ubuntu. However, with all things open source, there are plenty of alternatives should you find that OpenOffice.org does not meet your specific requirements. These include the popular

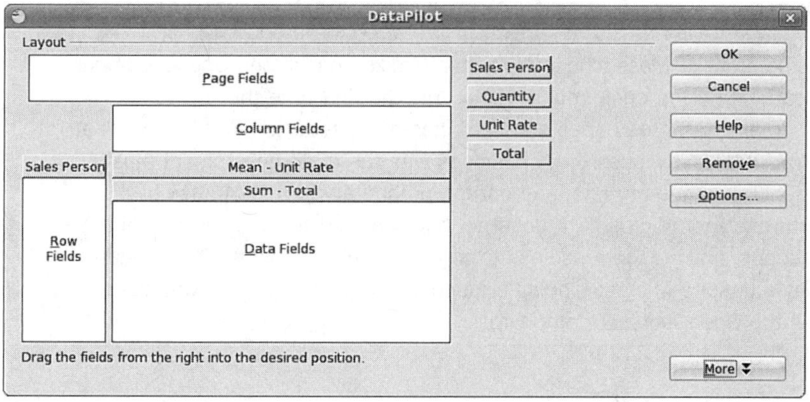

FIGURE 6.12   Lay your data pilot out as you want it.

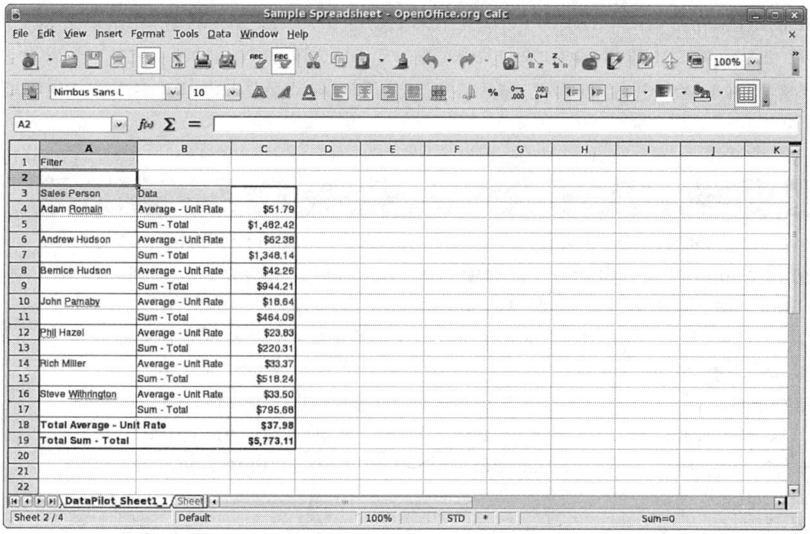

FIGURE 6.13   Summarize large volumes of numerical data with ease, using Calc's Data Pilot function.

Gnome Office and also KOffice, the default KDE productivity suite. You are more likely to hear more about OpenOffice.org, especially as more and more people wake up to the fact that it is compatible with Microsoft Office file formats. In fact, the state of Massachusetts recently elected to standardize on two file formats for use in government: the Adobe Acrobat PDF format and the OASIS OpenDocument format, both of which are supported natively in OpenOffice.org.

NOTE

The decision by the state of Massachusetts to standardize on PDF and OpenDocument has huge ramifications for the open source world. It is the first time that OpenDocument, an already-agreed open standard, has been specified in this way. What it means is that anyone who wishes to do business with the state government must use OpenDocument-based file formats, and not the proprietary formats in use by Microsoft. Unfortunately for Microsoft, it does not have support for OpenDocument in any of its applications, making them useless to anyone wishing to work with the state government. This is despite Microsoft being a founding member of OASIS, who developed and ratified the OpenDocument standard!

Working with Gnome Office

The other office suite available for GNOME is Gnome Office, which is a collection of individual applications. Unlike OpenOffice.org, Gnome Office does not have a coherent suite of applications, meaning that you have to get used to using a word processor that offers no integration with a spreadsheet, and that cannot work directly with a presentation package. However, if you need only one or two components, it is worthwhile investigating Gnome Office.

The GTK Widget Set

Open Source developers are always trying to make it easier for people to build applications and help in development. To this end, there are a number of widgets or toolkits that other developers can use to rapidly create and deploy GUI applications. These widgets control things such as drop-down lists, Save As dialogs, window buttons, and general look and feel. Unfortunately, whereas Windows and Apple developers have to worry about only one set of widgets each, Linux has a plethora of different widgets, including GTK+, QT, and Motif. What is worse is that these widgets are incompatible with one another, making it difficult to easily move a finished application from one widget set to another.

GTK is an acronym for *GIMP Tool Kit*. The GIMP (The GNU Image Manipulation Program) is a graphics application very similar to Adobe Photoshop. By using the GTK-based jargon, we save ourselves several hundred words of typing and help move along our discussion of GNOME Office. You might also see similar references to QT and Motif, as well as other widget sets, in these chapters.

Here are some of the primary components of the Gnome Office suite that are available in Ubuntu:

▶ **AbiWord**—This word processing program enables you to compose, format, and organize text documents and has some compatibility with the Microsoft Word file format. It uses plug-ins (programs that add functionality such as language translation) to enhance its functionality.

> ▶ **Gnumeric**—This spreadsheet program enables you to manipulate numbers in a spreadsheet format. Support for all but the most esoteric Microsoft Excel functions means that users should have little trouble trading spreadsheets with Excel users.

> ▶ **The GIMP**—This graphics application allows you to create images for general use. It can import and export all common graphic file formats. The GIMP is analogous to Adobe's Photoshop application and is described in Chapter 7, "Multimedia Applications."

> ▶ **Evolution**—Evolution is a mail client with an interface similar to Microsoft Outlook, providing email, scheduling, and calendaring. It is described in Chapter 5, "On the Internet."

The loose association of applications known as Gnome Office includes several additional applications that duplicate the functionality of applications already provided by Ubuntu. Those extra GNOME applications are not included in a default installation of Ubuntu to eliminate redundancy. They are all available from the Gnome Office website, at http://www.gnome.org/gnome-office/. Both The GIMP and Evolution are available with Ubuntu by default. You have to use synaptic to retrieve the remaining components.

Ubuntu provides the AbiWord editor, shown in Figure 6.14, as part of its Extras. AbiWord can import XML, Microsoft Word, RTF, UTF8, plain text, WordPerfect, KWord, and a few other formats. AbiWord is notable for its use of plug-ins, or integrated helper applications, that extend its capabilities. These plug-ins add language translation, HTML editing, a thesaurus, a Linux command shell, and an online dictionary, among other functions and features. If you just need a simple yet powerful word processing application, you should examine AbiWord.

AbiWord is not installed by default in Ubuntu so you'll need to install it either using apt-get or synaptic. The package is simply called abiword-gnome although you might want to install the meta-package gnome-office which will include the other Gnome Office applications.

After you've installed Abiword, it becomes available in the Applications menu, under the Office submenu. Simply click the icon to launch the application.

If you are familiar with Microsoft Works, the AbiWord interface will be familiar to you because its designers based the interface upon Works.

You can use the Gnumeric spreadsheet application to perform financial calculations and to graph data, as shown in Figure 6.15. It can import comma- or tab-separated files, text, or files in the Gnumeric XML format, saving files only as XML or text. You need to install Gnumeric using either apt-get or synaptic in the same way as Abiword. If you have already installed the gnome-office package then Gnumeric will be available under Applications, Office as Gnumeric Spreadsheet.

After you press Enter, the main Gnumeric window appears. You enter data in the spreadsheet by clicking a cell and then typing in the text box. To create a graph, you click and drag over the spreadsheet cells to highlight the desired data, and then you click the Graph Wizard icon in Gnumeric's toolbar. Gnumeric's graphing component launches and you are

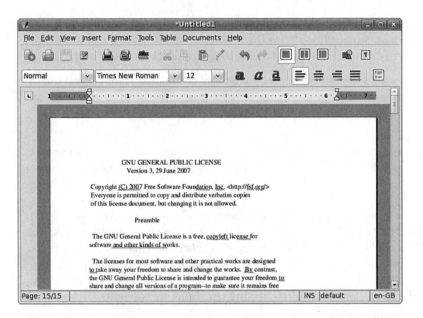

FIGURE 6.14 AbiWord is a word processing program for Ubuntu, GNOME, and X11. It handles some formats that OpenOffice.org cannot, but does not yet do well with Microsoft Word formats.

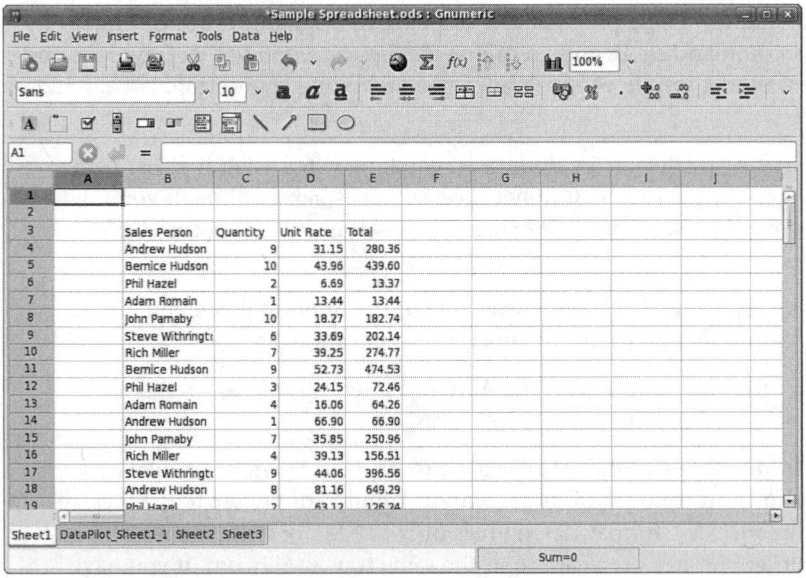

FIGURE 6.15 GNOME's Gnumeric is a capable financial data editor—here working with the same spreadsheet used earlier. OpenOffice.org also provides a spreadsheet application, as does KOffice.

guided through a series of dialogs to create a graph. When you are finished, you can click and drag a blank area of your spreadsheet, and the graph appears.

The Project Planner application is useful for tracking the progress of projects, much like its Windows counterpart, Microsoft Project. When the main window is displayed, you can start a new project or import an existing project. The application provides three views: Resources, Gantt Charts, and Tasks.

Working with KOffice

The KDE office suite KOffice was developed to provide tight integration with the KDE desktop. Integration enables objects in one application to be inserted in other applications via drag-and-drop, and all the applications can communicate with each other, so a change in an object is instantly communicated to other applications. The application integration provided by KDE is a significant enhancement to productivity. (Some GNOME desktop applications share a similar communication facility with each other.) If you use the KDE desktop instead of the default GNOME desktop, you can enjoy the benefits of this integration, along with the Konqueror web and file browser.

The word processor for KOffice is KWord. KWord is a frames-based word processor, meaning that document pages can be formatted in framesets that hold text, graphics, and objects in enclosed areas. Framesets can be used to format text on a page that includes text and images within columns that the text needs to flow around, making KWord an excellent choice for creating documents other than standard business letters, such as newsletters and brochures.

KWord and other components of KOffice are still under development and lack all the polished features of OpenOffice.org and AbiWord. However, it does have the ability to work with the OpenDocument format found in OpenOffice.org, as well as limited compatibility with Microsoft file formats.

You can access the KOffice components from the Office menu.

KWord asks you to select a document for your session. The KWord client, shown in Figure 6.16, offers sophisticated editing capabilities, including desktop publishing.

The KOffice KSpread client is a functional spreadsheet program that offers graphing capabilities. Like KWord, KSpread can be accessed from the Office menu.

KDE includes other productivity clients in its collection of KOffice and related applications. These clients include an address book, time tracker, calculator, notepad, and scheduler. One popular client is Kontact, which provides daily, weekly, work week, and monthly views of tasks, to-do lists, and scheduled appointments with background alarms. A journal, or diary, function is also supported within it, and you can synchronize information with your Palm Pilot. You can launch this client from the Office menu.

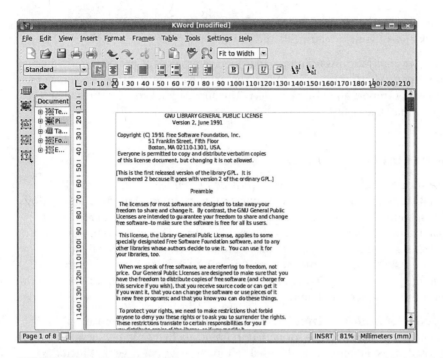

FIGURE 6.16 The KOffice KWord word processing component is a sophisticated frames-based WYSIWYG editor that is suitable for light desktop publishing, supporting several formats, including WordPerfect.

A typical Kontact window is shown in Figure 6.17.

Productivity Applications Written for Microsoft Windows

Microsoft Windows is fundamentally different from Linux, yet you can install and run some Microsoft Windows applications in Linux by using an application named Wine. Wine enables you to use Microsoft Windows and DOS programs on Unix-based systems. Wine includes a program loader that you can use to execute a Windows binary, along with a .dll library that implements Windows command calls, translating them to the equivalent Unix and X11 command calls. Because of frequent updates to the Wine code base, Wine is not included with Ubuntu. Download a current version of Wine from http://www. winehq.org/. To see whether your favorite application is supported by Wine, you can look at the Wine application database at http://appdb.winehq.org/appbrowse.php.

As well, there are other solutions to enable use of Microsoft productivity applications, primarily CodeWeavers' CrossOver Office. If you are after a painless way of running not only Microsoft Office, but also Apple iTunes and other software, you should really pay CodeWeavers a visit. CrossOver Office is one of the simplest programs you can use to get Windows-based programs to work. Check out www.codeweavers.com to download a trial

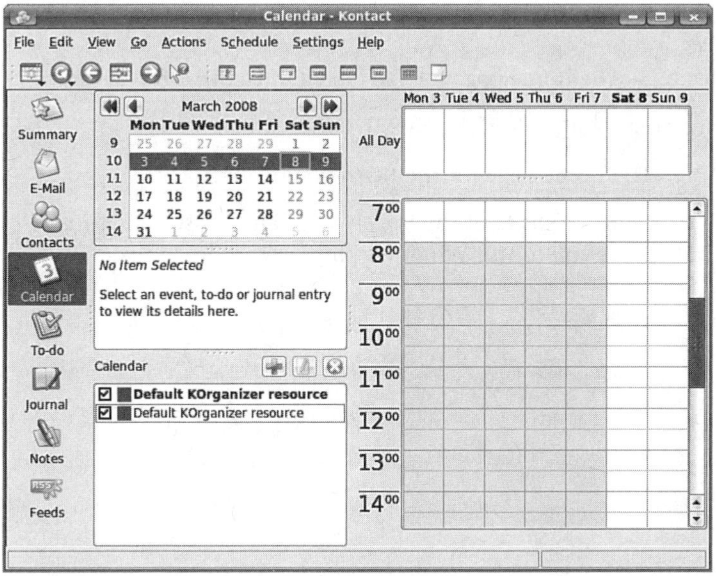

FIGURE 6.17   KDE's Kontact client supports editing of tasks and schedules that you can sync with your PDA. Shown here is the address book as well.

version of the latest software. It requires registration, but do not worry—the guys at CodeWeavers are great and will not misuse your details. The big plus is that you get a whole month to play around with the trial before you decide whether to buy it. Of course, you might get to the end of the 30 days and realize that Linux does what you want it to do and you don't want to go back to Windows. Do not be afraid; take the plunge!

Relevant Ubuntu Commands

The following commands give you access to productivity applications, tools, and processes in Ubuntu:

- ▶ oowriter—OpenOffice.org's Writer
- ▶ oocalc—OpenOffice.org's Calc
- ▶ ooimpress—OpenOffice.org's Impress
- ▶ koshell—KDE's KOffice office suite shell
- ▶ kspread—KDE's KSpread spreadsheet
- ▶ gimp—The GIMP (GNU Image Manipulation Package)
- ▶ gnumeric—A spreadsheet editor for GNOME
- ▶ planner—A project management client for GNOME
- ▶ abiword—A graphical word processor for GNOME

Reference

▶ http://www.openoffice.org—The home page for the OpenOffice.org office suite.

▶ http://www.gnome.org/gnome-office/—The GNOME Office site.

▶ http://www.koffice.org/—The home page for the KOffice suite.

▶ http://www.codeweavers.com/—Website of the hugely popular CrossOver Office from CodeWeavers that allows you to run Windows programs under Linux.

# CHAPTER 7

Multimedia Applications

The twenty-first century has become the century of the digital lifestyle, with millions of computer users around the world embracing new technologies, such as digital cameras, MP3 players, and other assorted multimedia gadgets. Whereas 10 years ago you might have had a collection of WAV files littering your Windows installation, nowadays you are more likely to have hundreds, if not thousands of MP3 files scattered across various computers. Along with video clips, animations, and other graphics, the demand for organizing and maintaining these vast libraries is driving development of applications. Popular proprietary applications such as iTunes and Google's Picasa are coveted by Linux users, but open source applications are starting to appear that provide real alternatives, and for some the final reasons they need to move to Linux full time.

This chapter provides an overview of some of the basic multimedia tools included with Ubuntu. You will see how to create your own CDs, watch TV, rip audio CDs into the open source Ogg audio format for playback, as well as manage your media library. You will also learn about how Ubuntu handles graphics and pictures.

Sound and Music

Linux historically had a reputation of lacking good support for sound and multimedia applications in general. However, great strides have been made in recent years to correct this, and support is now a lot better than it used to be. (It might make you smile to know that Microsoft no longer supports the Microsoft Sound Card, but Linux users still enjoy support for it, no doubt just to annoy the folks in

Redmond.) Unix, however, has always had good multimedia support as David Taylor, Unix author and guru, points out:

> The original graphics work for computers was done by Evans & Sutherland on Unix systems. The innovations at MIT's Media Lab were done on Unix workstations. In 1985, we at HP Labs were creating sophisticated multimedia immersive work environments on Unix workstations, so maybe Unix is more multimedia than suggested. Limitations in Linux support doesn't mean Unix had the same limitations. I think it was more a matter of logistics, with hundreds of sound cards and thousands of different possible PC configurations.

That last sentence sums it up quite well. Unix had a limited range of hardware to support; Linux has hundreds of sound cards. Sound card device driver support has been long lacking from manufacturers, and there is still no single standard for the sound subsystem in Linux.

In this section, you learn about sound cards, sound file formats, and the sound applications provided with Ubuntu.

Sound Cards

Ubuntu supports a wide variety of sound hardware and software. Two models of sound card drivers compete for prominence in today's market:

▶ ALSA, the Advanced Linux Sound Architecture, which is entirely open source

▶ OSS, the Open Sound System, which offers free and commercial drivers

Ubuntu uses ALSA because ALSA is the sound architecture for the 2.6 series kernels.

ALSA supports a long list of sound cards. You can review the list at http://www.alsa-project.org/alsa-doc/. If your sound card is not supported, it might be supported in the commercial version of OSS. You can download a trial version of commercial software and test your sound card at http://www.opensound.com/download.cgi.

Ubuntu detects most sound cards during the original installation and should detect any new additions to the system during boot up. To configure the sound card at any other time, use the sound preferences graphical tool found under System, Preferences, Sound.

In addition, since the 8.04 release, Ubuntu uses an additional layer of software called PulseAudio. PulseAudio is what is called a sound server and acts as a mediator between the various multimedia programs that have sound output and the ALSA kernel drivers. Over the years there have been many different sound servers used in Linux, each with different strengths, usability issues, and levels of documentation. These various sound servers have often been forced to run side by side on the same computer causing all sorts of confusion and issues. PulseAudio aims to replace all of them and work as a single handler to accept output from applications which use the APIs for any of the major sound servers already in use like ESD, OSS, Gstreamer, and aRts and route the various output streams together through one handler. This gives several advantages including the ability to control the output volume of various programs individually.

PulseAudio is still quite young and not all of ifs full potential has yet been realized, however it has already seen great improvements in the intervening releases and is better and more powerful than ever in 9.10. While there were stability issues and complaints in the first release that included PulseAudio, those don't seem to be a problem any more except in unusual hardware combinations and special cases and more and more features have been implemented. For more information about PulseAudio, please see http://www.pulseaudio.org/ .

Adjusting Volume

Ubuntu offers a handy utility that you can use to control the volumes for various outputs from your computer. For a simple master volume control, just click on the speaker icon in the top-right corner of the screen and move the slider up or down, as shown in Figure 7.1.

Alternatively you can control all the output volumes for the system to make sure that you have set everything to your taste, as shown in Figure 7.2. To access the volume control, right-click on the speaker icon and select Open Volume Control.

FIGURE 7.1   Control the master volume level with the volume slider.

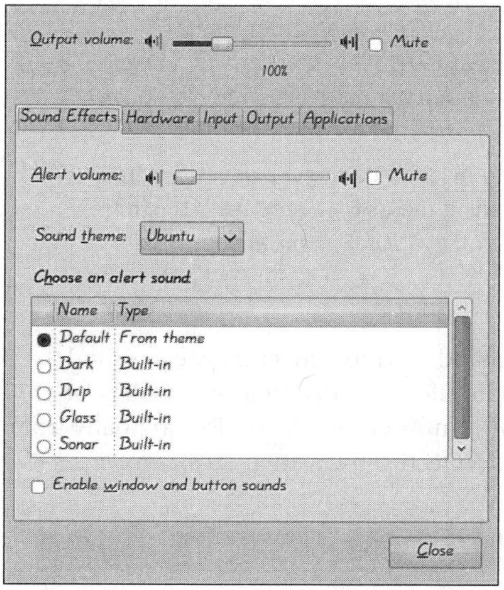

FIGURE 7.2   Use the volume control to manage volume settings for all your sound output devices.

Sound Formats

A number of formats exist for storing sound recordings. Some of these formats are associated with specific technologies, and others are used strictly for proprietary reasons. Ubuntu supports several of the most popular sound formats, including

▶ raw (`.raw`)—More properly known as *headerless format*, audio files using this format contain an amorphous variety of specific settings and encodings. All other sound files contain a short section of code at the beginning—a header—that identifies the format type.

▶ MP3 (`.mp3`)—A popular, but commercially licensed, format for the digital encoding used by many Linux and Windows applications. MP3 is not supported by any software included with Ubuntu (which advises you to use the open source Ogg-Vorbis format instead).

▶ WAV (`.wav`)—The popular uncompressed Windows audio-visual sound format. It is often used as an intermediate file format when encoding audio.

▶ Ogg-Vorbis (`.ogg`)—Ubuntu's preferred audio encoding format. You enjoy better compression and audio playback, and freedom from lawsuits when you use this open-source encoding format for your audio files.

NOTE

Because of patent and licensing issues, Ubuntu has removed support for the MPEG, MPEG2, and MPEG3 (MP3) file formats in Ubuntu Linux. Although we cannot offer any legal advice, it appears that individuals using MP3 software are okay; it is just that Ubuntu cannot distribute the code because it sells its distribution. It seems—at this point—perfectly all right for you to obtain an MP3-capable version of Xmms (for example), which is a Winamp clone that plays MPEG1/2/3 files. You can get Xmms directly from http://www.xmms.org/ because that group has permission to distribute the MP3 code.

You can also enable the MP3 codec within Ubuntu by downloading a plugin for gstreamer, the GNOME audio system. You do this by installing the `gstreamer0.10-plugins-ugly` package, which enables the MP3 codec in all the GNOME applications.

Ubuntu includes software (such as the sox command used to convert between sound formats) so that you can more easily listen to audio files provided in a wide variety of formats, such as AU (from NeXT and Sun), AIFF (from Apple and SGI), IFF (originally from Commodore's Amiga), RA (from Real Audio), and VOC (from Creative Labs).

TIP

To learn more about the technical details of audio formats, read Chris Bagwell's Audio Format FAQ at http://www.cnpbagwell.com/audio.html.

Ubuntu also offers utilities for converting sound files from one format to another. Conversion utilities come in handy when you want to use a sound in a format not accepted by your current application of choice. A repository of conversion utilities resides at http://ibiblio.org/pub/linux/apps/sound/convert/!INDEX.html and includes MP3 and music CD–oriented utilities not found in Ubuntu. You have to know how to compile and install from source, however.

Ubuntu does provide sox, a self-described sound translator that converts music among the AIFF, AU, VAR, DAT, Ogg, WAV, and other formats. It also can be used to change many other parameters of the sound files.

Timidity is a MIDI-to-WAV converter and player. If you are interested in MIDI and musical instruments, Timidity is a handy application; it handles karaoke files as well, displaying the words to accompany your efforts at singing.

Listening to Music

If you're anything like us, you might be a huge music fan. One of the downsides of having a fairly large music collection is the physical problem of having to store so many CDs. Wouldn't it be great if you could pack them all away somewhere, yet still have access to all the music when you want it? Some hi-fi manufacturers experimented with rather bulky jukeboxes that stored 250 CDs at once. The main downside with that was that finding a particular piece of music could take hours, having to cycle through each CD in the hope that it would match your mood.

Fortunately for you and me, Ubuntu is fantastic at working with CDs, even allowing you to rip all your CD collection into a vast searchable music library, letting you quickly create playlists and even giving you the ability to create your own customized CDs. Getting started couldn't be easier, mainly because Ubuntu comes preconfigured with everything you need to get started.

RhythmBox

A standard CD player application was supplied in previous versions of Ubuntu, but this has now been dropped largely due to the fact that other applications made it redundant. In its place is RhythmBox, a useful application that does more than just play CDs. If you insert an audio CD into your computer, RhythmBox will appear and attempt to obtain information about the CD from the Internet service MusicBrainz. If it's successful, then you'll see the name of the CD appear in the left window of RhythmBox, as shown in Figure 7.3.

When you're ready to play your CD, simply click the name of the CD under the devices section and click the Play button, as shown in Figure 7.4. You can also define whether the CD should just repeat itself until stopped, or whether you want to shuffle the music (randomize the playlist).

Of course, just listening to your CDs doesn't really change anything; RhythmBox acts just like a regular CD player, allowing you to listen to specific tracks and define how you want to listen to your music by using playlists or sorting it by artists. The real fun starts when you click the Copy to Library button in your toolbar. RhythmBox then starts to extract, or

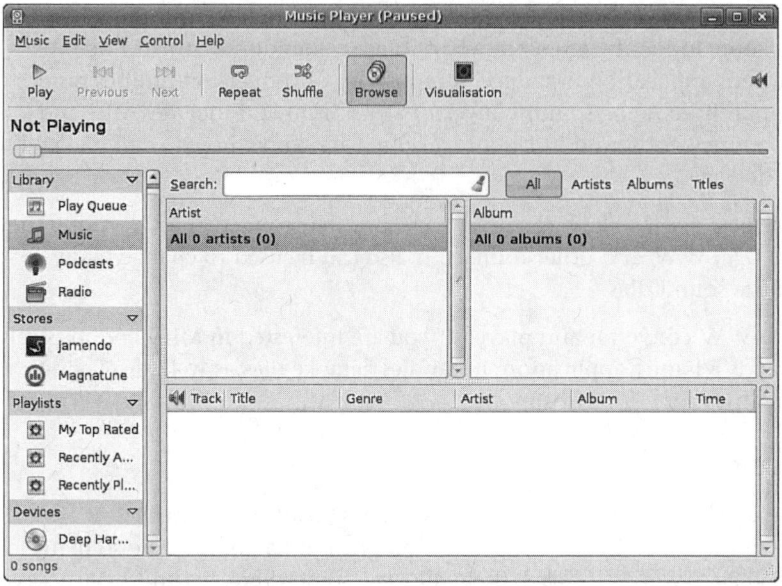

FIGURE 7.3   RhythmBox automatically downloads information about your CD, if it's available.

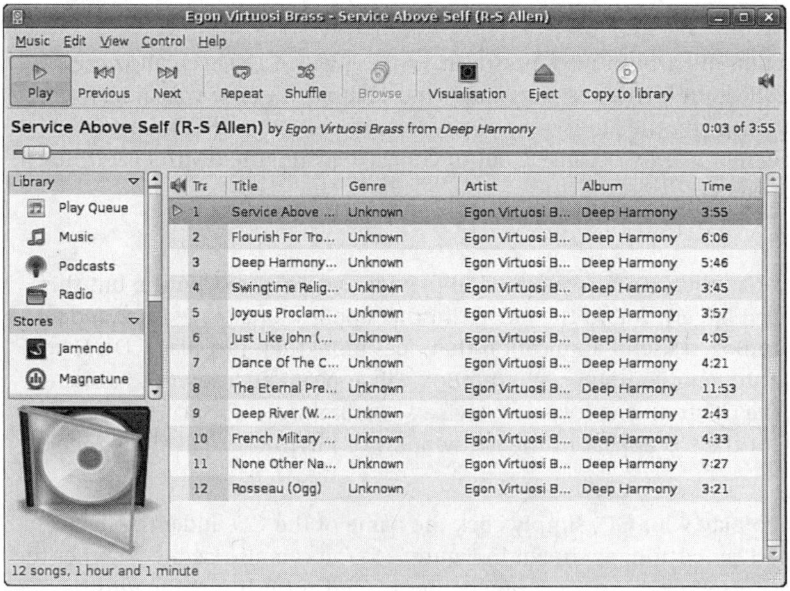

FIGURE 7.4   Just like the normal controls on a CD player, RhythmBox responds to your requests.

rip, the audio from your CD and store it within the Music directory that is found under your home directory. If you have already clicked this button, then go to the Places menu and select Music (see Figure 7.5) to see what's happening.

FIGURE 7.5   RhythmBox does a good job of keeping your newly ripped audio files organized.

Depending on the speed of your optical drive and the power of your computer, the ripping process can take up to 15 minutes to complete a full CD. As it goes along, RhythmBox automatically adds the files to your media library, which you can access by clicking the Music button on the left side of the RhythmBox screen, as you can see in Figure 7.6.

Within the RhythmBox interface you can easily browse through the list of artist names or album titles, which affects the track listing that appears at the bottom of the screen. The numbers after each artist and album tell you how many tracks are assigned to that specific entry, giving you a heads up before you click on them. Double-clicking on any entry automatically starts the music playing, so for example, double-clicking an artist's name causes the music tracks associated with that artist to start playing. When a track starts to play, RhythmBox automatically attempts to retrieve the CD artwork, which it then displays in the bottom-left corner of the screen, shown in Figure 7.7.

There's a lot more that you can do with RhythmBox, including downloading and listening to podcasts. A good place to start if you want to get hold of the latest podcasts is to head to the Linux Link (www.thelinuxlink.net) where you'll find a long list of Linux-related podcasts. All you have to do is right-click on the RSS link for the Ogg feed and select Copy Link Location. Now go to RhythmBox and press Ctrl+P, or go to Music, New Podcast Feed, paste the link into the field, and click the Add button. RhythmBox then contacts the

FIGURE 7.6   RhythmBox gives you a neat interface to browse through your burgeoning music collection.

FIGURE 7.7   A nice touch is RhythmBox's being able to automatically retrieve CD artwork from the Internet.

server and attempts to download the most recent episodes of your chosen podcast, which you can see happening in Figure 7.8.

FIGURE 7.8   Manage your podcasts using RhythmBox and never miss an episode again.

Banshee

Of course, other programs are available for listening to music within Ubuntu. One of our particular favorites is Banshee, another music application that can also handle ripping and playing back music. Banshee is not installed by default with Ubuntu, so you'll need to use synaptic to download and install it. After it's installed, you can access it under Applications, Sound and Video, as shown in Figure 7.9, complete with a selection of music.

Banshee can rip music in a similar way to RhythmBox; all you have to do is insert a CD and Banshee will detect it. If you want to import it into Banshee, simply select it in the left navigation pane and click the Import CD button. In Figure 7.10, you can see Banshee ripping a CD.

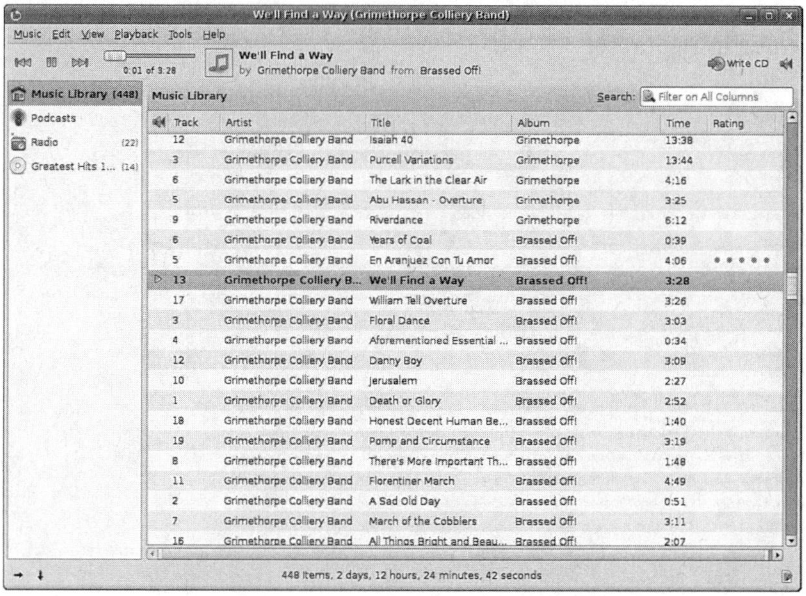

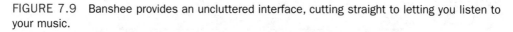

FIGURE 7.9 Banshee provides an uncluttered interface, cutting straight to letting you listen to your music.

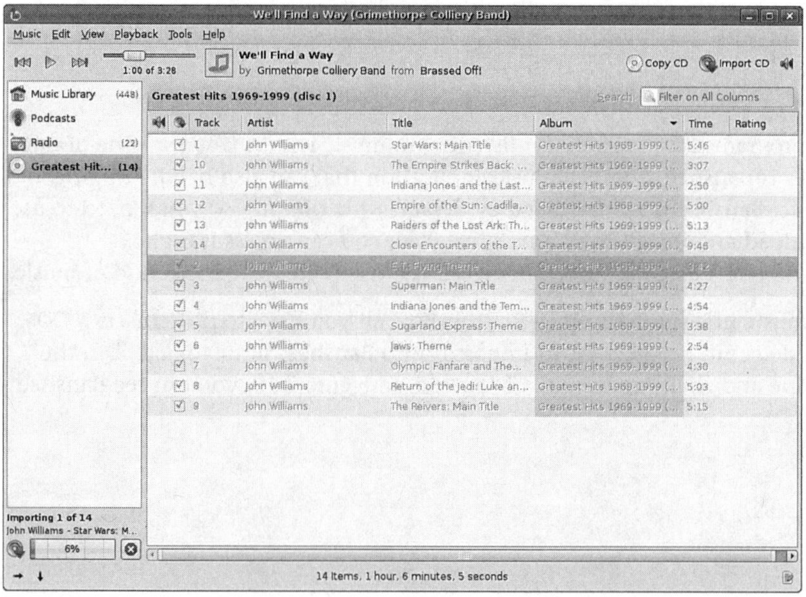

FIGURE 7.10 Banshee makes light work of ripping your CD collection.

Just as with RhythmBox, Banshee will attempt to download the cover art and track information for the CD that you're either playing or ripping.

Getting Music into Ubuntu with Sound Juicer

A handy utility that is included with Ubuntu is Sound Juicer, found under Applications, Sound and Video as the Audio CD Extractor. Sound Juicer automatically detects when you install a CD and attempt to retrieve the track details from the Internet. From there it will rip the CD tracks into Ogg files for storage on your filesystem. You can see Sound Juicer in action in Figure 7.11

FIGURE 7.11   Create your own digital music collection with Sound Juicer.

Graphics Manipulation

Over a very short space of time, digital cameras and digital imagery have become extremely popular, to the point where some traditional film camera manufacturers are switching solely to digital. This meteoric rise has led to an increase in the number of applications that can handle digital imagery. Linux, thanks to its rapid pace of development, is now highly regarded as a multimedia platform of choice for editing digital images.

This section of the chapter discusses The GIMP, a powerful graphics manipulation tool. You also learn about graphic file formats supported by Ubuntu, as well as some tools you can use to convert them if the application you want to use requires a different format.

The GNU Image Manipulation Program

One of the best graphics clients available is The GIMP. The GIMP is a free, GPLed image editor with sophisticated capabilities that can import and export more than 30 different graphics formats, including files created with Adobe Photoshop. It is often compared with

Photoshop, and The GIMP represents one of the GNU Projects' first significant successes. Many images in Linux were prepared with The GIMP.

The GIMP can be found under the Applications, Graphics menu as simply The GIMP.

You see an installation dialog box when The GIMP is started for the first time, and then a series of dialog boxes that display information regarding the creation and contents of a local GIMP directory. This directory can contain personal settings, preferences, external application resource files, temporary files, and symbolic links to external software tools used by the editor.

What Does Photoshop Have That Isn't in the GIMP?

Although The GIMP is powerful, it does lack two features Adobe Photoshop offers that are important to some graphics professionals.

The first of these is the capability to generate color separations for commercial press printers (CMYK for the colors cyan, magenta, yellow, and key [or black]). The GIMP uses RGB (red, green, and blue), which is great for video display, but not so great for printing presses. The second feature The GIMP lacks is the use of Pantone colors (a patented color specification) to ensure accurate color matching.

If these features are unimportant to you, The GIMP is an excellent tool. If you must use Adobe Photoshop, the current version of CodeWeavers' CrossOver Office will run Photoshop in Linux.

These deficiencies might not last long. A CMYK plug-in is in the works, and the Pantone issues are likely to be addressed in the near future as well.

After the initial configuration has finished, The GIMP's main windows and toolboxes appear. The GIMP's main window contains tools used for selecting, drawing, moving, view enlarging or reducing, airbrushing, painting, smudging, copying, filling, and selecting color. Depending on the version installed on your system, the toolbox can host more than 25 different tools.

The toolbox's File, Xtns, and Help menus are used for file operations (including sending the current image by electronic mail), image acquisition or manipulation, and documentation, respectively. If you right-click an open image window, you see the wealth of The GIMP's menus, as shown in Figure 7.12.

Using Scanners in Ubuntu

With the rise of digital photography, there has been an equal decline in the need for image scanners. However, there are still times that you want to use a scanner, and Ubuntu makes it easy.

You can also use many types of image scanners with The GIMP. In the past, the most capable scanners required a SCSI port. Today, however, most scanners work through a USB port. You must have scanner support enabled for Linux (usually through a loaded kernel module, scanner.o) before using a scanner with The GIMP.

FIGURE 7.12   Right-click on an image window to access The GIMP's cascading menus.

Although some scanners can work via the command line, you will enjoy more productive scanning sessions if you use a graphical interface because GUI features, such as previewing and cropping, can save time before actually scanning an image. Most scanners in use with Linux use the Scanner Access Now Easy (*SANE*) package, which supports and enables graphical scanning sessions.

SANE consists of two software components. A low-level driver enables the hardware support and is specific to each scanner. Next, a graphical scanner interface X client known as xsane is used as a plug-in or ancillary program (or script) that adds features to The GIMP.

NOTE

Although xsane is commonly used as a GIMP plug-in, it can also be used as a stand-alone program. Another useful program is Joerg Schulenburg's gocr client, used for optical character recognition (*OCR*). Although not a standalone application, it is included in the Kooka scanning application. This program works best with 300 dots per inch (*dpi*) scans in several different graphics formats. OCR is a resource-intensive task and can require hundreds of megabytes of disk storage!

A list of currently supported scanners can be found at http://www.sane-project.org/sane-supported-devices.html. Unfortunately, if your scanner doesn't appear on the list, you should not expect it to work with the SANE software. There is also a list on that same page for drivers not yet included, but you must be able to compile the application from source to use them.

Supported USB scanners are automatically detected and the appropriate driver is loaded automatically. The USB devices tell the USB system several pieces of information when they are connected—the most important of which are the vendor ID and the device ID. This identification is used to look up the device in a table and load the appropriate driver. You will find that Ubuntu successfully identifies and configures most modern USB-based scanners.

Many scanners are supported in Linux. If yours is not, it still might be possible to use it. The Kooka and Xsane scanner applications are included with Ubuntu and are fairly straightforward to use. They can both be found in the Graphics menu as the Scanner Tool.

Working with Graphics Formats

Image file formats are developed to serve a specific technical purpose (lossless compression, for example, where the file size is reduced without sacrificing image quality) or to meet a need for a proprietary format for competitive reasons. Many file formats are covered by one or more patents. For example, the GIF format had fallen into disfavor with the open-source crowd because the patent holder waited a while before deciding to enforce his patent rights rather than being upfront with requests for patent royalties.

If you want to view or manipulate an image, you need to identify the file format to choose the proper tool for working with the image. The file's extension is your first indicator of the file's format. The graphics image formats supported by the applications included with Ubuntu include

- ▶ .bmp—Bitmapped graphics, commonly used in Microsoft Windows
- ▶ .gif—CompuServe Graphics Interchange Format
- ▶ .jpg—Joint Photographic Experts Group
- ▶ .pcx—IBM Paintbrush
- ▶ .png—Portable Network Graphics
- ▶ .svg—Scalable Vector Graphics
- ▶ .tif—Tagged Image File format

An extensive list of image file extensions can be found in the man page for ImageMagick, an excellent application included with Ubuntu, which you learn more about in upcoming sections of this chapter.

TIP

Ubuntu includes dozens of graphics conversion programs that are accessible through the command line, and there are few, if any, graphics file formats that cannot be manipulated when using Linux. These programs can be called in Perl scripts, shell scripts, or command-line pipes to support many types of complex format conversion and image manipulation tasks. See the man pages for the ppm, pbm, pnm, and pgm families of commands. Also see the man page for the convert command, which is part of a suite of extremely capable programs included with the ImageMagick suite.

Often, a file you want to manipulate in some way is in a format that cannot be used by either your graphics application or the final application. The solution is to convert the image file—sometimes through several formats. The convert utility from ImageMagick is useful, as is the netpbm family of utilities. If it is not already installed, ImageMagick can be installed with the Add Remove Software GUI found in the System Settings menu; the netpbm tools are always installed by default.

The convert utility converts between image formats recognized by ImageMagick. Color depth and size also can be manipulated during the conversion process. You can use ImageMagick to append images, surround them with borders, add labels, rotate and shade them, and perform other manipulations well suited to scripting. Commands associated with ImageMagick include display, animate, identify, and import. The application supports more than 130 different image formats—(all listed in the man page for ImageMagick).

The netpbm tools are installed by default because they compose the underpinnings of graphics format manipulation. The man page for each image format lists related conversion utilities; the number of those utilities gives you some indication of the way that format is used and shows how one is built on another:

- ▶ The man page for ppm, the portable pixmap file format, lists 47 conversion utilities related to ppm. This makes sense because ppm, or *portable pixmap*, is considered the lowest common denominator for color image files. It is therefore often used as an intermediate format.

- ▶ The man page for pgm, the portable graymap file format, lists 22 conversion utilities. This makes sense because pgm is the lowest common denominator for grayscale image files.

- ▶ The man page for pnm, the portable anymap file format, lists 31 conversion utilities related to it. However, there is no format associated with PNM because it operates in concert with ppm, pgm, and pbm.

- ▶ An examination of the man page for pbm, the portable bitmap file format, reveals no conversion utilities. It's a monochrome format and serves as the foundation of the other related formats.

Capturing Screen Images

You can use graphics manipulation tools to capture images that are displayed on your computer screen. Although this technique was used for the production of this book, it has broader uses; there is truth to the cliché that a picture is worth a thousand words. Sometimes it is easier to show an example than it is to describe it.

A captured screen image (also called a *screen grab* or a *screenshot*) can be used to illustrate an error in the display of an application (a font problem, for example) or an error dialog that is too complex to copy down by hand. You might just want to share an image of your beautifully crafted custom desktop configuration with your friends or illustrate your written documents.

When using the GNOME desktop, you can take advantage of the built-in screenshot mechanism (gnome-panel-screenshot). Access this tool by pressing the Print Screen key. (Alt+Print Screen takes a screenshot of only the window that has focus on a desktop.) Captured images are saved in .png format.

Using Digital Cameras with Ubuntu

Most digital cameras used in connection with Ubuntu fall into one of two categories: webcams (small, low-resolution cameras connected to the computer's interface) or hand-held digital cameras that record image data on disks or memory cards for downloading and viewing on a PC. Ubuntu supports both types. Other types of cameras, such as surveillance cameras that connect directly to a network via wired or wireless connections, need no special support (other than a network connection and viewing software) to be used with a Linux computer.

Ubuntu supports hundreds of different digital cameras, from early parallel-port (CPiA chipset-based) cameras to today's USB-based cameras. You can even use Intel's QX3 USB microscope with Ubuntu. If you prefer a standalone network-based webcam, explore the capabilities of Linux-based cameras from Axis (at http://www.axis.com/products/video/camera/productguide.htm). The following sections describe some of the more commonly used still camera hardware and software supported by Ubuntu.

Handheld Digital Cameras

Digital cameras are one of the major success stories of the last few years. Now you can take pictures and see previews of your pictures immediately. The pictures themselves are stored on discs or memory cards that can be easily plugged into Ubuntu for further manipulation, using The GIMP or other software. Unfortunately, most of the supplied software that comes with the cameras tend to be for Windows users only, making you reliant on the packages supplied with Ubuntu.

The good news, though, is that because of the good development carried out in Ubuntu and GNOME, you are now able to plug pretty much any camera into your computer through a USB interface and Ubuntu automatically recognizes the camera as a USB mass storage device. You can even set Ubuntu to recognize when a camera is plugged in so that it automatically imports your photographs for you.

To do this, you need to set up your settings for removable drives and media. You can find this in the System, Preferences menu. Click the Cameras tab and select the option to import digital photographs when connected (see Figure 7.13).

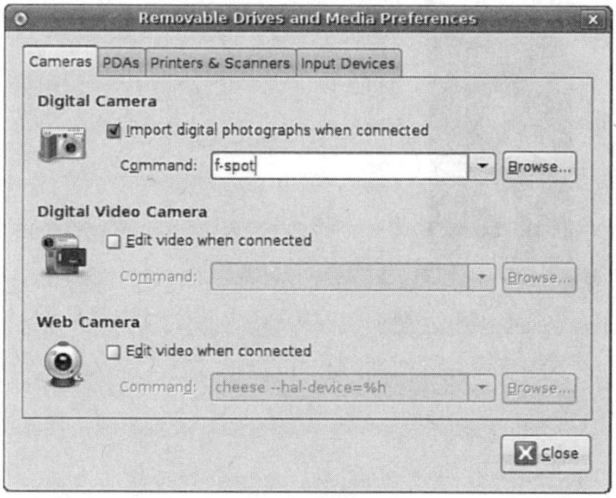

FIGURE 7.13   Use GNOME's intelligent handling of removable media by setting it to import your photographs automatically.

Now whenever you connect a digital camera to your computer GNOME automatically detects it (see Figure 7.14), and asks whether you want to import the photographs.

FIGURE 7.14   GNOME detects the presence of a digital camera and asks whether the photos should be imported.

Using F-Spot

Ubuntu has access to the superb F-Spot photo management application.

When F-Spot is installed, you can find it under the Applications, Graphics menu listed as F-Spot Photo Manager. If you have used the popular Google Picasa application, you will feel instantly at home with F-Spot because it is similar in many ways.

The first time you open F-Spot, you are asked to import your first batch of photographs, as shown in Figure 7.15. You can also assign a tag to them, if you want to track particular types of photographs. You might want to allow F-Spot to copy the photograph to a new directory, Photos—something that may help you organize your photos on the system.

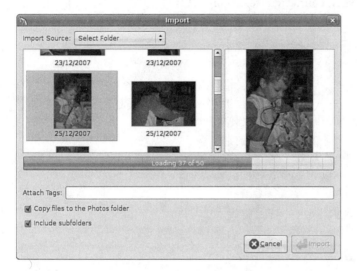

FIGURE 7.15   The versatile F-Spot makes adding photos to your library easy.

When you are ready, click Import to let F-Spot import the photos into the library. The pictures appear in the F-Spot library, and are stored according to the date they were taken. This information is given to F-Spot by the EXIF information that your camera stores each time you take a picture. In Figure 7.16, you can see the standard F-Spot window.

Use the timeline across the top of the window to browse through your photographs, and you can do some minor editing by double-clicking on any photograph. F-Spot is still in its infancy, but development is ongoing, so keep a eye open for any major updates.

Burning CDs and DVDs in Ubuntu

Linux is distributed across the Internet through the use of ISOs that are waiting to be written to CDs or DVDs. Therefore learning how to burn discs is essential if you have to download and install a Linux distribution. Not only that, but you are likely to want to use CDs and, more commonly, DVDs to back up your music, family pictures, or other important files. With DVD writers being so cheap, the format is now pervasive and more and more people use cheap DVDs as way of archiving simply due to the larger storage size available. Of course, you can use blank CD media, but they don't have anywhere near the capacity offered by DVDs albeit being slightly cheaper. Today's high-resolution digital cameras can occupy upward of 3MB per shot, and music files can be anything from 1MB to 10MB+ in size. These file sizes make DVD the obvious choice, but there are still occasions when you need to write to a CD. You can use CDs and DVDs to

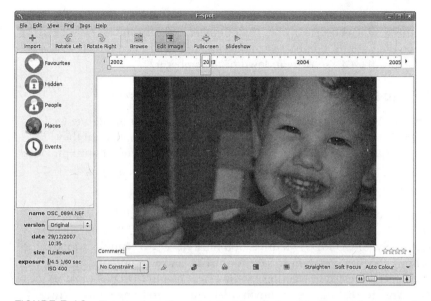

FIGURE 7.16   Browse through your extensive photo collection and correct minor problems using F-Spot.

- ▶ Record and store multimedia data, such as backup files, graphics images, and music.
- ▶ Rip audio tracks from music CDs (*ripping* refers to extracting music tracks from a music CD) and compile your own music CDs for your personal use.

Linux audio clients and programs support the creation and use of many different types of audio formats. Later sections of this chapter discuss sound formats, sound cards, music players, and much more. Because CD burning is used for many other purposes in Ubuntu, we cover the essentials of that process first in this chapter. To record multimedia data on a CD, you must have installed a drive with CD writing capabilities on your system. To make certain that your CD writer is working, use wodim -scanbus to get the information for using the CD drive under SCSI (small computer system interface) emulation:

```
# wodim -scanbus
scsibus0:
        0,0,0     0) 'HL-DT-ST' 'RW/DVD GCC-4120B' '2.01' Removable CD-ROM
        0,1,0     1) *
        0,2,0     2) *
        0,3,0     3) *
        0,4,0     4) *
        0,5,0     5) *
        0,6,0     6) *
        0,7,0     7) *
```

Here, you can see that the CD writer (in this example, a CD writer/DVD reader) is present and is known by the system as device 0,0,0. The numbers represent the scsibus/target/lun (logical unit number) of the device. You need to know this device number when you burn the CD, so write it down or remember it.

Creating CDs and DVDs with Ubuntu's Graphical Clients

Although adequate for quick burns and use in shell scripting, the command-line technique for burning CDs and DVDs is an awkward choice for many people until they become proficient at it and learn all the arcane commands. Fortunately, Ubuntu provides several graphical clients.

Nautilus

With Ubuntu, enhanced functionality has been included in the default file browser Nautilus. Under the Places menu item is a CD/DVD Creator selection. To use it, insert a blank CD or DVD into your CD-R/DVD-R drive. You must have two Nautilus windows open: one that shows the files you want to save to the CD, and a second one open to the CD/DVD Creator Folder (accessed in Nautilus by the Places menu, CD/DVD Creator) location. Click on the Write to Disc button as shown in Figure 7.17 to bring up the Write dialog; at the next dialog box, choose the format to which you want to write the disc. Nautilus CD/DVD Creator supports writing to a disc image file, commonly known as *ISO*. You can also give your new disc a label and tell Nautilus at what speed you want to write the disc. Finally, click the Write button to start the burning process—it is that simple!

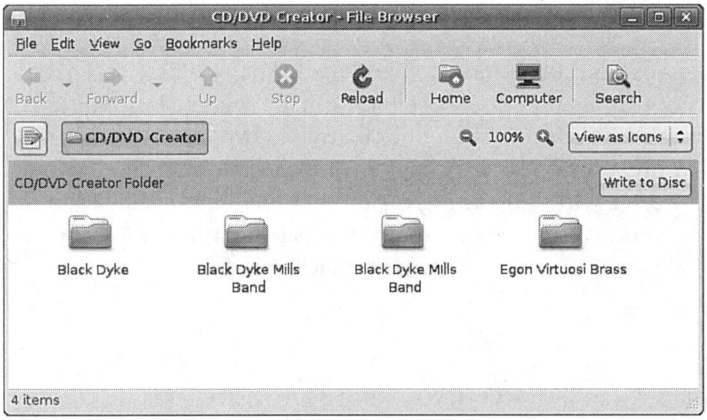

FIGURE 7.17   Creating a CD or DVD using the Nautilus browser is made easy with the drag-and-drop features it provides.

Brasero

A relatively new addition to the Ubuntu default distribution is Brasero, an easy-to-use graphical CD and DVD burning application. Installed as part of the standard Live CD installation, Brasero is found under Applications, Sound and Video as Brasero Disc Burning.

Brasero takes a project-based approach to disc burning, opening up with a wizard that allows you to select from four different tasks that you'll commonly want to do. You can see the opening screen in Figure 7.18. Brasero also remembers previous "projects" allowing you to quickly create several copies of a disc, which is ideal if you're planning on passing on copies of Ubuntu to your friends and family.

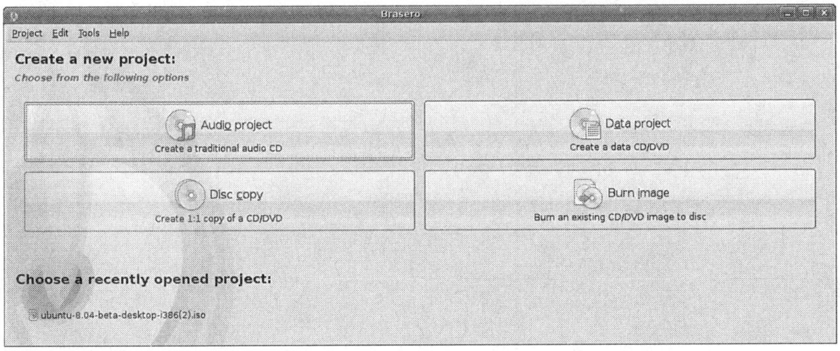

FIGURE 7.18   A new but welcome addition is Brasero, giving you an intuitive way to create data and audio CDs and DVDs.

Burning a Data CD or DVD is as easy as selecting the option in the opening screen and dragging and dropping the files you want to include from the directory tree on the left to the drop area on the right. Brasero keeps an eye on the disc size, and tells you when you exceed the limits. By default it selects a 4.3GB DVD, but you can change this by using the CD icon toward the bottom of the screen (shown in Figure 7.19). Brasero also allows you the option to overburn a CD or DVD. Overburning makes use of extra space on recordable media by squeezing a little extra onto your disc. It can add up to an additional 10% of the disc's capacity, but it runs the risk of making the disc incompatible with CD or DVD drives because overburning does not adhere to established standards.

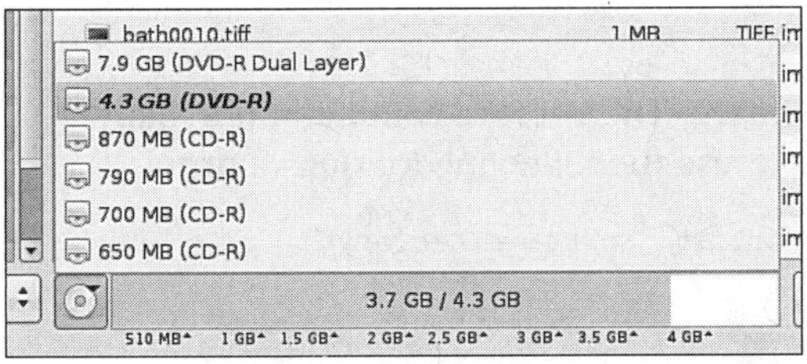

FIGURE 7.19   Brasero can write to a selection of recordable media, even accommodating over-burning if you want to use it.

When you're ready to create your disc, simply click the Burn button and Brasero will ask you to choose a label for the disc. You're also able to choose whether you want to create an image (very useful if you plan to make multiple copies of the same disc although not at the same time). You can do this by selecting File, image in the drop-down menu on the Burn screen (see Figure 7.20). To ensure that your disc image can be used with your friends and colleagues who use Windows, you should choose the Increase compatibility with Windows systems option.

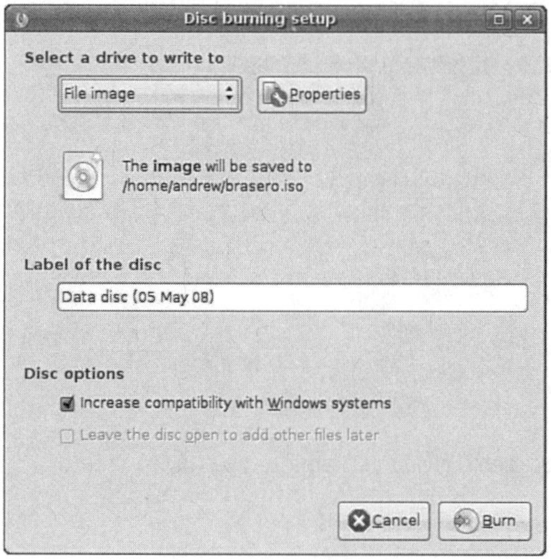

FIGURE 7.20   If you're creating an image for use with Windows, use the compatibility option to ensure it will work.

Finally, click the Burn button to start the process and Brasero will start creating your new CD or DVD. How long it takes depends on the amount of data you are writing and also the speed of your drive.

Creating CDs from the Command Line

In Linux, creating a CD at the command line is a two-step process. You first create the iso9660-formatted image, and you then burn or write the image onto the CD. The iso9660 is the default file system for CD-ROMs.

Use the mkisofs command to create the ISO image. The mkisofs command has many options (see the man page for a full listing), but use the following for quick burns:

```
$ mkisofs -r -v -J -l -o /tmp/our_special_cd.iso /source_directory
```

The options used in this example are as follows:

▶ -r—Sets the permission of the files to more useful values. UID and GID (individual and group user ID requirements) are set to zero, all files are globally readable and searchable, and all files are set as executable (for Windows systems).

▶ -v—Displays verbose messages (rather than terse messages) so that you can see what is occurring during the process; these messages can help you resolve problems if they occur.

▶ -J—Uses the Joliet extensions to ISO9660 so that your Windows-using buddies can more easily read the CD. The Joliet (for Windows), Rock Ridge (for Unix), and HSF (for Mac) extensions to the iso9660 standard are used to accommodate long filenames rather than the eight-character DOS filenames that the iso9660 standard supports.

▶ -l—Allows 31-character filenames; DOS does not like it, but everyone else does.

▶ -o—Defines the directory where the image will be written (that is, the output) and its name. The /tmp directory is convenient for this purpose, but the image could go anywhere you have write permissions.

▶ /source_directory—Indicates the path to the source directory; that is, the directory containing the files you want to include. There are ways to append additional paths and exclude directories (and files) under the specified path—it is all explained in the man page, if you need that level of complexity. The simple solution is to construct a new directory tree and populate it with the files you want to copy, and then make the image using that directory as the source.

Many more options are available, including options to make the CD bootable.

After you have created the ISO image, you can write it to the CD with the cdrecord command:

```
$ cdrecord -eject -v speed=12 dev=0,0,0 /tmp/our_special_cd.iso
```

The options used in this example are as follows:

▶ -eject—Ejects the CD when the write operation is finished.

▶ -v—Displays verbose messages.

▶ speed=—Sets the speed; the rate depends on the individual drive's capabilities. If the drive or the recordable medium is poor, you can use lower speeds to get a good burn.

▶ dev=—Specifies the device number of the CD writer (the number I told you to write down earlier).

NOTE

You can also use the blank= option with the cdrecord command to erase CD-RW disks. The cdrecord command has fewer options than mkisofs does, but it offers the -multi option, which enables you to make multisession CDs. A multisession CD enables you to write a data track, quit, and then add more data to the CD later. A single-session CD can be written to only once; any leftover CD capacity is wasted. Read about other options in the cdrecord man page.

Current capacity for CD media is 700MB of data or 80 minutes of music. (There are 800MB/90 minute CDs, but they are rare.) Some CDs can be overburned; that is, recorded to a capacity in excess of the standard. The cdrecord command is capable of overburning if your CD-RW drive supports it. You can learn more about overburning CDs at http://www.cdmediaworld.com/hardware/cdrom/cd_oversize.shtml/.

Creating DVDs from the Command Line

There are several competing formats for DVD, and with prices rapidly falling, it is more likely that DVD-writing drives will become commonplace. The formats are as follows:

▶ DVD+R

▶ DVD-R

▶ DVD+RW

▶ DVD-RW

Differences in the + and – formats have mostly to do with how the data is modulated onto the DVD itself, with the + format having an edge in buffer underrun recovery. How this is achieved impacts the playability of the newly created DVD on any DVD player. The DVD+ format also has some advantages in recording on scratched or dirty media. Most drives support the DVD+ format. As with any relatively new technology, your mileage may vary.

We focus on the DVD+RW drives because most drives support that standard. The software supplied with Ubuntu has support for writing to DVD-R/W (rewritable) media as well. It will be useful for you to review the DVD+RW/+R/-R[W] for Linux HOWTO at http://fy.chalmers.se/~appro/linux/DVD+RW/ before you attempt to use dvd+rw-tools, which you need to install to enable DVD creation (also known as *mastering*) as well as the cdrtools package. You can ignore the discussion in the HOWTO about kernel patches and compiling the tools.

TIP

The 4.7GB size of DVD media is measured as 1000 megabytes per gigabyte, instead of the more commonly used 1024 megabytes per gigabyte, so do not be surprised when the actual formatted capacity, about 4.4GB, is less than you anticipated. dvd+rw-tools does not allow you to exceed the capacity of the disk.

You need to have the dvd+rw-tools package installed (as well as the cdrtools package). The dvd+rw-tools package contains the growisofs application (that acts as a front end to mkisofs) as well as the DVD formatting utility.

You can use DVD media to record data in two ways. The first way is much the same as that used to record CDs in a session, and the second way is to record the data as a true file system, using packet writing.

Session Writing

To record data in a session, you use a two-phase process:

1. Format the disk with dvd+rw-format /dev/scd0 (only necessary the first time you use a disk).

2. Write your data to the disk with growisofs -Z /dev/scd0 -R -J /your_files.

The `growisofs` command simply streams the data to the disk. For subsequent sessions, use the `-M` argument instead of `-Z`. The `-Z` argument is used only for the initial session recording; if you use the `-Z` argument on an already used disk, it erases the existing files.

CAUTION

Some DVDs come preformatted; formatting them again when you use them for the first time can make the DVD useless. Always be sure to carefully read the packaging your DVD comes in to ensure that you are not about to create another coaster!

TIP

Writing a first session of at least 1GB helps maintain compatibility of your recorded data with other optical drives. DVD players calibrate themselves by attempting to read from specific locations on the disk; you need data there for the drive to read it and calibrate itself.

Also, because of limitations to the ISO9660 file system in Linux, do not start new sessions of a multisession DVD that would create a directory past the 4GB boundary. If you do so, it causes the offsets used to point to the files to "wrap around" and point to the wrong files.

Packet Writing

Packet writing treats the CD or DVD disk like a hard drive in which you create a file system (like ext3) and format the disk, and then write to it randomly as you would to a conventional hard drive. This method, although commonly available on Windows-based computers, is still experimental for Linux and is not yet covered in detail here.

TIP

DVD+RW media are capable of only about 1,000 writes, so it is very useful to mount them with the `noatime` option to eliminate any writing to update their inodes or simply mount them read-only when it's not necessary to write to them.

It is possible to pipe data to the `growisofs` command:

```
# your_application | growisofs -Z /dev/scd0=/dev/fd/0
```

It is also possible to burn from an existing image (or file, named pipe, or device):

```
# growisofs -Z /dev/scd0=image
```

The `dvd+rw-tools` documentation, found at `/usr/share/doc/dvd+rw-tools-*/index.html`, is required reading before your first use of the program. We also suggest that you experiment with DVD-RW (rewritable) media first, as if you make mistakes then you will still be able to reuse the disk, rather than creating several new coasters for your coffee mug.

Viewing Video

You can use Ubuntu tools and applications to view movies and other video presentations on your PC. This section presents some TV and motion picture video software tools included with the Ubuntu distribution you received with this book.

TV and Video Hardware

To watch TV and video content on your PC, you must install a supported TV card or have a video/TV combo card installed. A complete list of TV and video cards supported by Ubuntu is at http://www.exploits.org/v4l/.

Freely available Linux support for TV display from video cards that have a TV-out jack is poor. That support must come from the X driver, not from a video device that Video4Linux supports with a device driver. Some of the combo TV-tuner/video display cards have support, including the Matrox Marvel, the Matrox Rainbow Runner G-Series, and the RivaTV cards. Many other combo cards lack support, although an independent developer might have hacked something together to support his own card. Your best course of action is to perform a thorough Internet search with Google.

Many of the TV-only PCI cards are supported. In Linux, however, they are supported by the video chipset they use, and not by the name some manufacturer has slapped on a generic board (the same board is typically sold by different manufacturers under different names). The most common chipset is the Brooktree Bt*** series of chips; they are supported by the bttv device driver.

If you have a supported card in your computer, it should be detected during installation. If you add it later, the Kudzu hardware detection utility should detect it and configure it. You can always configure it by hand.

To determine what chipset your card has, use the lspci command to list the PCI device information, find the TV card listing, and look for the chipset that the card uses. For example, the lspci output for my computer shows

```
$ lspci
00:00.0 Host bridge: Advanced Micro Devices [AMD] AMD-760 [IGD4-1P] System Con-
troller (rev 13)
00:01.0 PCI bridge: Advanced Micro Devices [AMD] AMD-760 [IGD4-1P] AGP Bridge
00:07.0 ISA bridge: VIA Technologies, Inc. VT82C686 [Apollo Super South] (rev 40)
00:07.1 IDE interface: VIA Technologies, Inc. VT82C586B PIPC Bus Master IDE (rev 06)
00:07.2 USB Controller: VIA Technologies, Inc. USB (rev 1a)
00:07.3 USB Controller: VIA Technologies, Inc. USB (rev 1a)
00:07.4 SMBus: VIA Technologies, Inc. VT82C686 [Apollo Super ACPI] (rev 40)
00:09.0 Multimedia audio controller: Ensoniq 5880 AudioPCI (rev 02)
00:0b.0 Multimedia video controller: Brooktree Corporation Bt878 Video Capture (rev 02)
00:0b.1 Multimedia controller: Brooktree Corporation Bt878 Audio Capture (rev 02)
00:0d.0 Ethernet controller: Realtek Semiconductor Co., Ltd. RTL-8029(AS)
```

```
00:0f.0 FireWire (IEEE 1394): Texas Instruments TSB12LV23 IEEE-1394 Controller
00:11.0 Network controller: Standard Microsystems Corp [SMC] SMC2602W EZConnect
01:05.0 VGA compatible controller: nVidia Corporation NV15 [GeForce2 Ti] (rev a4)
```

Here, the lines listing the multimedia video controller and multimedia controller say that this TV board uses a Brooktree Bt878 Video Capture chip and a Brooktree Bt878 Audio Capture chip. This card uses the Bt878 chipset. Your results will be different, depending on what card and chipset your computer has. This card happened to be an ATI All-in-Wonder VE (also known as ATI TV-Wonder). (The VE means *Value Edition*; hence, there is no TV-out connector and no radio chip on the card; what a value!) The name of the chipset says that the card uses the bttv driver.

In the documentation directory is a file named CARDLIST, and in that file is the following entry, among others:

```
card=64 - ATI TV-Wonder VE
```

There are 105 cards listed, as well as 41 radio cards, including

```
card=0 -  *** UNKNOWN/GENERIC ***
```

which is what you could have used had you not known the manufacturer's name for the card.

The file named Modules.conf, located in the same directory, offers the following example of information to place in the /etc/modules.conf file:

```
$ i2c
alias char-major-89      i2c-dev
options i2c-core         i2c_debug=1
options i2c-algo-bit     bit_test=1
```

```
$ bttv
alias char-major-81      videodev
alias char-major-81-0    bttv
options bttv             card=2 radio=1
options tuner            debug=1
```

All you need do is enter this information into /etc/modules.conf and change the value for card=2 to card=64 to match your hardware. Youcan delete the reference to the radio card (radio=2) because there isn't one and leave the other values alone. Then you must execute

```
$ sudo depmod -a
```

to rebuild the modules dependency list so that all the modules are loaded automatically. When finished, all you need do is execute

```
$ sudo modprobe bttv
```

and your TV card should be fully functional. All the correct modules will be automatically loaded every time you reboot. Ubuntu is clever enough to detect and configure a supported TV card that is present during installation.

TIP

Other useful documentation can be found in /usr/src/linux-2.6/Documentation/_video4linux. After you have identified a driver for a device, it does not hurt to look at the source code for it because so little formal documentation exists for many drivers; much of it is in the source code comments.

The development of support for TV cards in Linux has coalesced under the Video4Linux project. The Video4Linux software provides support for video capture, radio, and teletext devices in Ubuntu.

Video Formats

Ubuntu recognizes a variety of video formats. The formats created by the MPEG group, Apple, and Microsoft dominate, however. At the heart of video formats are the *codecs*—the encoders and decoders of the video and audio information. These codecs are typically proprietary, but free codecs do exist. Here is a list of the most common video formats and their associated file extensions:

▶ .mpeg—The MPEG video format; also known as .mpg

▶ .qt—The QuickTime video format from Apple

▶ .mov—Another QuickTime video format

▶ .avi—The Windows audio visual format

TIP

An RPM that provides a Divx codec for Linux can be found at http://www.freshrpms. net/. Divx is a patented MPEG-4 video codec that is the most widely used codec of its type. It allows for compression of MPEG-2 video by a factor of 8. See http://www.divx. com/ for more information.

The GetCodecs application is a Python script with a GUI interface that downloads, installs, and configures your Ubuntu system with multimedia codecs not provided by Ubuntu, such as MP3, Divx, and DVD codecs. The script can be obtained from http:/ /sourceforge.net/projects/getcodecs/.

If you need to convert video from one format to another, you use encoder applications called *grabbers*. These applications take raw video data from a video device such as a camera or TV card, and convert it to one of the standard MPEG formats or to a still image format, such as JPEG or GIF. Ubuntu does not supply any encoder applications (other than

ppmtompeg, which encodes MPEG-1 video), but you can find them at http://www.
freshrpms.net/ or another online source (see the "Reference" section at the end of this
chapter).

Viewing Video in Linux

Out of the box, Ubuntu does not support any of the proprietary video codecs due to
licensing restrictions. However this functionality can be restored if you install the full
version of the applications described in this section from the Universe repository. There
you can find multimedia applications such as Ogle, Xine, AlsaPlayer, Gstreamer, Grip,
Mplayer, VCDImager, VideoLAN-client, Xmms, and Zapping.

You can use Linux software to watch TV, save individual images (take snapshots) from a
televised broadcast, save a series of snapshots to build animation sequences, or capture
video, audio, or both. The following sections describe some of the ways in which you can
put Linux multimedia software to work for you.

You can watch MPEG and DVD video with Xine. Xine is a versatile and popular media
player that is not included with Ubuntu. Xine is used to watch AVI, QuickTime, Ogg, and
MP3 files (the latter is disabled in Ubuntu).

Adobe Flash

The Adobe Flash plug-in for the Firefox browser is a commercial multimedia application
that isn't provided with Ubuntu out of the box, but many people find it useful. Adobe
Flash enables you to view Flash content at websites that support it. The easiest way of
getting hold of the official version of Flash is to install the `flashplugin-nonfree` package either using `apt-get` or `synaptic`. Once you've done this, any flash animations will
play quite happily within any Firefox-based browsers.

Another interesting video viewer application is MPlayer (not provided by Ubuntu), a
movie player for Linux. MPlayer can use Win32 codecs and it supports a wider range of
video formats than Xine, including Divx and some RealMedia files. MPlayer also uses
some special display drivers that support Matrox, 3Dfx, and Radeon cards and can make
use of some hardware MPEG decoder boards for better MPEG decoding. Look for Ubuntu
packages at http://www.mplayerhq.hu; a Win32 codec package is also available, as well as
other codec packages and a GUI interface.

Personal Video Recorders

The best reason to attach a television antenna to your computer, however, is to use the
video card and the computer as a personal video recorder.

The commercial personal video recorder, TiVo, uses Linux running on a PowerPC processor to record television programming with a variety of customizations. TiVo has a clever
interface and wonderful features, including a record/playback buffer, programmed recording and pause, slow motion, and reverse effects. Ubuntu does not provide any of the
many applications that attempt to mimic the TiVo functionality on a desktop PC running

Linux. However, several such applications, including DVR, The Linux TV Project, and OpenPVR, are listed at http://www.exploits.org/v4l/. These projects are in development and do not provide .rpm files, so you have to know how to download from CVS and compile your own binaries. For something a little easier, check out MythTV at http://www.mythtv.org/; a Ubuntu .rpm file should be available from ATRpms.

Linux, TiVo, and PVRs

Some TiVo users say that using this Linux-based device has changed their lives. Indeed, the convenience of using a personal video recorder (PVR) can make life a lot easier for inveterate channel surfers. Although PVR applications are not included with Ubuntu, open source developers are working on newer and better versions of easy-to-install and easy-to-use PVR software for Linux. For more information about TiVo, which requires a monthly charge and a phone line (or broadband connection with a newer TiVo2), browse to http://www.tivo.com/. Unrepentant Linux hardware hackers aiming to disembowel or upgrade a TiVo can browse to http://www.9thtee.com/tivoupgrades.htm or read the TiVo Hack FAQ at http://www.tivofaq.com/. A PVR makes viewing television a lot more fun!

A number of Linux sites are devoted to PVR software development. Browse to the DVR project page at http://www.pierrox.net/dvr/.

DVD and Video Players

You can now easily play DVDs with Ubuntu as long as you install the appropriate software. (Ubuntu doesn't provide any.) Browse to http://www.videolan.org/, and then download, build, and install the vlc client.

You must have a CPU of at least 450MHz and a working sound card to use a DVD player. The default Ubuntu kernel supports the DVD CD-ROM file system. As mentioned earlier, Xine and MPlayer do a great job of playing DVD files.

NOTE

The VideoLAN HOWTO found at http://videolan.org/ discusses the construction of a network for streaming video. Although you might not want to create a network, a great deal of useful information about the software and hardware involved in the enterprise can be generalized for use elsewhere, so it is worth a look. The site also contains a link to a HOWTO about cross-compiling on Linux to produce a Windows binary.

Reference

▶ http://www.cdcopyworld.com/—A resource for technical information about CD media and CD writers.

▶ http://hardware.redhat.com/hcl/—A database of supported hardware.

▶ http://www.opensound.com/download.cgi—The commercial OSS sound driver trial version download.

▶ http://www.xmms.org/—Home to the Xmms audio player.

▶ http://www.thekompany.com/projects/tkcoggripper/—A free (but not GPL) Ogg CD ripper.

▶ http://faceprint.com/code/—An MP3 to Ogg converter named mp32ogg.

▶ http://www.ibiblio.org/pub/linux/apps/sound/convert/!INDEX.html—Home to several sound conversion utilities.

▶ http://linux-sound.org/—An excellent resource for Linux music and sound.

▶ http://www.cnpbagwell.com/audio.html—The Audio Format FAQ.

▶ http://www.icecast.org/—A streaming audio server.

▶ http://www.linuxnetmag.com/en/issue4/m4icecast1.html—An Icecast tutorial.

▶ http://linuxselfhelp.com/HOWTO/MP3-HOWTO-7.html—The MP3 HOWTO contains brief descriptions of many audio applications and, although it focuses on the MP3 format, the information is easily generalized to other music formats.

▶ http://www.exploits.org/v4l/—Video for Linux resources.

▶ http://fame.sourceforge.net/—Video encoding tools.

▶ http://teletext.mb21.co.uk/faq.shtml—The Teletext FAQ.

▶ http://xine.sourceforge.net/—Home of the Xine DVD/video player.

▶ http://www.MPlayerHQ.hu/homepage/—Home to the MPlayer video player.

▶ http://www.videolan.org/—A VideoLAN project with good documentation.

▶ http://fy.chalmers.se/~appro/linux/DVD+RW/—The DVD+RW/+R/-R[W] for Linux, a HOWTO for creating DVDs under Linux.

▶ http://www.gimp.org—Home page of The GIMP (Gnu Image Manipulation Program.

▶ http://f-spot.org—Home page of the F-Spot project.

▶ http://www.linuxformat.co.uk—Website of Linux Format, home of a long-running GIMP tutorial by Michael J Hammel.

▶ http://www.exif.org—More information on EXIF and how it is used in digital cameras.

▶ http://www.sane-project.org—Home page of the SANE (*Scanner Access Now Easy*) project.

▶ http://www.imagemagick.org—Home page for ImageMagick.

▶ http://www.codeweavers.com—Home of the popular crossover office; required if you want to try to run Photoshop under Linux.

▶ http://gimp.net/tutorials/—Official tutorials for The GIMP.

# CHAPTER 8

Printing with Ubuntu

From the word *go*, Ubuntu provides support for a huge range of printers from many different manufacturers. This chapter looks at how to get your printer connected and talking to Ubuntu, as well as at the software that Ubuntu uses to manage printers and print jobs.

In keeping with most of the other Linux distributions, Ubuntu uses CUPS (*Common Unix Printing System*) to handle printers. Other systems are supported, such as LPRng, but you do not have access to some of the graphical management tools from within Ubuntu.

The Internet Printing Protocol

CUPS supports the Internet Printing Protocol, known as *IPP*, and offers a number of unique features, such as network printer directory (printer browsing) services, support for encryption, and support for PostScript Printer Description (.ppd) files.

According to the Internet Engineering Task Force (*IETF*), IPP grew out of a 1996 proposal by Novell to create a printing protocol for use over the Internet. Since then, the system has been developed and has matured into a stable print system for use on a variety of Linux and Unix-like operating platforms.

Overview of Ubuntu Printing

Ubuntu's print filter system is the main engine that enables the printing of many types of documents. The heart of that engine is the GNU GPL version of Aladdin's Ghostscript interpreter, the gs client. The system administrator's printer configuration tool is the system-config-printer client.

> **NOTE**
>
> Ubuntu's print system can be used to print to local (attached) or remote (network) print-ers. If you use a local printer, it is represented by a printer device, such as /dev/lp0 or /dev/usb/lp0 (if you have a USB printer). Local and remote printers use print *queues* defined in your system's printer capabilities database, /etc/printcap. A docu-ment being printed is known as a print *job*, and you can view and control your list, or queue, of current print jobs in the spool directory, which is /var/spool/cups. Note that you may control only your print jobs; only the root operator can control print jobs of any user on the system.

To add a printer to your system, you use the system-config-printer client to create, configure, and save the printer's definition.

CUPS maintains its own database of defined printers under the /etc/cups directory in a file named printers.conf. For example, an associated printer defined in /etc/printcap previously might have the following entry in /etc/cups/printers.conf:

```
<DefaultPrinter lp>
Info Created by system-config-printer 0.7.x
DeviceURI parallel:/dev/lp0
Location HP P135 local printer
State Idle
Accepting Yes
JobSheets none none
QuotaPeriod 0
PageLimit 0
KLimit 0
</Printer>
```

This example shows the definition for the printer named lp, along with its associated device, description, state, and other information. The various possible fields and entries in this file are documented in the printer.conf man page.

CUPS uses a print server (daemon) named cupsd, also called a *scheduler* in the CUPS docu-mentation. The server can be controlled, like other Ubuntu services, by the /etc/init.d/cupsys command or system-config-services client. How the server works on a system is determined by settings in its configuration file, cupsd.conf, found under the /etc/cups directory. CUPS executables are found under the /usr/lib/cups directory.

The cupsd.conf man page documents more than 80 different settings for the server, which you can configure to match your system, network, or printing environment. Default CUPS-related files and directories are stored under the /usr/share/cups directory. Logging can be set to seven different levels, with information about access and errors stored in log files under the /var/log/cups directory.

Resource requirements can be tailored through other settings, such as MaxCopies to set the maximum number of copies of a print job by a user, MaxJobs to set a limit on the number of active print jobs, and MaxJobsPerUser to set a limit on the number of active jobs per user. The RIPCache setting (8MB by default) controls the amount of memory used for graphics cache during printing.

For example, if you want to limit printing to 20 copies of a document or page at a time and only 10 simultaneous print jobs per user, use settings such as

```
MaxCopies 20
MaxJobsPerUser 10
```

> **TIP**
>
> Don't forget to restart the CUPS server after making any changes to its configuration file. Changes are activated only when the service is restarted (when the daemon rereads its configuration file). See the "GUI-Based Printer Configuration Quickstart" section later in this chapter.

Configuring and Managing Print Services

Your task as a system administrator (or root operator of your workstation) is to properly define local or remote printers and to ensure that printing services are enabled and running properly. Fortunately, Ubuntu includes a graphical print service configuration tool that makes this job easy. You should use these tools to configure printing, as you learn in this section of the chapter. But first, take a moment to read through a quick overview of the configuration process.

You can configure printing services using the system-config-printer graphical interface. Most of the detailed information in this chapter refers to the use of the GUI. The overview sections that follow, however, give you a solid foundation in both configuration approaches. You learn the details of these processes in later sections of the chapter.

GUI-Based Printer Configuration Quickstart

Configuring a printer for Ubuntu is easy using the system-config-printer tool, found under System, Administration, Printing. If you're not sure whether cupsd is running, you can quickly drop to a terminal and use the /etc/init.d/cupsys command with the status keyword like so:

```
$ sudo /etc/init.d/cupsys status
```

You will see either

```
Status of Common Unix Printing System: cupsd is not running.
```

8

or, if cupsd is running, an acknowledgement such as

```
Status of Common Unix Printing System: cupsd is running.
```

If cupsd is installed but not running, start the daemon like so:

```
$ sudo /etc/init.d/cups start
```

to access the GUI select System, Administration, Printing.

You then simply follow the prompts to define your printer and add local or remote print-ing services. You should print a test page before saving your changes. Use the printer configuration client or the File menu's Print menu item from a GNOME or KDE client.

> **NOTE**
>
> The system-config-printer utility is a replacement for gnome-cups-manager, which was previously the default printer configuration tool for Ubuntu. This new utility was actually originally developed for Fedora and has been adopted by Ubuntu.

Managing Printing Services

After defining a printer, you can use the command line to view and control your print jobs, or if root, all print jobs and printers on your system. Table 8.1 contains a partial list of CUPS and related printing commands and drivers included with Ubuntu.

TABLE 8.1   Print-Related Commands and Drivers

Name	Description
a2ps	Formats text files for PostScript printing
accept	Controls CUPS print job destinations
cancel	Cancels a CUPS print job
disable	Controls CUPS printers
dvi[lj, lj4l, lj2p, lj4]	Converts TeX DVI files to specific PCL format
enable	Controls CUPS printers
encscript	Converts text files to PostScript
escputil	Epson Stylus inkjet printer utility

Most Linux systems use PostScript as the default document format for printing. Ubuntu uses the gs command along with CUPS to manage local and remote print jobs and the type of data transferred during a print job. The gs command is used to translate the document stream into a format accepted by the destination printer (which most likely uses HPCL).

You can use the Ghostscript interpreter gs to display its built-in printer devices by using the gs interpreter with its --help command-line option like this:

```
# gs --help
```

NOTE

Ubuntu includes graphical clients you can use to view many different types of documents. For example, to display PostScript documents (including compressed PostScript documents) or PostScript images, use the gv client. To display Portable Document Format (PDF) documents, you can use gv or the xpdf client.

The gs command outputs many lines of help text on command-line usage and then lists built-in printer and graphics devices. Another way to get this information is to start gs and then use the devicenames == command like this:

```
# gs
GPL Ghostscript SVN PRE-RELEASE 8.61 (2007-08-02)

Copyright (C) 2007 Artifex Software, Inc.  All rights reserved.

This software comes with NO WARRANTY: see the file PUBLIC for details.

GS>devicenames ==

[/epson /pnggray /lp3000c /epl2050 /pgnm /ljet4d\
 /cljet5pr /pbmraw /lips4v /cdj550 /mag16 /laserjet\
 /bj200 /dfaxhigh /ibmpro /alc8500 /bmpgray\
 /hpdj600 /tiffgray /hpdj310 /pswrite\
...
```

Not all the devices are listed in this example.

Aladdin or GNU?

At least two versions of Ghostscript are available for Linux. One version is named AFPL Ghostscript, which formerly went by the name Aladdin Ghostscript. This version is licensed under the Aladdin Free Public License, which disallows commercial distribution. The other version is called GNU Ghostscript, which is distributed under the GNU General Public License. For details about the different versions or for answers to questions regarding licensing, see the Ghostscript home page at http://www.cs.wisc.edu/ ~ghost/.

8

Creating and Configuring Local Printers

Creating a local printer for your Ubuntu system can be accomplished in a few easy steps. The cupsd daemon should also be running before you begin (start the daemon manually as shown earlier in this chapter).

To launch system-config-printer, go to System, Administration and choose the Printing menu option.

Creating the Print Queue

The Ubuntu `system-config-printer` tool walks you through a process to create a new printer. To begin configuration of a local (attached) printer, click the New Printer toolbar button in `system-config-printer`'s main window. The first screen that appears allows you to choose the type of connection that the printer will use, as shown in Figure 8.1. Select the connection type that is appropriate for you. You can select a number of different connection types, depending on your specific requirements. Normally you will use the LPT#1 option if your printer is connected by a standard Parallel (or what used to be called Centronics) cable. Alternatively, if you are connecting to a printer that has a JetDirect port (most HP network-capable printers fit in this category) then select the appropriate option and enter the network address for the printer.

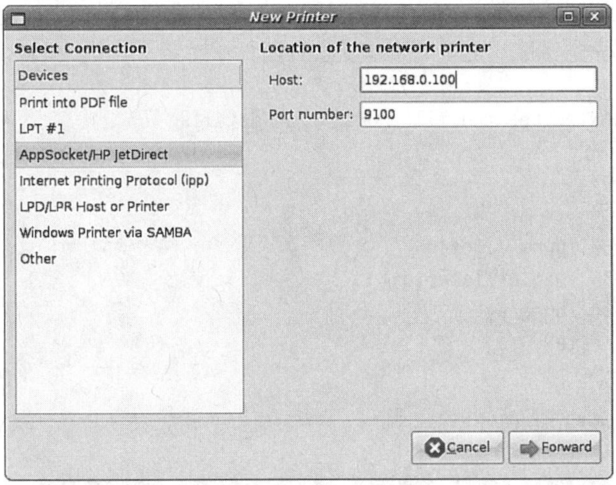

FIGURE 8.1   Select the appropriate connection method for your printer and enter the relevant details.

Next you need to select the make/manufacturer of the printer that you are setting up, shown in Figure 8.2.

Note that you can configure a printer for Ubuntu even if it is not attached to your computer. After you select your printer's manufacturer, a list of printers from that manufacturer (such as HP, as shown in Figure 8.3) appears. Select your printer from the list, and then click the Forward button.

Do not worry if you do not see your printer listed in the selection; it is possible to select a related, although different, printer model and still be able to print to your printer. For example, many HP printers can be used by selecting the DeskJet 500 for monochrome or 500C model for color printing.

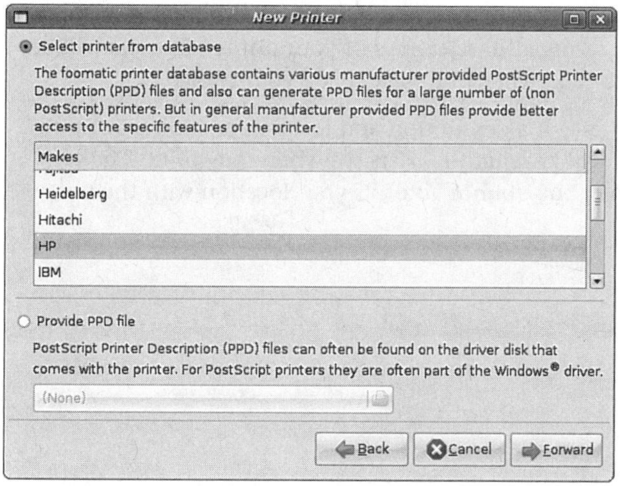

FIGURE 8.2   Select the make or manufacturer of your printer from this dialog box to help Ubuntu narrow down the driver options.

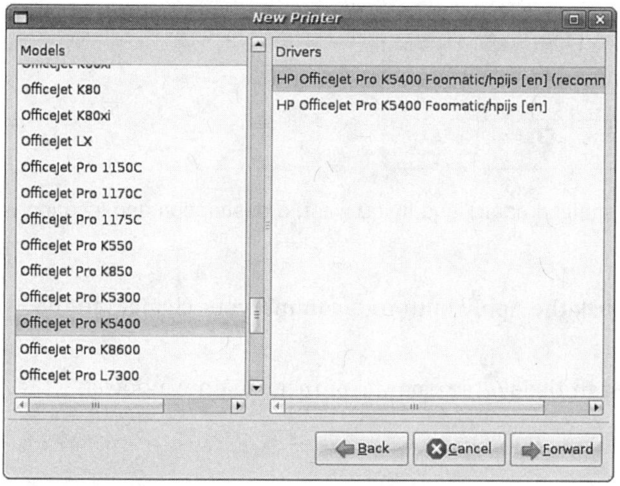

FIGURE 8.3   Select your printer from the list and click the Forward button to continue the configuration.

NOTE

You can also browse to http://www.linuxprinting.org/ to find out what drivers to use with your printer or to see a cross-referenced listing of printers supported by each driver. You might also find new and improved drivers for the latest printers on the market.

You can experiment to see which printer selection works best for your printer if its model is not listed. You might not be able to use all the features of your printer, but you will be able to set up printing service. Click Next when you have made your choice.

Now you can name the printer and give it a description and location as shown in Figure 8.4. The name is important, as this will be what the users see when they print. The description and location are optional, but Ubuntu autofills your location with the hostname of your computer.

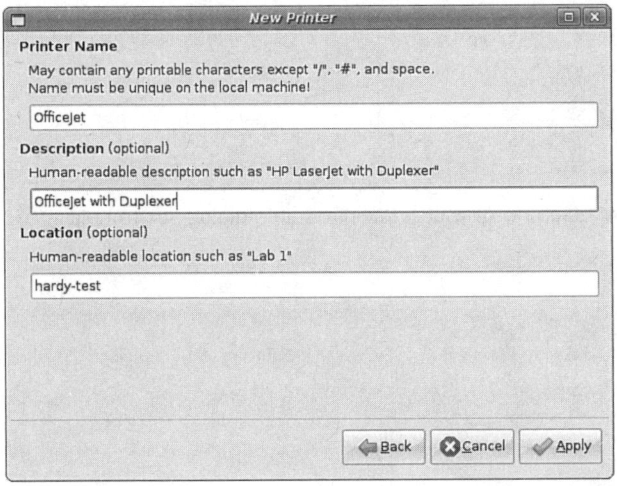

FIGURE 8.4   Give your printer a meaningful name, and if you want, a description and location.

If you are happy with the details, click the Apply button to commit your changes to the system.

You can see the new printer defined in the system-config-printer main window as shown in Figure 8.5.

Editing Printer Settings

You also use the system-config-printer tool to edit the newly defined printers. To edit the printer settings, highlight the printer's listing in the printer browser window. You can then select specific settings related to that printer by using the tabs that appear in the right side of the dialog box. The Settings dialog is shown in Figure 8.6.

The first tab in this dialog enables you to assign a new name for the printer. In this example, the printer has the name OfficeJet. Other tabs in this dialog enable you to change the queue type or queue options (such as whether to print a banner page or set

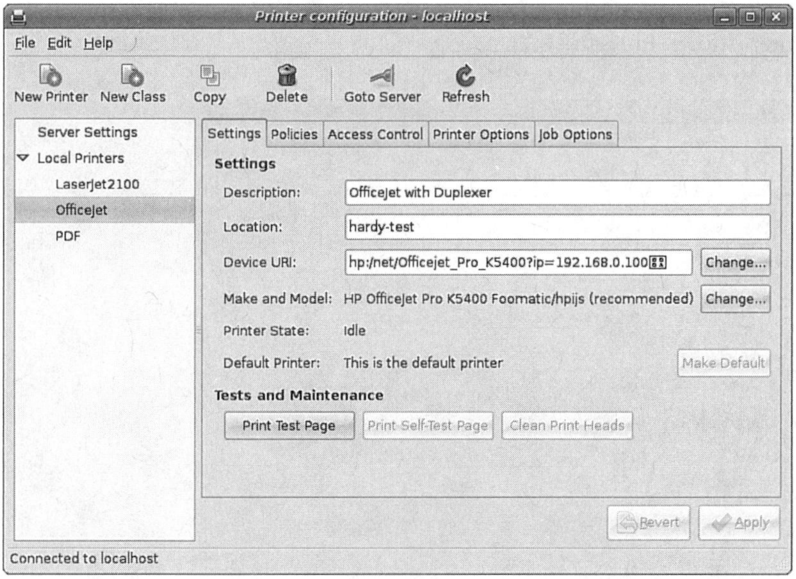

FIGURE 8.5   New printer entries displayed in `system-config-printer`'s main window.

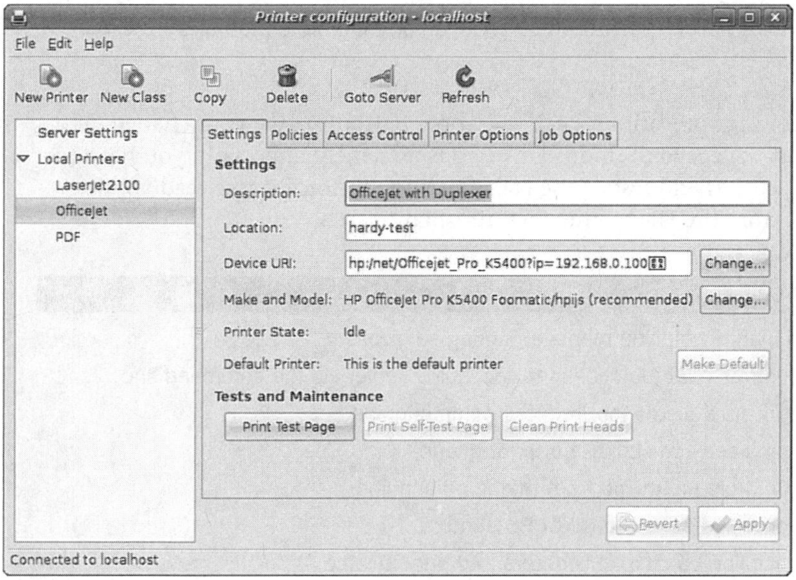

FIGURE 8.6   Edit a printer's settings by using tabs in `system-config-printer`.

the image area of a page), to select or update the driver, or to choose available print options for the printer (shown in Figure 8.7).

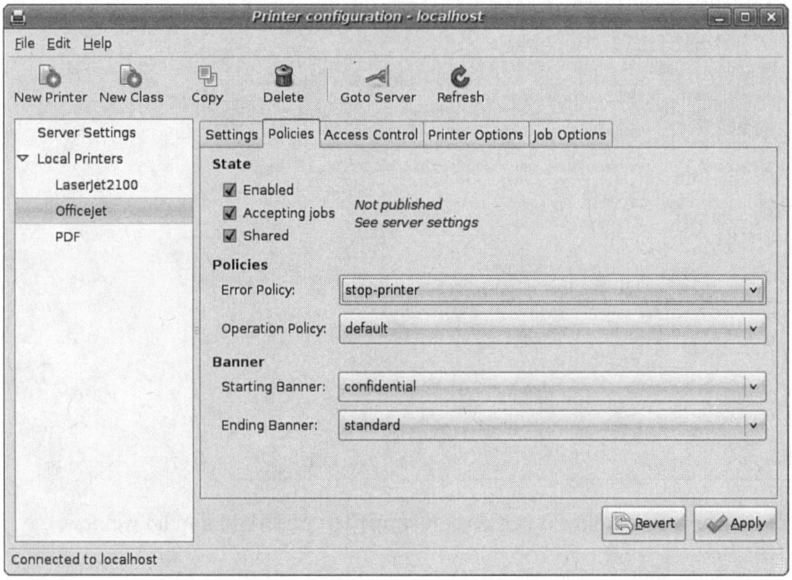

FIGURE 8.7   A printer's policy options can be changed on the Policies tab of `system-config-printer`.

When you finish editing your printer click the Apply button to save your changes and automatically restart the `cupsd` daemon. This step is extremely important; you have to update the printer settings and restart the `cupsd` daemon to force it to reread your new settings. Click Quit from the File menu when finished.

Related Ubuntu and Linux Commands

The following commands help you manage printing services:

- `accept`—Controls print job access to the CUPS server via the command line
- `cancel`—Cancels a print job from the command line
- `cancel`—Command-line control of print queues
- `disable`—Controls printing from the command line
- `enable`—Command-line control CUPS printers
- `lp`—Command-line control of printers and print service
- `lpc`—Displays status of printers and print service at the console
- `lpq`—Views print queues (pending print jobs) at the console
- `lprm`—Removes print jobs from the print queue via the command line
- `lpstat`—Displays printer and server status
- `system-config-printer`—Ubuntu's graphical printer configuration tool

Reference

▶ http://www.linuxprinting.org/—Browse here for specific drivers and information about USB and other types of printers.

▶ http://www.hp.com/wwsolutions/linux/products/printing_imaging/index.html—Short but definitive information from HP regarding printing product support under Linux.

▶ http://www.cups.org/—A comprehensive repository of CUPS software, including versions for Ubuntu.

▶ http://www.pwg.org/ipp/—Home page for the Internet Printing Protocol standards.

▶ http://www.linuxprinting.org/cups-doc.html—Information about the Common UNIX Printing System (CUPS).

▶ http://www.cs.wisc.edu/~ghost/—Home page for the Ghostscript interpreter.

CHAPTER 9

Games

Whether your boss likes it or not, gaming is a huge part of computing. For any operating system to have true mass market appeal, it must have the ability to play games. From the humble card games that entertain millions during their coffee breaks, to the heavily involved first-person shooters that involve players dotted around the globe, Linux offers a gaming platform that may surprise even the hardened Windows fanboy.

In this chapter we'll explore some of the common games available for you to download and install. We'll even show you how to get your Windows-based games running under Linux.

Linux Gaming

A number of games come as part of Ubuntu, and they are divided into three distinct camps: KDE games, GNOME games, and X games. Our favorites are Planet Penguin Racer and Torc (see Figure 9.1), but there are a few others for you to choose from. The best part, of course, is trying each one and seeing what you think. Many other free games are available across the Web, so go to Google and see what you come up with.

However, games for Linux do not stop there—a few versions of popular Windows-based games have been across to the Linux platform, including DOOM 3, Unreal Tournament 2004, and Quake 4. These three popular games have native Linux support and in some cases can run at similar, if not better, speeds than their Windows counterparts. There's even an emulator available that enables you to play classic adventure games, such as the Secret of Monkey Island, natively under Linux.

FIGURE 9.1   Sliding around corners in the high-speed Torc.

Finally, an implementation of the Wine code called Cedega is optimized especially for games. This uses application interfaces to make Windows games believe they are running on a Windows platform and not a Linux platform. Bear in mind that Wine stands for *wine is not an emulator*, so do not start thinking of it as such—the community can get quite touchy about it!

A major gripe of Linux users has been the difficulty involved in getting modern 3D graphics cards to work. Thankfully, both AMD/ATI and Nvidia support Linux, albeit by using closed-source drivers. This means that Ubuntu does not ship with native 3D drivers activated for either graphics card.

Installing Proprietary Video Drivers

Unfortunately, both Nvidia and AMD/ATI still produce proprietary drivers, meaning that the source code is not open and available for developers to look at. This means that it is hard for some Linux distros to include them as part of their standard package manifest. However, Ubuntu have taken the pragmatic approach of including both Nvidia and AMD/ATI drivers within the main Ubuntu distro, albeit disabled by default. That way the end user can, if they so wish, activate those drivers to take advantage of them.

NOTE

Don't think that proprietary drivers are the only way on Linux, as there is a lot of development going into providing totally free and open source drivers for slightly older graphics cards. Ubuntu will automatically select the best "free" driver for your system and allow you to switch the proprietary driver should you want to. Although the open source drivers will provide 3D acceleration, this support doesn't always extend to the more recent graphics cards.

It's very easy to activate the proprietary driver if you need to; all you have to do is use the Hardware Drivers Manager found under System, Administration and which is shown in Figure 9.2.

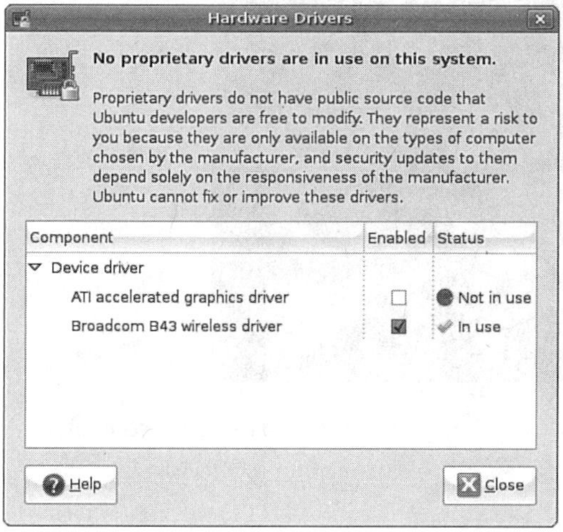

FIGURE 9.2   Use the Hardware Drivers Manager to activate or deactivate the appropriate proprietary graphics driver for your graphics card.

You will be prompted for your password before you proceed, as you will be setting a system-wide option. Once the Hardware Drivers Manager has opened up, look for the entry that says ATI (or Nvidia) Accelerated Graphics Driver and check the box. Ubuntu will confirm that you want to use the proprietary driver and, if you agree, will automatically download and configure the relevant driver. In order to activate the driver you will need to log out of GNOME by going to System, Log Off. The next time you log in, Ubuntu will automatically switch to the proprietary driver.

Installing Games in Ubuntu

In this section we'll take a look at how to install some of the more popular games for Ubuntu. Alongside the usual shoot-'em-up games, you'll also find one or two strategy-focused titles.

DOOM 3

The follow-up to the infamous DOOM and DOOM II was released in the second half of
2004 (see Figure 9.3), and it provides a way to run it under Linux. Although it's almost
four years old it is still an impressive game in its own right. You still have to purchase the
Windows version because you need some of the files that are on the CDs. The rest of the
files are available from id Software at http://zerowing.idsoftware.com/linux/doom.

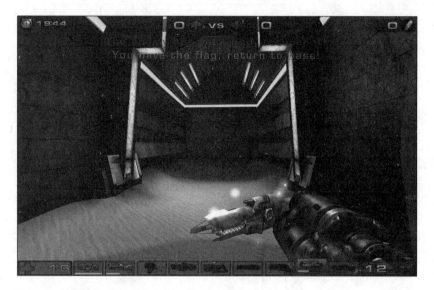

FIGURE 9.3   Descending into the pits of hell. DOOM 3 is one of the most graphic computer
games available.

You can download the file doom3-linux-1.1.1286-demo.x86.run from the id Software FTP
server or by using BitTorrent. When that's finished, open a terminal and change to the
directory in which you saved the file. Type the following command_FIRST:

```
$ sudo sh doom3-linux-*.run
```

This begins the installation of the demo. As with other commercial games, you must agree
to an EULA before you can install. Follow the installation procedure. When it finishes,
you need to get the Windows CDs ready.

The files you need to copy across are the following:

- pak000.pk4
- pak001.pk4
- pak002.pk4
- pak003.pk4
- pak004.pk4

They must be saved in the /usr/local/games/doom3/base/ directory. After you copy the files, you can start the game by typing **doom3** or start the dedicated server for multiplayer games by typing **doom3-dedicated**.

Unreal Tournament 2004

Unreal Tournament 2004 (or *UT2004*, as it is affectionately known) from Epic natively supports Linux in both its 32-bit and 64-bit incarnations (see Figure 9.4). Be aware that if you run the 64-bit version, you need to ensure that your graphics drivers are supported under 64-bit mode.

FIGURE 9.4   Unreal Tournament 2004 builds on the classic deathmatch scenario with more enemies and more combatants!

Installation is easy, and there are two ways to do it. You can insert the DVD and mount it, or you can open the DVD in GNOME and double-click the linux-installer.sh icon. When you are asked whether you want to run it or display its contents, click Run in Terminal to launch the graphical installer. As with DOOM 3, you must read and accept the terms of the EULA before you are allowed to install UT2004. You are given the option of where you want to install the software; the default is in your home directory. After you select the destination directory, click Begin Install; UT2004 does the rest.

The alternative way to access the graphical installer is via the command line. Change directory to /media/cdrom/ and type the following_FIRST:

```
$ sudo sh linux-install.sh
```

This brings up the installer. Continue through this and, when finished, you should find Unreal Tournament 2004 in /home/username/ut2004.

If you want to uninstall UT2004, you can use the uninstall script in the ut2004 directory. Type this_FIRST:

```
$ sudo sh uninstall.sh
```

After confirmation, Unreal Tournament removes itself from your system.

Quake 4

Being based on the DOOM 3 engine, you could almost expect Quake 4 (seen in Figure 9.5) to ship with a good deal of support for Linux. To get started, you must have the Windows version of the software because you need several files as well as the CD key to be able to play the game. First things first, though. Head on over to http://zerowing.idsoftware.com/ linux/quake4/ to download the required Linux installer (quake4-linux-1.0*.run) by either direct FTP or the more bandwidth-friendly BitTorrent.

FIGURE 9.5   Based on the popular DOOM 3 engine, Quake 4 pits you against the evil Strogg. Get out there and frag 'em!

After you download the file, drop down to a command line and type the following:[[STYLE_FIRST]]

```
$ sudo sh quake4-linux-1.0*.run
```

Then press Enter. The installer starts up and asks you a couple questions. After you answer these, the installer creates the necessary files and folders. All you need to do is to copy several files from the /quake4/qbase directory on the DVD to /usr/local/bin/quake4/qbase. You can start the game by typing **quake4** at a command prompt.

Wolfenstein: Enemy Territory

Whereas the earlier Return to Castle Wolfenstein was both single- and multiplayer, the freely available Wolfenstein: Enemy Territory is multiplayer only (see Figure 9.6). Available in Win32 and Linux native versions, you can download it from http://www. SplashDamage.com/. After you download the 260MB file named et-linux-2.55.x86.run, install the game by typing the following:

```
$sudo sh et-linux-2.55.x86.run
```

FIGURE 9.6   Teamwork is the key to victory in this lush but hostile graphical environment.

Then accept the defaults. A symlink exists in /usr/local/bin to the script that loads the game.

Battle for Wesnoth

Of course, there is more to Linux gaming than just first-person shooters. One of the most popular games currently available for Linux is Battle for Wesnoth (see Figure 9.7), a strategy game much in the vein of Age of Empires. Based in a fantasy land, you are responsible for building armies to wage war against your foes.

FIGURE 9.7   Flex your strategic brain by playing Battle for Wesnoth—a rich and full land of fantasy of adventure

Battle for Wesnoth is easy to install with Ubuntu. You need to select the wesnoth package using either synaptic or aptitude. When installed, you launch it from the command line by entering the following:

```
$ wesnoth
```

Playing Windows Games with Cedega

As mentioned earlier, the key to mass-market appeal of an operating system is in the applications available for it. A group of developers saw that the vast majority of the computing world was using Windows-based productivity and gaming software and decided to develop a way to run this software on Linux, thereby giving Linux users access to this large application base. The developers came up with a program called Wine, which has been updated regularly and forms the basis of the gaming variant called Cedega. This is a commercial product available from developers TransGaming Technologies (http://www.transgaming.com/), so you cannot retrieve it using `aptitude`.

However, Cedega is a popular and up-to-date product with support for recent releases such as Elder Scrolls IV: Oblivion and World of Warcraft. Because the state of Cedega is constantly changing, TransGaming Technologies has a subscription service, which means that you get updates for the code when they are released—ensuring that you are able to enjoy not only the games of today, but also those of tomorrow.

So, if you cannot wait for Linux to become more popular with game developers, use Cedega as a stop-gap until they can be persuaded to support Linux directly.

> **TIP**
>
> The keys to successful gaming in Linux are to always read the documentation thoroughly, always investigate the Internet resources thoroughly, and always understand your system. Installing games is a great way to learn about your system because the reward of success is so much fun.

Reference

▶ http://www.transgaming.com/—The official TransGaming Technologies website provides details of games that are directly supported under Cedega.

▶ http://www.linuxgames.com/—A good source of up-to-date information about the state of Linux gaming.

▶ http://zerowing.idsoftware.com/linux/doom/—Includes a complete how-to and troubleshooting guide for running DOOM 3 under Linux.

▶ http://www.unrealtournament.com/—The official site of Unreal Tournament.

▶ http://www.nvnews.net/vbulletin/forumdisplay.php?f=14—The Official Nvidia Linux driver support forum.

▶ http://www.nvidia.com/object/linux.html—Home page for the Nvidia Linux drivers.

▶ http://tinyurl.com/3pm2v—Home page for the ATI Linux drivers (courtesy of tinyurl.com).

PART III

System Administration

IN THIS PART

CHAPTER 10

Managing Users

If it weren't for users then system administrators would have a quiet life! However, it's impossible for you have a system with absolutely no users, so it is important that you learn how to effectively manage and administer your users as they work with your system. Whether you are creating a single user account or modifying a group that holds hundreds of user accounts, the fundamentals of user administration are the same.

User management and administration includes looking after allocating and managing home directories, putting in place good password policies and applying an effective security policy including disk quotas and file and directory access permissions. We will take a look at all of these areas within this chapter, as well as taking a look at the different types of user that you are likely to find on an average Linux system.

User Accounts

You can normally find three types of users on all Linux systems: the super user, the day to day user and the system user. Each type of user is essential to the smooth running of your system and learning the differences between the three is essential if you are to work efficiently and safely within your Linux environment.

All users who access your system must have accounts on the system itself. Ubuntu uses the /etc/passwd file to store information on the user accounts that are present on the system. All users, regardless of their type, have a one line entry in this file which contains their username (typically used for logging in to the system), a password field (which contains an x to denote that a password is present), a User ID (commonly referred to as the UID) and a Group ID (commonly referred to as the GID). The last two fields show the location of the home directory (usually /home/username) and the default shell for the user (/bin/bash is the default for new users).

> **NOTE**
>
> Just because the password field contains an x doesn't mean that this is your password! All passwords are actually encrypted and stored in /etc/shadow for safe keeping. Ubuntu automatically refers to this file whenever a password is required.

In keeping with other UNIX-based operating systems, Linux and Ubuntu make use of the established UNIX file ownership and permission system. All files (which can include directories and devices) can be assigned one or more of read, write and/or execute permissions. These three 'flags' can also be assigned to the owner of the file, a member of a group or anyone on the system. The security for a file is drawn from these permissions and also file ownership. As the system administrator (more commonly referred to as the super user) it is your responsibility to manage these settings effectively and ensure that the users have proper UIDs and GIDS. Perhaps most importantly you will need to lock away sensitive files from users who should not have access to them, through file permissions.

The Super User/Root User

No matter how many system administrators there are for a system, there can ever only be one super user account. The super user account, more commonly referred to as the root user, has total and complete control over all aspects of the system. They can go anywhere in the filesystem, grant and revoke access to files and directories, and can carry out any operation on the system, including destroying it if they so wish. The root user is unique in that it has a UID of 0 and GID of 0.

As you can probably guess by now, the root user has supreme power over your system. With this in mind, it's important that you do not work as root all the time as you may inadvertently cause serious damage to your system, perhaps even making it totally unusable. Instead, you should rely on root only when you need to make specific changes to your system that require root privileges. As soon as you've finished your work you can switch back to your normal user account to carry on working.

Within Ubuntu you execute a command with root privileges by way of the sudo command like so:

```
$sudo apt-get update
```

You will be prompted for your password so you should enter this. Ubuntu will then carry out the command (in this case updating information about available software) as if you were running it as root.

The Root User

If you've used other Linux distros then you are likely to be a little puzzled by the use of the sudo command. In short, Ubuntu allows the first user on the system access to full root privileges through the sudo command. It also disables the root account so no one can actually login with the username root.

In other Linux distros you would change to the root user by issuing the command su - followed by the root password. This will land you at the root prompt, which is shown as a pound sign (#). From here you are able to execute any command you wish. To get to a root prompt in Ubuntu you need to execute the command sudo -i which, after you enter your password, will give you the prompt so familiar to other Linux distros. When you've finished working as root just type exit and hit Enter to get back to a normal user prompt ($).

A regular user is someone who logs on to the system to make use of it for nonadministrative tasks such as word processing or email. These users do not need to make systemwide changes or manage other users. However, they might want to be able to change settings specific to them (for instance, a desktop background). Of course, depending on how draconian the root user is, regular users might not even be able to do that!

The super user grants privileges to regular users by means of file and directory permissions (as covered in Chapter 4, "Command Line Quickstart"). For example, if the super user does not want you to change your settings in ~/.profile (the ~ is a shell shortcut representing your home directory), root can alter the permissions so that you may read from, but not write to, that file.

CAUTION

Because of the potential for making a catastrophic error as the super user (using the command rm -rf /* is the classic example, but do not ever try it!), always use your system as a regular user and become root only temporarily to do sysadmin duties. While you are on a multiuser system, consider this advice an absolute rule; if root were to delete the wrong file or kill the wrong process, the results could be disastrous for the business. On your home system, you can do as you please, and running as root makes many things easier, but less safe. In any setting, however, the risks of running as root are significant and we cannot stress how important it is to be careful when working as root.

The third type of user is the system user. The system user is not a person, but rather an administrative account that the system uses during day-to-day running of various services. For example, the system user named apache owns the apache web server and all the associated files. Only itself and root can have access to these files—no one else can access or make changes to these files. System users do not have a home directory or password, nor do they permit access to the system through a login prompt.

You will find a list of all the users on a system in the /etc/passwd file. Ubuntu refers to these users as the *standard users* because they are found on every Ubuntu computer as the default set of system (or logical) users provided during the initial installation. This "standard" set differs among Linux distributions.

User IDs and Group IDs

A computer is, by its very nature, a number-oriented machine. It identifies users and groups by numbers known as the *user ID (UID)* and *group ID (GID)*. The alphabetic names display on your screen just for the your ease of use.

As previously mentioned, the root user is UID 0. Numbers from 1 through 499 and 65,534 are the system, or logical, users. Regular users have UIDs beginning with 1,000; Ubuntu assigns them sequentially beginning with this number.

With only a few exceptions, the GID is the same as the UID.

Ubuntu creates a private GID for every UID of 1,000 and greater. The system administrator can add other users to a GID or create a totally new group and add users to it. Unlike Windows NT and some UNIX variants, a group cannot be a member of another group in Linux.

File Permissions

As you learned in Chapter 4, permissions are of three types: read, write, and execute (r, w, x). For any file or directory, permissions can be established in three categories: user, group, and global. In this section, we focus on group permissions, but there is a highlight of the commands used to change the group, user, or access permissions of a file or directory: Seth

- ▶ chgrp—Changes the group ownership of a file or directory
- ▶ chown—Changes the owner of a file or directory
- ▶ chmod—Changes the access permissions of a file or directory

These commands, which modify file ownerships and permissions, can be used to model organizational structures and permissions in the real world onto your Ubuntu system (see the next section, "Managing Groups"). For example, a human resources department can share health-benefit memos to all company employees by making the files readable (but not writable) by anyone in an accessible directory. On the other hand, programmers in the company's research and development section, although able to access each other's source code files, would not have read or write access to HR pay-scale or personnel files (and certainly would not want HR or marketing poking around R&D).

These commands are used to easily manage group and file ownerships and permissions from the command line. It is essential that you know these commands because sometimes you might have only a command-line interface to work with; perhaps some idiot system administrator set incorrect permissions on X11, for example, rendering the system incapable of working with a graphical interface.

User Stereotypes

As is the case in many professions, exaggerated characterizations (**stereotypes** or **caricatures**) have emerged for users and system administrators. Many stereotypes contain elements of truth mixed with generous amounts of hyperbole and humor and serve to assist us in understanding the characteristics of and differences in the stereotyped subjects. The stereotypes of the "luser" and the "BOFH" (users and administrators, respectively) also serve as cautionary tales describing what behavior is acceptable and unacceptable in the computing community.

Understanding these stereotypes allows you to better define the appropriate and inappropriate roles of system administrators, users, and others. You can find a good reference for both at Wikipedia: http://en.wikipedia.org/wiki/BOFH and http://en.wikipedia.org/wiki/Luser.

Managing Groups

Groups can make managing users a lot easier. Instead of having to assign individual permissions to every user, you can use groups to grant or revoke permissions to a large number of users quickly and easily. Setting group permissions allows you to set up workspaces for collaborative working and to control what devices can be used, such as external drives or DVD writers. This approach also represents a secure method of limiting access to system resources to only those users who need them. As an example, the sysadmin could put the users andrew, paul, michael, bernice, mark, and john in a new group named unleashed. Those users could each create files intended for their group work and chgrp those files to unleashed.

Now, everyone in the unleashed group—but no one else except root—can work with those files. The sysadmin would probably create a directory owned by that group so that its members could have an easily accessed place to store those files. The sysadmin could also add other users such as bernice and ildiko to the group and remove existing users when their part of the work is done. The sysadmin could make the user andrew the group administrator so that andrew could decide how group membership should be changed. You could also put restrictions on the DVD writer so that only andrew could burn DVDs, thus protecting sensitive material from falling into the wrong hands.

Different UNIX operating systems implement the group concept in various ways. Ubuntu uses a scheme called *UPG*, the *user private group*, in which all users are assigned to a group with their own name by default. (The user's username and group name are identical.) All the groups are listed in /etc/group file.

Here is a partial list of a sample /etc/group file:

```
$ sudo cat /etc/group
```

10

```
root:x:0:
daemon:x:1:
bin:x:2:
sys:x:3:

mail:x:8:
news:x:9:
...
gdm:x:111:
andrew:x:1000:
admin:x:112:andrew
```

This example contains a number of groups, mostly for services (mail, news, and so on) and devices (floppy, disk, and so on). As previously mentioned, the system services groups enable those services to have ownership and control of their files. For example, adding postfix to the mail group, as shown previously, enables the postfix application to access mail's files in the manner that mail would decide for group access to its file. Adding a regular user to a device's group permits the regular user to use the device with permissions granted by the group owner. Adding user andrew to the group cdrom, for example, would allow andrew to use the optical drive device. You learn how to add and remove users from groups in the next section.

Group Management Tools

Ubuntu provides several command-line tools for managing groups, but also provides graphical tools for such. Many experienced sysadmins prefer the command-line tools because they are quick and easy to use and can be included in scripts if the sysadmin desires to script a repetitive task.

Here are the most commonly used group management command-line tools:

- groupadd—This command creates and adds a new group.

- groupdel—This command removes an existing group.

- groupmod—This command creates a group name or GIDs but doesn't add or delete members from a group.

- gpasswd—This command creates a group password. Every group can have a group password and an administrator. Use the -A argument to assign a user as group administrator.

- useradd -G—The -G argument adds a user to a group during the initial user creation. (More arguments are used to create a user.)

- usermod -G—This command allows you to add a user to a group so long as the user is not logged in at the time.

- grpck—A command for checking the /etc/group file for typos.

As an example, there is a DVD-RW device (/dev/scd0) on our computer that the sysadmin wants a regular user named john to have access to. To grant john that access, we would follow these steps:

1. Add a new group with the groupadd command:

   # **groupadd dvdrw**

2. Change the group ownership of the device to the new group with the chgrp command:

   # **chgrp dvdrw /dev/scd0**

3. Add the approved user to the group with the usermod command:

   # **usermod -G dvdrw john**

4. Make user john the group administrator with the gpasswd command so that she can add new users to the group:

   # **gpasswd -A john**

Now, the user john has permission to use the DVD-RW drive, as would anyone else added to the group by the super user or john because she is now also the group administrator and can add users to the group.

The sysadmin can also use the graphical interface that Ubuntu provides, as shown in Figure 10.1. It is accessed under System, Administration as the Users and Groups entry.

FIGURE 10.1   Use the manage groups option to allow you to assign users to groups.

10

Note that the full set of group commands and options are not available from the graphical interface, limiting the usefulness of the GUI to a subset of the most frequently used commands. You learn more about using the Ubuntu User Manager GUI in the next section of this chapter.

Managing Users

We have mentioned users previously, but in this section we look at how the sysadmin can actually manage the users. Users must be created, assigned a UID, provided a home directory, provided an initial set of files for their home directory, and assigned to groups so that they can use the system resources securely and efficiently. The system administrator might elect to restrict a user's access not only to files, but to the amount of disk space they use, too.

User Management Tools

Ubuntu provides several command-line tools for managing users, but also provides graphical tools too. Many experienced sysadmins prefer the command-line tools because they are quick and easy to use and they can be included in scripts if the sysadmin prefers to script a repetitive task. Here are the most frequently used commands used to manage users:

▶ useradd—This command is used to add a new user account to the system. Its options permit the sysadmin to specify the user's home directory and initial group or to create the user with the default home directory and group assignments.

▶ useradd -D—This command sets the system defaults for creating the user's home directory, account expiration date, default group, and command shell. See the specific options in man useradd. Used without any arguments, it displays the defaults for the system. The default set of files for a user are found in /etc/skel.

> **NOTE**
>
> The set of files initially used to populate a new user's home directory are kept in /etc/skel. This is convenient for the system administrator because any special files, links, or directories that need to be universally applied can be placed in /etc/skel and will be duplicated automatically with appropriate permissions for each new user.
>
> ```
> $ ls -al /etc/skel
> total 20
>
> drwxr-xr-x   2 root root 4096 2007-08-09 00:59 .
>
> drwxr-xr-x 111 root root 4096 2007-08-20 09:54 ..
> ```

```
-rw-r--r--   1 root root   220 2007-05-17 12:59 .bash_logout

-rw-r--r--   1 root root  2298 2007-05-17 12:59 .bashrc

lrwxrwxrwx   1 root root    26 2007-08-13 19:42 Examples \
-> /usr/share/example-content

-rw-r--r--   1 root root   566 2007-05-17 12:59 .profile
```

Each line provides the file permissions, the number of files housed under that file or directory name, the file owner, the file group, the file size, the creation date, and the filename.

As you can see, root owns every file here, but the adduser command (a symbolic link to the actual command named useradd) copies everything in /etc/skel to the new home directory and resets file ownership and permissions to the new user.

Certain user files might exist that the system administrator doesn't want the user to change; the permissions for those files in /home/username can be reset so that the user can read them but can't write to them.

- ▶ userdel—This command completely removes a user's account (thereby eliminating that user's home directory and all files it contains).

- ▶ passwd—This command updates the "authentication tokens" used by the password management system.

TIP

To lock a user out of his account, use the following command:

```
# passwd -l username
```

This prepends an ! (exclamation point, also called a bang) to the user's encrypted password; the command to reverse the process uses the -u option. This is a more elegant and preferred solution to the problem than the traditional UNIX way of manually editing the file.

- ▶ usermod—This command changes several user attributes. The most commonly used arguments are -s to change the shell and -u to change the UID. No changes can be made while the user is logged in or running a process.

▶ chsh—This command changes the user's default shell. For Ubuntu, the default shell is /bin/bash, known as the *Bash,* or *Bourne Again Shell.*

Adding New Users

The command-line approach to adding this user is actually quite simple and can be accomplished on a single line. In the example shown here, the sysadmin uses the useradd command to add the new user bernice. The command adduser (a variant found on some UNIX systems) is a symbolic link to useradd, so both commands work the same. In this example, we use the -p option to set the password the user requested; we use the -s to set his special shell, and the -u option to specify her UID. (If we create a user with the default settings, we do not need to use these options.) All we want to do can be accomplished on one line:

```
# useradd bernice -p sTitcher -s /bin/zsh -u 1002
```

The sysadmin can also use the graphical interface that Ubuntu provides, as shown in Figure 10.2. It is accessed as the Users and Groups item from the Administration menu. Here, the sysadmin is adding a new user to the system where user bernice uses the bash command shell.

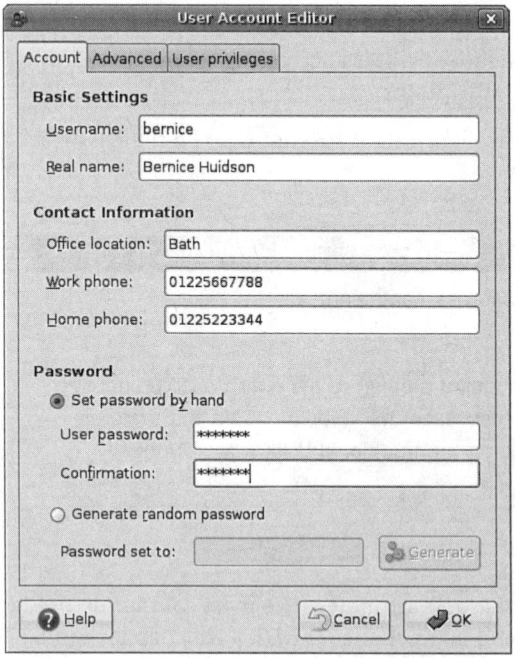

FIGURE 10.2   Adding a new user is simple. The GUI provides a more complete set of commands for user management than for group management.

These are the steps we used to add the same account as shown in the preceding command, but using the graphical User Manager interface:

1. Launch the Ubuntu User Manager graphical interface by clicking on the Users and Groups menu item found in the System Settings menu.

2. Click the Add User button to bring up the Add User dialog window.

3. Fill in the form with the appropriate information as requested, ensuring you create a good password.

4. Click the Advanced tab and open the drop-down Shell menu to select the bash shell.

5. Using the arrows found in the UID dialog, increment the UID to 1413.

6. Click OK to save the settings.

Note that the user is being manually assigned the UID of 1413 because that is her UID on another system machine that will be connected to this machine. Because the system only knows her as 1001 and not as bernice, the two machines would not recognize bernice as the same user if two different UIDs were assigned.

NOTE

A Linux username can be any alphanumeric combination that does not begin with a special character reserved for shell script use (see Chapter 11, "Automating Tasks," for disallowed characters, mostly punctuation characters). In Chapter 4, we told you that usernames are typically the user's first name plus the first initial of her last name. That is a common practice on larger systems with many users because it makes life simpler for the sysadmin, but is neither a rule nor a requirement.

Monitoring User Activity on the System

Monitoring user activity is part of the sysadmin's duties and an essential task in tracking how system resources are being used. The w command tells the sysadmin who is logged in, where he is logged in, and what he is doing. No one can hide from the super user. The w command can be followed by a specific user's name to show only that user.

The ac command provides information about the total connect time of a user measured in hours. It accesses the /var/log/wtmp file for the source of its information. The ac command proves most useful in shell scripts to generate reports on operating system usage for management review. Note that in order to use the ac command you will have to install the acct package using either synaptic or apt-get.

TIP

Interestingly, a phenomenon known as **timewarp** can occur in which an entry in the wtmp files jumps back into the past and ac shows unusual amounts of time accounted for users. Although this can be attributed to some innocuous factors having to do with the system clock, it is worthy of investigation by the sysadmin because it can also be the result of a security breach.

10

The `last` command searches through the `/var/log/wtmp` file and lists all the users logged in and out since that file was first created. The user `reboot` exists so that you might know who has logged in since the last reboot. A companion to `last` is the command `lastb`, which shows all failed, or bad, logins. It is useful for determining whether a legitimate user is having trouble or a hacker is attempting access.

> **NOTE**
>
> The accounting system on your computer keeps track of usage user statistics and is kept in the current `/var/log/wtmp` file. That file is managed by the `init` and `login` processes. If you want to explore the depths of the accounting system, use the GNU info system: `info accounting`.

Managing Passwords

Passwords are an integral part of Linux security, and they are the most visible part to the user. In this section, you learn how to establish a minimal password policy for your system, where the passwords are stored, and how to manage passwords for your users.

System Password Policy

An effective password policy is a fundamental part of a good system administration plan. The policy should cover the following:

- ▶ Allowed and forbidden passwords
- ▶ Frequency of mandated password changes
- ▶ Retrieval or replacement of lost or forgotten passwords
- ▶ Password handling by users

The Password File

The password file is `/etc/passwd`, and it is the database file for all users on the system. The format of each line is as follows:

```
username:password:uid:gid:gecos:homedir:shell
```

The fields are self-explanatory except for the `gecos` field. This field is for miscellaneous information about the user, such as the users' full name, his office location, office and home phone numbers, and possibly a brief text message. For security and privacy reasons, this field is little used nowadays, but the system administrator should be aware of its existence because the `gecos` field is used by traditional UNIX programs such as `finger` and `mail`. For that reason, it is commonly referred to as the *finger information field*. The data in this field will be comma delimited; the `gecos` field can be changed with the `cgfn` (change finger) command.

Note that a colon separates all fields in the /etc/passwd file. If no information is available for a field, that field is empty, but all the colons remain.

If an asterisk appears in the password field, that user will not be permitted to log on. Why does this feature exist? So that a user can be easily disabled and (possibly) reinstated later without having to be created all over again. The system administrator manually edits this field, which is the traditional UNIX way of accomplishing this task. Ubuntu provides improved functionality with the passwd -l command mentioned earlier.

Several services run as pseudo-users, usually with root permissions. These are the system, or logical, users mentioned previously. You would not want these accounts available for general login for security reasons, so they are assigned /sbin/nologin as their shell, which prohibits any logins from those "users."

A list of /etc/passwd reveals the following:

```
$ cat /etc/passwd
root:x:0:0:root:/root:/bin/bash
daemon:x:1:1:daemon:/usr/sbin:/bin/sh
bin:x:2:2:bin:/bin:/bin/sh
sys:x:3:3:sys:/dev:/bin/sh
sync:x:4:65534:sync:/bin:/bin/sync
games:x:5:60:games:/usr/games:/bin/sh
man:x:6:12:man:/var/cache/man:/bin/sh
lp:x:7:7:lp:/var/spool/lpd:/bin/sh
mail:x:8:8:mail:/var/mail:/bin/sh
news:x:9:9:news:/var/spool/news:/bin/sh
...
hplip:x:106:7:HPLIP system user,,,:/var/run/hplip:/bin/false
andrew:x:1000:1000:Andrew Hudson,17,01225112233,01225445566:\
/home/andrew:/bin/bash
beagleindex:x:107:65534::/var/cache/beagle:/bin/false
```

Note that all the password fields do not show a password, but contain an x because they are *shadow passwords*, a useful security enhancement to Linux, discussed in the following section.

Shadow Passwords

It is considered a security risk to keep any password in /etc/passwd because anyone with read access can run a cracking program on the file and obtain the passwords with little trouble. To avoid this risk, *shadow passwords* are used so that only an x appears in the password field of /etc/passwd; the real passwords are kept in /etc/shadow, a file that can only be read by the sysadmin (and *PAM*, the *Pluggable Authentication Modules* authentication manager; see the "PAM Explained" sidebar for an explanation of PAM).

Special versions of the traditional password and login programs must be used to enable shadow passwords. Shadow passwords are automatically enabled during the installation phase of the operating system on Ubuntu systems.

Let's examine a listing of the shadow companion to /etc/passwd, the /etc/shadow file:

```
# cat /etc/shadow
root:*:13299:0:99999:7:::
daemon:*:13299:0:99999:7:::
bin:*:13299:0:99999:7:::
...
haldaemon:!:13299:0:99999:7:::
gdm:!:13299:0:99999:7:::
hplip:!:13299:0:99999:7:::
andrew:$1$6LT/qkWL$sPJPp.2QkpC8JPtpRk906/:13299:0:99999:7:::
beagleindex:!:13299:0:99999:7:::
```

The fields are separated by colons and are, in order:

- ▶ The user's login name.

- ▶ The encrypted password for the user.

- ▶ The day of which the last password change occurred, measured in the number of days since January 1, 1970. This date is known in UNIX circles as the *epoch*. Just so you know, the billionth second since the epoch occurred was in September 2001; that was the UNIX version of Y2K—as with the real Y2K, nothing much happened.

- ▶ The number of days before the password can be changed (prevents changing a password and then changing it back to the old password right away—a dangerous security practice).

- ▶ The number of days after which the password must be changed. This can be set to force the change of a newly issued password known to the system administrator.

- ▶ The number of days before the password expiration that the user is warned it will expire.

- ▶ The number of days after the password expires that the account is disabled (for security).

- ▶ Similar to the password change date, although this is the number of days since January 1, 1970 that the account has been disabled.

- ▶ The final field is a "reserved" field and is not currently allocated for any use.

Note that password expiration dates and warnings are disabled by default in Ubuntu. These features are not used on home systems and usually not used for small offices. It is the sysadmin's responsibility to establish and enforce password expiration policies.

The permissions on the /etc/shadow file should be set so that it is not writable or readable by regular users: The permissions should be 600.

PAM Explained

Pluggable Authentication Modules (PAM) is a system of libraries that handle the tasks of authentication on your computer. It uses four management groups: account management, authentication management, password management, and session management. This allows the system administrator to choose how individual applications will authenticate users. Ubuntu has preinstalled and preconfigured all the necessary PAM files for you.

The configuration files in Ubuntu are found in /etc/pam.d. These files are named for the service they control, and the format is as follows:

```
type control module-path module-arguments
```

The type field is the management group that the rule corresponds to. The control field tells PAM what to do if authentication fails. The final two items deal with the PAM module used and any arguments it needs. Programs that use PAM typically come packaged with appropriate entries for the /etc/pam.d directory. To achieve greater security, the system administrator can modify the default entries. Misconfiguration can have unpredictable results, so back up the configuration files before you modify them. The defaults provided by Ubuntu are adequate for home and small office users.

An example of a PAM configuration file with the formatted entries as described previously is shown next. Here are the contents of /etc/pam.d/gdm:

```
#%PAM-1.0

auth     requisite       pam_nologin.so

auth     required        pam_env.so readenv=1

auth     required        pam_env.so readenv=1 envfile=/etc/default/locale

@include common-account

session required        pam_limits.so

@include common-session

@include common-password
```

Amusingly, even the PAM documents state that you do not really need (or want) to know a lot about PAM to use it effectively.

You will likely need only the PAM system administrator's guide. You can find it at http://www.kernel.org/pub/linux/libs/pam/Linux-PAM-html/Linux-PAM_SAG.html

Managing Password Security for Users

Selecting appropriate user passwords is always an exercise in trade-offs. A password such as *password* (do not laugh, it has been used too often before in the real world with devastating consequences) is just too easy to guess by an intruder as are simple words or number combinations (a street address, for example). A security auditor for one of my former employers used to take the cover sheet from an employee's personnel file (which contained the usual personal information of name, address, birth date, and so on) and then attempt to log on to a terminal with passwords constructed from that information—and often succeeded in logging on.

On the other hand, a password such as 2a56u'"F($84u&#^Hiu44Ik%$([#EJD is sure to present great difficulty to an intruder (or an auditor). However, that password is so difficult to remember that it would be likely that the password owner would write that password down and tape it next to her keyboard. I worked for a company in which the entry code to one of the buildings was etched into the cigarette bin outside the door; we never found out who did this, but quickly changed the security number. This is but one of many examples of poor security in the field.

The sysadmin has control, with settings in the /etc/shadow file, over how often the password must be changed. The settings can be changed using a text editor, the change command, or a configuration tool such as Ubuntu's User Manager, as shown previously in Figure 10.1. Click on the Password Info tab under that particular user's Properties to set individual password policies.

Changing Passwords in a Batch

On a large system, there might be times when a large number of users and their passwords need some attention. The super user can change passwords in a batch by using the chpasswd command, which accepts input as a name/password pair per line in the following form:

```
$ sudo chpasswd username:password
```

Passwords can be changed *en masse* by redirecting a list of name and password pairs to the command. An appropriate shell script can be constructed with the information gleaned from Chapter 11.

However, Ubuntu also provides the newusers command to add users in a batch from a text file. This command also allows a user to be added to a group, and a new directory can be added for the user, too.

Granting System Administrator Privileges to Regular Users

On occasion, it is necessary for regular users to run a command as if they were the root user. They usually do not need these powers, but they might on occasion—for example, to temporarily access certain devices or run a command for testing purposes.

There are two ways to run commands with root privileges: The first is useful if you are the super user and the user; the second if you are not the regular user (as on a large, multiuser network).

Temporarily Changing User Identity with the su Command

What if you are also root but are logged on as a regular user because you are performing nonadministrative tasks and you need to do something that only the super user can do? The su command is available for this purpose.

> **NOTE**
>
> A popular misconception is that the su command is short for *super user*; it just means *substitute user*. An important but often overlooked distinction is that between su and su -. In the former instance, you become that user but keep your own environmental variables (such as paths). In the latter, you inherit the environment of that user. This is most noticeable when you use su to become the super user, root. Without appending the -, you do not inherit the path variable that includes /bin or /sbin, so you must always enter the full path to those commands when you just su to root.
>
> Don't forget that on a standard Ubuntu system, the first created user is classed as root, whilst the true root account is disabled. To enable the root account, enter the command sudo passwd at the command line and enter your password and a new root password. Once this has been completed then you can su to root.

Because almost all Linux file system security revolves around file permissions, it can be useful to occasionally become a different user with permission to access files belonging to other users or groups or to access special files (such as the communications port /dev/ttyS0 when using a modem or the sound device /dev/audio when playing a game). You can use the su command to temporarily switch to another user identity, and then switch back.

> **TIP**
>
> It is never a good idea to use an **Internet Relay Chat (IRC)** client as the root user, and you might not want to run it using your regular user account. Simply create a special new user just for IRC and su to that user in a terminal widow to launch your IRC client.

The su command spawns a new shell, changing both the UID and GID of the existing user and automatically changes the environmental variables associated with that user, known as *inheriting the environment*. Refer to Chapter 4 for more information on environmental variables.

The syntax for the su command is as follows:

```
$ su option username arguments
```

The man page for su gives more details, but some highlights of the su command are here:

```
-c, --command COMMAND
```

10

```
        pass a single COMMAND to the shell with -c

-m, --preserve-environment
        do not reset environment variables

-l    a full login simulation for the substituted user,
        the same as specifying the dash alone
```

You can invoke the su command in different ways that yield diverse results. By using su alone, you can become root, but you keep your regular user environment. This can be verified by using the printenv command before and after the change. Note that the working directory (you can execute pwd as a command line to print the current working directory) has not changed. By executing the following, you become root and inherit root's environment:

```
$ su -
```

By executing the following, you become that user and inherit the super user's environment—a pretty handy tool. (Remember: Inheriting the environment comes from using the dash in the command; omit that, and you keep your "old" environment.) To become another user, specify a different user's name on the command line:

```
$ su - other_user
```

When leaving an identity to return to your usual user identity, use the exit command. For example, while logged on as a regular user,

```
$ su - root
```

the system prompts for a password:

```
Password:
```

When the password is entered correctly, the root user's prompt appears:

```
#
```

To return to the regular user's identity, just type

```
# exit
```

This takes you to the regular user's prompt:

```
$
```

If you need to allow other users access to certain commands with root privileges, you must give them the root password so that they can use su—that definitely is not a secure solution. The next section describes a more flexible and secure method of allowing normal users to perform selected root tasks.

Granting Root Privileges on Occasion—The sudo Command

It is often necessary to delegate some of the authority that root wields on a system. For a large system, this makes sense because no single individual will always be available to perform super user functions. The problem is that UNIX permissions come with an all-or-nothing authority. Enter sudo, an application that permits the assignment of one, several, or all of the root-only system commands.

> **NOTE**
>
> As mentioned earlier, the sudo command is pervasive in Ubuntu, because it is used by default. If you want to get to a root shell, and thereby removing the need to type **sudo** for every command, just enter sudo -i to get the root prompt. To return to a normal user prompt, enter exit and press Return.

After it is configured, using sudo is simple. An authorized user merely precedes the super user authority-needed command with the sudo command, like so:

```
$ sudo command
```

After getting the user's password, sudo checks the /etc/sudoers file to see whether that user is authorized to execute that particular command; if so, sudo generates a "ticket" for a specific length of time that authorizes the use of that command. The user is then prompted for his password (to preserve accountability and provide some measure of security), and then the command is run as if root had issued it. During the life of the ticket, the command can be used again without a password prompt. If an unauthorized user attempts to execute a sudo command, a record of the unauthorized attempt is kept in the system log and a mail message is sent to the super user.

Three man pages are associated with sudo: sudo, sudoers, and visudo. The first covers the command itself, the second the format of the /etc/sudoers file, and the third the use of the special editor for /etc/sudoers. You should use the special editing command because it checks the file for parse errors and locks the file to prevent others from editing it at the same time. The visudo command uses the vi editor, so you might need a quick review of the vi editing commands found in Chapter 4, "Command Line Quickstart," in the section "Working with vi." You begin the editing by executing the visudo command with this:

```
$ sudo visudo
```

The default /etc/sudoers file looks like this:

```
# /etc/sudoers
#
# This file MUST be edited with the 'visudo' command as root.
```

```
#
# See the man page for details on how to write a sudoers file.
# Host alias specification

# User alias specification

# Cmnd alias specification

# Defaults

Defaults        !lecture,tty_tickets,!fqdn

# User privilege specification
root    ALL=(ALL) ALL

# Members of the admin group may gain root privileges
%admin  ALL=(ALL) ALL
```

The basic format of a sudoers line in the file is as follows:

```
user host_computer=command
```

The user can be an individual user or a group (prepended by a % to identify the name as a group). The host_computer is normally ALL for all hosts on the network and localhost for the local machine, but the host computer can be referenced as a subnet or any specific host. The command in the sudoers line can be ALL, a list of specific commands, or a restriction on specific commands (formed by prepending a ! to the command). A number of options are available for use with the sudoers line, and aliases can be used to simplify the assignment of privileges. Again, the sudoers man page will give the details, but here are a few examples:

If we uncomment the line

```
# %wheel       ALL=(ALL)       NOPASSWD: ALL
```

any user we add to the wheel group can execute any command without a password.

Suppose that we want to give a user john permission across the network to be able to add users with the graphical interface. We would add the line

```
john ALL=/users-admin
```

or perhaps grant permission only on her local computer:

```
john 192.168.1.87=/usr/bin/users-admin
```

If we want to give the editor group systemwide permission with no password required to delete files

```
%editors ALL=NOPASSWD: /bin/rm
```

If we want to give every user permission with no password required to mount the CD drive on the `localhost`

```
ALL localhost=NOPASSWD:/sbin/mount /dev/scd0 /mnt/cdrom /sbin/umount /mnt/cdrom
```

It is also possible to use wildcards in the construction of the sudoers file. Aliases can be used, too, to make it easier to define users and groups. Although the man page for `sudoers` contains some examples, http://www.komar.org/pres/sudo/toc.html provides illustrative notes and comments of `sudo` use at a large aerospace company. The sudo home page at http://www.sudo.ws/ is also a useful resource for additional explanations and examples.

The following command presents users with a list of the commands they are entitled to use:

```
$ sudo -l
```

Adding Extra Sudo Users

As mentioned earlier, by default Ubuntu grants the first created user full root access through the sudo command. If you need to add this capability for other users, then you can do this easily by adding each user to the admin group or by using the User Manager tool to allow them to Administer the System, which can be found in the User Privileges tab when you edit the properties for a user.

Disk Quotas

On large systems with many users, you need to control the amount of disk space a user has access to. Disk quotas are designed specifically for this purpose. Quotas, managed per each partition, can be set for both individual users as well as groups; quotas for the group need not be as large as the aggregate quotas for the individuals in the groups.

When files are created, both a user and a group own them; ownership of the files is always part of the metadata about the files. This makes quotas based on both users and groups easy to manage.

NOTE

Disk quota management is never done on a home system and rarely, if ever, done on a small office system.

To manage disk quotas, you must have the `quota` and `quotatool` packages installed on your system. Quota management with Ubuntu is not enabled by default and has traditionally been enabled and configured manually by system administrators. Sysadmins use the family of quota commands, such as `quotacheck` to initialize the quota database files, `edquota` to set and edit user quotas, `setquota` to configure disk quotas, and `quotaon` or

quotaoff to control the service. (Other utilities include warnquota for automatically
sending mail to users over their disk space usage limit.)

Implementing Quotas

To reiterate, quotas might not be enabled by default, even if the quota software package is
installed on your system. When quotas are installed and enabled, you can see which partitions have either user quotas, group quotas, or both by looking at the fourth field in the
/etc/fstab file. For example, one line in /etc/fstab shows that quotas are enabled for
the /home partition:

```
/dev/hda5      /home    ext3      defaults,usrquota,grpquota 1 1
```

The root of the partition with quotas enabled will have the files quota.user or
quota.group in them (or both files, if both types of quotas are enabled), and the files will
contain the actual quotas. The permissions of these files should be 600 so that users
cannot read or write to them. (Otherwise, users would change them to allow ample space
for their music files and Internet art collections.) To initialize disk quotas, the partitions
must be remounted. This is easily accomplished with the following:

```
# mount -o ro,remount partition_to_be_remounted mount_point
```

The underlying console tools (complete with man pages) are

- quotaon, quotaoff—Toggles quotas on a partition

- repquota—A summary status report on users and groups

- quotacheck—Updates the status of quotas (compares new and old tables of disk
  usage); it is run after fsck

- edquota—A basic quota management command

Manually Configuring Quotas

Manual configuration of quotas involves changing entries in your system's file system
table, /etc/fstab, to add the usrquota mount option to the desired portion of your file
system. As an example in a simple file system, quota management can be enabled like
this:

```
LABEL=/          /          ext3      defaults,usrquota      1 1
```

Group-level quotas can also be enabled by using the grpquota option. As the root operator, you must then create a file (using our example of creating user quotas) named
quota.user in the designated portion of the file system, like so:

```
# touch /quota.user
```

You should then turn on the use of quotas using the quotaon command:

```
# quotaon -av
```

You can then edit user quotas with the edquota command to set hard and soft limits on file system use. The default system editor (vi unless you change your EDITOR environment variable) will be launched when editing a user's quota.

Any user can find out what their quotas are with

```
$ quota -v
```

NOTE

Ubuntu does not support any graphical tools that enable you to configure disk quotas. A Quota mini-HOWTO is maintained at http://www.tldp.org/HOWTO/mini/Quota.html.

Related Ubuntu Commands

You will use these commands to manage user accounts in Ubuntu:

- ac—A user account-statistics command
- change—Sets or modifies user password expiration policies
- chfn—Creates or modifies user finger information in /etc/passwd
- chgrp—Modifies group memberships
- chmod—Changes file permissions
- chown—Changes file ownerships
- chpasswd—Batch command to modify user passwords
- chsh—Modifies a user's shell
- groups—Displays existing group memberships
- logname—Displays a user's login name
- newusers—Batches user management command
- passwd—Creates or modifies user passwords
- su—Executes shell or command as another user
- sudo—Manages selected user execution permissions
- useradd—Creates, modifies, or manages users
- usermod—Edits a user's login profile

10

Reference

▶ http://www.ibiblio.org/pub/Linux/docs/HOWTO/other-formats/html_single/_User-Authentication-HOWTO.html—The User-Authentication HOWTO describes how user and group information is stored and used for authentication.

▶ http://www.ibiblio.org/pub/Linux/docs/HOWTO/other-formats/html_single/Shadow-Password-HOWTO.html—The Shadow-Password HOWTO delves into the murky depths of shadow passwords and even discusses why you might not want to use them.

▶ http://www.ibiblio.org/pub/Linux/docs/HOWTO/other-formats/html_single/_Security-HOWTO.html—A must-read HOWTO, the Security HOWTO is a good overview of security issues. Especially applicable to this chapter are sections on creating accounts, file permissions, and password security.

▶ http://www.secinf.net/unix_security/Linux_Administrators_Security_Guide/—A general guide, the Linux System Administrator's Security Guide has interesting sections on limiting and monitoring users.

▶ http://www.ibiblio.org/pub/Linux/docs/HOWTO/other-formats/html_single/Config-HOWTO.html—How can you customize some user-specific settings? The Config HOWTO Software Configuration gives some advice.

▶ http://www.ibiblio.org/pub/Linux/docs/HOWTO/other-formats/html_single/Path.html—How can one know the true path? The Path HOWTO sheds light on this issue. You need to understand paths if you want to guide the users to their data and applications.

▶ http://www.courtesan.com/sudo/—The SUperuser DO command is a powerful and elegant way to delegate authority to regular users for specific commands.

▶ http://www.kernel.org/pub/linux/libs/pam/index.html—The Pluggable Authentication Modules suite contains complex and highly useful applications that provide additional security and logging for passwords. PAM is installed by default in Ubuntu. It isn't necessary to understand the intricacies of PAM to use it effectively.

CHAPTER **11**

Automating Tasks

In this chapter you learn about the five ways to automate tasks on your system: making them services that run as your system starts, making them services you start and stop by hand, scheduling them to run at specific times, connecting multiple commands together on the shell, and writing custom scripts that group everything together under one command.

After you turn on the power switch, the boot process begins with the computer executing code stored in a chip called the BIOS; this process occurs no matter what operating system you have installed. The Linux boot process begins when the code known as the boot loader starts loading the Linux kernel and ends only when the login prompt appears.

As a system administrator, you will use the skills you learn in this chapter to control your system's services and manage runlevels on your computer. Understanding the management of the system services and states is essential to understanding how Linux works (especially in a multi-user environment) and will help untangle the mysteries of a few of your Ubuntu system's configuration files. Furthermore, a good knowledge of the cron daemon that handles task scheduling is essential for administrators at all skill levels.

This chapter is also an introduction to the basics of creating *shell scripts*, or executable text files written to conform to shell syntax. Shell scripts run like any other command under Linux and can contain complex logic or a simple series of Linux command-line instructions. You can also run other shell scripts from within a shell program. The features and functions for several Linux shells are discussed in this chapter after a short introduction to working from the shell command line. You learn how to write and execute a simple shell program using bash, one of the most popular Linux shells.

Running Services at Bootup

Although most people consider a computer to be either on or off, in Ubuntu there are a number of states in between. Known as *runlevels*, they control what system services are started upon bootup. These services are simply applications running in the background that provide some needed function to your system, such as getting information from your mouse and sending it to the display; or a service could monitor the partitions to see whether they have enough free space left on them. Services are typically loaded and run (also referred to as being started) during the boot process, in the same way as Microsoft Windows services are. Internally, Ubuntu uses a system known as Upstart for fast booting, but this has a special backward compatibility layer that uses runlevels in the way that Linux veterans are accustomed.

You can manage nearly every aspect of your computer and how it behaves after booting via configuring and ordering boot scripts, as well as by using various system administration utilities included with Ubuntu. In this chapter, you learn how to work with these boot scripts and system administration utilities. This chapter also offers advice for troubleshooting and fixing problems that might arise with software configuration or the introduction or removal of various types of hardware from your system.

Beginning the Boot Loading Process

Although the actual boot loading mechanism for Linux varies on different hardware platforms (such as the SPARC, Alpha, or PowerPC systems), Intel-based PCs running Ubuntu most often use the same mechanism throughout product lines. This process is accomplished through a Basic Input Output System, or BIOS. The BIOS is an application stored in a chip on the motherboard that initializes the hardware on the motherboard (and often the hardware that's attached to the motherboard). The BIOS gets the system ready to load and run the software that we recognize as the operating system.

As a last step, the BIOS code looks for a special program known as the boot loader or boot code. The instructions in this little bit of code tell the BIOS where the Linux kernel is located, how it should be loaded into memory, and how it should be started.

If all goes well, the BIOS looks for a bootable volume such as a floppy disk, CD-ROM, hard drive, RAM disk, or other media. The bootable volume contains a special hexadecimal value written to the volume by the boot loader application (likely either GRUB or LILO, although LILO is not provided with Ubuntu) when the boot loader code was first installed in the system's drives. The BIOS searches volumes in the order established by the BIOS settings (for example, the floppy first, followed by a CD-ROM, and then a hard drive) and then boots from the first bootable volume it finds. Modern BIOS's allow considerable flexibility in choosing the device used for booting the system.

11

> **NOTE**
>
> If the BIOS detects a hardware problem, the boot process will fail and the BIOS will generate a few beeps from the system speaker. These "beep codes" indicate the nature of the problem the BIOS has encountered. The codes vary among manufacturers, and the diagnosis of problems occurring during this phase of the boot process is beyond the scope of this book and does not involve Linux. If you encounter a problem, you should consult the motherboard manual or contact the manufacturer of the motherboard.

Next, the BIOS looks on the bootable volume for boot code in the partition boot sector also known as the Master Boot Record (MBR) of the first hard disk. The MBR contains the boot loader code and the partition table—think of it as an index for a book, plus a few comments on how to start reading the book. If the BIOS finds a boot loader, it loads the boot loader code into memory. At that point, the BIOS's job is completed, and it passes control of the system to the boot loader.

The boot loader locates the Linux kernel on the disk and loads it into memory. After that task is completed, the boot loader passes control of the system to the Linux kernel. You can see how one process builds on another in an approach that enables many different operating systems to work with the same hardware.

> **NOTE**
>
> Linux is very flexible and can be booted from multiple images on a CD-ROM, over a network using PXE (pronounced "pixie") or NetBoot, or on a headless server with the console display sent over a serial or network connection. Work is even underway to create a special Linux BIOS at http://www.coreboot.org/ that will expedite the boot process because Linux does not need many of the services offered by the typical BIOS.
>
> This kind of flexibility enables Linux to be used in a variety of ways, such as remote servers or diskless workstations, which are not generally seen in personal home use.

Loading the Linux Kernel

In a general sense, the kernel manages the system resources. As the user, you do not often interact with the kernel, but instead just the applications that you are using. Linux refers to each application as a process, and the kernel assigns each process a number called a *process ID (PID)*. First, the Linux kernel loads and runs a process named init, which is also known as the "father of all processes" because it starts every subsequent process.

> **NOTE**
>
> Details about the sequence of events that occur when the Linux kernel is loaded can be found in the file /usr/src/linux-2.6/init/main.c if you have installed the Linux kernel documentation.

This next step of the boot process begins with a message that the Linux kernel is loading, and a series of messages will be printed to the screen, giving you the status of each command. A failure should display an error message. The -quiet option may be passed to the kernel at boot time to suppress many of these messages.

If the boot process were halted at this point, the system would just sit idle and the screen would be blank. In order to make the system useful for users, we need to start the system services. Those services are some of the applications that allow us to interact with the system.

System Services and Runlevels

The init command boots Ubuntu to a specific system state, commonly referred to as its runlevel.

Runlevels determine which of the many available system services are started, as well as in which order they start. A special runlevel is used to stop the system, and a special runlevel is used for system maintenance. As you will see, there are other runlevels for special purposes.

You will use runlevels to manage the system services running on your computer. All these special files and scripts are set up during your installation of Ubuntu Linux, and they receive their initial values based on your choices during the installation—as described in Chapter 3, "Installing Ubuntu," and Chapter 4, "Post-Installation Configuration." You can change and control them manually, as you learn later in this chapter using tools of varying sophistication.

Runlevel Definitions

The Ubuntu runlevels are defined for the Ubuntu system in /etc/init.d.

Each runlevel tells the init command what services to start or stop. Although runlevels might all have custom definitions, Ubuntu has adopted some standards for runlevels:

- **Runlevel 0**—Known as "halt," this runlevel is used to shut down the system.

- **Runlevel 1**—This is a special runlevel, defined as "single," which boots Ubuntu to a root access shell prompt where only the root user may log in. It has networking, X, and multi-user access turned off. This is the maintenance or rescue mode. It allows the system administrator to perform work on the system, make backups, or repair configuration or other files.

- **Runlevel 2**—This is the default runlevel for Ubuntu.

- **Runlevels 3–5**—These runlevels aren't used in Ubuntu but are often used in other Linux distributions.

- **Runlevel 6**—This runlevel is used to reboot the system.

Runlevel 1 (also known as single-user mode or maintenance mode) is most commonly used to repair file systems and change the root password on a system when the password has been forgotten. Trespassers with physical access to the machine can also use runlevel 1 to access your system.

> **CAUTION**
>
> Never forget that uncontrolled physical access is virtually a guarantee of access to your data by an intruder.

Booting into the Default Runlevel

Ubuntu boots into runlevel 2 by default, which means it starts the system as normal and leaves you inside the X Window System looking at the Gnome login prompt. It knows what runlevel 2 needs to load by looking in the rc*.d directories in /etc. Ubuntu contains directories for rc0.d through to rc5.d and rcS.d.

Assuming that the value is 1, the rc script then executes all the scripts under the /etc/rc.1 directory and then launches the graphical login.

If Ubuntu is booted to runlevel 1, for example, scripts beginning with the letter K followed by scripts beginning with the letter S under the /etc/rc1.d directory are then executed:

```
# ls /etc/rc1.d/
K01gdm        K19hplip      K20laptop-mode    K20vsftpd    K80slapd
K01usplash        K20acpi-support    K20makedev    k21acpid    K86ppp
...etc...
K19cupsys    K20inetutils-inetd    K20ssh    K74-bluez-utils    S20single
```

These scripts, as with all scripts in the rc*.d directories, are actually symbolic links to system service scripts under the /etc/init.d directory.

The rc1.d links are prefaced with a letter and number, such as K15 or S10. The (K) or (S) in these prefixes indicate whether or not a particular service should be killed (K) or started (S) and pass a value of stop or start to the appropriate /etc/init.d script. The number in the prefix executes the specific /etc/init.d script in a particular order. The symlinks have numbers to delineate the order in which they are started. Nothing is sacred about a specific number, but some services need to be running before others are started. You would not want your Ubuntu system to attempt, for example, to mount a remote Network File System (NFS) volume without first starting networking and NFS services.

Booting to a Non-Default Runlevel with GRUB

There might come a time when you do not want to boot into the default runlevel, such as when you want to repair the X server or install a new graphics driver. You'll need to follow several specific steps to boot to a non-default runlevel if you use the default boot loader for Ubuntu, GRUB.

> **NOTE**
>
> If you have enabled a GRUB password, you must first press **p,** type your password, and then press Enter before using this boot method.

The GRUB boot loader passes arguments, or commands, to the kernel at boot time. These arguments are used, among other things, to tell GRUB where the kernel is located and also to pass specific parameters to the kernel, such as how much memory is available or how special hardware should be configured.

To override the default runlevel, you can add an additional kernel argument to GRUB as follows:

1. At the graphical boot screen, press **e** (for edit), scroll down to select the kernel, and press **e** again.

2. Press the spacebar, type `single` or **1** (Ubuntu allows **S** and **s** as well), and press Enter.

3. Finally, press **b** to boot, and you'll boot into runlevel 1 instead of the default runlevel listed in /etc/inittab.

Understanding `init` Scripts and the Final Stage of Initialization

Each /etc/init.d script, or init script, contains logic that determines what to do when receiving a start or stop value. The logic might be a simple switch statement for execution, as in this example:

```
case "$1" in
  start)
        start
        ;;
  stop)
        stop
        ;;
  restart)
        restart
        ;;
  reload)
        reload
        ;;
  status)
        rhstatus
        ;;
  condrestart)
        [ -f /var/lock/subsys/smb ] && restart ¦¦ :
        ;;
  *)
        echo $"Usage: $0 {start¦stop¦restart¦status¦condrestart}"
```

```
    exit 1
esac
```

Although the scripts can be used to customize the way that the system runs from power-on, absent the replacement of the kernel, this script approach also means that the system does not have to be halted in total to start, stop, upgrade, or install new services.

Note that not all scripts will use this approach, and that other messages might be passed to the service script, such as restart, reload, or status. Also, not all scripts will respond to the same set of messages (with the exception of start and stop, which they all have to accept by convention) because each service might require special commands.

After all the system scripts have been run, your system is configured and all the necessary system services have been started. If you are using a runlevel other than 5, the final act of the init process is to launch the user shell—bash, tcsh, zsh, or any of the many command shells available. The shell launches and you see a login prompt on the screen.

Controlling Services at Boot with Administrative Tools

In the Services dialog (shown in Figure 11.1) Ubuntu lists all the services that you can have automatically start at boot time. They are usually all enabled by default, but you can simply uncheck the ones you don't want and click OK. It is not recommended that you disable services randomly "to make things go faster." Some services might be vital for the continuing operation of your computer, such as the graphical login manager and the system communication bus.

FIGURE 11.1   You can enable and disable Ubuntu's boot-up services by toggling the check-boxes in the Services dialog.

Changing Runlevels

After making changes to system services and runlevels, you can use the `telinit` command to change runlevels on-the-fly on a running Ubuntu system. Changing runlevels this way allows system administrators to alter selected parts of a running system in order to make changes to the services or to put changes into effect that have already been made (such as reassignment of network addresses for a networking interface).

For example, a system administrator can quickly change the system to maintenance or single-user mode by using the `telinit` command with its **S** option like this:

```
# telinit S
```

The `telinit` command uses the `init` command to change runlevels and shut down currently running services.

After booting to single-user mode, you can then return to multi-user mode, like this:

```
# telinit 2
```

TIP

Linux is full of shortcuts: If you exit the single-user shell by typing **exit** at the prompt, you will go back to the default runlevel without worrying about using `telinit`.

Troubleshooting Runlevel Problems

Reordering or changing system services during a particular runlevel is rarely necessary when using Ubuntu unless some disaster occurs. But system administrators should have a basic understanding of how Linux boots and how services are controlled in order to perform troubleshooting or to diagnose problems. By using additional utilities such as the **dmesg ¦ less** command to read kernel output after booting or by examining system logging with **cat /var/log/messages ¦ less**, it is possible to gain a bit more detail about what is going on when faced with troublesome drivers or service failure.

To better understand how to troubleshoot service problems in Ubuntu, look at the diagnosis and resolution of a typical service-related issue.

In this example, X will not start: You don't see a desktop displayed, nor does the computer seem to respond to keyboard input. The X server might either be hung in a loop, repeatedly failing, or might exit to a shell prompt with or without an error message.

The X server only attempts to restart itself in runlevel 2, so to determine whether the X server is hung in a loop, try switching to runlevel 1.

TIP

If you are working on a multi-user system and might inadvertently interrupt the work of other users, ask them to save their current work; then change to a safer runlevel, such as single user mode.

Change to runlevel 1 by running the command **telinit 1.** This switch to runlevel 1 will stop the X server from attempting to restart itself.

Now you can easily examine the error and attempt to fix it.

First, try to start the X server "naked" (without also launching the window manager). If you are successful, you will get a gray screen with a large X in the middle. If so, kill X with the Ctrl+Alt+Backspace key combination, and look at your window manager configuration. (This configuration varies according to which window manager you have chosen.)

Let us assume that X won't run "naked." If we look at the log file for Xorg (it's clearly identified in the /var/log directory), we'll pay attention to any line that begins with (EE), the special error code. We can also examine the error log file, .xsessions-error, in our home directory if such a file exists.

If we find an error line, the cause of the error might or might not be apparent to us. The nice thing about the Linux community is that it is very unlikely that you are the first person to experience that error. Enter the error message (or better, a unique part of it) into http://www.google.com/linux and discover what others have had to say about the problem. You might need to adjust your search to yield usable results, but that level of detail is beyond the scope of this chapter. Make adjustments and retest as before until you achieve success.

Fix the X configuration and start X with **startx.** Repeat as necessary.

CAUTION

Before making any changes to any configuration file, always make a backup copy of the original, unmodified file. Our practice is to append the extension .original to the copy because that is a unique and unambiguous identifier.

If you need to restore the original configuration file, do not rename it, but copy it back to its original name.

Starting and Stopping Services Manually

If you change a configuration file for a system service, it is usually necessary to stop and restart the service to make it read the new configuration. If you are reconfiguring the X server, it is often convenient to change from runlevel 2 to runlevel 1 to make testing easier and then switch back to runlevel 2 to re-enable the graphical login. If a service is improperly configured, it is easier to stop and restart it until you have it configured correctly than it is to reboot the entire machine.

The traditional way to manage a service (as root) is to call the service's /etc/init.d name on the command line with an appropriate keyword, such as start, status, or stop. For example, to start the Apache web server, call the /etc/init.d/apache2 script like this:

```
sudo /etc/init.d/apache2 start
Starting apache 2.2 web server                          [  OK  ]
```

The script will execute the proper program(s) and report the status of it. Stopping services is equally easy, using the stop keyword.

Scheduling Tasks

There are three ways to schedule commands in Ubuntu, all of which work in different ways. The first is the at command, which specifies a command to run at a specific time and date relative to today. The second is the batch command, which is actually a script that redirects you to the at command with some extra options set so your command runs when the system is quiet. The last option is the cron daemon, which is the Linux way of executing tasks at a given time.

Using at and batch to Schedule Tasks for Later

If there is a time-intensive task you want to run, but you do not want to do it while you are still logged in, you can tell Ubuntu to run it later with the at command. To use at, you need to tell it the time at which you want to run and then press Enter. You will then see a new prompt that starts with at>, and everything you type there until you press Ctrl+D will be the commands you want at to run.

When the designated time arrives, at will perform each action individually and in order, which means later commands can rely on the results of earlier commands. In this next example, run at just after 5 p.m., at is used to download and extract the latest Linux kernel at a time when the network should be quiet:

```
[paul@caitlin ~]$ at now + 7 hours
at> wget http://www.kernel.org/pub/linux/kernel/v2.6/linux-2.6.10.tar.bz2
at> tar xvfjp linux-2.6.10.tar.bz2
at> <EOT>
job 2 at 2005-01-09 17:01
```

Specifying now + 7 hours as the time does what you would expect: at was run at 5 p.m., so the command will run just after midnight that night. When your job has finished, at will send you an email with a full log of your job's output; type mail at the console to bring up your mailbox and then press the relevant number to read at's mail.

If you have a more complex job, you can use the -f parameter to have at read its commands from a file, like this:

```
echo wget http://www.kernel.org/pub/linux/kernel/v2.6/linux-2.6.10.tar.bz2\;
tar xvfjp linux-2.6.10.tar.bz2 > myjob.job
at -f myjob.job tomorrow
```

As you can see, at is flexible about the time format it takes; you can specify it in three ways:

▶ Using the now parameter, you can specify how many minutes, hours, days, or weeks relative to the current time—for example, now + 4 weeks would run the command one month from today.

▶ You can also specify several special times, including tomorrow, midnight, noon, or teatime (4 p.m.). If you do not specify a time with tomorrow, your job is set for precisely 24 hours from the current time.

▶ You can specify an exact date and time using HH:MM MM/DD/YY format—for example, 16:40 22/12/05 for 4:40 p.m. on the 22nd of December 2005.

When your job is submitted, at will report the job number, date, and time that the job will be executed; the queue identifier; plus the job owner (you). It will also capture all your environment variables and store them along with the job so that, when your job runs, it can restore the variables, preserving your execution environment.

The job number and job queue identifier are both important. When you schedule a job using at, it is placed into queue "a" by default, which means it runs at your specified time and takes up a normal amount of resources.

There is an alternative command, batch, which is really just a shell script that calls at with a few extra options. These options (-q b -m now, if you were interested) set at to run on queue b (-q b), mailing the user on completion (-m), and running immediately (now). The queue part is what is important: Jobs scheduled on queue b will only be executed when system load falls below 0.8—that is, when the system is not running at full load. Furthermore, it will run with a lower niceness, meaning a queue jobs usually have a niceness of 2, whereas b queue jobs have a niceness of 4.

Because batch always specifies now as its time, you need not specify your own time; it will simply run as soon as the system is quiet. Having a default niceness of 4 means that batched commands will get less system resources than a queue job's (at's default) and less system resources than most other programs. You can optionally specify other queues using at. Queue c runs at niceness 6, queue d runs at niceness 8, and so on. However, it is important to note that the system load is only checked before the command is run. If the load is lower than 0.8, your batch job will be run. If the system load subsequently rises beyond 0.8, your batch job will continue to run, albeit in the background, thanks to its niceness value.

When you submit a job for execution, you will also be returned a job number. If you forget this or just want to see a list of other jobs you have scheduled to run later, use the atq command with no parameters. If you run this as a normal user, it will print only your jobs; running it as a superuser will print everyone's jobs. The output is in the same format as when you submit a job, so you get the ID number, execution time, queue ID, and owner of each job.

If you want to delete a job, use the atrm command followed by the ID number of the job you want to delete. This next example shows atq and atrm being used to list jobs and delete one:

```
[paul@caitlin ~]$ atq
14      2005-01-20 23:33 a paul
16      2005-02-03 22:34 a paul
17      2005-01-25 22:34 a paul
15      2005-01-22 04:34 a paul
18      2005-01-22 01:35 b paul
[paul@caitlin ~]$ atrm 16
[paul@caitlin ~]$ atq
14      2005-01-20 23:33 a paul
17      2005-01-25 22:34 a paul
15      2005-01-22 04:34 a paul
18      2005-01-22 01:35 b paul
```

In that example, job 16 is deleted using atrm, and so it does not show up in the second call to atq.

The default configuration for at and batch is to allow everyone to use it, which is not always the desired behavior. Access is controlled through two files: /etc/at.allow and /etc/at.deny. By default, at.deny exists but is empty, which allows everyone to use at and batch. You can enter usernames into at.deny, one per line, to stop those users scheduling jobs.

Alternatively, you can use the at.allow file; this does not exist by default. If you have a blank at.allow file, no one except root is allowed to schedule jobs. As with at.deny, you can add usernames to at.allow one per line, and those users will be able to schedule jobs. You should use either at.deny or at.allow: When someone tries to run at or batch, Ubuntu checks for her username in at.allow. If it is in there, or if at.allow does not exist, Ubuntu checks for her username in at.deny. If her username is in at.deny or at.deny does not exist, she is not allowed to schedule jobs.

Using `cron` to Run Jobs Repeatedly

The at and batch commands work well if you just want to execute a single task at a later date, but they are less useful if you want to run a task frequently. Instead, there is the crond daemon for running tasks repeatedly based upon system—and user—requests. Cron has a similar permissions system to at: Users listed in the cron.deny file are not allowed to use Cron, and users listed in the cron.allow file are. An empty cron.deny file—the default—means everyone can set jobs. An empty cron.allow file means that no one (except root) can set jobs.

There are two types of jobs: system jobs and user jobs. Only root can edit *system* jobs, whereas any user whose name appears in cron.allow or does not appear in cron.deny can run *user* jobs. System jobs are controlled through the /etc/crontab file, which by default looks like this:

```
SHELL=/bin/sh
PATH=/usr/local/sbin:/usr/local/bin:/sbin:/bin:/usr/sbin:/usr/bin

# m h dom mon dow user command
17 * * * * root run-parts —report /etc/cron.hourly
25 6 * * * root test -x /usr/sbin/anacron ¦¦ run-parts —report /etc/cron.daily
47 6 * * 7 root test -x /usr/sbin/anacron ¦¦ run-parts —report /etc/cron.weekly

52 6 1 * * root test -x /usr/sbin/anacron ¦¦ run-parts —report /etc/cron.monthly
```

The first two lines specify which shell should be used to execute the job (defaults to the shell of the user who owns the crontab file, usually /bin/bash), and the search path for executables that will be used. It's important that you avoid using environment variables in this path statement, as they may not be set when the job runs.

The next line starts with a pound sign (#) and so is treated as a comment and ignored. The next four lines are the important parts: They are the jobs themselves.

Each job is specified in seven fields that define the time to run, owner, and command. The first five commands specify the execution time in quite a quirky order: minute (0–59), hour (0–23), day of the month (1–31), month of the year (1–12), and day of the week (0–7). For day of the week, both 0 and 7 are Sunday, which means that 1 is Monday, 3 is Wednesday, and so on. If you want to specify "all values" (that is, every minute, every hour, every day, and so on), use an asterisk, *.

The next field specifies the username of the owner of the job. When a job is executed, it uses the username specified here. The last field is the command to execute.

So, the first job runs at minute 17, every hour of every day of every month and executes the command run-parts /etc/cron.hourly. The run-parts command is a simple script that runs all programs inside a given directory—in this case, /etc/cron.hourly. So, in this case, the job will execute at 00:17 (17 minutes past midnight), 01:17, 02:17, 03:17, and so on, and will use all the programs listed in the cron.hourly directory.

The next job runs at minute 25 and hour 6 of every day of every month, running run-parts /etc/cron.daily. Because of the hour limitation, this script will run only once per day, at 6:25 a.m. Note that it uses minute 25 rather than minute 17 so that daily jobs do not clash with hourly jobs. You should be able to guess what the next two jobs do, simply by looking at the commands they run!

Inside each of those four directories (cron.hourly, cron.daily, cron.weekly, and cron.monthly) are a collection of shell scripts that will be run by run-parts. For example, in cron.daily you will have scripts like logrotate, which handles backing up of log files, and makewhatis, which updates the whatis database. You can add other system tasks to these directories if you want to, but you should be careful to ensure your scripts are correct.

CAUTION

The cron daemon reads all the system crontab files and all user crontab files once a minute (on the minute, i.e. at 6:00:00, 6:01:00, and so on) to check for changes. However, any new jobs it finds will not be executed until at least 1 minute has passed.

For example, if it is 6:01:49 (that is, 49 seconds past 1 minute past 6 a.m.) and you set a cron job to run at 6:02, it will not execute. At 6:02, the cron daemon will reread its configuration files and see the new job, but it will not be able to execute it. If you set the job to run at 6:02 a.m. every day, it will be executed the following morning and every subsequent morning.

This same situation exists when deleting jobs. If it is 6:01:49 and you have a job scheduled to run at 6:02, deleting it will make no difference: cron will run it before it rereads the crontab files for changes. However, after it has reread the crontab file and noticed the job is no longer there, it will not be executed in subsequent days.

There are alternative ways of specifying dates. For example, you can use sets of dates and times by using hyphens of commas, such as hours 9–15 would execute at 9, 10, 11, 12, 13, 14, and 15 (from 9 a.m. to 3 p.m.), whereas 9,11,13,15 would miss out at the even hours. Note that it is important you do not put spaces into these sets because the cron daemon will interpret them as the next field. You can define a step value with a slash (/) to show time division: */4 for hours means "every four hours all day", and 0-12/3 means "every three hours from midnight to noon." You can also specify day and month names rather than numbers, using three-character abbreviations: Sun, Mon, Tue, Fri, Sat for days, or Jan, Feb, Mar, Oct, Nov, Dec for months.

As well as system jobs, there are also user jobs for those users who have the correct permissions. User jobs are stored in the /var/spool/cron directory, with each user having his own file in his named after his username—for instance, /var/spool/cron/paul or /var/spool/cron/root. The contents of these files contain the jobs the user wants to run and take roughly the same format as the /etc/crontab file, with the exception that the owner of the job should not be specified because it will always be the same as the file-name.

To edit your own `crontab` file, type **crontab -e.** This brings up a text editor (`vim` by default, but you can set the `EDITOR` environment variable to change that) where you can enter your entries. The format of this file is a little different from the format for the main `crontab` because this time there is no need to specify the owner of the job—it is always you.

So, this time each line is made up of six fields: minute (0–59), hour (0–23), day of the month (1–31), month of the year (1–12), day of the week (0–7), and then the command to run. If you are using `vim` and are new to it, press `i` to enter insert mode to edit your text; then press Esc to exit insert mode. To save and quit, type a colon followed by `wq` and press Enter.

When programming, we tend to use a `sandbox` subdirectory in our home directory where we keep all sorts of temporary files that we were just playing around with. We can use a personal job to empty that directory every morning at 6 a.m. so that we get a fresh start each morning. Here is how that would like in our `crontab` file:

```
0 6 * * * rm -rf /home/paul/sandbox/*
```

If you are not allowed to schedule jobs, you will be stopped from editing your `crontab` file.

Once your jobs are placed, you can use the command `crontab -1` to list your jobs. This just prints the contents of your `crontab` file, so its output will be the same as the line you just entered.

If you want to remove just one job, the easiest thing to do is type `crontab -e` to edit your `crontab` file in `vim`; then, after having moved the cursor to the job you want to delete, type `dd` (two *d*s) to delete that line. If you want to delete all your jobs, you can use `crontab -r` to delete your `crontab` file.

TABLE 11.1   Shells with Ubuntu

Name	Description	Location
bash	The Bourne Again SHell	/bin/bash
ksh	The Korn shell	/bin/ksh, /usr/bin/ksh
pdksh	A symbolic link to ksh	/usr/bin/pdksh
rsh	The restricted shell (for network operation)	/usr/bin/rsh
sh	A symbolic link to bash	/bin/sh
tcsh	A csh-compatible shell	/bin/tcsh
zsh	A compatible csh, ksh, and sh shell	/bin/zsh

Basic Shell Control

Ubuntu includes a rich assortment of capable, flexible, and powerful shells. Each shell is different but has numerous built-in commands and configurable command-line prompts and might include features such as command-line history, the ability to recall and use a previous command line, and command-line editing. As an example, the bash shell is so powerful that it is possible to write a minimal web server entirely in bash's language using 114 lines of script (see the link at the end of this chapter).

Although there are many shells to choose from, most people stick with the default, bash. This is because bash does everything most people need to do, and more. Only change your shell if you really need to.

Table 11.1 lists each shell, along with its description and location, in your Ubuntu file system.

Learning More About Your Shell

All the shells listed in Table 11.1 have accompanying man pages, along with other documentation under the /usr/share/doc directory. Some of the documentation can be quite lengthy, but it is generally much better to have too much documentation than too little! The bash shell includes more than 100 pages in its manual, and the zsh shell documentation is so extensive that it includes the zshall meta man page (use man zshall to read this overview)!

The Shell Command Line

Having a basic understanding of the capabilities of the shell command line can help you write better shell scripts. If, once you have finished reading this short introduction, you want to learn more about the command line, check out Chapter 33, "Command Line Masterclass." You can use the shell command line to perform a number of different tasks, including

▶ Searching files or directories with programs using pattern-matching, or *expressions*; these commands include the GNU gawk (linked as awk) and the grep family of commands, including egrep and fgrep.

▶ Getting data from and sending data to a file or command, known as *input* and *output redirection*.

▶ Feeding or filtering a program's output to another command (called using *pipes*).

A shell can also have built-in *job-control* commands to launch the command line as a background process, suspend a running program, selectively retrieve or kill running or suspended programs, and perform other types of process control.

Multiple commands can be run on a single command line using a semicolon to separate commands:

```
$ w ; free ; df
  6:02pm  up 4 days, 24 min,  1 user,  load average: 0.00, 0.00, 0.00
USER     TTY      FROM              LOGIN@   IDLE   JCPU   PCPU  WHAT
bball    pts/0    shuttle.home.org 1:14pm  0.00s  0.57s  0.01s  w
total        used       free     shared    buffers     cached
Mem:        190684     184420       6264         76      17620     142820
-/+ buffers/cache:       23980     166704
Swap:      1277156       2516    1274640
Filesystem          1k-blocks     Used Available Use% Mounted on
/dev/hda1           11788296   4478228   6711248  41% /
none                   95340         0     95340   0% /dev/shm
```

This example displays the output of the w, free, and df commands. Long shell command lines can be extended inside shell scripts or at the command line by using the backslash character (\). For example,

```
$ echo ""this is a long \
> command line and"" ; echo ""shows that multiple commands \
> may be strung out.""
this is a long command line and
shows that multiple commands may be strung out.
```

The first three lines of this example are a single command line. In that single line are two instances of the echo command. Note that when you use the backslash as a line-continuation character, it must be the last character on the command line (or in your shell script, as you will see later on in this chapter).

Using the basic features of the shell command line is easy, but mastering use of all features can be difficult. Entire books have been devoted to using shells, writing shell scripts, and using pattern-matching expressions. The following sections provide an overview of some features of the shell command line relating to writing scripts.

Grokking grep

If you plan to develop shell scripts to expand the capabilities of pattern-matching commands such as grep, you will benefit from learning more about using expressions. One of the definitive guides to using the pattern-matching capabilities of Unix and Linux commands is *Mastering Regular Expressions* by Jeffrey E. F. Freidl (O'Reilly), ISBN: 0-596-52812-4.

Shell Pattern-Matching Support

The shell command line allows you to use strings of specially constructed character patterns for wildcard matches. This is a different simpler capability than that supported by GNU utilities such as grep, which can use more complex patterns, known as *expressions*, to search through files or directories or to filter data input to or out of commands.

The shell's pattern strings can be simple or complex, but even using a small subset of the available characters in simple wildcards can yield constructive results at the command line. Some common characters used for shell pattern matching are

▶ *—Matches any character. For example, to find all files in the current directory ending in .txt, you could use

```
$ ls *.txt
```

▶ ?—Matches a single character. For example, to find all files in the current directory ending in the extension .d?c (where ? could be 0–9, a–z, or A–Z),

```
$ ls *.d?c
```

▶ [xxx] or [x-x]—Matches a range of characters. For example, to list all files in a directory with names containing numbers,

```
$ ls *[0-9]*
```

▶ \x—Matches or escapes a character such as ? or a tab character. For example, to create a file with a name containing question mark,

```
$ touch foo\?
```

Note that the shell might not interpret some characters or regular expressions in the same manner as a Linux command, and mixing wildcards and regular expressions in shell scripts can lead to problems unless you're careful. For example, finding patterns in text is best left to regular expressions used with commands such as grep; simple wildcards should be used for filtering or matching filenames on the command line. And although both Linux command expressions and shell scripts can recognize the backslash as an escape character in patterns, the dollar sign ($) will have two wildly different meanings (single-character pattern matching in expressions and variable assignment in scripts).

CAUTION

Make sure you read your command carefully when using wildcards; an all-too-common error is to type something like `rm -rf * .txt` with a space between the `*` and the `.txt`. By the time you wonder why the command is taking so long, Bash will already have deleted most of your files. The problem is that it will treat the `*` and the `.txt` separately. `*` will match everything, so Bash will delete all your files.

Redirecting Input and Output

You can create, overwrite, and append data to files at the command line, using a process called *input* and *output redirection*. The shell recognizes several special characters for this process, such as >, <, or >>.

In this example, the output of the `ls` command is redirected to create a file named `textfiles.listing`:

```
$ ls *.txt >textfiles.listing
```

Use output redirection with care because it is possible to overwrite existing files. For example, specifying a different directory but using the same output filename will overwrite the existing `textfiles.listing`:

```
$ ls /usr/share/doc/mutt-1.4/*.txt >textfiles.listing
```

Fortunately, most shells are smart enough to recognize when you might do something foolish. Here, the `bash` shell warns that the command is attempting to redirect output to a directory:

```
$ mkdir foo
$ ls >foo
bash: foo: Is a directory
```

Output can be appended to a file without overwriting existing content by using the append operator, >>. In this example, the directory listing will be appended to the end of `textfiles.listing` instead of overwriting its contents:

```
$ ls /usr/share/doc/mutt-1.4/*.txt >>textfiles.listing
```

You can use *input redirection* to feed data into a command by using the < like this:

```
$ cat < textfiles.listing
```

You can use the shell *here* operator, <<, to specify the end of input on the shell command line:

```
$ cat >simple_script <<DONE
> echo ""this is a simple script""
> DONE
$ cat simple_script
echo ""this is a simple script""
```

In this example, the shell will feed the cat command you are typing (input) until the pattern DONE is recognized. The output file simple_script is then saved and its contents verified. This same technique can be used in scripts to create content based on the output of various commands and define an end-of-input or delimiter.

Piping Data

Many Linux commands can be used in concert in a single, connected command line to transform data from one form to another. Stringing Linux commands together in this fashion is known as using or creating *pipes*. Pipes are created on the command line with the bar operator (¦). For example, a pipe can be used to perform a complex task from a single command line like this:

```
$ find /d2 -name '*.txt' -print ¦ xargs cat ¦ \
tr ' ' '\n' ¦ sort ¦ uniq >output.txt
```

This example takes the output of the find command to feed the cat command (via xargs) the name all text files under the /d2 command. The content of all matching files is then fed through the tr command to change each space in the data stream into a carriage return. The stream of words is then sorted, and identical adjacent lines are removed using the uniq command. The output, a raw list of words, is then saved in the file named output.txt.

Background Processing

The shell allows you to start a command and then launch it into the background as a process by using an ampersand (&) at the end of a command line. This technique is often used at the command line of an X terminal window to start a client and return to the command line. For example, to launch another terminal window using the xterm client,

```
$ xterm &
[3] 1437
```

The numbers echoed back show a number (3 in this example), which is a *job* number, or reference number for a shell process, and a *Process ID* number, or PID (1437 in this example). The xterm window session can be killed by using the shell's built-in kill command, along with the job number like this:

```
$ kill %3
```

Or the process can be killed by using the `kill` command, along with the PID, like so:

```
$ kill 1437
```

Background processing can be used in shell scripts to start commands that take a long time, such as backups:

```
# tar -czf /backup/home.tgz /home &
```

Writing and Executing a Shell Script

Why should you write and use shell scripts? Shell scripts can save you time and typing, especially if you routinely use the same command lines multiple times every day. Although you could also use the history function (press the Up or Down keys while using bash or use the `history` command), a shell script can add flexibility with command-line argument substitution and built-in help.

Although a shell script won't execute faster than a program written in a computer language such as C, a shell program can be smaller in size than a compiled program. The shell program does not require any additional library support other than the shell or, if used, existing commands installed on your system. The process of creating and testing shell scripts is also generally simpler and faster than the development process for equivalent C language commands.

> **NOTE**
>
> Hundreds of commands included with Ubuntu are actually shell scripts, and many other good shell script examples are available over the Internet—a quick search will yield numerous links to online tutorials and scripting guides from fellow Linux users and developers. For example, the `startx` command, used to start an X Window session from the text console, is a shell script used every day by most users. To learn more about shell scripting with bash, see the Advanced Bash-Scripting Guide, listed in the "Reference" section at the end of this chapter. You'll also find *Sams Teach Yourself Shell Programming in 24 Hours* a helpful guide to learning more about using the shell to build your own commands.

When you are learning to write and execute your first shell scripts, start with scripts for simple, but useful tasks. Begin with short examples, and then expand the scripts as you build on your experience and knowledge. Make liberal use of comments (lines preceded with a pound # sign) to document each section of your script. Include an author statement and overview of the script as additional help, along with a creation date or version number. Write shell scripts using a text editor such as `vi` because it does not automatically wrap lines of text. Line wrapping can break script syntax and cause problems. If you use the nano editor, include its -w flag to disable line wrap.

In this section, you learn how to write a simple shell script to set up a number of *aliases* (command synonyms) whenever you log on. Instead of typing all the aliases every time you log on, you can put them in a file by using a text editor, such as vi, and then execute the file. Normally these changes are saved in systemwide shell configuration files under the /etc directory to make the changes active for all users or in your .bashrc, .cshrc (if you use tcsh), or .bash_profile files in your home directory.

Here is what is contained in myenv, a sample shell script created for this purpose (for bash):

```
#!/bin/sh
alias ll='ls -l'
alias ldir='ls -aF'
alias copy='cp'
```

This simple script creates command *aliases*, or convenient shorthand forms of commands, for the ls and cp commands. The ll alias provides a long directory listing: The ldir alias is the ls command, but prints indicators (for directories or executable files) in listings. The copy alias is the same as the cp command. You can experiment and add your own options or create aliases of other commands with options you frequently use.

You can execute myenv in a variety of ways under Linux. As shown in this example, you can make myenv executable by using the chmod command and then execute it as you would any other native Linux command:

```
$ chmod +x myenv
```

This line turns on the executable permission of myenv, which can be checked with the ls command and its -l option like this:

```
$ ls -l myenv
-rwxrwxr-x   1 winky    winky        11 Aug 26 17:38 myenv
```

Running the New Shell Program

You can run your new shell program in several ways. Each method will produce the same results, which is a testament to the flexibility of using the shell with Linux. One way to run your shell program is to execute the file myenv from the command line as if it were a Linux command:

```
$ ./myenv
```

A second way to execute `myenv` under a particular shell, such as `pdksh`, is as follows:

```
$ pdksh myenv
```

This invokes a new `pdksh` shell and passes the filename `myenv` as a parameter to execute the file. A third way will require you to create a directory named `bin` in your home directory, and to then copy the new shell program into this directory. You can then run the program without the need to specify a specific location or to use a shell. You do this like so:

```
$ mkdir bin
$ mv myenv bin
$ myenv
```

This works because Ubuntu is set up by default to include the executable path `$HOME/bin` in your shell's environment. You can view this environment variable, named `PATH`, by piping the output of the `env` command through `fgrep` like so:

```
$ env ¦ fgrep PATH
/usr/kerberos/bin:/usr/local/bin:/bin:/usr/bin: \
/usr/X11R6/bin:/sbin:/home/paul/bin
```

As you can see, the user (`paul` in this example) can use the new `bin` directory to hold executable files. Another way to bring up an environment variable is to use the `echo` command along with the variable name (in this case, `$PATH`):

```
$ echo $PATH
/usr/kerberos/bin:/usr/local/bin:/usr/bin:/bin:/usr/X11R6/bin:/home/bball/bin
```

> **CAUTION**
>
> Never put . in your $PATH in order to execute files or a command in the current directory—this presents a serious security risk, especially for the root operator, and even more so if . is first in your $PATH search order. Trojan scripts placed by crackers in directories such as /tmp can be used for malicious purposes, and will be executed immediately if the current working directory is part of your $PATH.

Storing Shell Scripts for Systemwide Access

After you execute the command `myenv`, you should be able to use `ldir` from the command line to get a list of files under the current directory and `ll` to get a list of files with attributes displayed. However, the best way to use the new commands in `myenv` is to put them into your shell's login or profile file. For Ubuntu, and nearly all Linux users, the default shell is bash, so you can make these commands available for everyone on your system by putting them in the /etc/bashrc file. Systemwide aliases for tcsh are contained in files with the extension .csh under the /etc/profile.d directory. The pdksh shell can use these command aliases as well.

> **NOTE**
>
> To use a shell other than bash after logging in, use the chsh command from the command line or the system-config-users client during an X session. You'll be asked for your password (or the root password if using system-config-users), as well as the location and name of the new shell (refer to Table 11.1). The new shell will become your default shell, but only if its name is in the list of acceptable system shells in /etc/shells.

Interpreting Shell Scripts Through Specific Shells

The majority of shell scripts use a *shebang line* (#!) at the beginning to control the type of shell used to run the script; this bang line calls for an sh-incantation of bash:

```
#!/bin/sh
```

A shebang line (it is short for "sharp" and "bang", two names for # and !) tells the Linux kernel that a specific command (a shell, or in the case of other scripts, perhaps awk or Perl) is to be used to interpret the contents of the file. Using a shebang line is common practice for all shell scripting. For example, if you write a shell script using bash, but want the script to execute as if run by the Bourne shell, sh, the first line of your script will contain #!/bin/sh, which is a link to the bash shell. Running bash as sh will cause bash to act as a Bourne shell. This is the reason for the symbolic link sh, which points to bash.

> **The Shebang Line**
>
> The shebang line is a magic number, as defined in /usr/share/magic—a text database of magic numbers for the Linux file command. Magic numbers are used by many different Linux commands to quickly identify a type of file, and the database format is documented in the section five manual page named magic (read by using man 5 magic). For example, magic numbers can be used by the Linux file command to display the identity of a script (no matter what filename is used) as a shell script using a specific shell or other interpreter such as awk or Perl.

You might also find different or new environment variables available to your scripts by using different shells. For example, if you launch csh from the bash command line, you will find several new variables or variables with slightly different definitions, such as

```
$ env
...
VENDOR=intel
MACHTYPE=i386
HOSTTYPE=i386-linux
HOST=thinkpad.home.org
```

On the other hand, bash might provide these variables or variables of the same name with a slightly different definition, such as

```
$ env
...
HOSTTYPE=i386
HOSTNAME=thinkpad.home.org
```

Although the behavior of a shebang line is not defined by POSIX, variations of its use can be helpful when you are writing shell scripts. For example, as described in the wish man page, you can use a shell to help execute programs called within a shell script without needing to hard code pathnames of programs. The wish command is a windowing Tool Control Language (tcl) interpreter that can be used to write graphical clients. Avoiding the use of specific pathnames to programs increases shell script portability because not every Unix or Linux system has programs in the same location.

For example, if you want to use the wish command, your first inclination might be to write

```
#!/usr/local/bin/wish
```

Although this will work on many other operating systems, the script will fail under Linux because wish is located under the /usr/bin directory. However, if you write the command line this way,

```
#!/bin/sh
exec wish "$@"
```

You can use the wish command (as a binary or a shell script itself); your first inclination might be to write in Linux.

Using Variables in Shell Scripts

When writing shell scripts for Linux, you work with three types of variables:

▶ **Environment variables**—Part of the system environment, you can use them in your shell program. New variables can be defined, and some of them, such as PATH, can also be modified within a shell program.

▶ **Built-in variables**—These are variables such as options used on the command (interpreted by the shell as a *positional argument*) are provided by Linux. Unlike environment variables, you cannot modify them.

▶ **User variables**—Defined by you when you write a shell script. You can use and modify them at will within the shell program.

A major difference between shell programming and other programming languages is that in shell programming, variables are not *typed*—that is, you do not have to specify whether a variable is a number or a string, and so on.

Assigning a Value to a Variable

Say that you want to use a variable called lcount to count the number of iterations in a loop within a shell program. You can declare and initialize this variable as follows:

Command	Environment
lcount=0	pdksh and bash
set lcount=0	tcsh

> **NOTE**
>
> Under pdksh and bash, you must ensure that the equal sign (=) does not have spaces before and after it.

To store a string in a variable, you can use the following:

Command	Environment
myname=Sanjiv	pdksh and bash
set myname=Sanjiv	tcsh

Use the preceding variable form if the string doesn't have embedded spaces. If a string has embedded spaces, you can do the assignment as follows:

Command	Environment
myname="Sanjiv Guha"	pdksh and bash
set myname="Sanjiv Guha"	tcsh

Accessing Variable Values

You can access the value of a variable by prefixing the variable name with a $ (dollar sign). That is, if the variable name is var, you can access the variable by using $var.

If you want to assign the value of var to the variable lcount, you can do so as follows:

Command	Environment
lcount=$var	pdksh and bash
set lcount=$var	tcsh

Positional Parameters

It is possible to pass options from the command line or from another shell script to your shell program.

These options are supplied to the shell program by Linux as *positional parameters*, which have special names provided by the system. The first parameter is stored in a variable called 1 (number 1) and can be accessed by using $1 within the program. The second parameter is stored in a variable called 2 and can be accessed by using $2 within the program, and so on. One or more of the higher numbered positional parameters can be omitted while you're invoking a shell program.

Understanding how to use these positional parameters and how to access and use variables retrieved from the command line is necessary when developing more advanced shell programs.

A Simple Example of a Positional Parameter

For example, if a shell program mypgm expects two parameters—such as a first name and a last name—you can invoke the shell program with only one parameter, the first name. However, you cannot invoke it with only the second parameter, the last name.

Here is a shell program called mypgm1, which takes only one parameter (a name) and displays it on the screen:

```
#!/bin/sh
#Name display program
if [ $# -eq 0 ]
then
    echo "Name not provided"
else
    echo "Your name is "$1
fi
```

If you execute mypgm1, as follows,

```
$ bash  mypgm1
```

you get the following output:

```
Name not provided
```

However, if you execute mypgm1, as follows,

```
$ bash  mypgm1 Sanjiv
```

you get the following output:

```
Your name is Sanjiv
```

The shell program mypgm1 also illustrates another aspect of shell programming: the built-in variables provided to the shell by the Linux kernel. In mypgm1, the built-in variable $# provides the number of positional parameters passed to the shell program. You learn more about working with built-in variables in the next major section of this chapter.

Using Positional Parameters to Access and Retrieve Variables from the Command Line

Using positional parameters in scripts can be helpful if you need to use command lines with piped commands requiring complex arguments. Shell programs containing positional parameters can be even more convenient if the commands are infrequently used. For example, if you use your Ubuntu system with an attached voice modem as an answering machine, you can write a script to issue a command that retrieves and plays the voice messages. The following lines convert a saved sound file (in .rmd or voice-phone format) and pipe the result to your system's audio device:

```
#!/bin/sh
# play voice message in /var/spool/voice/incoming
rmdtopvf /var/spool/voice/incoming/$1 ¦ pvfspeed -s 8000 ¦ \
pvftobasic >/dev/audio
```

A voice message can then easily be played back using this script (perhaps named pmm):

```
$ pmm name_of_message
```

Shell scripts that contain positional parameters are often used for automating routine and mundane jobs, such as system log report generation, file system checks, user resource accounting, printer use accounting, and other system, network, or security administration tasks.

Using a Simple Script to Automate Tasks

You could use a simple script, for example, to examine your system log for certain keywords. If the script is run via your system's scheduling table, /etc/crontab, it can help automate security monitoring. By combining the output capabilities of existing Linux commands with the language facilities of the shell, you can quickly build a useful script to perform a task normally requiring a number of command lines. For example, you can create a short script, named greplog, like this:

```
#!/bin/sh
#    name:  greplog
#     use:  mail grep of designated log using keyword
# version:  v.01 08aug02
#
#  author: bb
#
# usage: greplog [keyword] [logpathname]
#
#  bugs: does not check for correct number of arguments

# build report name using keyword search and date
log_report=/tmp/$1.logreport.`date '+%m%d%y'`

# build report header with system type, hostname, date and time
echo "=============================================================" \
      >$log_report
echo "          S Y S T E M   M O N I T O R   L O G" >>$log_report
echo uname -a >>$log_report
echo "Log report for" `hostname -f` "on" `date '+%c'`       >>$log_report
echo "=============================================================" \
      >>$log_report ; echo "" >>$log_report

# record log search start
echo "Search for->" $1 "starting" `date '+%r'` >>$log_report
echo "" >>$log_report

# get and save grep results of keyword ($1) from logfile ($2)
grep -i $1 $2 >>$log_report

# build report footer with time
echo "" >>$log_report
echo "End of" $log_report at `date '+%r'` >>$log_report
```

```
# mail report to root
mail -s "Log Analysis for $1" root <$log_report

# clean up and remove report
rm $log_report
exit 0
```

In this example, the script creates the variable $log_report, which will be the filename of the temporary report. The keyword ($1) and first argument on the command line is used as part of the filename, along with the current date (with perhaps a better approach to use $$ instead of the date, which will append the script's PID as a file extension). Next, the report header containing some formatted text, the output of the uname command, and the hostname and date is added to the report. The start of the search is then recorded, and any matches of the keyword in the log are added to the report. A footer containing the name of the report and the time is then added. The report is mailed to root with the search term as the subject of the message, and the temporary file is deleted.

You can test the script by running it manually and feeding it a keyword and a pathname to the system log, /var/log/messages, like this:

```
# greplog FAILED /var/log/messages
```

Note that your system should be running the syslogd daemon. If any login failures have occurred on your system, the root operator might get an email message that looks like this:

```
Date: Thu, 23 Oct 2003 16:23:24 -0400
From: root <root@stinkpad.home.org>
To: root@stinkpad.home.org
Subject: FAILED


================================================================
              S Y S T E M   M O N I T O R   L O G
Linux stinky 2.4.22-1.2088.nptl #1 Thu Oct 9 20:21:24 EDT 2003 i686 i686 i386
+GNU/Linux
Log report for stinkpad.home.org on Thu 23 Oct 2003 04:23:24 PM EDT
================================================================

Search for-> FAILED starting 04:23:24 PM

Oct 23 16:23:04 stinkpad login[1769]: FAILED LOGIN 3 FROM (null) FOR bball,
+Authentication failure

End of /tmp/FAILED.logreport.102303 at 04:23:24 PM
```

To further automate the process, you can include command lines using the script in another script to generate a series of searches and reports.

Built-In Variables

Built-in variables are special variables provided to shell by Linux that can be used to make decisions within a shell program. You cannot modify the values of these variables within the shell program.

Some of these variables are

- ▶ $#—Number of positional parameters passed to the shell program
- ▶ $?—Completion code of the last command or shell program executed within the shell program (returned value)
- ▶ $0—The name of the shell program
- ▶ $*—A single string of all arguments passed at the time of invocation of the shell program

To show these built-in variables in use, here is a sample program called mypgm2:

```
#!/bin/sh
#my test program
echo "Number of parameters is $#"
echo "Program name is $0"
echo "Parameters as a single string is $*"
```

If you execute mypgm2 from the command line in pdksh and bash as follows,

```
$ bash mypgm2 Sanjiv Guha
```

you get the following result:

```
Number of parameters is 2
Program name is mypgm2
Parameters as a single string is Sanjiv Guha
```

Special Characters

Some characters have special meaning to Linux shells; these characters represent commands, denote specific use for surrounding text, or provide search parameters. Special characters provide a sort of shorthand by incorporating these rather complex meanings into a simple character. Some special characters are shown in Table 11.2.

TABLE 11.2   Special Shell Characters

Character	Explanation
$	Indicates the beginning of a shell variable name
¦	Pipes standard output to next command
#	Starts a comment
&	Executes a process in the background
?	Matches one character
*	Matches one or more characters
>	Output redirection operator
<	Input redirection operator
`	Command substitution (the backquote or backtick—the key above the Tab key on most keyboards)
>>	Output redirection operator (to append to a file)
<<	Wait until following end-of-input string (HERE operator)
[ ]	Range of characters
[a-z]	All characters a through z
[a,z] or [az]	Characters a or z
Space	Delimiter between two words

Special characters are very useful to you when you're creating shell scripts, but if you inadvertently use a special character as part of variable names or strings, your program will behave incorrectly. As you learn in later parts of this section, you can use one of the special characters in a string if you precede it with an *escape character* (/, or backslash) to indicate that it isn't being used as a special character and shouldn't be treated as such by the program.

A few special characters deserve special note. They are the double quotes ("), the single quotes ('), the backslash (\), and the backtick (`)—all discussed in the following sections.

Use Double Quotes to Resolve Variables in Strings with Embedded Spaces

If a string contains embedded spaces, you can enclose the string in double quotes (") so that the shell interprets the whole string as one entity instead of more than one.

For example, if you assigned the value of abc def (abc followed by one space, followed by def) to a variable called x in a shell program as follows, you would get an error because the shell would try to execute def as a separate command:

Command	Environment
x="abc def"	pdksh and bash
set x = "adb def"	tcsh

The shell will execute the string as a single command if you surround the string in double quotes as follows:

Command	Environment
x=abc def	pdksh and bash
set x=abc def	tcsh

The double quotes resolve all variables within the string. Here is an example for pdksh and bash:

```
var="test string"
newvar="Value of var is $var"
echo $newvar
```

Here is the same example for tcsh:

```
set var="test string"
set newvar="Value of var is $var"
echo $newvar
```

If you execute a shell program containing the preceding three lines, you get the following result:

```
Value of var is test string
```

Using Single Quotes to Maintain Unexpanded Variables

You can surround a string with single quotes (') to stop the shell from expanding variables and interpreting special characters. When used for the latter purpose, the single quote is an *escape character*, similar to the backslash, which you learn about in the next section. Here, you learn how to use the single quote to avoid expanding a variable in a shell script. An unexpanded variable maintains its original form in the output.

In the following examples, the double quotes in the preceding examples have been changed to single quotes.

pdksh and bash:

```
var='test string'
newvar='Value of var is $var'
echo $newvar
```

tcsh:

```
set var = 'test string'
set newvar = 'Value of var is $var'
echo $newvar
```

If you execute a shell program containing these three lines, you get the following result:

```
Value of var is $var
```

As you can see, the variable var maintains its original format in the results, rather than having been expanded.

Using the Backslash as an Escape Character

As you learned earlier, the backslash (\) serves as an escape character that stops the shell from interpreting the succeeding character as a special character. Say that you want to assign a value of $test to a variable called var. If you use the following command, the shell reads the special character $ and interprets $test as the value of the variable test. No value has been assigned to test; a null value is stored in var as follows:

Command	Environment
var=$test	pdksh and bash
set var=$test	tcsh

Unfortunately, this assignment may work for bash and pdksh, but it returns an error of "undefined variable" if you use it with tcsh. Use the following commands to correctly store $test in var:

Command	Environment
var=`wc -l test.txt`	pdksh and bash
set var = `wc -l test.txt`	tcsh

The backslash before the dollar sign (\$) signals the shell to interpret the $ as any other ordinary character and not to associate any special meaning to it. You could also use single quotes (') around the $test variable to get the same result.

Using the Backtick to Replace a String with Output

You can use the backtick (`) character to signal the shell to replace a string with its output when executed. This special character can be used in shell programs when you want the result of the execution of a command to be stored in a variable. For example, if you want to count the number of lines in a file called test.txt in the current directory and store the result in a variable called var, you can use the following command:

Command	Environment
var=\$test	pdksh and bash
set var = \$test	tcsh

Comparison of Expressions in pdksh and bash

Comparing values or evaluating the differences between similar bits of data—such as file information, character strings, or numbers—is a task known as *comparison of expressions*. Comparison of expressions is an integral part of using logic in shell programs to accomplish tasks. The way the logical comparison of two operators (numeric or string) is done varies slightly in different shells. In pdksh and bash, a command called test can be used to achieve comparisons of expressions. In tcsh, you can write an expression to accomplish the same thing.

The following section covers comparison operations using the pdksh or bash shells. Later in the chapter, you learn how to compare expressions in the tcsh shell.

The pdksh and bash shell syntax provide a command named test to compare strings, numbers, and files. The syntax of the test command is as follows:

```
test expression
```

or

```
[ expression ]
```

Both forms of the test commands are processed the same way by pdksh and bash. The test commands support the following types of comparisons:

▶ String comparison

▶ Numeric comparison

▶ File operators

▶ Logical operators

String Comparison
The following operators can be used to compare two string expressions:

▶ =—To compare whether two strings are equal

▶ !=—To compare whether two strings are not equal

▶ -n—To evaluate whether the string length is greater than zero

▶ -z—To evaluate whether the string length is equal to zero

Next are some examples using these operators when comparing two strings, string1 and string2, in a shell program called compare1:

```
#!/bin/sh
string1="abc"
string2="abd"
```

```
if [ $string1 = $string2 ]; then
   echo "string1 equal to string2"
else
   echo "string1 not equal to string2"
fi

if [ $string2 != string1 ]; then
   echo "string2 not equal to string1"
else
   echo "string2 equal to string2"
fi

if [ $string1 ]; then
   echo "string1 is not empty"
else
   echo "string1 is empty"
fi

if [ -n $string2 ]; then
   echo "string2 has a length greater than zero"
else
   echo "string2 has length equal to zero"
fi

if [ -z $string1 ]; then
   echo "string1 has a length equal to zero"
else
  echo "string1 has a length greater than zero"
fi
```

If you execute compare1, you get the following result:

```
string1 not equal to string2
string2 not equal to string1
string1 is not empty
string2 has a length greater than zero
string1 has a length greater than zero
```

If two strings are not equal in size, the system pads out the shorter string with trailing spaces for comparison. That is, if the value of string1 is abc and that of string2 is ab, string2 will be padded with a trailing space for comparison purposes—it will have a value of ab.

Number Comparison

The following operators can be used to compare two numbers:

▶ -eq—To compare whether two numbers are equal

▶ -ge—To compare whether one number is greater than or equal to the other number

▶ -le—To compare whether one number is less than or equal to the other number

▶ -ne—To compare whether two numbers are not equal

▶ -gt—To compare whether one number is greater than the other number

▶ -lt—To compare whether one number is less than the other number

The following shell program compares three numbers, number1, number2, and number3:

```
#!/bin/sh
number1=5
number2=10
number3=5

if [ $number1 -eq $number3 ]; then
    echo "number1 is equal to number3"
else
    echo "number1 is not equal to number3"
fi

if [ $number1 -ne $number2 ]; then
    echo "number1 is not equal to number2"
else
    echo "number1 is equal to number2"
fi

if [ $number1 -gt $number2 ]; then
    echo "number1 is greater than number2"
else
    echo "number1 is not greater than number2"
fi

if [ $number1 -ge $number3 ]; then
    echo "number1 is greater than or equal to number3"
else
    echo "number1 is not greater than or equal to number3"
fi

if [ $number1 -lt $number2 ]; then
    echo "number1 is less than number2"
else
    echo "number1 is not less than number2"
fi

if [ $number1 -le $number3 ]; then
    echo "number1 is less than or equal to number3"
else
    echo "number1 is not less than or equal to number3"
fi
```

When you execute the shell program, you get the following results:

```
number1 is equal to number3
number1 is not equal to number2
number1 is not greater than number2
number1 is greater than or equal to number3
number1 is less than number2
number1 is less than or equal to number3
```

File Operators

The following operators can be used as file comparison operators:

- ▶ -d—To ascertain whether a file is a directory
- ▶ -f—To ascertain whether a file is a regular file
- ▶ -r—To ascertain whether read permission is set for a file
- ▶ -s—To ascertain whether a file exists and has a length greater than zero
- ▶ -w—To ascertain whether write permission is set for a file
- ▶ -x—To ascertain whether execute permission is set for a file

Assume that a shell program called compare3 is in a directory with a file called file1 and a subdirectory dir1 under the current directory. Assume that file1 has a permission of r-x (read and execute permission) and dir1 has a permission of rwx (read, write, and execute permission). The code for the shell program would look like this:

```
#!/bin/sh
if [ -d $dir1 ]; then
    echo "dir1 is a directory"
else
    echo "dir1 is not a directory"
fi

if [ -f $dir1 ]; then
    echo "dir1 is a regular file"
else
    echo "dir1 is not a regular file"
fi

if [ -r $file1 ]; then
    echo "file1 has read permission"
else
    echo "file1 does not have read permission"
fi
```

```
if [ -w $file1 ]; then
   echo "file1 has write permission"
else
   echo "file1 does not have write permission"
fi

if [ -x $dir1 ]; then
   echo "dir1 has execute permission"
else
   echo "dir1 does not have execute permission"
fi
```

If you execute the shell program, you get the following results:

```
dir1 is a directory
file1 is a regular file
file1 has read permission
file1 does not have write permission
dir1 has execute permission
```

Logical Operators

Logical operators are used to compare expressions using Boolean logic, which compares values using characters representing NOT, AND, and OR.

- ▶ !—To negate a logical expression

- ▶ -a—To logically AND two logical expressions

- ▶ -o—To logically OR two logical expressions

This example named logic uses the file and directory mentioned in the previous compare3 example.

```
#!/bin/sh
if [ -x file1 -a -x dir1 ]; then
   echo file1 and dir1 are executable
else
   echo at least one of file1 or dir1 are not executable
fi

if [ -w file1 -o -w dir1 ]; then
   echo file1 or dir1 are writable
else
   echo neither file1 or dir1 are executable
fi
```

```
if [ ! -w file1 ]; then
   echo file1 is not writable
else
   echo file1 is writable
fi
```

If you execute logic, it will yield the following result:

```
file1 and dir1 are executable
file1 or dir1 are writable
file1 is not writable
```

Comparing Expressions with tcsh

As stated earlier, the method for comparing expressions in tcsh is different from the method used under pdksh and bash. The comparison of expression demonstrated in this section uses the syntax necessary for the tcsh shell environment.

String Comparison

The following operators can be used to compare two string expressions:

▶ ==—To compare whether two strings are equal

▶ !=—To compare whether two strings are not equal

The following examples compare two strings, string1 and string2, in the shell program compare1:

```
#!/bin/tcsh
set string1 = "abc"
set string2 = "abd"

if  (string1 == string2)  then
   echo "string1 equal to string2"
else
   echo "string1 not equal to string2"
endif

if  (string2 != string1)  then
   echo "string2 not equal to string1"
else
   echo "string2 equal to string1"
endif
```

If you execute compare1, you get the following results:

```
string1 not equal to string2
string2 not equal to string1
```

Number Comparison

These operators can be used to compare two numbers:

- ► >=—To compare whether one number is greater than or equal to the other number
- ► <=—To compare whether one number is less than or equal to the other number
- ► >—To compare whether one number is greater than the other number
- ► <—To compare whether one number is less than the other number

The next examples compare two numbers, number1 and number2, in a shell program called compare2:

```
#!/bin/tcsh
set number1=5
set number2=10
set number3=5

if  ($number1 > $number2)  then
    echo "number1 is greater than number2"
else
    echo "number1 is not greater than number2"
endif

if  ($number1 >= $number3) then
    echo "number1 is greater than or equal to number3"
else
    echo "number1 is not greater than or equal to number3"
endif

if  ($number1 < $number2)  then
    echo "number1 is less than number2"
else
    echo "number1 is not less than number2"
endif

if  ($number1 <= $number3) then
    echo "number1 is less than or equal to number3"
else
    echo "number1 is not less than or equal to number3"
endif
```

When executing the shell program compare2, you get the following results:

```
number1 is not greater than number2
number1 is greater than or equal to number3
number1 is less than number2
number1 is less than or equal to number3
```

File Operators

These operators can be used as file comparison operators:

- ▶ -d—To ascertain whether a file is a directory
- ▶ -e—To ascertain whether a file exists
- ▶ -f—To ascertain whether a file is a regular file
- ▶ -o—To ascertain whether a user is the owner of a file
- ▶ -r—To ascertain whether read permission is set for a file
- ▶ -w—To ascertain whether write permission is set for a file
- ▶ -x—To ascertain whether execute permission is set for a file
- ▶ -z—To ascertain whether the file size is zero

The following examples are based on a shell program called compare3, which is in a directory with a file called file1 and a subdirectory dir1 under the current directory. Assume that file1 has a permission of r-x (read and execute permission) and dir1 has a permission of rwx (read, write, and execute permission).

The following is the code for the compare3 shell program:

```
#!/bin/tcsh
if  (-d dir1) then
   echo "dir1 is a directory"
else
   echo "dir1 is not a directory"
endif

if (-f dir1)  then
   echo "file1 is a regular file"
else
   echo "file1 is not a regular file"
endif

if (-r file1) then
   echo "file1 has read permission"
else
   echo "file1 does not have read permission"
endif

if (-w file1) then
   echo "file1 has write permission"
else
   echo "file1 does not have write permission"
endif
```

```
if (-x dir1) then
    echo "dir1 has execute permission"
else
    echo "dir1 does not have execute permission"
endif

if (-z file1) then
    echo "file1 has zero length"
else
    echo "file1 has greater than zero length"
endif
```

If you execute the file compare3, you get the following results:

```
dir1 is a directory
file1 is a regular file
file1 has read permission
file1 does not have write permission
dir1 has execute permission
file1 has greater than zero length
```

Logical Operators

Logical operators are used with conditional statements. These operators are used to negate a logical expression or to perform logical ANDs and ORs:

- !—To negate a logical expression

- &&—To logically AND two logical expressions

- ¦¦—To logically OR two logical expressions

This example named logic uses the file and directory mentioned in the previous compare3 example.

```
#!/bin/tcsh
if ( -x file1 && -x dir1 ) then
    echo file1 and dir1 are executable
else
    echo at least one of file1 or dir1 are not executable
endif

if ( -w file1 ¦¦ -w dir1 ) then
    echo file1 or dir1 are writable
else
    echo neither file1 or dir1 are executable
endif
```

```
if ( ! -w file1 ) then
    echo file1 is not writable
else
    echo file1 is writable
endif
```

If you execute logic, it will yield the following result:

```
file1 and dir1 are executable
file1 or dir1 are writable
file1 is not writable
```

The for **Statement**

The for statement is used to execute a set of commands once each time a specified condition is true. The for statement has a number of formats. The first format used by pdksh and bash is as follows:

```
for curvar in list
do
    statements
done
```

This form should be used if you want to execute statements once for each value in list. For each iteration, the current value of the list is assigned to vcurvar. list can be a variable containing a number of items or a list of values separated by spaces. The second format is as follows:

```
for curvar
do
    statements
done
```

In this form, the statements are executed once for each of the positional parameters passed to the shell program. For each iteration, the current value of the positional parameter is assigned to the variable curvar.

This form can also be written as follows:

```
for curvar in $
do
    statements
done
```

Remember that $@ gives you a list of positional parameters passed to the shell program, quoted in a manner consistent with the way the user originally invoked the command.

Under tcsh, the for statement is called foreach. The format is as follows:

```
foreach curvar (list)
    statements
end
```

In this form, statements are executed once for each value in list, and, for each iteration, the current value of list is assigned to curvar.

Suppose that you want to create a backup version of each file in a directory to a subdirectory called backup. You can do the following in pdksh and bash:

```
#!/bin/sh
for filename in *
do
    cp $filename backup/$filename
    if [ $? -ne 0 ]; then
        echo "copy for $filename failed"
    fi
done
```

In the preceding example, a backup copy of each file is created. If the copy fails, a message is generated.

The same example in tcsh is as follows:

```
#!/bin/tcsh
foreach filename (`/bin/ls`)
    cp $filename backup/$filename
    if ($? != 0) then
        echo "copy for $filename failed"
    endif
end
```

The while **Statement**

The while statement can be used to execute a series of commands while a specified condition is true. The loop terminates as soon as the specified condition evaluates to false. It is possible that the loop will not execute at all if the specified condition initially evaluates to false. You should be careful with the while command because the loop will never terminate if the specified condition never evaluates to false.

Endless Loops Have Their Place in Shell Programs

Endless loops can sometimes be useful. For example, you can easily construct a simple command that constantly monitors the 802.11b link quality of a network interface by using a few lines of script:

```
#!/bin/sh
```

```
while :
do
    /sbin/iwconfig eth0 | grep Link | tr '\n' '\r'
done
```

The script outputs the search, and then the `tr` command formats the output. The result is a simple animation of a constantly updated single line of information:

```
Link Quality:92/92  Signal level:-11 dBm  Noise level:-102 dBm
```

This technique can also be used to create a graphical monitoring client for X that outputs traffic information and activity about a network interface:

```
#!/bin/sh
xterm -geometry 75x2 -e \
bash -c \
"while :; do \
    /sbin/ifconfig eth0 | \
    grep 'TX bytes' | \
    tr '\n' '\r' ; \
done"
```

The simple example uses a bash command-line script (enabled by `-c`) to execute a command line repeatedly. The command line pipes the output of the `ifconfig` command through `grep`, which searches `ifconfig`'s output and then pipes a line containing the string `"TX bytes"` to the `tr` command. The `tr` command then removes the carriage return at the end of the line to display the information inside an `/xterm` X11 terminal window, automatically sized by the `-geometry` option:

```
RX bytes:4117594780 (3926.8 Mb)  TX bytes:452230967 (431.2 Mb)
```

Endless loops can be so useful that Linux includes a command that will repeatedly execute a given command line. For example, you can get a quick report about a system's hardware health by using the `sensors` command. But instead of using a shell script to loop the output endlessly, you can use the `watch` command to repeat the information and provide simple animation:

```
$ watch "sensors -f | cut -c 1-20"
```

In pdksh and bash, the following format is used for the `while` flow control construct:

```
while expression
do
    statements
done
```

In tcsh, the following format is used:

```
while (expression)
```

```
    Statements
end
```

If you want to add the first five even numbers, you can use the following shell program in pdksh and bash:

```
#!/bin/bash
loopcount=0
result=0
while [ $loopcount -lt 5 ]
do
    loopcount=`expr $loopcount + 1`
    increment=`expr $loopcount \* 2`
    result=`expr $result + $increment`
done

echo "result is $result"
```

In tcsh, this program can be written as follows:

```
#!/bin/tcsh
set loopcount = 0
set result = 0
while ($loopcount < 5)
    set loopcount = `expr $loopcount + 1`
    set increment = `expr $loopcount \* 2`
    set result = `expr $result + $increment`

end

echo "result is $result"
```

The until **Statement**

The until statement can be used to execute a series of commands until a specified condition is true.

The loop terminates as soon as the specified condition evaluates to True.

In pdksh and bash, the following format is used:

```
until expression
do
    statements
done
```

As you can see, the format of the until statement is similar to that of the while state-ment, but the logic is different: In a while loop, you execute until an expression is False, but in an until loop, you loop until the expression is True.

If you want to add the first five even numbers, you can use the following shell program in pdksh and bash:

```
#!/bin/bash
loopcount=0
result=0
until [ $loopcount -ge 5 ]
do
    loopcount=`expr $loopcount + 1`
    increment=`expr $loopcount \* 2`
    result=`expr $result + $increment`
done

echo "result is $result"
```

The example here is identical to the example for the while statement, except that the condition being tested is just the opposite of the condition specified in the while statement.

The tcsh shell does not support the until statement.

The repeat Statement (tcsh)

The repeat statement is used to execute only one command a fixed number of times.

If you want to print a hyphen (-) 80 times with one hyphen per line on the screen, you can use the following command:

```
repeat  80 echo '-'
```

The select Statement (pdksh)

The select statement is used to generate a menu list if you are writing a shell program that expects input from the user online. The format of the select statement is as follows:

```
select  item in itemlist
do
    Statements
done
```

itemlist is optional. If it isn't provided, the system iterates through the item entries one at a time. If itemlist is provided, however, the system iterates for each entry in itemlist and the current value of itemlist is assigned to item for each iteration, which then can be used as part of the statements being executed.

If you want to write a menu that gives the user a choice of picking a Continue or a Finish, you can write the following shell program:

```
#!/bin/ksh
select  item in Continue Finish
do
    if [ $item = "Finish" ]; then
        break
    fi
done
```

When the select command is executed, the system displays a menu with numeric choices to the user—in this case, 1 for Continue and 2 for Finish. If the user chooses 1, the variable item contains a value of Continue; if the user chooses 2, the variable item contains a value of Finish. When the user chooses 2, the if statement is executed and the loop terminates.

The shift Statement

The shift statement is used to process the positional parameters, one at a time, from left to right. As you'll remember, the positional parameters are identified as $1, $2, $3, and so on. The effect of the shift command is that each positional parameter is moved one position to the left and the current $1 parameter is lost.

The shift statement is useful when you are writing shell programs in which a user can pass various options. Depending on the specified option, the parameters that follow can mean different things or might not be there at all.

The format of the shift command is as follows:

```
shift  number
```

The parameter number is the number of places to be shifted and is optional. If not specified, the default is 1; that is, the parameters are shifted one position to the left. If specified, the parameters are shifted number positions to the left.

The if Statement

The if statement evaluates a logical expression to make a decision. An if condition has the following format in pdksh and bash:

```
if [ expression ]; then
    Statements
elif [ expression ]; then
    Statements
else
    Statements
fi
```

The if conditions can be nested. That is, an if condition can contain another if condition within it. It isn't necessary for an if condition to have an elif or else part. The else part is executed if none of the expressions that are specified in the if statement and are optional if subsequent elif statements are true. The word fi is used to indicate the end of the if statements, which is very useful if you have nested if conditions. In such a case, you should be able to match fi to if to ensure that all if statements are properly coded.

In the following example for bash or pdksh, a variable var can have either of two values: Yes or No. Any other value is invalid. This can be coded as follows:

```
if [ $var = "Yes" ]; then
    echo "Value is Yes"
elif [ $var = "No" ]; then
    echo "Value is No"
else
    echo "Invalid value"
fi
```

In tcsh, the if statement has two forms. The first form, similar to the one for pdksh and bash, is as follows:

```
if (expression) then
    Statements
else if (expression) then
    Statements
else
    Statements
endif
```

The if conditions can be nested—that is, an if condition can contain another if condition within it. It isn't necessary for an if condition to have an else part. The else part is executed if none of the expressions specified in any of the if statements are true. The optional if part of the statement (else if (expression) then) is executed if the condition following it is true and the previous if statement is not true. The word endif is used to indicate the end of the if statements, which is very useful if you have nested if conditions. In such a case, you should be able to match endif to if to ensure that all if statements are properly coded.

Using the example of the variable var having only two values, Yes and No, here is how it would be coded with tcsh:

```
if ($var == "Yes") then
    echo "Value is Yes"
else if ($var == "No" ) then
    echo "Value is No"
else
```

```
      echo "Invalid value"
endif
```

The second form of the if condition for tcsh is as follows:

```
if (expression) command
```

In this format, only a single command can be executed if the expression evaluates to true.

The case **Statement**

The case statement is used to execute statements depending on a discrete value or a range of values matching the specified variable. In most cases, you can use a case statement instead of an if statement if you have a large number of conditions.

The format of a case statement for pdksh and bash is as follows:

```
case str in
    str1 ¦ str2)
       Statements;;
    str3¦str4)
       Statements;;
    *)
       Statements;;
esac
```

You can specify a number of discrete values—such as str1, str2, and so on—for each condition, or you can specify a value with a wildcard. The last condition should be * (asterisk) and is executed if none of the other conditions are met. For each of the specified conditions, all the associated statements until the double semicolon (;;) are executed.

You can write a script that will echo the name of the month if you provide the month number as a parameter. If you provide a number that isn't between 1 and 12, you will get an error message. The script is as follows:

```
#!/bin/sh


case $1 in
    01 ¦ 1) echo "Month is January";;
    02 ¦ 2) echo "Month is February";;
    03 ¦ 3) echo "Month is March";;
    04 ¦ 4) echo "Month is April";;
    05 ¦ 5) echo "Month is May";;
    06 ¦ 6) echo "Month is June";;
    07 ¦ 7) echo "Month is July";;
```

```
08 ¦ 8) echo "Month is August";;
09 ¦ 9) echo "Month is September";;
10) echo "Month is October";;
11) echo "Month is November";;
12) echo "Month is December";;
*) echo "Invalid parameter";;
esac
```

You need to end the statements under each condition with a double semicolon (;;). If you do not, the statements under the next condition will also be executed.

The format for a case statement for tcsh is as follows:

```
switch (str)
    case str1¦str2:
       Statements
       breaksw
    case str3¦str4:
       Statements
       breaksw
    default:
       Statements
       breaksw
endsw
```

You can specify a number of discrete values—such as str1, str2, and so on—for each condition, or you can specify a value with a wildcard. The last condition should be default and is executed if none of the other conditions are met. For each of the specified conditions, all the associated statements until breaksw are executed.

The example that echoes the month when a number is given, shown earlier for pdksh and bash, can be written in tcsh as follows:

```
#!/bin/tcsh

set month = 5
switch ( $month )
    case 1: echo "Month is January" ;  breaksw
    case 2: echo "Month is February" ;  breaksw
    case 3: echo "Month is March" ;  breaksw
    case 4: echo "Month is April" ;  breaksw
    case 5: echo "Month is May" ;  breaksw
    case 6: echo "Month is June" ;  breaksw
    case 7: echo "Month is July" ;  breaksw
    case 8: echo "Month is August"  ;  breaksw
```

```
    case 9: echo "Month is September" ;  breaksw
    case 10: echo "Month is October" ;  breaksw
    case 11: echo "Month is November" ;  breaksw
    case 12: echo "Month is December" ;  breaksw
    default: echo "Oops! Month is Octember!" ;  breaksw
endsw
```

You need to end the statements under each condition with breaksw. If you do not, the statements under the next condition will also be executed.

The break and exit Statements

You should be aware of two other statements: the break statement and the exit statement.

The break statement can be used to terminate an iteration loop, such as a for, until, or repeat command.

exit statements can be used to exit a shell program. You can optionally use a number after exit. If the current shell program has been called by another shell program, the calling program can check for the code (the $? or $status variable, depending on shell) and make a decision accordingly.

Using Functions in Shell Scripts

As with other programming languages, shell programs also support functions. A function is a piece of a shell program that performs a particular process; you can reuse the same function multiple times within the shell program. Functions help eliminate the need for duplicating code as you write shell programs.

The following is the format of a function in pdksh and bash:

```
func(){
    Statements
}
```

You can call a function as follows:

```
func param1 param2 param3
```

The parameters param1, param2, and so on are optional. You can also pass the parameters as a single string—for example, $@. A function can parse the parameters as if they were positional parameters passed to a shell program from the command line as command-line arguments, but instead use values passed inside the script. For example, the following script uses a function named Displaymonth() that displays the name of the month or an error message if you pass a month number out of the range 1 to 12. This example works with pdksh and bash:

```
#!/bin/sh
Displaymonth() {
    case $1 in
        01 ¦ 1) echo "Month is January";;
        02 ¦ 2) echo "Month is February";;
        03 ¦ 3) echo "Month is March";;
        04 ¦ 4) echo "Month is April";;
        05 ¦ 5) echo "Month is May";;
        06 ¦ 6) echo "Month is June";;
        07 ¦ 7) echo "Month is July";;
        08 ¦ 8) echo "Month is August";;
        09 ¦ 9) echo "Month is September";;
        10) echo "Month is October";;
        11) echo "Month is November";;
        12) echo "Month is December";;
        *) echo "Invalid parameter";;
    esac
}
Displaymonth 8
```

The preceding program displays the following output:

```
Month is August
```

Related Ubuntu and Linux Commands

You can use these commands and tools when using the shell or writing shell scripts:

▶ chsh—Command used to change one's login shell

▶ kibitz—Allows two-person interaction with a single shell

▶ mc—A visual shell named the GNU Midnight Commander

▶ nano—An easy-to-use text editor for the console

▶ shar—Command used to create shell archives

▶ vi—The vi (actually vim) text editor

Reference

► http://www.linuxgazette.com/issue70/ghosh.html—A Linux Gazette article on "Bootstrapping Linux," which includes much detail on the BIOS and MBR aspects of the boot process.

► http://www.lostcircuits.com/advice/bios2/1.shtml—the LostCircuits BIOS guide; much detail on the meaning of all those BIOS settings.

► http://www.rojakpot.com/default.aspx?location=1—The BIOS Optimization Guide; details on tweaking those BIOS settings to your heart's content.

► http://www-106.ibm.com/developerworks/linux/library/l-slack.html—A link through IBM's website to an article on booting Slackware Linux, along with a sidebar about the history of System V versus BSD init scripts.

► /usr/src/linux/init/main.c—The best place to learn about how Linux boots. Fascinating reading, really. Get it from the source!

► http://sunsite.dk/linux-newbie/—Home page for the Linux Newbie Administrator Guide—A gentle introduction to Linux System Administration.

► The GRUB Manual—The still yet-to-be-completed manual can be found at http://www.gnu.org/software/grub/manual/. On your Ubuntu system, info grub provides a plethora of information and a sample grub.conf file (/boot/grub/menu.lst is a symbolic link to /boot/grub/grub.conf; use either name) can be found in /usr/doc/grub.

► "LILO User's Guide"—Werner Almesberger's definitive technical tome on the LInux LOader, or LILO, and how it works on Intel-based PCs. Look under the /usr/share/doc/lilo*/doc directory for the file User_Guide.ps, which can be viewed using the gv client. LILO has been dropped from Ubuntu; GRUB is now the default boot loader supported in the distribution.

► "Grub, Glorious Grub"—Hoyt Duff, *Linux Format*, August 2001; pp. 58–61. A tutorial on the GRUB boot leader.

► http://www.linuxbase.org/spec/refspecs/LSB_1.0.0/gLSB/sysinit.html—The Linux Standard Base description of system initialization; this is the standard.

► http://www.gnu.org/software/bash/bash.html—The bash home page at the GNU Software Project.

► http://www.tldp.org/LDP/abs/html/—Mendel Cooper's "Advanced Bash-Scripting Guide."

► http://www.linuxnewbie.org/nhf/intel/shells/basic.html—Learn basic shell commands at this site.

► http://www.cs.princeton.edu/~jlk/lj/—"The New Korn Shell—ksh93," an article by David G. Korn, Charles J. Northrup, and Jeffery Korn regarding the korn shell.

▶ http://web.cs.mun.ca/~michael/pdksh/—The pdksh home page.

▶ http://lug.umbc.edu/~mabzug1/bash-httpd.html—The Bash-httpd FAQ, with links to the latest version of the bash web server, bash-httpd-0.02.

▶ http://www.tcsh.org/—Find out more about tcsh here.

▶ http://www.zsh.org/—Examine zsh in more detail here.

# CHAPTER 12

System-Monitoring Tools

To keep your system in optimum shape, you need to be able to monitor it closely. Such monitoring is imperative in a corporate environment where uptime is vital and any system failures can cost real money. Whether it is checking processes for any errant daemons, or keeping a close eye on CPU and memory usage, Ubuntu provides a wealth of utilities designed to give you as little or as much feedback as you want. This chapter looks at some of the basic monitoring tools, along with some tactics designed to keep your system up longer. Some of the monitoring tools cover network connectivity, memory, and hard drive usage, but all should find a place in your sysadmin toolkit. Finally you will learn how to manipulate active system processes, using a mixture of graphical and command-line tools.

Console-Based Monitoring

Those familiar with Unix system administration already know about the ps or process display command commonly found on most flavors of Unix. Because Linux is closely related to Unix, it also benefits from this command and allows you to quickly see the current running processes on the system, as well as who owns them and how resource-hungry they are.

Although the Linux kernel has its own distinct architecture and memory management, it also benefits from enhanced use of the /proc file system, the virtual file system found on many Unix flavors. Through the /proc file system you can communicate directly with the kernel to get a deep view of what is currently happening. Developers tend to use the /proc file system as a way of getting information out from the kernel and for their programs to manipulate it into more human readable formats. The /proc file system is beyond the scope of this book, but if you want to get a better idea of what it contains you should head on over to http://en. tldp.org/LDP/Linux-Filesystem-Hierarchy/html/proc.html for an excellent and very in-depth guide.

Processes can also be controlled at the command line, which is important because you might sometimes have only a command-line interface. Whenever an application or command is launched, either from the command line or a clicked icon, the process that comes from the kernel is assigned an identification number called a *process ID* or *PID* for short. This number is shown in the shell if the program is launched via the command line.

```
$ gedit &
```

```
[1] 6193
```

In this example, gedit has been launched in the background, and the (bash) shell reported a shell job number ([1] in this case). A job number or job control is a shell-specific feature that allows a different form of process control, such as sending or suspending programs to the background and retrieving background jobs to the foreground (see your shell's man pages for more information if you are not using bash).

The second number displayed (6193 in this example) represents the process ID. You can get a quick list of your processes by using the ps command like this:

```
# ps
  PID TTY          TIME CMD

 6176 pts/0     00:00:00 bash

 6193 pts/0     00:00:00 gedit

 6197 pts/0     00:00:00 ps
```

Note that not all output from the display is shown here. But as you can see, the output includes the process ID, abbreviated as PID, along with other information, such as the name of the running program. As with any Unix command, many options are available; the proc man page has a full list. A most useful option is aux, which provides a friendly list of all the processes. You should also know that ps works not by polling memory, but through the interrogation of the Linux /proc or process file system. (ps is one of the inter-faces mentioned at the beginning of this section.)

The /proc directory contains quite a few files—some of which include constantly updated hardware information (such as battery power levels, and so on). Linux administrators often pipe the output of ps through a member of the grep family of commands to display information about a specific program, perhaps like this:

```
$ ps aux ¦ grep system-config-display
andrew    6193  0.4  1.4  42772 14992 pts/0     S    20:27   0:00 gedit
```

This example returns the owner (the user who launched the program) and the PID, along with other information, such as the percentage of CPU and memory usage, size of the command (code, data, and stack), time (or date) the command was launched, and name of the command. Processes can also be queried by PID like this:

```
$ ps 6193
  PID TTY      STAT   TIME COMMAND

 6193 pts/0    S      0:00 gedit
```

You can use the PID to stop a running process by using the shell's built-in `kill` command. This command asks the kernel to stop a running process and reclaim system memory. For example, to stop the `system-config-display` client in the example, use the `kill` command like this:

```
$ kill 6193
```

After you press Enter (or perhaps press Enter again), the shell might report

```
[1]+  Terminated              gedit
```

Note that users can `kill` only their own processes, but root can kill them all. Controlling any other running process requires root permission, which should be used judiciously (especially when forcing a `kill` by using the `-9` option); by inadvertently killing the wrong process through a typo in the command, you could bring down an active system.

Using the `kill` Command to Control Processes

The `kill` command is a basic Unix system command. You can communicate with a running process by entering a command into its interface, such as when you type into a text editor. But some processes (usually system processes rather than application processes) run without such an interface, and you need a way to communicate with them as well, so we use a system of signals. The `kill` system accomplishes that by sending a signal to a process, and you can use it to communicate with any process. The general format of the `kill` command is

```
# kill option PID
```

A number of signal options can be sent as words or numbers, but most are of interest only to programmers. One of the most common is

```
# kill PID
```

This tells the process with PID to stop; you supply the actual PID.

```
# kill -9 PID
```

is the signal for `kill` (9 is the number of the SIGKILL signal); use this combination when the plain `kill` shown previously does not work.

```
# kill -SIGHUP PID
```

is the signal to "hang up"—stop—and then clean up all associated processes as well. (Its number is -1.)

As you become proficient at process control and job control, you will learn the utility of a number of `kill` options. A full list of signal options can be found in the `signal` man page.

Using Priority Scheduling and Control

No process can make use of the system's resources (CPU, memory, disk access, and so on) as it pleases. After all, the kernel's primary function is to manage the system resources equitably. It does this by assigning a priority to each process so that some processes get better access to system resources and some processes might have to wait longer until their turn arrives. Priority scheduling can be an important tool in managing a system support-ing critical applications or in a situation in which CPU and RAM usage must be reserved or allocated for a specific task. Two legacy applications included with Ubuntu include the `nice` and `renice` commands. (`nice` is part of the GNU `sh-utils` package, whereas `renice` is inherited from BSD Unix.)

The `nice` command is used with its -n option, along with an argument in the range of -20 to 19, in order from highest to lowest priority (the lower the number, the higher the priority). For example, to run the `gkrellm` client with a low priority, use the `nice` command like this:

```
$ nice -n 12 gkrellm &
```

The `nice` command is typically used for disk- or CPU-intensive tasks that might be obtru-sive or cause system slowdown. The `renice` command can be used to reset the priority of running processes or control the priority and scheduling of all processes owned by a user. Regular users can only numerically increase process priorities (that is, make tasks less important) with this command, but the root operator can use the full `nice` range of sched-uling (-20 to 19).

System administrators can also use the `time` command to get an idea of how much time and what proportion of a system's resources are required for a task, such as a shell script. (Here, `time` is used to measure the duration of elapsed time; the command that deals with civil and sidereal time is the `date` command.) This command is used with the name of another command (or script) as an argument like this:

```
# time -p find / -name core -print
/dev/core
/proc/sys/net/core

real 61.23

user 0.72
```

`sys 3.33`

Output of the command displays the time from start to finish, along with the user and system time required. Other factors you can query include memory, CPU usage, and file system input/output (I/O) statistics. See the `time` command's man page for more details.

Nearly all graphical process-monitoring tools include some form of process control or management. Many of the early tools ported to Linux were clones of legacy Unix utilities. One familiar monitoring (and control) program is `top`. Based on the `ps` command, the `top` command provides a text-based display of constantly updated console-based output showing the most CPU-intensive processes currently running. It can be started like this:

$ **top**

After you press Enter, you see a display as shown in Figure 12.1. The `top` command has a few interactive commands: Pressing **h** displays the help screen; pressing k prompts you to enter the `pid` of a process to kill; pressing **n** prompts you to enter the `pid` of a process to change its nice value. The `top` man page describes other commands and includes a detailed description of what all the columns of information `top` can display actually represent; have a look at top's well-written man page.

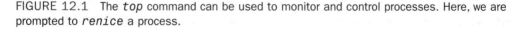

```
                          andrew@Ubuntu: ~                          _ □ ×
File  Edit  View  Terminal  Tabs  Help
top - 20:38:13 up 16 min,  2 users,  load average: 0.02, 0.24, 0.28
Tasks: 117 total,   1 running, 116 sleeping,   0 stopped,   0 zombie
Cpu(s):  2.5%us,  1.1%sy,  0.1%ni, 89.1%id,  6.8%wa,  0.3%hi,  0.1%si,  0.0%st
Mem:   1026048k total,   800364k used,   225684k free,   132804k buffers
Swap:  1646620k total,        0k used,  1646620k free,   361140k cached
PID to renice:
  PID USER      PR  NI  VIRT  RES  SHR S %CPU %MEM    TIME+  COMMAND
    1 root      18   0  2952 1852  532 S    0  0.2  0:02.11 init
    2 root      12  -5     0    0    0 S    0  0.0  0:00.00 kthreadd
    3 root      RT  -5     0    0    0 S    0  0.0  0:00.00 migration/0
    4 root      34  19     0    0    0 S    0  0.0  0:00.00 ksoftirqd/0
    5 root      RT  -5     0    0    0 S    0  0.0  0:00.00 watchdog/0
    6 root      RT  -5     0    0    0 S    0  0.0  0:00.00 migration/1
    7 root      34  19     0    0    0 S    0  0.0  0:00.00 ksoftirqd/1
    8 root      RT  -5     0    0    0 S    0  0.0  0:00.00 watchdog/1
    9 root      10  -5     0    0    0 S    0  0.0  0:00.01 events/0
   10 root      10  -5     0    0    0 S    0  0.0  0:00.00 events/1
   11 root      11  -5     0    0    0 S    0  0.0  0:00.00 khelper
   31 root      12  -5     0    0    0 S    0  0.0  0:00.02 kblockd/0
   32 root      10  -5     0    0    0 S    0  0.0  0:00.00 kblockd/1
   33 root      10  -5     0    0    0 S    0  0.0  0:00.00 kacpid
   34 root      12  -5     0    0    0 S    0  0.0  0:00.00 kacpi_notify
  172 root      10  -5     0    0    0 S    0  0.0  0:00.02 kseriod
  199 root      16   0     0    0    0 S    0  0.0  0:00.00 pdflush
```

FIGURE 12.1   The *top* command can be used to monitor and control processes. Here, we are prompted to *renice* a process.

The `top` command displays quite a bit of information about your system. Processes can be sorted by PID, age, CPU or memory usage, time, or user. This command also provides process management, and system administrators can use its k and r keypress commands to kill and reschedule running tasks, respectively.

The top command uses a fair amount of memory, so you might want to be judicious in its use and not leave it running all the time. When you've finished with it, simply press **q to** quit top.

Displaying Free and Used Memory with free

Although top includes some memory information, the free utility displays the amount of free and used memory in the system in kilobytes (the -m switch displays in megabytes). On one system, the output looks like this:

```
$ free

              total      used      free    shared   buffers    cached

Mem:        1026048    808388    217660         0    132896    362360

-/+ buffers/cache:      313132    712916

Swap:       1646620         0   1646620

andrew@Ubuntu:~$
```

This output describes a machine with 1GB of RAM memory and a swap partition of 1.6GB. Note that none of the swap is being used, and that the machine is not heavily loaded. Linux is very good at memory management and "grabs" all the memory it can in anticipation of future work.

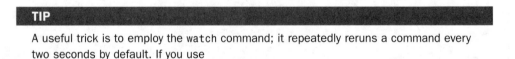

TIP

A useful trick is to employ the watch command; it repeatedly reruns a command every two seconds by default. If you use

```
#  watch free
```

you can see the output of the free command updated every two seconds.

Another useful system-monitoring tool is vmstat (*virtual memory statistics*). This command reports on processes, memory, I/O, and CPU, typically providing an average since the last reboot; or you can make it report usage for a current period by telling it the time interval in seconds and the number of iterations you desire, like

```
$ vmstat 5 10
```

which runs vmstat every five seconds for 10 iterations.

Use the uptime command to see how long it has been since the last reboot and to get an idea of what the load average has been; higher numbers mean higher loads.

Disk Space

As well as system load it's important to keep an eye on the amount of free hard drive space that your computer has remaining.

It's very easy to do this, mainly by using the df command, like so:

```
$ df
```

Just using the command as is can give you a lot of gobbldegook like so,

```
Filesystem           1K-blocks     Used Available Use% Mounted on

/dev/sda1             36835176  6829896  28134112  20% /

varrun                  513024      160    512864   1% /var/run

varlock                 513024        0    513024   0% /var/lock

udev                    513024       72    512952   1% /dev

devshm                  513024        0    513024   0% /dev/shm

lrm                     513024    34696    478328   7% /lib/modules/\
2.6.22-12-generic/volatile
```

Here you can see each drive as mounted on your system, as well as the used space, the available space, the percentage of the total usage of the disk, and finally where it is mounted on your system.

Unless you're good at math, you may find it difficult to work out exactly what the figures mean in megabytes and gigabytes, so it's recommended that you use the -h switch to make the output human readable, like so:

```
Filesystem      Size  Used Avail Use% Mounted on

/dev/sda1        36G  6.6G   27G  20% /

varrun          501M  160K  501M   1% /var/run

varlock         501M     0  501M   0% /var/lock

udev            501M   72K  501M   1% /dev

devshm          501M     0  501M   0% /dev/shm

lrm             501M   34M  468M   7% /lib/modules/2.6.22-12-generic/volatile
```

Disk Quotas

Disk quotas are a way to restrict the usage of disk space either by user or by groups. Although rarely—if ever—used on a local or standalone workstation, quotas are definitely a way of life at the enterprise level of computing. Usage limits on disk space not only conserve resources, but also provide a measure of operational safety by limiting the amount of disk space any user can consume.

Disk quotas are more fully covered in Chapter 10, "Managing Users."

Graphical Process and System Management Tools

The GNOME and KDE desktop environments offer a rich set of network and system-monitoring tools. Graphical interface elements, such as menus and buttons, and graphical output, including metering and real-time load charts, make these tools easy to use. These clients, which require an active X session and (in some cases) root permission, are included with Ubuntu.

If you view the graphical tools locally while they are being run on a server, you must have X properly installed and configured on your local machine. Although some tools can be used to remotely monitor systems or locally mounted remote file systems, you have to properly configure pertinent X11 environment variables, such as $DISPLAY, to use the software or use the ssh client's -X option when connecting to the remote host.

A good graphical process and system management tool is GKrellM, which provides a neat interface and a host of additional plugins. You have to use this command to retrieve GKrellM:

```
$ sudo apt-get install gkrellm
```

or you can use synaptic and after installed it can be found under Applications, System Tools. GKrellM is shown in Figure 12.2.

Some of the graphical system- and process-monitoring tools that come with Ubuntu include the following:

- ▶ vncviewer—AT&T's open source remote session manager (part of the Xvnc package), which can be used to view and run a remote desktop session locally. This software (discussed in more detail in Chapter 15, "Remote Access with SSH and Telnet") requires an active, background, X session on the remote computer.

- ▶ gnome-nettool—A GNOME-developed tool that enables system administrators to carry out a wide range of diagnostics on network interfaces, including port scanning and route tracing.

- ▶ ethereal—This graphical network protocol analyzer can be used to save or display packet data in real time and has intelligent filtering to recognize data signatures or patterns from a variety of hardware and data captures from third-party data capture programs, including compressed files. Some protocols include AppleTalk, Andrew File System (AFS), AOL's Instant Messenger, various Cisco protocols, and many more.

FIGURE 12.2   GKrellM allows you to monitor most system processes on Ubuntu.

▶ gnome-system-monitor—This tool is a simple process monitor offering three views: a list view, a moving graph, and a storage status overview. To access it choose System, Administration, System Monitor (see Figure 12.3).

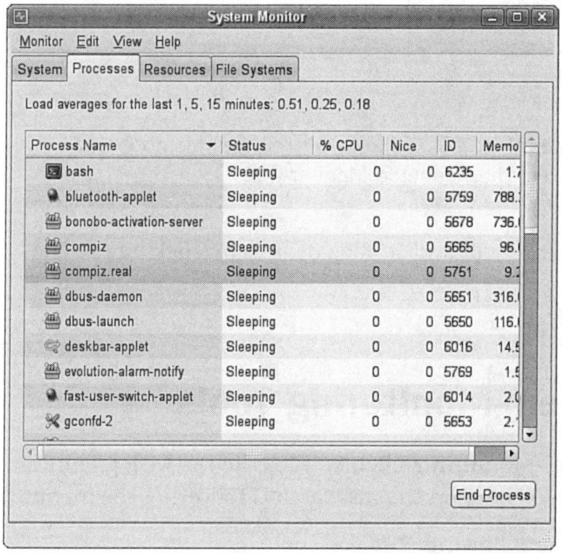

FIGURE 12.3   The Process Listing view of the System Monitor.

From the Process Listing view (chosen via the Processes tab in the upper-left portion of the window), select a process and click on More Info at the bottom left of the screen to display details on that process at the bottom of the display. You can select from three views to filter the display, available in the drop-down View list: All Processes, My Processes (those you alone own), or Active Processes (all processes that are active).

Choose Hidden Processes under the Edit command accessible from the top of the display to show any hidden processes (those that the kernel does not enable the normal monitoring tools to see). Select any process and kill it with End Process.

You can renice the processes by selecting Edit, Change Priority. The View selection from the menu bar also provides a memory map. In the Resource Monitor tab, you can view a moving graph representing CPU and memory usage (see Figure 12.4).

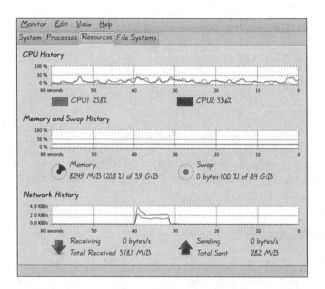

FIGURE 12.4   The Graph view of the System Monitor. It shows CPU usage, Memory/Swap usage, and disk usage. To get this view, select the Resource Monitor tab.

Finally, you can see the status of your file system and storage devices by clicking the File Systems tab shown in Figure 12.5.

KDE Process- and System-Monitoring Tools

KDE provides several process- and system-monitoring clients. Integrate the KDE graphical clients into the desktop taskbar by right-clicking on the taskbar and following the menus.

These KDE monitoring clients include the following:

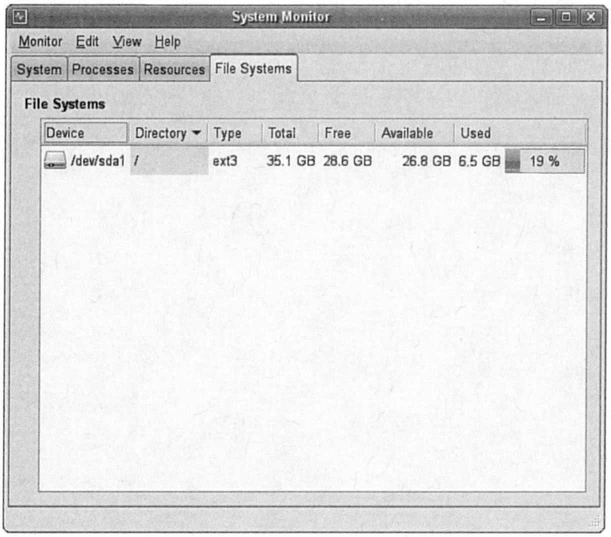

FIGURE 12.5   Keep a close eye on your free disk space.

▶ kdf—A graphical interface to your system's file system table that displays free disk space and enables you to mount and unmount file systems with a pointing device.

▶ ksysguard—Another panel applet that provides CPU load and memory use information in animated graphs.

Reference

▶ http://and.sourceforge.net/—Home page of the and auto-nice daemon, which can be used to prioritize and reschedule processes automatically.

▶ http://sourceforge.net/projects/schedutils/—Home page for various projects offering scheduling utilities for real-time scheduling.

▶ http://freetype.sourceforge.net/patents.html—A discussion of the FreeType bytecode interpreter patents.

▶ http://www.ethereal.com/—Home page for the Ethereal client.

▶ http://www.realvnc.com/—The home page for the Virtual Network Computing remote desktop software, available for a variety of platforms, including Ubuntu. This software has become so popular that it is now included with nearly every Linux distribution.

CHAPTER 13

Backing Up

This chapter examines the practice of safeguarding data through backups, restoring that same data if necessary, and recovering data in case of a catastrophic hardware or software failure. After reading this chapter, you will have a full understanding of the reasons for sound backup practices. You can use the information in this chapter to make intelligent choices about which strategies are best for you. The chapter also shows you how to perform some types of data recovery and system restoration on your own and when to seek professional assistance.

Choosing a Backup Strategy

Backups are always trade-offs. Any backup will consume time, money, and effort on an ongoing basis; backups must be monitored, validated, indexed, stored, and new media continuously purchased. Sound expensive? The cost of not having backups is the loss of your critical data. Re-creating the data from scratch will cost time and money, and if the cost of doing it all again is greater than the cost associated with backing up, you should be performing backups. At the where-the-rubber-meets-the-road level, backups are nothing more than insurance against financial loss for you or your business.

Your first step in formulating and learning to use an effective backup strategy is to choose the strategy that is right for you. First, you must understand some of the most common (and not so common) causes of data loss so that you are better able to understand the threats your system faces. Then, you need to assess your own system, how it is used and by whom, your available hardware and software resources, and your budget constraints. The following sections look at each of these issues in detail, as well as offering some sample backup systems and discussing their use.

Why Data Loss Occurs

Files disappear for any number of reasons: They can be lost because the hardware fails and causes data loss; your attention might wander and you accidentally delete or overwrite a file. Some data loss occurs as a result of natural disasters and other circumstances beyond your control. A tornado, flood, or earthquake could strike, the water pipes could burst, or the building could catch on fire. Your data, as well as the hardware, would likely be destroyed in such a disaster. A disgruntled employee might destroy files or hardware in an attempt at retribution. And any equipment might fail, and it all will fail at some time— most likely when it is extremely important for it not to fail.

A Case in Point

A recent Harris poll of Fortune 500 executives found that roughly two-thirds of them had problems with their backups and disaster-recovery plans. How about you?

Data can also be lost because of malfunctions that corrupt the data as it attempts to write to the disk. Other applications, utilities, and drivers might be poorly written, buggy (the phrase most often heard is "still beta quality"), or might suffer some corruption and fail to correctly write that all-important data you have just created. If that happened, the contents of your data file would be indecipherable garbage of no use to anyone.

All of these accidents and disasters offer important reasons for having a good backup strategy; however, the most frequent cause of data loss is human error. Who among us has not overwritten a new file with an older version or unintentionally deleted a needed file? This applies not only to data files, but also to configuration files and binaries. While perusing the mail lists or the Usenet newsgroup postings, stories about deleting entire directories such as /home, /usr, or /lib seem all too common. Incorrectly changing a configuration file and not saving the original in case it has to be restored (which it does more often than not because the person reconfigured it incorrectly) is another common error.

TIP

To make a backup of a configuration file you are about to edit, use the cp command:

```
$ cp filename filename.original
```

And to restore it:

```
$ cp filename.original filename
```

Never edit or move the *.original file, or the original copy will be lost.

Proper backups can help you recover from these problems with a minimum of hassle, but you have to put in the effort to keep backups current, verify their intactness, and practice restoring the data in different disaster scenarios.

Assessing Your Backup Needs and Resources

By now you have realized that some kind of plan is needed to safeguard your data, and, like most people, you are overwhelmed by the prospect. Entire books, as well as countless articles and whitepapers, have been written on the subject of backing up and restoring data. What makes the topic so complex is that each solution is truly individual.

Yet, the proper approach to making the decision is very straightforward. You start the process by asking

- ▶ What data must be safeguarded?

- ▶ How often does the data change?

The answers to these two questions determine how important the data is, determine the volume of the data, and determine the frequency of the backups. This in turn will determine the backup medium. Only then can the software be selected that will accommodate all these considerations. (You learn about choosing backup software, hardware, and media later in this chapter.)

Available resources are another important consideration when selecting a backup strategy. Backups require time, money, and personnel. Begin your planning activities by determining what limitations you face for all of these resources. Then, construct your plan to fit those limitations, or be prepared to justify the need for more resources with a careful assessment of both backup needs and costs.

13

TIP

If you are not willing or capable of assessing your backup needs and choosing a back-up solution, there exists a legion of consultants, hardware vendors, and software vendors who would love to assist you. The best way to choose one in your area is to query other Unix and Linux system administrators (located through user groups, discussion groups, or mail lists) who are willing to share their experiences and make recommendations. If you cannot get a referral, ask the consultant for references and check them out.

Many people also fail to consider the element of time when formulating their plan. Some backup devices are faster than others, and some recovery methods are faster than others. You need to consider that when making choices.

To formulate your backup plan, you need to determine the frequency of backups. The necessary frequency of backups should be determined by how quickly the important data on your system changes. On a home system, most files never change, a few change daily, and some change weekly. No elaborate strategy needs to be created to deal with that. A good strategy for home use is to back up (to any kind of removable media) critical data frequently and back up configuration and other files weekly.

At the enterprise level on a larger system with multiple users, a different approach is called for. Some critical data is changing constantly, and it could be expensive to re-create;

this typically involves elaborate and expensive solutions. Most of us exist somewhere in between these extremes. Assess your system and its use to determine where you fall in this spectrum.

Backup schemes and hardware can be elaborate or simple, but they all require a workable plan and faithful follow-through. Even the best backup plan is useless if the process is not carried out, data is not verified, and data restoration is not practiced on a regular basis. Whatever backup scheme you choose, be sure to incorporate in it these three principles:

- ▶ **Have a plan**—Design a plan that is right for your needs and have equipment appropriate to the task. This involves assessing all the factors that affect the data you are backing up. We will get into more detail later in the chapter.

- ▶ **Follow the plan**—Faithfully complete each part of your backup strategy, and then verify the data stored in the backups. Backups with corrupt data are of no use to anyone. Even backup operations can go wrong.

- ▶ **Practice your skills**—Practice restoring data from your backup systems from time to time, so when disaster strikes, you are ready (and able) to benefit from the strength of your backup plan. (For restoring data, see the section "Using Backup Software.") Keep in mind that it is entirely possible that the flaws in your backup plan will only become apparent when you try restoring!

Sound Practices

You have to create your own best-backup plan, but here are some building blocks that go into the foundation of any sound backup program:

- ▶ Maintain more than one copy of critical data.
- ▶ Label the backups.
- ▶ Store the backups in a climate-controlled and secure area.
- ▶ Use secure, offsite storage of critical data. Many companies choose bank vaults for their offsite storage, and this is highly recommended.
- ▶ Establish a backup policy that makes sense and can be followed religiously. Try to back up your data when the system is consistent (that is, no data is being written), which is usually overnight.
- ▶ Keep track of who has access to your backup media, and keep the total number of people as low as possible. If you can, allow only trusted personnel near your backups.
- ▶ Routinely verify backups and practice restoring data from them.
- ▶ Routinely inspect backup media for defects and regularly replace them (after destroying the data on them if it is sensitive).

Evaluating Backup Strategies

Now that you are convinced you need backups, you need a strategy. It is difficult to be specific about an ideal strategy because each user or administrator's strategy will be highly individualized, but here are a few general examples:

▶ **Home user**—At home, the user has the Ubuntu installation DVD that takes an hour or so to reinstall, so the time issue is not a major concern. The home user will want to back up any configuration files that have altered, keep an archive of any files that have been downloaded, and keep an archive of any data files created while using any applications. Unless the home user has a special project in which constant backups are useful, a weekly backup is adequate. The home user will likely use a DVD-RW drive or other removable media for backups.

▶ **Small office**—Many small offices tend to use the same strategy as the home user, but are more likely to back up critical data daily and use manually changed tape drives. If they have a tape drive with adequate storage, they will likely have a full system backup as well because restoring from the tape is quicker than reinstalling from the CDs. They also might be using CD-RW or DVD writers for backups. Although they will use scripts to automate backups, most of it is probably done by hand.

▶ **Small enterprise**—Here is where backups begin to require higher-end equipment such as autoloading tape drives with fully automated backups. Commercial backup software usually makes an introduction at this level, but a skillful system administrator on a budget can use one of the basic applications discussed in this chapter. Backups are highly structured and supervised by a dedicated system administrator.

▶ **Large enterprise**—These are the most likely settings for the use of expensive, proprietary, highly automated backup solutions. At this level, data means money, lost data means lost money, and delays in restoring data means money lost as well. These system administrators know that backups are necessary insurance and plan accordingly.

Does all this mean that enterprise-level backups are better than those done by a home user? Not at all. The "little guy" with Ubuntu can do just as well as the enterprise operation at the expense of investing more time in the process. By examining the higher-end strategies, we can apply useful concepts across the board.

NOTE

If you are a new sysadmin, you might be inheriting an existing backup strategy. Take some time to examine it and see if it meets the current needs of the organization. Think about what backup protection your organization really needs, and determine if the current strategy meets that need. If it does not, change the strategy. Consider whether the current policy is being practiced by the users, and, if not, why it is not.

Backup Levels

Unix uses the concept of backup levels as a shorthand way of referring to how much data is backed up in relation to a previous backup. It works this way:

A level 0 backup is a full backup. The next backup level would be 1.

Backups at the other numbered levels will back up everything that has changed since the last backup at that level or a numerically higher level (the dump command, for example, offers 10 different backup levels). For example, a level 3 followed by a level 4 will generate an incremental backup from the full backup, whereas a level 4 followed by a level 3 will generate a differential backup between the two.

The following sections examine a few of the many strategies in use today. Many strategies are based on these sample schemes; one of them can serve as a foundation for the strategy you construct for your own system.

Simple Strategy

If you need to back up just a few configuration files and some small data files, copy them to a USB stick, engage the write-protect tab, and keep it someplace safe. If you need just a bit more backup storage capacity, you can copy the important files to a Zip disk (100,250 and 750MB in size), CD-RW disk (up to 700MB in size), or DVD-RW disk (up to 8GB for data).

In addition to configuration and data files, you should archive each user's home directory, as well as the entire /etc directory. Between the two, that backup would contain most of the important files for a small system. Then, you can easily restore this data from the backup media device you have chosen, after a complete reinstall of Ubuntu, if necessary.

Experts believe that if you have more data than can fit on a floppy disk, you really need a formal backup strategy. Some of those are discussed in the following sections. We use a tape media backup as an example.

Full Backup on a Periodic Basis

This backup strategy involves a backup of the complete file system on a weekly, bi-weekly, or other periodic basis. The frequency of the backup depends on the amount of data being backed up, the frequency of changes to the data, and the cost of losing those changes.

This backup strategy is not complicated to perform, and it can be accomplished with the swappable disk drives discussed later in the chapter. If you are connected to a network, it is possible to mirror the data on another machine (preferably offsite); the rsync tool is particularly well suited to this task. Recognize that this does not address the need for archives of the recent state of files; it only presents a snapshot of the system at the time the update is done.

Full Backups with Incremental Backups

This scheme involves performing a full backup of the entire system once a week, along with a daily incremental backup of only those files that have changed in the previous day, and it begins to resemble what a sysadmin of a medium to large system would tradition-ally use.

This backup scheme can be advanced in two ways. In one way, each incremental backup can be made with reference to the original full backup. In other words, a level 0 backup is followed by a series of level 1 backups. The benefit of this backup scheme is that a restoration requires only two tapes (the full backup and the most recent incremental backup). But because it references the full backup, each incremental backup might be large (and grow ever larger) on a heavily used system.

Alternatively, each incremental backup could reference the previous incremental backup. This would be a level 0 backup followed by a level 1, followed by a level 2, and so on. Incremental backups are quicker (less data each time), but require every tape to restore a full system. Again, it is a classic trade-off decision.

Modern commercial backup applications such as Amanda or BRU assist in organizing the process of managing complex backup schedules and tracking backup media. Doing it yourself using the classic dump or employing shell scripts to run tar requires that the system administrator handle all the organization herself. For this reason, complex backup situations are typically handled with commercial software and specialized hardware that are packaged, sold, and supported by vendors.

Mirroring Data or RAID Arrays

Given adequate (and often expensive) hardware resources, you can always mirror the data somewhere else, essentially maintaining a real-time copy of your data on hand. This is often a cheap, workable solution if no large amounts of data are involved. The use of RAID arrays (in some of their incarnations) provides for a recovery if a disk fails.

Note that RAID arrays and mirroring systems will just as happily write corrupt data as valid data. Moreover, if a file is deleted, a RAID array will not save it. RAID arrays are best suited for protecting the current state of a running system, not for backup needs.

Making the Choice

Only you can decide what is best for your situation. After reading about the backup options in this book, put together some sample backup plans; run through a few likely scenarios and assess the effectiveness of your choice.

In addition to all the other information you have learned about backup strategies, here are a couple of good rules of thumb to remember when making your choice:

▶ If the backup strategy and policy is too complicated (and this holds true for most security issues), it will eventually be disregarded and fall into disuse.

▶ The best scheme is often a combination of strategies; use what works.

Choosing Backup Hardware and Media

Any device that can store data can be used to back it up, but that is like saying that anything with wheels can take you on a cross-country trip. Trying to fit a gigabyte worth of data on a big stack of CD-RWs is an exercise in frustration, and using an expensive automated tape device to save a single copy of an email is a waste of resources.

Many people use what hardware they already have for their backup operations. Many consumer-grade workstations have a CD-RW drive, but they typically do not have the abundant free disk space necessary for performing and storing multiple full backups.

In this section, you learn about some of the most common backup hardware available and how to evaluate its appropriateness for your backup needs. With large storage devices becoming increasingly affordable (160GB IDE drives can be had for around $100) and prices falling on DVD recorders, decisions about backup hardware for the small business and home users have become more interesting.

Removable Storage Media

Choosing the right media for you isn't as easy as it used to be back when floppy drives were the only choice. Today, most machines have CD-ROM drives that can read but not write CDs, which rules them out for backup purposes. Instead, USB hard drives and solid-state "pen" drives have taken over the niche previously held by floppy drives: you can get a 256MB drive for under $10, and you can even get capacities up to 16GB for good prices if you shop around. If your machine supports them (or if you have purchased a card reader), you can also use Compact Flash devices, which come in sizes up to 8GB in the Flash memory versions and 4GB for Hitachi Microdrives. Both USB hard drives and solid-state drives are highly portable. Support for these drives under Ubuntu is very good, accommodating these drives by emulating them as SCSI drives—the system usually sees them as /dev/scd1. Watch for improved support and ever falling prices in the future. A 500GB USB hard drive will cost about $150. The biggest benefits of USB drives are data transfer speed and portability.

FireWire Drives

FireWire (IEEE-1394) hard drives are similar to USB drives; they just use a different interface to your computer. Many digital cameras and portable MP3 players use FireWire. Kernel support is available if you have this hardware. The cost of FireWire devices is now essentially the same as USB because many external drives come with both USB and FireWire standard.

CD-RW and DVD+RW/-RW Drives

Compared to floppy drives and some removable drives, CD-RW drives and their cousins, DVD+RW/-RW drives, can store large amounts of data and are useful for a home or small business. Once very expensive, CD writers and media are at commodity prices today, although automated CD changing machines, necessary for automatically backing up large amounts of data, are still quite costly. A benefit of CD and DVD storage over tape devices is that the archived uncompressed file system can be mounted and its files accessed randomly just like a hard drive (you do this when you create a data CD, refer to Chapter 10, "Multimedia Applications"), making the recovery of individual files easier.

Each CD-RW disk can hold 650MB–700MB of data (the media comes in both capacities at roughly the same cost); larger chunks of data can be split to fit on multiple disks. Some backup programs support this method of storage. Once burned and verified, the shelf life for the media is at least a decade or longer. Prices increase with writing speed, but a serviceable CD-RW drive can be purchased for less than $100.

DVD+RW/-RW is similar to CD-RW, but it is more expensive and can store up to 8GB of uncompressed data per disk. These drives are selling for less than $50.

Network Storage

For network backup storage, remote arrays of hard drives provide one solution to data storage. With the declining cost of mass storage devices and the increasing need for larger storage space, network storage (NAS, or Network Attached Storage) is available and supported in Linux. These are cabinets full of hard drives and their associated controlling circuitry, as well as special software to manage all of it. These NAS systems are connected to the network and act as a huge (and expensive) mass storage device.

More modest and simple network storage can be done on a remote desktop-style machine that has adequate storage space (up to eight 250GB IDE drives is a lot of storage space, easily accomplished with off-the-shelf parts), but then that machine (and the local system administrator) has to deal with all the problems of backing up, preserving, and restoring its own data, doesn't it? Several hardware vendors offer such products in varying sizes.

Tape Drive Backup

Tape drives have been used in the computer industry from the beginning. Tape drive storage has been so prevalent in the industry that the `tar` command (the most commonly used command for archiving) is derived from the words Tape ARchive. Modern tape drives use tape cartridges that can hold 70GB of data (or more in compressed format). Capacities and durability of tapes vary from type to type and range from a few gigabytes to hundreds of gigabytes with commensurate increases in cost for the equipment and media. Autoloading tape-drive systems can accommodate archives that exceed the capacity of the file systems.

TIP

Older tape equipment is often available in the used equipment market and might be useful for smaller operations that have outgrown more limited backup device options.

Tape equipment is well supported in Linux and, when properly maintained, is extremely reliable. The tapes themselves are inexpensive, given their storage capacity and the ability to reuse them. Be aware, however, that tapes do deteriorate over time and, being mechanical, tape drives can and will fail.

> **CAUTION**
>
> Neglecting to clean, align, and maintain tape drives puts your data at risk. The tapes themselves are also susceptible to mechanical wear and degradation. Hardware maintenance is part of a good backup policy. Do not ever forget that it is a question of when—not if—hardware will fail.

Using Backup Software

Because there are thousands of unique situations requiring as many unique backup solutions, it comes as no surprise that Linux offers many backup tools. Along with command-line tools such as tar and dd, Ubuntu also provides a graphical archiving tool, File Roller, that can create and extract files from archives. Finally, Ubuntu provides support for the Amanda backup application—a sophisticated backup application that works well over network connections and can be configured to automatically back up all the computers on your network. Amanda works with drives as well as tapes. The book *Unix Backup and Recovery* by W. Curtis Preston includes a whole chapter on setting up and using Amanda, and this chapter is available online at http://www.backupcentral.com/amanda.html.

> **NOTE**
>
> The software in a backup system must support the hardware, and this relationship can determine which hardware or software choices you make. Many sysadmins choose a particular backup software not because they prefer it to other options, but because it supports the hardware they own.
>
> The price seems right for free backup tools, but consider the software's ease of use and automation when assessing costs. If you must spend several hours implementing, debugging, documenting, and otherwise dealing with overly elaborate automation scripts, the real costs go up.

tar: **The Most Basic Backup Tool**

The tar tool, the bewhiskered old man of archiving utilities, is installed by default. It is an excellent tool for saving entire directories full of files. For example, here is the command used to back up the /etc directory:

```
sudo tar cvf etc.tar /etc
```

Here, the options use tar to create an archive, be verbose in the message output, and use the filename etc.tar as the archive name for the contents of the directory /etc.

Alternatively, if the output of tar is sent to the standard output and redirected to a file, the command appears as follows:

```
sudo tar cv /etc > etc.tar
```

and the result is the same.

All files in the /etc directory will be saved to a file named etc.tar. With an impressive array of options (see the man page), tar is quite flexible and powerful in combination with shell scripts. With the -z option, it can even create and restore gzip compressed archives while the -j option works with bzipped files.

Creating Full and Incremental Backups with tar

If you want to create a full backup,

```
sudo tar cjvf fullbackup.tar.bz2 /
```

will create a bzip2 compressed tarball (the j option) of the entire system.

To perform an incremental backup, you must locate all the files that have been changed since the last backup. For simplicity, assume that you do incremental backups on a daily basis. To locate the files, use the find command:

```
sudo find / -newer name_of_last_backup_file ! -a –type f –print
```

When run alone, find will generate a list of files systemwide and print it to the screen. The ! -a -type eliminates everything but regular files from the list; otherwise, the entire directory would be sent to tar even if the contents was not all changed.

Pipe the output of our find command to tar as follows:

```
sudo find / -newer name_of_last_backup_file ! –type d -print ¦\
 tar czT - backup_file_name_or_device_name
```

Here, the T - option gets the filenames from a buffer (where the - is the shorthand name for the buffer).

NOTE

The tar command can back up to a raw device (one with no file system) as well as a formatted partition. For example,

```
sudo tar cvzf /dev/hdd  /boot  /etc /home
```

backs up those directories to device /dev/hdd (not /dev/hda1, but to the unformatted device itself).

The tar command can also back up over multiple floppy disks:

```
sudo tar czvMf /dev/fd0 /home
```

will back up the contents of /home and spread the file out over multiple floppies, prompting you with this message:

```
Prepare volume #2 for '/dev/fd0' and hit return:
```

Restoring Files from an Archive with tar

The xp option in tar will restore the files from a backup and preserve the file attributes as well, and tar will create any subdirectories it needs. Be careful when using this option because the backups might have been created with either relative or absolute paths. You should use the tvf option with tar to list the files in the archive before extracting them so that you will know where they will be placed.

For example, to restore a tar archive compressed with bzip2,

```
sudo tar xjvf ubuntutest.tar.bz2
```

To list the contents of a tar archive compressed with bzip2,

```
sudo tar tjvf ubuntutest.tar.bz2
drwxrwxr-x paul/paul        0 2003-09-04 18:15:05 ubuntutest/
-rw-rw-r— paul/paul       163 2003-09-03 22:30:49
                           ‹ubuntutest/ubuntu_screenshots.txt
-rw-rw-r— paul/paul       840 2003-09-01 19:27:59
                           ‹ubuntutest/a_guideline.txt
-rw-rw-r— paul/paul      1485 2003-09-01 18:14:23 ubuntutest/style-sheet.txt
-rw-rw-r— paul/paul       931 2003-09-01 19:02:00 ubuntutest/ubuntu_TOC.txt
```

Note that because the pathnames do not start with a backslash, they are relative pathnames and will install in your current working directory. If they were absolute pathnames, they would install exactly where the paths state.

The GNOME File Roller

The GNOME desktop file archiving graphical application File Roller (file-roller) will view, extract, and create archive files using tar, gzip, bzip, compress, zip, rar, lha, and several other compression formats. Note that File Roller is only a front-end to the command-line utilities that actually provide these compression formats; if they are not installed, File Roller cannot use that format.

CAUTION

File Roller will not complain if you select a compression format that is not supported by installed software until after you attempt to create the archive. Install any needed compression utilities first.

File Roller is well-integrated with the GNOME desktop environment to provide convenient drag-and-drop functionality with the Nautilus file manager. To create a new archive, select Archive, New to open the New Archive dialog box and navigate to the directory where you want the archive to be kept. Type your archive's name in the Selection: /root text box at the bottom of the New Archive dialog box. Use the Archive type drop-down menu to select a compression method. Now, drag the files that you want to be included from

Nautilus into the empty space of the File Roller window, and the animated icons will show that files are being included in the new archive. When you are done, a list of files will be shown in the previously blank File Roller window (see Figure 13.1). To save the archive, simply select Archive, Close. Opening an archive is as easy as using the Archive, Open dialog to select the appropriate archive file.

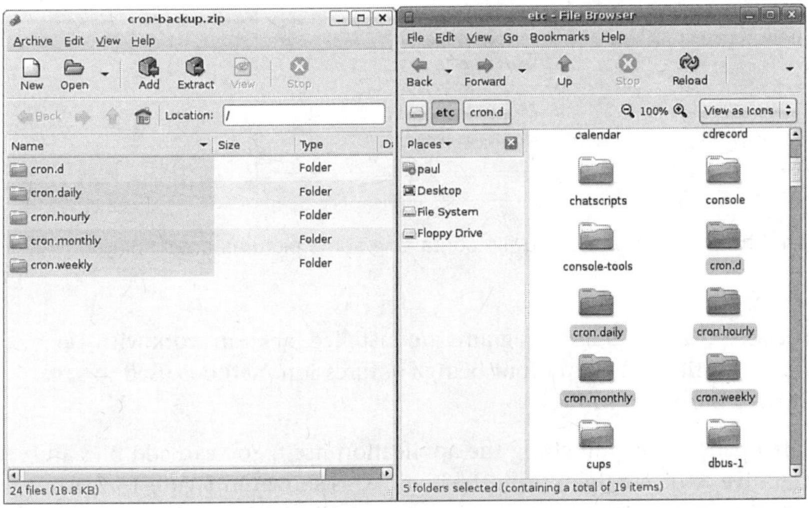

FIGURE 13.1   Drag and drop files to build an archive with the GNOME File Roller.

Ubuntu provides you with the KDE ark and kdat GUI tools for backups; they are installed only if you select the KDE desktop during installation, but you can search through Synaptic to find them. Archiving has traditionally been a function of the system administrator and not seen as a task for the individual user, so no elaborate GUI was believed necessary. Backing up has also been seen as a script driven, automated task in which a GUI is not as useful. Although that's true for sysadmins, home users usually want something a little more attractive and easier to use, and that's the exact gap filled by ark.

The KDE ark Archiving Tool
You launch ark by launching it from the command line. It is integrated with the KDE desktop (like File Roller is with GNOME), so it might be a better choice if you use KDE. This application provides a graphical interface to viewing, creating, adding to, and extracting from archived files as shown in Figure 13.2. Several configuration options are available with ark to ensure its compatibility with MS Windows. You can drag and drop from the KDE desktop or Konqueror file browser to add or extract files, or you can use the ark menus.

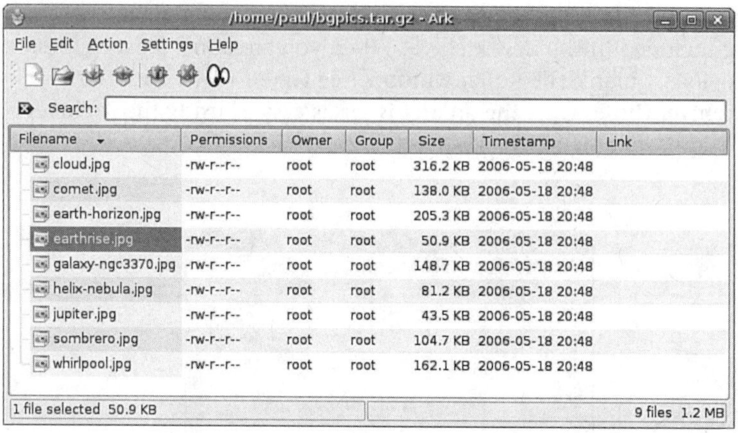

FIGURE 13.2   Here, the contents of a `.zip` file containing some pictures are displayed.

As long as the associated command-line programs are installed, ark can work with tar, gzip, bzip2, zip, and lha files (the latter four being compression methods used to save space by compaction of the archived files).

Existing archives are opened after launching the application itself. You can add files and directories to the archive or delete them from the archive, as shown in Figure 13.3. After opening the archive, you can extract all of its contents or individual files. You can also perform searches using patterns (all *.jpg files, for example) to select files.

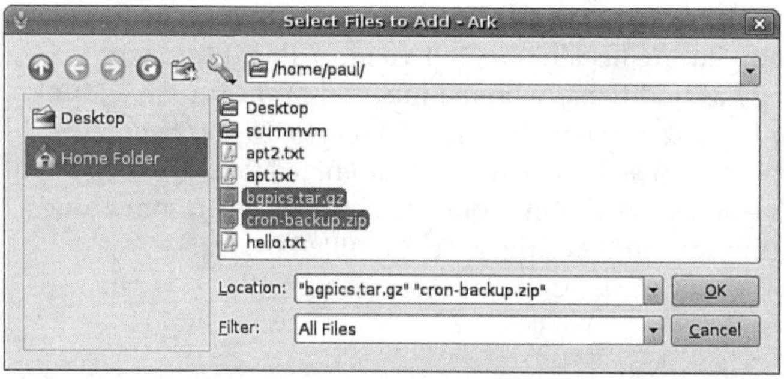

FIGURE 13.3   Adding files to ark is a matter of selecting them in the usual Open File dialog. Here, several files are being selected to add to the new archive.

Choosing New from the File menu creates new archives. You then type the name of the archive, providing the appropriate extension (.tar, .gz, and so on), and then proceed to add files and directories as you desire.

Using the Amanda Backup Application

Provided with Ubuntu, Amanda is a powerful, network backup application created by the University of Maryland at College Park. Amanda is a robust backup and restore application best suited to unattended backups with an autoloading tape drive of adequate capacity. It benefits from good user support and documentation.

Amanda's features include compression and encryption. It is intended for use with high-capacity tape drives, floptical, CD-R, and CD-RW devices.

Amanda uses GNU tar and dump; it is intended for unattended, automated tape backups, and is not well-suited for interactive or ad hoc backups. The support for tape devices in Amanda is robust, and file restoration is relatively simple. Although Amanda does not support older Macintosh clients, it will use Samba to back up Microsoft Windows clients, as well as any UNIX client that can use GNU tools (which includes Mac OS X). Because Amanda runs on top of standard GNU tools, file restoration can be made using those tools on a recovery disk even if the Amanda server is not available. File compression can be done on either the client or server, thus lightening the computational load on less powerful machines that need backing up.

> **CAUTION**
>
> Amanda does not support dump images larger than a single tape and requires a new tape for each run. If you forget to change a tape, Amanda continues to attempt backups until you insert a new tape, but those backups will not capture the data as you intended them to. Do not use too small a tape or forget to change a tape, or you will not be happy with the results.

There is no GUI interface for Amanda. Configuration is done in the time-honored UNIX tradition of editing text configuration files located in /etc/amanda. The default installation in Ubuntu includes a sample cron file because it is expected that you will be using cron to run Amanda regularly. The client utilities are installed with the package am-utils; the Amanda server must be obtained from the Amanda website. As far as backup schemes are concerned, Amanda calculates an optimal scheme on-the-fly and schedules it accordingly. It can be forced to adhere to a traditional scheme, but other tools are possibly better suited for that job.

The man page for Amanda (the client is amdump) is well written and useful, explaining both the configuration of Amanda as well as detailing the several programs that actually make up Amanda. The configuration files found in /etc/amanda are well commented; they provide a number of examples to assist you in configuration.

The program's home page is http://www.amanda.org. There, you will find information on subscribing to the mail list, as well as links to Amanda-related projects and a FAQ.

Alternative Backup Software

Commercial and other freeware backup products do exist; BRU and Veritas are good examples of effective commercial backup products. Here are some useful free software backup tools that are not installed with Ubuntu:

- ▶ flexbackup—This backup tool is a large file of Perl scripts that makes dump and restore easier to use. flexbackup's command syntax can be accessed by using the command with the -help argument. It also can use afio, cpio, and tar to create and restore archives locally or over a network using rsh or ssh if security is a concern. Its home page is http://www.flexbackup.org/.

- ▶ afio—This tool creates cpio-formatted archives, but handles input data corruption better than cpio (which does not handle data input corruption very well at all). It supports multi-volume archives during interactive operation and can make compressed archives. If you feel the need to use cpio, you might want to check out afio at http://freshmeat.net/projects/afio/.

- ▶ cdbackup—Designed for the home or small office user, cdbackup will work with any backup and will restore software that can read from stdin, write to stdout, and can handle linear devices such as tape drives. It makes it easier to use CD-Rs as the storage medium. Similar applications are available elsewhere as well; the home page for this application is at http://www.muempf.de/index.html.

Many other alternative backup tools exist, but covering all of them is beyond the scope of this book. Two good places to look for free backup software are Freshmeat (http://www.freshmeat.net) and Google (http://www.google.com/linux).

Copying Files

Often, when you have only a few files that you need to protect from loss or corruption, it might make better sense to simply copy the individual files to another storage medium rather than to create an archive of them. You can use the tar, cp, rsync, or even the cpio commands to do this, as well as a handy file management tool known as mc. Using tar is the traditional choice because older versions of cp did not handle symbolic links and permissions well at times, causing those attributes (characteristics of the file) to be lost; tar handled those file attributes in a better manner. cp has been improved to fix those problems, but tar is still more widely used. rsync has recently been added to Ubuntu and is an excellent choice for mirroring sets of files, especially when done over a network.

To illustrate how to use file copying as a backup technique, the examples here show how to copy (not archive) a directory tree. This tree includes symbolic links and files that have special file permissions we need to keep intact.

Copying Files Using `tar`

One choice for copying files into another location would be to use the `tar` command where you would create a `tar` file that would be piped to tar to be uncompressed in the new location. To accomplish this, first change to the source directory. Then, the entire command resembles

```
sudo tar cvf - files ¦ (cd target_directory ; tar xpf -)
```

where *files* are the filenames you want to include; use * to include the entire current directory.

Here is how the command shown works: You have already changed to the source directory and executed tar with the `cvf` - arguments that tell tar to

- ▶ c—Create an archive.
- ▶ v—Verbose; lists the files processed so we can see that it is working.
- ▶ f—The filename of the archive will be what follows. (In this case, it is -.)
- ▶ - —A buffer; a place to hold our data temporarily.

The following `tar` commands can be useful for creating file copies for backup purposes:

- ▶ l—Stay in the local file system (so you do not include remote volumes).
- ▶ `atime-preserve`—Do not change access times on files, even though you are accessing them now, to preserve the old access information for archival purposes.

The contents of the `tar` file (held for us temporarily in the buffer, which is named -) are then piped to the second expression, which will extract the files to the target directory. In shell programming (refer to Chapter 15, "Automating Tasks"), enclosing an expression in parentheses causes it to operate in a subshell and be executed first.

First we change to the target directory, and then

- ▶ x—Extract files from a `tar` archive.
- ▶ p—Preserve permissions.
- ▶ f—The filename will be -, the temporary buffer that holds the `tar`ed files.

Compressing, Encrypting, and Sending `tar` Streams

The file copy techniques using the tar command in the previous section can also be used to quickly and securely copy a directory structure across a LAN or the Internet (using the ssh command). One way to make use of these techniques is to use the following command line to first compress the contents of a designated directory, and then decompress the compressed and encrypted archive stream into a designated directory on a remote host:

```
$ tar cvzf - data_folder ¦ ssh remote_host '( cd ~/mybackup_dir; tar xvzf - )'
```

The tar command is used to create, list, and compress the files in the directory named data_folder. The output is piped through the ssh (secure shell) command and sent to the remote computer named *remote_host*. On the remote computer, the stream is then extracted and saved in the directory named */mybackup_dir*. You will be prompted for a password in order to send the stream.

Copying Files Using cp

To copy files, we could use the cp command. The general format of the command when used for simple copying is

```
$ cp -a source_directory target_directory
```

The -a argument is the same as giving -dpR, which would be

- ▸ -d—Dereferences symbolic links (never follows symbolic links) and copies the files that they point to instead of copying the links.

- ▸ -p—Preserves all file attributes if possible. (File ownership might interfere.)

- ▸ -R—Copies directories recursively.

The cp command can also be used to quickly replicate directories and retain permissions by using the -avR command-line options. Using these options preserves file and directory permissions, gives verbose output, and recursively copies and re-creates subdirectories. A log of the backup can also be created during the backup by redirecting the standard output like this:

```
sudo cp -avR directory_to_backup destination_vol_or_dir 1>/root/backup_log.txt
```

or

```
sudo cp -avR ubuntu /test2 1>/root/backup_log.txt
```

This example makes an exact copy of the directory named /ubuntu on the volume named /test2, and saves a backup report named backup_log.txt under /root.

Copying Files Using mc

The Midnight Commander (available in the Universe repository, under the package "mc"; see Chapter 7, "Managing Software" for how to enable the Universe and Multiverse repositories) is a command-line file manager that is useful for copying, moving, and archiving files and directories. The Midnight Commander has a look and feel similar to the Norton Commander of DOS fame. By executing mc at a shell prompt, a dual-pane view of the files is displayed. It contains drop-down menu choices and function keys to manipulate files. It also uses its own virtual file system, enabling it to mount FTP directories and display the contents of tar files, gzipped tar files (.tar.gz or .tgz), bzip files, DEB files, and RPM files, as well as extract individual files from them. As if that was not enough, mc contains a File Undelete virtual file system for ext2/3 partitions. By using cd to "change directories" to an FTP server's URL, you can transfer files using the FTP protocol. The default font chosen for Ubuntu makes the display of mc ugly when used in a tty console (as opposed to an xterm), but does not affect its performance.

Figure 13.4 shows a shot of the default dual-panel display. Pressing the F9 key drops down the menu, and pressing F1 displays the Help file. A "feature" in the default GNOME terminal intercepts the F10 key used to exit mc, so use F9 instead to access the menu item to quit, or simply click on the menu bar at the bottom with your mouse. The configuration files are well documented, and it would appear easy to extend the functionality of mc for your system if you understand shell scripting and regular expressions. It is an excellent choice for file management on servers not running X.

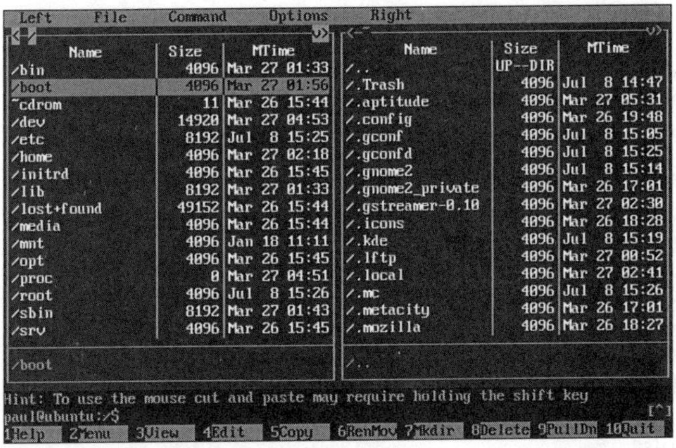

FIGURE 13.4   The Midnight Commander is a highly versatile file tool. If it does not display properly on your screen, launch it with the -a argument to force ASCII mode.

System Rescue

There will come a time when you need to engage in system rescue efforts. This need arises when the system will not even start Linux so that you can recover any files. This problem is most frequently associated with the boot loader program or partition table, but it could be that critical system files have been inadvertently deleted or corrupted. If you have been making backups properly, these kinds of system failures are easily, though not quickly, recoverable through a full restore. Still, valuable current data might not have been backed up since the last scheduled backup, and the backup archives are found to be corrupt, incomplete, or missing. A full restore also takes time you might not have. If the problem causing the system failure is simply a damaged boot loader, a damaged partition table, a missing library, or misconfiguration, a quick fix can get the system up and running and the data can then be easily retrieved.

In this section, we will first examine a way to back up and restore the boot loader itself or, having failed to do that, restore it by hand. Then we will look at a few alternatives to booting the damaged system so that we can inspect it, fix it, or retrieve data from it.

The Ubuntu Rescue Disc

Ubuntu provides a rescue disc hidden in the installation DVD. To use it, insert the disc and reboot the computer, booting from the DVD just as you did when you installed Ubuntu originally.

If necessary, you can perform all the operations discussed in this section from rescue mode.

Backing Up and Restoring the Master Boot Record

The Master Boot Record (MBR) is the first 512 bytes of a hard disk. It contains the boot loader code in the first 446 bytes and the partition table in the next 64 bytes; the last two bytes identify that sector as the MBR. The MBR can become corrupted, so it makes sense to back it up.

This example uses the dd command as root to back up the entire MBR. If the boot loader code changes from the time you make this image and restore the old code, the system will not boot when you restore it all; it is easy enough to keep a boot floppy handy and then re-run LILO if that is what you are using.

To copy the entire MBR to a file, use this:

```
sudo dd if=/dev/hda of=/tmp/hdambr bs=512 count=1
```

To restore the entire MBR, use this:

```
sudo dd if=/tmp/hdambr of=/dev/hda bs=512 count=1
```

To restore only the partition table, skipping the boot loader code, use this:

```
sudo dd if=/tmp/hdambr of=/dev/hda bs=1 skip=446 count=66
```

Of course, it would be prudent to move the copy of the MBR to a floppy or other appropriate storage device. (The file is only 512 bytes in size.) You will need to be able to run dd on the system in order to restore it (which means that you will be using the Ubuntu rescue disc as described later, or any equivalent to it).

Booting the System from a Generic Boot Floppy

If you failed to make a boot floppy or cannot locate the one you did make, any Linux boot floppy (a slightly older version or one borrowed from a friend) can be pressed into service as long as it has a reasonably similar kernel version. (The major and minor numbers match—for example, 2.6.5 would likely work with any 2.6 system, but not with a 2.4 system.) You would boot your system by manually specifying the root and boot partitions as described previously. Although you are almost guaranteed to get some error messages, you might at least be able to get a base system running enough to replace files and recover the system.

TIP

In both preceding cases, it is assumed that you do not need any special file system or device drivers to access the root partition. If you do, add the `initrd=` argument to the LILO line pointing to the appropriate initrd file on your system. If you do not know the exact name of the `initrd` file, you are out of luck with LILO, so learn to use a GRUB boot floppy as well.

Using a GRUB Boot Floppy

The GRand Unified Boot loader (GRUB) can attempt to boot a system from a floppy without a viable custom-made boot floppy. The image for the floppy can be downloaded from ftp://alpha.gnu.org/gnu/grub/grub-0.95-i386-pc.ext2fs and copied to a floppy using dd. (`rawrite.exe` would be used on a Microsoft system.) Or, if you have a boot floppy from an existing system using GRUB, that one will work as well.

GRUB has its own command shell, file system drivers, and search function (much like command completion in the bash shell). It is possible to boot using the GRUB floppy, examine the drive partitions, and search for the kernel and initrd image as well, using them to boot the system. Worthy of a chapter all its own, the GRUB documentation is extensive: In addition to `info grub` (the `info` system is similar to the `man` system for documentation), the GRUB documents contain a tutorial worth reading. The GRUB boot loader is shown in Figure 13.5.

```
 GRUB  version 0.5.96.1  (637K lower / 64512K upper memory)

┌────────────────────────────────────────────────────────────────┐
│ GNU/Hurd (sd0s1 multi-user)                                      │
│ GNU/Hurd (sd0s1 single-user)                                     │
│ GNU/Hurd (hd0s1 multi-user)                                      │
│ GNU/Hurd (hd0s1 single-user)                                     │
│ Install GRUB from hard disk into MBR                             │
│ GNU/Linux (hd0s2)                                                │
│ DOS, Windows, or OS/2 (hd0s3)                                    │
│                                                                  │
│                                                                  │
└────────────────────────────────────────────────────────────────┘

     Use the ↑ and ↓ keys to select which entry is highlighted.
     Press enter to boot the selected OS, 'e' to edit the
     commands before booting, or 'c' for a command-line.
```

FIGURE 13.5   The GRUB boot loader gives you incredible flexibility in booting even unfamiliar systems.

Using the Recovery Facility

As your computer starts, Ubuntu will show a message prompting you to press Escape to see the GRUB menu. If you do that, you'll see a list of bootable operating systems, which will include Recovery Mode options for your Ubuntu install. If you boot into recovery mode, you'll get automatic root access to your machine where can fix your problems safely.

Alternatively, you can insert your Ubuntu installation disc and use the recovery mode from there. Keep in mind that these recovery modes are designed to be text-only systems for serious system recovery purposes; don't expect them to be hand-held, and don't expect much in the way of ease of use!

Relevant Ubuntu Commands

The following commands are useful in performing backup, recovery, and restore operations in Ubuntu:

▶ amdump—Amanda is a network-based backup system, consisting of 18 separate commands, for use with Linux.

▶ ark—A KDE desktop GUI archiving utility.

▶ cp—The copy command.

▶ scp—The secure shell copy command.

▶ cpio—A data archive utility.

▶ dd—A data copy and conversion utility.

▶ gzip—The GNU compression utility.

▶ tar—The GNU tape archive utility.

Reference

▶ http://www.tldp.org/LDP/solrhe/Securing-Optimizing-Linux-RH-Edition-v1.3/whywhen.html—A thorough discussion with examples of using dump and restore for backups.

▶ http://en.tldp.org/LDP/solrhe/Securing-Optimizing-Linux-RH-Edition-v1.3/chap29sec306.html—Making automatic backups with tar using cron.

▶ http://kmself.home.netcom.com/Linux/FAQs/backups.html—The Linux Backups mini FAQ contains some useful, although brief, comments on backup media, compression, encryption, and security.

▶ http://www.tldp.org/—The Linux Documentation Project offers several useful HOWTO documents that discuss backups and disk recovery.

▶ http://www.ibiblio.org/pub/Linux/docs/HOWTO/other-formats/html_single/ Bootdisk-HOWTO.html#AEN1483—Here is a list of LILO Boot error codes to help you debug a cranky system that will not boot.

▶ http://www.ibiblio.org/pub/Linux/docs/HOWTO/other-formats/html_single/Ftape-HOWTO.html—This is a HOWTO for the floppy tape device driver.

▶ http://www.linux-usb.org/USB-guide/x498.html—The USB Guide for mass storage devices. If you have a USB device and need to know if it is supported, check here.

▶ http://www.backupcentral.com/amanda.html—This is the Amanda chapter of *Unix Backup and Recovery* (written by John R. Jackson and published by O'Reilly and Associates). The chapter is available online and covers every aspect of using Amanda. The site features a handy search tool for the chapter.

▶ http://twiki.org/cgi-bin/view/Wikilearn/RsyncingALargeFileBeginner—Rsyncing a large file to "repair" a local ISO image that does not pass the md5sum check.

▶ http://www.lycoris.org/sections.php?op=viewarticle&artid=8—Lycoris ISO rsync mini HOWTO. A step-by-step tutorial on using rsync to sync files.

▶ http://www.mikerubel.org/computers/rsync_snapshots/—Automated snapshot-style backups using rsync.

▶ http://www.mondorescue.org/—Mondo Rescue is a bare-metal backup/rescue tool independent of Ubuntu, using CD, DVD, tape, or NFS; it can produce bootable CDs to restore the system.

▶ http://www.ccp14.ac.uk/ccp14admin/linux-server/mondorescue/dvd_mondo.html— A HOWTO for using MondoRescue to back up on a DVD.

▶ http://www.linuxorbit.com/modules.php?op=modload&name=Sections&file=index &req=viewarticle&artid=222&page=1—A HOWTO using split and mkisofs to manually back up large archives to CD.

13

CHAPTER 14

Networking

One of the benefits of open source technology in general and Linux is particular is that it can be used effortlessly across several different networking environments as well as the Internet. With strong support for the standard internet protocol TCP/IP, Linux can also talk to all of the UNIX flavors, including Mac OS X, Windows (with the help of Samba), NetWare (IPX) and even older protocols such as DECNET and Banyan Vines. Many organizations use Linux as an Internet gateway, allowing many different clients to access the Internet through Linux, as well as communicate via email and instant messaging. Most important is its built-in support for IPv6, which should start to see a significant uptake through 2009. It's safe to say that whatever networking protocol you'll come across, Linux will be able to work with it in some way.

This chapter covers network and Internet connectivity, as most networks invariably end up connected to the Internet in some shape or form. You will learn about how to get the basics right, including configuration and management of network cards (*NICs*) and other network services with Ubuntu. You will also find out how to manage network services from the command line—again an important lesson in case you are ever confined to a command prompt. We will also look at connectivity options, both for inbound and outbound network traffic and the importance of PPP (*Point to Point Protocol*). Also included is an overview of graphical network management clients for Ubuntu, which are becoming more and more popular.

Laying the Foundation: The `localhost` Interface

The first thing that needs to be in place before you can successfully connect to a network or even to the Internet is a `localhost` interface, sometimes also called a *loopback interface*, but more commonly referenced as `lo`. The TCP/IP protocol (see "Networking with TCP/IP" later on in this chapter) uses this interface to assign an IP address to your computer and is needed for Ubuntu to establish a PPP interface.

Checking for the Availability of the Loopback Interface

You should not normally have to manually create a loopback interface as Ubuntu creates one automatically for you during installation. To check that one is set up, you can use the `ifconfig` command to show something similar to this:

```
$ ifconfig
lo        Link encap:Local Loopback
          inet addr:127.0.0.1  Mask:255.0.0.0
          inet6 addr: ::1/128 Scope:Host
          UP LOOPBACK RUNNING  MTU:16436  Metric:1
          RX packets:13 errors:0 dropped:0 overruns:0 frame:0
          TX packets:13 errors:0 dropped:0 overruns:0 carrier:0
          collisions:0 txqueuelen:0
          RX bytes:832 (832.0 b)  TX bytes:832 (832.0 b)
```

What you see in this example is evidence that the loopback interface is present and active. The `inet addr` is the IP number assigned to the `localhost`, typically `127.0.0.1` along with the broadcast mask of `255.255.255.0` and that there has been little activity on this interface (`RX` = receive and `TX` = transmit). If your output does not look like the one above, you must hand-configure the `localhost` interface after you finish the rest of this section. You can also see the Ipv6 address that is assigned to `lo`, which is `::1/128`, referred to as the `inet6 addr`.

Configuring the Loopback Interface Manually

The `localhost` interface's IP address is specified in a text configuration file that is used by Ubuntu to keep record of various network wide IP addresses. The file is called `/etc/hosts` and usually exists on a system, even if it is empty. The file is used by the Linux kernel and other networking tools to enable them to access local IP addresses and hostnames. If you have not configured any other networking interfaces then you may find that the file looks something like this:

```
127.0.0.1      localhost
127.0.0.1      hardy-laptop
# The following lines are desirable for IPv6 capable hosts

::1     ip6-localhost ip6-loopback
```

```
fe00::0 ip6-localnet
```

```
ff00::0 ip6-mcastprefix
```

```
ff02::1 ip6-allnodes
```

```
ff02::2 ip6-allrouters
```

The first line defines the special localhost interface and assigns it an IP address of 127.0.0.1. You might hear or read about terms such as *localhost*, *loopback*, and *dummy interface*; all these terms refer to the use of the IP address *127.0.0.1*. The term *loopback interface* indicates that to Linux networking drivers, it looks as though the machine is talking to a network that consists of only one machine; the kernel sends network traffic to and from itself on the same computer. *Dummy interface* indicates that the interface doesn't really exist as far as the outside world is concerned; it exists only for the local machine.

Each networked Ubuntu machine on a LAN will use this same IP address for its localhost. If for some reason a Ubuntu computer does not have this interface, edit the /etc/hosts file to add the localhost entry, and then use the ifconfig and route commands using your sudo permissions to create the interface like this:

```
$ sudo /sbin/ifconfig lo 127.0.0.1
$ sudo /sbin/route add 127.0.0.1 lo
```

These commands will create the localhost interface in memory (all interfaces, such as eth0 or ppp0, are created in memory when using Linux), and then add the IP address 127.0.0.1 to an internal (in-memory) table so that the Linux kernel's networking code can keep track of routes to different addresses.

Use the ifconfig command as shown previously to test the interface.

You should now be able to use ping to check that the interface is responding properly like this (using either localhost or its IP address):

```
$ ping -c 3 localhost
PING localhost (127.0.0.1) 56(84) bytes of data.
64 bytes from localhost (127.0.0.1): icmp_seq=1 ttl=64 time=0.036 ms
64 bytes from localhost (127.0.0.1): icmp_seq=2 ttl=64 time=0.028 ms
64 bytes from localhost (127.0.0.1): icmp_seq=3 ttl=64 time=0.028 ms

--- localhost ping statistics ---
3 packets transmitted, 3 received, 0% packet loss, time 1999ms
rtt min/avg/max/mdev = 0.028/0.030/0.036/0.007 ms
```

The -c option is used to set the number of pings, and the command, if successful (as it was previously), returns information regarding the round-trip speed of sending a test packet to the specified host.

14

The second line in the /etc/hosts file uses the actual hostname of the computer and assigns it to a similar private IP address that is unique to that computer. In the earlier code example, you can see that 127.0.1.1 is assigned to hardy-laptop, which is the computer on which that hosts file resides.

The remaining lines are used for IPv6 and can be ignored with the exception of the line that begins ::1—this is used to define the localhost connection for IPv6, which you can text with the ping6 command at the terminal like so:

```
$ ping6 ::1
PING ::1(::1) 56 data bytes

64 bytes from ::1: icmp_seq=1 ttl=64 time=0.037 ms

64 bytes from ::1: icmp_seq=2 ttl=64 time=0.045 ms

64 bytes from ::1: icmp_seq=3 ttl=64 time=0.048 ms

--- ::1 ping statistics ---

3 packets transmitted, 3 received, 0% packet loss, time 1998ms

rtt min/avg/max/mdev = 0.037/0.043/0.048/0.007 ms
```

Networking with TCP/IP

The basic building block for any network based on Unix hosts is the Transport Control Protocol/Internet Protocol (*TCP/IP*) suite of three protocols. The suite consists of the Internet Protocol (*IP*), Transport Control Protocol (*TCP*), and Universal Datagram Protocol (*UDP*). IP is the base protocol. The TCP/IP suite is *packet*-based, which means that data is broken into little chunks on the transmit end for transmission to the receiving end. Breaking data up into manageable packets allows for faster and more accurate transfers. In TCP/IP, all data travels via IP packets, which is why addresses are referred to as IP addresses. It is the lowest level of the suite.

TCP is also a connection-based protocol. Before data is transmitted between two machines, a connection is established between them. When a connection is made, a stream of data is sent to the IP to be broken into the packets that are then transmitted. At the receiving end, the packets are put back in order and sent to the proper application port. TCP/IP forms the basis of the Internet; without it the Internet would be a very different place indeed, if it even existed!

On the other hand, UDP is a connectionless protocol. Applications using this protocol just choose their destination and start sending. UDP is normally used for small amounts of data or on fast and reliable networks. If you are interested in the internals of TCP/IP, see the "Reference" section at the end of this chapter for places to look for more information.

Ubuntu and Networking

Chances are that your network card was configured during the installation of Ubuntu. You can however, use the ifconfig command at the shell prompt or Ubuntu's graphical network configuration tools, such as network-admin, to edit your system's network device information or to add or remove network devices on your system. Hundreds of networking commands and utilities are included with Ubuntu—far too many to cover in this chapter and more than enough for coverage in two or three volumes.

Nearly all ethernet cards can be used with Linux, along with many PCMCIA wired and wireless network cards. The great news is that many USB wireless networking devices also work just fine with Linux, and more will be supported with upcoming versions of the Linux kernel. Check the Linux USB Project at http://www.linux-usb.org/ for the latest developments or to verify support for your device.

After reading this chapter, you might want to learn more about other graphical network clients for use with Linux. The GNOME ethereal client, for example, can be used to monitor all traffic on your LAN or specific types of traffic. Another client, NmapFE, can be used to scan a specific host for open ports and other running services.

TCP/IP Addressing

To understand networking with Linux, you need to know the basics of TCP/IP addressing. Internet IP addresses (also known as *public* IP addresses) are different from those used internally on a local area network, or *LAN*. Internet IP addresses are assigned (for the United States and some other hosts) by the American Registry for Internet Numbers, available at http://www.arin.net/. Entities that need an Internet address apply to this agency to be assigned an address. The agency assigns Internet service providers (*ISPs*) one or more blocks of IP addresses, which the ISPs can then assign to their subscribers.

You will quickly recognize the current form of TCP/IP addressing, known as IPv4 (IP version 4). In this method, a TCP/IP address is expressed of a series of four decimal numbers—a 32-bit value expressed in a format known as dotted decimal format, such as 192.168.0.1. Each set of numbers is known as an *octet* (eight ones and zeros, such as 10000000 to represent 128) and ranges from zero to 255.

The first octet usually determines what *class* the network belongs to. There are three classes of networks. The classes are

- ▶ **Class A**—Consists of networks with the first octet ranging from 1 to 126. There are only 126 Class A networks—each composed of up to 16,777,214 hosts. (If you are doing the math, there are potentially 16,777,216 addresses, but no host portion of an address can be all zeros or 255s.) The "10." network is reserved for local network use, and the "127." network is reserved for the loopback address of 127.0.0.1. Loopback addressing is used by TCP/IP to enable Linux network-related client and server programs to communicate on the same host. This address will not appear and is not accessible on your LAN.

NOTE

Notice that zero is not included in Class A. The zero address is used for network-to-network broadcasts. Also, note that there are two other classes of networks, Classes D and E. Class D networks are reserved for multicast addresses and not for use by network hosts. Class E addresses are deemed experimental, and thus are not open for public addressing.

- ▶ **Class B**—Consists of networks defined by the first two octets with the first ranging from 128 to 191. The "128." network is also reserved for local network use. There are 16,382 Class B networks—each with 65,534 possible hosts.

- ▶ **Class C**—Consists of a network defined by the first three octets with the first ranging from 192 to 223. The "192." network is another that is reserved for local network use. There are a possible 2,097,150 Class C networks of up to 254 hosts each.

No host portion of an IP address can be all zeros or 255s. These addresses are reserved for broadcast addresses. IP addresses with all zeros in the host portion are reserved for network-to-network broadcast addresses. IP addresses with all 255s in the host portion are reserved for local network broadcasts. Broadcast messages are not typically seen by users.

These classes are the standard, but a *netmask* also determines what class your network is in. The netmask determines what part of an IP address represents the network and what part represents the host. Common netmasks for the different classes are

- ▶ **Class A**—255.0.0.0
- ▶ **Class B**—255.255.0.0
- ▶ **Class C**—255.255.255.0

Because of the allocation of IP addresses for Internet hosts, it is now impossible to get a Class A network. It is also nearly impossible to get a Class B network (all the addresses have been given out, but some companies are said to be willing to sell theirs), and Class C network availability is dropping rapidly with the continued growth of Internet use worldwide. See the following sidebar.

Limits of Current IP Addressing

The current IPv4 address scheme is based on 32-bit numbering and limits the number of available IP addresses to about 4.1 billion. Many companies and organizations (particularly in the United States) were assigned very large blocks of IP addresses in the early stages of the growth of the Internet, which has left a shortage of "open" addresses. Even with careful allocation of Internet-connected host IP addresses and the use of *network address translation* (*NAT*) to provide communication to and from machines behind an Internet-connected computer, the Internet might run out of available addresses.

To solve this problem, a newer scheme named IPv6 (IP version 6) is being implemented. It uses a much larger addressing solution based on 128-bit addresses, with enough room to include much more information about a specific host or device, such as global positioning server (GPS) or serial numbering. Although the specific details about the entire contents of the an IPv6 address have yet to be finalized, all Internet-related organizations appear to agree that something must be done to provide more addresses. According to Vint Cerf, one of the primary developers of the TCP/IP protocol, "There will be nearly 2.5 billion devices on the Internet by 2006, and by 2010 half the world's population will have access to the Internet."

You can get a good overview of the differences between IPv4 and IPv6 policies regarding IP address assignments, and the registration process of obtaining IP addresses, by browsing to http://www.arin.net/library/index.html. Read the Linux IPv6 HOWTO by browsing to http://tldp.org/HOWTO/Linux+IPv6-HOWTO/.

Ubuntu supports the use of IPv6 and includes a number of networking tools conforming to IPv6 addressing.

Migration to IPv6 is slow in coming, however, because the majority of computer operating systems, software, hardware, firmware, and users are still in the IPv4 mindset. Supporting IPv6 will require rewrites to many networking utilities, portions of operating systems currently in use, and firmware in routing and firewall hardware.

Using IP Masquerading in Ubuntu

Three blocks of IP addresses are reserved for use on internal networks and hosts not directly connected to the Internet. The address ranges are from 10.0.0.0 to 10.255.255.255, or 1 Class A network; from 172.16.0.0 to 172.31.255.255, or 16 Class B networks; and from 192.168.0.0 to 192.168.255.255, or 256 Class C networks. Use these IP addresses when building a LAN for your business or home. Which class you choose can depend on the number of hosts on your network.

Internet access for your internal network can be provided by a PC running Ubuntu or other broadband or dial-up router. The host or device is connected to the Internet and is used as an Internet gateway to forward information to and from your LAN. The host should also be used as a firewall to protect your network from malicious data and users while functioning as an Internet gateway.

A PC used in this fashion typically has at least two network interfaces. One is connected to the Internet with the other connected to the computers on the LAN (via a hub or switch). Some broadband devices also incorporate four or more switching network interfaces. Data is then passed between the LAN and the Internet using *network address translation*, or *NAT*, better known in Linux circles as *IP masquerading*.

NOTE

Do not rely on a single point of protection for your LAN, especially if you use wireless networking, provide dial-in services, or allow mobile (laptop or PDA) users internal or external access to your network. Companies, institutions, and individuals relying on a "moat mentality" have often discovered to their dismay that such an approach to security is easily breached. Make sure that your network operation is accompanied by a security policy that stresses multiple levels of secure access, with protection built into every server and workstation—something easily accomplished when using Linux.

Ports

Most servers on your network have more than one task. For example, web servers have to serve both standard and secure pages. You might also be running an FTP server on the same host. For this reason, applications are provided *ports* to use to make "direct" connections for specific software services. These ports help TCP/IP distinguish services so that data can get to the correct application. If you check the file /etc/services, you will see the common ports and their usage. For example, for FTP, HTTP, and Post Office Protocol (email retrieval server), you will see

```
ftp        21/tcp
http       80/tcp      http         # WorldWideWeb HTTP
pop3       110/tcp     pop-3          # POP version 3
```

The ports defined in /etc/services in this example are 21 for FTP, 80 for HTTP, and 110 for POP3. Other common port assignments are 25 for *simple mail transport protocol (SMTP)* and 22 for *secure shell (SSH)* remote login. Note that these ports are not set in stone, and you can set up your server to respond to different ports. For example, although port 22 is listed in /etc/services as a common default for SSH, the sshd server can be configured to listen on a different port by editing its configuration file /etc/ssh/sshd_config. The default setting (commented out with a pound sign) looks like this:

```
#Port 22
```

Edit the entry to use a different port, making sure to select an unused port number, such as

```
Port 2224
```

Save your changes, and then restart the sshd server. (Refer to Chapter 11, "Automating Tasks," to see how to restart a service.) Remote users must now access the host through port 2224, which can be done using ssh's -p (port) option like so:

```
$ ssh -p 2224 remote_host_name_or_IP
```

Network Organization

Properly organizing your network addressing process grows more difficult as the size of your network grows. Setting up network addressing for a Class C network with fewer than 254 devices is simple. Setting up addressing for a large, worldwide company with a Class A network and many different users can be extremely complex. If your company has fewer than 254 *hosts* (meaning any device that requires an IP address, including computers, printers, routers, switches, and other devices) and all your workgroups can share information, a single Class C network will be sufficient.

Subnetting

Within Class A and B networks, there can be separate networks called *subnets*. Subnets are considered part of the host portion of an address for network class definitions. For example, in the 128. Class B network, you can have one computer with an address of 128.10.10.10 and another with an address of 128.10.200.20; these computers are on the same network (128.10.), but they have different subnets (128.10.10. and 128.10.200.). Because of this, communication between the two computers requires either a router or a switch. Subnets can be helpful for separating workgroups within your company.

Often subnets can be used to separate workgroups that have no real need to interact with or to shield from other groups' information passing among members of a specific workgroup. For example, if your company is large enough to have its own HR department and payroll section, you could put those departments' hosts on their own subnet and use your router configuration to limit the hosts that can connect to this subnet. This configuration prevents networked workers who are not members of the designated departments from being able to view some of the confidential information the HR and payroll personnel work with.

Subnet use also enables your network to grow beyond 254 hosts and share IP addresses. With proper routing configuration, users might not even know they are on a different subnet from their co-workers. Another common use for subnetting is with networks that cover a wide geographic area. It is not practical for a company with offices in Chicago and London to have both offices on the same subnet, so using a separate subnet for each office is the best solution.

Subnet Masks

Subnet masks are used by TCP/IP to show which part of an IP address is the network portion and which part is the host. Subnet masks are usually referred to as *netmasks*. For a pure Class A network, the netmask would be 255.0.0.0; for a Class B network, the netmask would be 255.255.0.0; and for a Class C network, the netmask would be 255.255.255.0. Netmasks can also be used to deviate from the standard classes.

By using customized netmasks, you can subnet your network to fit your needs. For example, your network has a single Class C address. You have a need to subnet your network. Although this is not possible with a normal Class C subnet mask, you can change the mask to break your network into subnets. By changing the last octet to a number greater than zero, you can break the network into as many subnets as you need.

For more information on how to create customized subnet masks, see Day 6, "The Art of Subnet Masking," in *Sams Teach Yourself TCP/IP Network Administration in 21 Days*. That chapter goes into great detail on how to create custom netmasks and explains how to create an addressing cheat sheet for hosts on each subnet. You can also browse to the Linux Network Administrator's Guide and read about how to create subnets at http://www.tldp.org/LDP/nag2/index.html.

Broadcast, Unicast, and Multicast Addressing

Information can get to systems through three types of addresses: unicast, multicast, and broadcast. Each type of address is used according to the purpose of the information being sent, as explained here:

▶ **Unicast**—Sends information to one specific host. Unicast addresses are used for Telnet, FTP, SSH, or any other information that needs to be shared in a one-to-one exchange of information. Although it is possible that any host on the subnet/network can see the information being passed, only one host is the intended recipient and will take action on the information being received.

▶ **Multicasting**—Broadcasts information to groups of computers sharing an application, such as a video conferencing client or online gaming application. All the machines participating in the conference or game require the same information at precisely the same time to be effective.

▶ **Broadcasting**—Transmits information to all the hosts on a network or subnet. *Dynamic Host Configuration Protocol (DHCP)* uses broadcast messages when the DHCP client looks for a DHCP server to get its network settings, and *Reverse Address Resolution Protocol (RARP)* uses broadcast messages for hardware address to IP address resolution. Broadcast messages use .255 in all the host octets of the network IP address. (10.2.255.255 will broadcast to every host in your Class B network.)

Hardware Devices for Networking

As stated at the beginning of this chapter, networking is one of the strong points of the Linux operating system. This section covers the classes of devices used for basic networking. Note that this section talks about hardware devices, and not Linux networking devices, which are discussed in the section, "Using Network Configuration Tools."

Network Interface Cards

A computer must have a *network interface card (NIC)* to connect to a network. Currently, there are several topologies (ways of connecting computers) for network connections. These topologies range from the old and mostly outdated 10BASE-2 to the much newer and popular wireless Wi-Fi or 802.11 networking.

Each NIC has a unique address (the hardware address, known as *media access control*, or MAC), which identifies that NIC. This address is six pairs of hexadecimal bits separated by colons (:). A MAC address looks similar to this: 00:60:08:8F:5A:D9. The hardware address is used by DHCP (see "Dynamic Host Configuration Protocol" later in this chapter) to identify a specific host. It is also used by the *Address Resolution Protocol (ARP)* and *Reverse Address Resolution Protocol (RARP)* to map hosts to IP addresses.

This section covers some of the different types of NIC used to connect to your network.

Token Ring

Token ring networking was developed by IBM. As the name implies, the network is set up in a ring. A single "token" is passed from host to host, indicating the receiving host's permission to transmit data.

Token ring has a maximum transfer rate of 16Mbps (16 million bits per second). Unlike 10BASE-2 and 10BASE-5, token ring uses what is called *unshielded twisted pair (UTP)* cable. This cable looks a lot like the cable that connects your phone to the wall. Almost all token ring NICs are recognized by Linux.

10BASE-T

10BASE-T was the standard for a long time. A large number of networks still use it. 10BASE-T also uses UTP cable. Instead of being configured in a ring, 10BASE-T mostly uses a star architecture. In this architecture, the hosts all connect to a central location (usually a hub, which you learn about later in the section titled "Hubs and Switches"). All the data is sent to all hosts, but only the destination host takes action on individual packets. 10BASE-T has a transfer rate of 10Mbps.

10BASE-T has a maximum segment length of 100 meters. There are many manufacturers of 10BASE-T NICs, and most are recognized by Ubuntu.

100BASE-T

100BASE-T was popular around the turn of the millennium, keeping the same ease of administration as 10BASE-T while increasing the speed by a factor of 10. For most networks, the step from 10BASE-T to 100BASE-T is as simple as replacing NICs and hubs. Most 100BASE-T NICs and hubs can also handle 10BASE-T and can automatically detect which is in use. This allows for a gradual network upgrade and usually does not require rewiring your whole network. Nearly every known 100BASE-T NIC and most generic NICs are compatible with Linux, thanks to Donald Becker of http://www.scyld.com/. 100BASE-T requires category 5 unshielded twisted pair cabling.

1000BASE-T

1000BASE-T—usually referred to as *gigabit ethernet*—is the accepted standard in enterprise networking, with most NICs being detected and configured correctly by Ubuntu. Like 100BASE-T NICs, gigabit NICs automatically downgrade if they are plugged in to a slower network. Also like 100BASE-T, gigabit NICs require category 5 unshielded twisted pair cabling; however, many institutions are now deploying category 6 cables because they have much longer range and so are often worth the extra cost. You will find that many newer computers tend to be fitted with gigabit NICs as standard.

Fiber Optic and Gigabit Ethernet

Fiber optic is more commonly used in newer and high-end installations because the cost of upgrading can be prohibitive for older sites.

Fiber optics were originally used on *fiber distributed data interface (FDDI)* networks, similar to token ring in structure except that there are two rings—one is primary, whereas the other is secondary. The primary ring is used exclusively, and the secondary sits idle until there is a break in the primary ring. At this point, the secondary ring takes over, keeping the network alive. FDDI has a speed of 100Mbps and has a maximum ring length of 62 miles. FDDI uses several tokens at the same time that, along with the faster speed of fiber optics, account for the drastic increase in network speed.

As stated, switching to a fiber optic network can be very costly. To make the upgrade, the whole network has to be rewired (as much as U.S. $150 per network connection), and all NICs must be replaced at the same time. Most FDDI NICs are recognized by Linux.

Fiber-related gigabit is termed 1000BASE-X, whereas 1000BASE-T gigabit ethernet uses twisted-pair (see the "Unshielded Twisted Pair" section, later in this chapter).

Wireless Network Interfaces

Wireless networking, as the name states, works without network cables and is an extremely popular option, particularly for those whose spouses do not like wires trailing everywhere! Upgrading is as easy as replacing network cards and equipment, such as routers and switches. Wireless networking equipment can also work along with the traditional wired networking using existing equipment.

It might not be practical to upgrade a desktop or large server to wireless just yet if the wiring is already in place. Wireless networking is still generally slower than a traditional wired network. However, this situation is changing with wider adoption of newer protocols, such as 802.11g (supporting the common 802.11b and faster but less popular 802.11a), along with the introduction of more compliant and inexpensive wireless NICs.

Some 802.11g NICs work at up to 108Mbps, which appears faster than 100BASE-T wired networking on the surface. However, in practice, it is a great deal slower: Unless your networking environment has paper-thin walls, you can usually halve the reported speed of Wi-Fi network devices. 108Mbps works about half the speed of 100BASE-T.

With each new version of Linux, more and more wireless NICs are compatible. That said, it is usually better to get brand name wireless NICs, because you have a better chance of compatibility. Check the http://www.hpl.hp.com/personal/Jean_Tourrilhes/Linux/ web page for more specific hardware compatibility information. More on wireless networking is discussed later in this chapter.

Network Cable

Currently, three types of network cable exist: coaxial, unshielded twisted pair (UTP), and fiber. Coaxial cable (rarely used today) looks a lot like the coaxial cable used to connect your television to the cable jack or antenna. UTP looks a lot like the cable that runs from your phone to the wall jack (the jacks are a bit wider). Fiber cable looks sort of like the RCA cables used on your stereo or like the cable used on your electrical appliances in your house (two separate segments connected together). The following sections discuss UTP and fiber network cable in more detail.

Unshielded Twisted Pair

Unshielded twisted pair (UTP) uses color-coded pairs of thin copper wire to transmit data. Six categories of UTP exist—each serving a different purpose:

- **Category 1 (Cat1)**—Used for voice transmissions such as your phone. Only one pair is used per line—one wire to transmit and one to receive. An RJ-11 plug is used to connect the cable to your phone and the wall.

- **Category 2 (Cat2)**—Used in early token ring networks. Has a transmission rate of 4Mbps (million bits per second) and has the slowest data transfer rate. An RJ-11 plug is also used for cable connections.

- **Category 3 (Cat3)**—Used for 10BASE-T networks. It has a transmission rate of 10Mbps. Three pairs of cables are used to send and receive signals. RJ-11 or RJ-45 plugs can be used for Cat3 cables, usually deferring to the smaller RJ-11. RJ-45 plugs are similar in design to RJ-11, but are larger to handle up to four pairs of wire and are used more commonly on Cat5 cables.

- **Category 4 (Cat4)**—Used in modern token ring networks. It has a transmission rate of 16Mbps and is less and less common as companies are switching to better alternatives. RJ-45 plugs are used for cable connections.

- **Category 5 (Cat5)**—The fastest of the UTP categories with a transmission rate of up to 1000Mbps. It is used in both 100BASE-T and 1000BASE-T networks and uses four pairs of wire. Cat5 cable came out just as 10BASE-T networks were becoming popular and isn't much more expensive than Cat3 cable. As a result, most 10BASE-T networks use Cat5 UTP instead of Cat3. Cat5 cable uses RJ-45 plugs.

▶ **Category 6 (Cat6)**—Also rated at 1000Mbps, this cable is available in two forms: stranded for short runs (25-meter) and solid for up to 100-meter runs, but which should not be flexed.

Fiber Optic Cable

Fiber optic cable (fiber) is usually orange or red in color. The transmission rate is 100Mbps and has a maximum length of 62 miles. Fiber uses a two-pronged plug to connect to devices. A couple of advantages to fiber are that because it uses light instead of electricity to transmit its signal, it is free from the possibility of electromagnetic interference and is also more difficult to tap into and eavesdrop.

Hubs and Switches

Hubs and switches are used to connect several hosts together on a star architecture network. They can have any number of connections; the common sizes are 4, 8, 16, 24, and 48 connections (ports)—each port has a light that comes on when a network connection is made (link light). Their use enables you to expand your network easily; you can just add new hubs or switches when you need to add new connections. Each unit can connect to the other hubs or switches on the network, typically, through a port on the hub or switch called an *uplink* port. This enables two hubs or switches, connected by their uplink ports, to act as one hub or switch. Having a central location where all the hosts on your network can connect allows for easier troubleshooting of problems. If one host goes down, none of the other hosts are affected (depending on the purpose of the downed host). Because hubs and switches are not directly involved with the Linux operating system, compatibility is not an issue.

If you are constructing a small to mid-size network, it is important to consider whether you intend to use either hubs or switches. Hubs and switches are visually the same in that they have rows of network ports. However, under the hood, the difference is quite important. Data is sent as packets of information across the network; with a hub the data is transmitted simultaneously to all the network ports, irrespective of which port the destination computer is attached to.

Switches, however, are more intelligent because they can direct packets of information directly to the correct network port that leads to the destination computer. They do this by "learning" the MAC addresses of each computer that is attached to them. In short, using switches minimizes excess packets being sent across the network, thus increasing network bandwidth. In a small network with a handful of computers, the use of hubs might be perfectly acceptable and you will find that hubs are generally cheaper than switches. However, for larger networks of 15 computers or more, you should consider implementing a switched network.

TIP

Troubleshooting network connections can be a challenge, especially on large networks. If a user complains that he has lost his network connection, the hub or switch is a good place to start. If the link light for the user's port is lit, chances are the problem is with the user's network configuration. If the link light is not on, the host's NIC is bad, the cable is not inserted properly, or the cable has gone bad for some reason.

Routers and Bridges

Routers and bridges are used to connect different networks to your network and to connect different subnets within your network. Routers and bridges both serve the same purpose of connecting networks and subnets, but they do so with different techniques. The information in the following sections will help you choose the connection method that best suits your needs.

Bridges

Bridges are used within a network to connect different subnets. A bridge blindly relays all information from one subnet to another without any filtering and is often referred to as a *dumb gateway*. This can be helpful if one subnet in your network is becoming overburdened and you need to lighten the load. A bridge is not very good for connecting to the Internet, however, because it lacks filtering. You really do not want all traffic traveling the Internet to be able to get through to your network.

Routers

Routers can pass data from one network to another, and they allow for filtering of data. Routers are best suited to connect your network to an outside network, such as the Internet. If you have a web server for an internal intranet that you do not want people to access from the Internet, for example, you can use a router's filter to block port 80 from your network. These filters can be used to block specific hosts from accessing the Internet as well. For these reasons, routers are also called *smart gateways*.

Routers range in complexity and price from a Cisco brand router that can cost thousands of dollars to other brands that can be less than a hundred dollars.

Initializing New Network Hardware

All the initial network configuration and hardware initialization for Ubuntu is normally done during installation. At times, however, you will have to reconfigure networking on your system, such as when a host needs to be moved to a different subnet or a different network, or if you replace any of your computer's networking hardware.

Linux creates network interfaces in memory when the kernel recognizes that a NIC or other network device is attached to the system. These interfaces are unlike other Linux interfaces, such as serial communications ports, and do not have a corresponding device file in the /dev directory. Unless support for a particular NIC is built in to your kernel, Linux must be told to load a specific kernel module to support your NIC. More than 100 such modules are located in the /lib/modules/2.6.*XX-XX*/kernel/net directory (where *XX-XX* is your version of the kernel).

You can initialize a NIC in several ways when using Linux. When you first install Ubuntu, automatic hardware probing detects and configures your system to use any installed NICs. If you remove the original NIC and replace it with a different make and model, your system will not automatically detect and initialize the device unless you configure Ubuntu to use automatic hardware detection when booting. Ubuntu should detect the absence of the old NIC and the presence of the new NIC at boot time.

If you do not use automatic hardware detection and configuration, you can initialize network hardware by

▶ Manually editing the /etc/modprobe.conf file to prompt the system to recognize and support the new hardware upon reboot

▶ Manually loading or unloading the new device's kernel module with the modprobe command

The following sections explain the first and last of the preceding methods.

Editing the /etc/modprobe.conf **File**

This file may not be present when you first look for it, so you may need to create a blank file in a text editor. You can manually edit the /etc/modprobe.conf file to add a module dependency entry (also known as a *directive*) to support a new NIC or other network device. This entry includes the device's name and its corresponding kernel module. After you add this entry, the Linux kernel recognizes your new networking hardware upon reboot. Ubuntu runs a module dependency check upon booting.

For example, if your system uses a RealTek NIC, you could use an entry like this:

```
alias eth0 8139too
```

The example entry tells the Linux kernel to load the 8139too.o kernel module to support the eth0 network device. On the other hand, if you have an Intel Ethernet Pro NIC installed, you would use an entry like this:

```
alias eth0 eepro100
```

Other parameters can be passed to a kernel module using one or more option entries, if need be, to properly configure your NIC. See the modprobe.conf man page for more information on using entries. For more specifics regarding NIC kernel modules, examine the module's source code because no man pages exist (a good opportunity for anyone willing to write the documentation).

> **TIP**
>
> Linux kernel and network tools can be used to diagnose problems or troubleshoot problematic NICs. However, if you browse to Don Becker's Linux Ethercard Status, Diagnostic and Setup Utilities page at http://www.scyld.com/ethercard_diag.html, you will find more than two dozen hardware-specific utilities for a variety of PCI and legacy ISA Ethernet network cards. These tools can be extremely helpful if you run into trouble during NIC recognition or configuration.

Using modprobe to Manually Load Kernel Modules

You do not have to use an /etc/modprobe.conf entry to initialize kernel support for your new network device. As root (using sudo), you can manually load or unload the device's kernel module using the modprobe command, along with the module's name. For example, use the following command line to enable the example RealTek NIC:

```
$ sudo modprobe 8139too
```

After you press Enter, you will see this device reported from the kernel's ring buffer messages, which can be displayed by the dmesg command. Here's a portion of that command's output:

```
$ dmesg
...
eth0: RealTek RTL8139 Fast Ethernet at 0xce8ee000, 00:30:1b:0b:07:0d, IRQ 11
eth0: Identified 8139 chip type 'RTL-8139C'
eth0: Setting half-duplex based on auto-negotiated partner ability 0000.
...
```

Note that at this point, an IP address or other settings have not been assigned to the device. Linux can use multiple ethernet interfaces, and the first ethernet device will be numbered eth0, the second eth1, and so on. Each different ethernet device recognized by the kernel might have additional or different information reported, depending on its kernel module. For example,

```
$ dmesg
...
eepro100.c:v1.09j-t 9/29/99 Donald Becker http://cesdis.gsfc.nasa.gov/linux/drive
rs/eepro100.html
eepro100.c: $Revision: 1.36 $ 2000/11/17 Modified by Andrey V. Savochkin
➥<saw@saw.sw.com.sg> and others
PCI: Found IRQ 10 for device 00:0d.0
eth0: Intel Corporation 82557 [Ethernet Pro 100], 00:90:27:91:92:B5, IRQ 10.
  Board assembly 721383-007, Physical connectors present: RJ45
  Primary interface chip i82555 PHY #1.
  General self-test: passed.
  Serial sub-system self-test: passed.
  Internal registers self-test: passed.
```

14

```
ROM checksum self-test: passed (0x04f4518b).
...
```

In this example, an Intel Ethernet Pro 100 NIC has been recognized. To disable support for a NIC, the kernel module can be unloaded, but usually only after the device is no longer in use. Read the next section to learn how to configure a NIC after it has been recognized by the Linux kernel and how to control its behavior.

Using Network Configuration Tools

If you add or replace networking hardware after your initial installation, you must configure the new hardware. You can do so using either the command line or the graphical configuration tools. To configure a network client host using the command line, you can use a combination of commands or edit specific files under the /etc directory. To configure the hardware through a graphical interface, you can use Ubuntu's graphical tool for X called network-admin. This section introduces command-line and graphical software tools you can use to configure a network interface and network settings on your Ubuntu system. You'll see how to control your NIC and manage how your system interacts with your network.

Using the command-line configuration tools can seem difficult if you are new to Linux. For anyone new to networking, the network-admin graphical tool is the way to go. Both manual and graphical methods require root access to work. If you do not have root access, get it before trying any of these actions. You should not edit any scripts or settings files used by graphical network administration tools on your system. Your changes will be lost the next time the tool, such as network-admin, is run! Either use a manual approach and write your own network setup script, or stick to using graphical configuration utilities.

Command-Line Network Interface Configuration

You can configure a network interface from the command line using the basic Linux networking utilities. You configure your network client hosts with the command line by using commands to change your current settings or by editing a number of system files. Two commands, ifconfig and route, are used for network configuration. The netstat command displays information about the network connections.

/sbin/ifconfig

ifconfig is used to configure your network interface. You can use it to

▶ Activate or deactivate your NIC or change your NIC's mode

▶ Change your machine's IP address, netmask, or broadcast address

▶ Create an IP alias to allow more than one IP address on your NIC

▶ Set a destination address for a point-to-point connection

You can change as many or as few of these options as you'd like with a single command. The basic structure for the command is as follows:

```
ifconfig [network device] options
```

Table 14.1 shows a subset of `ifconfig` options and examples of their uses.

TABLE 14.1 **ifconfig** Options

Use	Option	Example
Create alias	–[*network device*]	ifconfig eth0:0_:[number] 10.10.10.10
Change IP address		ifconfig eth0 10.10.10.12
Change the netmask	netmask [*netmask*]	fconfig eth0 netmask 255.255.255.0
Change the broadcast	broadcast [*address*]	–ifconfig eth0 broadcast 10.10.10.255
Take interface down	down	ifconfig eth0 down
Bring interface up	up (*add IP address*)	–ifconfig eth0 up (ifconfig eth0 10.10.10.10)
Set NIC promiscuous	[-]promisc	ifconfig eth0 promisc mode on
	[ifconfig eth0 - promisc]	[off]
Set multicasting mode	[-]allmulti	ifconfig eth0_on [off]
		allmulti [ifconfig eth0 -allmulti]
Enable [disable] [address]	[-]pointopoint eth0_pointopoint	ifconfig_point-to-point address 10.10.10.20 [ifconfig eth0 pointopoint_10.10.10.20]

The `ifconfig` man page shows other options that enable your machine to interface with a number of network types such as AppleTalk, Novell, IPv6, and others. Again, read the man page for details on these network types.

NOTE

Promiscuous mode causes the NIC to receive all packets on the network. It is often used to sniff a network. Multicasting mode enables the NIC to receive all multicast traffic on the network.

If no argument is given, ifconfig displays the status of active interfaces. For example, the output of ifconfig, without arguments and one active and configured NIC, looks similar to this:

```
$ ifconfig
```

```
eth0      Link encap:Ethernet  HWaddr 00:0F:EA:B2:53:85
          inet addr:192.168.2.5  Bcast:192.168.2.255  Mask:255.255.255.0
          inet6 addr: fe80::20f:eaff:feb2:5385/64 Scope:Link
          UP BROADCAST RUNNING MULTICAST  MTU:1500  Metric:1
          RX packets:471 errors:0 dropped:0 overruns:0 frame:0
          TX packets:695 errors:0 dropped:0 overruns:0 carrier:0
          collisions:0 txqueuelen:1000
          RX bytes:160637 (156.8 KiB)  TX bytes:86193 (84.1 KiB)
          Interrupt:185 Base address:0x6000

lo        Link encap:Local Loopback
          inet addr:127.0.0.1  Mask:255.0.0.0
          inet6 addr: ::1/128 Scope:Host
          UP LOOPBACK RUNNING  MTU:16436  Metric:1
          RX packets:19 errors:0 dropped:0 overruns:0 frame:0
          TX packets:19 errors:0 dropped:0 overruns:0 carrier:0
          collisions:0 txqueuelen:0
          RX bytes:1336 (1.3 KiB)  TX bytes:1336 (1.3 KiB)
```

The output is easily understood. The inet entry displays the IP address for the interface. UP signifies that the interface is ready for use, BROADCAST denotes that the interface is connected to a network that supports broadcast messaging (ethernet), RUNNING means that the interface is operating, and LOOPBACK shows which device (lo) is the loopback address. The *maximum transmission unit (MTU)* on eth0 is 1500 bytes. This determines the size of the largest packet that can be transmitted over this interface (and is sometimes "tuned" to other values for performance enhancement). Metric is a number from 0 to 3 that relates to how much information from the interface is placed in the routing table. The lower the number, the smaller the amount of information.

The ifconfig command can be used to display information about or control a specific interface using commands as listed in Table 14.1. For example, to deactivate the first Ethernet device on a host, use the ifconfig command, the interface name, and the command down like so:

```
$ sudo ifconfig eth0 down
```

You can also configure and activate the device by specifying a hostname or IP address and network information. For example to configure and activate ("bring up") the eth0 interface with a specific IP address, use the ifconfig command like this:

```
$ sudo ifconfig eth0 192.168.2.9 netmask 255.255.255.0 up
```

If you have a host defined in your system's /etc/hosts file (see the section "Network Configuration Files" later in this chapter), you can configure and activate the interface according to the defined hostname like this:

```
$ sudo ifconfig eth0 dogdog.hudson.com up
```

Read the next section to see how to configure your system to work with your LAN.

/sbin/route

The second command used to configure your network is the route command. route is used to build the routing tables (in memory) implemented for routing packets as well as displaying the routing information. It is used after ifconfig has initialized the interface. route is normally used to set up static routes to other networks via the gateway or to other hosts. The command configuration is like this:

```
$ route [options] [commands] [parameters]
```

To display the routing table, use the route command with no options. The display will look similar to this:

```
$ route
Kernel IP routing table
Destination     Gateway          Genmask          Flags Metric Ref    Use Iface
192.168.2.0     *                255.255.255.0    U     0      0        0 eth0
default         .                0.0.0.0          UG    0      0        0 eth0
```

In the first column, Destination is the IP address (or, if the host is in /etc/hosts or /etc/networks, the hostname) of the receiving host. The default entry is the default gateway for this machine. The Gateway column lists the gateway that the packets must go through to reach their destination. An asterisk (*) means that packets go directly to the host. Genmask is the netmask. The Flags column can have several possible entries. In our example, U verifies that the route is enabled and G specifies that Destination requires the use of a gateway. The Metric column displays the distance to the Destination. Some daemons use this to figure the easiest route to the Destination. The Ref column is used by some UNIX flavors to convey the references to the route. It isn't used by Linux. The Use column indicates the number of times this entry has been looked up. Finally, the Iface column is the name of the interface for the corresponding entry.

Using the -n option to the route command will give the same information, substituting IP addresses for names and asterisks (*), and looks like this:

```
# /sbin/route -n
Kernel IP routing table
Destination     Gateway          Genmask          Flags Metric Ref    Use Iface
192.168.2.0     0.0.0.0          255.255.255.0    U     0      0        0 eth0
0.0.0.0         192.168.2.1      0.0.0.0          UG    0      0        0 eth0
```

The route command can add to the table using the add option. With the add option, you can specify a host (-host) or a network (-net) as the destination. If no option is used, the route command assumes that you are configuring the host issuing the command. The most common uses for the route command are to add the default gateway for a host, for a host that has lost its routing table, or if the gateway address has changed. For example, to add a gateway with a specific IP address, you could use the following:

```
$ sudo route add default gw 149.112.50.65
```

Note that you could use a hostname instead of an IP address if desired. Another common use is to add the network to the routing table right after using the ifconfig command to configure the interface. Assuming that the 208.59.243.0 entry from the previous examples was missing, replace it using the following command:

```
$ sudo route add -net 208.59.243.0 netmask 255.255.255.0 dev eth0
```

You also can use route to configure a specific host for a direct (point-to-point) connection. For example, say that you have a home network of two computers. One of the computers has a modem through which it connects to your business network. You typically work at the other computer. You can use the route command to establish a connection through specific hosts using the following command:

```
$ sudo route add -host 198.135.62.25 gw 149.112.50.65
```

The preceding example makes the computer with the modem the gateway for the computer you are using. This type of command line is useful if you have a gateway or firewall connected to the Internet. There are many additional uses for the route command, such as manipulating the default packet size. See the man page for those uses.

/bin/netstat

The netstat command is used to display the status of your network. It has several parameters that can display as much or as little information as you prefer. The services are listed by *sockets* (application-to-application connections between two computers). You can use netstat to display the information in Table 14.2.

TABLE 14.2 **netstat** Options

Option	Output
-g	Displays the multicast groups configured
-i	Displays the interfaces configured by ifconfig
-s	Lists a summary of activity for each protocol
-v	Gives verbose output, listing both active and inactive sockets
-c	Updates output every second (good for testing and troubleshooting)
-e	Gives verbose output for active connections only
-C	Displays information from the route cache and is good for looking at past connections

Several other options are available for this command, but they are used less often. As with the route command, the man page can give you details about all options and parameters.

Network Configuration Files

As previously stated, five network configuration files can be modified to make changes to basic network interaction of your system. The files are

- ▶ /etc/hosts—A listing of addresses, hostnames, and aliases

- ▶ /etc/services—Network service and port connections

- ▶ /etc/nsswitch.conf—Linux network information service configuration

- ▶ /etc/resolv.conf—Domain name service domain (search) settings

- ▶ /etc/host.conf—Network information search order (by default, /etc/hosts and then DNS)

After these files are modified, the changes are active. As with most configuration files, comments can be added with a hash mark (#) preceding the comment. All of these files have a man page written about them for more information.

Adding Hosts to /etc/hosts

The /etc/hosts file is a map of IP to hostnames. If you are not using DNS or another naming service, and you are connected to a large network, this file can get quite large and can be a real headache to manage. A small /etc/hosts file can look something like this:

```
127.0.0.1       localhost
127.0.1.1       optimus


# The following lines are desirable for IPv6 capable hosts
::1     ip6-localhost ip6-loopback
fe00::0 ip6-localnet
ff00::0 ip6-mcastprefix
ff02::1 ip6-allnodes
ff02::2 ip6-allrouters
ff02::3 ip6-allhosts
```

The first entry is for the loopback entry. The second is for the name of the machine. If no naming service is in use on the network, the only host that myhost will recognize by name is yourhost. (IP addresses on the network can still be used.)

Service Settings in /etc/services

The /etc/services file maps port numbers to services. The first few lines look similar to this (the /etc/services file can be quite long, more than 500 lines):

```
# Each line describes one service, and is of the form:
#
# service-name port/protocol [aliases ...]   [# comment]
```

```
tcpmux      1/tcp           # TCP port service multiplexer
tcpmux      1/udp           # TCP port service multiplexer
rje         5/tcp           # Remote Job Entry
rje         5/udp           # Remote Job Entry
echo        7/tcp
echo        7/udp
discard     9/tcp       sink null
discard     9/udp       sink null
systat      11/tcp      users
```

Typically, there are two entries for each service because most services can use either TCP or UDP for their transmissions. Usually after /etc/services is initially configured, you will not need to change it.

Using /etc/nsswitch.conf After Changing Naming Services

This file was initially developed by Sun Microsystems to specify the order in which services are accessed on the system. A number of services are listed in the /etc/nsswitch.conf file, but the most commonly modified entry is the hosts entry. A portion of the file can look like this:

```
passwd:         compat
group:          compat
shadow:         compat

hosts:          files dns mdns
networks:       files

protocols:      db files
services:       db files
ethers:         db files
rpc:            db files

netgroup:       nis
```

This tells services that they should consult standard Unix/Linux files for passwd, shadow, and group (/etc/passwd, /etc/shadow, /etc/group, respectively) lookups. For host lookups, the system checks /etc/hosts and if there is no entry, it checks DNS. The commented hosts entry lists the possible values for hosts. Edit this file only if your naming service has changed.

Setting a Name Server with /etc/resolv.conf

/etc/resolv.conf is used by DNS, the domain name service. The following is an example of resolv.conf:

```
nameserver 192.172.3.8
nameserver 192.172.3.9
search mydomain.com
```

This sets the nameservers and the order of domains for DNS to use. The contents of this file will be set automatically if you use Dynamic Host Configuration Protocol, or DHCP (see the section on "Dynamic Host Configuration Protocol" later in this chapter).

Setting DNS Search Order with `/etc/host.conf`

The `/etc/host.conf` file lists the order in which your machine will search for hostname resolution. The following is the default `/etc/host.conf` file:

```
order hosts, bind
```

In this example, the host checks the `/etc/hosts` file first and then performs a DNS lookup. A couple more options control how the name service is used. The only reason to modify this file is if you use NIS for your name service or you want one of the optional services. The `nospoof` option can be a good option for system security. It compares a standard DNS lookup to a reverse lookup (host-to-IP then IP-to-host) and fails if the two don't match. The drawback is that often when proxy services are used, the lookup fails, so you want to use this with caution.

Using Graphical Configuration Tools

Ubuntu has made some big improvements to how desktop users may configure networking using graphical configuration tools. For most people, all you will need to know is contained in Chapter 2, "Post-Installation Configuration," in the section about Network Manager. For others, you may configure your network connections by right clicking the networking icon on your top panel and choosing "Edit Connections.." from the menu as in Figure 14.1. From the Network Connections window that opens, you may select from various types of connections to configure; Wired, Wireless, Mobile Broadband, VPN and DSL as in Figure 14.2. By default, each is set to auto configure and most users will never need to change the settings available here. For those who require doing so, choosing the appropriate tab and clicking the "Add" button will give the opportunity to configure and fine tune settings as needed, such as in the wireless connection example in Figure 14.3. .

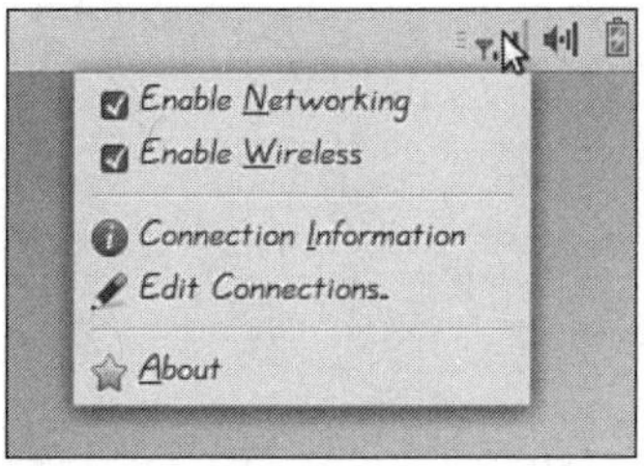

FIGURE 14.1   Use network-admin to configure your network devices.

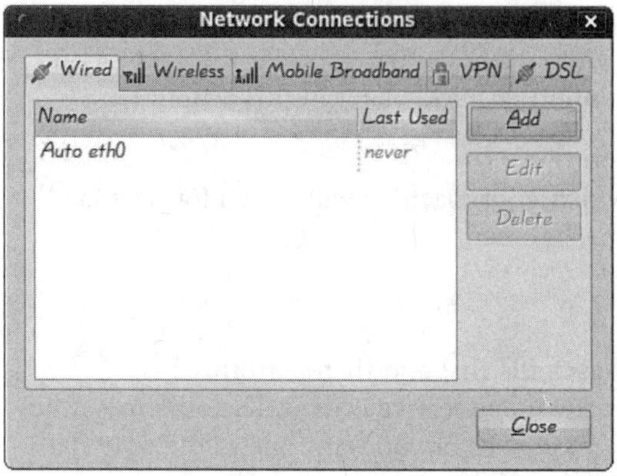

FIGURE 14.2   Highlight an existing entry, and then click the Properties button to change
/etc/hosts entries in the Hosts tab of the Network Configuration screen.

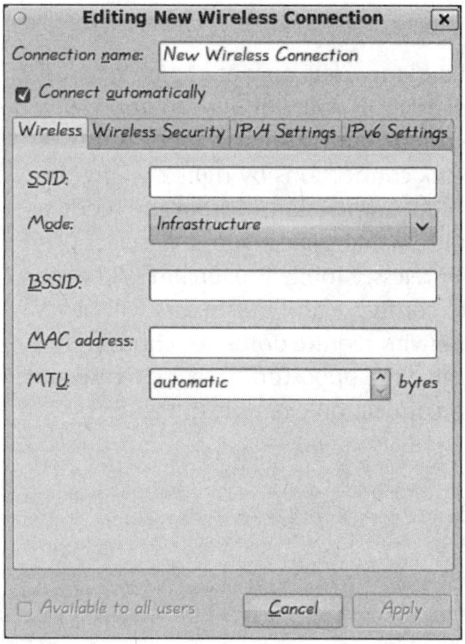

FIGURE 14.3   Assign a static IP address to a network interface.

Dynamic Host Configuration Protocol

As its name implies, *Dynamic Host Configuration Protocol (DHCP)* configures hosts for connection to your network. DHCP allows a network administrator to configure all TCP/IP parameters for each host as he connects to the network after activation of a NIC. These parameters include automatically assigning an IP address to a NIC, setting name server entries in /etc/resolv.conf, and configuring default routing and gateway information for a host. This section first describes how to use DHCP to obtain IP address assignment for your NIC, and then how to quickly set up and start a DHCP server using Ubuntu.

> **NOTE**
>
> You can learn more about DHCP by reading RFC2131 "Dynamic Host Configuration Protocol." Browse to http://www.ietf.org/rfc/rfc2131.txt.

How DHCP Works

DHCP provides persistent storage of network parameters by holding identifying information for each network client that might connect to the network. The three most common pairs of identifying information are

▸ **Network subnet/host address**—Used by hosts to connect to the network at will

▸ **Subnet/hostname**—Enables the specified host to connect to the subnet

▸ **Subnet/hardware address**—Enables a specific client to connect to the network after getting the hostname from DHCP

DHCP also allocates to clients temporary or permanent network (IP) addresses. When a temporary assignment, known as a *lease*, elapses, the client can request to have the lease extended, or, if the address is no longer needed, the client can relinquish the address. For hosts that will be permanently connected to a network with adequate addresses available, DHCP allocates infinite leases.

DHCP offers your network some advantages. First, it shifts responsibility for assigning IP addresses from the network administrator (who can accidentally assign duplicate IP addresses) to the DHCP server. Second, DHCP makes better use of limited IP addresses. If a user is away from the office for whatever reason, the user's host can release its IP address for use by other hosts.

Like most things in life, DHCP is not perfect. Servers cannot be configured through DHCP alone because DNS does not know what addresses that DHCP assigns to a host. This means that DNS lookups are not possible on machines configured through DHCP alone; therefore, services cannot be provided. However, DHCP can make assignments based on DNS entries when using subnet/hostname or subnet/hardware address identifiers.

> **NOTE**
>
> The problem of using DHCP to configure servers using registered hostnames is being addressed by Dynamic DNS which, when fully developed, will enable DHCP to register IP addresses with DNS. This will allow you, for example, to register a domain name (such as imalinuxuser.com) and be able to easily access that domain's web server without needing to use static IP addressing of a specific host. The largest hurdle to overcome is the security implication of enabling each host connecting to the system to update DNS. A few companies, such as http://www.dyndns.org/, are already offering Dynamic DNS services and have clients for Linux.

Activating DHCP at Installation and Boot Time

Ubuntu automatically defaults your network interfaces to using DHCP, as it is the simplest way of setting up a network interface. With *dynamic*, or DHCP-assigned IP addressing schemes for your NIC, the broadcast address is set at 255.255.255.255 because dhclient, the DHCP client used for IP configuration, is initially unaware of where the DHCP server is located, so the request must travel every network until a server replies.

The instruction to use DHCP for your NIC can be found under /etc/network/interfaces, with a line that says dhcp.

Other settings specific to obtaining DHCP settings are saved in the file named dhclient.conf under the /etc/dhcp3/dhclient.conf directory and are documented in the dhclient.conf man page. More than 100 options are also documented in the dhcp-options man page.

However, using DHCP is not that complicated. If you want to use DHCP and know that there is a server on your network, you can quickly configure your NIC by using the dhclient like so:

```
# dhclient
Internet Systems Consortium DHCP Client V3.0.6
Copyright 2004-2007 Internet Systems Consortium.
All rights reserved.
For info, please visit http://www.isc.org/sw/dhcp/
```

```
SIOCSIFFLAGS: No such file or directory
SIOCSIFFLAGS: No such file or directory
Listening on LPF/eth1/00:11:50:3c:fe:21
Sending on   LPF/eth1/00:11:50:3c:fe:21
Listening on LPF/eth0/00:0f:ea:b2:53:85
Sending on   LPF/eth0/00:0f:ea:b2:53:85
Sending on   Socket/fallback
receive_packet failed on eth1: Network is down
DHCPDISCOVER on eth1 to 255.255.255.255 port 67 interval 7
send_packet: Network is down
DHCPDISCOVER on eth0 to 255.255.255.255 port 67 interval 7
DHCPOFFER from 192.168.0.1
DHCPREQUEST on eth0 to 255.255.255.255 port 67
DHCPACK from 192.168.0.1
bound to 192.168.0.7 — renewal in 118148 seconds.
```

In this example, the first ethernet device, eth0, has been assigned an IP address of 192.168.0.7 from a DHCP server at 192.168.0.1. The renewal will take place in about 33 hours.

DHCP Software Installation and Configuration

Installation of the DHCP client and server is fairly straightforward, mainly because Ubuntu already includes dhclient in a default installation, but also because installing software is easy using synaptic or apt-get.

DHCP dhclient

DHCP is automatically enabled when you install Ubuntu, so you don't need to worry about having to enable it. The DHCP client, dhclient, sends a broadcast message that the DHCP server replies to with networking information for your host. Once it has this, you're done!

You can however, fine-tune how dhclient works, and where and how it obtains or looks for DHCP information. You probably will not need to take this additional effort; but if you do, you can create and edit a file named dhclient.conf, and save it in the /etc directory with your settings.

CAUTION

You shouldn't just go ahead and overwrite your dhclient.conf with any old file, as it could lead you to painful networking problems. Instead, copy the file like so:

```
sudo cp /etc/dhcp3/dhclient.conf/ etc/dhcp3/dhclient.conf.backup
```

That way, if anything goes wrong, you can then copy it back to restore the original settings.

A few of the `dhclient.conf` options include

▶ `timeout` *time* ;—How long to wait before giving up trying (60 seconds is the default)

▶ `retry` *time* ;—How long to wait before retrying (five minutes is the default)

▶ `select-timeout time` ;—How long to wait before selecting a DHCP offer (zero seconds is the default)

▶ `reboot time` ;—How long to wait before trying to get a previously set IP (10 seconds is the default)

▶ `renew date` ;—When to renew an IP lease, where `date` is in the form of *<weekday>* *<year>*/*<month>*/*<day>* *<hour>*:*<minute>*:*<second>*, such as `4 2004/1/1 22:01:01` for Thursday, January 4, 2004 at 10:01 p.m.

See the `dhclient.conf` man page for more information on additional settings.

DHCP Server

Again, the easiest way to install the DHCP server on your computer is to use either `synaptic` or `apt-get` to retrieve the dhcp3-server package. If you are so inclined, you can go to the Internet Software Consortium (ISC) website and download and build the source code yourself (http://www.isc.org/).

If you decide to install from a source downloaded from the ISC website, the installation is very straightforward. Just unpack your `tar` file, run `./configure` from the root of the source directory, run `make`, and finally, if there are no errors, run `make install`. This puts all the files used by the DHCP daemon in the correct places. If you have the disk space, it is best to leave the source files in place until you are sure that DHCP is running correctly; otherwise, you can delete the source tree.

NOTE

For whichever installation method you choose, be sure that a file called `/etc/dhcp3/dhcpd.leases` is created. The file can be empty, but it does need to exist in order for dhcpd to start properly.

Using DHCP to Configure Network Hosts

Configuring your network with DHCP can look difficult, but is actually easy if your needs are simple. The server configuration can take a bit more work if your network is more complex and depending on how much you want DHCP to do.

Configuring the server takes some thought and a little bit of work. Luckily, the work involves editing only a single configuration file, `/etc/dhcp3/dhcpd.conf`. To start the server at boot time, use the `service`, `ntsysv`, or `bum` commands.

The `/etc/dhcp3/dhcpd.conf` file contains all the information needed to run `dhcpd`. Ubuntu includes a sample `dhcpd.conf` in `/usr/share/doc/dhcp*/dhcpd.conf.sample`. The DHCP server source files also contain a sample `dhcpd.conf` file.

The `/etc/dhcp3/dhcpd.conf` file can be looked at as a three-part file. The first part contains configurations for DHCP itself. The configurations include

- **Setting the domain name**—`option domain-name "example.org"`.

- **Setting DNS servers**—`option domain-name-servers ns1.example.org, ns2.example.org` (IP addresses can be substituted.)

- **Setting the default and maximum lease times**—`default-lease-time 3600` and `max-lease-time 14400`.

Other settings in the first part include whether the server is the primary (authoritative) server and what type of logging DHCP should use. These settings are considered defaults and can be overridden by the subnet and host portion of the configuration in more complex situations.

NOTE

The `dhcpd.conf` file requires semicolons (`;`) after each command statement. If your configuration file has errors or runs improperly, check for this.

The next part of the `dhcpd.conf` deals with the different subnets that your DHCP server serves; this section is quite straightforward. Each subnet is defined separately and can look like this:

```
subnet 10.5.5.0 netmask 255.255.255.224 {
 range 10.5.5.26 10.5.5.30;
 option domain-name-servers ns1.internal.example.org;
 option domain-name "internal.example.org";
 option routers 10.5.5.1;
 option broadcast-address 10.5.5.31;
 default-lease-time 600;
 max-lease-time 7200;
}
```

This defines the IP addressing for the `10.5.5.0` subnet. It defines the IP address ranging from `10.5.5.26` through `10.5.5.30` to be dynamically assigned to hosts that reside on that subnet. This example shows that any TCP/IP option can be set from the subnet portion of the configuration file. It shows which DNS server the subnet will connect to, which can be good for DNS server load balancing, or which can be used to limit the hosts that can be reached through DNS. It defines the domain name, so you can have more than one domain on your network. It can also change the default and maximum lease time.

If you want your server to ignore a specific subnet, the following entry can be used to accomplish this:

```
subnet 10.152.187.0 netmask 255.255.255.0 {
}
```

This defines no options for the 10.152.187.0 subnet; therefore, the DHCP server ignores it.

The last part of your dhcp.conf is for defining hosts. This can be good if you want a computer on your network to have a specific IP address or other information specific to that host. The key to completing the host section is to know the hardware address of the host. As you learned in "Hardware Devices for Networking," earlier in this chapter, the hardware address is used to differentiate the host for configuration. Your hardware address can be obtained by using the ifconfig command as described previously. The hardware address is on the eth0 line labeled "Hwaddr".

```
host prowl {
  hardware ethernet 08:00:07:26:c0:a5;
  fixed-address prowl.hudson.com;
}
```

This example takes the host with the hardware address 08:00:07:26:c0:a5 and does a DNS lookup to assign the IP address for prowl.hudson.com to the host.

DHCP can also define and configure booting for diskless clients like this:

```
host bumblebee {
  hardware ethernet 0:0:c0:5d:bd:95;
  filename "vmunix.bumblebee";
  server-name "optimus.hudson.com";
}
```

The diskless host bumblebee will get its boot information from server optimus.hudson. com and use vmunix.bumblebee kernel. All other TCP/IP configuration can also be included.

CAUTION

Remember, only one DHCP server should exist on a local network to avoid problems. Your DHCP might not work correctly on a LAN with hosts running outdated legacy operating systems. Often Windows NT servers will have the Windows DHCP server installed by default. Because there is no configuration file for NT to sort through, that DHCP server configures your host before the Linux server if both machines are on the same LAN. Check your NT servers for this situation and disable DHCP on the NT server; afterward, your other DHCP-enabled hosts should configure correctly. Also, check to make sure that there are no conflicts if you use a cable or DSL modem, wireless access point (WAP), or other intelligent router on your LAN that can provide DHCP.

Other Uses for DHCP

A whole host of options can be used in dhcpd.conf: Entire books are dedicated to DHCP. The most comprehensive book is *The DHCP Handbook*, available at http://www.dhcp-hand-book.com/. You can define NIS domains, configure NETBIOS, set subnet masks, and define time servers, or many other types of servers—to name a few of the DHCP options you can use. The preceding example will get your DHCP server and client up and running.

The DHCP server distribution contains an example of the dhcpd.conf file that you can use as a template for your network. The file shows a basic configuration that can get you started with explanations for the options used.

Wireless Networking

As stated earlier, Linux has had support for wireless networking since the first standards were developed in the early 1990s. With computers getting smaller and smaller, the uses for wireless networking increased; meanwhile, the transmission speeds are increasing all the time. There are several different ways to create a wireless network. The following sections introduce you to several Linux commands you can use to initialize, configure, and manage wireless networking on your Ubuntu system.

Support for Wireless Networking in Ubuntu

The Linux kernel that ships with Ubuntu provides extensive support for wireless networking. Related wireless tools for configuring, managing, or displaying information about a wireless connection include

- ▶ iwconfig—Sets the network name, encryption, transmission rate, and other features of a wireless network interface

- ▶ iwlist—Displays information about a wireless interface, such as rate, power level, or frequency used

- ▶ iwpriv—Uses i to set optional features, such as roaming, of a wireless network interface

- ▶ iwspy—Shows wireless statistics of a number of nodes

Support varies for wireless devices, but most modern (that is, post-2005) wireless devices should work with Ubuntu. In general, Linux wireless device software (usually in the form of a kernel module) support the creation of an ethernet device that can be managed by traditional interface tools such as ifconfig—with wireless features of the device managed by the various wireless software tools.

For example, when a wireless networking device is first recognized and initialized for use, the driver will most likely report a new device:

```
zd1211rw 5-4:1.0: firmware version 4725
```

```
zd1211rw 5-4:1.0: zd1211b chip 050d:705c v4810 \
high 00-17-3f AL2230_RF pa0 g—NS

zd1211rw 5-4:1.0: eth2

usbcore: registered new interface driver zd1211rw
```

This output (from the dmesg command) shows that the eth2 device has been reported. If DHCP is in use, the device should automatically join the nearest wireless subnet and be automatically assigned an IP address. If not, the next step is to use a wireless tool such as iwconfig to set various parameters of the wireless device. The iwconfig command, along with the device name (eth2 in this example), will show the status:

```
$ iwconfig eth2
eth2      IEEE 802.11b/g  ESSID:"SKY35120"  Nickname:"zd1211"
          Mode:Managed  Frequency:2.462 GHz  \
Access Point: 00:18:4D:06:8E:2A
          Bit Rate=24 Mb/s
          Encryption key:0EFD-C1AF-5C8D-B2C6-7A89-3790-07A7-AC64-0AB5\
-C36E-D1E9-A230-1DB9-D227-2EB6-D6C8    Security mode:open
          Link Quality=100/100  Signal level=82/100
          Rx invalid nwid:0  Rx invalid crypt:0  Rx invalid frag:0
          Tx excessive retries:0  Invalid misc:0    Missed beacon:0
```

This example shows a 24Mbps connection to a network named SKY35120. To change a parameter, such as the transmission rate, use a command-line option with the iwconfig command like so:

```
$ sudo iwconfig eth0 rate 11M
```

Other options supported by the iwconfig command include essid, used to set the NIC to connect to a specific network by named; mode, used to enable the NIC to automatically retrieve settings from an access point or connect to another wireless host; or freq, to set a frequency to use for communication. Additional options include channel, frag, enc (for encryption), power, and txpower. Details and examples of these options are in the iwconfig manual page.

You can then use the ifconfig command or perhaps a graphical Ubuntu tool to set the device networking parameters, and the interface will work as on a hardwired LAN. One handy output of the iwconfig command is the link quality output, which can be used in shell scripts or other graphical utilities for signal monitoring purposes.

Advantages of Wireless Networking

Advantages of wireless networking are its mobility and potential range. If you have a large enough antenna network, your network can stretch many miles. This would be an expensive network, but one that would easily break out of the brick and mortar confines of the office.

Wireless networking would also be a great advantage to college campuses to eliminate the need to tear through walls to install cabling because more and more students expect to have a network connection in their dorm rooms. Wireless networking cards are very reasonable in price and can easily be issued to each student as he requires them.

Home networkers can also benefit from wireless networking. For those who cannot do wired network modifications to their homes, wireless networking removes the unsightly wires running along baseboards and ceilings that are required to connect computers in different rooms. With a wireless home network, you are not even confined to inside the house. Depending on the transmit power of your router, you can sit out in your backyard and watch clouds drifting by as you type away.

Choosing the right types of wireless devices is an important decision. The next sections discuss some of the basic differences between current protocols used for wireless networking.

Choosing from Among Available Wireless Protocols

The Institute of Electrical and Electronics Engineers (IEEE) started to look seriously at wireless networking in 1990. This is when the 802.11 Standard was first introduced by the Wireless Local Area Networks Standards Working Group. The group based the standard roughly around the architecture used in cellular phone networks. The wireless network is controlled by a base station, which can be just a transmitter attached to the network or, more commonly these days, a router.

Larger networks can use more than one base station. Networks with more than one base station are usually referred to as *distribution systems*. A distribution system can be used to increase coverage area and support roaming of wireless hosts. You can also employ external omnidirectional antennas to increase coverage area, or if required, use point-to-point, or directional antennas to connect distant computers or networks. Right now, the least expensive wireless Linux networks are built using devices (such as access points or NICs) supporting 802.11b, although the faster 802.11g devices tend to get more shelf space. Devices are starting to appear marketed as Pre-N, meaning that they implement a draft standard, while the IEEE carry on debating the full N standard. Significantly more power throughput and range are promised by hardware that supports Pre-N, but this specification has yet to be formally agreed upon and is still some time off.

An early standard, 802.11a, offers greater transmission rates than 802.11b, and a number of 802.11a wireless NICs are available (some products provide up to 72Mbps, but will not work with 802.11b devices). Wireless networking devices based on 802.11g, which has the speed improvement of 802.11a and is compatible with 802.11b, are becoming more widely available. Other wireless protocols include Bluetooth, which provides up to 720Kbps data transfers. Bluetooth is intended for short-range device communications (such as for a printer) and supports a typical range of only 10 meters. Bluetooth is unlike IrDA, which requires line-of-sight (devices that are aimed at each other). Bluetooth use conflicts with 802.11 networks because it also uses the 2.4GHz band. You can find out more by browsing to http://www.bluetooth.com/.

The 802.11 standard specifies that wireless devices use a frequency range of 2400–2483.5MHz. This is the standard used in North America and Europe. In Japan, however, wireless networks are limited to a frequency range of 2471MHz–2479MHz because of Japanese regulations. Within these ranges, each network is given up to 79 non-overlapping frequency channels to use. This reduces the chance of two closely located wireless networks using the same channel at the same time. It also allows for channel hopping, which can be used for security.

Beyond the Network and onto the Internet

Ubuntu supports Internet connections and the use of Internet resources in many different ways. You will find a wealth of Internet-related software included with this book's version of Ubuntu, and you can download hundreds of additional free utilities from a variety of sources. To use them, you must have a working Internet connection.

In this section, you learn how to set up an Internet connection in Ubuntu using a modem and Point-to-Point Protocol (PPP) as well as other connection methods, including Digital Subscriber Line (DSL) and cable modem services. Just a few years ago, getting a dial-up connection working was difficult—hence, an entire chapter of this book was devoted to it. Nowadays, as long as you have a hardware modem, dial-up configuration is simple. The Ubuntu developers and the wider Linux community have made great progress in making connectivity easier.

Although many experienced Linux users continue to use manual scripts to establish their Internet connectivity, new users and experienced system administrators alike will find Ubuntu's graphical network configuration interface, the Internet Connection Wizard, much easier to use. You learn how to use the Internet Connection Wizard in this chapter, as well as how to configure Ubuntu to provide dial-in PPP support. The chapter also describes how to use Roaring Penguin's DSL utilities for managing connectivity through a cable modem connection.

Common Configuration Information

Although Ubuntu enables great flexibility in configuring Internet connections, that flexibility comes at the price of an increase in complexity. To configure Internet connectivity in Ubuntu, you must know more about the details of the connection process than you can learn from the information typically provided by your Internet service provider (ISP). In this section of the chapter, you learn what to ask about and how to use the information.

Some ISPs are unaware of Linux or unwilling to support its use with their service. Fortunately, that attitude is rapidly changing, and the majority of ISPs offer services using standard protocols that are compatible with Linux, even if they (or their technical support people) aren't aware that their own ISPs are Linux-friendly. You just need to press a little for the information you require.

If you are using a dial-up modem account (referred to in Linux as *PPP* for the Point-to-Point Protocol it uses), your ISP will provide your computer with a static or dynamic IP (Internet Protocol) address. A dynamic IP address changes each time you dial in, whereas a static IP address remains the same. The ISP also might automatically provide your computer with the names of the Domain Name Service (DNS) servers. You need to know the telephone number that your computer will dial in to for making the connection; your ISP supplies that number, too. You will also need a working modem and need to know the device name of the modem (usually /dev/modem).

NOTE

Most IP addresses are dynamically assigned by ISPs; ISPs have a pool of addresses, and you get whatever address is available. From the ISP's viewpoint, a small number of addresses can serve a large number of people because not everyone will be online at the same time. For most Internet services, a dynamic IP works well because it is the ISP's job to route that information to you, and it sits in the middle—between you and the service you want to use. But a dynamic IP address changes, and if someone needs to find you at the same address (if you run a website or a file transfer site, for example), an IP that changes every time you log on will not work well. For that, you need a static IP. Because your ISP cannot reuse that IP with its other customers, it will likely charge you more for a static IP than a dynamic IP. The average consumer doesn't need the benefit of a static IP, so he is happy paying less for a dynamically assigned IP. Also, the DNS information can be provided automatically by the ISP by the Dynamic Host Configuration Protocol, or DHCP.

If you are using DSL access or a cable modem, you might have a dynamic IP provided through DHCP, or you might be assigned a static IP. You might automatically be provided with the names of the DNS servers if you use DHCP, or you might have to set up DNS manually (in which case, you have to know the IP addresses of the DNS servers).

In all cases, you have to know your username, your password, and for the configuration of other services, the names of the mail servers and the news server. This information can be obtained from your ISP if you specifically ask for it.

> **NOTE**
>
> The information in this book will help you understand and avoid many connection issues, but you might experience connection problems. Keep the telephone number of the technical help service for your ISP on hand in case you are not able to establish a connection. But be aware that few ISPs offer Linux support, and you might need to seek help from a Linux-savvy friend or a Linux user's group if your special circumstances cannot be handled from the knowledge you gain from this book. Of course, the best place to look is on the Internet. Use Google's Linux page (http://www.google.com/linux/) to research the problem and see if any other users have found fixes or workarounds.

Configuring Digital Subscriber Line Access

Ubuntu also supports the use of a digital subscriber line (DSL) service. Although it refers to the different types of DSL available as xDSL, that name includes ADSL, IDSL, SDSL, and other flavors of DSL service; they can all be configured using the Internet Connection Wizard. DSL service generally provides 256Kbps to 24Mbps transfer speeds and transmits data over copper telephone lines from a central office to individual subscriber sites (such as your home). Many DSL services provide asymmetric speeds with download speeds greater than upload speeds.

> **NOTE**
>
> DSL service is an "always-on" type of Internet service, although you can turn off the connection under Ubuntu using the network configuration tool found under System, Administration, Network. An always-on connection exposes your computer to malicious abuse from crackers who trawl the Internet attempting to gain access to other computer systems. In addition to the capability to turn off such connections, Ubuntu is also preconfigured to not listen on any network ports, which means that any attempts to gain access to your computer will fail as Ubuntu will reject the request. This is the Ubuntu equivalent of putting up a 12-foot steel fence surrounding your computer.

A DSL connection requires that you have an ethernet network interface card (sometimes a USB interface that is not easily supported in Linux) in your computer or notebook. Many users also configure a gateway, firewall, or other computer with at least two network interface cards in order to share a connection with a LAN. We looked at the hardware and protocol issues earlier on in this chapter. Advanced configuration of a firewall or router, other than what was addressed during your initial installation of Ubuntu, is beyond the scope of this book.

Understanding Point-to-Point Protocol over Ethernet

Establishing a DSL connection with an ISP providing a static IP address is easy. Unfortunately, many DSL providers use a type of PPP protocol named Point-to-Point Protocol over Ethernet (*PPPoE*) that provides dynamic IP address assignment and authentication by encapsulating PPP information inside ethernet frames. Roaring Penguin's rp-pppoe clients are available from the Roaring Penguin site (www.roaringpenguin.com/penguin/pppoe/rp-pppoe-3.8.tar.gz), and these clients make the difficult-to-configure PPPoE connection much easier to deal with. You can download and install newer versions (see the Roaring Penguin link in the "Reference" section at the end of this chapter).

14

NOTE

ADSL modems were frequently supplied by ISPs when they originally started to roll out ADSL services. Nowadays however, these modems are optional, which is a good thing as many people choose to purchase a router with an in-built modem to create a dedicated connection. Using a router can save many headaches and will allow you to easily connect more than one computer to an Internet connection. Note that if you are using a cable connection then they usually come with an ethernet cable, in which case you just need a router. Check with your ISP before buying to ensure that whatever router you do end up with can be supported by them. You might find that your ISP even supplies a router as part of the package!

Configuring a PPPoE Connection Manually

You should only need to use these steps if you are using a modem supplied by your ISP, and not a router. The basic steps involved in manually setting up a DSL connection using Ubuntu involve connecting the proper hardware, and then running a simple configuration script if you use rp-pppoe from Roaring Penguin.

First, connect your DSL modem to your telephone line, and then plug in your ethernet cable from the modem to your computer's network interface card. If you plan to share your DSL connection with the rest of your LAN, you need at least two network cards—designated eth0 (for your LAN) and eth1 (for the DSL connection).

The following example assumes that you have more than one computer and will share your DSL connection on a LAN.

First, log in as root, and ensure that your first eth0 device is enabled and up (perhaps using the ifconfig command). Next, bring up the other interface, but assign a null IP address like this:

```
$ sudo /sbin/ifconfig eth1 0.0.0.0 up
```

Now use the adsl-setup command to set up your system. Type the command like this:

```
$ sudo /sbin/adsl-setup
```

You will be presented with a text script and be asked to enter your username and the Ethernet interface used for the connection (such as eth1). You will then be asked to use "on demand" service or have the connection stay up all the time (until brought down by the root operator). You can also set a timeout in seconds, if desired. You'll then be asked to enter the IP addresses of your ISP's DNS servers if you haven't configured the system's /etc/resolv.conf file.

After that, you will be prompted to enter your password two times, and have to choose the type of firewall and IP masquerading to use. (You learned about IP masquerading in the "Using IP Masquerading in Ubuntu" section, earlier in this chapter.) The actual configuration is done automatically. Using a firewall is essential nowadays, so you should choose this option unless you intend to craft your own set of firewall rules—a discussion of which is beyond the scope of this book. After you have chosen your firewall and IP masquerading setup, you will be asked to confirm, save, and implement your settings. You are also given a choice to allow users to manage the connection, a handy option for home users.

Changes will be made to your system's /etc/sysconfig/network-scripts/ifcfg-ppp0, /etc/resolv.conf, /etc/ppp/pap-secrets, and /etc/ppp/chap-secrets files.

After configuration has finished, use the adsl-start command to start a connection and DSL session, like this:

```
$ sudo /sbin/adsl-start
```

The DSL connection should be nearly instantaneous, but if problems occur, check to make sure that your DSL modem is communicating with the phone company's central office by examining the status LEDs on the modem. Because this varies from modem to modem, consult your modem user's manual.

Check to make certain that all cables are properly attached, that your interfaces are properly configured, and that you have entered the correct information to the setup script.

If IP masquerading is enabled, other computers on your LAN on the same subnet address (such as 192.168.0.XXX) can use the Internet, but must have the same /etc/resolv.conf name server entries and a routing entry with the DSL-connected computer as a gateway. For example, if the host computer with the DSL connection has an IP address of 192.168.0.1, and other computers on your LAN use addresses in the 192.168.0.XXX range, use the route command on each computer like this:

```
# /sbin/route add default gw 192.168.0.1
```

Note that you can also use a hostname instead if each computer has an /etc/hosts file with hostname and IP address entries for your LAN. To stop your connection, use the adsl-stop command like this:

```
# /sbin/adsl-stop
```

Configuring Dial-Up Internet Access

Most ISPs provide dial-up connections supporting PPP because it is a fast and efficient protocol for using TCP/IP over serial lines. PPP is designed for two-way networking; TCP/IP provides the transport protocol for data. One hurdle faced by new Ubuntu users is how to set up PPP and connect to the Internet. It is not necessary to understand the details of the PPP protocol in order to use it, and setting up a PPP connection is easy. You can configure the PPP connections manually using the command line or graphically during an X session using Ubuntu's Network Configuration Tool. Each approach produces the same results.

PPP uses several components on your system. The first is a daemon called pppd, which controls the use of PPP. The second is a driver called the high-level data link control (*HDLC*), which controls the flow of information between two machines. A third component of PPP is a routine called chat that dials the other end of the connection for you when you want it to. Although PPP has many "tunable" parameters, the default settings work well for most people.

Configuring a Dial-Up Connection Manually

Ubuntu includes some useful utilities to get your dial-up connection up and running. In this section we will take a look at two options that will have you on the Internet in no time.

The first way is to configure a connection using `pppconfig`, a command line utility to help you to configure specific dial-up connection settings.

Enter the following command:

```
$ sudo pppconfig
```

Before you connect for the first time you need to add yourself to both the dip and dialout groups by using the commands:

```
$ sudo adduser YOURNAMEHERE dip
$ sudo adduser YOURNAMEHERE dialout
```

Once this has been done it is just a simple matter of issuing the `pon` command to connect, and the `poff` command to disconnect. You can create as many different profiles as you need, and can launch specific ones by using the command `pon profilename`, again using the `poff` command to disconnect.

Troubleshooting Connection Problems

The Linux Documentation Project at http://www.tldp.org/ offers many in-depth resources for configuring and troubleshooting these connections. The Internet search engine Google is also an invaluable tool for dealing with specific questions about these connections. For many other useful references, see the "Reference" section at the end of this chapter.

Here are a few troubleshooting tips culled from many years of experience:

▶ If your modem connects and then hangs up, you are probably using the wrong password or dialing the wrong number. If the password and phone number are correct, it is likely an authentication protocol problem.

▶ If you get connected but cannot reach websites, it is likely a domain name resolver problem, meaning that DNS is not working. If it worked yesterday and you haven't "adjusted" the associated files, it is probably a problem at the ISP's end. Call and ask.

▶ Always make certain that everything is plugged in. Check again—and again.

▶ If the modem works in Windows, but not in Linux no matter what you do, it is probably a software modem no matter what it said on the box.

▶ If everything just stops working (and you do not see smoke), it is probably a glitch at the ISP or the telephone company. Take a break and give them some time to fix it.

▶ Never configure a network connection when you have had too little sleep or too much caffeine; you will just have to redo it tomorrow.

Related Ubuntu and Linux Commands

You will use these commands when managing network connectivity in your Ubuntu system:

- `dhclient`—Automatically acquire, and then set IP info for a NIC
- `ethereal`—GNOME graphical network scanner
- `firestarter`—Ubuntu's basic graphical firewalling tool for X
- `ifconfig`—Displays and manages Linux networking devices
- `iwconfig`—Displays and sets wireless network device parameters
- `route`—Displays and manages Linux kernel routing table
- `ssh`—The OpenSSH remote-login client and preferred replacement for `telnet`
- `network-admin`—Ubuntu's GUI for configuring network connections

Reference

The following websites and books are great resources for more information on the topics covered in this chapter. Networking is complex. The more you take the time to learn, the easier setting up and maintaining your network will be.

Websites

- http://www.ietf.org/rfc.html—Go here to search for, or get a list of, Request for Comments (RFC).

- http://www.oth.net/dyndns.html—For a list of Dynamic DNS service providers, go to this site.

- http://www.isc.org/products/DHCP/dhcpv3-README.html—The DHCP README is available at this site.

- http://www.ieee.org—The Institute of Electrical and Electronics Engineers (IEEE) website.

- http://www.mozillaquest.com/Network_02/Wireless_Network_Technology_03_Story-01.html—Wireless networking with Red Hat 7.2.

Books

▶ *Sams Teach Yourself TCP/IP Network Administration in 21 Days*, Sams Publishing, ISBN: 0-672-31250-6

▶ *TCP/IP Network Administration*, O'Reilly Publishing, ISBN: 1-56592-322-7

▶ *Practical Networking*, Que Publishing, ISBN: 0-7897-2252-6

▶ *Samba Unleashed*, Sams Publishing, ISBN: 0-672-31862-8

▶ *The DHCP Handbook*, Sams Publishing, ISBN: 0-672-32327-3

# CHAPTER 15

Remote Access with SSH and Telnet

The ability to control your system remotely is one of the high points of Ubuntu—you can connect from any Linux box to another Linux box in a variety of ways. If you just want to check something quickly or if you have limited bandwidth, you have the option of using only the command line, but you can also connect directly to the X server and get full graphical control.

Understanding the selection of tools available is largely a history lesson. For example, Telnet was an earlier way of connecting to another computer through the command line, but that has since been superseded by SSH. That is not to say that you should ignore Telnet; you need to know how to use it so you have it as a fallback. However, SSH is preferred because it is more secure. We cover both in this chapter.

Setting Up a Telnet Server

You will find the Telnet server installation packages in Synaptic under the telnetd package. Once installed, select Administration, Services and enable Telnet. Note your IP address while you are here (run ifconfig with sudo).

With that done, you can now fire up your other Linux box and type **telnet <your IP>**. You are prompted to enter your username and password. The whole conversation should look like this:

```
[paul@susannah ~]$ telnet 10.0.0.1
Trying 10.0.0.1...
Connected to 10.0.0.1 (10.0.0.1)
```

```
Escape character is '^]'.

Welcome to Caitlin
Running Ubuntu

* All access is logged *

login: paul
Password:
Last login: Sat Jul 9 12:05:41 from 10.0.0.5
[paul@caitlin ~]$
```

TIP

Note that the server responds with Welcome to Caitlin, running Ubuntu, which is
a customized message. Your machine will probably respond with Ubuntu and some version information. This is insecure: giving away version numbers is never a smart move.
In fact, even saying Ubuntu is questionable. Edit the issue and issue.net files in your
/etc directory to change these messages.

Running the w command now shows you as connecting from the external IP address.

Telnet Versus SSH

Although Telnet is worth keeping around as a fail-safe, last resort option, SSH is superior
in virtually every way. Telnet is fast but also insecure. It sends all your text, including your
password, in plain text that can be read by anyone with the right tools. SSH, on the other
hand, encrypts all your communication and so is more resource-intensive but secure—
even a government security agency sniffing your packets for some reason would still have
a hard time cracking the encryption.

Andy Green, posting to the fedora-list mailing list, summed up the Telnet situation
perfectly when he said, "As Telnet is universally acknowledged to encourage evil, the
service telnetd is not enabled by default." It is worthwhile taking the hint: Use Telnet as a
last resort only.

Setting Up an SSH Server

If not installed already, the OpenSSH server can be installed through Synaptic by adding
the openssh-server package. If you have disabled it, you can re-enable it by selecting
System, Administration, Services and selecting the Remote Shell Server box. As you might
have gathered, sshd is the name for the SSH server daemon.

Two different versions of SSH exist, called SSH1 and SSH2. The latter is newer, is more secure, comes with more features, and is the default in Ubuntu. Support for SSH1 clients is best left disabled so older clients can connect. This is set up in the /etc/ssh/sshd_config file on this line:

```
#Protocol 2,1
```

For maximum security, that line should read:

```
Protocol 2
```

This removes the comment sign (#) and tells sshd that you want it to only allow SSH2 connections. Save the file and exit your editor. The next step is to tell sshd to reread its configuration file, by executing this command:

```
kill -HUP 'cat /var/run/sshd.pid'
```

If this returns cat: /var/run/sshd.pid: No such file or directory, it means you didn't have sshd running. Next time you start it, it reads the configuration file and uses SSH2 only.

You can test this change by trying to connect to your SSH server in SSH1 mode. From the same machine, type this:

```
ssh -1 localhost
```

The -1 switch forces SSH1 mode. If you successfully forced the SSH2 protocol, you should get the message Protocol major versions differ: 1 vs. 2.

The SSH Tools

To the surprise of many, OpenSSH actually comprises a suite of tools. We have already seen ssh, the secure shell command that connects to other machines, and sshd, the SSH server daemon that accepts incoming SSH connections. However, there is also sftp, a replacement for ftp, and scp, a replacement for rcp.

You should already be familiar with the ftp command because it is the lowest-common-denominator system for handling FTP file transfers. Like Telnet, though, ftp is insecure: It sends your data in plain text across the network and anyone can sniff your packets to pick out a username and password. The SSH replacement, sftp, puts FTP traffic over an SSH link, thus securing it.

The rcp command might be new to you, largely because it is not used much anymore. Back in its day, rcp was the primary way of copying a single file to another server. As with ftp, scp replaces rcp by simply channeling the data over a secure SSH connection. The difference between sftp and scp is that the former allows you to copy many files, whereas the latter just sends one.

Using `scp` to Copy Individual Files Between Machines

The most basic use of the `scp` command is to copy a file from your current machine to a remote machine. You can do that with the following command:

```
scp test.txt 10.0.0.1:
```

The first parameter is the name of the file you want to send, and the second is the server to which you want to send it. Note that there is a colon at the end of the IP address. This is where you can specify an exact location for the file to be copied. If you have nothing after the colon, as in the previous example, `scp` copies the file to your home directory. As with SSH, `scp` prompts you for your password before copying takes place.

You can rewrite the previous command so you copy `test.txt` from the local machine and save it as `newtest.txt` on the server:

```
scp test.txt 10.0.0.1:newtest.txt
```

Alternatively, if there is a directory where you want the file to be saved, you can specify it like this:

```
scp test.txt 10.0.0.1:subdir/stuff/newtest.txt
```

The three commands so far have all assumed that your username on your local machine is the same as your username on the remote machine. If this is not the case, you need to specify your username before the remote address, like this:

```
scp test.txt japhnewtest.txt
```

You can use `scp` to copy remote files locally, simply by specifying the remote file as the source and the current directory (.) as the destination:

```
scp 10.0.0.1:remote.txt .
```

The `scp` command is nominally also capable of copying files from one remote machine to another remote machine, but this functionality has yet to be properly implemented in Ubuntu. If a patch is released—and we hope one is eventually—the correct command to use would be this:

```
scp 10.0.0.1:test.txt 10.0.0.2:remotetest.txt
```

That copies `test.txt` from `10.0.0.1` to `remotetest.txt` on `10.0.0.2`. If this works, you are asked for passwords for both servers.

Using `sftp` to Copy Many Files Between Machines

`sftp` is a mix between `ftp` and `scp`. Connecting to the server uses the same syntax as `scp`—you can just specify an IP address to connect using your current username, or you can specify a username using *username@ipaddress*. You can optionally add a colon and a directory, as with scp. After you are connected, the commands are the same as ftp: cd, put, mput, get, quit, and so on.

In one of the scp examples, we copied a remote file locally. You can do the same thing with sftp with the following conversation:

```
[paul@susannah ~]$ sftp 10.0.0.1
Connecting to 10.0.0.1...
paul@10.0.0.1's password:
sftp> get remote.txt
Fetching /home/paul/remote.txt to remote.txt
/home/paul/remote.txt      100%  23   0.0KB/s    00:00
sftp> quit
paul@susannah ~]$
```

Although FTP remains prominent because of the number of systems that do not have support for SSH (Windows, specifically), SFTP is gaining in popularity. Apart from the fact that it secures all communications between client and server, SFTP is popular because the initial connection between the client and server is made over port 22 through the sshd daemon. Someone using SFTP connects to the standard sshd daemon, verifies himself, and then is handed over to the SFTP server. The advantage to this is that it reduces the attack vectors because the SFTP server cannot be contacted directly and so cannot be attacked as long as the sshd daemon is secure.

Using ssh-keygen to Enable Key-based Logins

There is a weak link in the SSH system, and, inevitably, it lies with users. No matter what lengths system administrators go to in training users to be careful with their passwords, monitors around the world have Post-it notes attached to them with "pAssw0rd" written on. Sure, it has a mix of letters and numbers, but it can be cracked in less than a second by any brute-force method. *Brute-forcing* is the method of trying every password possibility, starting with likely words (such as *password* and variants, or *god*) and then just trying random letters (for example, *a*, *aa*, *ab*, *ac*, and so on).

Even very strong passwords are no more than about 16 characters; such passwords take a long time to brute-force but can still be cracked. The solution is to use key-based logins, which generate a unique, 1024-bit private and public key pair for your machine. These keys take even the fastest computers a lifetime to crack, and you can back them up with a password to stop others from using them.

Creating an SSH key is done through the ssh-keygen command, like this:

```
ssh-keygen -t dsa
```

Press Enter when it prompts you where to save your key, and enter a passphrase when it asks you to. This passphrase is just a password used to protect the key—you can leave it blank if you want to, but doing so would allow other people to use your account to connect to remote machines if they manage to log in as you.

After the key is generated (it might take up to 30 seconds depending on the speed of your machine), change the directory to .ssh (cd ~/.ssh), which is a hidden directory where your key is stored and also where it keeps a list of safe SSH hosts. There you will see the files id_dsa and id_dsa.pub. The first is your private key and should never be given out. The second is your public key, which is safe for distribution. You need to copy the public key to each server you want to connect to via key-based SSH.

Using scp, you can copy the public key over to your server, like this:

```
scp id_dsa.pub 10.0.0.1:
```

This places id_dsa.pub in your home directory on 10.0.0.1. The next step is to SSH into 10.0.0.1 normally and set up that key as an authorized key. So, you can SSH in as yourself and then type

```
touch .ssh/authorized_keys
cat id_dsa.pub >> .ssh/authorized_keys
chmod 400 .ssh/authorized_keys
```

The touch command creates the authorized_keys file (if it does not exist already); then you use cat to append the contents of id_dsa.pub to the list of already authorized keys. Finally, chmod is used to make authorized_keys read only.

With that done, you can type exit to disconnect from the remote machine and return to your local machine. Then you can try running ssh again. If you are prompted for your passphrase, you have successfully configured key-based authentication.

That is the current machine secured, but what about every other machine? It is still possible to log in from another machine using only a password, which means your remote machine is still vulnerable.

The solution to this is to switch to root and edit the /etc/ssh/sshd_config file. Look for the PasswordAuthentication line and make sure it reads no (and that it is not commented out with a #). Save the file, and run kill -HUP 'cat /var/run/sshd.pid' to have sshd reread its configuration files. With that done, sshd accepts only connections from clients with authorized keys, which stops crackers from brute-forcing their way in.

TIP

For extra security, consider setting PermitRootLogin to no in /etc/ssh/sshd_config. When this is set, it becomes impossible to SSH into your machine using the root account—you must connect with a normal user account and then use su or sudo to switch to root. This is advantageous because most brute-force attempts take place on the root account because it is the only account that is guaranteed to exist on a server.

Also, even if a cracker knows your user account, she has to guess both your user password and your root password to take control of your system.

Remote X

Everything we have looked at so far has been about command-line remoting, with no mention so far of how to bring up a graphical user interface. There are two ways of doing this in Linux: the X Display Manager Control Protocol (XDMCP) and Virtual Network Computing (VNC). The former is specific to X Windows and is very tightly integrated with the rest of the graphical system but is also very insecure. VNC is more modern and very widespread but insecure in some implementations. Both are being used with Ubuntu, so we will cover both here.

XDMCP

Unless you have Ubuntu configured to log in a specific user automatically, you will be familiar with the user login screen that appears at bootup. What you are seeing is the Gnome Display Manager (GDM), which runs your X sessions, checks passwords, and so forth. What you are doing is logging in to the local machine because that is the default configuration.

However, GDM is also equipped to allow other network users to connect to your machine through the XDMCP protocol. There are various reasons for using XDMCP, of which the most popular is that many modern machines are large and noisy. They have big hard drives, CPUs with huge fans, and powerful graphics cards, and so do not fit into a peaceful living room. On the flip side, a thin client (a machine with very little CPU power and no hard disk of its own) is silent but not powerful enough to run Gnome or OpenOffice.org.

The solution is to have your powerful machine locked away in a cupboard somewhere with a Wi-Fi connection attached and your quiet thin client sitting in the lounge also on the Wi-Fi link. The thin client connects to the powerful machine and runs all its programs from there, with all the graphics being relayed over the network.

With Ubuntu, this is easy to do. Starting with the server side first, select System > Administration > Login Window; then select the Remote tab and change the Style option to "Plain with face browser". On the client side, go to the same dialog and make sure the Show Actions Menu box is checked from the Local tab.

Now, from the client side, log out from your desktop so you return to the Ubuntu login screen. When it prompts you for your username, look for the Options button and select Remote Login with XDMCP. A new dialog box appears with a list of local XDMCP servers that are willing to accept your connection—you should see your server in there. Select it and click Connect; you will see a login screen from that server, inviting you to log in. You will, of course, need a valid account on the server to be able to log in; however, that is the only thing you need.

As you can see, because XDMCP is so core to the X Windows system, it is easy to set up. However, as you will find as you use it, XDMCP is very slow—even on a Gigabit Ethernet network, it will chew up a substantial percentage of bandwidth. It is also insecure. Anyone can monitor what you are doing with very little work. Because of these two flaws, XDMCP should never be used outside a trusted network.

15

VNC

The next step up from XDMCP is VNC, which was developed at AT&T's Cambridge Research Laboratory in England. VNC is widespread in the Linux world and, to a lesser extent, in the Windows world. Its main advantage is its widespread nature: Nearly all Linux distros bundle VNC, and clients are available for a wide selection of platforms.

To set up VNC, start Synaptic and install the vnc-common and xvncviewer packages. With that done, all that remains is to tell Ubuntu who should be allowed to connect to your session. This is done from the Remote Desktop option on the Preferences menu. By default, your desktop is not shared, so check Allow Other Users to View Your Desktop to share it. You should also check Allow Other Users to Control Your Desktop; otherwise, people will be able to see what you are doing but not interact with the desktop—which is not very helpful.

The second set of options on that screen is important. If you are using this as a remote way to connect to your own desktop, deselect Ask You for Confirmation. If this is not done, when you try to connect from your remote location, Ubuntu will pop up a message box on the local machine asking Should this person be allowed to connect? Because you are not there to click Yes, the connection will fail. If you want to let someone else remotely connect to your system, keep this box enabled so you know when people are connecting. You should always enter a password, no matter who it is that will connect. VNC, like XDMCP, should not be considered secure over the Internet, or even on untrusted networks.

Reference

▶ http://www.openssh.com—The home page of the OpenSSH implementation of SSH that Ubuntu uses. It is run by the same team as OpenBSD, a secure BSD-based operating system.

▶ http://www.realvnc.com—The home page of the team that made VNC at AT&T's Cambridge Research Laboratory. It has since started RealVNC Ltd., a company dedicated to developing and supporting VNC.

▶ http://www.tightvnc.com—Here you can find an alternative to VNC called TightVNC that has several key advances over the stock VNC release. The most important feature is that TightVNC can use SSH for encryption, guaranteeing security.

▶ http://www.nomachine.com/—Another alternative to VNC is in the pipeline, called NX. The free implementation, FreeNX, is under heavy development at the time of writing but promises to work much faster than VNC.

One book on SSH that stands out from the crowd is known as "The Snail Book" because of the picture on the cover. It covers all the SSH suite and is called *SSH: The Secure Shell* (O'Reilly), ISBN: 0-596-00011-1.

PART IV

Ubuntu as a Server

IN THIS PART

CHAPTER 16

File and Print

In the early days of computing, file and printer sharing was pretty much impossible because of the lack of good networking standards and interoperability. If you wanted to use a printer connected to another computer, you had to save the file to a floppy disk and walk over.

Nowadays, both file and printer sharing have become second nature in a world where it is not unusual for someone to own more than one computer. Whether it be for sharing photographs among various computers or having a central repository available for collaboration, file sharing is an important part of our information age. Alongside this is the need to be able to share printers; after all, no one wants to have to plug and unplug a computer to a printer just so he can print out a quick letter.

Whatever your reasons for needing to share files and printers across a network, you find out how to do both in this chapter. We look at how you can share files using the popular UNIX NFS protocol and the more Windows-friendly Samba system. You also find out how to configure network-attached printers with interfaces such as JetDirect. We look at both graphical and command-line tools, so you should find something to suit the way you work.

> **CAUTION**
>
> By default, Ubuntu ships with all its network ports blocked. That is, it does not listen to any requests on any ports when it is first installed. To configure the firewall, you must retrieve and install Firestarter using either `synaptic` or `apt-get`. After you have installed this, you can use it to configure the firewall to open specific ports relating to the topics covered in this chapter.
>
> You can find detailed documentation about Firestarter at http://www.fs-security.com/docs/.

Using the Network File System

Network File System (NFS) is the protocol developed by Sun Microsystems that allows computers to use a remote file system as if it were a real part of the local machine. A common use of NFS is to allow users home directories to appear on every local machine they use, thus eliminating the need to have physical home directories. This opens up hot desking and other flexible working arrangements, especially because no matter where the user is, his home directory follows him around.

Another popular use for NFS is to share binary files between similar computers. If you have a new version of a package that you want all machines to have, you have to the upgrade only on the NFS server, and all hosts running the same version of Ubuntu will have the same upgraded package.

Installing and Starting or Stopping NFS

NFS is not installed by default on Ubuntu, so you need to install the `nfs-common`, `nfs-kernel-server`, and `portmap` packages. NFS itself consists of several programs that work together to provide the NFS server service. One is `rpc.portmapper`, which maps NFS requests to the correct daemon. Two others are `rpc.nfsd`, which is the NFS daemon, and `rpc.mountd`, which controls the mounting and unmounting of file systems.

Ubuntu automatically adds NFS to the system startup scripts, so it will always be available after you have configured it. To check this, use the command `sudo /etc/init.d/nfs-kernel-server status` and it will show you that the service is running. If you need to manually start the NFS server, use the following command:

```
$ sudo /etc/init.d/nfs-kernel-server start
Starting NFS services:                     [ OK ]
Starting NFS quotas:                       [ OK ]
Starting NFS daemon:                       [ OK ]
Starting NFS mountd:                       [ OK ]
```

In this example, NFS has been started. Use the `stop` keyword instead to stop the service, or `restart` to restart the server. This approach to controlling NFS proves handy, especially after configuration changes have been made. See the next section on how to configure NFS support on your Ubuntu system.

NFS Server Configuration

You can configure the NFS server by editing the /etc/exports file. This file is similar to the /etc/fstab file in that it is used to set the permissions for the file systems being exported. The entries look like this:

```
/file/system yourhost(options) *.yourdomain.com(options) 192.168.0.0/24(options)
```

This shows three common clients to which to share /file/system. The first, yourhost, shares /file/system to just one host. The second, .yourdomain.com, uses the asterisk (*) as a wildcard to enable all hosts in yourdomain.com to access /file/system. The third share enables all hosts of the Class C network, 192.168.0.0, to access /file/share. For security, it is best not to use shares like the last two across the Internet because all data will be readable by any network the data passes by.

Table 16.1 shows some common options.

TABLE 16.1   /etc/fstab Options

Option	Purpose
rw	Gives read and write access
ro	Gives read-only access
async	Writes data when the server, not the client, feels the need
sync	Writes data as it is received

16

The following is an example of an /etc/exports file:

```
# /etc/exports: the access control list for filesystems which may be exported
#               to NFS clients.  See exports(5).
/home/andrew 192.168.0.0/24(rw,no_root_squash)
```

This file exports (makes available) /home/ahudson to any host in 192.168.0.* and allows users to read from and write to /home/andrew.

After you have finished with the /etc/exports file, the following command

```
$ sudo exportfs -a
```

exports all the file systems in the /etc/exports file to a list named xtab under the /var/lib/nfs directory, which is used as a guide for mounting when a remote computer asks for a directory to be exported. The -r option to the command reads the entire /etc/exports file and mounts all the entries. You can also use the exportfs command to export specific files temporarily. Here's an example using exportfs to export a file system:

```
/usr/sbin/exportfs -o async yourhost:/usr/tmp
```

This command exports /usr/tmp to yourhost with the async option.

Be sure to restart the NFS server after making any changes to /etc/exports. If you prefer, you can use Ubuntu's shares-admin graphical client to set up NFS while using the X Window System. Start the client by clicking the System menu and then selecting the Shared Folders menu item from the Administration menu.

After you press Enter, you are prompted for your password. Type in the password and click OK; the main window will then display. Click the Add button to open the Add Share dialog box, as shown in Figure 16.1.

FIGURE 16.1   You can use Ubuntu's share-admin client to quickly set up local directories for export using NFS.

In the Path drop-down box, choose the directory that you want to share; in the Share drop-down box, choose NFS. Click the Add Host button that appears to specify which hosts, IP addresses, or networks to be allowed access to the directory. By default, a directory is exported as read/write, but you can choose read-only by ticking the Read Only option. When finished, click the OK button, click the Apply button, and then use the File menu to quit.

NFS Client Configuration

To configure your host as an NFS client (to acquire remote files or directories), you need to ensure that you have the nfs-common package installed, in order to be able to access NFS shares. Once you've installed this using either synaptic or apt-get, edit the /etc/fstab file as you would to mount any local file system. However, instead of using a device name to be mounted (such as /dev/sda1), enter the remote hostname and the desired file system to be imported. For example, one entry might look like this:

```
# Device            Mount Point  Type  Options      Freq Pass
yourhost:/usr/local  /usr/local   nfs   nfsvers=3,ro  0    0
```

> **NOTE**
>
> If you use `autofs` on your system, you need to use proper `autofs` entries for your remote NFS mounts. See the `section` 5 man page for `autofs`.

The Options column uses the same options as standard `fstab` file entries with some additional entries, such as `nfsvers=3`, which specifies the third version of NFS. You can also use the `mount` command, as root, to quickly attach a remote directory to a local file system by using a remote host's name and exported directory. For example:

```
$ sudo mount -t nfs 192.168.2.67:/music /music
```

After you press Enter, the entire remote directory appears on your file system. You can verify the imported file system using the `df` command, as follows:

```
$ df
Filesystem            1k-blocks      Used Available Use% Mounted on
/dev/hda2             18714368   9642600   8121124  55% /
/dev/hda1                46636     13247     30981  30% /boot
none                    120016         0    120016   0% /dev/shm
192.168.2.67:/music   36875376  20895920  14106280  60% /music
```

Make sure that the desired mount point exists before using the `mount` command. When finished using the directory (perhaps for copying backups), you can use the `umount` command to remove the remote file system. Note that if you specify the root directory (`/`) as a mount point, you cannot unmount the NFS directory until you reboot (because Linux complains that the file system is in use).

Putting Samba to Work

Samba uses the *Session Message Block (SMB)* protocol to enable the Windows operating system (or any operating system) to access Linux files. Using Samba, you can make your Ubuntu machine look just like a Windows computer to other Windows computers on your network. You do not need to install Windows on your PC.

Samba is a complex program—the Samba man page (when converted to text) for just the configuration file is 330KB and 7,226 lines long. Although Samba is complex, setting it up and using it does not have to be difficult. There are many options, which accounts for some of Samba's complexity. Depending on what you want, Samba's use can be as easy or as difficult as you would like it to be.

Fortunately, Ubuntu includes the *Samba Web Administration Tool (SWAT)*, which you can use to configure Samba by using the Mozilla web browser. SWAT provides an easy way to start and stop the Samba server; set up printing services; define remote access permissions; and create Samba usernames, passwords, and shared directories. This section delves into the basics of configuring Samba, and you should first read how to manually configure Samba to get an understanding of how the software works. At the end of this section, you will see how to enable, start, and use SWAT to set up simple file sharing.

Like most of the software that comes with Ubuntu, Samba is licensed under the GPL and is free. Installation is straightforward and the software can be installed using either synaptic or apt-get. Regardless of which route you take, you should snag the samba and swat packages.

Installing from source code can be more time-consuming. If you do not want to install using Ubuntu's default locations, however, installing from the source code is a more configurable method. Just download the source from http://www.samba.org/ and unpack the files. Change into the source directory and, as root, run the command ./configure along with any changes from the defaults. Then run make, make test (if you want), followed by make install to install Samba in the specified locations.

NOTE

If you haven't done so, you might need to install a meta-package (a single package that provides several related packages) called build-essential. This package automatical-ly installs all the make tools, plus other development utilities that you will need to com-pile software from source code.

When you install Samba, it is a good idea to also install the samba-doc and samba-doc-pdf packages because they contain extensive documentation in text, PDF, and HTML format. After you install it, you can find this documentation in /usr/share/doc/samba*/doc. If you install Samba using your Ubuntu disc, you can find a large amount of documentation in the directory tree starting at /usr/share/doc/samba-doc or /usr/share/doc/samba-doc-pdf in several formats, including PDF, HTML, and text, among others. Altogether, almost 3MB of documentation is included with the source code.

After installing Samba, you can either create the file /etc/samba/smb.conf or use the smb.conf file supplied with Samba, which is located by default under the /etc/samba directory with Ubuntu. You can find nearly a dozen sample configuration files under the /usr/share/doc/samba*/examples directory.

NOTE

Depending on your needs, smb.conf can be a simple file of fewer than 20 lines or a huge file spanning many pages of text. If your needs are complex, I suggest you browse through The Official Samba Howto and Reference Guide, or TOSHARG. This helpful guide can be found at http://samba.org/samba/docs/man/Samba3-HOWTO/.

Manually Configuring Samba with `/etc/samba/smb.conf`

The `/etc/samba/smb.conf` file is broken into sections. Each section is a description of the resource shared (share) and should be titled appropriately. The three special sections are as follows:

- ▶ `[global]`—Establishes the global configuration settings (defined in detail in the `smb.conf` man page and Samba documentation, found under the `/usr/share/doc/samba/docs` directory)

- ▶ `[homes]`—Shares users' home directories and specifies directory paths and permissions

- ▶ `[printers]`—Handles printing by defining shared printers and printer access

Each section in your `/etc/samba/smb.conf` configuration file should be named for the resource being shared. For example, if the resource `/usr/local/programs` is being shared, you could call the section `[programs]`. When Windows sees the share, it is called by whatever you name the section (`programs` in this example). The easiest and fastest way to set up this share is with the following example from `smb.conf`:

```
[programs]
path = /usr/local/programs
writeable = true
```

This bit shares the `/usr/local/programs` directory with any valid user who asks for it and makes that directory writable. It is the most basic share because it sets no limits on the directory.

Here are some parameters you can set in the sections:

- ▶ Requiring a user to enter a password before accessing a shared directory

- ▶ Limiting the hosts allowed to access the shared directory

- ▶ Altering permissions users are allowed to have on the directory

- ▶ Limiting the time of day during which the directory is accessible

The possibilities are almost endless. Any parameters set in the individual sections override the parameters set in the `[global]` section. The following section adds a few restrictions to the `[programs]` section:

```
[programs]
path = /usr/local/programs
writeable = true
valid users = ahudson
browseable = yes
```

16

```
create mode = 0700
```

The valid users entry limits userid to just ahudson. All other users can browse the directory because of the browseable = yes entry, but only ahudson can write to the directory.
Any files created by ahudson in the directory give ahudson full permissions, but no one
else will have access to the file. This is exactly the same as setting permissions with the
chmod command. Again, there are numerous options, so you can be as creative as you
want to when developing sections.

Setting Global Samba Behavior with the [global] Section

The [global] section set parameters establishes configuration settings for all of Samba. If a
given parameter is not specifically set in another section, Samba uses the default setting in
the [global] section. The [global] section also sets the general security configuration for
Samba. The [global] section is the only section that does not require the name in brackets.

Samba assumes that anything before the first bracketed section not labeled [global] is
part of the global configuration. (Using bracketed headings in /etc/samba/smb.conf
makes your configuration file more readable.) The following sections discuss common
Samba settings to share directories and printers. You will then see how to test your Samba
configuration.

Sharing Home Directories Using the [homes] Section

The [homes] section shares out Ubuntu home directories for the users. The home directory
is shared automatically when a user's Windows computer connects to the Linux server
holding the home directory. The one problem with using the default configuration is that
the user sees all the configuration files (such as .profile and others with a leading period
in the filename) that he normally wouldn't see when logging on through Linux. One
quick way to avoid this is to include a path option in the [homes] section. To use this
solution, each user who requires a Samba share of his home directory needs a separate
"home directory" to act as his Windows home directory.

For example, this pseudo home directory could be a directory named share in each user's
home directory on your Ubuntu system. You can specify the path option when using
SWAT by using the %u option when specifying a path for the default homes shares (see the
section "Configuring Samba Using SWAT" later in this chapter). The complete path setting
would be this:

```
/home/%u/share
```

This setting specifies that the directory named share under each user's directory is the
shared Samba directory. The corresponding manual smb.conf setting to provide a separate
"home directory" looks like this:

```
[homes]
        comment = Home Directories
        path = /home/%u/share
        valid users = %S
```

```
read only = No
create mask = 0664
directory mask = 0775
browseable = No
```

If you have a default [homes] section, the share shows up in the user's Network Neighborhood as the user's name. When the user connects, Samba scans the existing sections in smb.conf for a specific instance of the user's home directory. If there is not one, Samba looks up the username in /etc/passwd. If the correct username and password have been given, the home directory listed in /etc/passwd is shared out at the user's home directory. Typically, the [homes] section looks like this (the browseable = no entry prevents other users from being able to browse your home directory and is a good security practice):

```
[homes]
browseable = no
writable = yes
```

This example shares out the home directory and makes it writable to the user. Here's how you specify a separate Windows home directory for each user:

```
[homes]
browseable = no
writable = yes
path = /path/to/windows/directories
```

Sharing Printers by Editing the [printers] Section

The [printers] section works much like the [homes] section but defines shared printers for use on your network. If the section exists, users have access to any printer listed in your Ubuntu /etc/printcap file.

Like the [homes] section, when a print request is received, all the sections are scanned for the printer. If no share is found (with careful naming, there should not be unless you create a section for a specific printer), the /etc/printcap file is scanned for the printer name that is then used to send the print request.

For printing to work properly, you must correctly set up printing services on your Ubuntu computer. A typical [printers] section looks like the following:

```
[printers]
comment = Ubuntu Printers
browseable = no
printable = yes
path = /var/spool/samba
```

The /var/spool/samba is a spool path set just for Samba printing.

16

Testing Samba with the `testparm` Command

After you have created your /etc/smb.conf file, you can check it for correctness by using the testparm command. This command parses through your /etc/smb.conf file and checks for any syntax errors. If none are found, your configuration file will probably work correctly. It does not, however, guarantee that the services specified in the file will work. It is merely making sure that the file is correctly written.

As with all configuration files, if you are modifying an existing, working file, it is always prudent to copy the working file to a different location and modify that file. Then, you can check the file with the testparm utility. The command syntax is as follows:

```
$ sudo testparm /path/to/smb.conf.back-up
Load smb config files from smb.conf.back-up
Processing section "[homes]"
Processing section "[printers]"
Loaded services file OK.
```

This output shows that the Samba configuration file is correct, and, as long as all the services are running correctly on your Ubuntu machine, Samba should be working correctly. Now copy your old smb.conf file to a new location, put the new one in its place, and restart Samba with the command /etc/init.d/smb restart. Your new or modified Samba configuration should now be in place.

Starting the `smbd` Daemon

Now that your smb.conf file is correctly configured, you can start your Samba server daemon. This can be done with the /usr/sbin/smbd command, which (with no options) starts the Samba server with all the defaults. The most common option you will change in this command is the location of the smb.conf file; you change this option if you don't want to use the default location /etc/smb/smb.conf. The -s option allows you to change the smb.conf file Samba uses; this option is also useful for testing whether a new smb.conf file actually works. Another useful option is the -l option, which specifies the log file Samba uses to store information.

To start, stop, or restart Samba from the command line, use the /etc/init.d/samba script with a proper keyword, such as start, like so:

```
$ sudo /etc/init.d/samba start
```

Using the `smbstatus` Command

The smbstatus command reports on the current status of your Samba connections. The syntax is as follows:

```
/usr/bin/smbstatus [options]
```

Table 16.2 shows some of the available options.

TABLE 16.2 **mbstatus** Options

Option	Result
-b	Brief output
-d	Verbose output
-s /path/to/config	Used if the configuration file used at startup is not the standard one
-u username	Shows the status of a specific user's connection
-p	Lists current smb processes, which can prove useful in scripts

Connecting with the smbclient Command

The smbclient command allows users on other Linux hosts to access your smb shares. You cannot mount the share on your host, but you can use it in a way that is similar to an FTP client. Several options can be used with the smbclient command. The most frequently used is -I followed by the IP address of the computer to which you are connecting. The smbclient command does not require root access to run:

```
smbclient -I 10.10.10.20 -Uusername%password
```

This gives you the following prompt:

```
smb: <current directory on share>
```

From here, the commands are almost identical to the standard UNIX/Linux FTP commands. Note that you can omit a password on the smbclient command line. You are then prompted to enter the Samba share password.

Mounting Samba Shares

There are two ways to mount Samba shares to your Linux host. Mounting a share is the same as mounting an available media partition or remote NFS directory except that the Samba share is accessed using SMB. The first method uses the standard Linux mount command:

```
$ sudo mount -t smbfs //10.10.10.20/homes /mount/point -o
username=ahudson,dmask=777,\
 fmask=777
```

NOTE

You can substitute the IP address for hostname if your name service is running or the host is in your /etc/hosts file.

This command mounts ahudson's home directory on your host and gives all users full permissions to the mount. The permissions are equal to the permissions on the chmod command.

The second method produces the same results using the smbmount command, as follows:

```
$ sudo smbmount //10.10.10.20/homes /mount/point -o username=ahudson,dmask-777,\
  fmask=777
```

To unmount the share, use the following standard command:

```
$ sudo umount /mount/point
```

You can also use these mount commands to mount true Windows client shares to your Ubuntu host. Using Samba, you can configure your server to provide any service Windows can serve, and no one but you will ever know.

Configuring Samba Using SWAT

The Samba team of developers has made administering Samba much easier with the *Samba Web Administration Tool (SWAT)*. SWAT is a web-based configuration and maintenance interface that gets as close to a point-and-click Samba environment as possible. This section provides a simple example of how to use SWAT to set up SMB access to a user's home directory and how to share a directory.

> **NOTE**
>
> Using SWAT requires you to install the openbsd_inetd and swat packages, so make sure you have these before proceeding.
>
> Also you need to enable the root account by giving it a password by using the command sudo passwd root. Not enabling the root account prevents you from using SWAT effectively.

You need to perform a few steps before you can start using SWAT. First, make sure you have the Samba and the swat packages installed. You then enable SWAT access to your system by editing the /etc/inetd.conf file by changing the following lines to remove the #<off># comments if present:

```
#<off># swat   stream  tcp  nowait.400  root\
  /usr/sbin/tcpd  /isr/sbin/swat
```

Save the file, and then restart the openbsd_inetd daemon using the following command:

```
$ sudo /etc/init.d/openbsd-inetd restart
```

Next, start an X session, launch Firefox, and browse to the http://localhost:901 *uniform resource locator (URL)*. You are presented a login prompt. Enter the root username and password, and then click the OK button. The screen clears, and you see the main SWAT page, as shown in Figure 16.2.

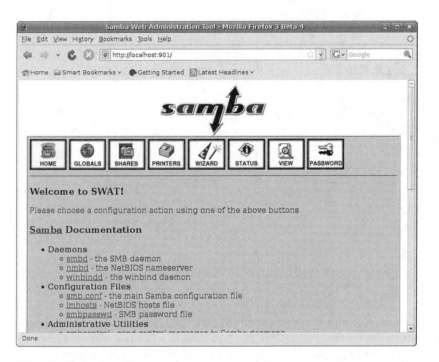

FIGURE 16.2   You can use SWAT to easily configure and administer Samba on your system.

TIP

You can also configure Samba using Ubuntu's `shares-admin` client. Launch the client from the command line of an X terminal window or select the System, Administration, Shared Folders menu item (as shown later in Figure 16.9).

First, click the Globals icon in SWAT's main page. You see a page similar to the one shown in Figure 16.3. Many options are in the window, but you can quickly set up access for hosts from your LAN by simply entering one or more IP addresses or a subnet address (such as 192.168.0.—note the trailing period, which allows access for all hosts; in this example, on the 192.168.0 subnet) in the Hosts Allow field under the Security Options section. If you need help on how to format the entry, click the Help link to the left of the field. A new web page appears with the pertinent information.

16

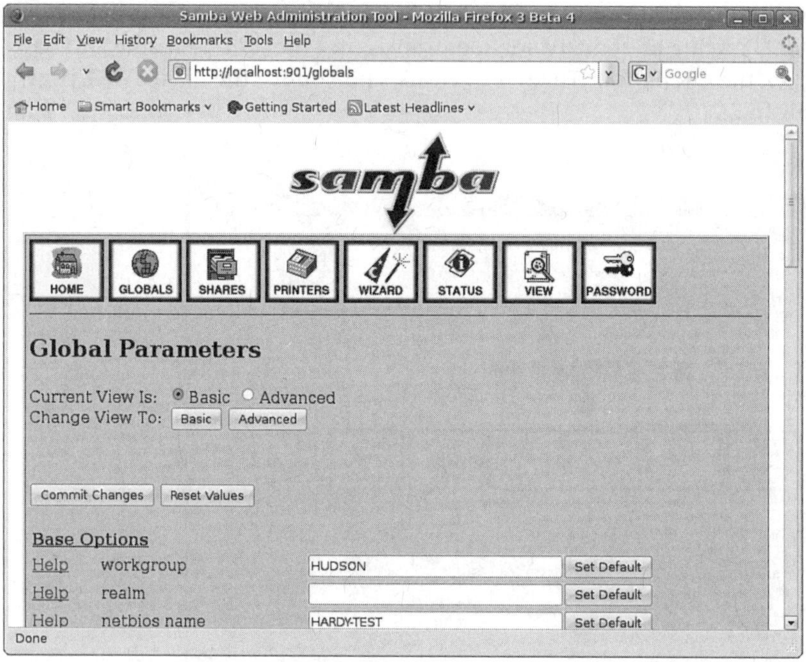

FIGURE 16.3   Configure Samba to allow access from specific hosts or subnets on your LAN.

When finished, click the Commit Changes button to save the global access settings. The next step is to create a Samba user and set the user's password. Click the Password icon on the main SWAT page (refer to Figure 16.2). The Server Password Management page opens, as shown in Figure 16.4. Type a new username in the User Name field; then type a password in the New Password and Re-type New Password fields.

NOTE

You must supply a username of an existing system user, but the password used for Samba access does not have to match the existing user's password.

When finished, click the Add New User button. SWAT then creates the username and password and displays Added user *username* (where *username* is the name you entered). The new Samba user should now be able to gain access to the home directory from any allowed host if the Samba (smb) server is running.

For example, if you have set up Samba on a host named mini that has a user named andrew, the user can access the home directory on mini from any remote host (if allowed by the Globals settings), perhaps by using the smbclient command like so:

```
$ smbclient //mini/andrew -U andrew
```

```
added interface ip=192.168.0.68 bcast=192.168.0.255 nmask=255.255.255.0
Password:
Domain=[MYGROUP] OS=[Unix] Server=[Samba 3.0.28]
smb: \> pwd
Current directory is \\mini\andrew\
smb: \> quit
```

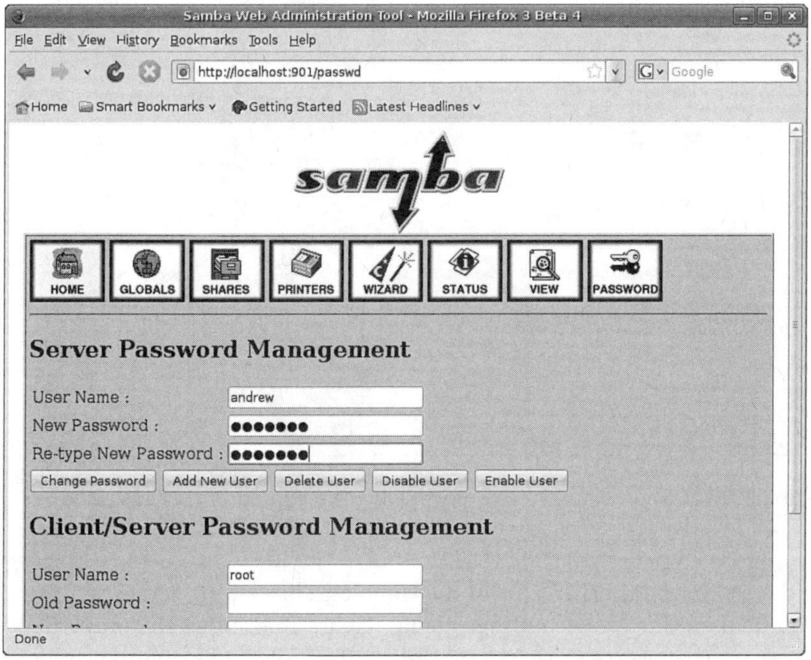

FIGURE 16.4   Enter a Samba username and password in the SWAT Password page.

Click the Status icon (as shown in Figure 16.2 or 16.4) to view Samba's status or to start, stop, or restart the server. You can use various buttons on the resulting web page to control the server and view periodic or continuous status updates.

You can also use SWAT to share a Linux directory. First, click the Shares icon in the toolbar at the top of the main Samba page (refer to Figure 16.2). Then, type a share name in the Create Shares field, and then click the Create Shares button. The SWAT Shares page displays the detailed configuration information in a dialog box, as shown in Figure 16.5, providing access to detailed configuration for the new Samba share.

Type the directory name (such as /music) you want to share in the Path field under the Base options. Select No or Yes in the Read Only field under Security options to allow or deny read and write access. Select Yes in the Guest OK option to allow access from other users and specify a hostname, IP address, or subnet in the Hosts Allow field to allow access. Click the Commit Changes button when finished. Remote users can then access the shared volume. This is how a Linux server running Samba can easily mimic shared volumes in a mixed computing environment!

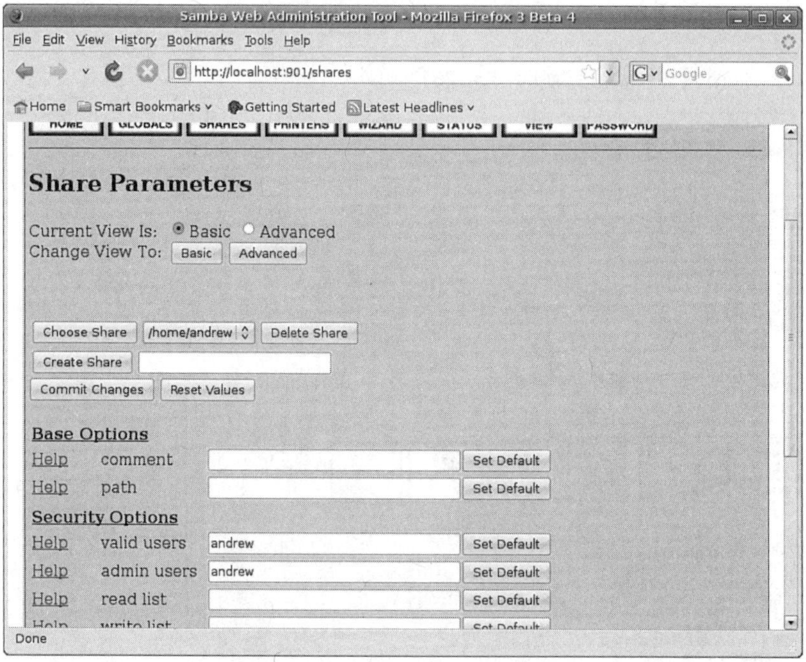

FIGURE 16.5   Use the SWAT Shares page to set up sharing of a portion of your Linux file system.

Alternatively, use the shares-admin client (from the command line or the Server Settings Samba Server menu item on the System Settings menu). Figure 16.6 shows the properties of a shared directory named /home/andrew/music. Unlock the tool by clicking the Unlock button, use the Add button to create new shares, and use the Properties button to edit the share's access options.

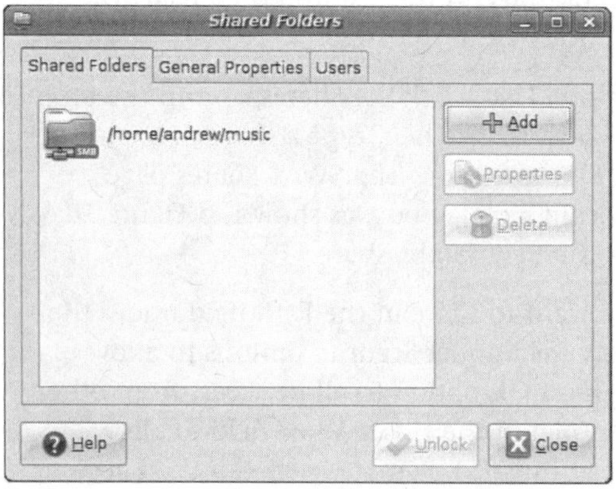

FIGURE 16.6   Configure a Samba share by editing the share defaults.

Network and Remote Printing with Ubuntu

Chapter 8, "Printing with Ubuntu," discussed how to set up and configure local printers and the associated print services. This section covers configuring printers for sharing and access across a network.

Offices all over the world benefit from using print servers and shared printers. In my office, I have two printers connected to the network via a Mac mini with Ubuntu PPC so that my wife can print from downstairs using a wireless link, and I can print from my three computers in my office. It is a simple thing to do and can bring real productivity benefits, even in small settings.

Creating Network Printers

Setting up remote printing service involves configuring a print server and then creating a remote printer entry on one or more computers on your network. This section introduces a quick method of enabling printing from one Linux workstation to another Linux computer on a LAN. You also learn about SMB printing using Samba and its utilities. Finally, this section discusses how to configure network-attached printers and use them to print single or multiple documents.

Enabling Network Printing on a LAN

If the computer with an attached printer is using Ubuntu and you want to set up the system for print serving, again use the `system-config-printer` client to create a new printer.

To enable sharing, you must follow a few steps, because by default CUPS is not set up to share printers across a network.

First, edit your `/etc/cups/cupsd.conf` file using the following command:

```
$ sudo gedit /etc/cups/cupsd.conf
```

In this example I have used `gedit`, but feel free to substitute in your favorite text editor.

Then, look for the section that begins with `<Location />` and modify it so that it reads as follows:

```
<Location />
Order Deny,Allow
Deny From All
Allow From 127.0.0.1
Allow From 192.168.0.*
```

```
</Location>
```

This tells CUPS to share your printers across the network 192.168.0.*, for example. Make sure and change this to match your own network settings.

Next you need to look in the same file for the section that starts

```
Listen localhost:631
```

and modify it to show this:

```
Listen 631
```

This tells CUPS to listen on port 631 for any printer requests.

Session Message Block Printing

Printing to an SMB printer requires Samba, along with its utilities such as the `smbclient` and associated `smbprint` printing filter. You can use the Samba software included with Ubuntu to print to a shared printer on a Windows network or set up a printer attached to your system as an SMB printer. This section describes how to create a local printer entry to print to a remote shared printer using SMB.

Setting up an SMB or shared printer is usually accomplished under Windows operating systems through configuration settings using the Control Panel's Network device. After enabling print sharing, reboot the computer. In the My Computer, Printers folder, right-click the name or icon of the printer you want to share and select Sharing from the pop-up menu. Set the Shared As item, and then enter a descriptive shared name, such as **HP2100**, and a password.

You must enter a shared name and password to configure the printer when running Linux. You also need to know the printer's workgroup name, IP address, and printer name and have the username and password on hand. To find this information, select Start, Settings, Printers; then right-click the shared printer's listing in the Printers window and select Properties from the pop-up window.

You can use CUPS to configure Samba to use your printers by editing the `smb.conf` file.

In the global section enter the following lines, if they are not already there:

```
...
load printers = yes
printing = cups
printcap name = cups
```

This tells Samba to use CUPS to provide printing services. Next you need to create a new section in the `smb.conf` file at the end of the file, as follows:

```
[printers]
comment = Use this for All Printers
path = /var/spool/samba
```

```
browseable = no
public = yes
guest ok = yes
writable = no
printable = yes
printer admin = root, andrew
```

This publishes your printers to the network and allows others to connect to them via Windows clients.

Make sure you restart the Samba service using the command shown earlier to make Samba pick up the changes to the configuration file.

Using the Common UNIX Printing System GUI

You can use CUPS to create printer queues, get print server information, and manage queues by launching a browser (such as Firefox) and browsing to http://localhost:631. CUPS provides a web-based administration interface, as shown in Figure 16.7.

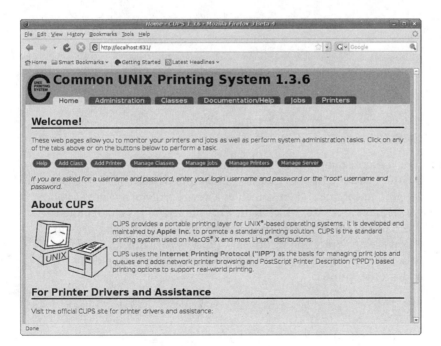

FIGURE 16.7   Use the web-based CUPS administrative interface to configure and manage printing.

If you click the Administration tab in the browser page, you can start configuring your printers, as shown in Figure 16.8.

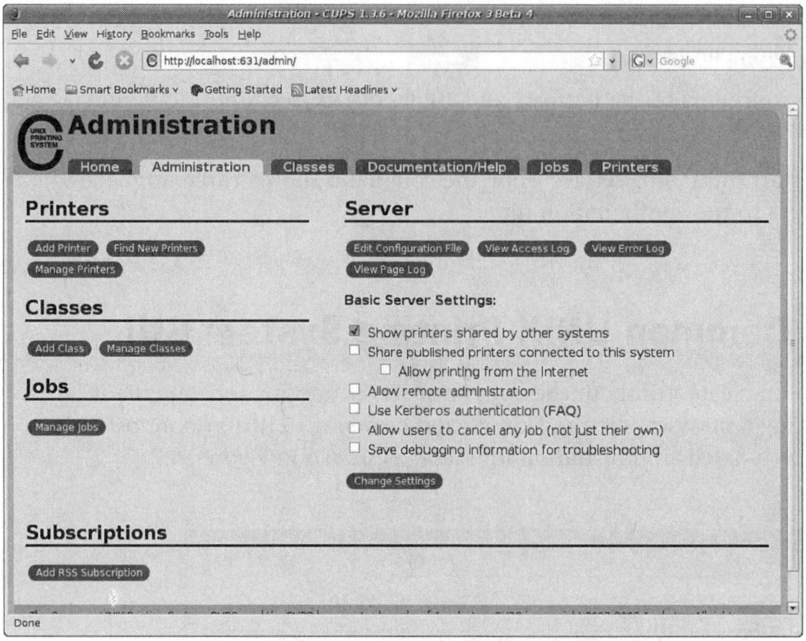

FIGURE 16.8   Enter the root password to perform printer administration with CUPS.

Creating a CUPS Printer Entry

This section provides a short example of creating a Linux printer entry using CUPS's web-based interface. Use the CUPS interface to create a printer and device queue type (such as local, remote, serial port, or Internet); then you enter a device *uniform resource identifier (URI)*, such as lpd://192.168.2.35/lp, which represents the IP address of a remote UNIX print server, and the name of the remote print queue on the server. You also need to specify the model or make of printer and its driver. A Printers page link allows you to print a test page, stop the printing service, manage the local print queue, modify the printer entry, or add another printer.

In the Admin page, click the Add Printer button and then enter a printer name in the Name field (such as 1p), a physical location of the printer in the Location field, and a short note about the printer (such as its type) in the Description field. Figure 16.9 shows a sample entry for an HP 2100 LaserJet.

Click the Continue button. You can then select the type of printer access (local, remote, serial port, or Internet) in the Device page, as shown in Figure 16.10. For example, to configure printing to a local printer, select LPT1 or, for a remote printer, select the LPD/LPR Host or Printer entry.

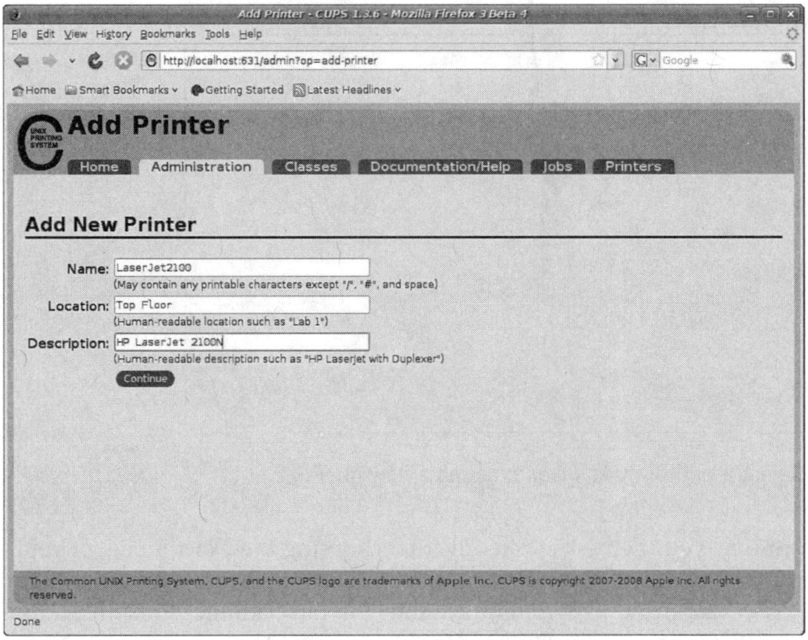

FIGURE 16.9   Use CUPS to create a new printer queue.

Again click Continue and select a printer make as requested in the dialog box shown in Figure 16.10.

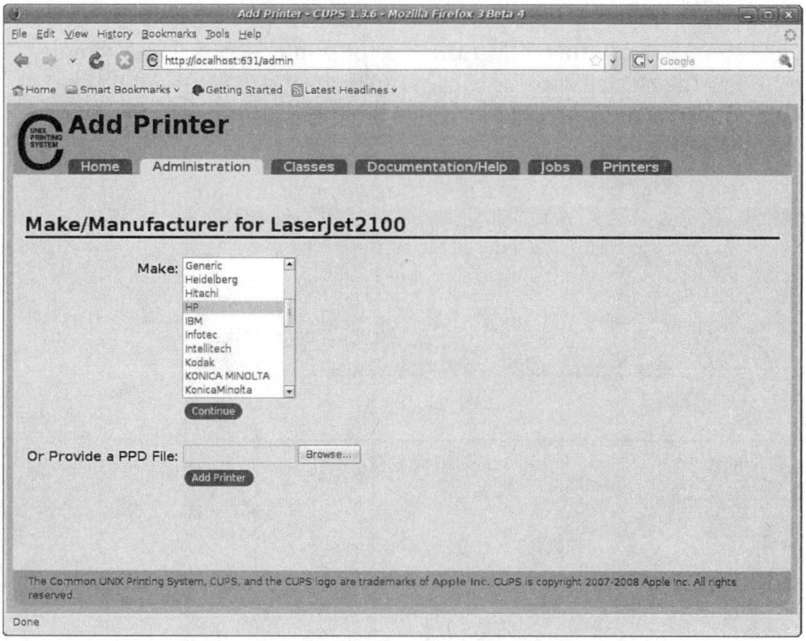

FIGURE 16.10   Select a printer make when creating a new queue.

After you click Continue, you then select the driver by choosing the exact model of your printer from the list provided. Finish by clicking the Add Printer button, and you will be prompted for your user name and password (make sure you have admin rights linked to your account) before the printer is actually added to the system. After creating the printer, you can then use the Printer page, as shown in Figure 16.11, to print a test page, stop printing service, manage the local print queue, modify the printer entry, or add another printer.

CUPS offers many additional features and after it is installed, configured, and running, provides transparent traditional UNIX printing support for Ubuntu.

> **NOTE**
>
> To learn more about CUPS and to get a basic overview of the system, browse to http://www.cups.org/.

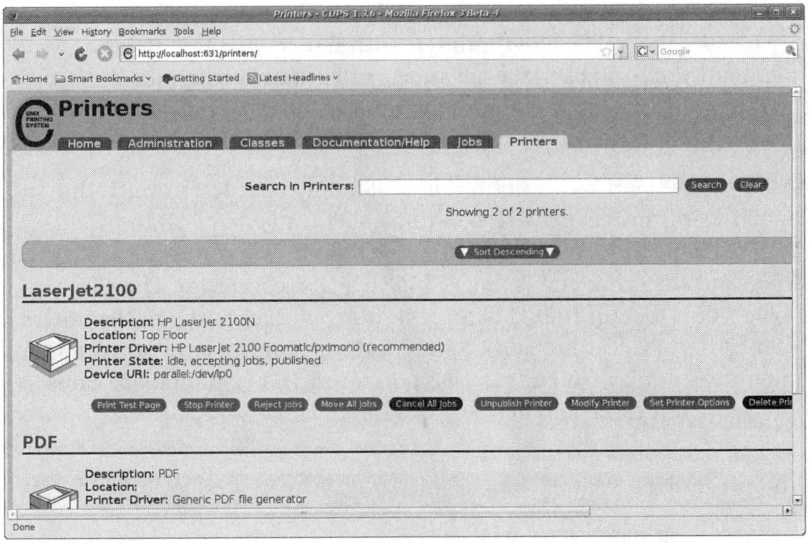

FIGURE 16.11   Manage printers easily using the CUPS Printer page.

Avoiding Printer Support Problems

Troubleshooting printer problems can prove frustrating, especially if you find that your new printer is not working properly with Linux. Keep in mind, however, that nearly all printers on the market today work with Linux. That said, some vendors have higher batting averages in the game of supporting Linux. If you care to see a scorecard, browse to http://www.linuxprinting.org/vendors.html.

All-in-One (Print/Fax/Scan) Devices

Problematic printers, or printing devices that might or might not work with Ubuntu, include multifunction (or *all-in-one*) printers that combine scanning, faxing, and printing services. You should research any planned purchase and avoid any vendor unwilling to support Linux with drivers or development information.

One shining star in the field of Linux support for multifunction printers is the HP support of the HP OfficeJet Linux driver project at http://hpoj.sourceforge.net/. Printing and scanning are supported on many models, with fax support in development.

Using USB and Legacy Printers

Other problems can arise because of a lack of a printer's USB vendor and device ID information—a problem shared by some USB scanners under Linux. For information regarding USB printer support, check with the Linux printing folks (at the URL in the start of this section) or with the Linux USB project at http://www.linux-usb.org/.

16

Although many newer printers require a *universal serial bus (USB)* port, excellent support still exists for legacy parallel-port (IEEE-1284) printers with Linux, enabling sites to continue to use older hardware. You can take advantage of Linux workarounds to set up printing even if the host computer does not have a traditional parallel printer port or if you want to use a newer USB printer on an older computer.

For example, to host a parallel-port-based printer on a USB-only computer, attach the printer to the computer using an inexpensive USB-to-parallel converter. USB-to-parallel converters typically provide a Centronics connector; one end of that connector is plugged in to the older printer, and the other end is plugged in to a USB connector. The USB connector is then plugged in to your hub, desktop, or notebook USB port. On the other hand, you can use an add-on PCI card to add USB support for printing (and other devices) if the legacy computer does not have a built-in USB port. Most PCI USB interface cards add at least two ports, and you can chain devices via a hub.

Related Ubuntu and Linux Commands

The following commands help you manage printing services:

▶ accept—Controls print job access to the CUPS server via the command line

▶ cancel—Cancels a print job from the command line

▶ disable—Control printing from the command line

▶ enable—Controls CUPS printers

▶ lp—Sends a specified file to the printer and allows control of the prince service

▶ lpc—Displays the status of printers and print service at the console

▶ lpq—Views print queues (pending print jobs) at the console

▶ lprm—Removes print jobs from the print queue via the command line

▶ lpstat—Displays printer and server status

Reference

▶ http://www.linuxprinting.org/—Browse here for specific drivers and information about USB and other types of printers.

▶ http://www.hp.com/wwsolutions/linux/products/printing_imaging/index.html—Short but definitive information from HP regarding printing product support under Linux.

▶ http://www.linuxdoc.org/HOWTO/Printing-HOWTO/—Grant Taylor's Printing HOWTO, with information on using various print services under Linux.

▶ http://www.cups.org/—A comprehensive repository of CUPS software, including versions for Red Hat Linux.

▶ http://www.pwg.org/ipp/—Home page for the Internet Printing Protocol standards.

▶ http://www.linuxprinting.org/cups-doc.html—Information about CUPS.

▶ http://www.cs.wisc.edu/~ghost/—Home page for the Ghostscript interpreter.

▶ http://www.samba.org/—Base entry point for getting more information about Samba and using the SMB protocol with Linux, UNIX, Mac OS, and other operating systems.

▶ In addition, an excellent book on Samba to help you learn more is *Samba Unleashed* (Sams Publishing, 2000, ISBN: 0-672-31862-8).

▶ If you are after more recent coverage of Samba, we would also recommend *Using Samba, 3rd Edition* (O'Reilly & Associates, 2007, ISBN: 0-596-00769-8).

16

Apache Web Server Management

This chapter covers the configuration and management of the Apache web server. The chapter includes an overview of some of the major components of the server and discussions of text-based and graphical server configuration. You will see how to start, stop, and restart Apache using the command line. The chapter begins with some introductory information about this popular server and then shows you how to install, configure, and start using Apache.

About the Apache Web Server

Apache is the most widely used web server on the Internet today, according to a Netcraft survey of active websites in June 2007, which is shown in Table 17.1.

Note that these statistics do not reflect Apache's use on internal networks, known as *intranets*.

The name *Apache* appeared during the early development of the software because it was "a patchy" server, made up of patches for the freely available source code of the NCSA HTTPd web server. For a while after the NCSA HTTPd project was discontinued, a number of people wrote a variety of patches for the code, to either fix bugs or add features they wanted. A lot of this code was floating around and people were freely sharing it, but it was completely unmanaged.

After a while, Brian Behlendorf and Cliff Skolnick set up a centralized repository of these patches, and the Apache project was born. The project is still composed of a small core group of programmers, but anyone is welcome to submit patches to the group for possible inclusion in the code.

TABLE 17.1   Netcraft Survey Results (June 2007)

Web Server	Number	Percentage
Apache	65,588,298	53.76%
Microsoft*	38,836,030	31.83%
Google	4,872,765	3.99%
SunONE	2,273,173	1.86%
lighttpd	1,470,930	1.21%

*All web server products

There has been a surge of interest in the Apache project over the past several years, partially buoyed by a new interest in open source on the part of enterprise-level information services. It's also due in part to crippling security flaws found in Microsoft's Internet Information Services (IIS); the existence of malicious web task exploits; and operating system and networking vulnerabilities to the now-infamous Code Red, Blaster, and Nimda worms. IBM made an early commitment to support and use Apache as the basis for its web offerings and has dedicated substantial resources to the project because it makes more sense to use an established, proven web server.

In mid-1999, The Apache Software Foundation was incorporated as a nonprofit company. A board of directors, who are elected on an annual basis by the ASF members, oversees the company. This company provides a foundation for several open-source software development projects, including the Apache Web Server project.

The best places to find out about Apache are the Apache Group's website, http://www.apache.org/, and the Apache Week website, http://www.apacheweek.com/, where you can subscribe to receive Apache Week by email to keep up on the latest developments in the project, keep abreast of security advisories, and research bug fixes.

TIP

You'll find an overview of Apache in its frequently asked questions (FAQs) at http:/ /httpd.apache.org/docs-2.0/faq/. In addition to extensive online documentation, you'll also find the complete documentation for Apache in the HTML directory of your Apache server. You can access this documentation by looking at http://localhost/manual/index.html on your new Ubuntu system with one of the web browsers included on your system. You'll need to have Apache running on your system!

Ubuntu ships with Apache 2, and the server (named apache2) is included on this book's DVD. You can obtain the latest version of Apache as a package file from an Ubuntu FTP server, through Synaptic, or by getting the source code from the Apache website and, in true Linux tradition, build it for yourself.

To determine the version of Apache included with your system, use the web server's -V command-line option like this:

```
$ /usr/sbin/apache2 -V
Server version: Apache/2.0.50
Server built:   Jun 29 2004 11:11:55
Server's Module Magic Number: 20020903:8
Architecture:   32-bit
Server compiled with....
```

The output displays the version number, build date and time, platform, and various options used during the build. You can use the -v option to see terser version information.

Installing the Apache Server

You can install Apache through APT or build it yourself from source code. The Apache source builds on just about any UNIX-like operating system and on Win32.

If you are about to install a new version of Apache, you should shut down the old server. Even if it's unlikely that the old server will interfere with the installation procedure, shutting it down ensures that there will be no problems. If you do not know how to stop Apache, see the "Starting and Stopping Apache" section later in this chapter.

Installing with APT

You can find the Apache package in the default Ubuntu software repository, on the Ubuntu FTP server, or at one of its many mirror sites. Updated packages usually contain important bug and security fixes. When an updated version is released, install it as quickly as possible to keep your system secure.

> **NOTE**
>
> Check the Apache site for security reports. Browse to http://httpd.apache.org/security_report.html for links to security vulnerabilities for Apache 1.3, 2.0, and 2.2. Subscribe to a support list or browse through up-to-date archives of all Apache mailing lists at http://httpd.apache.org/mail/ (for various articles) or http://httpd.apache.org/lists.html (for comprehensive and organized ·archives).

> **CAUTION**
>
> You should be wary of installing experimental packages, and never install them on production servers (that is, servers used in "real life"). Very carefully test the packages beforehand on a host that is not connected to a network!

17

The easiest way to use APT is through Synaptic, which is under the System > Administration menu. Search for apache2 and select it, and Synaptic will add the required dependencies.

The Apache package installs files in the following directories:

▶ /etc/apache2—This directory contains the Apache configuration file, apache2.conf.

▶ /etc/init.d/—The tree under this directory contains the system startup scripts. The Apache package installs a startup script named apache2 for the web server under the /etc/init.d directory. This script, which you can use to start and stop the server from the command line, also automatically starts and stops the server when the computer is halted, started, or rebooted.

▶ /var/www—The package installs the default server icons, Common Gateway Interface (CGI) programs, and HTML files in this location. If you want to keep web content elsewhere, you can do so by making the appropriate changes in the server configuration files.

▶ /var/www/manual/—If you've installed the apache-manual package, you'll find a copy of the Apache documentation in HTML format here. You can access it with a web browser by going to http://localhost/manual/.

▶ /usr/share/man—Ubuntu's Apache package also contains manual pages, which are placed underneath this directory. For example, the apache2 man page is in section 8 of the man directory.

▶ /usr/sbin—The executable programs are placed in this directory. This includes the server executable itself, as well as various utilities.

▶ /usr/bin—Some of the utilities from the Apache package are placed here—for example, the htpasswd program, which is used for generating authentication password files.

▶ /var/log/apache2—The server log files are placed in this directory. By default, there are two important log files (among several others): access_log and error_log. However, you can define any number of custom logs containing a variety of information. See the section "Logging," later in this chapter, for more detail.

When Apache is being run, it also creates the file apache2.pid, containing the process ID of Apache's parent process in the /var/run/ directory.

NOTE

If you are upgrading to a newer version of Apache, APT does not write over your current configuration files.

Building the Source Yourself

You can download the source directly from http://www.apache.org/. The latest version at the time of this writing (2.2.8) is a 6MB compressed tape archive, and the latest pre-2.0 version of Apache is 1.3.34. Although many sites continue to use the older version (for script and other compatibility reasons), many new sites are migrating to or starting out using the latest stable version.

After you have the tar file, you must unroll it in a temporary directory, such as /tmp. Unrolling this tar file creates a directory called apache_*version_number*, where *version_number* is the version you have downloaded (for example, apache_1.3.34).

There are two ways to compile the source—the old, familiar way (at least, to those of us who have been using Apache for many years) by editing Makefile templates, and the new, easy way using a configure script. You will first see how to build Apache from source the easy way. The configure script offers a way to have the source software automatically configured according to your system. However, manually editing the configuration files before building and installing Apache provides more control over where the software is installed and which capabilities or features are built in to Apache.

> **TIP**
>
> As with many software packages distributed in source code form for Linux and other UNIX-like operating systems, extracting the source code results in a directory that contains a README and an INSTALL file. Be sure to peruse the INSTALL file before attempting to build and install the software.

Using ./configure to Build Apache

To build Apache the easy way, run the ./configure script in the directory just created. You can provide it with a --prefix argument to install it in a directory other than the default, which is /usr/local/apache/. Use this command:

```
# ./configure --prefix=/preferred/directory/
```

This generates the Makefile that is used to compile the server code.

Next, type **make** to compile the server code. After the compilation is complete, type **make install** as root to install the server. You can now configure the server via the configuration files. See the "Runtime Server Configuration Settings" section for more information.

> **TIP**
>
> A safer way to install a new version of Apache from source is to use the ln command to create symbolic links of the existing file locations (listed in the "Installing with APT" section earlier in this chapter) to the new locations of the files. This method is safer because the default install locations are different from those used when the package installs the files. Failure to use this installation method could result in your web server process not being started automatically at system startup.
>
> Another safe way to install a new version of Apache is to first back up any important configuration directories and files (such as /etc/apache2) and then use the apt-get command to remove the server. You can then install and test your new version and, if needed, easily restore your original server and settings.

17

It is strongly recommended that you use Ubuntu's version of Apache until you really know what happens at system startup. No "uninstall" option is available when installing Apache from source!

Apache File Locations After a Build and Install

Files are placed in various subdirectories of /usr/local/apache (or whatever directory you specified with the --prefix parameter) if you build the server from source.

The following is a list of the directories used by Apache, as well as brief comments on their usage:

▶ /usr/local/apache/conf—This contains several subdirectories and the Apache configuration file, httpd.conf. Debian-based systems such as Ubuntu often rename this to apache2.conf, so your mileage may vary. See the section "Editing apache2.conf" later in this chapter to learn more about configuration files.

▶ /usr/local/apache—The cgi-bin, icons, and htdocs subdirectories contain the CGI programs, standard icons, and default HTML documents, respectively.

▶ /usr/local/apache/bin—The executable programs are placed in this directory.

▶ /usr/local/apache/logs—The server log files are placed in this directory. By default, there are two log files—access_log and error_log—but you can define any number of custom logs containing a variety of information (see the "Logging" section later in this chapter). The default location for Apache's logs as installed by Ubuntu is /var/log/apache2.

A Quick Guide to Getting Started with Apache

Setting up, testing a web page, and starting Apache using Ubuntu can be accomplished in just a few steps. First, make sure that Apache is installed on your system. Either select it during installation or install the server and related package files (refer to Chapter 31 if you need to install the server software) .

Next, set up a home page for your system by editing (as root) the file named index.html under the /var/ www directory on your system. Make a backup copy of the original page or www directory before you begin so you can restore your web server to its default state if necessary.

> Start Apache through the Services window (under System, Administration from the menu bar), making sure to enable "Web Server".

You can also use the apache2 script under the /etc/init.d/ directory, like this:

> sudo /etc/init.d/apache2 start

You can then check your home page by running a favorite browser and using localhost, your system's hostname, or its Internet Protocol (IP) address in the URL. For example, with the links text browser, use a command line like this:

> # links http://localhost/

For security reasons, you should not start and run Apache as root if your host is connected to the Internet or a company intranet. Fortunately, Apache is set to run as the user and group www-data no matter how it is started (by the User and Group settings in /etc/apache2/apache2.conf). Despite this safe default, Apache should be started and managed by the user named apache, defined in /etc/passwd as

    www-data:x:33:33:www-data:/var/www:/sbin/nologin

After you are satisfied with your website, use the Services configuration dialog to ensure that Apache is started.

Starting and Stopping Apache

At this point, you have installed your Apache server with its default configuration. Ubuntu provides a default home page named index.html as a test under the /var/www/ directory. The proper way to run Apache is to set system initialization to have the server run after booting, network configuration, and any firewall configuration. See Chapter 11, "Automating Tasks," for more information about how Ubuntu boots.

It is time to start it up for the first time. The following sections show how to either start and stop Apache or configure Ubuntu to start or not start Apache when booting.

Starting the Apache Server Manually

You can start Apache from the command line of a text-based console or X terminal window, and you must have root permission to do so. The server daemon, apache2, recognizes several command-line options you can use to set some defaults, such as specifying where apache2 reads its configuration directives. The Apache apache2 executable also understands other options that enable you to selectively use parts of its configuration file, specify a different location of the actual server and supporting files, use a different configuration file (perhaps for testing), and save startup errors to a specific log. The -v option causes Apache to print its development version and quit. The -V option shows all the settings that were in effect when the server was compiled.

The -h option prints the following usage information for the server (assuming that you are running the command through sudo):

```
sudo apache2 -h
Usage: apache2 [-D name] [-d directory] [-f file]
               [-C "directive"] [-c "directive"]
               [-k start¦restart¦graceful¦stop]
               [-v] [-V] [-h] [-l] [-L] [-t]
Options:
  -D name            : define a name for use in <IfDefine name> directives
```

```
 -d directory       : specify an alternate initial ServerRoot
 -f file            : specify an alternate ServerConfigFile
 -C "directive"     : process directive before reading config files
 -c "directive"     : process directive after reading config files
 -e level           : show startup errors of level (see LogLevel)
 -E file            : log startup errors to file
 -v                 : show version number
 -V                 : show compile settings
 -h                 : list available command line options (this page)
 -l                 : list compiled in modules
 -L                 : list available configuration directives
 -t -D DUMP_VHOSTS  : show parsed settings (currently only vhost settings)
-t                  : run syntax check for config files
```

Other options include listing Apache's *static modules*, or special, built-in independent parts of the server, along with options that can be used with the modules. These options are called *configuration directives* and are commands that control how a static module works. Note that Apache also includes nearly 50 *dynamic modules*, or software portions of the server that can be optionally loaded and used while the server is running.

The -t option is used to check your configuration files. It's a good idea to run this check before restarting your server, especially if you've made changes to your configuration files. Such tests are important because a configuration file error can result in your server shutting down when you try to restart it.

NOTE

When you build and install Apache from source, start the server manually from the command line through sudo (such as when testing). You do this for two reasons:

▶The standalone server uses the default HTTP port (port 80), and only the superuser can bind to Internet ports that are lower than 1024.

▶Only processes owned by root can change their UID and GID as specified by Apache's User and Group directives. If you start the server under another UID, it runs with the permissions of the user starting the process.

Note that although some of the following examples show how to start the server through sudo, you should do so only for testing after building and installing Apache.

Using /etc/init.d/apache2

Ubuntu uses the scripts in the /etc/init.d directory to control the startup and shutdown of various services, including the Apache web server. The main script installed for the Apache web server is /etc/init.d/apache2, although the actual work is done by the apache2ctl shell script included with Apache.

NOTE

/etc/init.d/apache2 is a shell script and is not the same as the Apache server located in /usr/sbin. That is, /usr/sbin/apache2 is the program executable file (the server); /etc/init.d/apache2 is a shell script that uses another shell script, apache2ctl, to control the server. See Chapter 11 for a description of some service scripts under /etc/init.d and how the scripts are used to manage services such as apache2.

You can use the /etc/init.d/apache2 script and the following options to control the web server:

▶ start—The system uses this option to start the web server during bootup. You, through sudo, can also use this script to start the server.

▶ stop—The system uses this option to stop the server gracefully. You should use this script, rather than the kill command, to stop the server.

▶ reload—You can use this option to send the HUP signal to the apache2 server to have it reread the configuration files after modification.

▶ restart—This option is a convenient way to stop and then immediately start the web server. If the apache2 server isn't running, it is started.

▶ condrestart—The same as the restart parameter, except that it restarts the apache2 server only if it is actually running.

▶ status—This option indicates whether the server is running; if it is, it provides the various PIDs for each instance of the server.

For example, to check on the status of your server, use the command

```
sudo /etc/init.d/apache2 status
```

This prints the following for me:

```
apache2 (pid 15997 1791 1790 1789 1788 1787 1786 1785 1784 1781) is running...
```

This indicates that the web server is running; in fact, 10 instances of the server are currently running in this configuration.

In addition to the previous options, the apache2 script also offers these features:

▶ help—Prints a list of valid options to the apache2 script (which are passed onto the server as if called from the command line).

▶ configtest—A simple test of the server's configuration, which reports Status OK if the setup is correct. You can also use apache2's -t option to perform the same test, like this:

```
audo apache2 -t
```

17

▶ `fullstatus`—Displays a verbose status report.

▶ `graceful`—The same as the `restart` parameter, except that the `configtest` option is used first and open connections are not aborted.

TIP

Use the `reload` option if you are making many changes to the various server configuration files. This saves time when you are stopping and starting the server by having the system simply reread the configuration files.

Runtime Server Configuration Settings

At this point, the Apache server will run, but perhaps you want to change a behavior, such as the default location of your website's files. This section talks about the basics of configuring the server to work the way you want it to work.

Runtime configurations are stored in just one file—`apache2.conf`, which is found under the `/etc/apache2` directory. This configuration file can be used to control the default behavior of Apache, such as the web server's base configuration directory (`/etc/apache2`), the name of the server's process identification (PID) file (`/var/run/apache2.pid`), or its response timeout (300 seconds). Apache reads the data from the configuration file when started (or restarted). You can also cause Apache to reload configuration information with the command `/etc/init.d/apache2 reload`, which is necessary after making changes to its configuration file. (You learned how to accomplish this in the earlier section, "Starting and Stopping Apache.")

Runtime Configuration Directives

You perform runtime configuration of your server with configuration directives, which are commands that set options for the `apache2` daemon. The directives are used to tell the server about various options you want to enable, such as the location of files important to the server configuration and operation. Apache supports nearly 300 configuration directives using the following syntax:

```
directive option option...
```

Each directive is specified on a single line. See the following sections for some sample directives and how to use them. Some directives only set a value such as a filename, whereas others enable you to specify various options. Some special directives, called sections, look like HTML tags. Section directives are surrounded by angle brackets, such as `<directive>`. Sections usually enclose a group of directives that apply only to the directory specified in the section:

```
<Directory somedir/in/your/tree>
  directive option option
  directive option option
</Directory>
```

All sections are closed with a matching section tag that looks like this: `</directive>`. Note that section tags, like any other directives, are specified one per line.

Editing `apache2.conf`

Most of the default settings in the config file are okay to keep, particularly if you've installed the server in a default location and aren't doing anything unusual on your server. In general, if you do not understand what a particular directive is for, you should leave it set to the default value.

The following sections describe some of the configuration file settings you *might* want to change concerning operation of your server.

ServerRoot

The `ServerRoot` directive sets the absolute path to your server directory. This directive tells the server where to find all the resources and configuration files. Many of these resources are specified in the configuration files relative to the `ServerRoot` directory.

Your `ServerRoot` directive should be set to `/etc/apache2` if you installed the Ubuntu package or `/usr/local/apache` (or whatever directory you chose when you compiled Apache) if you installed from the source.

Listen

The `Listen` directive indicates on which port you want your server to run. By default, this is set to 80, which is the standard HTTP port number. You might want to run your server on another port—for example, when running a test server that you don't want people to find by accident. Do not confuse this with real security! See the "File System Authentication and Access Control" section for more information about how to secure parts of your web server.

User **and** Group

The `User` and `Group` directives should be set to the UID and group ID (GID) the server will use to process requests.

In Ubuntu, set these configurations to a user with few or no privileges. In this case, they're set to user apache and group apache—a user defined specifically to run Apache. If you want to use a different UID or GID, be aware that the server will run with the permissions of the user and group set here. That means in the event of a security breach, whether on the server or (more likely) in your own CGI programs, those programs will run with the assigned UID. If the server runs as `root` or some other privileged user, someone can exploit the security holes and do nasty things to your site. Always think in terms of the specified user running a command such as `rm -rf /` because that would wipe all files from your system. That should convince you that leaving apache as a user with no privileges is probably a good thing.

Instead of specifying the User and Group directives using names, you can specify them using the UID and GID numbers. If you use numbers, be sure that the numbers you specify correspond to the user and group you want and that they're preceded by the pound (#) symbol.

Here's how these directives look if specified by name:

```
User apache
Group apache
```

Here's the same specification by UID and GID:

```
User #48
Group #48
```

TIP

If you find a user on your system (other than root) with a UID and GID of 0, your system has been compromised by a malicious user.

ServerAdmin

The ServerAdmin directive should be set to the address of the webmaster managing the server. This address should be a valid email address or alias, such as webmaster@gnulix.org, because this address is returned to a visitor when a problem occurs on the server.

ServerName

The ServerName directive sets the hostname the server will return. Set it to a fully qualified domain name (FQDN). For example, set it to www.your.domain rather than simply www. This is particularly important if this machine will be accessible from the Internet rather than just on your local network.

You don't need to set this unless you want a name other than the machine's canonical name returned. If this value isn't set, the server will figure out the name by itself and set it to its canonical name. However, you might want the server to return a friendlier address, such as www.your.domain. Whatever you do, ServerName should be a real domain name service (DNS) name for your network. If you're administering your own DNS, remember to add an alias for your host. If someone else manages the DNS for you, ask that person to set this name for you.

DocumentRoot

Set this directive to the absolute path of your document tree, which is the top directory from which Apache will serve files. By default, it's set to /var/www/. If you built the source code yourself, DocumentRoot is set to /usr/local/apache/htdocs (if you did not choose another directory when you compiled Apache).

UserDir

The UserDir directive disables or enables and defines the directory (relative to a local user's home directory) where that user can put public HTML documents. It is relative because each user has her own HTML directory. This setting is disabled by default but can be enabled to store user web content under any directory.

The default setting for this directive, if enabled, is public_html. Each user can create a directory called public_html under her home directory, and HTML documents placed in that directory are available as http://*servername*/~*username*, where *username* is the username of the particular user.

DirectoryIndex

The DirectoryIndex directive indicates which file should be served as the index for a directory, such as which file should be served if the URL http://*servername*/_*SomeDirectory*/ is requested.

It is often useful to put a list of files here so that if index.html (the default value) isn't found, another file can be served instead. The most useful application of this is to have a CGI program run as the default action in a directory. If you have users who make their web pages on Windows, you might want to add index.htm as well. In that case, the directive would look like DirectoryIndex index.html index.cgi index.htm.

Apache Multiprocessing Modules

Apache version 2.0 and greater now uses a new internal architecture supporting multiprocessing modules (MPMs). These modules are used by the server for a variety of tasks, such as network and process management, and are compiled into Apache. MPMs enable Apache to work much better on a wider variety of computer platforms, and they can help improve server stability, compatibility, and scalability.

Apache can use only one MPM at any time. These modules are different from the base set included with Apache (see the "Apache Modules" section later in this chapter) but are used to implement settings, limits, or other server actions. Each module in turn supports numerous additional settings, called *directives*, which further refine server operation.

The internal MPM modules relevant for Linux include

▶ mpm_common—A set of 20 directives common to all MPM modules

▶ prefork—A nonthreaded, preforking web server that works similar to earlier (1.3) versions of Apache

▶ worker—Provides a hybrid multiprocess multithreaded server

MPM enables Apache to be used on equipment with fewer resources yet still handle massive numbers of hits and provide stable service. The worker module provides directives to control how many simultaneous connections your server can handle.

17

> **NOTE**
>
> Other MPMs are available for Apache related to other platforms, such as mpm_netware for NetWare hosts and mpm_winnt for NT platforms. An MPM named perchild, which provides user ID assignment to selected daemon processes, is under development. For more information, browse to the Apache Software Foundation's home page at http:/ /www.apache.org.

Using `.htaccess` Configuration Files

Apache also supports special configuration files, known as .htaccess files. Almost any directive that appears in apache2.conf can appear in a .htaccess file. This file, specified in the AccessFileName directive in apache2.conf sets configurations on a per-directory (usually in a user directory) basis. As the system administrator, you can specify both the name of this file and which of the server configurations can be overridden by the contents of this file. This is especially useful for sites in which there are multiple content providers and you want to control what these people can do with their space.

To limit which server configurations the .htaccess files can override, use the AllowOverride directive. AllowOverride can be set globally or per directory. For example, in your apache2.conf file, you could use the following:

```
# Each directory to which Apache has access can be configured with respect
# to which services and features are allowed and/or disabled in that
# directory (and its subdirectories).
#
# First, we configure the "default" to be a very restrictive set of
# permissions.
#
<Directory />
    Options FollowSymLinks
    AllowOverride None
</Directory>
```

Options Directives

To configure which configuration options are available to Apache by default, you must use the Options directive. Options can be None; All; or any combination of Indexes, Includes, FollowSymLinks, ExecCGI, and MultiViews. MultiViews isn't included in All and must be specified explicitly. These options are explained in Table 17.2.

TABLE 17.2   Switches Used by the Options Directive

Switch	Description
None	None of the available options are enabled for this directory.
All	All the available options, except for MultiViews, are enabled for this directory.

TABLE 17.2   Switches Used by the `Options` Directive

Switch	Description
Indexes	In the absence of an `index.html` file or another `DirectoryIndex` file, a listing of the files in the directory is generated as an HTML page for display to the user.
Includes	Server-side includes (SSIs) are permitted in this directory. This can also be written as `IncludesNoExec` if you want to allow includes but don't want to allow the `exec` option in them. For security reasons, this is usually a good idea in directories over which you don't have complete control, such as `UserDir` directories.
FollowSymLinks	Allows access to directories that are symbolically linked to a document directory. You should never set this globally for the whole server and only rarely for individual directories. This option is a potential security risk because it allows web users to escape from the document directory and could potentially allow them access to portions of your file system where you really don't want people poking around.
ExecCGI	CGI programs are permitted in this directory, even if it is not a directory defined in the `ScriptAlias` directive.
MultiViews	This is part of the `mod_negotiation` module. When a client requests a document that can't be found, the server tries to figure out which document best suits the client's requirements. See `http://localhost/manuals/mod/_mod_negotiation.html` for your local copy of the Apache documentation.

NOTE

These directives also affect all subdirectories of the specified directory.

`AllowOverrides` **Directives**

The `AllowOverrides` directives specify which configuration options .`htaccess` files can override. You can set this directive individually for each directory. For example, you can have different standards about what can be overridden in the main document root and in `UserDir` directories.

This capability is particularly useful for user directories, where the user does not have access to the main server configuration files.

`AllowOverrides` can be set to `All` or any combination of `Options`, `FileInfo`, `AuthConfig`, and `Limit`. These options are explained in Table 17.3.

TABLE 17.3   Switches Used by the `AllowOverrides` Directive

Switch	Description
Options	The .`htaccess` file can add options not listed in the `Options` directive for this directory.

FileInfo	The .htaccess file can include directives for modifying document type information.
AuthConfig	The .htaccess file might contain authorization directives.
Limit	The .htaccess file might contain allow, deny, and order directives.

File System Authentication and Access Control

You're likely to include material on your website that isn't supposed to be available to the public. You must be able to lock out this material from public access and provide designated users with the means to unlock the material. Apache provides two methods for accomplishing this type of access: authentication and authorization. You can use different criteria to control access to sections of your website, including checking the client's IP address or hostname, or requiring a username and password. This section briefly covers some of these methods.

> **CAUTION**
>
> Allowing individual users to put web content on your server poses several important security risks. If you're operating a web server on the Internet rather than on a private network, you should read the WWW Security FAQ at http://www.w3.org/Security/Faq/www-security-faq.html.

Restricting Access with allow and deny

One of the simplest ways to limit access to website material is to restrict access to a specific group of users, based on IP addresses or hostnames. Apache uses the allow and deny directives to accomplish this.

Both directives take an address expression as a parameter. The following list provides the possible values and use of the address expression:

- ▶ all can be used to affect all hosts.

- ▶ A hostname or domain name, which can either be a partially or a fully qualified domain name; for example, test.gnulix.org or gnulix.org.

- ▶ An IP address, which can be either full or partial; for example, 212.85.67 or 212.85.67.66.

- ▶ A network/netmask pair, such as 212.85.67.0/255.255.255.0.

- ▶ A network address specified in classless inter-domain routing (CIDR) format; for example, 212.85.67.0/24. This is the CIDR notation for the same network and netmask that were used in the previous example.

If you have the choice, it is preferable to base your access control on IP addresses rather than hostnames. Doing so results in faster performance because no name lookup is necessary—the IP address of the client is included with each request.

You also can use `allow` and `deny` to provide or deny access to website material based on the presence or absence of a specific environment variable. For example, the following statement denies access to a request with a context that contains an environment variable named NOACCESS:

```
deny from env=NOACCESS
```

The default behavior of Apache is to apply all the `deny` directives first and then check the `allow` directives. If you want to change this order, you can use the `order` statement. Apache might interpret this statement in three different ways:

- ► `Order deny,allow`—The deny directives are evaluated before the `allow` directives. If a host is not specifically denied access, it is allowed to access the resource. This is the default ordering if nothing else is specified.

- ► `Order allow,deny`—All `allow` directives are evaluated before `deny` directives. If a host is not specifically allowed access, it is denied access to the resource.

- ► `Order mutual-failure`—Only hosts that are specified in an `allow` directive and at the same time do not appear in a `deny` directive are allowed access. If a host does not appear in either directive, it is not granted access.

Consider this example. Suppose you want to allow only persons from within your own domain to access the `server-status` resource on your web. If your domain were named `gnulix.org`, you could add these lines to your configuration file:

```
<Location /server-status>
    SetHandler server-status
    Order deny,allow
    Deny from all
    Allow from gnulix.org
</Location>
```

Authentication

Authentication is the process of ensuring that visitors really are who they claim to be. You can configure Apache to allow access to specific areas of web content only to clients who can authenticate their identity. There are several methods of authentication in Apache; Basic Authentication is the most common (and the method discussed in this chapter).

Under Basic Authentication, Apache requires a user to supply a username and a password to access the protected resources. Apache then verifies that the user is allowed to access the resource in question. If the username is acceptable, Apache verifies the password. If the password also checks out, the user is authorized and Apache serves the request.

HTTP is a stateless protocol; each request sent to the server and each response is handled individually, and not in an intelligent fashion. Therefore, the authentication information must be included with each request. That means each request to a password-protected area is larger and therefore somewhat slower. To avoid unnecessary system use and delays, protect only those areas of your website that absolutely need protection.

17

To use Basic Authentication, you need a file that lists which users are allowed to access the resources. This file is composed of a plain text list containing name and password pairs. It looks very much like the /etc/passwd user file of your Linux system.

CAUTION

Do not use /etc/passwd as a user list for authentication. When you're using Basic Authentication, passwords and usernames are sent as base64-encoded text from the client to the server—which is just as readable as plain text. The username and password are included in each request that is sent to the server. So, anyone who might be snooping on Net traffic would be able to get this information!

To create a user file for Apache, use the htpasswd command. This is included with the Apache package. If you installed using the packages, it is in /usr/bin. Running htpasswd without any options produces the following output:

```
Usage:
        htpasswd [-cmdps] passwordfile username
        htpasswd -b[cmdps] passwordfile username password

        htpasswd -n[mdps] username
        htpasswd -nb[mdps] username password
 -c  Create a new file.
 -n  Don't update file; display results on stdout.
 -m  Force MD5 encryption of the password.
 -d  Force CRYPT encryption of the password (default).
 -p  Do not encrypt the password (plaintext).
 -s  Force SHA encryption of the password.
 -b  Use the password from the command line rather than prompting for it.
 -D  Delete the specified user.
On Windows, TPF and NetWare systems the '-m' flag is used by default.
On all other systems, the '-p' flag will probably not work.
```

As you can see, it isn't a very difficult command to use. For example, to create a new user file named gnulixusers with a user named wsb, you need to do something like this:

```
sudo htpasswd -c gnulixusers wsb
```

You would then be prompted for a password for the user. To add more users, you would repeat the same procedure, only omitting the -c flag.

You can also create user group files. The format of these files is similar to that of /etc/groups. On each line, enter the group name, followed by a colon, and then list all users, with each user separated by spaces. For example, an entry in a user group file might look like this:

```
gnulixusers: wsb pgj jp ajje nadia rkr hak
```

Now that you know how to create a user file, it's time to look at how Apache might use this to protect web resources.

To point Apache to the user file, use the `AuthUserFile` directive. `AuthUserFile` takes the file path to the user file as its parameter. If the file path is not absolute—that is, beginning with a /—it is assumed that the path is relative to the `ServerRoot`. Using the `AuthGroupFile` directive, you can specify a group file in the same manner.

Next, use the `AuthType` directive to set the type of authentication to be used for this resource. Here, the type is set to `Basic`.

Now you need to decide to which realm the resource will belong. Realms are used to group different resources that will share the same users for authorization. A realm can consist of just about any string. The realm is shown in the Authentication dialog box on the user's web browser. Therefore, you should set the realm string to something informative. The realm is defined with the `AuthName` directive.

Finally, state which type of user is authorized to use the resource. You do this with the `require` directive. The three ways to use this directive are as follows:

▶ If you specify `valid-user` as an option, any user in the user file is allowed to access the resource (that is, provided she also enters the correct password).

▶ You can specify a list of users who are allowed access with the `users` option.

▶ You can specify a list of groups with the `group` option. Entries in the group list, as well as the user list, are separated by a space.

Returning to the `server-status` example you saw earlier, instead of letting users access the `server-status` resource based on hostname, you can require the users to be authenticated to access the resource. You can do so with the following entry in the configuration file:

```
<Location /server-status>
    SetHandler server-status
    AuthType Basic
    AuthName "Server status"
    AuthUserFile "gnulixusers"
    Require valid-user
</Location>
```

Final Words on Access Control

If you have host-based as well as user-based access protection on a resource, the default behavior of Apache is to require the requester to satisfy both controls. But assume that you want to mix host-based and user-based protection and allow access to a resource if either method succeeds. You can do so using the `satisfy` directive. You can set the `satisfy` directive to `All` (this is the default) or `Any`. When set to `All`, all access control methods must be satisfied before the resource is served. If `satisfy` is set to `Any`, the resource is served if any access condition is met.

Here's another access control example, again using the previous server-status example. This time, you combine access methods so all users from the Gnulix domain are allowed access and those from outside the domain must identify themselves before gaining access. You can do so with the following:

```
<Location /server-status>
    SetHandler server-status
    Order deny,allow
    Deny from all
    Allow from gnulix.org
    AuthType Basic
    AuthName "Server status"
    AuthUserFile "gnulixusers"
    Require valid-user
    Satisfy Any
</Location>
```

There are more ways to protect material on your web server, but the methods discussed here should get you started and will probably be more than adequate for most circumstances. Look to Apache's online documentation for more examples of how to secure areas of your site.

Apache Modules

The Apache core does relatively little; Apache gains its functionality from modules. Each module solves a well-defined problem by adding necessary features. By adding or removing modules to supply the functionality you want Apache to have, you can tailor Apache server to suit your exact needs.

Nearly 50 core modules are included with the basic Apache server. Many more are available from other developers. The Apache Module Registry is a repository for add-on modules for Apache, and it can be found at http://modules.apache.org/. The modules are stored in the /usr/lib/apache2/modules directory (your list might look different):

mod_access.so	mod_cern_meta.so	mod_log_config.so	mod_setenvif.so
mod_actions.so	mod_cgi.so	mod_mime_magic.so	mod_speling.so
mod_alias.so	mod_dav_fs.so	mod_mime.so	mod_ssl.so
mod_asis.so	mod_dav.so	mod_negotiation.so	mod_status.so
mod_auth_anon.so	mod_dir.so	mod_perl.so	mod_suexec.so
mod_auth_dbm.so	mod_env.so	mod_proxy_connect.so	mod_unique_id.so
mod_auth_digest.so	mod_expires.so	mod_proxy_ftp.so	mod_userdir.so
mod_auth_mysql.so	mod_headers.so	mod_proxy_http.so	mod_usertrack.so
mod_auth_pgsql.so	mod_imap.so	mod_proxy.so	mod_vhost_alias.so

```
mod_auth.so        mod_include.so      mod_python.so          mod_autoindex.so
mod_info.so        mod_rewrite.so
```

Each module adds new directives that can be used in your configuration files. As you might guess, there are far too many extra commands, switches, and options to describe them all in this chapter. The following sections briefly describe a subset of those modules available with Ubuntu's Apache installation.

mod_access

mod_access controls access to areas on your web server based on IP addresses, hostnames, or environment variables. For example, you might want to allow anyone from within your own domain to access certain areas of your web. Refer to the "File System Authentication and Access Control" section for more information.

mod_alias

mod_alias manipulates the URLs of incoming HTTP requests, such as redirecting a client request to another URL. It also can map a part of the file system into your web hierarchy. For example,

```
Alias /images/ /home/wsb/graphics/
```

fetches contents from the /home/wsb/graphics directory for any URL that starts with /images/. This is done without the client knowing anything about it. If you use a redirection, the client is instructed to go to another URL to find the requested content. More advanced URL manipulation can be accomplished with mod_rewrite.

mod_asis

mod_asis is used to specify, in fine detail, all the information to be included in a response. This completely bypasses any headers Apache might have otherwise added to the response. All files with an .asis extension are sent straight to the client without any changes.

As a short example of the use of mod_asis, assume you've moved content from one location to another on your site. Now you must inform people who try to access this resource that it has moved, as well as automatically redirect them to the new location. To provide this information and redirection, you can add the following code to a file with a .asis extension:

```
Status: 301 No more old stuff!
Location: http://gnulix.org/newstuff/
```

```
Content-type: text/html

<HTML>
 <HEAD>
  <TITLE>We've moved...</TITLE>
 </HEAD>
 <BODY>
   <P>We've moved the old stuff and now you'll find it at:</P>
   <A HREF="http://gnulix.org/newstuff/">New stuff</A>!.
 </BODY>
</HTML>
```

mod_auth

mod_auth uses a simple user authentication scheme, referred to as Basic Authentication, which is based on storing usernames and encrypted passwords in a text file. This file looks very much like UNIX's /etc/passwd file and is created with the htpasswd command. Refer to the "File System Authentication and Access Control" section earlier in this chapter for more information about this subject.

mod_auth_anon

The mod_auth_anon module provides anonymous authentication similar to that of anonymous FTP. The module enables you to define user IDs of those who are to be handled as guest users. When such a user tries to log on, he is prompted to enter his email address as his password. You can have Apache check the password to ensure that it's a (more or less) proper email address. Basically, it ensures that the password contains an @ character and at least one . character.

mod_auth_dbm

mod_auth_dbm uses Berkeley DB files instead of text for user authentication files.

mod_auth_digest

An extension of the basic mod_auth module, instead of sending the user information in plain text, mod_auth_digestis sent via the MD5 Digest Authentication process. This authentication scheme is defined in RFC 2617. Compared to using Basic Authentication, this is a much more secure way of sending user data over the Internet. Unfortunately, not all web browsers support this authentication scheme.

To create password files for use with mod_auth_dbm, you must use the htdigest utility. It has more or less the same functionality as the htpasswd utility. See the man page of htdigest for further information.

mod_autoindex

The mod_autoindex module dynamically creates a file list for directory indexing. The list is rendered in a user-friendly manner similar to those lists provided by FTP's built-in ls command.

mod_cgi

mod_cgi allows execution of CGI programs on your server. CGI programs are executable files residing in the /var/www/cgi-bin directory and are used to dynamically generate data (usually HTML) for the remote browser when requested.

mod_dir **and** mod_env

The mod_dir module is used to determine which files are returned automatically when a user tries to access a directory. The default is index.html. If you have users who create web pages on Windows systems, you should also include index.htm, like this:

```
DirectoryIndex index.html index.htm
```

mod_env controls how environment variables are passed to CGI and SSI scripts.

mod_expires

mod_expires is used to add an expiration date to content on your site by adding an Expires header to the HTTP response. Web browsers or cache servers won't cache expired content.

mod_headers

mod_headers is used to manipulate the HTTP headers of your server's responses. You can replace, add, merge, or delete headers as you see fit. The module supplies a Header directive for this. Ordering of the Header directive is important. A set followed by an unset for the same HTTP header removes the header altogether. You can place Header directives almost anywhere within your configuration files. These directives are processed in the following order:

1. Core server
2. Virtual host
3. <Directory> and .htaccess files
   <Location>
   <Files>

mod_include

mod_include enables the use of server-side includes on your server, which were quite popular before PHP took over this part of the market.

mod_info **and** mod_log_config

mod_info provides comprehensive information about your server's configuration. For example, it displays all the installed modules, as well as all the directives used in its configuration files.

mod_log_config defines how your log files should look. See the "Logging" section for further information about this subject.

mod_mime **and** mod_mime_magic

The mod_mime module tries to determine the MIME type of files from their extensions.

The mod_mime_magic module tries to determine the MIME type of files by examining portions of their content.

mod_negotiation

Using the mod_negotiation module, you can select one of several document versions that best suits the client's capabilities. There are several options to select which criteria to use in the negotiation process. You can, for example, choose among different languages, graphics file formats, and compression methods.

mod_proxy

mod_proxy implements proxy and caching capabilities for an Apache server. It can proxy and cache FTP, CONNECT, HTTP/0.9, and HTTP/1.0 requests. This isn't an ideal solution for sites that have a large number of users and therefore have high proxy and cache requirements. However, it's more than adequate for a small number of users.

mod_rewrite

mod_rewrite is the Swiss army knife of URL manipulation. It enables you to perform any imaginable manipulation of URLs using powerful regular expressions. It provides rewrites, redirection, proxying, and so on. There is very little that you can't accomplish using this module.

> **TIP**
>
> See http://localhost/manual/misc/rewriteguide.html for a cookbook that gives you an in-depth explanation of what the mod_rewrite module is capable of.

mod_setenvif

mod_setenvif allows manipulation of environment variables. Using small snippets of text-matching code known as *regular expressions*, you can conditionally change the content of environment variables. The order in which SetEnvIf directives appear in the configuration files is important. Each SetEnvIf directive can reset an earlier SetEnvIf directive when used on the same environment variable. Be sure to keep that in mind when using the directives from this module.

mod_speling

mod_speling is used to enable correction of minor typos in URLs. If no file matches the requested URL, this module builds a list of the files in the requested directory and extracts those files that are the closest matches. It tries to correct only one spelling mistake.

mod_status

You can use mod_status to create a web page containing a plethora of information about a running Apache server. The page contains information about the internal status as well as statistics about the running Apache processes. This can be a great aid when you're trying to configure your server for maximum performance. It's also a good indicator of when something's amiss with your Apache server.

mod_ssl

mod_ssl provides Secure Sockets Layer (version 2 and 3) and transport layer security (version 1) support for Apache. At least 30 directives exist that deal with options for encryption and client authorization and that can be used with this module.

mod_unique_id

mod_unique_id generates a unique request identifier for every incoming request. This ID is put into the UNIQUE_ID environment variable.

mod_userdir

The mod_userdir module enables mapping of a subdirectory in each user's home directory into your web tree. The module provides several ways to accomplish this.

mod_usertrack

mod_usertrack is used to generate a cookie for each user session. This can be used to track the user's click stream within your web tree. You must enable a custom log that logs this cookie into a log file.

mod_vhost_alias

mod_vhost_alias supports dynamically configured mass virtual hosting, which is useful for Internet service providers (ISPs) with many virtual hosts. However, for the average user, Apache's ordinary virtual hosting support should be more than sufficient.

There are two ways to host virtual hosts on an Apache server. You can have one IP address with multiple CNAMEs, or you can have multiple IP addresses with one name per address. Apache has different sets of directives to handle each of these options. (You learn more about virtual hosting in Apache in the next section of this chapter.)

Again, the available options and features for Apache modules are too numerous to describe completely in this chapter. You can find complete information about the Apache modules in the online documentation for the server included with Ubuntu or at the Apache Group's website.

Virtual Hosting

One of the more popular services to provide with a web server is to host a virtual domain. Also known as a *virtual host*, a virtual domain is a complete website with its own domain name, as if it were a standalone machine, but it's hosted on the same machine as other websites. Apache implements this capability in a simple way with directives in the apache2.conf configuration file.

Apache now can dynamically host virtual servers by using the mod_vhost_alias module you read about in the preceding section of the chapter. The module is primarily intended for ISPs and similar large sites that host a large number of virtual sites. This module is for more advanced users and, as such, it is outside the scope of this introductory chapter. Instead, this section concentrates on the traditional ways of hosting virtual servers.

Address-Based Virtual Hosts

After you've configured your Linux machine with multiple IP addresses, setting up Apache to serve them as different websites is simple. You need only put a VirtualHost directive in your apache2.conf file for each of the addresses you want to make an independent website:

```
<VirtualHost 212.85.67.67>
ServerName gnulix.org
DocumentRoot /home/virtual/gnulix/public_html
TransferLog /home/virtual/gnulix/logs/access_log
ErrorLog /home/virtual/gnulix/logs/error_log
</VirtualHost>
```

Use the IP address, rather than the hostname, in the VirtualHost tag.

You can specify any configuration directives within the <VirtualHost> tags. For example, you might want to set AllowOverrides directives differently for virtual hosts than you do for your main server. Any directives that aren't specified default to the settings for the main server.

Name-Based Virtual Hosts

Name-based virtual hosts enable you to run more than one host on the same IP address. You must add the names to your DNS as CNAMEs of the machine in question. When an HTTP client (web browser) requests a document from your server, it sends with the request a variable indicating the server name from which it's requesting the document. Based on this variable, the server determines from which of the virtual hosts it should serve content.

Some older browsers are unable to see name-based virtual hosts because this is a feature of HTTP 1.1 and the older browsers are strictly HTTP 1.0–compliant. However, many other older browsers are partially HTTP 1.1–compliant, and this is one of the parts of HTTP 1.1 that most browsers have supported for a while.

Name-based virtual hosts require just one step more than IP address-based virtual hosts. You must first indicate which IP address has the multiple DNS names on it. This is done with the NameVirtualHost directive:

```
NameVirtualHost 212.85.67.67
```

You must then have a section for each name on that address, setting the configuration for that name. As with IP-based virtual hosts, you need to set only those configurations that must be different for the host. You must set the ServerName directive because it's the only thing that distinguishes one host from another:

```
<VirtualHost 212.85.67.67>
ServerName bugserver.gnulix.org
ServerAlias bugserver
DocumentRoot /home/bugserver/htdocs
ScriptAlias /home/bugserver/cgi-bin
TransferLog /home/bugserver/lcgs/access_log
</VirtualHost>

<VirtualHost 212.85.67.67>
ServerName pts.gnulix.org
ServerAlias pts
DocumentRoot /home/pts/htdocs
ScriptAlias /home/pts/cgi-bin
TransferLog /home/pts/logs/access_log
ErrorLog /home/pts/logs/error_log
</VirtualHost>
```

17

If you are hosting websites on an intranet or internal network, users will likely use the shortened name of the machine rather than the FQDN. For example, users might type http://bugserver/index.html in their browser location field rather than http://bugserver.gnulix.org/index.html. In that case, Apache would not recognize that those two addresses should go to the same virtual host. You could get around this by setting up VirtualHost directives for both bugserver and bugserver.gnulix.org, but the easy way around it is to use the ServerAlias directive, which lists all valid aliases for the machine:

```
ServerAlias bugserver
```

For more information about `VirtualHost`, refer to the help system on http://localhost/_manual.

Logging

Apache provides logging for just about any web access information you might be interested in. Logging can help with

- System resource management, by tracking usage
- Intrusion detection, by documenting bad HTTP requests
- Diagnostics, by recording errors in processing requests

Two standard log files are generated when you run your Apache server: `access_log` and `error_log`. They are found under the `/var/log/apache2` directory. (Others include the SSL logs `ssl_access_log`, `ssl_error_log` and `ssl_request_log`.) All logs except for the `error_log` (by default, this is just the `access_log`) are generated in a format specified by the `CustomLog` and `LogFormat` directives. These directives appear in your `apache2.conf` file.

A new log format can be defined with the `LogFormat` directive:

```
LogFormat "%h %l %u %t \"%r\" %>s %b" common
```

The `common` log format is a good starting place for creating your own custom log formats. Note that most of the available log analysis tools assume you're using the `common` log format or the `combined` log format—both of which are defined in the default configuration files.

The following variables are available for `LogFormat` statements:

- `%a` Remote IP address.
- `%A` Local IP address.
- `%b` Bytes sent, excluding HTTP headers. This is shown in Apache's Combined Log Format (CLF). For a request without any data content, a `-` is shown instead of `0`.
- `%B` Bytes sent, excluding HTTP headers.
- `%{VARIABLE}e` The contents of the environment variable `VARIABLE`.
- `%f` The filename of the output log.
- `%h` Remote host.
- `%H` Request protocol.
- `%{HEADER}i` The contents of `HEADER`; header line(s) in the request sent to the server.
- `%l` Remote log name (from `identd`, if supplied).
- `%m` Request method.
- `%{NOTE}n` The contents of note `NOTE` from another module.

- ▶ %{HEADER}o The contents of HEADER; header line(s) in the reply.

- ▶ %p The canonical port of the server serving the request.

- ▶ %P The process ID of the child that serviced the request.

- ▶ %q The contents of the query string, prepended with a ? character. If there's no query string, this evaluates to an empty string.

- ▶ %r The first line of request.

- ▶ %s Status. For requests that were internally redirected, this is the status of the original request—%>s for the last.

- ▶ %t The time, in common log time format.

- ▶ %{format}t The time, in the form given by format, which should be in strftime(3) format. See the section "Basic SSI Directives" later in this chapter for a complete list of available formatting options.

- ▶ %T The seconds taken to serve the request.

- ▶ %u Remote user from auth; this might be bogus if the return status (%s) is 401.

- ▶ %U The URL path requested.

- ▶ %V The server name according to the UseCanonicalName directive.

- ▶ %v The canonical ServerName of the server serving the request.

You can put a conditional in front of each variable to determine whether the variable is displayed. If the variable isn't displayed, - is displayed instead. These conditionals are in the form of a list of numerical return values. For example, %!401u displays the value of REMOTE_USER unless the return code is 401.

You can then specify the location and format of a log file using the CustomLog directive:

```
CustomLog logs/access_log common
```

If it is not specified as an absolute path, the location of the log file is assumed to be relative to the ServerRoot.

Other Web Servers for Use with Ubuntu

To determine the best web server for your use, consider the needs of the website you manage. Does it need heavy security (for e-commerce), multimedia (music, video, and pictures), or the capability to download files easily? How much are you willing to spend for the software? Do you need software that is easy to maintain and troubleshoot or that includes tech support? The answers to these questions might steer you to something other than Apache.

The following sections list some of the more popular alternatives to using Apache as your web server.

Sun ONE Web Server

Despite the Netcraft numbers shown previously in Table 17.1, there is evidence that the Sun Java System Web Server (formerly known as the iPlanet Web Server, and subsequently Sun ONE Web Server) might be even more popular than Apache in strictly corporate arenas. The server got its start as the Netscape Enterprise Server—one of the first powerful web servers ever to hit the market. Sun ONE Web Server comes in many flavors, and all of them are big. In addition to the enterprise-level web server that can be run on Ubuntu, the software features application, messaging, calendar, and directory servers—just to name a few.

Sun ONE Web Server is great for handling big web needs, and it comes with an appropriately big price tag. It's definitely not something to run the school website—unless your school happens to be a major state university with several regional campuses. For more information on Sun Java System Web Server, you can visit its website (http://wwws.sun.com/software/products/web_srvr/home_web_srvr.html).

Zope

Zope is another open-source web server. Although it is still relatively young and might not have as much flexibility as Apache, it is making strong inroads in the web server market.

What makes Zope different from Apache is the fact that it is managed through a completely web-based graphic interface. This has broad appeal for those who are not enthused about a command-line–only interface.

Zope is a product of the Zope Corporation (formerly Digital Creations), the same firm that made the Python programming language. And, like all things open source, it is free. Information on Zope can be found at both http://www.zope.com (for the commercial version) and http://www.zope.org (for the open-source version).

Zeus Web Server

Ubuntu sites can also use the Zeus Web Server from Zeus Technology. This server offers a scalable SSL implementation, security settings across multiple websites, and an online administration server. The current price is $1,700 for a host platform with up to two CPUs, but load balancing via the Zeus Load Balancer costs $12,000 (at the time of writing) for each pair of load-balancing computers.

You can get more information about the Zeus Web Server at http://www.zeus.com/products/zws/.

Related Ubuntu and Linux Commands

You will use these commands when managing your Apache web Server in Ubuntu:

▶ `apache2ctl`—Server control shell script included with Apache

▶ `apache2`—The Apache web server

▶ `konqueror`—KDE's graphical web browser

▶ `elinks`—A text-based, graphical menu web browser

▶ `firefox`—The premier open-source web browser

Reference

There is a plethora of Apache documentation online. For more information about Apache and the subjects discussed in this chapter, look at some of the following resources:

▶ http://news.netcraft.com/archives/web_server_survey.html—A statistical graph of web server usage by millions of servers. The research points out that Apache is by far the most widely used server for Internet sites.

▶ http://www.apache.org/—Extensive documentation and information about Apache are available at The Apache Project website.

▶ http://www.apacheweek.com/—You can obtain breaking news about Apache and great technical articles at the Apache Week site.

▶ http://apachetoday.com/—Another good Apache site. Original content as well as links to Apache-related stories on other sites can be found at Apache Today's site.

▶ http://www.hwg.org/—HTML, CGI, and related subjects are available at The HTML Writers Guild site.

▶ http://modules.apache.org/—Available add-on modules for Apache can be found at The Apache Module Registry website.

There are several good books about Apache. For example, *Apache Server Unleashed* (Sams Publishing), ISBN 0-672-31808-3.

For more information on Zope, see *The Zope Book* (New Riders Publishing), ISBN 0-7357-11372.

17

CHAPTER 18

Remote File Serving with FTP

*F*ile *Transfer Protocol (FTP)* was once considered the primary method used to transfer files over a network from computer to computer. FTP is still heavily used today, although many graphical FTP clients now supplement the original text-based interface command. As computers have evolved, so has FTP, and Ubuntu includes many ways with which to use a graphical interface to transfer files over FTP.

This chapter contains an overview of the available FTP software included with Ubuntu, along with some details concerning initial setup, configuration, and use of FTP-specific clients. Ubuntu also includes an FTP server software package named vsftpd, the Very Secure FTP Daemon, and a number of associated programs you can use to serve and transfer files with the FTP protocol.

Choosing an FTP Server

FTP uses a client/server model. As a client, FTP accesses a server, and as a server, FTP provides access to files or storage. Just about every computer platform available has software written to enable a computer to act as an FTP server, but Ubuntu provides the average user with the capability do this without paying hefty licensing fees and without regard for client usage limitations.

There are two types of FTP servers and access: anonymous and standard. A *standard* FTP server requires an account name and password from anyone trying to access the server. *Anonymous* servers allow anyone to connect to the server to retrieve files. Anonymous servers provide the most flexibility, but they can also present a security risk. Fortunately, as you will read in this chapter, Ubuntu is set up to use proper file and directory permissions and common-sense default configuration, such as disallowing root to perform an FTP login.

> **NOTE**
>
> Many Linux users now use OpenSSH and its suite of clients, such as the sftp command, for a more secure solution when transferring files. The OpenSSH suite provides the sshd daemon and enables encrypted remote logins (see Chapter 15 for more information).

Choosing an Authenticated or Anonymous Server

When you are preparing to set up your FTP server, you must first make the decision to install either the authenticated or anonymous service. *Authenticated* service requires the entry of a valid username and password for access. As previously mentioned, *anonymous* service allows the use of the username anonymous and an email address as a password for access.

Authenticated FTP servers are used to provide some measure of secure data transfer for remote users, but will require maintenance of user accounts as usernames and passwords are used. Anonymous FTP servers are used when user authentication is not needed or necessary, and can be helpful in providing an easily accessible platform for customer support or public distribution of documents, software, or other data.

If you use an anonymous FTP server in your home or business Linux system, it is vital that you properly install and configure it to retain a relatively secure environment. Generally, sites that host anonymous FTP servers place them outside the firewall on a dedicated machine. The dedicated machine contains only the FTP server and should not contain data that cannot be restored quickly. This dedicated-machine setup prevents malicious users who compromise the server from obtaining critical or sensitive data. For an additional, but by no means more secure setup, the FTP portion of the file system can be mounted read-only from a separate hard drive partition or volume, or mounted from read-only media, such as CD-ROM, DVD, or other optical storage.

Ubuntu FTP Server Packages

The Very Secure vsftpd server, like wu-ftpd (also discussed in this chapter), is licensed under the GNU GPL. The server can be used for personal or business purposes. The wu-ftpd and vsftpd servers are covered in the remainder of this chapter.

Other FTP Servers

One alternative server is NcFTPd, available from http://www.ncftp.com. This server operates independently of inetd (typically used to enable and start the wu-ftp server) and provides its own optimized daemon. Additionally, NcFTPd has the capability to cache directory listings of the FTP server in memory, thereby increasing the speed at which users can obtain a list of available files and directories. Although NcFTPd has many advantages over wu-ftpd, NcFTPd is not GPL-licensed software, and its licensing fees vary according to the maximum number of simultaneous server connections ($199 for 51 or more concurrent users and $129 for up to 50 concurrent users, but free to education institutions with a compliant domain name).

> **NOTE**
>
> Do not confuse the ncftp client with ncftpd. The ncftp-3.1 package included with Ubuntu is the client software, a replacement for ftp-0.17, and includes the ncftpget and ncftpput commands for transferring files via the command line or by using a remote file uniform resource locator (URL) address. ncftpd is the FTP server, which can be downloaded from www.ncftpd.com.

Another FTP server package for Linux is ProFTPD, licensed under the GNU GPL. This server works well with most Linux distributions and has been used by a number of Linux sites, including ftp.kernel.org and ftp.sourceforge.net. ProFTPD is actively maintained and updated for bug fixes and security enhancements. Its developers recommend that you use the latest release (1.2.10 at the time of this writing) to avoid exposure to exploits and vulnerabilities. Browse to http://www.proftpd.org to download a copy.

Yet another FTP server package is Bsdftpd-ssl, which is based on the BSD ftpd (and distributed under the BSD license). Bsdftpd-ssl offers simultaneous standard and secure access using security extensions; secure access requires a special client. For more details, browse to http://bsdftpd-ssl.sc.ru.

Finally, another alternative is to use Apache (and the HTTP protocol) for serving files. Using a web server to provide data downloads can reduce the need to monitor and maintain a separate software service (or directories) on your server. This approach to serving files also reduces system resource requirements and gives remote users a bit more flexibility when downloading (such as enabling them to download multiple files at once). See Chapter 17, "Apache Web Server Management," for more information about using Apache.

Installing FTP Software

As part of the standard installation, the client software for FTP is already installed. You can verify that FTP-related software is installed on your system by using dpkg, grep, and sort commands in this query:

```
$ dpkg --get-selections ¦ grep ftp ¦ sort
```

The example results might differ, depending on what software packages are installed. In your Ubuntu file system, you will find the /usr/bin/pftp file symbolically linked to /usr/bin/netkit-ftp as well as the vsftpd server under the /usr/sbin directory. Other installed packages include additional text-based and graphical FTP clients.

In this chapter we will discuss two seperate FTP server applications, wu-ftpd and vsftpd. It's important to note that both applications cannot be installed at the same time.

If vsftpd is not installed, you can install it via the command line by running the following command: sudo apt-get install vsftpd.

Alternatively, you can install wu-ftpd by running the following command: sudo apt-get install wu-ftpd.

> **NOTE**
>
> If you host an FTP server connected to the Internet, make it a habit to always check the Ubuntu site for up-to-date system errata and security and bug fixes for your server software.

You can find packages for a wide variety of FTP tools, including wu-ftpd, in Synaptic. Again, just make sure you have the Universe repository enabled.

The FTP User

After installing Ubuntu, an FTP user is created. This user is not a normal user per se, but a name for anonymous FTP users. The FTP user entry in /etc/passwd looks like this:

```
ftp:x:14:50:FTP User:/home/ftp:/bin/false
```

> **NOTE**
>
> The FTP user, as discussed here, applies to anonymous FTP configurations and server setup.
>
> Also, note that other Linux distributions might use a different default directory, such as /usr/local/ftp, for FTP files and anonymous users.

This entry follows the standard /etc/passwd entry: username, password, User ID, Group ID, comment field, home directory, and shell. To learn more about /etc/password, see the section "The Password File" in Chapter 10, "Managing Users."

Each of the items in this entry is separated by colons. In the preceding example, you can see that the Ubuntu system hosting the server uses shadowed password because an x is present in the traditional password field. The shadow password system is important because it adds an additional level of security to Ubuntu; the shadow password system is normally installed during the Ubuntu installation.

The FTP server software uses this user account to assign permissions to users connecting to the server. By using a default shell of /bin/false for anonymous FTP users versus /bin/bash or some other standard, interactive shell, an anonymous FTP user, will be unable to log in as a regular user. /bin/false is not a shell, but a program usually assigned to an account that has been locked. As root inspection of the /etc/shadow file shows (see Listing 18.2), it is not possible to log in to this account, denoted by the * as the password.

LISTING 18.1   Shadow Password File ftp User Entry

```
# cat /etc/shadow
```

```
bin:*:11899:0:99999:7:::
daemon:*:11899:0:99999:7:::
adm:*:11899:0:99999:7:::
lp:*:11899:0:99999:7:::
...
ftp:*:12276:0:99999:7:::
...
```

The shadow file (only a portion of which is shown in Listing 18.1) contains additional information not found in the standard /etc/passwd file, such as account expiration, password expiration, whether the account is locked, and the encrypted password. The * in the password field indicates that the account is not a standard login account; thus, it does not have a password.

Although shadow passwords are in use on the system, passwords are not transmitted in a secure manner when using FTP. Because FTP was written before the necessity of encryption and security, it does not provide the mechanics necessary to send encrypted passwords. Account information is sent in plain text on FTP servers; anyone with enough technical knowledge and a network sniffer can find the password for the account you connect to on the server. Many sites use an anonymous-only FTP server specifically to prevent normal account passwords from being transmitted over the Internet.

Figure 18.1 shows a portion of a wireshark capture of an FTP session. The wireshark client is a graphical browser used to display network traffic in real time, and it can be used to watch packet data, such as an FTP login on a LAN.

Quick and Dirty FTP Service

Conscientious Linux administrators will take the time to carefully install, set up, and configure a production FTP server before offering public service or opening up for business on the Internet. However, you can set up a server very quickly on a secure LAN by following a few simple steps:

1. Ensure that the FTP server package is installed, networking is enabled, and firewall rules on the server allow FTP access. See Chapter 14, "Networking," to learn about firewalling.

2. If anonymous access to server files is desired, populate the /home/ftp/pub directory. Do this by mounting or copying your content, such as directories and files, under this directory.

3. Edit and then save the appropriate configuration file (such as /etc.vsftpd.conf for vsftpd) to enable access.

4. If you are using wu-ftpd, you must then restart the server like so: /etc/init.d/wu-ftpd restart. Alternatively, if you are using vsftpd, you must then start or restart the server like so: /etc/init.d/vsftpd restart.

18

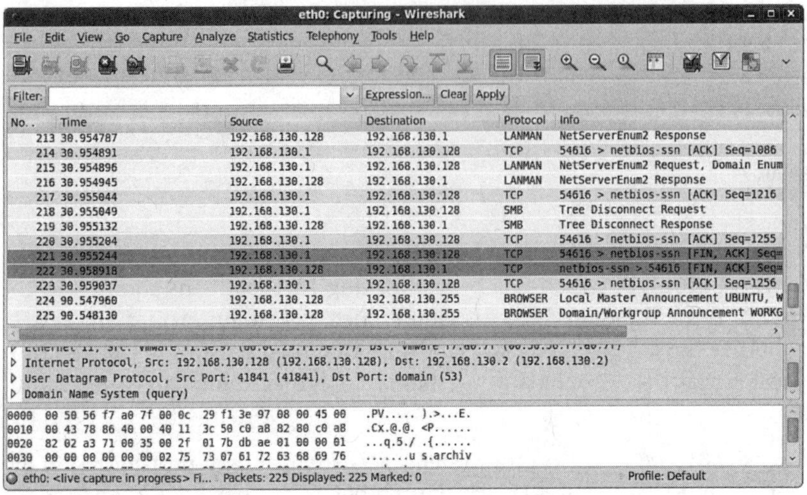

FIGURE 18.1   The Wireshark client can filter and sniff FTP sessions to capture usernames and passwords.

Starting the Very Secure FTP Server (`vsftpd`) Package

You can use the shell script named `vsftp` under the `/etc/init.d` directory to start, stop, restart, and query the `vsftpd` server. You must have root permission to use the `vsftpd` script to control the server, but any user can query the server (to see if it is running and to see its process ID number) using the `status` keyword, like this:

```
$ /etc/init.d/vsftpd status
```

Be sure not to run two FTP servers on your system at the same time!

Configuring the Very Secure FTP Server

The `server` offers simplicity, security, and speed. It has been used by a number of sites, such as ftp.debian.org, ftp.gnu.org, rpmfind.net, and ftp.gimp.org. Note that despite its name, the Very Secure FTP server does not enable use of encrypted usernames or passwords.

Its main configuration file is `vsftpd.conf`, which resides under the `/etc` directory. The server has a number of features and default policies, but these can be overridden by changing the installed configuration file.

By default, anonymous logins are enabled, but users are not allowed to upload files, create new directories, or delete or rename files. The configuration file installed by Ubuntu allows local users (that is, users with a login and shell account) to log in and then access their home directory. This configuration presents potential security risks because usernames and passwords are passed without encryption over a network. The best policy is to deny your users access to the server from their user accounts. The standard vsftpd configuration disables this feature.

Controlling Anonymous Access

Toggling anonymous access features for your FTP server is done by editing the `vsftpd.conf` file and changing related entries to YES or NO in the file. Settings to control how the server works for anonymous logins include:

- `anonymous_enable`—Enabled by default. Use a setting of NO, and then restart the server to turn off anonymous access.

- `anon_mkdir_write_enable`—Allows or disallows creating of new directories.

- `anon_other_write_enable`—Allows or disallows deleting or renaming of files and directories.

- `anon_upload_enable`—Controls whether anonymous users can upload files (also depends on the global `write_enable` setting). This is a potential security and liability hazard and should rarely be used; if enabled, consistently monitor any designated upload directory.

18

▶ anon_world_readable_only—Allows only anonymous users to download files with world-readable (444) permission.

After making any changes to your server configuration file, make sure to restart the server; this forces vsftpd to reread its settings.

Other vsftpd Server Configuration Files

You can edit vsftpd.conf to enable, disable, and configure many features and settings of the vsftpd server, such as user access, filtering of bogus passwords, and access logging. Some features might require the creation and configuration of other files, such as:

▶ /etc/vsftpd.user_list—Used by the userlist_enable and/or the userlist_deny options; the file contains a list of usernames to be denied access to the server.

▶ /etc/vsftpd.chroot_list—Used by the chroot_list_enable and/or chroot_local_user options, this file contains a list of users who are either allowed or denied access to a home directory. An alternate file can be specified by using the chroot_list_file option.

▶ /etc/vsftpd.banned_emails—A list of anonymous password entries used to deny access if the deny_email_enable setting is enabled. An alternative file can be specified by using the banned_email option.

▶ /var/log/vsftpd.log—Data transfer information is captured to this file if logging is enabled using the xferlog_enable setting.

TIP

Whenever editing the FTP server files, make a backup file first. Also, it is always a good idea to comment out (using a pound sign at the beginning of a line) what is changed instead of deleting or overwriting entries. Follow these comments with a brief description explaining why the change was made. This leaves a nice audit trail of what was done, by whom, when, and why. If you have any problems with the configuration, these comments and details can help you troubleshoot and return to valid entries if necessary. You can use the dpkg command or other Linux tools (such as mc) to extract a fresh copy of a configuration file from the software's package archive. Be aware, however, that the extracted version will replace the current version and overwrite your configuration changes.

Default vsftpd Behaviors

The contents of a file named .message (if it exists in the current directory) are displayed when a user enters the directory. This feature is enabled in the installed configuration file, but disabled by the daemon. FTP users are also not allowed to perform recursive directory listings, which can help reduce bandwidth use.

The PASV data connection method is enabled to let external users know the IP address of the FTP server. This is a common problem when using FTP from behind a firewall/gateway using IP masquerading or when incoming data connections are disabled because without passive mode, the remote server tries to form a connection to your local host and gets blocked. For example, here is a connection to an FTP server (running ProFTPD), an attempt to view a directory listing, and the resulting need to use ftp's internal passive command:

```
$ ftp ftp.tux.org
Connected to gwyn.tux.org.
220 ProFTPD 1.2.5rc1 Server (ProFTPD on ftp.tux.org) [gwyn.tux.org]
500 AUTH not understood.
KERBEROS_V4 rejected as an authentication type
Name (ftp.tux.org:gbush): gbush
331 Password required for gbush.
Password:
230 User gbush logged in.
Remote system type is UNIX.
Using binary mode to transfer files.
ftp> cd public_html
250 CWD command successful.
ftp> ls
500 Illegal PORT command.
ftp: bind: Address already in use
ftp>
ftp> pass
Passive mode on.
ftp> ls
227 Entering Passive Mode (204,86,112,12,187,89).
150 Opening ASCII mode data connection for file list
-rw-r—r—  1 gbush    gbush         8470 Jan 10  2000 LinuxUnleashed.gif
-rw-r—r—  1 gbush    gbush         4407 Oct  4  2001 RHU72ed.gif
-rw-r—r—  1 gbush    gbush         6732 May 18  2000 SuSEUnleashed.jpg
-rw-r—r—  1 gbush    gbush         6175 Jan 10  2000 TYSUSE.gif
-rw-r—r—  1 gbush    gbush         3135 Jan 10  2000 TZones.gif
...
```

18

> **NOTE**
>
> Browse to http://slacksite.com/other/ftp.html for a detailed discussion regarding active and passive FTP modes and the effect of firewall blocking of service ports on FTP server and client connections.

Other default settings are that specific user login controls are not set, but you can configure the controls to deny access to one or more users.

The data transfer rate for anonymous client access is unlimited, but you can set a maximum rate (in bytes per second) by using the anon_max_rate setting in vsftpd.conf.

This can be useful for throttling bandwidth use during periods of heavy access. Another default is that remote clients will be logged out after five minutes of idle activity or a stalled data transfer. You can set idle and transfer timeouts (stalled connections) separately.

Other settings that might be important for managing your system's resources (networking bandwidth or memory) when offering FTP access include the following:

- ▶ dirlist_enable—Toggles directory listings on or off.
- ▶ dirmessage_enable—Toggles display of a message when the user enters a directory. A related setting is ls_recurse_enable, which can be used to disallow recursive directory listings.
- ▶ download_enable—Toggles downloading on or off.
- ▶ max_clients—Sets a limit on the maximum number of connections.
- ▶ max_per_ip—Sets a limit on the number of connections from the same IP address.

Configuring the wu-ftpd Server

Wu-FTP uses a number of configuration files to control how it operates, including the following:

- ▶ ftpaccess—Contains the majority of server configuration settings
- ▶ ftpconversions—Contains definitions of file conversions during transfers
- ▶ ftphosts—Settings to control user access from specific hosts

These files may be created in the /etc/wu-ftpd directory during installation of the wu-ftpd application. The following sections describe each of these files and how to use the commands they contain to configure the Wu-FTP server so that it is accessible to all incoming requests.

CAUTION

When configuring an anonymous FTP server, it is extremely important to ensure that all security precautions are taken to prevent malicious users from gaining privileged-level access to the server. Although this chapter shows you how to configure your FTP server for secure use, all machines connected to the Internet are potential targets for malicious attacks. Vulnerable systems can be a source of potential liability, especially if anyone accesses and uses them to store illegal copies of proprietary software—even temporarily.

Using Commands in the ftpaccess File to Configure wu-ftpd

The ftpaccess file contains most of the server configuration details. Each line contains a definition or parameter that is passed to the server to specify how the server is to operate. The directives can be broken down into the following categories, including:

- ▶ **Access Control**—Settings that determine who can access the FTP server and how it is accessed

- ▶ **Information**—Settings that determine what information is provided by the server or displayed to a user

- ▶ **Logging**—Settings that determine whether logging is enabled and what information is logged

- ▶ **Permission Control**—Settings that control the behavior of users when accessing the server; in other words, what actions users are allowed to perform, such as create a directory, upload a file, delete a file or directory, and so on

---

TIP

Many more options can be specified for the wu-ftpd FTP server in its ftpaccess file. The most common commands have been covered here. A full list of configuration options can be found in the ftpaccess man page after you install the server.

You can edit the ftpaccess file at the command line to make configuration changes in any of these categories. The following sections describe some configuration changes and how to edit these files to accomplish them.

Configure Access Control

Controlling which users can access the FTP server and how they can access it is a critical part of system security. Use the following entries in the ftpaccess file to specify to which group the user accessing the server is assigned.

Limit Access for Anonymous Users

This command imposes increased security on the anonymous user:

```
autogroup <groupname> <class> [<class>]
```

If the anonymous user is a member of a group, he will only be allowed access to files and directories owned by him or his group. The group must be a valid group from /etc/groups.

Define User Classes

This command defines a class of users by the address to which the user is connected:

```
class <class> <typelist> <addrglob> [<addrglob>]
```

There might be multiple members for a class of users, and multiple classes might apply to individual members. When multiple classes apply to one user, the first class that applies will be used.

The typelist field is a comma-separated list of the keywords anonymous, guest, and real. anonymous applies to the anonymous user, and guest applies to the guest access account, as specified in the guestgroup directive. real defines those users who have a valid entry in the /etc/passwd file.

The addrglob field is a regular expression that specifies addresses to which the class is to be applied. The (*) entry specifies all hosts.

Block a Host's Access to the Server

Sometimes it is necessary to block access to the server to entire hosts. This can be useful to protect the system from individual hosts or entire blocks of IP addresses, or to force the use of other servers. Use this command to do so:

```
deny <addrglob> <message_file>
```

deny will always deny access to hosts that match a given address.

addrglob is a regular expression field that contains a list of addresses, either numeric or a DNS name. This field can also be a file reference that contains a listing of addresses. If an address is a file reference, it must be an absolute file reference; that is, starting with a /. To ensure that IP addresses can be mapped to a valid domain name, use the !nameserver parameter.

A sample deny line resembles the following:

```
deny *.exodous.net /home/ftp/.message_exodous_deny
```

This entry denies access to the FTP server from all users who are coming from the exodous.net domain, and displays the message contained in the .message_exoduous_deny file in the /home/ftp directory.

ftpusers File Purpose Now Implemented in ftpaccess

Certain accounts for the system to segment and separate tasks with specific permissions are created during Linux installation. The ftpusers file (located in /etc/ftpusers) is where accounts for system purposes are listed. It is possible that the version of wu-ftp you use with Ubuntu deprecates the use of this file, and instead implements the specific functionality of this file in the ftpaccess file with the commands of deny-uid/deny-gid.

Restrict Permissions Based on Group IDs

The guestgroup line assigns a given group name or group names to behave exactly like the anonymous user. Here is the command:

```
guestgroup <groupname> [<groupname>]
```

This command confines the users to a specific directory structure in the same way anonymous users are confined to /var/ftp. This command also limits these users to access files for which their assigned group has permissions.

The groupname parameter can be the name of a group or that group's corresponding Group ID (*GID*). If you use a GID as the groupname parameter, put a percentage symbol (%)

in front of it. You can use this command to assign permissions to a range of group IDs, as in this example:

```
guestgroup %500-550
```

This entry restricts all users with the group IDs 500–550 to being treated as a guest group, rather than individual users. For guestgroup to work, you must set up the user's home directories with the correct permissions, exactly like the anonymous FTP user.

Limit Permissions Based on Individual ID

The guestuser line works exactly like the guestgroup command you just read about, except it specifies a User ID (*UID*) instead of a group ID. Here's the command:

```
guestuser <username> [<username>]
```

This command limits the guest user to files for which the user has privileges. Generally, a user has more privileges than a group, so this type of assignment can be less restrictive than the guestgroup line.

Restrict the Number of Users in a Class

The limit command restricts the number of users in a class during given times. Here is the command, which contains fields for specifying a class, a number of users, a time range, and the name of a text file that contains an appropriate message:

```
limit <class> <n> <times> <message_file>
```

If the specified number of users from the listed class is exceeded during the given time period, the user sees the contents of the file given in the message_file parameter.

The times parameter is somewhat terse. Its format is a comma-delimited string in the form of days, hours. Valid day strings are Su, Mo, Tu, We, Th, Fr, Sa, and Any. The hours are formatted in a 24-hour format. An example is as follows:

```
limit anonymous 10 MoTuWeThFr,Sa0000-2300 /home/ftp/.message_limit_anon_class
```

This line limits the anonymous class to 10 concurrent connections on Monday through Friday, and on Saturday from midnight to 11:00 p.m. If the number of concurrent connections is exceeded or at 11:00 p.m. on Saturday, the users will see the contents of the file /home/ftp/.message_limit_anon_class.

Syntax for finer control over limiting user connections can be found in the ftpaccess man page.

Limit the Number of Invalid Password Entries

This line allows control over how many times a user can enter an invalid password before the FTP server terminates the session:

```
loginfails <number>
```

The default for `loginfails` is set to 5. This command prevents users without valid passwords from experimenting until they "get it right."

Configure User Information

Providing users with information about the server and its use is a good practice for any administrator of a public FTP server. Adequate user information can help prevent user problems and eliminate tech support calls. You also can use this information to inform users of restrictions governing the use of your FTP server. User information gives you an excellent way to document how your FTP server should be used.

You can use the commands detailed in the following sections to display messages to users as they log in to the server or as they perform specific actions. The following commands enable messages to be displayed to users when logging in to the server or when an action is performed.

Display a Prelogin Banner

This command is a reference to a file that is displayed before the user receives a login prompt from the FTP server:

```
banner <path>
```

This file generally contains information to identify the server. The path is an absolute pathname relative to the system root (/), not the base of the anonymous FTP user's home. The entry might look like this:

```
banner /etc/uftp.banner
```

This example uses the file named `uftp.banner` under the `/etc` directory. The file can contain one or more lines of text, such as:

```
Welcome to Widget, Inc.'s Red Hat Linux FTP server.
This server is only for use of authorized users.
Third-party developers should use a mirror site.
```

When an FTP user attempts to log in, the banner is displayed like so:

```
$ ftp shuttle2
Connected to shuttle2.home.org.
220-Welcome to Widget, Inc.'s FTP server.
220-This server is only for use of authorized users.
220-Third-party developers should use a mirror site.
220-
220-
220 shuttle2 FTP server (Version wu-2.6.2-8) ready.
504 AUTH GSSAPI not supported.
504 AUTH KERBEROS_V4 not supported.
KERBEROS_V4 rejected as an authentication type
```

```
Name (shuttle2:phudson):
```

Note that the banner does not replace the greeting text that, by default, displays the hostname and server information, such as:

```
220 shuttle2 FTP server (Version wu-2.6.2-8) ready.
```

To hide version information, use the greeting command in ftpaccess with a keyword, such as terse, like so:

```
greeting terse
```

FTP users then see a short message like this as part of the login text:

```
220 FTP server ready.
```

Also, not all FTP clients can handle multiline responses from the FTP server. The banner <path> command is how the banner line passes the file contents to the client. If clients cannot interrupt multiline responses, the FTP server is useless to them. You should also edit the default banner to remove identity and version information.

Display a File

This line specifies a text file to be displayed to the user during login and when the user issues the cd command:

```
message <path> {<when> {<class> ...}}
```

The optional when clause can be LOGIN or CWD=(dir), where dir is the name of a directory that is current. The optional class parameter enables messages to be shown to only a given class or classes of users.

Using messages is a good way to give information about where things are on your site as well as information that is system dependent, such as alternative sites, general policies regarding available data, server availability times, and so on.

You can use magic cookies to breathe life into your displayed messages. *Magic cookies* are symbolic constants that are replaced by system information. Table 18.1 lists the message command's valid magic cookies and their representations.

TABLE 18.1   Magic Cookies and Their Descriptions

Cookie	Description
%T	Local time (form Thu Nov 15 17:12:42 1990)
%F	Free space in partition of CWD (kilobytes)
	[Not supported on all systems]
%C	Current working directory
%E	Maintainer's email address as defined in ftpaccess
%R	Remote hostname

18

TABLE 18.1   Magic Cookies and Their Descriptions

Cookie	Description
%L	Local hostname
%u	Username as determined via RFC931 authentication
%U	Username given at login time
%M	Maximum allowed number of users in this class
%N	Current number of users in this class
%B	Absolute limit on disk blocks allocated
%b	Preferred limit on disk blocks
%Q	Current block count
%I	Maximum number of allocated inodes (+1)
%i	Preferred inode limit
%q	Current number of allocated inodes
%H	Time limit for excessive disk use
%h	Time limit for excessive files
Ratios	
%xu	Uploaded bytes
%xd	Downloaded bytes
%xR	Upload/download ratio (1:*n*)
%xc	Credit bytes
%xT	Time limit (minutes)
%xE	Elapsed time since login (minutes)
%xL	Time left
%xU	Upload limit
%xD	Download limit

To understand how this command works, imagine that you want to display a welcome message to everyone who logs in to the FTP server. An entry of:

```
message /home/ftp/welcome.msg    login
message /welcome.msg             login
```

shows the contents of the welcome.msg file to all real users who log in to the server. The second entry shows the same message to the anonymous user.

The welcome.msg file is not created with the installation of the package, but you can create it using a text editor. Type the following:

```
Welcome to the anonymous ftp service on %L!


There are %N out of %M users logged in.
```

```
Current system time is %T

Please send email to %E if there are
any problems with this service.

Your current working directory is %C
```

Save this file as `/var/ftp/welcome.msg`. Verify that it works by connecting to the FTP server:

```
220 FTP server ready.
504 AUTH GSSAPI not supported.
504 AUTH KERBEROS_V4 not supported.
KERBEROS_V4 rejected as an authentication type
Name (shuttle:phudson): anonymous
331 Guest login ok, send your complete e-mail address as password.
Password:
230-Welcome to the anonymous ftp service on shuttle.home.org!
230-
230-There are 1 out of unlimited users logged in.
230-
230-Current system time is Mon Nov  3 10:57:06 2003
230-
230-Please send email to root@localhost if there are
230-any problems with this service.
230-Your current working directory is /
```

Display Administrator's Email Address

This line sets the email address for the FTP administrator:

```
email <name>
```

This string is printed whenever the %E magic cookie is specified. This magic cookie is used in the messages line or in the shutdown file. You should display this string to users in the login banner message so that they know how to contact you (the administrator) in case of problems with the FTP server.

> **CAUTION**
>
> Do not use your live email address in the display banner; you want others to be able to access user emails as necessary. Instead, use an alias address that routes the messages to the appropriate IT department or other address.

Notify User of Last Modification Date

The `readme` line tells the server whether a notification should be displayed to the user when a specific file was last modified. Here's the command:

```
readme <path> {<when {<class>}}
```

The path parameter is any valid path for the user. The optional when parameter is exactly as seen in the message line. class can be one or more classes as defined in the class file. The path is absolute for real users. For the anonymous user, the path is relative to the anonymous home directory, which is /var/ftp by default.

Configure System Logging

Part of any system administration involves reviewing log files for what the server is doing, who accessed it, what files were transferred, and other pieces of important information. You can use a number of commands within /etc/ftpaccess to control your FTP server logging actions.

Redirect Logging Records

This line allows the administrator to redirect where logging information from the FTP server is recorded:

```
log <syslog>{+<xferlog>}
```

By default, the information for commands is stored in /var/log/messages, although the man pages packaged in some packages state that this information is written to /var/log/xferlog. Check your server's settings for information regarding the location of your file transfer logs.

Log All User-Issued Commands

This line enables logging for all commands issued by the user:

```
log commands [<typelist>]
```

typelist is a comma-separated list of anonymous, guest, and real. If no typelist is given, commands are logged for all users. Some wu-ftpd packages set the logging of all file transfers to /var/log/xferlog (see the next section). However, you can add the log command to ftpaccess with the commands keyword to capture user actions. Logging is then turned on and user actions are captured in /var/log/messages. Here is a sample log file:

```
Oct  6 12:21:42 shuttle2 ftpd[5229]: USER anonymous
Oct  6 12:21:51 shuttle2 ftpd[5229]: PASS phudson@widget.com
Oct  6 12:21:51 shuttle2 ftpd[5229]: ANONYMOUS FTP LOGIN FROM 192.168.2.31
➥[192.168.2.31], phudson@widget.com
Oct  6 12:21:51 shuttle2 ftpd[5229]: SYST
Oct  6 12:21:54 shuttle2 ftpd[5229]: CWD pub
Oct  6 12:21:57 shuttle2 ftpd[5229]: PASV
Oct  6 12:21:57 shuttle2 ftpd[5229]: LIST
Oct  6 12:21:59 shuttle2 ftpd[5229]: QUIT
Oct  6 12:21:59 shuttle2 ftpd[5229]: FTP session closed
```

The sample log shows the username and password entries for an anonymous login. The CWD entry shows that a cd command is used to navigate to the pub directory. Note that the commands shown do not necessarily reflect the syntax the user typed, but instead list corresponding system calls the FTP server received. For example, the LIST entry is actually the ls command.

Log Security Violations and File Transfers

Two other logging commands are useful in the /etc/ftpaccess configuration file. This line enables the logging of security violations:

```
log security [<typelist>]
```

Violations are logged for anonymous, guest, and real users, as specified in the typelist—the same as other log commands. If you do not specify a typelist, security violations for all users are logged.

This line writes a log of all files transferred to and from the server:

```
log transfers [<typelist> [<directions>]]
```

typelist is the same as seen in log commands and log security lines. directions is a comma-separated list of the keywords inbound for uploaded files and outbound for downloaded files. If no directions are given, both uploaded and downloaded files are logged. Inbound and outbound logging is turned on by default.

Configure Permission Control

Controlling user activity is an important component of securing your system's server. The ftpaccess file includes a number of commands that enable you to determine what users can and cannot execute during an FTP session. You can use these permission controls to allow users to change file permissions, delete or overwrite files, rename files, and create new files with default permissions. You learn how to use all these ftpaccess file command lines in the following sections.

18

> **NOTE**
>
> By default, all the ftpaccess file command lines prohibit anonymous users from executing actions and enable authorized users to do so.

Allow Users to Change File Permissions

The chmod line determines whether a user has the capability to change a file's permissions. Here is the command line:

```
chmod <yes¦no> <typelist>
```

This command acts the same as the standard chmod command.

The yes¦no parameter designates whether the command can be executed. typelist is a comma-delimited string of the keywords anonymous, guest, and real. If you do not specify a `typelist` string, the command is applied to all users. An exhaustive description of its purpose and parameters can be found in the man page.

Assign Users File-Delete Permission
The `delete` line determines whether the user can delete files with the `rm` command. Here's the command line:

```
delete<yes¦no> <typelist>
```

The `yes¦no` parameter is used to turn this permission on or off, and `typelist` is the same as the `chmod` command.

Assign Users File-Overwrite Permission
This command line of the `ftpaccess` file allows or denies users the ability to overwrite an existing file. Here's the command line:

```
overwrite <yes¦no> <typelist>
```

The FTP client determines whether users can overwrite files on their own local machines; this line specifically controls overwrite permissions for uploads to the server. The `yes¦no` parameter toggles the permission on or off, and `typelist` is the same as seen in the `chmod` line.

Allow Users to Rename Files
You can enable or prevent a user from renaming files by using this command line:

```
rename <yes¦no> <typelist>
```

The `yes¦no` parameter toggles the permission on or off, and `typelist` is the same comma-delimited string as seen in `chmod`.

Allow Users to Compress Files
This line determines whether the user is able to use the `compress` command on files:

```
compress <yes¦no> [<classglob>]
```

The `yes¦no` parameter toggles the permission on or off, and `classglob` is a regular expression string that specifies one or more defined classes of users. The conversions that result from the use of this command are specified in the `ftpconversions` file, which contains directions on what compression or extraction command is to be used on a file with a specific extension, such as `.Z` for the `compress` command, `.gz` for the `gunzip` command, and so on. See the section "Configuring FTP Server File-Conversion Actions" later in this chapter.

Assign or Deny Permission to Use `tar`
This line determines whether the user is able to use the `tar` (tape archive) command on files:

```
tar <yes¦no> [<classglob> ...]
```

The yes|no parameter toggles the permission on or off, and classglob is a regular expression string that specifies one or more defined classes of users. Again, the conversions that result from the use of this command are specified in the ftpconversions file.

Determine What Permissions Can Apply to User-Created Upload Files

This line is a bit different from the other commands in the permission control section. The umask command determines with what permissions a user can create new files; here it is.

umask <yes¦no> <typelist>

The yes¦no parameter toggles based on whether a user is allowed to create a file with his default permissions when uploading a file. Like the overwrite command you read about earlier in this section, this command line is specific to uploaded files because the client machine determines how new files are created from a download.

Configure Commands Directed Toward the cdpath

This alias command allows the administrator to provide another name for a directory other than its standard name:

alias <string> <dir>

The alias line applies to only the cd command. This line is particularly useful if a popular directory is buried deep within the anonymous FTP user's directory tree. The following is a sample entry:

alias linux-386 /pub/slackware/11/i386/

This line would allow the user to type cd linux-386 and be automatically taken to the /pub/slackwase/11/i386 directory.

The cdpath <dir> line specifies the order in which the cd command looks for a given user-entered string. The search is performed in the order in which the cdpath lines are entered in the ftpacess file.

For example, if the following cdpath entries are in the ftpaccess file,

cdpath /pub/slackware/
cdpath /pub/linux/

and the user types cd i386, the server searches for an entry in any defined aliases, first in the /pub/slackware directory and then in the /pub/linux directory. If a large number of aliases are defined, it is recommended that symbolic links to the directories be created instead of aliases. Doing so reduces the amount of work on the FTP server and decreases the wait time for the user.

18

Structure of the `shutdown` File

The `shutdown` command tells the server where to look for the `shutdown` message generated by the `ftpshut` command or by the user. The `shutdown` command is used with a pathname to a shutdown file, such as:

```
shutdown /etc/uftpshutdown
```

If this file exists, the server checks the file to see when the server should shut down. The syntax of this file is as follows:

```
<year> <month> <day> <hour> <minute> <deny_offset> <disc_offset> <text>
```

year can be any year after 1970 (called the *epoch*), month is from 0–11, hour is 0–23, and minute is 0–59. `deny_offset` is the number of minutes before shutdown in which the server will disable new connections. `disc_offset` is the number of minutes before connected users are disconnected, and `text` is the message displayed to the users at login. In addition to the valid magic cookies defined in the messages section, those listed in Table 18.2 are also available.

TABLE 18.2   Magic Cookies for the `Shutdown` File

Cookie	Description
%s	The time the system will be shut down
%r	The time new connections will be denied
%d	The time current connections will be dropped

Configuring FTP Server File-Conversion Actions

The FTP server can convert files during transfer to compress and uncompress files automatically. Suppose that the user is transferring a file to his Microsoft Windows machine that was TARed and GZIPed on a Linux machine. If the user does not have an archive utility installed to uncompress these files, he cannot access or use the files.

As the FTP server administrator, you can configure the FTP server to automatically unarchive these files before download should the site support users who might not have unarchive capabilities. Additionally, you can configure an upload area for the users, and then configure the FTP server to automatically compress any files transferred to the server.

The structure of the format of the `ftpconversions` file is:

```
1:2:3:4:5:6:7:8
```

where 1 is the strip prefix, 2 is the strip postfix, 3 is the add-on prefix, 4 is the add-on postfix, 5 is the external command, 6 is the types, 7 is the options, and 8 is the description.

Strip Prefix

The *strip prefix* is one or more characters at the beginning of a filename that should be automatically removed by the server when the file is requested. By specifying a given prefix to strip in a conversions rule, such as devel, the user can request the file devel_procman.tar.gz by the command get procman.tar.gz, and the FTP server performs any other rules that apply to that file and retrieve it from the server. Although this feature is documented, as of version 2.6.2, it has yet to be implemented.

Strip Postfix

The *strip postfix* works much the same as the strip prefix, except that one or more characters are taken from the end of the filename. This feature is typically used to strip the .gz extension from files that have been TARed and GZIPed when the server is performing automatic decompression before sending the file to the client.

Add-On Prefix

The *add-on* prefix conversion instructs the server to insert one or more characters to a filename before it is transferred to the server or client. For example, a user requests the file procman.tar.gz. The server has a conversion rule to add a prefix of gnome to all .tar.gz files; therefore the server would append this string to the file before sending it to the client. The user would receive a file called gnome_procman.tar.gz. Keywords such as uppercase and lowercase can be used in this function to change the case of the filename for those operating systems in which case makes a difference. Similar to the strip prefix conversion, this feature is not yet implemented in version 2.6.2.

Add-On Postfix

An *add-on* postfix instructs the server to append one or more characters to the end of a filename during the transfer or reception of a file. A server can contain TARed packages of applications that are uncompressed. If an add-on postfix conversion was configured on the server, the server could compress the file, append a .gz extension after the file was compressed, and then send that file to the client. The server could also do the same action for uncompressed files sent to the server. This would have the effect of conserving disk space on the server.

External Command

The *external command* entries in the ftpconversions file contain the bulk of the FTP server conversion rules. The external command entry tells the server what should be done with a file after it is transferred to the server. The specified conversion utility can be any command on the server, although generally it is a compression utility. As the file is sent, the server passes the file through the external command. If the file is being uploaded to the server, the command needs to send the result to standard in, whereas a download sends the command to standard out. For example, here is an entry specifying the tar command:

```
:    : :.tar:/bin/tar -c -f - %s:T_REG¦T_DIR:O_TAR:TAR
```

The following sections describe the fields in a conversion entry.

Types

You must use the types field of the ftpconversions file to tell the server what types of files the conversion rules apply to. Separate the file type entries with the (¦) character, and give each type a value of T_REG, T_ASCII, and T_DIR.

T_REG signifies a regular file, T_ASCII an ASCII file, and T_DIR a directory. A typical entry is T_REG ¦ T_ASCII, which signifies a regular ASCII file.

Options

The options field informs the server what action is being done to the file. Similar to the types file, options are separated by the (¦) character. Here are the valid ranges you can assign to items in the options field:

- ▶ O_COMPRESS to compress the file

- ▶ O_UNCOMPRESS to uncompress the file

- ▶ O_TAR to tar the file

An example of this field is O_COMPRESS ¦ O_TAR, where files are both compressed and TARed.

Description

The description field allows an administrator to quickly understand what the rule is doing. This field does not have any syntax restriction, although it is usually a one-word entry—such as TAR, TAR+COMPRESS, or UNCOMPRESS—which is enough to get the concept across.

An Example of Conversions in Action

Crafting complex conversion entries is a task perhaps best left to the Linux/Unix expert, but the sample ftpconversions file included with wu-ftpd provides more than enough examples for the average administrator. Building your own simple conversion entry is not really too difficult, so let's examine and decode an example:

```
:.Z:   : :/bin/compress -d -c %s:T_REG¦T_ASCII:O_UNCOMPRESS:UNCOMPRESS
```

In this example, the strip prefix (field 1) is null because it is not yet implemented, so this rule does not apply to prefixes. The second field of this rule contains the .Z postfix; therefore it deals with files that have been compressed with the compress utility. The rule does not address the add-on prefix or postfix, so fields 3 and 4 are null. Field 5, the external command field, tells the server to run the compress utility to decompress all files that have the .Z extension, as the -d parameter signifies. The -c option tells compress to write the output of the compress utility to the standard out, which is the server in this case. The %s is the name of the file against which the rule was applied. Field 6 specifies that this file is a regular file in ASCII format. Field 7, the options field, tells the server that this command uncompresses the file. Finally, the last field is a comment that gives the administrator a quick decode of what the conversion rule is doing—that is, uncompressing the file.

Examples

Several conversion rules may be specified in wu-ftpd's default ftpconversions file. Additional examples, such as for Sun's Solaris operating system, might also be available in additional wu-ftpd documentation.

Using the `ftphosts` File to Allow or Deny FTP Server Connection

The purpose of the `ftphosts` file is to allow or deny specific users or addresses from connecting to the FTP server. The format of the file is the word `allow` or `deny`, optionally followed by a username, followed by an IP or a DNS address.

```
allow username address
deny username address
```

Listing 18.3 shows a sample configuration of this file.

LISTING 18.3   `ftphosts` Configuration File for Allowing or Denying Users

```
# Example host access file
#
# Everything after a '#' is treated as comment,
# empty lines are ignored
allow tdc 128.0.0.1
allow tdc 192.168.101.*
allow tdc insanepenguin.net
allow tdc *.exodous.net
 deny anonymous 201.*
deny anonymous *.pilot.net
```

The * is a wildcard that matches any combination of that address. For example, allow tdc `*.exodous.net` allows the user `tdc` to log in to the FTP server from any address that contains the domain name exodous.net. Similarly, the anonymous user is not allowed to access the FTP if he is coming from a 201 public class C IP address.

Changes made to your system's FTP server configuration files only become active after you restart `inetd` because configuration files are only parsed at startup. To restart `inetd` as root, issue the command `/etc/init.d/inetutils-inetd restart`. This makes a call to the same shell script that is called at system startup and shutdown for any runlevel to start or stop the `inet` daemon. `inetd` should report its status as

```
# /etc/init.d/inetutils-inetd restart
```

```
Stopping internet superserver inetd:                              [  OK  ]
Starting internet superserver inetd:                              [  OK  ]
```

Once restarted, the FTP server is accessible to all incoming requests.

Using Commands for Server Administration

wu-ftp provides a few commands to aid in server administration. Those commands are:

- ▶ ftpwho—Displays information about current FTP server users

- ▶ ftpcount—Displays information about current server users by class

- ▶ ftpshut—Provides automated server shutdown and user notification

- ▶ ftprestart—Provides automated server restart and shutdown message removal

Each of these commands must be executed with superuser privileges because they reference the ftpaccess configuration file to obtain information about the FTP server.

Display Information About Connected Users

The ftpwho command provides information about who are users currently connected to the FTP server. Here's the command line:

/usr/bin/ftpwho

Table 18.3 shows the format of the output ftpwho displays.

TABLE 18.3   ftpwho Fields

Name	Description
Process ID	The process ID of the FTP server process.
TTY	The terminal ID of the process. This is always a ? because the FTP daemon is not an interactive login.
Status	The status of the FTP process. The values are
	S: Sleeping
	Z: Zombie, indicating a crash
	R: Running
	N: Normal process
Time	The elapsed processor time the process has used in minutes and seconds.
Details	Tells from what host the process is connecting, the user who connected, and the currently executing command.

Listing 18.4 shows a typical output of this command. It lists the process ID for the ftp daemon handling requests, the class to which the particular user belongs, the total time connected, the connected username, and the status of the session.

In addition to the information given about each connected user, ftpwho also displays the total number of users connected out of any maximum that might have been set in the ftpaccess file. This information can be used to monitor the use of your FTP server.

You can pass one parameter to ftpwho. (You can find the parameter by using the ftpwho--help command.) The single parameter you can pass to ftpwho is -v. This parameter prints out version and licensing information for wu-ftp, as shown here:

```
# ftpwho
Service class all:
10447 ?         SN     0:00 ftpd: localhost: anonymous/winky IDLE
1 users (no maximum)
```

The output of ftpwho, using the -V option, which shows version information, is shown in Listing 18.4.

LISTING 18.4   ftpwho -V Command Output

```
Copyright © 1999,2000,2001 WU-FTPD Development Group.
All rights reserved.

Portions Copyright © 1980, 1985, 1988, 1989, 1990, 1991, 1993, 1994
 The Regents of the University of California.
Portions Copyright © 1993, 1994 Washington University in Saint Louis.
Portions Copyright © 1996, 1998 Berkeley Software Design, Inc.
Portions Copyright © 1989 Massachusetts Institute of Technology.
Portions Copyright © 1998 Sendmail, Inc.
Portions Copyright © 1983, 1995, 1996, 1997 Eric P.  Allman.
Portions Copyright © 1997 by Stan Barber.
Portions Copyright © 1997 by Kent Landfield.
Portions Copyright © 1991, 1992, 1993, 1994, 1995, 1996, 1997
Free Software Foundation, Inc.

Use and distribution of this software and its source code are governed
by the terms and conditions of the WU-FTPD Software License ("LICENSE").

If you did not receive a copy of the license, it may be obtained online
at http://www.wu-ftpd.org/license.html.
Version wu-2.6.2-8
```

Count the Number of Connections

/usr/bin/ftpcount counts the number of connected users to the FTP server and the maximum number of users allowed. This same information is found at the end of the output for the ftpwho command. This command takes only one parameter, -V, which displays the same output as the previous ftpwho example.

```
# ftpcount
Service class all                    -   4 users (no maximum)
```

Use /usr/sbin/ftpshut to Schedule FTP Server Downtime

As with any public server administration, it is always good practice to let users of the FTP server know about upcoming outages, when the server will be updated, and other relevant site information. The ftpshut command allows the administrator to let the FTP server do much of this automatically.

The ftpshut command enables the administrator to take down the FTP server at a specific time, based on some parameters passed to it. The format of the command is as follows and is documented in the ftpshut man page:

```
ftpshut [ -V ] [ -l min] [ -d min] time [ warning-message ... ]
```

The -V parameter displays the version information of the command. The time parameter is the time when the ftpshut command will stop the FTP servers. This parameter takes either a + number for the number of minutes from the current time, or a specific hour and minute in 24-hour clock format with the syntax of *HH:MM*.

The -l parameter enables the FTP server administrator to specify how long, in minutes, before shutdown the server will disable new connections. The default for this is 10 minutes. If the time given to shut down the servers is less than 10 minutes, new connections will be disabled immediately.

The -d parameter is similar to the -l parameter, but controls when the FTP server terminates the current connections. By default, this occurs five minutes before the server shuts down. If the shutdown time is less than five minutes, the server terminates the current connections immediately.

When you execute this command, the FTP server creates a file containing the shutdown information in the location specified under the shutdown section in the ftpaccess file. The default configuration for this file is /etc/shutmsg. If you execute the ftpshut command with warning messages, the messages are displayed when the user logs in to the server.

```
Name (pheniox:tdc): anonymous
331 Guest login ok, send your complete e-mail address as password.
Password:
230-system doing down at Mon Sep  3 06:23:00 2001
230-0 users of unlimited on pheniox.
230 Guest login ok, access restrictions apply.
Remote system type is UNIX.
Using binary mode to transfer files.
```

Here is a sample `ftpshut` command:

```
ftpshut -l 5 -d 5 +10 "system going down at %s %N users of %M on %R"
```

This command tells the FTP server to disconnect new connections in 5 minutes, drop all current connections in 5 minutes, shut down the server in 10 minutes, and display a warning message to the users at login. The message can be a mixture of text and magic cookies defined in Table 18.4. It is important to keep in mind that the message can only be a maximum of 75 characters in length. Additionally, it is not important to know how many characters the magic cookies will take because the system knows this information and truncates the message at 75 characters.

TABLE 18.4   Magic Cookies for the **ftpshut** Command

Cookie	Description
%S	Time the system will be shut down
%r	Time new connections will be denied
%d	Time current connections will be dropped
%C	Current working directory
%E	Server administrator's email address as specified in the `ftpaccess` file
%F	Available free space in the current working directories partition, in kilobytes
%L	Local host time
%M	Maximum number of allowed connections in this user class
%N	Current number of connections for this user class
%R	Remote hostname
%T	Local time, in the form of `Fri Aug 31 21:04:00 2001`
%U	Username given at login

When `ftpshut` is issued to the system, it creates a file that stores the necessary information. The `ftprestart` command removes this file for all servers, either canceling the impending shutdown or removing the shutdown file and restarting the FTP server. The `ftprestart` has only one optional argument, `-V`, to show version information.

Use `/var/log/xferlog` to View a Log of Server Transactions

The `xferlog` file gives a log of what transactions have occurred with the FTP server. Depending on the settings in the `/etc/ftpaccess` file, the contents of this file can contain the files sent or received, by whom, with a date stamp. Table 18.5 lists the fields of this file. The same information can also be found in the corresponding man page included in the `wu-ftp`.

18

TABLE 18.5   **/var/log/**xferlog Fields

Field	Description
current-time	Current local time in the form of *DDD MMM dd hh:mm:ss YYYY*, where DDD is the day of the week, *MMM* is the month, *dd* is the day of the month, *hh* is the hour, *mm* is the minutes, ss is the seconds, and *YYYY* is the year.
transfer-time	Total time in seconds for the transfer.
remote-host	Remote hostname.
file-size	Size of the transferred file in bytes.
filename	Name of the file.
transfer-type	A single character indicating the transfer type. The types are
	a for ASCII transfers
	b for binary transfers
special-action-flag	One or more character flags indicating any special action taken by the server. The values are
	C for compressed files
	U for uncompressed files
	T for TARed files
	- for no special action taken
direction	Indicates whether the file was sent from or received by the server.
access-mode	The way in which the user logged in to the server. The values are
	a for an anonymous guest user
	g for a guest user, corresponding to the guestgroup command in the /etc/ftpaccess file
	r for a real user on the local machine
username	If logged in as a real user, the username.
	If the access mode was guest, the password is given.
service-name	The name of the service used, usually FTP.
authentication-method	Type of authentication used. The values are 0 for none

TABLE 18.5 **/var/log**/xferlog Fields

Field	Description
	1 for RFC931 authentication (a properly formed email address)
authenticated-user-id	This is the user ID returned to the server based on the authentication method used to access the server. An * is used when an authenticated user ID cannot be found.
completion-status	A single-character field indicating the status of the transfer. The values are
	c for a completed transfer
	i for an incomplete transfer

An example of this file is seen in Listing 18.5.

LISTING 18.5 Sample /var/log/xferlog File with Inbound and Outbound Logging

```
Mon Sep  3 07:13:05 2001 1 localhost.localdomain 100
 /var/ftp/pub/README b   o a testing@test.com ftp 0 * c
Mon Sep  3 02:35:35 2001 1 helios 8 /var/ftp/pub/configuration a
_ o a testing@test.com ftp 0 * c
Mon Sep  3 02:35:35 2001 1 helios 8 /var/ftp/pub/temp.txt a  o a
testing@test.com ftp 0 * c
Mon Sep  3 02:35:35 2001 1 helios 8 /var/ftp/pub/tftp-server-
0.17-14.i386.rpm a  o a testing@test.com ftp 0 * c
Mon Sep  3 02:35:35 2001 1 helios 8 /var/ftp/pub/wu-ftpd-2.6.1-
22.i386.rpm a  o a testing@test.com ftp 0 * c
```

18

Related Ubuntu and Linux Commands

You use these commands to install, configure, and manage FTP services in Ubuntu:

▶ epiphany—A graphical GNOME browser supporting FTP

▶ ftp—A text-based interactive FTP command

▶ ftpcopy—Copy directories and files from an FTP server

▶ ftpcp—Retrieve data from a remote FTP server, but do not overwrite existing local files

▶ gftp—A graphical FTP client for GNOME

▶ konqueror—KDE's graphical web browser

▶ lftp—An advanced text-based FTP program

▶ nautilus—Gnome's graphical file explorer and browser

▶ ncftp—A sophisticated, text-based FTP program

▶ sftp—Secure file transfer program

▶ smbclient—Samba FTP client to access SMB/CIFS resources on servers

▶ vsftpd—The Very Secure FTP daemon

▶ webcam—A webcam-oriented FTP client included with xawtv

Reference

▶ http://www.wu-ftpd.org/—Official Wu-FTP website.

▶ http://www.cert.org/—Computer Emergency Response Team.

▶ http://www.openssh.com/—The OpenSSH home page and source for the latest version of OpenSSH and its component clients, such as sftp.

▶ http://www.cert.org/tech_tips/anonymous_ftp_config.html—CERT Anonymous FTP configuration guidelines.

▶ http://vsftpd.beasts.org/—Home page for the vsftd FTP server.

▶ ftp://vsftpd.beasts.org/users/cevans/—Download site for the latest releases of the vsftpd server.

# CHAPTER 19

Handling Electronic Mail

Email is still the dominant form of communication over the Internet. It is fast, free, and easy to use. However, much of what goes on behind the scenes is extremely complicated and would appear scary to anyone who does not know much about how email is handled. Ubuntu comes equipped with a number of powerful applications that will help you build anything from a small email server, right through to large servers able to handle thousands of messages.

This chapter shows you how to configure Ubuntu to act as an email server. We look at the options available in Ubuntu and examine the pros and cons of each one. You will also learn how mail is handled in Linux, and to a lesser extent, UNIX.

How Email Is Sent and Received

Email is transmitted as plain text across networks around the world using the *SMTP* protocol (*Simple Mail Transfer Protocol*). As the name implies, the protocol itself is fairly basic, and it has been extended to add further authentication and error reporting/messaging to satisfy the growing demands of modern email. Mail *transfer agents*, or MTAs, work in the background transferring email from server to server allowing emails to be sent all over the world. You may have come across such MTA software such as Sendmail, Postfix, Fetchmail, Exim, or Qmail.

SMTP allows each computer that the email passes through to forward it in the right direction to the final destination. When you consider the millions of email servers across the world, you have to marvel at how simple it all seems.

Here is a simplified example of how email is successfully processed and sent to its destination:

1. andrew@hudson.org composes and sends an email message to paul@hudzilla.org.

2. The MTA at hudson.org receives Andrew's email message and queues it for delivery behind any other messages that are also waiting to go out.

3. The MTA at hudson.org contacts the MTA at hudzilla.org on port 24. After hudzilla.org acknowledges the connection, the MTA at hudson.org sends the mail message. After hudzilla.org accepts and acknowledges receipt of the message, the connection is closed.

4. The MTA at hudzilla.org places the mail message into Paul's incoming mailbox; Paul is notified that he has new mail the next time he logs on.

Of course, several things can go wrong during this process. Here are a few examples:

> What if Paul does not exist at hudzilla.org? In this case, the MTA at hudzilla.org will reject the email and notify the MTA at hudson.org of what the problem is. The MTA at hudson.org will then generate an email message and send it to andrew@hudson.org, informing him that no Paul exists at hudzilla.org (or perhaps just silently discard the message and give the sender no indication of the problem, depending on how the email server is configured).

> What happens if hudzilla.org doesn't respond to hudson.org's connection attempts? (Perhaps the server is down for maintenance.) The MTA at hudson.org notifies the sender that the initial delivery attempt has failed. Further attempts will be made at intervals decided by the server administrator until the deadline is reached, and the sender will be notified that the mail is undeliverable.

The Mail Transport Agent

Several MTAs are available for Ubuntu, each with its pros and cons. Normally they are hidden under the skin of Ubuntu, silently moving mail between servers all over the world with need for little or no maintenance. Some MTAs are extremely powerful, being able to cope with hundreds of thousands of messages each day, whereas some are more geared toward smaller installations. Other MTAs are perhaps not as powerful, but are packed full with features. In the next section, we take a look at some of the more popular MTAs available for Ubuntu.

Postfix

Postfix has its origins as the IBM Secure Mailer, but was released to the community by IBM. Compared to Sendmail, it is much easier to administer and has a number of speed advantages. Postfix offers a pain-free replacement for Sendmail, and you are able to literally replace Sendmail with Postfix without the system breaking a sweat. In fact, the applications that rely on Sendmail will automatically use Postfix instead and carry on working correctly (because Postfix uses a Sendmail wrapper, which deceives other programs into thinking that Postfix is Sendmail). This wrapper, or more correctly interface, makes switching to Postfix extremely easy if you are already running Sendmail. Postfix also happens to be the MTA of choice for Ubuntu, so it is this one that we spend more time on later in this chapter.

For enhanced security, many Postfix processes used to use the chroot facility (which restricts access to only specific parts of the file system) for improved security, and there are no setuid components in Postfix. With the current release of Ubuntu, a chroot configuration is *no longer used* and is, in fact, discouraged by the Postfix author. You can manually reconfigure Postfix to a chroot configuration, but that is no longer supported by Ubuntu.

If you are starting from scratch, Postfix is considered a better choice than Sendmail.

Sendmail

Sendmail handles the overwhelming majority of emails transmitted over the Internet today. It is extremely popular across the Linux/UNIX/BSD world and is well supported. A commercial version is available that has a GUI interface for ease of configuration.

As well as being popular, Sendmail is particularly powerful compared to some of the other MTAs. However, it is not without its downsides, and you will find that other MTAs can handle more email per second in a larger environment. The other issue with Sendmail is that it can be extremely complicated to set it up exactly as you want it. A few books are available specifically for Sendmail, but the most popular one has more than a thousand pages, reflecting the complex nature of Sendmail configuration.

We can be thankful, however, that the default configuration for Sendmail works fine for most basic installations out of the box, making further configurations unnecessary. Even if you want to use it as a basic email server, you only need to do some minor tweaks. The level of complexity associated with Sendmail often leads to system administrators replacing it with one of the other alternatives that is easier to configure.

Qmail and Exim

Qmail is a direct competitor to Postfix but is not provided with Ubuntu. Qmail is designed to be easier to use than Sendmail, as well as faster and more secure. However, Qmail isn't a drop-in replacement for Sendmail, so migrating an existing Sendmail installation to Qmail is not quite as simple as migrating from Sendmail to Postfix. Qmail is relatively easy to administer, and it integrates with a number of software add-ons, including web mail systems and POP3 servers. Qmail is available from http://www.qmail.org/.

Exim is yet another MTA, and it is available at http://www.exim.org/. Exim is considered faster and more secure that Sendmail or Postfix, but is much different to configure that either of those. Exim and Qmail use the maildir format rather than mbox, so both are considered "NFS safe" (see the following sidebar).

19

MDIR Versus Mailbox

Qmail also introduced maildir, which is an alternative to the standard UNIX method of storing incoming mail. maildir is a more versatile system of handling incoming email, but it requires your email clients to be reconfigured, and it is not compatible with the traditional UNIX way of storing incoming mail. You will need to use mail programs that recognize the maildir format. (The modern programs do.)

The traditional mbox format keeps all mail assigned to a folder concatenated as a single file and maintains an index of individual emails. With maildir, each mail folder has three subfolders: /cur, /new, and /tmp. Each email is kept in a separate, unique file. If you are running a mail server for a large number of people, you should select a file system that can efficiently handle a large number of small files.

mbox does offer one major disadvantage. While you are accessing the monolithic mbox file that contains all your email, suppose that some type of corruption occurs, either to the file itself or to the index. Recovery from this problem can prove difficult. The mbox files are especially prone to problems if the files are being accessed over a network and can result in file corruption; one should avoid accessing mbox mail mounted over NFS, the Network File System, because file corruption can occur.

Depending on how you access your mail, maildir does permit the simultaneous access of maildir files by multiple applications; mbox does not.

The choice of a *mail user agent (MUA)*, or email client, also affects your choice of mail directory format. For example, the pine program does not cache any directory information and must reread the mail directory any time it accesses it. If you are using pine, maildir is a poor choice. More-advanced email clients perform caching, so maildir might be a good choice, although the email client cache can get out of synchronization. It seems that no perfect choice exists.

Ubuntu provides you with mail alternatives that have both strong and weak points. Be aware of the differences among the alternatives and frequently reevaluate your selection to make certain that it is the best one for your circumstances.

Choosing an MTA

Other MTAs are available for use with Ubuntu, but those discussed in the previous sections are the most popular. Which one should you choose? That depends on what you need to do. Postfix's main strengths is that it scales well and can handle large volumes of email at high speeds, not to mention that it is much easier to configure than the more cryptic Sendmail. However, you may find that there are specific things that you need that only Sendmail can provide. It is easy to switch between MTAs when you need to.

The Mail Delivery Agent

SMTP is a server-to-server protocol that was designed to deliver mail to systems that are always connected to the Internet. Dial-up systems only connect at the user's command; they connect for specific operations, and are frequently disconnected. To accommodate this difference, many mail systems also include a *mail delivery agent*, or *MDA*. The MDA transfers mail to systems without permanent Internet connections. The MDA is similar to an MTA (see the following note), but does not handle deliveries between systems and does not provide an interface to the user.

> **NOTE**
>
> Procmail or Spamassassin are examples of MTAs; both provide filtering services to the MTA while they store messages locally and then make them available to the MUA or email client for reading by the user.

The MDA uses the POP3 or IMAP protocols for this process. In a manner similar to a post office box at the post office, POP3 and IMAP implement a "store and forward" process that alleviates the need to maintain a local mail server if all you want to do is read your mail. For example, dial-up Internet users can intermittently connect to their ISP's mail server to retrieve mail using Fetchmail—the MDA recommended by Ubuntu (see the section "Using Fetchmail to Retrieve Mail" later in this chapter).

The Mail User Agent

The *mail user agent*, or *MUA*, is another necessary part of the email system. The MUA is a mail client, or mail reader, that allows the user to read and compose email and provides the user interface. (It is the email application itself that most users are familiar with as "email.") Some popular UNIX command-line MUAs are `elm`, `pine`, and `mutt`. Ubuntu also provides modern GUI MUAs: Evolution, Thunderbird, Mozilla Mail, Balsa, Sylpheed, and KMail. For comparison, common non-UNIX MUAs are Microsoft Outlook, Outlook Express, Pegasus, Eudora, and Netscape Messenger.

The Microsoft Windows and Macintosh MUAs often include some MTA functionality; UNIX does not. For example, Microsoft Outlook can connect to your Internet provider's mail server to send messages. On the other hand, UNIX MUAs generally rely on an external MTA such as Sendmail. This might seem like a needlessly complicated way to do things, and it is if used to connect a single user to her ISP. For any other situation, however, using an external MTA allows you much greater flexibility because you can use any number of external programs to handle and process your email functions and customize the service. Having the process handled by different applications gives you great control over how you provide email service to users on your network, as well as to individual and *small office/home office* (SOHO) users.

For example, you could do the following:

- ▶ Use Evolution to read and compose mail
- ▶ Use Sendmail to send your mail
- ▶ Use xbiff to notify you when you have new mail
- ▶ Use Fetchmail to retrieve your mail from a remote mail server
- ▶ Use Procmail to automatically sort your incoming mail based on sender, subject, or many other variables
- ▶ Use Spamassassin to eliminate the unwanted messages before you read them

19

Basic Postfix Configuration and Operation

Because Postfix is the Ubuntu-recommended MTA, the following sections provide a brief explanation and examples for configuring and operating your email system. As mentioned earlier, however, Postfix is an extremely complex program with many configuration options. As such, this chapter only covers some of the basics. For more information on Postfix, as well as other MTAs, see the "Reference" section at the end of this chapter.

Postfix configuration is handled by files in the /etc/postfix directory with much of the configuration being handled by the file main.cf. The actual syntax of the configuration file, main.cf, is fairly easy to read (see the following example):

```
# See /usr/share/postfix/main.cf.dist for a commented, more complete version
# Debian specific:  Specifying a file name will cause the first
# line of that file to be used as the name.  The Debian default
# is /etc/mailname.
#myorigin = /etc/mailname

smtpd_banner = $myhostname ESMTP $mail_name (Ubuntu)
biff = no

# appending .domain is the MUA's job.
append_dot_mydomain = no

# Uncomment the next line to generate "delayed mail" warnings
#delay_warning_time = 4h

# TLS parameters
smtpd_tls_cert_file=/etc/ssl/certs/ssl-cert-snakeoil.pem
smtpd_tls_key_file=/etc/ssl/private/ssl-cert-snakeoil.key
smtpd_use_tls=yes
smtpd_tls_session_cache_database = btree:${queue_directory}/smtpd_scache
smtp_tls_session_cache_database = btree:${queue_directory}/smtp_scache

# See /usr/share/doc/postfix/TLS_README.gz in the postfix-doc package for
# information on enabling SSL in the smtp client.

myhostname = optimus
alias_maps = hash:/etc/aliases
alias_database = hash:/etc/aliases
mydestination = optimus, localhost.localdomain, , localhost
relayhost =
mynetworks = 127.0.0.0/8
mailbox_size_limit = 0
recipient_delimiter = +
inet_interfaces = all
```

Complicated email server setup is beyond the scope of this book, and we would point you in the direction of *Postfix: The Definitive Guide* by Dent. This is a great reference, and rather unusual because it only runs to just under 300 pages. However, if you want to know something about Postfix, this is the book to read.

However, the following five sections address some commonly used advanced options.

Configuring Masquerading

Sometimes you might want to have Postfix masquerade as a host other than the actual hostname of your system. Such a situation could occur if you have a dial-up connection to the Internet and your ISP handles all your mail for you. In this case, you will want Postfix to masquerade as the domain name of your ISP. For example

```
masquerade_domains = hudson.com
```

will strip any messages that come from `andrew.hudson.com` to just `hudson.com`.

Using Smart Hosts

If you do not have a full-time connection to the Internet, you will probably want to have Postfix send your messages to your ISP's mail server and let it handle delivery for you. Without a full-time Internet connection, you could find it difficult to deliver messages to some locations (such as some underdeveloped areas of the world where email services are unreliable and sporadic). In those situations, you can configure Postfix to function as a smart host by passing email on to another sender instead of attempting to deliver the email directly. You can use a line such as the following in the `main.cf` file to enable a smart host:

```
relayhost = mail.isp.net
```

This line causes Postfix to pass any mail it receives to the server `mail.isp.net` rather than attempt to deliver it directly. Smart hosting will not work for you if your ISP, like many others, blocks any mail relaying. Some ISPs block relaying because it is frequently used to disseminate spam.

Setting Message Delivery Intervals

As mentioned earlier, Postfix typically attempts to deliver messages as soon as it receives them, and again at regular intervals after that. If you have only periodic connections to the Internet, as with a dial-up connection, you likely would prefer that Sendmail hold all messages in the queue and attempt to deliver them whenever you connect to your ISP. You can configure Postfix to do so by adding the following line to `/etc/ppp/peers/ppp0`:

```
/usr/sbin/sendmail =q
```

This line causes Postifix to automatically send all mail when connecting to your ISP.

However, Postfix will still attempt to send mail regardless of whether the computer is on or off line, meaning that your computer may dial out just to send email. To disable this, you need to enter the following line into `mail.cf`:

```
defer_transports = smtp
```

This stops any unwanted telephone calls from being placed!

> **TIP**
>
> If you use networking over a modem, there is a configuration file for pppd called ppp0, which is located in /etc/ppp/peers. Any commands in this file automatically run each time the PPP daemon is started. You can add the line sendmail -q to this file to have your mail queue automatically processed each time you dial up your Internet connection.

Mail Relaying

By default, Postfix will not relay mail that did not originate from the local domain. This means that if a Postfix installation running at hudson.org receives mail intended for hudzilla.org, and that mail did not originate from hudson.org, the mail will be rejected and will not be relayed. If you want to allow selected domains to relay through you, add an entry for the domain to the `main.cf` file like so:

```
mynetworks = 192.168.2.0/24, 10.0.0.2/24, 127.0.0.0/8
```

The IP address needs to be specified in CIDR format. For a handy calculator, head on over to http://www.subnet-calculator/cidr.php. You must restart Postfix for this change to take effect.

> **CAUTION**
>
> You need a good reason to relay mail; otherwise, do not do it. Allowing all domains to relay through you will make you a magnet for spammers who will use your mail server to send spam. This can lead to your site being blacklisted by many other sites, which then will not accept any mail from you or your site's users—even if the mail is legitimate!

Forwarding Email with Aliases

Aliases allow you to have an infinite number of valid recipient addresses on your system, without having to worry about creating accounts or other support files for each address. For example, most systems have "postmaster" defined as a valid recipient, but do not have an actual login account named "postmaster." Aliases are configured in the file `/etc/aliases`. Here is an example of an alias entry:

```
postmaster: root
```

This entry forwards any mail received for "postmaster" to the root user. By default, almost all the aliases listed in the `/etc/aliases` file forward to root.

> **CAUTION**
>
> Reading email as root is a security hazard; a malicious email message can exploit an email client and cause it to execute arbitrary code as the user running the client. To avoid this danger, you can forward all of root's mail to another account and read it from there. You can choose one of two ways for doing this.
>
> You can add an entry to the /etc/aliases file that sends root's mail to a different account. For example, root: foobar would forward all mail intended for root to the account foobar.
>
> The other way is to create a file named .forward in root's home directory that contains the address that the mail should forward to.

Anytime you make a change to the /etc/aliases file, you will need to rebuild the aliases database before that change will take effect. This is done with the following:

```
$ sudo newaliases
```

Using Fetchmail to Retrieve Mail

SMTP is designed to work with systems that have a full-time connection to the Internet. What if you are on a dial-up account? What if you have another system store your email for you and then you log in to pick it up once in awhile? (Most users who are not setting up servers will be in this situation.) In this case, you cannot easily receive email using SMTP, and you need to use a protocol, such as POP3 or IMAP, instead.

> **NOTE**
>
> Remember when we said that some mail clients can include some MTA functionality? Microsoft Outlook and Outlook Express can be configured to use SMTP and, if you use a dial-up connection, will offer to start the connection and then use SMTP to send your mail, so a type of MTA functionality is included in those mail clients.

Unfortunately, many MUAs do not know anything about POP3 or IMAP. To eliminate that problem, you can use a program called Fetchmail to contact mail servers using POP3 or IMAP, download mail off the servers, and then inject those messages into the local MTA just as if they had come from a standard SMTP server. The following sections explain how to install, configure, and use the Fetchmail program.

Installing Fetchmail

Similar to other packages, Fetchmail can be installed using either synaptic or apt-get.

You can get the latest version of Fetchmail at http://www.catb.org/~esr/fetchmail.

Configuring Fetchmail

After you have installed Fetchmail, you must create the file `.fetchmailrc` in your home directory, which provides the configuration for the Fetchmail program.

You can create and subsequently edit the `.fetchmailrc` file by using any text editor. The configuration file is straightforward and quite easy to create; the following sections explain the manual method for creating and editing the file. The information presented in the following sections does not discuss all the options available in the `.fetchmailrc` file, but covers the most common ones needed to get a basic Fetchmail installation up and running. You must use a text editor to create the file to include entries like the ones shown as examples—modified for your personal information, of course. For advanced configuration, see the man page for Fetchmail. The man page is well written and documents all the configuration options in detail.

> **CAUTION**
>
> The `.fetchmailrc` file is divided into three different sections: global options, mail server options, and user options. It is important that these sections appear in the order listed. Do not add options to the wrong section. Putting options in the wrong place is one of the most common problems that new users make with Fetchmail configuration files.

Configuring Global Options

The first section of `.fetchmailrc` contains the global options. These options affect all the mail servers and user accounts that you list later in the configuration file. Some of these global options can be overridden with local configuration options, as you learn later in this section. Here is an example of the options that might appear in the global section of the `.fetchmailrc` file:

```
set daemon 600
set postmaster foobar
set logfile ./.fetchmail.log
```

The first line in this example tells Fetchmail that it should start in daemon mode and check the mail servers for new mail every 600 seconds, or 10 minutes. Daemon mode means that after Fetchmail starts, it will move itself into the background and continue running. Without this line, Fetchmail would check for mail once when it started and would then terminate and never check again.

The second option tells Fetchmail to use the local account foobar as a last-resort address. In other words, any email that it receives and cannot deliver to a specified account should be sent to foobar.

The third line tells Fetchmail to log its activity to the file `./.fetchmail.log`. Alternatively, you can use the line `set syslog`—in which case, Fetchmail will log through the `syslog` facility.

Configuring Mail Server Options

The second section of the `.fetchmailrc` file contains information on each of the mail servers that should be checked for new mail. Here is an example of what the mail section might look like:

```
poll mail.samplenet.org
proto pop3
no dns
```

The first line tells Fetchmail that it should check the mail server mail.samplenet.org at each poll interval that was set in the global options section (which was 600 seconds in our example). Alternatively, the first line can begin with skip. If a mail server line begins with skip, it will not be polled as the poll interval, but will only be polled when it is specifically specified on the Fetchmail command line.

The second line specifies the protocol that should be used when contacting the mail server. In this case, we are using the POP3 protocol. Other legal options are IMAP, APOP, and KPOP. You can also use

AUTO here—in which case, Fetchmail will attempt to automatically determine the correct protocol to use with the mail server.

The third line tells Fetchmail that it should not attempt to do a *Dynamic Name Server (DNS)* lookup. You will probably want to include this option if you are running over a dial-up connection.

Configuring User Accounts

The third and final section of `.fetchmailrc` contains information about the user account on the server specified in the previous section. Here is an example:

```
user foobar
pass secretword
fetchall
flush
```

The first line, of course, simply specifies the username that is used to log in to the email server, and the second line specifies the password for that user. Many security conscious people cringe at the thought of putting clear-text passwords in a configuration file, and they should if it is group or world readable. The only protection for this information is to make certain that the file is readable only by the owner; that is, with file permissions of 600.

The third line tells Fetchmail that it should fetch all messages from the server, even if they have already been read.

The fourth line tells Fetchmail that it should delete the messages from the mail server after it has completed downloading them. This is the default, so we would not really have to specify this option. If you want to leave the messages on the server after downloading them, use the option no flush.

19

The configuration options you just inserted configured the entire .fetchmailrc file to look like this:

```
set daemon 600
set postmaster foobar
set logfile ./.fetchmail.log

poll mail.samplenet.org
proto pop3
no dns

user foobar
pass secretword
fetchall
flush
```

This file tells Fetchmail to do the following:

- ▶ Check the POP3 server mail.samplenet.org for new mail every 600 seconds.

- ▶ Log in using the username foobar and the password secretword.

- ▶ Download all messages off the server.

- ▶ Delete the messages from the server after it has finished downloading them.

- ▶ Send any mail it receives that cannot be delivered to a local user to the account foobar.

As mentioned before, many more options can be included in the .fetchmailrc file than are listed here. However, these options will get you up and running with a basic configuration.

For additional flexibility, you can define multiple .fetchmailrc files to retrieve mail from different remote mail servers while using the same Linux user account. For example, you can define settings for your most often used account and save them in the default .fetchmailrc file. Mail can then quickly be retrieved like so:

```
$ fetchmail -a
1 message for andrew at mail.ourphotos.me.uk (1108 octets).
reading message 1 of 1 (1108 octets) . flushed
```

By using Fetchmail's -f option, you can specify an alternative resource file and then easily retrieve mail from another server, as follows:

```
$ fetchmail -f .myothermailrc
2 messages for andrew at anrew.hudson.com (5407 octets).
reading message 1 of 2 (3440 octets) ... flushed
reading message 2 of 2 (1967 octets) . flushed
You have new mail in /var/spool/mail/andrew
```

By using the -d option, along with a time interval (in seconds), you can use Fetchmail in its daemon, or background mode. The command will launch as a background process and retrieve mail from a designated remote server at a specified interval. For more-advanced options, see the Fetchmail man page, which is well written and documents all options in detail.

> **CAUTION**
>
> Because the .fetchmailrc file contains your mail server password, it should be read-able only by you. This means that it should be owned by you and should have permis-sions no greater than 600. Fetchmail will complain and refuse to start if the .fetchmailrc file has permissions greater than this.

Choosing a Mail Delivery Agent

Because of the modular nature of mail handling, it is possible to use multiple applications to process mail and accomplish more than simply deliver it. Getting mail from the storage area and displaying it to the user is the purpose of the MDA. MDA functionality can be found in some of the mail clients (MUAs), which can cause some confusion to those still unfamiliar with the concept of UNIX mail. As an example, the Procmail MDA provides filtering based on rulesets; KMail and Evolution, both MUAs, provide filtering, but the MUAs pine, mutt, and Balsa do not. Some MDAs perform simple sorting, and other MDAs are designed to eliminate unwanted emails, such as spam and viruses.

You would choose an MDA based on what you want to do with your mail. We will look at five MDAs that offer functions you might find useful in your particular situation. If you have simple needs (just organizing mail by rules), one of the MUAs that offers filter-ing might be better for your needs. Ubuntu provides the Evolution MUA as the default selection (and it contains some MDA functionality as previously noted), so try that first and see whether it meets your needs. If not, investigate one of the following MDAs provided by Ubuntu.

Unless otherwise noted, all the MDA software is provided through synaptic and apt-get. Chapter 31, "Managing Software," details the general installation of any software.

Procmail

As a tool for advanced users, the Procmail application acts as a filter for email as it is retrieved from a mail server. It uses rulesets (known as *recipes*) as it reads each email message. No default configuration is provided; you must manually create a ~/.procmail file for each user, or each user can create her own.

There is no systemwide default configuration file. The creation of the rulesets is not trivial and requires an understanding of the use of regular expressions that is beyond the scope of this chapter. Ubuntu does provide three examples of the files in /usr/share/doc/procmail/examples, as well as a fully commented example in the /usr/share/doc/procmail directory, which also contains a README and FAQ. Details for the rulesets can be found in the man page for Procmail as well as the man pages for procmailrc, procmailsc, and procmailex, which contain examples of Procmail recipes.

Spamassassin

If you have used email for any length of time, you have likely been subjected to spam—unwanted email sent to thousands of people at the same time. Ubuntu provides an MDA named Spamassassin to assist you in reducing and eliminating unwanted emails. Easily integrated with Procmail and Sendmail, it can be configured for both systemwide and individual use. It uses a combination of rulesets and blacklists (Internet domains known to mail spam).

Enabling Spamassassin is simple. You must first have installed and configured Procmail. The README file found in /usr/share/doc/spamassasin provides details on configuring the .procmail file to process mail through Spamassassin. It will tag probable spam with a unique header; you can then have Procmail filter the mail in any manner you choose. One interesting use of Spamassasin is to use it to tag email received at special email accounts established solely for the purpose of attracting spam. This information is then shared with the Spamassassin site where these "spam trap" generated hits help the authors fine-tune the rulesets.

Squirrelmail

Perhaps you do not want to read your mail in an MUA. If you use your web browser often, it might make sense to read and send your mail via a web interface, such as the one used by Hotmail or Yahoo! Mail. Ubuntu provides Squirrelmail for just that purpose. Squirrelmail is written in the PHP 4 language and supports IMAP and SMTP with all pages rendering in HTML 4.0 without using Java. It supports MIME attachments, as well as an address book and folders for segregating email.

You must configure your web server to work with PHP 4. Detailed installation instructions can be found in /usr/share/doc/squirrelmail/INSTALL. Once configured, point your web browser to http://www.yourdomain.com/squirellmail/ to read and send email.

Virus Scanners

Although the currently held belief is that Linux is immune to email viruses targeted at Microsoft Outlook users, it certainly makes no sense for UNIX mail servers to permit infected email to be sent through them. Although Ubuntu does not provide a virus scanner, one of the more popular of many such scanners is MailScanner, available from http://www.sng.ecs.soton.ac.uk/mailscanner/; a Ubuntu DEB package is available as well as the source code. It supports Sendmail and Exim, but not Postfix or Qmail. A hunt through `synaptic` using the search terms "virus" and "scanner" should yield some other options for you to try out.

Mail Daemons

Biff is a small daemon that monitors your mail folder and notifies you when a message has been placed there. It is common to include `biff y` in the `.login` or `.profile` files to automatically start it upon user login if you want to use Biff.

> **NOTE**
>
> Autoresponders automatically generate replies to received messages; they are commonly used to notify others that the recipient is out of the office. Mercifully, Ubuntu does not include one, but you can find and install an autoresponder at Freshmeat.net. If you are subscribed to a mailing list, be aware that automatic responses from your account can be very annoying to others on the list. Please unsubscribe from mail lists before you leave the office with your autoresponder activated.

Alternatives to Microsoft Exchange Server

One of the last areas in which a Microsoft product has yet to be usurped by open-source software is a replacement for Microsoft Exchange Server. Many businesses use Microsoft Outlook and Microsoft Exchange Server to access email, as well as to provide calendaring, notes, file sharing, and other collaborative functions. General industry complaints about Exchange Server center around scalability, administration (backup and restore in particular), and licensing fees.

A "drop-in" alternative needs to have compatibility with Microsoft Outlook because it's intended to replace Exchange Server in an environment in which there are Microsoft desktops in existence using Outlook. A "work-alike" alternative provides similar features to Exchange Server, but does not offer compatibility with the Microsoft Outlook client itself; the latter is typical of many of the open-source alternatives.

Several "drop-in" alternatives exist, none of which are fully open source because some type of proprietary connector is needed to provide the services to Microsoft Outlook clients (or provide Exchange services to the Linux Evolution client). For Outlook compatibility, the key seems to be the realization of a full, open implementation of *MAPI*, the Microsoft *Messaging Application Program Interface*. That goal is going to be difficult to achieve because MAPI is a poorly documented Microsoft protocol. For Linux-only solutions, the missing ingredient for many alternatives is a usable group calendaring/scheduling system similar in function to that provided by Exchange Server/Outlook.

Of course, independent applications for these functions abound in the open-source world, but one characteristic of "groupware" is its central administration; another is that all components can share information.

19

The following sections examine several of the available servers, beginning with Microsoft Exchange Server itself and moving toward those applications that have increasing incompatibility with it. None of these servers are provided with Ubuntu.

Microsoft Exchange Server/Outlook Client

Exchange Server and Outlook seem to be the industry benchmark because of their widespread deployment. They offer a proprietary server providing email, contacts, scheduling, public folders, task lists, journaling, and notes using Microsoft Outlook as the client and MAPI as the API. If you consider what Microsoft Exchange offers as the "full" set of features, no other replacement offers 100% of the features exactly as provided by Microsoft Exchange Server—even those considered "drop-in" replacements. The home page for the Microsoft Exchange server is http://www.microsoft.com/exchange/.

CommuniGate Pro

CommuniGate Pro is a proprietary, drop-in alternative to Microsoft Exchange Server, providing, email, webmail, LDAP directories, a web server, file server, contacts, calendaring (third party), Voice over IP, and a list server. The CommuniGate Pro MAPI Connector provides access to the server from Microsoft Outlook and other MAPI-enabled clients. The home page for this server is http://www.stalker.com/.

Oracle Collaboration Suite

This is probably the closest that you will get to an Exchange replacement, allowing you to collaborate by instant messaging, email, sharing files (workspaces), calendaring, and other tools. It provides an Outlook Connector for users who have to have the familiarity of Outlook. OCS is available for Linux platforms and its homepage is http://www.oracle.com/collabsuite/.

Bynari

Bynari provides a proprietary group of servers to act as a drop-in replacement for Microsoft Exchange Server for email, calendaring, public folders, scheduling, address book, webmail, and contacts. Although it runs on Linux, it offers no Linux clients although it can be used with Evolution and Thunderbird, and the connector provides services to Microsoft Outlook only. The home page is http://www.bynari.net/.

Open-Xchange

Open-Xchange has a great pedigree having been owned and developed by Novell/SUSE until being spun off by itself into its own company. Working with open standards, it provides a number of collaboration options and is firmly based on Linux. It can work with a wide variety of protocols, making it one of the best connected suites available. You can get the open source version at http://www.open-xchange.com.

phpgroupware

phpgroupware is an open-source application written in PHP (and used with MySQL or postgresql plus a web server and an IMAP mail server). phpgroupware provides a web-based calendar, task list, address book, email, news headlines, and a file manager. Its modular nature enables you to plug in various components (around 50 at the last count) as you need them. The home page is http://www.phpgroupware.org/.

PHProjekt

PHProjekt is open-source software written in PHP (used with MySQL, postgresql, Oracle, Informix, or MS-sql). PHProjekt provides calendaring, contact manager, time card system, project management, online chat, threaded discussion forum, trouble ticket system, email, public files, notes bookmarks, voting system, task lists, reminders, site search, and integration with the PostNuke news site application. It provides no Exchange/Outlook compatibility whatsoever. The home page is http://www.PHProjekt.com/.

Horde

Horde is a PHP-based application framework. When combined with an HTTP server (Apache, Microsoft IIS, Netscape) and MySQL database, IMP/Horde offers modules that provide webmail, contact manager, calendar, CVS viewer, file manager, time tracking, email filter rules manager, notes, tasks, chat, newsgroups, forms, bug tracking, FAQ repository, and presentations. The home page is http://www.horde.org/.

Relevant Ubuntu and Linux Commands

You will use the following commands to manage electronic mail in Ubuntu:

- ▶ balsa—A GNOME mail user agent for X
- ▶ biff—A console-based mail notification utility
- ▶ evolution—A comprehensive and capable Ximian GNOME mail PIM for X
- ▶ fetchmail—A console-based and daemon-mode mail retrieval command for Linux
- ▶ fetchmailconf—A graphical fetchmail configuration client for X
- ▶ kmail—A graphical mail user client for KDE and X
- ▶ korn—A biff applet for KDE and X
- ▶ mutt—A console-based mail user agent
- ▶ sendmail—A comprehensive mail transport agent for UNIX and Linux
- ▶ xbiff—A mail notification X client

19

Reference

The following references are recommended reading for email configuration. Of course, not all references will apply to you. Select the ones that apply to the email server that you are using.

Web Resources

▶ http://www.sendmail.org/—This is the Sendmail home page. Here you will find configuration information and FAQs regarding the Sendmail MTA.

▶ http://www.postfix.org/—This is the Postfix home page. If you are using the Postfix MTA, you can find documentation and sample configurations at this site.

▶ http://www.qmail.org/—This is the home page for the Qmail MTA. It contains documentation and links to other resources on Qmail.

▶ http://www.linuxgazette.com/issue35/jao.html—IMAP on Linux: A Practical Guide. The Internet Mail Access Protocol allows a user to access his email stored on a remote server rather than a local disk.

▶ http://www.imap.org/about/whatisIMAP.html—This page describes IMAP.

▶ http://www.rfc-editor.org/—A repository of RFCs—Request for Comments—that define the technical "rules" of modern computer usage.

▶ http://www.procmail.org/—The Procmail home page.

▶ http://www.moongroup.com/docs/procmail/—The Procmail FAQ, which includes suggestions for troubleshooting problems. The page also references a page of links that, in turn, reference other link collections as well as tidbits from the Procmail mail list.

▶ http://www.ibiblio.org/pub/Linux/docs/HOWTO/other-formats/html_single/Qmail-VMailMgr-Courier-imap-HOWTO.html—If you want some help configuring a mail system based on the lesser-used applications, this HOWTO will help.

Books

▶ *Sendmail* (O'Reilly Publishing)—This is the de facto standard guide for everything Sendmail. It is loaded with more than 1,000 pages, which gives you an idea of how complicated Sendmail really is.

▶ *Postfix* (Sams Publishing)—An excellent book from Sams Publishing that covers the Postfix MTA.

▶ *Running Qmail* (Sams Publishing)—This is similar to the Postfix book from Sams Publishing except that it covers the Qmail MTA.

CHAPTER 20

Proxying and Reverse Proxying

You can never have enough of two things in this world: time and bandwidth. Ubuntu comes with a proxy server—Squid—that enables you to cache web traffic on your server so that websites load faster and users consume less bandwidth.

What Is a Proxy Server?

A *proxy server* lies between client machines—the desktops in your company—and the Internet. As clients request websites, they do not connect directly to the Web and send the HTTP request. Instead, they connect to the local proxy server. The proxy then forwards their request on to the Web, retrieves the result, and hands it back to the client. At its simplest, a proxy server really is just an extra layer between client and server, so why bother?

The three main reasons for deploying a proxy server are as follows:

▶ **Content control**—You want to stop people whiling away their work hours reading the news or downloading MP3s.

▶ **Speed**—You want to cache common sites to make the most of your bandwidth.

▶ **Security**—You want to monitor what people are doing.

Squid is capable of all of these and more.

Installing Squid

Like most Ubuntu software, Squid installation is handled through synaptic. After Squid is installed, it is automatically enabled for each boot up. You can check this by running ps aux | grep squid when the machine boots. If for some reason you see nothing there, run /etc/init.d/squid start.

Configuring Clients

Before you configure your new Squid server, set up the local web browser to use it for its web access. Doing so enables you to test your rules as you are working with the configuration file.

To configure Firefox, select Preferences from the Edit menu. From the dialog that appears, click the Connection Settings button (near the bottom on the General tab) and select the option Manual Proxy Configuration. Check the box beneath it, Use the Same Proxy for All Protocols; then enter 127.0.0.1 as the IP address and 3128 as the port number. See Figure 20.1 for how this should look. If you are configuring a remote client, specify the IP address of the Squid server rather than 127.0.0.1.

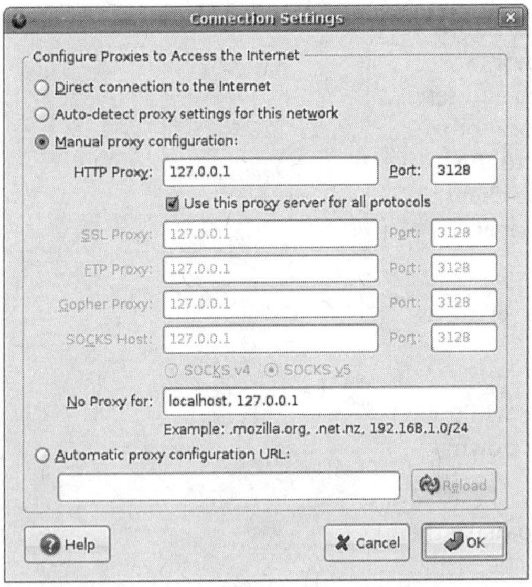

FIGURE 20.1   Setting up Firefox to use 127.0.0.1 routes all its web requests through Squid.

For Konqueror, go to the Settings menu and select Configure Konqueror. From the left tabs, scroll down to Proxy, select Manually Specify the Proxy Settings, and then click Setup. Enter 127.0.0.1 as the proxy IP address and 3128 as the port. As with Firefox, if you are configuring a remote client, specify the IP address of the Squid server rather than 127.0.0.1.

Internet Explorer proxy settings are in Tools/Internet Options. From the Connections tab, click the LAN Settings button and enable the Use a Proxy Server for Your LAN option. Enter the address as the IP of your Squid machine, and then specify **3128** as the port.

Access Control Lists

The main Squid configuration file is /etc/squid/squid.conf, and the default Ubuntu configuration file is full of comments to help guide you. The default configuration file allows full access to the local machine but denies the rest of your network. This is a secure place to start; we recommend you try all the rules on yourself (localhost) before rolling them out to other machines.

Before you start, open two terminal windows. In the first, change to the directory /var/log/squid and run this command:

```
sudo tail -f access.log cache.log
```

That reads the last few lines from both files and (thanks to the -f flag) follows them so that any changes appear in there. This allows you to watch what Squid is doing as people access it. We refer to this window as the "log window," so keep it open. In the other window (again, with sudo), bring up the file /etc/squid/squid.conf in your favorite editor. This window is referred to as the "config editor," and you should keep it open, too.

To get started, search for the string acl all—this brings you to the access control section, which is where most of the work needs to be done. You can configure a lot elsewhere, but unless you have unusual requirements, you can leave the defaults in place.

> **NOTE**
>
> The default port for Squid is 3128, but you can change that by editing the http_port line. Alternatively, you can have Squid listen on multiple ports by having multiple http_port lines: 80, 8000, and 8080 are all popular ports for proxy servers.

The acl lines make up your *access control lists (ACLs)*. The first 16 or so define the minimum recommended configuration that set up ports to listen to, and so on. You can safely ignore these. If you scroll down further (past another short block of comments), you come to the http_access lines, which are combined with the acl lines to dictate who can do what. You can (and should) mix and match acl and http_access lines to keep your configuration file easy to read.

Just below the first block of http_access lines is a comment like # INSERT YOUR OWN RULE(S) HERE TO ALLOW ACCESS FROM YOUR CLIENTS. This is just what we are going to do. First, though, scroll just a few lines further; you should see these two lines:

```
http_access allow localhost
http_access deny all
```

They are self-explanatory: The first says, "Allow HTTP access to the local computer, but deny everyone else." This is the default rule, as mentioned earlier. Leave that in place for now, and run `service squid start` to start the server with the default settings. If you have not yet configured the local web browser to use your Squid server, do so now so that you can test the default rules.

In your web browser (Firefox is assumed from here on, but it makes little difference), go to the URL http://www.ubuntulinux.org. You should see it appear as normal in the browser, but in the log window you should see a lot of messages scroll by as Squid downloads the site for you and stores it in its cache. This is all allowed because the default configuration allows access to the `localhost`.

Go back to the config editor window and add this before the last two `http_access` lines:

```
http_access deny localhost
```

So, the last three lines should look like this:

```
http_access deny localhost
http_access allow localhost
http_access deny all
```

Save the file and quit your editor. Then, run this command:

```
kill -SIGHUP 'cat /var/run/squid.pid'
```

That looks for the *process ID (PID)* of the Squid daemon and then sends the `SIGHUP` signal to it, which forces it to reread its configuration file while running. You should see a string of messages in the log window as Squid rereads its configuration files. If you now go back to Firefox and enter a new URL, you should see the Squid error page informing you that you do not have access to the requested site.

The reason you are now blocked from the proxy is because Squid reads its ACL lines in sequence, from top to bottom. If it finds a line that conclusively allows or denies a request, it stops reading and takes the appropriate action. So, in the previous lines, `localhost` is being denied in the first line and then allowed in the second. When Squid sees `localhost` asking for a site, it reads the `deny` line first and immediately sends the error page—it does not even get to the `allow` line. Having a `deny all` line at the bottom is highly recommended so that only those you explicitly allow are able to use the proxy.

Go back to editing the configuration file and remove the `deny localhost` and `allow localhost` lines. This leaves only deny all, which blocks everyone (including the `localhost`) from accessing the proxy. Now we are going to add some conditional allow statements: We want to allow `localhost` only if it fits certain criteria.

Defining access criteria is done with the `acl` lines, so above the `deny all` line, add this:

```
acl newssites dstdomain news.bbc.co.uk slashdot.org
http_access allow newssites
```

The first line defines an access category called `newssites`, which contains a list of domains (`dstdomain`). The domains are news.bbc.co.uk and slashdot.org, so the full line reads, "Create a new access category called newssites, that should filter on domain, and contain the two domains listed." It does *not* say whether access should be granted or denied to that category; that comes in the next line. The line `http_access allow newssites` means, "Allow access to the category `newssites` with no further restrictions." It is not limited to `localhost`, which means that applies to every computer connecting to the proxy server.

Save the configuration file and rerun the `kill -SIGHUP` line from before to restart Squid; then go back to Firefox and try loading http://www.ubuntulinux.org. You should see the same error as before because that was not in our `newssites` category. Now try http://news. bbc.co.uk, and it should work. However, if you try http://www.slashdot.org, it will *not* work, and you might also have noticed that the images did not appear on the BBC News website either. The problem here is that specifying slashdot.org as the website is specific: It means that http://slashdot.org will work, whereas http://www.slashdot.org will not. The BBC News site stores its images on the site http://newsimg.bbc.co.uk, which is why they do not appear.

Go back to the configuration file, and edit the `newssites` ACL to this:

```
acl newssites dstdomain .bbc.co.uk .slashdot.org
```

Putting the period in front of the domains (and in the BBC's case, taking the news off, too) means that Squid will allow any subdomain of the site to work, which is usually what you will want. If you want even more vagueness, you can just specify `.com` to match `*.com` addresses.

Moving on, you can also use time conditions for sites. For example, if you want to allow access to the news sites in the evenings, you can set up a time category using this line:

```
acl freetime time MTWHFAS 18:00-23:59
```

This time, the category is called freetime and the condition is `time`, which means we need to specify what time the category should contain. The seven characters following that are the days of the week: Monday, Tuesday, Wednesday, tHursday, Friday, sAturday, and Sunday. Thursday and Saturday use capital *H* and *A* so they do not clash with Tuesday and Sunday.

With that category defined, you can change the `http_access` line to include it, like this:

```
http_access allow newssites freetime
```

For Squid to allow access now, it must match both conditions—the request must be for either *.bbc.co.uk or slashdot.org, and during the time specified. If either condition does not match, the line is not matched and Squid continues looking for other matching rules beneath it. The times you specify here are inclusive on both sides, which means users in the `freetime` category will be able to surf from 18:00:00 until 23:59:59.

You can add as many rules as you like, although you should be careful to try to order them so that they make sense. Keep in mind that all conditions in a line must be matched for the line to be matched. Here is a more complex example:

▶ You want a category `newssites` that contains serious websites people need for their work.

▶ You want a category `playsites` that contains websites people do not need for their work.

▶ You want a category `worktime` that stretches from 09:00 to 18:00.

▶ You want a category `freetime` that stretches from 18:00 to 20:00, when the office closes.

▶ You want people to be able to access the news sites, but not the play sites, during working hours.

▶ You want people to be able to access both the news sites and the play sites during the free time hours.

To do that, you need the following rules:

```
acl newssites dstdomain .bbc.co.uk .slashdot.org
acl playsites dstdomain .tomshardware.com ubuntulinux.org
acl worktime time MTWHF 9:00-18:00
acl freetime time MTWHF 18:00-20:00
http_access allow newssites worktime
http_access allow newssites freetime
http_access allow playsites freetime
```

NOTE

The letter D is equivalent to MTWHF in meaning "all the days of the working week."

Notice that there are two `http_access` lines for the `newssites` category: one for `worktime` and one for `freetime`. This is because all the conditions must be matched for a line to be matched. Alternatively, you can write this:

```
http_access allow newssites worktime freetime
```

However, if you do that and someone visits news.bbc.co.uk at 2:30 p.m. (14:30) on a Tuesday, Squid will work like this:

▶ Is the site in the `newssites` category? Yes, continue.

▶ Is the time within the `worktime` category? Yes, continue.

▶ Is the time within the `freetime` category? No; do not match rule, and continue searching for rules.

It is because of this that two lines are needed for the `worktime` category.

One particularly powerful way to filter requests is with the `url_regex` ACL line. This allows you to specify a regular expression that is checked against each request: If the expression matches the request, the condition matches.

For example, if you want to stop people downloading Windows executable files, you would use this line:

```
acl noexes url_regex -i exe$
```

The dollar sign means "end of URL," which means it would match http://www.somesite.com/virus.exe but not http://www.executable.com/innocent.html. The `-i` part means "not case-sensitive," so the rule will match `.exe`, `.Exe`, `.EXE`, and so on. You can use the caret sign (^) for "start of URL."

For example, you could stop some pornography sites using this ACL:

```
acl noporn url_regex -i sex
```

Do not forget to run the `kill -SIGHUP` command each time you make changes to Squid; otherwise, it will not reread your changes. You can have Squid check your configuration files for errors by running `squid -k parse` as root. If you see no errors, it means your configuration is fine.

> **NOTE**
>
> It is critical that you run the command kill -SIGHUP and provide it the PID of your Squid daemon each time you change the configuration; without this, Squid will not reread its configuration files.

Specifying Client IP Addresses

The configuration options so far have been basic, and you can use many more to enhance the proxying system you want.

After you are past deciding which rules work for you locally, it is time to spread them out to other machines. You do so by specifying IP ranges that should be allowed or disallowed access, and you enter these into Squid using more ACL lines.

If you want to, you can specify all the IP addresses on your network, one per line. However, for networks of more than about 20 people or using *Dynamic Host Control Protocol (DHCP)*, that is more work than necessary. A better solution is to use *classless interdomain routing (CIDR)* notation, which allows you to specify addresses like this:

```
192.0.0.0/8
192.168.0.0/16
192.168.0.0/24
```

Each line has an IP address, followed by a slash and then a number. That last number defines the range of addresses you want covered and refers to the number of bits in an IP address. An IP address is a 32-bit number, but we are used to seeing it in dotted-quad notation: A.B.C.D. Each of those quads can be between 0 and 255 (although in practice some of these are reserved for special purposes), and each is stored as an 8-bit number.

The first line in the previous code covers IP addresses starting from 192.0.0.0; the /8 part means that the first 8 bits (the first quad, 192) is fixed and the rest is flexible. So, Squid treats that as addresses 192.0.0.0, 192.0.0.1, through to 192.0.0.255, then 192.0.1.0, 192.0.1.1, all the way through to 192.255.255.255.

The second line uses /16, which means Squid will allow IP addresses from 192.168.0.0 to 192.168.255.255. The last line has /24, which allows from 192.168.0.0 to 192.168.0.255.

These addresses are placed into Squid using the src ACL line, as follows:

```
acl internal_network src 10.0.0.0/24
```

That line creates a category of addresses from 10.0.0.0 to 10.0.0.255. You can combine multiple address groups together, like this:

```
acl internal_network src 10.0.0.0/24 10.0.3.0/24 10.0.5.0/24 192.168.0.1
```

That example allows 10.0.0.0 through 10.0.0.255, then 10.0.3.0 through 10.0.3.255, and finally the single address 192.168.0.1.

Keep in mind that if you are using the local machine and you have the web browser configured to use the proxy at 127.0.0.1, the client IP address will be 127.0.0.1, too. So, make sure you have rules in place for localhost.

As with other ACL lines, you need to enable them with appropriate http_access allow and http_access deny lines.

Example Configurations

To help you fully understand how Squid access control works, and to give you a head start developing your own rules, the following are some ACL lines you can try. Each line is preceded with one or more comment lines (starting with a #) explaining what it does:

```
# include the domains news.bbc.co.uk and slashdot.org
# and not newsimg.bbc.co.uk or www.slashdot.org.
acl newssites dstdomain news.bbc.co.uk slashdot.org

# include any subdomains or bbc.co.uk or slashdot.org
acl newssites dstdomain .bbc.co.uk .slashdot.org

# only include sites located in Canada
acl canadasites dstdomain .ca

# only include working hours
```

```
acl workhours time MTWHF 9:00-18:00

# only include lunchtimes
acl lunchtimes time MTWHF 13:00-14:00

# only include weekends
acl weekends time AS 00:00-23:59

# include URLs ending in ".zip". Note: the \ is important,
# because "." has a special meaning otherwise
acl zipfiles url_regex -i \.zip$

# include URLs starting with https
acl httpsurls url_regex -i ^https

# include all URLs that match "hotmail"
url_regex hotmail url_regex -i hotmail

# include three specific IP addresses
acl directors src 10.0.0.14 10.0.0.28 10.0.0.31

# include all IPs from 192.168.0.0 to 192.168.0.255
acl internal src 192.168.0.0/24

# include all IPs from 192.168.0.0 to 192.168.0.255
# and all IPs from 10.0.0.0 to 10.255.255.255
acl internal src 192.168.0.0/24 10.0.0.0/8
```

When you have your ACL lines in place, you can put together appropriate http_access lines. For example, you might want to use a multilayered access system so that certain users (for example, company directors) have full access, whereas others are filtered. For example:

```
http_access allow directors
http_access deny hotmail
http_access deny zipfiles
http_access allow internal lunchtimes
http_access deny all
```

Because Squid matches those in order, directors will have full, unfiltered access to the Web. If the client IP address is not in the directors list, the two deny lines are processed so that the user cannot download .zip files or read online mail at Hotmail. After blocking those two types of requests, the allow on line four allows internal users to access the Web, as long as they do so only at lunchtime. The last line (which is highly recommended) blocks all other users from the proxy.

20

Reference

▶ http://www.squid-cache.org/—The home page of the Squid Web Proxy Cache.

▶ http://squid-docs.sourceforge.net/latest/book-full.html—The home page of Squid: A User's Guide, a free online book about Squid.

▶ http://www.faqs.org/docs/securing/netproxy-squid.html—A brief online guide to configuring a local Squid server.

▶ http://squid.visolve.com/squid/index.htm/—The home page of a company that can provide commercial support and deployment of Squid.

▶ http://squid.visolve.com/squid/reverseproxy.htm—ViSolve's guide to setting up Squid to reverse proxy to cache a local web server for external visitors.

▶ As well as these URLs, there are two excellent books on the topic of web caching. The first is *Squid: The Definitive Guide* (O'Reilly) by Duane Wessels, ISBN: 0-596-00162-2. The second is *Web Caching* (O'Reilly) also by Duane Wessels, ISBN: 1-56592-536-X.

Of the two, the former is more practical and covers the Squid server in depth. The latter is more theoretical, discussing how caching is implemented. Wessels is one of the leading developers on Squid, so both books are of impeccable technical accuracy.

CHAPTER 21

Administering Database Services

This chapter is an introduction to MySQL and PostgreSQL, two database systems that are included with Ubuntu. You will learn what these systems do, how the two programs compare, and how to consider their advantages and disadvantages. This information can help you choose and deploy which one to use for your organization's database needs.

The database administrator (DBA) for an organization has several responsibilities, which vary according to the size and operations of the organization, supporting staff, and so on. Depending on the particular organization's structure, if you are the organization's DBA, your responsibilities might include the following:

▶ **Installing and maintaining database servers**—You might install and maintain the database software. Maintenance can involve installing patches as well as upgrading the software at the appropriate times. As DBA, you might need to have root access to your system and know how to manage software (see Chapter 7, "Managing Software"). You also need to be aware of kernel, file system, and other security issues.

▶ **Installing and maintaining database clients**—The database client is the program used to access the database (you'll learn more on that later in this chapter, in the section "Database Clients"), either locally or remotely over a network. Your responsibilities might include installing and maintaining these client programs on users' systems. This chapter discusses how to install and work with the clients from both the Linux command line and through its graphical interface database tools.

▶ **Managing accounts and users**—Account and user management include adding and deleting users from the database, assigning and administering passwords, and so on. In this chapter, you will learn how to grant and revoke user privileges and passwords for MySQL and PostgreSQL while using Ubuntu.

▶ **Ensuring database security**—To ensure database security, you need to be concerned with things such as access control, which ensures that only authorized people can access the database, and permissions, which ensure that people who can access the database cannot do things they should not do. In this chapter, you will learn how to manage Secure Shell (SSH), web, and local GUI client access to the database. Planning and overseeing the regular backup of an organization's database and restoring data from those backups is another critical component of securing the database.

▶ **Ensuring data integrity**—Of all the information stored on a server's hard disk storage, chances are the information in the database is the most critical. Ensuring data integrity involves planning for multiple-user access and ensuring that changes are not lost or duplicated when more than one user is making changes to the database at the same time.

A Brief Review of Database Basics

Database services under Linux that use the software discussed in this chapter are based on a *client/server* model. Database clients are often used to input data and to query or display query results from the server. You can use the command line or a graphical client to access a running server. Databases generally come in two forms: flat file and relational. A *flat file* database can be as simple as a text file with a space, tab, or some other character delimiting different parts of the information. One example of a simple flat file database is the Ubuntu /etc/passwd file. Another example could be a simple address book that might look something like this:

```
Doe~John~505 Some Street~Anytown~NY~12345~555-555-1212
```

You can use standard UNIX tools such as grep, awk, and perl to search for and extract information from this primitive database. Although this might work well for a small database such as an address book that only one person uses, flat file databases of this type have several limitations:

▶ **They do not scale well**—Flat file databases cannot perform random access on data. They can only perform sequential access. This means they have to scan each line in the file, one by one, to look for specific information. As the size of the database grows, access times increase and performance decreases.

▶ **Flat file databases are unsuitable for multi-user environments**—Depending on how the database is set up, it either enables only one user to access it at a time or allows two users to make changes simultaneously, and the changes could end up overwriting each other and cause data loss.

These limitations obviously make the flat file database unsuitable for any kind of serious work in even a small business—much less in an enterprise environment. Relational databases, or relational database management systems (RDBMSs) to give them their full name, are good at finding the relationships between individual pieces of data. An RDBMS stores data in tables with fields much like those in spreadsheets, making the data searchable and sortable. RDBMSs are the focus of this chapter.

Oracle, DB2, Microsoft SQL Server, and the freely available PostgreSQL and MySQL are all examples of RDBMSs. The following sections discuss how relational databases work and provide a closer look at some of the basic processes involved in administering and using databases. You will also learn about SQL, the standard language used to store, retrieve, and manipulate database data.

How Relational Databases Work

An RDBMS stores data in tables, which you can visualize as spreadsheets. Each column in the table is a field; for example, a column might contain a name or an address. Each row in the table is an individual record. The table itself has a name you use to refer to that table when you want to get data out of it or put data into it. Figure 21.1 shows an example of a simple relational database that stores name and address information.

last_name	first_name	address	city	state	zip	phone
Doe	John	501 Somestreet	Anytown	NY	55011	555-555-1212
Doe	Jane	501 Somestreet	Anytown	NY	55011	555-555-1212
Palmer	John	205 Anystreet	Sometown	NY	55055	123-456-7890
Johnson	Robert	100 Easystreet	Easytown	CT	12345	111-222-3333

FIGURE 21.1   In this visualization of how an RDBMS stores data, the database stores four records (rows) that include name and address information, divided into seven fields (columns) of data.

In the example shown in Figure 21.1, the database contains only a single table. Most RDBMS setups are much more complex than this, with a single database containing multiple tables. Figure 21.2 shows an example of a database named sample_database that contains two tables.

In the sample_database example, the phonebook table contains four records (rows) and each record hold three fields (columns) of data. The cd_collection table holds eight records, divided into five fields of data.

If you are thinking that there is no logical relationship between the phonebook table and the cd_collection table in the sample_database example, you are correct. In a relational database, users can store multiple tables of data in a single database—even if the data in one table is unrelated to the data in others.

For example, suppose you run a small company that sells widgets and you have a computerized database of customers. In addition to storing each customer's name, address, and

phonebook

last_name	first_name	phone
Doe	John	555-555-1212
Doe	Jane	555-555-1212
Palmer	John	555-123-4567
Johnson	Richard	555-111-4321

cd_collection

id	title	artist	year	rating
1	Mindbomb	The The	1989	4
2	For All You've Done	Hillsong	2004	
3	Trouser Jazz	Mr Scruff	2002	5
4	Natural Elements	Acoustic Alchemy	1988	3
5	Combat Rock	The Clash	1982	4
6	Life for Rent	Dido	2003	5
7	Adiemus 4	Karl Jenkins	2000	4
8	The Two Towers	Howard Shore	2002	5

FIGURE 21.2   A single database can contain two tables—in this case, phonebook and cd_collection.

phone number, you want to be able to look up outstanding order and invoice information for any of your customers. You could use three related tables in an RDBMS to store and organize customer data for just those purposes. Figure 21.3 shows an example of such a database.

customers

cid	last_name	first_name	shipping_address
1	Doe	John	505 Somestreet
2	Doe	Jane	505 Somestreet
3	Palmer	John	200 Anystreet
4	Johnson	Richard	1000 Another Street

orders

cid	order_num	stock_num	priority	shipped	date
1	1002	100,252,342	3	Y	8/31/01
1	1221	200,352	1	N	10/2/01
3	1223	200,121	2	Y	10/2/01
2	1225	221,152	1	N	10/3/01

overdue

cid	order_num	days_overdue	action
1	1002	32	sent letter

FIGURE 21.3   You can use three related tables to track customers, orders, and outstanding invoices.

In the example in Figure 21.3, we have added a customer ID field to each customer record. This field holds a customer ID number that is the unique piece of information that can be used to link all other information for each customer to track orders and invoices. Each customer is given an ID unique to him; two customers might have the same data in their name fields, but their ID field values will never be the same. The Customer ID field data in the Orders and Overdue tables replaces the Last Name, First Name, and Shipping Address field information from the Customers table. Now, when you want to run a search for any customer's order and invoice data, you can search based on one key rather than multiple keys. You get more accurate results in faster, easier-to-conduct data searches.

Now that you have an idea of how data is stored in an RDBMS and how the RDBMS structure enables you to work with that data, you are ready to learn how to input and output data from the database. This is where SQL comes in.

Understanding SQL Basics

SQL (pronounced "S-Q-L") is a database query language understood by virtually all RDBMSs available today. You use SQL statements to get data into and retrieve data from a database. As with statements in any language, SQL statements have a defined structure that determines their meanings and functions.

As a DBA, you should understand the basics of SQL, even if you will not be doing any of the actual programming yourself. Fortunately, SQL is similar to standard English, so learning the basics is simple.

Creating Tables

As mentioned previously, an RDBMS stores data in tables that look similar to spreadsheets. Of course, before you can store any data in a database, you need to create the necessary tables and columns to store the data. You do this by using the CREATE statement.

For example, the cd_collection table from Figure 21.2 has 5 columns, or fields: id, title, artist, year, and rating.

SQL provides several column types for data that define what kind of data will be stored in the column. Some of the available types are INT, FLOAT, CHAR, and VARCHAR. Both CHAR and VARCHAR hold text strings, with the difference being that CHAR holds a fixed-length string, whereas VARCHAR holds a variable-length string.

There are also special column types, such as DATE, that only take data in a date format, and ENUMs (enumerations), which can be used to specify that only certain values are allowed. If, for example, you wanted to record the genre of your CDs, you could use an ENUM column that accepts only the values POP, ROCK, EASY_LISTENING, and so on. You will learn more about ENUM later in this chapter.

Looking at the cd_collection table, you can see that three of the columns hold numerical data and the other two hold string data. In addition, the character strings are of variable length. Based on this information, you can discern that the best type to use for the text columns is type VARCHAR, and the best type to use for the others is INT. You should notice something else about the cd_collection table: One of the CDs is missing a rating, perhaps because we have not listened to it yet. This value, therefore, is optional; it starts empty and can be filled in later.

You are now ready to create a table. As mentioned before, you do this by using the CREATE statement, which uses the following syntax:

```
CREATE TABLE table_name (column_name column_type(parameters) options, ...);
```

You should know the following about the CREATE statement:

▶ **SQL commands are not case sensitive**—For example, CREATE TABLE, create table, and Create Table are all valid.

▶ **Whitespace is generally ignored**—This means you should use it to make your SQL commands clearer.

The following example shows how to create the table for the cd_collection database:

```
CREATE TABLE cd_collection
(
id INT NOT NULL,
title VARCHAR(50) NOT NULL,
artist VARCHAR(50) NOT NULL,
year VARCHAR(50) NOT NULL,
rating VARCHAR(50) NULL
);
```

Notice that the statement terminates with a semicolon. This is how SQL knows you are finished with all the entries in the statement. In some cases, the semicolon can be omitted, and we will point out these cases when they arise.

TIP

SQL has a number of reserved keywords that cannot be used in table names or field names. For example, if you keep track of CDs you want to take with you on vacation, you would not be able to use the field name select because that is a reserved keyword. Instead, you should either choose a different name (selected?) or just prefix the field name with an f, such as fselect.

Inserting Data into Tables

After you create the tables, you can put data into them. You can insert data manually with the INSERT statement, which uses the following syntax:

```
INSERT INTO table_name VALUES('value1', 'value2', 'value3', ...);
```

This statement inserts value1, value2, and so on into the table table_name. The values that are inserted constitute one row, or *record*, in the database. Unless specified otherwise, values are inserted in the order in which the columns are listed in the database table. If, for some reason, you want to insert values in a different order (or if you want to insert only a few values and they are not in sequential order), you can specify which columns you want the data to go in by using the following syntax:

```
INSERT INTO table_name (column1,column4) VALUES('value1', 'value2');
```

You can also fill multiple rows with a single INSERT statement, using syntax such as the following:

```
INSERT INTO table_name VALUES('value1', 'value2'),('value3', 'value4');
```

In this statement, *value1* and *value2* are inserted into the first row and *value3* and *value4* are inserted into the second row.

The following example shows how you would insert the Nevermind entry into the cd_collection table:

```
INSERT INTO cd_collection VALUES(9, 'Nevermind', ''Nirvana', '1991,
''NULL);
```

MySQL requires the NULL value for the last column (rating) if you do not want to include a rating. PostgreSQL, on the other hand, lets you get away with just omitting the last column. Of course, if you had columns in the middle that were null, you would need to explicitly state NULL in the INSERT statement.

Normally, INSERT statements are coded into a front-end program so users adding data to the database do not have to worry about the SQL statements involved.

Retrieving Data from a Database

Of course, the main reason for storing data in a database is so you can later look up, sort, and generate reports on that data. Basic data retrieval is done with the SELECT statement, which has the following syntax:

```
SELECT column1, column2, column3 FROM table_name WHERE search_criteria;
```

The first two parts of the statement—the SELECT and FROM parts—are required. The WHERE portion of the statement is optional. If it is omitted, all rows in the table table_name are returned.

The *column1, column2, column3* indicates the name of the columns you want to see. If you want to see all columns, you can also use the wildcard * to show all the columns that match the search criteria. For example, the following statement displays all columns from the cd_collection table:

```
SELECT * FROM cd_collection;
```

If you wanted to see only the titles of all the CDs in the table, you would use a statement such as the following:

```
SELECT title FROM cd_collection;
```

To select the title and year of a CD, you would use the following:

```
SELECT title, year FROM cd_collection;
```

If you wanted something a little fancier, you can use SQL to print the CD title followed by the year in parentheses, as is the convention. Both MySQL and PostgreSQL provide string concatenation functions to handle problems such as this. However, the syntax is different in the two systems.

In MySQL, you can use the CONCAT() function to combine the title and year columns into one output column, along with parentheses. The following statement is an example:

```
SELECT CONCAT(title," (",year, ")") AS TitleYear FROM cd_collection;
```

That statement lists both the title and year under one column that has the label TitleYear. Note that there are two strings in the CONCAT() function along with the fields—these add whitespace and the parentheses.

In PostgreSQL, the string concatenation function is simply a double pipe (¦¦). The following command is the PostgreSQL equivalent of the preceding MySQL command:

```
SELECT (genus¦¦'' ('¦¦species¦¦')') AS TitleYear FROM cd_collection;
```

Note that the parentheses are optional, but they make the statement easier to read. Once again, the strings in the middle and at the end (note the space between the quotes) are used to insert spacing and parentheses between the title and year.

Of course, more often than not, you do not want a list of every single row in the database. Rather, you only want to find rows that match certain characteristics. For this, you add the WHERE statement to the SELECT statement. For example, suppose you want to find all the CDs in the cd_collection table that have a rating of 5. You would use a statement like the following:

```
SELECT * FROM cd_collection WHERE rating = 5;
```

Using the table from Figure 21.2, you can see that this query would return the rows for *Trouser Jazz, Life for Rent,* and *The Two Towers.* This is a simple query, and SQL is capable of handling queries much more complex than this. Complex queries can be written using logical AND and logical OR statements. For example, suppose you want to refine the query so it lists only those CDs that were not released in 2003. You would use a query like the following:

```
SELECT * FROM cd_collection WHERE rating = 5 AND year != 2003;
```

In SQL, != means "is not equal to." So once again looking at the table from Figure 21.2, you can see that this query returns the rows for *Trouser Jazz* and *The Two Towers* but does not return the row for *Life for Rent* because it was released in 2003.

So, what if you want to list all the CDs that have a rating of 3 or 4 except those released in the year 2000? This time, you combine logical AND and logical OR statements:

```
SELECT * FROM cd_collection WHERE rating = 3 OR rating = 4 AND year != 2000;
```

This query would return entries for *Mind Bomb, Natural Elements,* and *Combat Rock.* However, it wouldn't return entries for *Adiemus 4* because it was released in 2000.

TIP

One of the most common errors among new database programmers is confusing logical AND and logical OR. For example, in everyday speech, you might say "Find me all CDs released in 2003 and 2004." At first glance, you might think that if you fed this statement to the database in SQL format, it would return the rows for *For All You've Done* and *Life for Rent*. In fact, it would return no rows at all. This is because the database interprets the statement as "Find all rows in which the CD was released in 2003 and was released in 2004." It is, of course, impossible for the same CD to be released twice, so this statement would never return any rows, no matter how many CDs were stored in the table. The correct way to form this statement is with an OR statement instead of an AND statement.

SQL is capable of far more than is demonstrated here. But as mentioned before, this section is not intended to teach you all there is to know about SQL programming; rather, it teaches you the basics so you can be a more effective DBA.

Choosing a Database: MySQL Versus PostgreSQL

If you are just starting out and learning about using a database with Linux, the first logical step is to research which database will best serve your needs. Many database software packages are available for Linux; some are free, and others cost hundreds of thousands of dollars. Expensive commercial databases, such as Oracle, are beyond the scope of this book. Instead, this chapter focuses on two freely available databases: MySQL and PostgreSQL.

Both of these databases are quite capable, and either one could probably serve your needs. However, each database has a unique set of features and capabilities that might serve your needs better or make developing database applications easier for you.

Speed

Until recently, the speed choice was simple: If the speed of performing queries was paramount to your application, you used MySQL. MySQL has a reputation for being an extremely fast database. Until recently, PostgreSQL was quite slow by comparison.

Newer versions of PostgreSQL have improved in terms of speed (when it comes to disk access, sorting, and so on). In certain situations, such as periods of heavy simultaneous access, PostgreSQL can be significantly faster than MySQL, as you will see in the next section. However, MySQL is still extremely fast when compared to many other databases.

Data Locking

To prevent data corruption, a database needs to put a lock on data while it is being accessed. As long as the lock is on, no other process can access the data until the first process has released the lock. This means that any other processes trying to access the data have to wait until the current process completes. The next process in line then locks the data until it is finished, and the remaining processes have to wait their turn, and so on.

Of course, operations on a database generally complete quickly, so in environments with a small number of users simultaneously accessing the database, the locks are usually of such short duration that they do not cause any significant delays. However, in environments in which many people are accessing the database simultaneously, locking can create performance problems as people wait their turn to access the database.

Older versions of MySQL lock data at the table level, which can be considered a bottleneck for updates during periods of heavy access. This means that when someone writes a row of data in the table, the entire table is locked so no one else can enter data. If your table has 500,000 rows (or records) in it, all 500,000 rows are locked any time 1 row is accessed. Once again, in environments with a relatively small number of simultaneous users, this doesn't cause serious performance problems because most operations complete so quickly that the lock time is extremely short. However, in environments in which many people are accessing the data simultaneously, MySQL's table-level locking can be a significant performance bottleneck.

PostgreSQL, on the other hand, locks data at the row level. In PostgreSQL, only the row currently being accessed is locked. The rest of the table can be accessed by other users. This row-level locking significantly reduces the performance impact of locking in environments that have a large number of simultaneous users. Therefore, as a general rule, PostgreSQL is better suited for high-load environments than MySQL.

The MySQL release bundled with Ubuntu gives you the choice of using tables with table-level or row-level locking. In MySQL terminology, MyISAM tables use table-level locking and InnoDB tables use row-level locking.

> **NOTE**
>
> MySQL's data locking methods are discussed in more depth at http://www.mysql.com/doc/en/Internal_locking.html.
>
> You can find more information on PostgreSQL's locking at http://www.postgresql.org/idocs/index.php?locking-tables.html.

ACID Compliance in Transaction Processing to Protect Data Integrity

Another way MySQL and PostgreSQL differ is in the amount of protection they provide for keeping data from becoming corrupted. The acronym ACID is commonly used to describe several aspects of data protection:

▶ **Atomicity**—This means that several database operations are treated as an indivisible (atomic) unit, often called a *transaction.* In a transaction, either all unit operations are carried out or none of them are. In other words, if any operation in the atomic unit fails, the entire atomic unit is canceled.

▶ **Consistency**—Ensures that no transaction can cause the database to be left in an inconsistent state. Inconsistent states can be caused by database client crashes, network failures, and similar situations. Consistency ensures that, in such a situation, any transaction or partially completed transaction that would cause the database to be left in an inconsistent state is *rolled back,* or undone.

▶ **Isolation**—Ensures that multiple transactions operating on the same data are completely isolated from each other. This prevents data corruption if two users try to write to the same record at the same time. The way isolation is handled can generally be configured by the database programmer. One way that isolation can be handled is through locking, as discussed previously.

▶ **Durability**—Ensures that, after a transaction has been committed to the database, it cannot be lost in the event of a system crash, network failure, or other problem. This is usually accomplished through transaction logs. Durability means, for example, that if the server crashes, the database can examine the logs when it comes back up and it can commit any transactions that were not yet complete into the database.

PostgreSQL is ACID-compliant, but again MySQL gives you the choice of using ACID-compliant tables or not. MyISAM tables are not ACID-compliant, whereas InnoDB tables are. Note that ACID compliancy is no easy task: All the extra precautions incur a performance overhead.

SQL Subqueries

Subqueries allow you to combine several operations into one atomic unit, and they enable those operations to access each other's data. By using SQL subqueries, you can perform some extremely complex operations on a database. In addition, using SQL subqueries eliminates the potential problem of data changing between two operations as a result of another user performing some operation on the same set of data. Both PostgreSQL and MySQL have support for subqueries in this release of Ubuntu, but this was not true in earlier releases.

Procedural Languages and Triggers

A *procedural language* is an external programming language that can be used to write functions and procedures. This allows you to do things that aren't supported by simple SQL. A *trigger* allows you to define an event that will invoke the external function or procedure you have written. For example, a trigger can be used to cause an exception if an INSERT statement containing an unexpected or out-of-range value for a column is given.

For example, in the CD tracking database, you could use a trigger to cause an exception if a user entered data that did not make sense. PostgreSQL has a procedural language called PL/pgSQL. Although MySQL has support for a limited number of built-in procedures and triggers, it does not have any procedural language. This means you cannot create custom procedures or triggers in MySQL, although the same effects can often be achieved through creative client-side programming.

Configuring MySQL

A free and stable version of MySQL is included with Ubuntu. MySQL is also available from the website http://www.mysql.com. The software is available in source code, binary, and APT format for Linux. You can use the Synaptic client to add the software to your system. See Chapter 7 for the details on adding (or removing) software.

After you have MySQL installed, you need to initialize the *grant tables* or permissions to access any or all databases and tables and column data within a database. You can do this by issuing mysql_install_db as root. This command initializes the grant tables and creates a MySQL root user.

CAUTION

The MySQL data directory needs to be owned by the user as which MySQL will run (changing ownership using the chown command). In addition, only this user should have any permissions on this directory. (In other words, the permissions should be set to 700 by using chmod.) Setting up the data directory any other way creates a security hole.

Running mysql_install_db should generate output similar to the following:

```
sudo mysql_install_db
Preparing db table
Preparing host table
Preparing user table
Preparing func table
Preparing tables_priv table
Preparing columns_priv table
Installing all prepared tables
020916 17:39:05 /usr/libexec/mysqld: Shutdown Complete
```

. . .

The command prepares MySQL for use on the system and reports helpful information. The next step is to set the password for the MySQL root user, which is discussed in the following section.

> **CAUTION**
>
> By default, the MySQL root user is created with no password. This is one of the first things you must change because the MySQL root user has access to all aspects of the database. The following section explains how to change the password of the user.

Setting a Password for the MySQL Root User

To set a password for the root MySQL user, you need to connect to the MySQL server as the root MySQL user; you can use the command `mysql -u root` to do so. This command connects you to the server with the MySQL client. When you have the MySQL command prompt, issue a command like the following to set a password for the root user:

```
mysql> SET PASSWORD FOR root = PASSWORD("secretword");
```

secretword should be replaced by whatever you want to be the password for the root user. You can use this same command with other usernames to set or change passwords for other database users.

After you enter a password, you can exit the MySQL client by typing `exit` at the command prompt.

Creating a Database in MySQL

In MySQL you create a database by using the `CREATE DATABASE` statement. To create a database, you connect to the server by typing **mysql -u root -p** and pressing Enter. After you do so, you are connected to the database as the MySQL root user and prompted for a password. After you enter the password, you are placed at the MySQL command prompt. Then you use the `CREATE DATABASE` command. For example, the following commands create a database called `animals`:

```
sudo mysql -u root -p
Enter password:
Welcome to the MySQL monitor. Commands end with ; or \g.
Your MySQL connection id is 1 to server version: 3.23.58

Type 'help;' or '\h' for help. Type '\c' to clear the buffer.

mysql> CREATE DATABASE animals;
Query OK, 1 row affected (0.00 sec)
mysql>
```

Another way to create a database is to use the `mysqladmin` command, as the root user, with the `create` keyword and the name of a new database. For example, to create a new database named reptiles, you use a command line like this:

```
# mysqladmin -u root -p create reptiles
```

Granting and Revoking Privileges in MySQL

You probably want to grant yourself some privileges, and eventually you will probably want to grant privileges to other users. Privileges, also known as *rights*, are granted and revoked on four levels:

▶ **Global-level**—These rights allow access to any database on a server.

▶ **Database-level**—These rights allow access to all tables in a database.

▶ **Table-level**—These rights allow access to all columns within a table in a database.

▶ **Column-level**—These rights allow access to a single column within a database's table.

> **NOTE**
>
> Listing all the available privileges is beyond the scope of this chapter. See the MySQL documentation for more information.

To add a user account, you connect to the database by typing `mysql -u root -p` and pressing Enter. You are then connected as the root user and prompted for a password. (You did set a password for the root user, as instructed in the last section, right?) After you enter the root password, you are placed at the MySQL command prompt.

To grant privileges to a user, you use the `GRANT` statement, which has the following syntax:

```
grant what_to_grant ON where_to_grant TO user_name IDENTIFIED BY 'password';
```

The first option, *what_to_grant*, is the privileges you are granting to the user. These privileges are specified with keywords. For example, the `ALL` keyword is used to grant global-, database-, table-, and column-level rights for a specified user.

The second option, *where_to_grant*, specifies the resources on which the privileges should be granted. The third option, *user_name*, is the username to which you want to grant the privileges. Finally, the fourth option, *password*, is a password that should be assigned to this user. If this is an existing user who already has a password and you are modifying permissions, you can omit the `IDENTIFIED BY` portion of the statement.

For example, to grant all privileges on a database named `sampledata` to a user named `foobar`, you could use the following command:

```
GRANT ALL ON animals.* TO foobar IDENTIFIED BY 'secretword';
```

The user foobar can now connect to the database sampledata by using the password secretword, and foobar has all privileges on the database, including the ability to create and destroy tables. For example, the user foobar can now log in to the server (by using the current hostname—shuttle2, in this example), and access the database like so:

```
$ mysql -h shuttle2 -u foobar -p animals
Enter password:
Welcome to the MySQL monitor. Commands end with ; or \g.
Your MySQL connection id is 43 to server version: 3.23.58

Type 'help;' or '\h' for help. Type '\c' to clear the buffer.

mysql>
```

> **NOTE**
>
> See the section "The MySQL Command-Line Client" for additional command-line options.

Later, if you need to revoke privileges from foobar, you can use the REVOKE statement. For example, the following statement revokes all privileges from the user foobar:

```
REVOKE ALL ON animals FROM foobar;
```

Advanced database administration, privileges, and security are very complex topics that are beyond the scope of this book. See the section "Reference" at the end of this chapter for links to online documentation. You can also check out Luke Welling's and Laura Thompson's book *PHP and MySQL* Development from Sams Publishing.

Configuring PostgreSQL

If you do not want to use the version of PostgreSQL bundled with Ubuntu, the latest PostgreSQL binary files and source are available at http://www.postgresql.org. The PostgreSQL packages are distributed as several files. At a minimum, you probably want the postgresql, postgresql-server, and postgresql-libs packages. You should see the README file in the FTP directory ftp://ftp.postgresql.org/pub/ to determine whether you need any other packages.

If you are installing from the Ubuntu package files, a necessary postgres user account (that is, an account with the name of the user running the server on your system) is created for you automatically:

```
$ fgrep postgres /etc/passwd
postgres:x:26:26:PostgreSQL Server:/var/lib/pgsql:/bin/bash
```

Otherwise, you need to create a user called postgres during the installation. This user shouldn't have login privileges because only root should be able to use su to become this user and no one will ever log in directly as the user. (See Chapter 10, "Managing Users," for more information on how to add users to an Ubuntu system.) After you have added the user, you can install each of the PostgreSQL packages you downloaded using the standard dpkg -i command for a default installation.

Initializing the Data Directory in PostgreSQL

After the packages have been installed, you need to initialize the data directory. To do so, you must first create the data directory and you must be the root user. The following example assumes that the data directory is /usr/local/pgsql/data.

Create the /usr/local/pgsql/data directory (using mkdir) and change the ownerships of the directory (using chown and chgrp) so it is owned by the user postgres. Then use su and, as the user postgres, issue the following commands:

```
# mkdir /usr/local/pgsql
# chown postgres /usr/local/pgsql
# chgrp postgres /usr/local/pgsql
# su - postgres
-bash-2.05b$ initdb -D /usr/local/pgsql/data
The files belonging to this database system will be owned by user "postgres".
This user must also own the server process.

The database cluster will be initialized with locale en_US.UTF-8.
This locale setting will prevent the use of indexes for pattern matching
operations.  If that is a concern, rerun initdb with the collation order
set to "C".  For more information see the Administrator's Guide.

creating directory /usr/local/pgsql/data... ok
creating directory /usr/local/pgsql/data/base... ok
creating directory /usr/local/pgsql/data/global... ok
creating directory /usr/local/pgsql/data/pg_xlog... ok
creating directory /usr/local/pgsql/data/pg_clog... ok
creating template1 database in /usr/local/pgsql/data/base/1... ok
creating configuration files... ok
initializing pg_shadow... ok
enabling unlimited row size for system tables... ok
initializing pg_depend... ok
creating system views... ok
loading pg_description... ok
creating conversions... ok
setting privileges on built-in objects... ok
vacuuming database template1... ok
```

```
copying template1 to template0... ok
```

```
Success. You can now start the database server using:
```

```
 /usr/bin/postmaster -D /usr/local/pgsql/data
or
 /usr/bin/pg_ctl -D /usr/local/pgsql/data -l logfile start
```

This initializes the database and sets the permissions on the data directory to their correct values.

CAUTION

The `initdb` program sets the permissions on the data directory to 700. You should not change these permissions to anything else to avoid creating a security hole.

You can start the `postmaster` program with the following command (make sure you are still the user `postgres`):

$ postmaster -D /usr/local/pgsql/data &

If you have decided to use a directory other than /usr/local/pgsql/data as the data directory, you should replace the directory in the `postmaster` command line with whatever directory you are using.

TIP

By default, Ubuntu makes the PostgreSQL data directory /var/lib/pgsql/data. This isn't a very good place to store the data, however, because most people do not have the necessary space in the /var partition for any kind of serious data storage. Note that if you do change the data directory to something else (such as /usr/local/pgsql/data, as in the examples in this section), you need to edit the PostgreSQL startup file (named postgres) located in /etc/init.d to reflect the change.

Creating a Database in PostgreSQL

Creating a database in PostgreSQL is straightforward, but it must be performed by a user who has permissions to create databases in PostgreSQL—for example, initially the user named `postgres`. You can then simply issue the following command from the shell prompt (not the PSQL client prompt, but a normal shell prompt):

```
# su - postgres
-bash-2.05b$ createdb database
```

where *database* is the name of the database you want to create.

The createdb program is actually a wrapper that makes it easier to create databases without having to log in and use psql. However, you can also create databases from within psql with the CREATE DATABASE statement. Here's an example:

```
CREATE DATABASE database;
```

You need to create at least one database before you can start the pgsql client program. You should create this database while you're logged in as the user postgres. To log in as this user, you need to use su to become root and then use su to become the user postgres. To connect to the new database, you start the psql client program with the name of the new database as a command-line argument, like so:

```
$ psql sampledata
```

If you don't specify the name of a database when you invoke psql, the command attempts to connect to a database that has the same name as the user as which you invoke psql (that is, the default database).

Creating Database Users in PostgreSQL

To create a database user, you use su to become the user postgres from the Linux root account. You can then use the PostgreSQL createuser command to quickly create a user who is allowed to access databases or create new database users, like this:

```
$ createuser phudson
Shall the new user be allowed to create databases? (y/n) y
Shall the new user be allowed to create more new users? (y/n) y
CREATE USER
```

In this example, the new user named phudson is created and allowed to create new databases and database users (you should carefully consider who is allowed to create new databases or additional users).

You can also use the PostgreSQL command-line client to create a new user by typing psql along with name of the database and then use the CREATE USER command to create a new user. Here is an example:

```
CREATE USER foobar ;
```

> **CAUTION**
>
> PostgreSQL allows you to omit the WITH PASSWORD portion of the statement. However, doing so causes the user to be created with no password. This is a security hole, so you should always use the WITH PASSWORD option when creating users.

> **NOTE**
>
> When you are finished working in the psql command-line client, you can type \q to get out of it and return to the shell prompt.

Deleting Database Users in PostgreSQL

To delete a database user, you use the dropuser command, along with the user's name, and the user's access is removed from the default database, like this:

```
$ dropuser msmith
DROP USER
```

You can also log in to your database by using psql and then use the DROP USER commands. Here's an example:

```
$ psql demodb
Welcome to psql, the PostgreSQL interactive terminal.

Type: \copyright for distribution terms
 \h for help with SQL commands
 \? for help on internal slash commands
 \g or terminate with semicolon to execute query
 \q to quit

demodb=# DROP USER msmith ;
DROP USER
demodb=# \q
$
```

Granting and Revoking Privileges in PostgreSQL

As in MySQL, granting and revoking privileges in PostgreSQL is done with the GRANT and REVOKE statements. The syntax is the same as in MySQL except that PostgreSQL doesn't use the IDENTIFIED BY portion of the statement because with PostgreSQL, passwords are assigned when you create the user with the CREATE USER statement, as discussed previously. Here is the syntax of the GRANT statement:

```
GRANT what_to_grant ON where_to_grant TO user_name;
```

The following command, for example, grants all privileges to the user foobar on the database sampledata:

```
GRANT ALL ON sampledata TO foobar;
```

To revoke privileges, you use the REVOKE statement. Here is an example:

```
REVOKE ALL ON sampledata FROM foobar;
```

This command removes all privileges from the user foobar on the database sampledata.

Advanced administration and user configuration are complex topics. This section cannot begin to cover all the aspects of PostgreSQL administration or of privileges and users. For more information on administering PostgreSQL, see the PostgreSQL documentation or consult a book on PostgreSQL, such as *PostgreSQL* (Sams Publishing).

Database Clients

Both MySQL and PostgreSQL use a client/server system for accessing databases. In the simplest terms, the database server handles the requests that come into the database and the database client handles getting the requests to the server as well as getting the output from the server to the user.

Users never interact directly with the database server even if it happens to be located on the same machine they are using. All requests to the database server are handled by a database client, which might or might not be running on the same machine as the database server.

Both MySQL and PostgreSQL have command-line clients. A command-line client is a very primitive way of interfacing with a database and generally isn't used by end users. As a DBA, however, you use the command-line client to test new queries interactively without having to write front-end programs for that purpose. In later sections of this chapter, you will learn a bit about the MySQL graphical client and the web-based database administration interfaces available for both MySQL and PostgreSQL.

The following sections examine two common methods of accessing a remote database, a method of local access to a database server, and the concept of web access to a database.

> **NOTE**
>
> You should consider access and permission issues when setting up a database. Should users be able to create and destroy databases? Or should they only be able to use existing databases? Will users be able to add records to the database and modify existing records? Or should users be limited to read-only access to the database? And what about the rest of the world? Will the general public need to have any kind of access to your database through the Internet? As DBA, you must determine the answers to these questions.

SSH Access to a Database

Two types of remote database access scenarios are briefly discussed in this section. In the first scenario, the user directly logs in to the database server through SSH (to take advantage of the security benefits of encrypted sessions) and then starts a program on the server to access the database. In this case, shown in Figure 21.4, the database client is running on the database server itself.

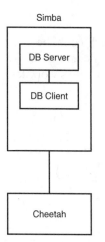

FIGURE 21.4   The user logs in to the database server located on host `simba` from the workstation (host `cheetah`). The database client is running on `simba`.

In the other scenario, shown in Figure 21.5, the user logs in to a remote host through SSH and starts a program on it to access the database, but the database is actually running on a different system. Three systems are now involved—the user's workstation, the remote host running the database client, and the remote host running the database server.

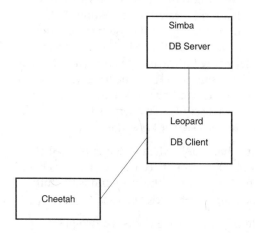

FIGURE 21.5   The user logs in to the remote host `leopard` from the workstation (host `cheetah`) and starts a database client on `leopard`. The client on `leopard` then connects to the database server running on host `simba`. The database client is running on `leopard`.

The important thing to note in Figure 21.5 is the middleman system leopard. Although the client is no longer running on the database server itself, it isn't running on the user's local workstation, either.

Local GUI Client Access to a Database

A user can log in to the database server by using a graphical client (which could be running on Windows, Macintosh, or a UNIX workstation). The graphical client then connects to the database server. In this case, the client is running on the user's workstation. Figure 21.6 shows an example.

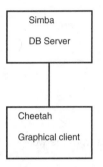

FIGURE 21.6   The user starts a GUI database program on his workstation (hostname cheetah). This program, which is the database client, then connects to the database server running on the host simba.

Web Access to a Database

In this section, we look at two basic examples of web access to the database server. In the first example, a user accesses the database through a form located on the World Wide Web. At first glance, it might appear that the client is running on the user's workstation. Of course, in reality it is not; the client is actually running on the web server. The web browser on the user's workstation simply provides a way for the user to enter the data that he wants to send to the database and a way for the results sent from the database to be displayed to the user. The software that actually handles sending the request to the database is running on the web server in the form of a CGI script; a Java servlet; or embedded scripting such as the PHP or Sun Microsystems, Inc.'s JavaServer Pages (JSP).

Often, the terms *client* and *front end* are used interchangeably when speaking of database structures. However, Figure 21.7 shows an example of a form of access in which the client and the front end aren't the same thing at all. In this example, the front end is the form displayed in the user's web browser. In such cases, the client is referred to as *middleware*.

In another possible web access scenario, it could be said that the client is a two-piece application in which part of it is running on the user's workstation and the other part is running on the web server. For example, the database programmer can use JavaScript in the web form to ensure that the user has entered a valid query. In this case, the user's query is partially processed on her own workstation and partially on the web server. Error

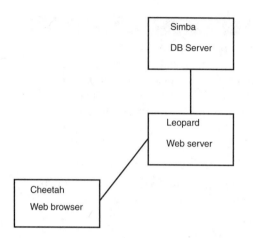

FIGURE 21.7   The user accesses the database through the World Wide Web. The front end is the user's web browser, the client is running on leopard, and the server is running on simba.

checking is done on the user's own workstation, which helps reduce the load on the server and also helps reduce network traffic because the query is checked for errors before being sent across the network to the server.

The MySQL Command-Line Client

The MySQL command-line client is mysql, and it has the following syntax:

```
mysql [options] [database]
```

Some of the available options for mysql are discussed in Table 21.1. *database* is optional, and if given, it should be the name of the database to which you want to connect.

TABLE 21.1   Command-Line Options to Use When Invoking mysql

Option	Action
-h *host-name*	Connects to the remote host *hostname* (if the database server isn't located on the local system).
-u *user-name*	Connects to the database as the user *username*.
-p	Prompts for a password. This option is required if the user you are connecting as needs a password to access the database. Note that this is a lowercase p.
-P *n*	Specifies *n* as the number of the port that the client should connect to. Note that this is an uppercase P.
-?	Displays a help message.

More options are available than are listed in Table 21.1, but these are the most common options. See the man page for mysql for more information on the available options.

> **CAUTION**
>
> Although `mysql` allows you to specify the password on the command line after the `-p` option, and thus allows you to avoid having to type the password at the prompt, you should never invoke the client this way. Doing so causes your password to display in the process list, and the process list can be accessed by any user on the system. This is a major security hole, so you should never give your password on the `mysql` command line.

You can access the MySQL server without specifying a database to use. After you log in, you use the help command to get a list of available commands, like this:

```
mysql> help
```

```
MySQL commands:
Note that all text commands must be first on line and end with ';'
help    (\h) Display this help.
?       (\?) Synonym for 'help'.
clear   (\c) Clear command.
connect (\r) Reconnect to the server. Optional arguments are db and host.
edit    (\e) Edit command with $EDITOR.
ego     (\G) Send command to mysql server, display result vertically.
exit    (\q) Exit mysql. Same as quit.
go      (\g) Send command to mysql server.
nopager (\n) Disable pager, print to stdout.
notee   (\t) Don't write into outfile.
pager   (\P) Set PAGER [to_pager]. Print the query results via PAGER.
print   (\p) Print current command.
quit    (\q) Quit mysql.
rehash  (\#) Rebuild completion hash.
source  (\.) Execute a SQL script file. Takes a file name as an argument.
status  (\s) Get status information from the server.
tee     (\T) Set outfile [to_outfile]. Append everything into given outfile.
use     (\u) Use another database. Takes database name as argument.
```

You can then access a database by using the use command and the name of a database that has been created (such as animals) and that you are authorized to connect to, like this:

```
mysql> use animals
Database changed
mysql>
```

The PostgreSQL Command-Line Client

You invoke the PostgreSQL command-line client with the command psql. Like mysql, psql can be invoked with the name of the database to which you would like to connect. Also like mysql, psql can take several options. These options are listed in Table 21.2.

TABLE 21.2   Command-Line Options to Use When Invoking psql

Option	Action
-h *host-name*	Connects to the remote host *hostname* (if the database server isn't located on the local system).
-p *n*	Specifies n as the number of the port that the client should connect to. Note that this is a lowercase p.
-U *user-name*	Connects to the database as the user *username*.
-W	Prompts for a password after connecting to the database. In PostgreSQL 7 and later, password prompting is automatic if the server requests a password after a connection has been established.
-?	Displays a help message.

Several more options are available in addition to those listed in Table 21.2. See the psql's man page for details on all the available options.

Graphical Clients

If you'd rather interact with a database by using a graphical database client than with the command-line clients discussed in the previous section, you're in luck: A few options are available.

MySQL has an official graphical client, called MySQLGUI. MySQLGUI is available in both source and binary formats from the MySQL website at http://www.mysql.com.

Web-based administration interfaces are also available for MySQL and PostgreSQL. phpMyAdmin and phpPgAdmin are two such products. Both of these products are based on the PHP-embedded scripting language and therefore require you to have PHP installed. Of course, you also need to have a web server installed.

Related Ubuntu and Database Commands

The following commands are useful for creating and manipulating databases in Ubuntu:

▶ `createdb`—Creates a new PostgreSQL database

▶ `createuser`—Creates a new PostgreSQL user account

▶ `dropdb`—Deletes a PostgreSQL database

▶ `dropuser`—Deletes a PostgreSQL user account

▶ `mysql`—Interactively queries the mysqld server

▶ `mysqladmin`—Administers the mysqld server

▶ `mysqldump`—Dumps or backs up MySQL data or tables

▶ `pgaccess`—Accesses a PostgreSQL database server

▶ `pg_ctl`—Controls a PostgreSQL server or queries its status

▶ `psql`—Accesses PostgreSQL via an interactive terminal

Reference

The following are references for the databases mentioned in this chapter:

▶ http://www.mysql.com—This is the official website of the MySQL database server. Here you can find the latest versions as well as up-to-date information and online documentation for MySQL. You can also purchase support contracts here. You might want to look into this if you will be using MySQL in a corporate setting. (Many corporations balk at the idea of using software for which the company has no support contract in place.)

▶ http://www.postgresql.org—This is the official website of the PostgreSQL database server. You are asked to select a mirror when you arrive at this site. After you select a mirror, you are taken to the main site. From there, you can find information on the latest versions of PostgreSQL and read the online documentation.

▶ http://www.postgresql.org/idocs/index.php?tutorial-start.html—This interactive HTML documentation tree is a great place to get started with learning how to use PostgreSQL.

▶ http://www.pgsql.com—This is a commercial company that provides fee-based support contracts for the PostgreSQL database.

CHAPTER 22

LDAP

The *Lightweight Directory Access Protocol* (LDAP, pronounced ell-dap) is one of those technologies that, while hidden, forms part of the core infrastructure in enterprise computing. Its job is simple: It stores information about users. However, its power comes from the fact that it can be linked into dozens of other services. LDAP can power login authentication, public key distribution, email routing, and address verification and, more recently, has formed the core of the push toward single-sign-on technology.

> **TIP**
>
> Most people find the concept of LDAP easier to grasp when they think of it as a highly specialized form of database server. Behind the scenes, Ubuntu uses a database for storing all its LDAP information; however, LDAP does not offer anything as straightforward as SQL for data manipulation!
>
> OpenLDAP uses Sleepycat *Software's Berkeley* DB (BDB), and sticking with that default is highly recommended. That said, there are alternatives if you have specific needs.

This chapter looks at a relatively basic installation of an LDAP server, including how to host a companywide directory service that contains the names and email addresses of employees. LDAP is a client/server system, meaning that an LDAP server hosts the data, and an LDAP client queries it. Ubuntu comes with OpenLDAP as its LDAP server, along with several LDAP-enabled email clients, including

Evolution and Mozilla Thunderbird. We cover all three of these applications in this chapter.

Because LDAP data is usually available over the Internet—or at least your local network—it is imperative that you make every effort to secure your server. This chapter gives specific instruction on password configuration for OpenLDAP, and we recommend you follow our instructions closely.

Configuring the Server

If you have been using LDAP for years, you will be aware of its immense power and flexibility. On the other hand, if you are just trying LDAP for the first time, it will seem like the most broken component you could imagine. LDAP has specific configuration requirements, is vastly lacking in graphical tools, and has a large number of acronyms to remember. On the bright side, all the hard work you put in will be worth it because, when it works, LDAP will hugely improve your networking experience.

The first step in configuring your LDAP server is to install the client and server applications. Start up Synaptic and install the slapd and `ldap-utils` packages. You'll be asked to enter an administrator password for slapd.

Now, use sudo to edit `/etc/ldap/slapd.conf` in the text editor of your choice. This is the primary configuration file for `slapd`, the OpenLDAP server daemon. Scroll down until you see the lines `database`, `suffix`, and `rootdn`.

This is the most basic configuration for your LDAP system. What is the name of your server? The `dc` stands for *domain component*, which is the name of your domain as stored in DNS—for example, example.com. For our examples, we used hudzilla.org. LDAP considers each part of a domain name (separated by a period) to be a domain component, so the domain hudzilla.org is made up of a domain component `hudzilla` and a domain component `org`.

Change the suffix line to match your domain components, separated by commas. For example:

```
suffix    "dc=hudzilla,dc=org"
```

The next line defines the root DN, which is another LDAP acronym meaning `distinguished name`. A DN is a complete descriptor of a person in your directory: her name and the domain in which she resides. For example

```
rootdn    "cn=root,dc=hudzilla,dc=org"
```

CN is yet another LDAP acronym, this time meaning common name. A `common name` is just that—the name a person is usually called. Some people have several common names. Andrew Hudson is a common name, but that same user might also have the common name Andy Hudson. In our `rootdn` line, we define a complete user: common name `root` at domain hudzilla.org. These lines are essentially read backward. LDAP goes to `org` first, searches `org` for `hudzilla`, and then searches `hudzilla` for `root`.

The `rootdn` is important because it is more than just another person in your directory. The root LDAP user is like the root user in Linux. It is the person who has complete control over the system and can make whatever changes he wants to.

Now comes a slightly more complex part: We need to give the LDAP root user a password. The easiest way to do this is to open a new terminal window alongside your existing one. Switch to root in the new terminal and type **slappasswd**. This tool generates password hashes for OpenLDAP using the SHA1 hash algorithm. Enter a password when it prompts you. When you have entered and confirmed your password, you should see output like this:

```
{SSHA}qMVxFT2K1UUmrA89Gd7z6EK3gRLDIo2W
```

That is the password hash generated from your password. Yours will differ from the one shown here, but what is important is that it has {SSHA} at the beginning to denote it uses SHA1. You now need to switch back to the other terminal (the one editing `slapd.conf`) and add this line below the rootdn line:

```
rootpw <your password hash>
```

You should replace <your password hash> with the full output from `slappaswd`, like this:

```
rootpw {SSHA}qMVxFT2K1UUmrA89Gd7z6EK3gRLDIo2W
```

That sets the LDAP root password to the one you just generated with `slappaswd`. That is the last change you need to make in the `slapd.conf` file, so save your changes and close your editor.

Back in the terminal, run the `slaptest` command. This checks your `slapd.conf` file for errors and ensures you edited it correctly. Presuming there are no errors, run `/etc/init.d/slapd` to start OpenLDAP.

Ubuntu automatically starts OpenLDAP each time you boot up, but that command starts it right now.

The final configuration step is to tell Ubuntu which DN it should use if none is specified. You do so by going to System Settings and selecting Authentication. In the dialog box that appears, check Enable LDAP Support in both the User Information tab and Authentication tab. Next, click the Configure LDAP button, enter your DCs (for example, `dc=hudzilla,dc=org`) for the LDAP Search Base DN, and enter **127.0.0.1** for the LDAP Server. Click OK, and then click OK again.

TIP

Checking Enable LDAP Support does not actually change the way in which your users log in. Behind the scenes, this forces Ubuntu to set up the `ldap.conf` file in `/etc/ldap` so that LDAP searches that do not specify a base search start point are directed to your DC.

Populating Your Directory

With LDAP installed, configured, and running, you can now fill the directory with people. This involves yet more LDAP acronyms and is by no means an easy task, so do not worry if you have to reread this several times before it sinks in.

First, create the file base.ldif. You will use this to define the base components of your system: the domain and the address book. LDIF is an acronym standing for *LDAP Data Interchange Format*, and it is the standard way of recording user data for insertion into an LDAP directory. Here are the contents we used for our example:

```
dn: dc=hudzilla,dc=org
objectClass: top
objectClass: dcObject
objectClass: organization
dc: hudzilla
o: Hudzilla Dot Org

dn: ou=People,dc=hudzilla,dc=org
ou: People
objectClass: top
objectClass: organizationalUnit
```

This file contains two individual entities, separated by an empty line. The first is our organization, hudzilla.org. The dn lines you know already, as they define each object uniquely in the scope of the directory. The objectClass directive specifies which attributes should be allowed for this entity and which attributes should be required. In this case, we use it to set the DC to hudzilla and to set o (the name of the organization) to Hudzilla Dot Org.

The next entity defines the address book, People, in which all our people will be stored. It is defined as an organizational unit, which is what the ou stands for. An *organizational unit* really is just an arbitrary partition of your company. You might have OUs for marketing, accounting, and management, for example.

You need to customize the file to your own requirements. Specifically, change the DCs to those you specified in your slapd.conf.

Next, create and edit a new file called people.ldif. This is where you will define entries for your address book, also using LDIF. Here are the people we used in our example:

```
dn: cn=Paul Hudson,ou=People,dc=hudzilla,dc=org
objectClass: inetOrgPerson
cn: Paul Hudson
cn: Hudzilla
mail: paul@hudzilla.org
jpegPhoto:< file:///home/paul/paulhudson.jpg
sn: Hudson
```

```
dn: cn=Andrew Hudson,ou=People,dc=hudzilla,dc=org
objectClass: inetOrgPerson
cn: Andrew Hudson
cn: IzAndy
mail: andrew@hudzilla.org
sn: Hudson

dn: cn=Nick Veitch,ou=People,dc=hudzilla,dc=org
objectClass: inetOrgPerson
cn: Nick Veitch
cn: CrackAttackKing
mail: nick@hudzilla.org

sn: Veitch
```

There are three entries there, again separated by empty lines. Each person has a DN that is made up of his common name (CN), organizational unit (OU), and domain components (DCs). He also has an `objectClass` definition, `inetOrgPerson`, which gives him standard attributes such as an email address, a photograph, and a telephone number. Entities of type `inetOrgPerson` must have a CN and an SN (*surname*) so you will see them in this code.

Note also that each person has two common names: his actual name and a nickname. Not all LDAP clients support more than one CN, but there is no harm in having several as long as the main one comes first and is listed in the DN.

TIP

Having multiple key/value pairs, like multiple CNs, is one of the defining features of LDAP. In today's interconnected world, few people can be defined using a single set of attributes, because people now have home phone numbers, work phone numbers, cell phone numbers, pager numbers, plus several email addresses, and potentially even a selection of offices where they hot desk. Using multiple CNs and other attributes allows you to properly record these complex scenarios.

The `jpegPhoto` attribute for the first entity has very particular syntax. Immediately after the colon, you use an opening angle bracket (<) followed by a space and then the location of the person's picture. Because the picture is local, it is prefixed with `file://`. It is in `/home/paul/paulhudson.jpg`, so the whole URL is file:///home/paul/paulhudson.jpg.

After you have edited the file to include the people in your organization, save it and close the editor. As root, issue these two commands:

```
ldapadd -x -W -D "cn=root,dc=hudzilla,dc=org" -f base.ldif
ldapadd -x -W -D "cn=root,dc=hudzilla,dc=org" -f people.ldif
```

The `ldapadd` command is used to convert LDIF into live directory content and, most important, can be executed while your LDAP server is running. The -x parameter means to use only basic authentication, which means you need to supply the root username and password. -W means to prompt you for the password. -D lets you specify a DN for your username; and immediately after the -D, we specify the root DN as set earlier in slapd.conf. Finally, -f means to use the LDIF from the following file.

When you run them, you are prompted for the root password you set earlier. Upon entering it, you should see confirmation messages as your entries are added, like this:

```
adding new entry "cn=Paul Hudson,ou=People,dc=hudzilla,dc=org"
```

If you see an error such as ldap_bind: Can't contact LDAP server (-1), you need to start the LDAP server by typing /etc/init.d/slapd start. The most likely sources of other errors are typing errors. LDIF is a precise format, even down to its use of whitespace.

To test that the directory has been populated and that your configuration settings are correct, run this command:

```
ldapsearch -x 'objectclass=*'
```

The ldapsearch command does what you might expect: It queries the LDAP directory from the command line. Again, -x means to use simple authentication, although in this situation you do not need to provide any credentials because you are only reading from the directory. The objectclass=* search specifies to return any entry of any objectclass, so the search will return all the entries in your directory.

You can amend the search to be more specific. For example:

```
ldapsearch -x 'cn=Ni*'
```

This command returns all people with a common name that begins with *Ni*. If you get results for your searches, you are ready to configure your clients.

TIP

OpenLDAP needs specific permissions for its files. The /var/lib/ldap directory should be owned by user ldap and group ldap, with permissions 600. If you experience problems, try running chmod 600 /var/lib/ldap.

Configuring Clients

Although Ubuntu comes with a selection of email clients, there is not enough room here to cover them all. So, we discuss the two most frequently used clients: Evolution, the default, and Thunderbird. Both are powerful messaging solutions and so both work well with LDAP. Of the two, Thunderbird seems to be the easier to configure. We have had various problems with Evolution in the past in situations where Thunderbird has worked the first time.

Evolution

To configure Evolution for LDAP, click the arrow next to the New button and select Address Book. A new screen appears, the first option of which prompts you for the type of address book to create. Select On LDAP Servers.

For Name, just enter **Address book**, and for Server, enter the IP address of your LDAP server (or **127.0.0.1** if you are working on the server), as shown in Figure 22.1. Leave the port as 389, which is the default for slapd. Switch to the Details tab, and set Search Base to be the DN for your address book—for example, ou=People,dc=hudzilla,dc=org. Set Search Scope to be Sub so that Evolution will perform a comprehensive search. To finish, click Add Address Book.

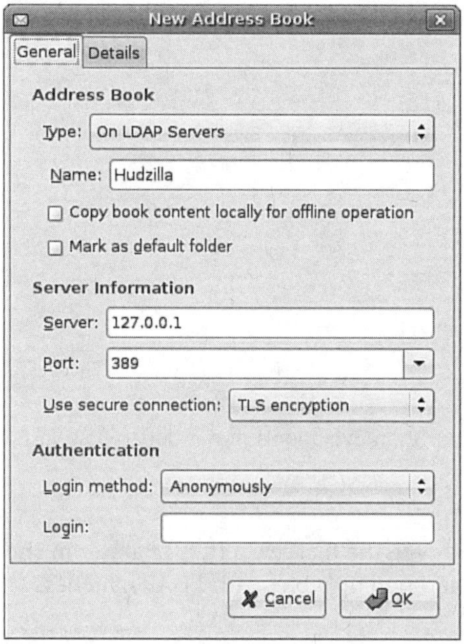

FIGURE 22.1   Configuring Evolution to use LDAP for addresses is easy for anonymous connections.

Although Evolution is now configured to use your directory, it will not use it for email address autocompletion just yet. To enable that, go to the Tools menu and click Settings.

From the options that appear on the left, click Autocompletion and select your LDAP server from the list. Click Close, and then create a new email message. If everything has worked, typing part of someone's name should pop up a box with LDAP matches.

Thunderbird

Thunderbird is a little easier to configure than Evolution and tends to work better, particularly with entries that have multiple CNs. To enable autocompletion, go to the Edit menu, click Preferences, and then select Composition from the tabs along the top.

From the Addressing subtab, check the Directory Server box and click the Edit Directories button to its right. From the dialog box that appears, click Add to add a new directory. You can give it any name you want because this is merely for display purposes. As shown in Figure 22.2, set the Hostname field to be the IP address of your LDAP server (or 127.0.0.1 if you are working on the server). Set the Base DN to be the DN for your address book (for instance, ou=People,dc=hudzilla,dc=org), and leave the port number as 389. Click OK three times to get back to the main interface.

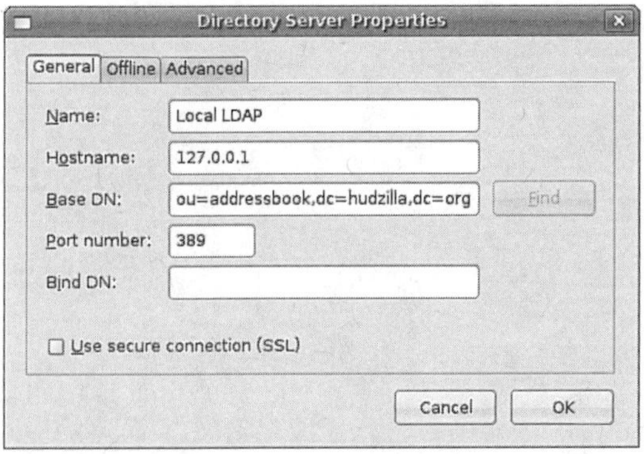

FIGURE 22.2   Thunderbird's options are buried deeper than Evolution's, but it does allow you to download the LDAP directory for offline use.

Now, click Write to create a new email message, and type the first few letters of a user in the To box. If everything has worked, Thunderbird should pop up a box with LDAP matches.

Administration

After you have your LDAP server and clients set up, they require little maintenance until something changes externally. Specifically, if someone in your directory changes jobs, changes her phone number, gets married (changing her last name [surname]), quits, or so forth, you need to be able to update your directory to reflect the change.

OpenLDAP comes with a selection of tools for manipulating directories, of which you have already met ldapadd. To add to that, you can use ldapdelete for deleting entries in your directory and `ldapmodify` for modifying entries. Both are hard to use but come with moderate amounts of documentation in their man pages.

A much smarter option is to use phpLDAPadmin, which is an LDAP administration tool that allows you to add and modify entries entirely through your web browser. You can learn more and download the product to try at http://www.phpldapadmin.com.

Reference

- ▶ http://www.openldap.org—The home page of the OpenLDAP project where you can download the latest version of the software and meet other users.

- ▶ http://www.kingsmountain.com/ldapRoadmap.shtml—A great set of links and resources across the Internet that explain various aspects of LDAP and its parent protocol, X500.

- ▶ http://ldap.perl.org/—The home of the Perl library for interacting with LDAP provides comprehensive documentation to get you started.

- ▶ http://www.ldapguru.com/—A gigantic portal for LDAP administrators around the world. From forums dedicated to LDAP to jobs specifically for LDAP admins, this site could very well be all you need.

- ▶ The definitive book on LDAP is *LDAP System Administration* (O'Reilly), ISBN: 1-56592-491-6. It is an absolute must for the bookshelf of any Linux LDAP administrator. For more general reading, try *LDAP Directories Explained* (Addison-Wesley), ISBN: 0-201-78792-X. It has a much stronger focus on the Microsoft Active Directory LDAP implementation, however.

PART V

Programming Linux

IN THIS PART

CHAPTER 23

Using Perl

*P*erl (the *Practical Extraction and Report Language*, or the *Pathologically Eclectic Rubbish Lister*, depending on who you speak to), a powerful scripting tool, enables you to manage files, create reports, edit text, and perform many other tasks when using Linux. Perl is included with Ubuntu and could be considered an integral part of the distribution because Ubuntu depends on Perl for many types of software services, logging activities, and software tools. If you do a full install from this book's disc, you will find nearly 150 software tools written in Perl installed under the /usr/bin and /usr/sbin directories.

Perl is not the easiest of programming languages to learn because it is designed for flexibility. This chapter shows how to create and use Perl scripts on your system. You will see what a Perl program looks like, how the language is structured, and where you can find modules of prewritten code to help you write your own Perl scripts. This chapter also includes several examples of Perl used to perform a few common functions on a computer system.

Using Perl with Linux

Although originally designed as a data-extraction and report-generation language, Perl appeals to many Linux system administrators because it can be used to create utilities that fill a gap between the capabilities of shell scripts and compiled C programs. Another advantage of Perl over other UNIX tools is that it can process and extract data from binary files, whereas sed and awk cannot.

> **NOTE**
>
> In Perl, "there is more than one way to do it." This is the unofficial motto of Perl, and it comes up so often that it is usually abbreviated as TIMTOWTDI.

You can use Perl at your shell's command line to execute one-line Perl programs, but most often the programs (usually ending in .pl) are run as a command. These programs generally work on any computer platform because Perl has been ported to just about every operating system. Perl is available by default when you install Ubuntu, and you will find its package files on the DVD included with this book.

Perl programs are used to support a number of Ubuntu services, such as system logging. For example, the logwatch.pl program is run every morning at 4:20 a.m. by the crond (scheduling) daemon on your system. Other Ubuntu services supported by Perl include the following:

▶ Amanda for local and network backups

▶ Fax spooling with the faxrunqd program

▶ Printing supported by Perl document filtering programs

▶ Hardware sensor monitoring setup using the sensors-detect Perl program

Perl Versions

As of this writing, the current production version of Perl is 5.8.8 (which is Perl version 5 point 8, patch level 8).

You can download the code from http://www.perl.com and build it yourself from source. You will occasionally find updated versions in APT format for Ubuntu, which can be installed by updating your system. See Chapter 7, "Managing Software," to see how to quickly get a list of available updates for Ubuntu.

You can determine what version of Perl you installed by typing **perl -v** at a shell prompt. If you are installing the latest Ubuntu distribution, you should have the latest version of Perl.

A Simple Perl Program

This section introduces a very simple sample Perl program to get you started using Perl. Although trivial for experienced Perl hackers, a short example is necessary for new users who want to learn more about Perl.

To introduce you to the absolute basics of Perl programming, Listing 23.1 illustrates a simple Perl program that prints a short message.

LISTING 23.1   A Simple Perl Program

```
#!/usr/bin/perl
print "Look at all the camels!\n";
```

Type that in and save it to a file called `trivial.pl`. Then make the file executable using the `chmod` command (see the following sidebar) and run it at the command prompt.

Command-Line Error

If you get the message `bash: trivial.pl: command not found` or `bash: ./trivial.pl: Permission denied`, you have either typed the command line incorrectly or forgotten to make `trivial.pl` executable (with the `chmod` command):

```
$ chmod +x trivial.pl
```

You can force the command to execute in the current directory as follows:

```
$ ./trivial.pl
```

Or you can use Perl to run the program like this:

```
$ perl trivial.pl
```

The sample program in the listing is a two-line Perl program. Typing in the program and running it (using Perl or making the program executable) shows how to create your first Perl program, a process duplicated by Linux users around the world every day!

NOTE

`#!` is often pronounced she-bang, which is short for sharp (the musicians name for the # character), and bang, which is another name for the exclamation point. This notation is also used in shell scripts. See Chapter 11, "Automating Tasks," for more information about writing shell scripts.

The `#!` line is technically not part of the Perl code at all. The # character indicates that the rest of the screen line is a comment. The comment is a message to the shell, telling it where it should go to find the executable to run this program. The interpreter ignores the comment line.

Exceptions to this practice include when the # character is in a quoted string and when it is being used as the delimiter in a regular expression. Comments are useful to document your scripts, like this:

```
#!/usr/bin/perl
# a simple example to print a greeting
print "hello there\n";
```

A block of code, such as what might appear inside a loop or a branch of a conditional statement, is indicated with curly braces ({}). For example, here is an infinite loop:

```
#!/usr/bin/perl
# a block of code to print a greeting forever
```

```
while (1) {
        print "hello there\n";
};
```

Perl statements are terminated with a semicolon. A Perl statement can extend over several actual screen lines because Perl is not concerned about whitespace.

The second line of the simple program prints the text enclosed in quotation marks. \n is the escape sequence for a newline character.

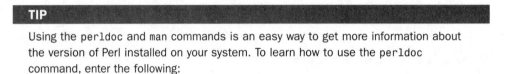

TIP

Using the perldoc and man commands is an easy way to get more information about the version of Perl installed on your system. To learn how to use the perldoc command, enter the following:

$ perldoc perldoc

To get introductory information on Perl, you can use either of these commands:

$ perldoc perl

$ man perl

For an overview or table of contents of Perl's documentation, use the perldoc command like this:

$ perldoc perltoc

The documentation is extensive and well organized. Perl includes a number of standard Linux manual pages as brief guides to its capabilities, but perhaps the best way to learn more about Perl is to read its perlfunc document, which lists all the available Perl functions and their usage. You can view this document by using the perldoc script and typing perldoc perlfunc at the command line. You can also find this document online at http://www.cpan.org/doc/manual/html/pod/perlfunc.html.

Perl Variables and Data Structures

Perl is a *weakly typed* language, meaning that it does not require that you declare a data type, such as a type of value (data) to be stored in a particular variable. C, for example, makes you declare that a particular variable is an integer, a character, a structure, or whatever the case may be. Perl variables are whatever type they need to be, and can change type when you need them to.

Perl Variable Types

Perl has three variable types: *scalars*, *arrays*, and *hashes*. A different character is used to signify each variable type.

Scalar variables are indicated with the $ *character*, as in $penguin. Scalars can be numbers or strings, and they can change type from one to the other as needed. If you treat a number like a string, it becomes a string. If you treat a string like a number, it is translated into a number if it makes sense to do so; otherwise, it usually evaluates to 0. For example, the string "76trombones" evaluates as the number 76 if used in a numeric calculation, but the string "polar bear" evaluates to 0.

Perl arrays are indicated with the @ character, as in @fish. An array is a list of values referenced by index number, starting with the first element numbered 0, just as in C and awk. Each element in the array is a scalar value. Because scalar values are indicated with the $ character, a single element in an array is also indicated with a $ character.

For example, $fish[2] refers to the third element in the @fish array. This tends to throw some people off, but is similar to arrays in C in which the first array element is 0.

Hashes are indicated with the % character, as in %employee. A *hash* is a list of name and value pairs. Individual elements in the hash are referenced by name rather than by index (unlike an array). Again, because the values are scalars, the $ character is used for individual elements.

For example, $employee{name} gives you one value from the hash. Two rather useful functions for dealing with hashes are *keys* and *values*. The keys function returns an array containing all the keys of the hash, and values returns an array of the values of the hash. Using this approach, the Perl program in Listing 23.2 displays all the values in your environment, much like typing the bash shell's env command.

LISTING 23.2   Displaying the Contents of the env Hash

```
#!/usr/bin/perl
foreach $key (keys %ENV)  {
  print "$key = $ENV{$key}\n";
}
```

Special Variables

Perl has a wide variety of special variables which usually look like punctuation— $_, $!, and $]—and are all extremely useful for shorthand code. $_ is the default variable, $! is the error message returned by the operating system, and $] is the Perl version number.

$_ is perhaps the most useful of these, and you will see that variable used often in this chapter. $_ is the Perl default variable, which is used when no argument is specified. For example, the following two statements are equivalent:

```
chomp;
chomp($_);
```

The following loops are equivalent:

```
for $cow (@cattle) {
        print "$cow says moo.\n";
}
```

```
for (@cattle)         {
        print "$_ says moo.\n";
}
```

For a complete listing of the special variables, you should see the `perlvar` document that comes with your Perl distribution (such as in the `perlvar` manual page), or you can go online to http://theoryx5.uwinnipeg.ca/CPAN/perl/pod/perlvar.html.

Operators

Perl supports a number of operators to perform various operations. There are *comparison* operators (used to compare values, as the name implies), *compound* operators (used to combine operations or multiple comparisons), *arithmetic* operators (to perform math), and special string constants.

Comparison Operators

The comparison operators used by Perl are similar to those used by C, `awk`, and the `csh` shells, and are used to specify and compare values (including strings). Most frequently, a comparison operator is used within an `if` statement or loop. Perl has comparison operators for numbers and strings. Table 23.1 shows the numeric comparison operators and their behavior.

TABLE 23.1   Numeric Comparison Operators in Perl

Operator	Meaning
==	Is equal to
<	Less than
>	Greater than
<=	Less than or equal to
>=	Greater than or equal to
<=>	Returns –1 if less than, 0 if equal, and 1 if greater than
!=	Not equal to
..	Range of >= first operand to <= second operand

Table 23.2 shows the string comparison operators and their behaviors.

TABLE 23.2   String Comparison Operators in Perl

Operator	Meaning
eq	Is equal to
lt	Less than
gt	Greater than
le	Less than or equal to
ge	Greater than or equal to
ne	Not equal to
cmp	Returns -1 if less than, 0 if equal, and 1 if greater than
=~	Matched by regular expression
!~	Not matched by regular expression

Compound Operators

Perl uses compound operators, similar to those used by C or awk, which can be used to combine other operations (such as comparisons or arithmetic) into more complex forms of logic. Table 23.3 shows the compound pattern operators and their behavior.

TABLE 23.3   Compound Pattern Operators in Perl

Operator	Meaning
&&	Logical AND
||	Logical OR
!	Logical NOT
()	Parentheses; used to group compound statements

Arithmetic Operators

Perl supports a wide variety of math operations. Table 23.4 summarizes these operators.

TABLE 23.4   Perl Arithmetic Operators

Operator	Purpose
x**y	Raises x to the y power (same as x^y)
x%y	Calculates the remainder of x/y
x+y	Adds x to y
x-y	Subtracts y from x
x*y	Multiplies x times y
x/y	Divides x by y
-y	Negates y (switches the sign of y); also known as the unary minus
++y	Increments y by 1 and uses value (prefix increment)
y++	Uses value of y and then increments by 1 (postfix increment)
—y	Decrements y by 1 and uses value (prefix decrement)
y—	Uses value of y and then decrements by 1 (postfix decrement)
x=y	Assigns value of y to x. Perl also supports operator-assignment operators (+=, -=, *=, /=, %=, **=, and others)

You can also use comparison operators (such as == or <) and compound pattern operators (&&, ¦¦, and !) in arithmetic statements. They evaluate to the value 0 for false and 1 for true.

Other Operators

Perl supports a number of operators that don't fit any of the prior categories. Table 23.5 summarizes these operators.

TABLE 23.5   Other Perl Operators

Operator	Purpose
~x	Bitwise not (changes 0 bits to 1 and 1 bits to 0)
x & y	Bitwise and
x ¦ y	Bitwise or
x ^ y	Bitwise exclusive or (XOR)
x << y	Bitwise shift left (shifts x by y bits)
x >> y	Bitwise shift right (shifts x by y bits)
x . y	Concatenate y onto x
a x b	Repeats string a for b number of times

x, y	Comma operator—evaluates x and then y
x ? y : z	Conditional expression—if x is true, y is evaluated; otherwise, z is evaluated

Except for the comma operator and conditional expression, these operators can also be used with the assignment operator, similar to the way addition (+) can be combined with assignment (=), giving +=.

Special String Constants

Perl supports string constants that have special meaning or cannot be entered from the keyboard.

Table 23.6 shows most of the constants supported by Perl.

TABLE 23.6   Perl Special String Constants

Expression	Meaning
\\	The means of including a backslash
\a	The alert or bell character
\b	Backspace
\cC	Control character (like holding the Ctrl key down and pressing the C character)
\e	Escape
\f	Formfeed
\n	Newline
\r	Carriage return
\t	Tab
\xNN	Indicates that NN is a hexadecimal number
\0NNN	Indicates that NNN is an octal (base 8) number

Conditional Statements: `if`/`else` and `unless`

Perl offers two conditional statements, `if` and `unless`, which function opposite one another. `if` enables you to execute a block of code only if certain conditions are met so that you can control the flow of logic through your program. Conversely, `unless` performs the statements when certain conditions are not met.

The following sections explain and demonstrate how to use these conditional statements when writing scripts for Linux.

if

The syntax of the Perl if/else structure is as follows:

```
if (condition) {
  statement or block of code
} elsif (condition) {
  statement or block of code
} else {
  statement or block of code
}
```

condition can be a statement that returns a true or false value.

Truth is defined in Perl in a way that might be unfamiliar to you, so be careful. Everything in Perl is true except 0 (the digit zero), "0" (the string containing the number 0), "" (the empty string), and an undefined value. Note that even the string "00" is a true value because it is not one of the four false cases.

The statement or block of code is executed if the test condition returns a true value.

For example, Listing 23.3 uses the if/else structure and shows conditional statements using the eq string comparison operator.

LISTING 23.3   if/elsif/else

```
if  ($favorite eq "chocolate") {
      print "I like chocolate too.\n";
} elsif ($favorite eq "spinach") {
      print "Oh, I don't like spinach.\n";
} else {
      print "Your favorite food is $favorite.\n";
}
```

unless

unless works just like if, only backward. unless performs a statement or block if a condition is false:

```
unless ($name eq "Rich")           {
  print "Go away, you're not allowed in here!\n";
}
```

NOTE

You can restate the preceding example in more natural language like this:

```
    print "Go away!\n" unless $name eq "Rich";
```

Looping

A *loop* is a way to repeat a program action multiple times. A very simple example is a countdown timer that performs a task (waiting for one second) 300 times before telling you that your egg is done boiling.

Looping constructs (also known as *control structures*) can be used to iterate a block of code as long as certain conditions apply, or while the code steps through (evaluates) a list of values, perhaps using that list as arguments.

Perl has four looping constructs: for, foreach, while, and until.

for

The for construct performs a *statement* (block of code) for a set of conditions defined as follows:

```
for (start condition; end condition; increment function) {
  statement(s)
}
```

The start condition is set at the beginning of the loop. Each time the loop is executed, the increment function is performed until the end condition is achieved. This looks much like the traditional for/next loop. The following code is an example of a for loop:

```
for ($i=1; $i<=10; $i++) {
    print "$i\n"
}
```

foreach

The foreach construct performs a statement block for each element in a list or array:

```
@names = ("alpha","bravo","charlie");
foreach $name (@names) {
  print "$name sounding off!\n";
}
```

The loop variable ($name in the example) is not merely set to the value of the array elements; it is aliased to that element. That means if you modify the loop variable, you're actually modifying the array. If no loop array is specified, the Perl default variable $_ may be used:

```
@names = ("alpha","bravo","charlie");
foreach (@names) {
  print "$_ sounding off!\n";

}
```

This syntax can be very convenient, but it can also lead to unreadable code. Give a thought to the poor person who'll be maintaining your code. (It will probably be you.)

> **NOTE**
>
> foreach is frequently abbreviated as for.

while

while performs a block of statements as long as a particular condition is true:

```
while ($x<10) {
    print "$x\n";
    $x++;
}
```

Remember that the condition can be anything that returns a true or false value. For example, it could be a function call:

```
while ( InvalidPassword($user, $password) )          {
        print "You've entered an invalid password. Please try again.\n";
        $password = GetPassword;
}
```

until

until is the exact opposite of the while statement. It performs a block of statements as long as a particular condition is false—or, rather, until it becomes true:

```
until (ValidPassword($user, $password))  {
  print "You've entered an invalid password. Please try again.\n";
  $password = GetPassword;
}
```

last **and** next

You can force Perl to end a loop early by using a last statement. last is similar to the C break command—the loop is exited. If you decide you need to skip the remaining contents of a loop without ending the loop itself, you can use next, which is similar to the C continue command. Unfortunately, these statements don't work with do ... while.

On the other hand, you can use redo to jump to a loop (marked by a label) or inside the loop where called:

```
$a = 100;
while (1) {
  print "start\n";
```

```
TEST: {
  if (($a = $a / 2) > 2) {
    print "$a\n";
    if (-$a < 2) {
      exit;
    }
    redo TEST;
  }
}
}
```

In this simple example, the variable $a is repeatedly manipulated and tested in an endless loop. The word *start* will only be printed once.

do ... while **and** do ... until

The while and until loops evaluate the conditional first. The behavior is changed by applying a do block before the conditional. With the do block, the condition is evaluated last, which results in the contents of the block always executing at least once (even if the condition is false). This is similar to the C language do ... while (conditional) statement.

Regular Expressions

Perl's greatest strength is in text and file manipulation, which is accomplished by using the regular expression (regex) library. Regexes, which are quite different from the wildcard-handling and filename-expansion capabilities of the shell (see Chapter 15), allow complicated pattern matching and replacement to be done efficiently and easily.

For example, the following line of code replaces every occurrence of the string bob or the string mary with fred in a line of text:

```
$string =~ s/bob|mary/fred/gi;
```

Without going into too many of the details, Table 23.7 explains what the preceding line says.

TABLE 23.7   Explanation of $string =~ s/bob|mary/fred/gi;

Element	Explanation
$string =~	Performs this pattern match on the text found in the variable called $string.
s	Substitute.
/	Begins the text to be matched.
bob¦mary	Matches the text bob or mary. You should remember that it is looking for the text mary, not the word mary; that is, it will also match the text mary in the word maryland.
/	Ends text to be matched; begins text to replace it.

TABLE 23.7   Explanation of $string =~ s/bob|mary/fred/gi;

Element	Explanation
fred	Replaces anything that was matched with the text fred.
/	Ends replace text.
g	Does this substitution globally; that is, replaces the match text wherever in the string you match it (and any number of times).
i	The search text is not case sensitive. It matches bob, Bob, or bOB.
;	Indicates the end of the line of code.

If you are interested in the details, you can get more information using the regex (7) section of the manual.

Although replacing one string with another might seem a rather trivial task, the code required to do the same thing in another language (for example, C) is rather daunting unless supported by additional subroutines from external libraries.

Access to the Shell

Perl can perform for you any process you might ordinarily perform by typing commands to the shell through the \\ syntax. For example, the code in Listing 23.4 prints a directory listing.

LISTING 23.4   Using Backticks to Access the Shell

```
$curr_dir = 'pwd';
@listing = 'ls -al';
print "Listing for $curr_dir\n";
foreach $file (@listing) {
    print "$file";
}
```

> **NOTE**
>
> The \\ notation uses the backtick found above the Tab key (on most keyboards), not the single quotation mark.

You can also use the Shell module to access the shell. Shell is one of the standard modules that comes with Perl; it allows creation and use of a shell-like command line. Look at the following code for an example:

```
use Shell qw(cp);
```

```
cp ("/home/httpd/logs/access.log", "/tmp/httpd.log");
```

This code almost looks like it is importing the command-line functions directly into Perl. Although that is not really happening, you can pretend that the code is similar to a command line and use this approach in your Perl programs.

A third method of accessing the shell is via the `system` function call:

```
$rc = 0xffff & system('cp /home/httpd/logs/access.log /tmp/httpd.log');
if ($rc == 0) {
  print "system cp succeeded \n";
} else {
  print "system cp failed $rc\n";
}
```

The call can also be used with the or die clause:

```
system('cp /home/httpd/logs/access.log /tmp/httpd.log') == 0
  or die "system cp failed: $?"
```

However, you can't capture the output of a command executed through the `system` function.

Modules and CPAN

A great strength of the Perl community (and the Linux community) is the fact that it is an open-source community. This community support is expressed for Perl via the *Comprehensive Perl Archive Network (CPAN)*, which is a network of mirrors of a repository of Perl code.

Most of CPAN is made up of *modules*, which are reusable chunks of code that do useful things, similar to software libraries containing functions for C programmers. These modules help speed development when building Perl programs and free Perl hackers from repeatedly reinventing the wheel when building a bicycle.

Perl comes with a set of standard modules installed. Those modules should contain much of the functionality that you will initially need with Perl. If you need to use a module not installed with Ubuntu, use the CPAN module (which is one of the standard modules) to download and install other modules onto your system. At http://www.perl.com/CPAN, you will find the CPAN Multiplex Dispatcher, which will attempt to direct you to the CPAN site closest to you.

Typing the following command will put you into an interactive shell that gives you access to CPAN. You can type `help` at the prompt to get more information on how to use the CPAN program:

```
$ perl -MCPAN -e shell
```

After installing a module from CPAN (or writing one of your own), you can load that module into memory where you can use it with the use function:

```
use Time::CTime;
```

use looks in the directories listed in the variable @INC for the module. In this example, use looks for a directory called Time, which contains a file called CTime.pm, which in turn is assumed to contain a package called Time::CTime. The distribution of each module should contain documentation on using that module.

For a list of all the standard Perl modules (those that come with Perl when you install it), see perlmodlib in the Perl documentation. You can read this document by typing **perldoc perlmodlib** at the command prompt.

Code Examples

The following sections contain a few examples of things you might want to do with Perl.

Sending Mail

You can get Perl to send email in several ways. One method that you see frequently is opening a pipe to the sendmail command and sending data to it (shown in Listing 23.5). Another method is using the Mail::Sendmail module (available through CPAN), which uses socket connections directly to send mail (as shown in Listing 23.6). The latter method is faster because it does not have to launch an external process. Note that sendmail must be running on your system for the Perl program in Listing 23.5 to work.

LISTING 23.5   Sending Mail Using Sendmail

```
#!/usr/bin/perl
open (MAIL, "| /usr/sbin/sendmail -t"); # Use -t to protect from users
print MAIL <<EndMail;
To: dpitts\
From: rbowen\
Subject: Email notification

David,
 Sending email from Perl is easy!
Rich
.

EndMail
close MAIL;
```

> **NOTE**
>
> Note that the @ sign in the email addresses must be escaped so that Perl does not try to evaluate an array of that name. That is, dpitts@mk.net will cause a problem, so you need to use dpitts\<indexterm startref="iddle2799" class="endofrange" signifi-cance="normal"/>:}]
>
> The syntax used to print the mail message is called a *here document*. The syntax is as follows:
>
>   print <<EndText;
>
>   .....
>
>   EndText
>
> The EndText value must be identical at the beginning and at the end of the block, including any whitespace.

LISTING 23.6   Sending Mail Using the `Mail::Sendmail` *Module*

```
#!/usr/bin/perl
use Mail::Sendmail;
%mail = ('To' => 'dpitts@mk.net',
  'From' => 'rbowen@mk.net'
  'Subject' => 'Email notification',
  'Message' => 'Sending email from Perl is easy!',
);
sendmail(%mail);
```

Perl ignores the comma after the last element in the hash. It is convenient to leave it there; if you want to add items to the hash, you don't need to add the comma. This is purely a style decision.

Using Perl to Install a CPAN Module

You can use Perl to interactively download and install a Perl module from the CPAN archives by using the -M and -e commands. Start the process by using a Perl like this:

```
# perl -MCPAN -e shell
```

After you press Enter, you will see some introductory information and be asked to choose an initial automatic or manual configuration, which is required before any download or install takes place. Type no and press Enter to have Perl automatically configure for the download and install process; or, if desired, simply press Enter to manually configure for downloading and installation. If you use manual configuration, you must answer a series of questions regarding paths, caching, terminal settings, program locations, and so on. Settings are saved in a directory named .cpan in current directory.

When finished, you will see the CPAN prompt:

```
cpan>
```

To have Perl examine your system and then download and install a large number of modules, use the `install` keyword, specify `Bundle` at the prompt, and then press Enter like this:

```
cpan> install Bundle::CPAN
```

To download a desired module (using the example in Listing 23.6), use the `get` keyword like so:

```
cpan> get Mail::Sendmail
```

The source for the module will be downloaded into the `.cpan` directory. You can then build and install the module using the `install` keyword, like this:

```
cpan> install Mail::Sendmail
```

The entire process of retrieving, building, and installing a module can also be accomplished at the command line by using Perl's -e option like this:

```
# perl -MCPAN  -e "install Mail::Sendmail"
```

Note also that the @ sign did not need to be escaped within single quotation marks (' '). Perl does not *interpolate* (evaluate variables) within single quotation marks, but does within double quotation marks and here strings (similar to << shell operations).

Purging Logs

Many programs maintain some variety of logs. Often, much of the information in the logs is redundant or just useless. The program shown in Listing 23.7 removes all lines from a file that contain a particular word or phrase, so lines that you know are not important can be purged. For example, you might want to remove all the lines in the Apache error log that originate with your test client machine because you know those error messages were produced during testing.

LISTING 23.7   Purging Log Files

```perl
#!/usr/bin/perl
# Be careful using this program!
# This will remove all lines that contain a given word
# Usage:  remove <word> <file>
$word=@ARGV[0];
$file=@ARGV[1];
if ($file)  {
  # Open file for reading
  open (FILE, "$file") or die "Could not open file: $!";      @lines=<FILE>;
  close FILE;
  # Open file for writing
  open (FILE, ">$file") or die "Could not open file for writing: $!";
  for (@lines)  {
    print FILE unless /$word/;
```

```
  } # End for
  close FILE;
} else {
  print "Usage:  remove <word> <file>\n";
}  #  End if...else
```

The code uses a few idiomatic Perl expressions to keep it brief. It reads the file into an array using the <FILE> notation; it then writes the lines back out to the file unless they match the pattern given on the command line.

The die function kills program operation and displays an error message if the open statements fail. $! in the error message, as mentioned in the section on special variables, is the error message returned by the operating system. It will likely be something like 'file not found' or 'permission denied'.

Posting to Usenet

If some portion of your job requires periodic postings to Usenet—a FAQ listing, for example—the following Perl program can automate the process for you. In the sample code, the posted text is read in from a text file, but your input can come from anywhere.

The program shown in Listing 23.8 uses the Net::NNTP module, which is a standard part of the Perl distribution. You can find more documentation on the Net::NNTP module by typing 'perldoc Net::NNTP' at the command line.

LISTING 23.8   Posting an Article to Usenet

```perl
#!/usr/bin/perl
# load the post data into @post
open (POST, "post.file");
@post = <POST>;
close POST;
# import the NNTP module
use Net::NNTP;
$NNTPhost = 'news';
# attempt to connect to the remote host;
# print an error message on failure
$nntp = Net::NNTP->new($NNTPhost)
  or die "Cannot contact $NNTPhost: $!";
# $nntp->debug(1);
$nntp->post()
  or die "Could not post article: $!";
# send the header of the post
$nntp->datasend("Newsgroups: news.announce\n");
$nntp->datasend("Subject: FAQ - Frequently Asked Questions\n");
$nntp->datasend("From: ADMIN <root\
$nntp->datasend("\n\n");
```

```
# for each line in the @post array, send it
for (@post)     {
  $nntp->datasend($_);
} #  End for
$nntp->quit;
```

One-Liners

One medium in which Perl excels is the one-liner. Folks go to great lengths to reduce tasks to one line of Perl code. Perl has the rather undeserved reputation of being unreadable. The fact is that you can write unreadable code in any language. Perl allows for more than one way to do something, and this leads rather naturally to people trying to find the most arcane way to do things.

Named for Randal Schwartz, a *Schwartzian Transform* is a way of sorting an array by something that is not obvious. The sort function sorts arrays alphabetically; that is pretty obvious. What if you want to sort an array of strings alphabetically by the third word? Perhaps you want something more useful, such as sorting a list of files by file size? A Schwartzian Transform creates a new list that contains the information that you want to sort by, referencing the first list. You then sort the new list and use it to figure out the order that the first list should be in. Here's a simple example that sorts a list of strings by length:

```
@sorted_by_length =
  map { $_ => [0] }             # Extract original list
  sort { $a=>[1] <=> $b=>[1] }  # Sort by the transformed value
  map { [$_, length($_)] }      # Map to a list of element lengths
  @list;
```

Because each operator acts on the thing immediately to the right of it, it helps to read this from right to left (or bottom to top, the way it is written here).

The first thing that acts on the list is the map operator. It transforms the list into a hash in which the keys are the list elements and the values are the lengths of each element. This is where you put in your code that does the transformation by which you want to sort.

The next operator is the sort function, which sorts the list by the values.

Finally, the hash is transformed back into an array by extracting its keys. The array is now in the desired order.

Command-Line Processing

Perl is great at parsing the output of various programs. This is a task for which many people use tools such as awk and sed. Perl gives you a larger vocabulary for performing these tasks. The following example is very simple, but illustrates how you might use Perl to chop up some output and do something with it. In the example, Perl is used to list only those files that are larger than 10KB:

```
$ ls -la ¦ perl -nae 'print "$F[8] is $F[4]\n" if $F[4] > 10000;'
```

The -n switch indicates that I want the Perl code run for each line of the output. The -a switch automatically splits the output into the @F array. The -e switch indicates that the Perl code is going to follow on the command line.

Related Ubuntu and Linux Commands

You will use these commands and tools when using Perl with Linux:

▶ a2p—A filter used to translate awk scripts into Perl

▶ find2perl—A utility used to create Perl code from command lines using the find command

▶ pcregrep—A utility used to search data using Perl-compatible regular expressions

▶ perlcc—A compiler for Perl programs

▶ perldoc—A Perl utility used to read Perl documentation

▶ s2p—A filter used to translate sed scripts into Perl

▶ vi—The vi (actually vim) text editor

Reference

The first place to look is in the Perl documentation and Linux man pages.

Perl, all of its documentation, and millions of lines of Perl programs are all available free on the Internet. A number of Usenet newsgroups are also devoted to Perl, as are shelves of books and a quarterly journal.

Books

Although your local bookstore might have dozens of titles on Perl, the following are some of the more highly recommended of these. You might also look at the *Camel Critiques* (Tom Christiansen; http://language.perl.com/critiques/index.html) for reviews of other available Perl books.

▶ *Advanced Perl Programming*, by Sriram Srinivasan, O'Reilly & Associates

▶ *Sams Teach Yourself Perl in 21 Days,* Second Edition, by Laura Lemay, Sams Publishing

▶ *Sams Teach Yourself Perl in 24 Hours,* Second Edition, by Clinton Pierce, Sams Publishing

▶ *Learning Perl, Third Edition*, by Randal L. Schwartz, Tom Phoenix, O'Reilly & Associates

▶ *Programming Perl,* Third Edition, by Larry Wall, Tom Christiansen, and Jon Orwant, O'Reilly & Associates

▶ *Effective Perl Programming: Writing Better Programs with Perl*, by Joseph Hall, Addison-Wesley Publishing Company

▶ *CGI Programming with Perl*, Second Edition, by Gunther Birznieks, Scott Guelich, Shishir Gundavaram, O'Reilly & Associates

▶ *Mastering Regular Expressions*, by Jeffrey Friedl, O'Reilly & Associates

Usenet

Check out the following on Usenet:

▶ comp.lang.perl.misc—Discusses various aspects of the Perl programming language. Make sure that your questions are Perl specific, not generic CGI programming questions. The regulars tend to flame folks who don't know the difference.

▶ comp.infosystems.www.authoring.cgi—Discusses authoring of CGI programs, so much of the discussion is Perl specific. Make sure that your questions are related to CGI programming, not just Perl. The regulars are very particular about staying on topic.

WWW

Check these sites on the World Wide Web:

▶ http://www.perl.com—Tom Christiansen maintains the Perl language home page. This is the place to find all sorts of information about Perl, from its history and culture to helpful tips. This is also the place to download the Perl interpreter for your system.

▶ http://www.perl.com/CPAN—This is part of the site just mentioned, but it merits its own mention. CPAN (Comprehensive Perl Archive Network) is the place for you to find modules and programs in Perl. If you write something in Perl that you think is particularly useful, you can make it available to the Perl community here.

▶ http://www.perl.com/pub/q/FAQs—Frequently Asked Questions index of common Perl queries; this site offers a handy way to quickly search for answers about Perl.

▶ http://learn.perl.org—One of the best places to start learning Perl online. If you master Perl, go to http://jobs.perl.org.

▶ http://www.hwg.org—The HTML Writers Guild is a not-for-profit organization dedicated to assisting web developers. One of its services is a plethora of mailing lists. The hwg-servers mailing list and the hwg-languages mailing list are great places for asking Perl-related questions.

▶ http://www.pm.org—The Perl Mongers are local Perl users groups. There might be one in your area. The Perl advocacy site is http://www.perl.org.

▶ http://www.tpj.com—*The Perl Journal* is "a reader-supported monthly e-zine" devoted to the Perl programming language. TPJ is always full of excellent, amusing, and informative articles, and is an invaluable resource to both new and experienced Perl programmers.

▶ http://www-106.ibm.com/developerworks/linux/library/l-p101—A short tutorial about one-line Perl scripts and code.

Other

Other valuable resources not falling into any of the preceding categories are Perl-related Internet Relay Chat channels. You can usually find several channels available on an IRC server. However, the questions, discussions, and focus of similarly named channels will vary from server to server.

For example, a #perlhelp channel is usually for general questions about installing, using, and learning about Perl. A #perl channel is generally for more advanced questions, but on some servers beginner questions might be welcomed. You might also find some helpful answers on #cgi and #html channels. Browse to http://perl-begin.berlios.de/irc for a list of servers.

23

Working with Python

As PHP has come to dominate the world of web scripting, Python is increasingly dominating the domain of command-line scripting. Python's precise and clean syntax makes it one of the easiest languages to learn, and it allows programmers to code more quickly and spend less time maintaining their code. Although PHP is fundamentally similar to Java and Perl, Python is closer to C and Modula-3, and so it might look unfamiliar at first.

Most of the other languages have a group of developers at their cores, but Python has Guido van Rossum—creator, father, and *Benevolent Dictator For Life (BDFL)*. Although Guido spends less time working on Python now, he still essentially has the right of veto changes to the language, which has enabled it to remain consistent over the many years of its development. The end result is that, in Guido's own words, "Even if you are in fact clueless about language design, you can tell that Python is a very simple language."

The following pages constitute a "quick-start" tutorial to Python designed to give you all the information you need to put together basic scripts and to point you toward resources that can take you further.

Python on Linux

Ubuntu comes with Python installed by default, as do many other versions of Linux and UNIX—even Mac OS X comes with Python preinstalled. Part of this is due to convenience because it is such a popular scripting language and it saves having to install it later if the user wants to run a script.

The Python binary is installed into /usr/bin/python; if you run that, you enter the Python interactive interpreter where you can type commands and have them executed immediately. Although PHP also has an interactive mode (use php -a to activate it), it is neither as powerful nor as flexible as Python's.

As with Perl, PHP, and other scripting languages, you can also execute Python scripts by adding a shebang line (#!) to the start of your scripts that point to /usr/bin/python and then setting the file to be executable.

The third and final way to run Python scripts is through mod_python, which you can install through synaptic.

For the purposes of this introduction, we use the interactive Python interpreter because it provides immediate feedback on commands as you type them.

Getting Interactive

We will be using the interactive interpreter for this chapter, so it is essential that you are comfortable using it. To get started, open a terminal and run the command python. You should see this:

```
[paul@caitlin ~]$ python
Python 2.4.3 (#2, Apr 27 2006, 14:43:58)
[GCC 4.0.3 (Ubuntu 4.0.3-1ubuntu5)] on linux2
Type "help", "copyright", "credits" or "license" for more information.
>>>
```

The >>> is where you type your input, and you can set and get a variable like this:

```
>>> python = 'great'
>>> python
'great'
>>>
```

On line one, the variable python is set to the text great, and on line two that value is read back from the variable simply by typing the name of the variable you want to read. Line three shows Python printing the variable; on line four you are back at the prompt to type more commands. Python remembers all the variables you use while in the interactive interpreter, which means you can set a variable to be the value of another variable.

When you are done, press Ctrl+D to exit. At this point, all your variables and commands are forgotten by the interpreter, which is why complex Python programs are always saved in scripts!

The Basics of Python

Python is a language wholly unlike most others, and yet it is so logical that most people can pick it up quickly. You have already seen how easily you can assign strings, but in Python nearly everything is that easy—as long as you remember the syntax!

Numbers

The way Python handles numbers is more precise than some other languages. It has all the normal operators—such as + for addition, - for subtraction, / for division, and * for multiplication—but it adds % for modulus (division remainder), ** for raise to the power, and // for floor division. It is also specific about which type of number is being used, as this example shows:

```
>>> a = 5
>>> b = 10
>>> a * b
50
>>> a / b
0
>>> b = 10.0
>>> a / b
0.5
>>> a // b
0.0
```

The first division returns 0 because both a and b are integers (whole numbers), so Python calculates the division as an integer, giving 0. By converting b to 10.0, Python considers it to be a floating-point number, and so the division is now calculated as a floating-point value, giving 0.5. Even with b being floating point, using //—floor division—rounds it down.

Using **, you can easily see how Python works with integers:

```
>>> 2 ** 30
1073741824
>>> 2 ** 31
2147483648L
```

The first statement raises 2 to the power of 30 (that is, $2 \times; 2 \times; 2 \times; 2 \times; 2 \times; ...$), and the second raises 2 to the power of 31. Notice how the second number has a capital *L* on the end of it—this is Python telling you that it is a long integer. The difference between long integers and normal integers is slight but important: Normal integers can be calculated using simple instructions on the CPU, whereas long integers—because they can be as big as you need them to be—need to be calculated in software and therefore are slower.

24

When specifying big numbers, you need not put the *L* at the end—Python figures it out for you. Furthermore, if a number starts off as a normal number and then exceeds its boundaries, Python automatically converts it to a long integer. The same is not true the other way around: If you have a long integer and then divide it by another number so that it could be stored as a normal integer, it remains a long integer:

```
>>> num = 999999999999999999999999999999999L
>>> num = num / 1000000000000000000000000000000
>>> num
999L
```

You can convert between number types using typecasting, like this:

```
>>> num = 10
>>> int(num)
10
>>> float(num)
10.0
>>> long(num)
10L
>>> floatnum = 10.0
>>> int(floatnum)
10
>>> float(floatnum)
10.0
>>> long(floatnum)
10L
```

You need not worry whether you are using integers or long integers; Python handles it all for you, so you can concentrate on getting the code right.

More on Strings

Python stores strings as an immutable sequence of characters—a jargon-filled way of saying that "it is a collection of characters that, once set, cannot be changed without creating a new string." Sequences are important in Python. There are three primary types, of which strings are one, and they share some properties. Mutability makes much sense when you learn about lists in the next section.

As you saw in the previous example, you can assign a value to strings in Python with just an equal sign, like this:

```
>>> mystring = 'hello';
>>> myotherstring = "goodbye";
>>> mystring
'hello'
>>> myotherstring;
'goodbye'
```

```
>>> test = "Are you really Bill O'Reilly?"
>>> test
"Are you really Bill O'Reilly?"
```

The first example encapsulates the string in single quotation marks, and the second and third in double quotation marks. However, printing the first and second strings show them both in single quotation marks because Python does not distinguish between the two. The third example is the exception—it uses double quotation marks because the string itself contains a single quotation mark. Here, Python prints the string with double quotation marks because it knows it contains the single quotation mark.

Because the characters in a string are stored in sequence, you can index into them by specifying the character you are interested in. Like most other languages, these indexes are zero based, which means you need to ask for character 0 to get the first letter in a string. For example:

```
>>> string = "This is a test string"
>>> string
'This is a test string'
>>> string[0]
'T'
>>> string [0], string[3], string [20]
('T', 's', 'g')
```

The last line shows how, with commas, you can ask for several indexes at the same time. You could print the entire first word using this:

```
>>> string[0], string[1], string[2], string[3]
('T', 'h', 'i', 's')
```

However, for that purpose you can use a different concept: slicing. A *slice* of a sequence draws a selection of indexes. For example, you can pull out the first word like this:

```
>>> string[0:4]
'This'
```

The syntax there means "take everything from position 0 (including 0) and end at position 4 (excluding it)." So, [0:4] copies the items at indexes 0, 1, 2, and 3. You can omit either side of the indexes, and it will copy either from the start or to the end:

```
>>> string [:4]
'This'
>>> string [5:]
'is a test string'
>>> string [11:]
'est string'
```

You can also omit both numbers, and it will give you the entire sequence:

```
>>> string [:]
'This is a test string'
```

Later you will learn precisely why you would want to do that, but for now there are a number of other string intrinsics that will make your life easier. For example, you can use the + and * operators to concatenate (join) and repeat strings, like this:

```
>>> mystring = "Python"
>>> mystring * 4
'PythonPythonPythonPython'
>>> mystring = mystring + " rocks! "
>>> mystring * 2
'Python rocks! Python rocks! '
```

In addition to working with operators, Python strings come with a selection of built-in methods. You can change the case of the letters with `capitalize()` (uppercases the first letter and lowercases the rest), `lower()` (lowercases them all), `title()` (uppercases the first letter in each word), and `upper()` (uppercases them all). You can also check whether strings match certain cases with `islower()`, `istitle()`, and `isupper()`; that also extends to `isalnum()` (returns `true` if the string is letters and numbers only) and `isdigit()` (returns `true` if the string is all numbers).

This example demonstrates some of these in action:

```
>>> string
'This is a test string'
>>> string.upper()
'THIS IS A TEST STRING'
>>> string.lower()
'this is a test string'
>>> string.isalnum()
False
>>> string = string.title()
>>> string
'This Is A Test String'
```

Why did `isalnum()` return `false`—our string contains only alphanumeric characters, doesn't it? Well, no. There are spaces in there, which is what is causing the problem. More important, we were calling `upper()` and `lower()` and they were not changing the contents of the string—they just returned the new value. So, to change our string from `This is a test string` to `This Is A Test String`, we actually have to assign it back to the string variable.

Lists

Python's built-in list data type is a sequence, like strings. However, they are mutable, which means they can be changed. Lists are like arrays in that they hold a selection of elements in a given order. You can cycle through them, index into them, and slice them:

```
>>> mylist = ["python", "perl", "php"]
>>> mylist
['python', 'perl', 'php']
>>> mylist + ["java"]
['python', 'perl', 'php', 'java']
>>> mylist * 2
['python', 'perl', 'php', 'python', 'perl', 'php']
>>> mylist[1]
'perl'
>>> mylist[1] = "c++"
>>> mylist[1]
'c++'
>>> mylist[1:3]
['c++', 'php']
```

The brackets notation is important: You cannot use parentheses, ((and)) or braces ({ and }) for lists. Using + for lists is different from using + for numbers. Python detects you are working with a list and appends one list to another. This is known as *operator overloading*, and it is one of the reasons Python is so flexible.

Lists can be *nested*, which means you can put a list inside a list. However, this is where mutability starts to matter, and so this might sound complicated! If you recall, the definition of an immutable string sequence is that it is a collection of characters that, once set, cannot be changed without creating a new string. Lists are mutable as opposed to immutable, which means you can change your list without creating a new list.

This becomes important because Python, by default, copies only a reference to a variable rather than the full variable. For example:

```
>>> list1 = [1, 2, 3]
>>> list2 = [4, list1, 6]
>>> list1
[1, 2, 3]
>>> list2
[4, [1, 2, 3], 6]
```

Here we have a nested list. list2 contains 4, then list1, then 6. When you print the value of list2, you can see it also contains list1. Now, proceeding on from that:

```
>>> list1[1] = "Flake"
```

```
>>> list2
[4, [1, 'Flake', 3], 6]
```

In line one, we set the second element in list1 (remember, sequences are zero based!) to be Flake rather than 2; then we print the contents of list2. As you can see, when list1 changed, list2 was updated, too. The reason for this is that list2 stores a reference to list1 as opposed to a copy of list1; they share the same value.

We can show that this works both ways by indexing twice into list2, like this:

```
>>> list2[1][1] = "Caramello"
>>> list1
[1, 'Caramello', 3]
```

The first line says, "Get the second element in list2 (list1) and the second element of that list, and set it to be 'Caramello'." Then list1's value is printed, and you can see it has changed. This is the essence of mutability: We are changing our list without creating a new list. On the other hand, editing a string creates a new string, leaving the old one unaltered. For example:

```
>>> mystring = "hello"
>>> list3 = [1, mystring, 3]
>>> list3
[1, 'hello', 3]
>>> mystring = "world"
>>> list3
[1, 'hello', 3]
```

Of course, this raises the question of how you copy without references when references are the default. The answer, for lists, is that you use the [:] slice, which we looked at earlier. This slices from the first element to the last, inclusive, essentially copying it without references. Here is how that looks:

```
>>> list4 = ["a", "b", "c"]
>>> list5 = list4[:]
>>> list4 = list4 + ["d"]
>>> list5
['a', 'b', 'c']
>>> list4
['a', 'b', 'c', 'd']
```

Lists have their own collections of built-in methods, such as sort(), append(), and pop(). The latter two add and remove single elements from the end of the list, with pop() also returning the removed element. For example:

```
>>> list5 = ["nick", "paul", "julian", "graham"]
>>> list5.sort()
>>> list5
```

```
['graham', 'julian', 'nick', 'paul']
>>> list5.pop()
'paul'
>>> list5
['graham', 'julian', 'nick']
>>> list5.append("Rebecca")
```

In addition, one interesting method of strings returns a list: split(). This takes a character to split by and then gives you a list in which each element is a chunk from the string. For example:

```
>>> string = "This is a test string";
>>> string.split(" ")
['This', 'is', 'a', 'test', 'string']
```

Lists are used extensively in Python, although this is slowly changing as the language matures.

Dictionaries

Unlike lists, *dictionaries* are collections with no fixed order. Instead, they have a *key* (the name of the element) and a *value* (the content of the element), and Python places them wherever it needs to for maximum performance. When defining dictionaries, you need to use braces ({ }) and colons (:). You start with an opening brace and then give each element a key and a value, separated by a colon, like this:

```
>>> mydict = { "perl" : "a language", "php" : "another language" }
>>> mydict
{'php': 'another language', 'perl': 'a language'}
```

This example has two elements, with keys perl and php. However, when the dictionary is printed, we find that php comes before perl—Python hasn't respected the order in which we entered them. We can index into a dictionary using the normal code:

```
>>> mydict["perl"]
'a language'
```

However, because a dictionary has no fixed sequence, we cannot take a slice, or index by position.

Like lists, dictionaries are mutable and can also be nested; however, unlike lists, you cannot merge two dictionaries by using +. This is because dictionary elements are located using the key. Therefore, having two elements with the same key would cause a clash. Instead, you should use the update() method, which merges two arrays by overwriting clashing keys.

You can also use the keys() method to return a list of all the keys in a dictionary.

Conditionals and Looping

So far, we have just been looking at data types, which should show you how powerful Python's data types are. However, you simply cannot write complex programs without conditional statements and loops.

Python has most of the standard conditional checks, such as, (greater than), <= (less than or equal to), and == (equal), but it also adds some new ones, such as in. For example, we can use in to check whether a string or a list contains a given character/element:

```
>>> mystring = "J Random Hacker"
>>> "r" in mystring
True
>>> "Hacker" in mystring
True
>>> "hacker" in mystring
False
```

The last example demonstrates how in is case sensitive. We can use the operator for lists, too:

```
>>> mylist = ["soldier", "sailor", "tinker", "spy"]
>>> "tailor" in mylist
False
```

Other comparisons on these complex data types are done item by item:

```
>>> list1 = ["alpha", "beta", "gamma"]
>>> list2 = ["alpha", "beta", "delta"]
>>> list1 > list2
True
```

list1's first element (alpha) is compared against list2's first element (alpha) and, because they are equal, the next element is checked. That is equal also, so the third element is checked, which is different. The *g* in gamma comes after the *d* in delta in the alphabet, so gamma is considered greater than delta and list1 is considered greater than list2.

Loops come in two types, and both are equally flexible. For example, the for loop can iterate through letters in a string or elements in a list:

```
>>> string = "Hello, Python!"
>>> for s in string: print s,
...
H e l l o ,   P y t h o n !
```

The for loop takes each letter in string and assigns it to s. This then is printed to the screen using the print command, but note the comma at the end; this tells Python not to insert a line break after each letter. The "..." is there because Python allows you to enter more code in the loop; you need to press Enter again here to have the loop execute.

The exact same construct can be used for lists:

```
>>> mylist = ["andi", "rasmus", "zeev"]
>>> for p in mylist: print p
...
andi
rasmus
zeev
```

Without the comma after the print statement, each item is printed on its own line.

The other loop type is the while loop, and it looks similar:

```
>> while 1: print "This will loop forever!"
...
This will loop forever!
This will loop forever!
This will loop forever!
This will loop forever!
This will loop forever!
(etc)
Traceback (most recent call last):
  File "<stdin>", line 1, in ?
KeyboardInterrupt
>>>
```

That is an infinite loop (it will carry on printing that text forever), so you need to press Ctrl+C to interrupt it and regain control.

If you want to use multiline loops, you need to get ready to use your Tab key: Python handles loop blocks by recording the level of indent used. Some people find this odious; others admire it for forcing clean coding on users. Most of us, though, just get on with programming!

For example:

```
>>> i = 0
>>> while i < 3:
...     j = 0
...     while j < 3:
...             print "Pos: " + str(i) + "," + str(j) + ")"
...             j += 1
...     i += 1
...
Pos: (0,0)
Pos: (0,1)
Pos: (0,2)
Pos: (1,0)
```

```
Pos: (1,1)
Pos: (1,2)
Pos: (2,0)
Pos: (2,1)
Pos: (2,2)
```

You can control loops using the break and continue keywords. break exits the loop and continues processing immediately afterward, and continue jumps to the next loop iteration.

Functions

Other languages—such as PHP—read and process an entire file before executing it, which means you can call a function before it is defined because the compiler reads the definition of the function before it tries to call it. Python is different: If the function definition has not been reached by the time you try to call it, you get an error. The reason behind this behavior is that Python actually creates an object for your function, and that in turns means two things. First, you can define the same function several times in a script and have the script pick the right one at runtime. Second, you can assign the function to another name just by using =.

Function definition starts with def, then the function name, then parentheses and a list of parameters, and then a colon. The contents of a function need to be indented at least one level beyond the definition. So, using function assignment and dynamic declaration, you can write a script that prints the right greeting in a roundabout manner:

```
>>> def hello_english(Name):
...     print "Hello, " + Name + "!"
...
>>> def hello_hungarian(Name):
...     print "Szia, " + Name + "!"
...
>>> hello = hello_hungarian
>>> hello("Paul")
Szia, Paul!
>>> hello = hello_english
>>> hello("Paul")
```

Notice that function definitions include no type information. Functions are typeless, like we said. The upside of this is that you can write one function to do several things:

```
>>> def concat(First, Second):
...     return First + Second
...
>>> concat(["python"], ["perl"])
['python', 'perl']
>>> concat("Hello, ", "world!")
```

```
'Hello, world!'
```

That demonstrates how the `return` statement sends a value back to the caller, but also how a function can do one thing with lists and another thing with strings. The magic here is being accomplished by the objects. We write a function that tells two objects to add themselves together, and the objects intrinsically know how to do that. If they don't—if, perhaps, the user passes in a string and an integer—Python catches the error for us. However, it is this hands-off, "let the objects sort themselves out" attitude that makes functions so flexible. Our `concat()` function could conceivably concatenate strings, lists, or *zonks*—a data type someone created herself that allows adding. The point is that we do not limit what our function can do—tacky as it might sound, the only limit is your imagination!

Object Orientation

After having read this far, you should not be surprised to hear that Python's object orientation is flexible and likely to surprise you if you have been using C-like languages for several years.

The best way to learn Python `object-oriented programming (OOP)` is to just do it. So, here is a basic script that defines a class, creates an object of that class, and calls a function:

```
class dog(object):
    def bark(self):
        print "Woof!"

fluffy = dog()
fluffy.bark()
```

Defining a class starts, predictably, with the `class` keyword followed by the name of the class you are defining and a colon. The contents of that class need to be indented one level so that Python knows where it stops. Note that the `object` inside parentheses is there for object inheritance, which is discussed later. For now, the least you need to know is that if your new class is not based on an existing class, you should put `object` inside parentheses as shown in the previous code.

Functions inside classes work in much the same way as normal functions do (although they are usually called *methods*), with the main difference being that they should all take at least one parameter, usually called `self`. This parameter is filled with the name of the object the function was called on, and you need to use it explicitly.

Creating an instance of a class is done by assignment. You do not need any `new` keyword, as in some other languages—you just provide empty parentheses. Calling a function of that object is done using a period, the name of the class to call, with any parameters being passed inside parentheses.

Class and Object Variables

Each object has its own set of functions and variables, and you can manipulate those variables independently of objects of the same type. In addition, some class variables are set to a default value for all classes and can be manipulated globally.

This script demonstrates two objects of the dog class being created, each with its own name:

```
class dog(object):
    name = "Lassie"
    def bark(self):
        print self.name + " says 'Woof!'"
    def setName(self, name):
        self.name = name
fluffy = dog()
fluffy.bark()
poppy = dog()
poppy.setName("Poppy")
poppy.bark()
```

That outputs the following:

```
Lassie says 'Woof!'
Poppy says 'Woof!'
```

There, each dog starts with the name Lassie, but it gets customized. Keep in mind that Python assigns by reference by default, meaning each object has a reference to the class's name variable, and as we assign that with the setName() method, that reference is lost. What this means is that any references we do not change can be manipulated globally. Thus, if we change a class's variable, it also changes in all instances of that class that have not set their own value for that variable. For example:

```
class dog(object):
    name = "Lassie"
    color = "brown"
fluffy = dog()
poppy = dog()
print fluffy.color
dog.color = "black"
print poppy.color
fluffy.color = "yellow"
print fluffy.color
print poppy.color
```

So, the default color of dogs is brown—both the fluffy and poppy dog objects start off as brown. Then, using dog.color, we set the default color to be black, and because neither of the two objects has set its own color value, they are updated to be black. The third to last line uses poppy.color to set a custom color value for the poppy object—poppy becomes yellow, while fluffy and the dog class in general remain black.

Constructors and Destructors

To help you automate the creation and deletion of objects, you can easily override two default methods: __init__ and __del__. These are the methods called by Python when a class is being instantiated and freed, known as the *constructor* and *destructor*, respectively.

Having a custom constructor is great for when you need to accept a set of parameters for each object being created. For example, you might want each dog to have its own name on creation, and you could implement that with this code:

```
class dog(object):
    def __init__(self, name):
        self.name = name
fluffy = dog("Fluffy")
print fluffy.name
```

If you do not provide a name parameter when creating the dog object, Python reports an error and stops. You can, of course, ask for as many constructor parameters as you want, although it is usually better to ask only for the ones you need and have other functions to fill in the rest.

On the other side of things is the destructor method, which allows you to have more control over what happens when an object is destroyed. Using the two, we can show the life cycle of an object by printing messages when it is created and deleted:

```
class dog(object):
    def __init__(self, name):
        self.name = name
        print self.name + " is alive!"
    def __del__(self):
        print self.name + " is no more!"
fluffy = dog("Fluffy")
```

The destructor is there to give you the chance to free up resources allocated to the object or perhaps log something to a file.

Class Inheritance

Python allows you to reuse your code by inheriting one class from one or more others. For example, lions, tigers, and bears are all mammals and so share a number of similar properties. In that scenario, you would not want to have to copy and paste functions between them; it would be smarter (and easier!) to have a mammal class that defines all the shared functionality and then inherit each animal from that.

Consider the following code:

```
class car(object):
    color = "black"
    speed = 0
```

```
    def accelerateTo(self, speed):
        self.speed = speed
    def setColor(self, color):
        self.color = color
mycar = car()
print mycar.color
```

That creates a car class with a default color and also provides a setColor() function so people can change their own colors. Now, what do you drive to work? Is it a car? Sure it is, but chances are it is a Ford, or a Dodge, or a Jeep, or some other make—you don't get cars without a make. On the other hand, you do not want to have to define a class Ford, give it the methods accelerateTo(), setColor(), and however many other methods a basic car has and then do exactly the same thing for Ferrari, Nissan, and so on.

The solution is to use inheritance: Define a car class that contains all the shared functions and variables of all the makes and then inherit from that. In Python, you do this by putting the name of the class from which to inherit inside parentheses in the class declaration, like this:

```
class car(object):
    color = "black"
    speed = 0
    def accelerateTo(self, speed):
        self.speed = speed
    def setColor(self, color):
        self.color = color

class ford(car): pass
class nissan(car): pass
mycar = ford()
print mycar.color
```

The pass directive is an empty statement—it means our class contains nothing new. However, because the ford and nissan classes inherit from the car class, they get color, speed, accelerateTo(), and setColor() provided by their parent class. Note that we do not need object after the class names for ford and nissan because they are inherited from an existing class: car.

By default, Python gives you all the methods the parent class has, but you can override that by providing new implementations for the classes that need them. For example:

```
class modelt(car):
    def setColor(self, color):
        print "Sorry, Model Ts only come in black!"

myford = ford()
ford.setColor("green")
```

```
mycar = modelt()
mycar.setColor("green")
```

The first car is created as a Ford, so `setColor()` will work fine because it uses the method from the car class. However, the second car is created as a Model T, which has its own `setColor()` method, so the call will fail.

This provides an interesting scenario: What do you do if you have overridden a method and yet want to call the parent's method also? If, for example, changing the color of a Model T was allowed but just cost extra, we would want to print a message saying, "You owe $50 more," but then change the color. To do this, we need to use the class object from which our current class is inherited—car in this example. Here's an example:

```
class modelt(car):
    def setColor(self, color):
        print "You owe $50 more"
        car.setColor(self, color)

mycar = modelt()
mycar.setColor("green")
print mycar.color
```

That prints the message and then changes the color of the car.

The Standard Library and the Vaults of Parnassus

A default Python install includes many modules (blocks of code) that enable you to inter-act with the operating system, open and manipulate files, parse command-line options, perform data hashing and encryption, and much more. This is one of the reasons most commonly cited when people are asked why they like Python so much—it comes stocked to the gills with functionality you can take advantage of immediately. In fact, the number of modules included in the Standard Library is so high that entire books have been written about them—try *Python Standard Library* (O'Reilly, ISBN: 0-596-00096-0) for a comprehensive, if slightly dated, list of them.

For unofficial scripts and add-ons for Python, the recommended starting place is called the Vaults of Parnassus: http://py.vaults.ca. There you can find about 20,000 public scripts and code examples for everything from mathematics to games.

Reference

The Python website (http://www.python.org) is packed with information and updated regularly. This should be your first stop, if only to read the latest Python news.

▶ http://www.zope.org—The home page of the Zope Content Management System (CMS), it's one of the most popular CMSes around and, more important, written entirely in Python.

▶ http://www.jython.org—Python also has an excellent Java-based interpreter to allow it to run on other platforms. If you prefer Microsoft .NET, try http://www. ironpython.com.

▶ http://www.pythonline.com—Guido van Rossum borrowed the name for his language from *Monty Python's Flying Circus*, and as a result many Python code examples use oblique *Monty Python* references. A visit to the official *Monty Python* site to hone your Python knowledge is highly recommended!

There are few truly great books about Python; however, you can find a list of what's on offer at http://www.python.org/moin/PythonBooks. If you are desperate to pick up a book immediately, you could do much worse than choose *Learning Python* (O'Reilly, ISBN: 0-596-00281-5).

Writing PHP Scripts

This chapter introduces you to the world of PHP programming, from the point of view of using it as a web scripting language and as a command-line tool. PHP originally stood for *personal home page* because it was a collection of Perl scripts designed to ease the creation of guest books, message boards, and other interactive scripts commonly found on home pages. However, since those early days, it has received two major updates (PHP 3 and PHP 4), plus a substantial revision in PHP 5, which is the version bundled with Ubuntu.

Part of the success of PHP has been its powerful integration with databases—its earliest uses nearly always took advantage of a database back end. In PHP 5, however, two big new data storage mechanisms were introduced: SQLite, which is a powerful and local database system, and SimpleXML, which is an *application programming interface (API)* designed to make XML parsing and querying easy. As you will see over time, the PHP developers did a great job: Both SQLite and SimpleXML are easy to learn and use.

> **NOTE**
>
> Many packages for PHP are available through `synaptic`. The basic package is just called php5, but you might also want to add extensions such as `php5-ldap`, `php5-mysql`, or `php5-pgsql`. Choose only the extensions you plan to use; otherwise, it will waste system resources.

Introduction to PHP

In terms of the way it looks, PHP is a cross between Java and Perl, having taken the best aspects of both and merged them successfully into one language. The Java parts include a powerful object-orientation system, the capability to throw program exceptions, and the general style of writing that both languages borrowed from C. Borrowed from Perl is the "it should just work" mentality where ease of use is favored over strictness. As a result, you will find a lot of "there is more than one way to do it" in PHP.

Entering and Exiting PHP Mode

Unlike PHP's predecessors, you embed your PHP code inside your HTML as opposed to the other way around. Before PHP, many websites had standard HTML pages for most of their content, linking to Perl CGI pages to do back-end processing when needed. With PHP, all your pages are capable of processing and containing HTML.

Each `.php` file is processed by PHP that looks for code to execute. PHP considers all the text it finds to be HTML until it finds one of four things:

- ► `<?php`

- ► `<?`

- ► `<%`

- ► `<script language="php">`

The first option is the preferred method of entering PHP mode because it is guaranteed to work.

When in PHP mode, you can exit it by using `?>` (for `<?php` and `<?`); `%>` for `<%`) or `</script>` (for `<script language="php">`). This code example demonstrates entering and exiting PHP mode:

```
In HTML mode
<?php
  echo "In PHP mode";
?>
In HTML mode
In <?php echo "PHP"; ?> mode
```

Variables

All variables in PHP start with a dollar sign ($). Unlike many other languages, PHP does not have different types of variable for integers, floating-point numbers, arrays, or Booleans. They all start with a $, and all are interchangeable. As a result, PHP is a weakly typed language, which means you do not declare a variable as containing a specific type of data; you just use it however you want to.

Save the code in Listing 25.1 into the script ubuntu1.php.

LISTING 25.1   Testing Types in PHP

```php
<?php
  $i = 10;
  $j = "10";
  $k = "Hello, world";
  echo $i + $j;
  echo $i + $k;
?>
```

To run that script, bring up a console and browse to where you saved it. Then type this command:

```
$ php ubuntu1.php
```

If PHP is installed correctly, you should see the output 2010, which is really two things. The 20 is the result of 10 + 10 ($i plus $j), and the 10 is the result of adding 10 to the text string Hello, world. Neither of those operations are really straightforward. Whereas $i is set to the number 10, $j is actually set to be the text value "10", which is not the same thing. Adding 10 to 10 gives 20, as you would imagine, but adding 10 to "10" (the string) forces PHP to convert $j to an integer on-the-fly before adding it.

Running $i + $k adds another string to a number, but this time the string is Hello, world and not just a number inside a string. PHP still tries to convert it, though, and converting any non-numeric string into a number converts it to 0. So, the second echo statement ends up saying $i + 0.

As you should have guessed by now, calling echo outputs values to the screen. Right now, that prints directly to your console, but internally PHP has a complex output mechanism that enables you to print to a console, send text through Apache to a web browser, send data over a network, and more.

Now that you have seen how PHP handles variables of different types, it is important that you understand the selection of types available to you.

Type	Stores
integer	Whole numbers; for example, 1, 9, or 324809873
float	Fractional numbers; for example, 1.1, 9.09, or 3.141592654
string	Characters; for example, "a", "sfdgh", or "Ubuntu Unleashed"
boolean	True or false
array	Several variables of any type
object	An instance of a class

Type	Stores
resource	Any external data

The first four can be thought of as simple variables, and the last three as complex variables. Arrays are simply collections of variables. You might have an array of numbers (the ages of all the children in a class); an array of strings (the names of all Wimbledon tennis champions); or even an array of arrays, known as a *multidimensional array*. Arrays are covered in more depth in the next section because they are unique in the way in which they are defined.

Objects are used to define and manipulate a set of variables that belong to a unique entity. Each object has its own personal set of variables, as well as functions that operate on those variables. Objects are commonly used to model real-world things. You might define an object that represents a TV, with variables such as $CurrentChannel (probably an integer), $SupportsHiDef (a Boolean), and so on.

Of all the complex variables, the easiest to grasp are resources. PHP has many extensions available to it that allow you to connect to databases, manipulate graphics, or even make calls to Java programs. Because they are all external systems, they need to have types of data unique to them that PHP cannot represent using any of the six other data types. So, PHP stores their custom data types in resources—data types that are meaningless to PHP but can be used by the external libraries that created them.

Arrays

Arrays are one of our favorite parts of PHP because the syntax is smart and easy to read and yet manages to be as powerful as you could want. There are four pieces of jargon you need to know to understand arrays:

▶ An array is made up of many *elements*.

▶ Each element has a *key* that defines its place in the array. An array can have only one element with a given key.

▶ Each element also has a *value*, which is the data associated with the key.

▶ Each array has a *cursor*, which points to the current key.

The first three are used regularly; the last one less so. The array cursor is covered later in this chapter in the section "Basic Functions," but we will look at the other three now. With PHP, your keys can be virtually anything: integers, strings, objects, or other arrays. You can even mix and match the keys so that one key is an array, another is a string, and so on. The one exception to all this is floating-point numbers: You cannot use floating-point numbers as keys in your arrays.

There are two ways of adding values to an array: with the [] operator, which is unique to arrays; and with the array() pseudo-function. You should use [] when you want to add items to an existing array and use array() to create a new array.

To sum all this up in code, Listing 25.2 shows a script that creates an array without specifying keys, adds various items to it both without keys and with keys of varying types, does a bit of printing, and then clears the array.

LISTING 25.2   Manipulating Arrays

```php
<?php
  $myarr = array(1, 2, 3, 4);

  $myarr[4] = "Hello";
  $myarr[] = "World!";
  $myarr["elephant"] = "Wombat";
  $myarr["foo"] = array(5, 6, 7, 8);

  echo $myarr[2];
  echo $myarr["elephant"];
  echo $myarr["foo"][1];

  $myarr = array();
?>
```

The initial array is created with four elements, to which we assign the values 1, 2, 3, and 4. Because no keys are specified, PHP automatically assigns keys for us starting at 0 and counting upward—giving keys 0, 1, 2, and 3. Then we add a new element with the [] operator, specifying 4 as the key and "Hello" as the value. Next, [] is used again to add an element with the value "World!" and no key and then again to add an element with the key "elephant" and the value "wombat". The line after that demonstrates using a string key with an array value—an array inside an array (a multidimensional array).

The next three lines demonstrate reading back from an array, first using a numeric key, then using a string key, and then using a string key and a numeric key. Remember, the "foo" element is an array in itself, so that third reading line retrieves the array and then prints the second element (arrays start at 0, remember). The last line blanks the array by simply using array() with no parameters, which creates an array with elements and assigns it to $myarr.

The following is an alternative way of using array() that allows you to specify keys along with their values:

```php
$myarr = array("key1" => "value1", "key2" => "value2",
7 => "foo", 15 => "bar");
```

Which method you choose really depends on whether you want specific keys or want PHP to pick them for you.

Constants

Constants are frequently used in functions that require specific values to be passed in. For example, a popular function is extract(), which takes all the values in an array and places them into variables in their own right. You can choose to change the name of the variables as they are extracted using the second parameter—send it a 0 and it overwrites variables with the same names as those being extracted, send it a 1 and it skips variables with the same names, send it 5 and it prefixes variables only if they exist already, and so on. Of course, no one wants to have to remember a lot of numbers for each function, so you can instead use EXTR_OVERWRITE for 0, EXTR_SKIP for 1, EXTR_PREFIX_IF_EXISTS for 5, and so on, which is much easier.

You can create constants of your own by using the define() function. Unlike variables, constants do not start with a dollar sign, which makes the code to define a constant look like this:

```php
<?php
  define("NUM_SQUIRRELS", 10);
  define("PLAYER_NAME", "Jim");
  define("NUM_SQUIRRELS_2", NUM_SQUIRRELS);
  echo NUM_SQUIRRELS_2;
?>
```

That script demonstrates how you can set constants to numbers, strings, or even the value of other constants, although that doesn't really get used much!

References

Using the equal sign (=) copies the value from one variable to another so they both have their own copy of the value. Another option here is to use references, which is where a variable does not have a value of its own; instead, it points to another variable. This enables you to share values and have variables mutually update themselves.

To copy by reference, use the & symbol, as follows:

```php
<?php
  $a = 10;
  $b = &$a;
  echo $a . "\n";
  echo $b . "\n";

  $a = 20;
  echo $a . "\n";
  echo $b . "\n";
```

```
  $b = 30;
  echo $a . "\n";
  echo $b . "\n";
?>
```

If you run that script, you will see that updating $a also updates $b, but also that updating $b updates $a, too.

Comments

Adding short comments to your code is recommended and usually a requirement in larger software houses. In PHP you have three options for commenting style: //, /* */, and #. The first option (two slashes) instructs PHP to ignore everything until the end of the line. The second (a slash and an asterisk) instructs PHP to ignore everything until it reaches */. The last (a hash symbol) works like // and is included because it is common among shell scripting languages.

This code example demonstrates the difference between // and /* */:

```
<?php
  echo "This is printed!";
  // echo "This is not printed";
  echo "This is printed!";
  /* echo "This is not printed";
  echo "This is not printed either"; */
?>
```

It is generally preferred to use // because it is a known quantity. On the other hand, it is easy to introduce coding errors with /* */ by losing track of where a comment starts and ends.

> **NOTE**
>
> Contrary to popular belief, having comments in your PHP script has almost no effect on the speed at which the script executes. What little speed difference exists is wholly removed if you use a code cache.

Escape Sequences

Some characters cannot be typed, and yet you will almost certainly want to use some of them from time to time. For example, you might want to use an ASCII character for new line, but you can't type it. Instead, you need to use an escape sequence: \n. Similarly, you can print a carriage return character with \r. It's important to know both of these because, on the Windows platform, you need to use \r\n to get a new line. If you do not plan to run your scripts anywhere else, you need not worry about this!

Going back to the first script we wrote, recall that it printed 2010 because we added 10 + 10 and then 10 + 0. We can rewrite that using escape sequences, like this:

```php
<?php
  $i = 10;
  $j = "10";
  $k = "Hello, world";
  echo $i + $j;
  echo "\n";
  echo $i + $k;
  echo "\n";
?>
```

This time PHP prints a new line after each of the numbers, making it obvious that the output is 20 and 10 rather than 2010. Note that the escape sequences must be used in double quotation marks because they will not work in single quotation marks.

Three common escape sequences are \\, which means "ignore the backslash"; \", which means "ignore the double quote"; and \', which means "ignore the single quote." This is important when strings include quotation marks inside them. If we had a string such as "are you really Bill O'Reilly?", which has a single quotation mark in, this code would not work:

```php
<?php
  echo 'Are you really Bill O'Reilly?';
?>
```

PHP would see the opening quotation mark, read all the way up to the *O* in O'Reilly, and then see the quotation mark following the *O* as being the end of the string. The Reilly? part would appear to be a fragment of text and would cause an error. You have two options here: You can either surround the string in double quotation marks or escape the single quotation mark with \'.

If you choose the escaping route, it will look like this:

```php
echo 'Are you really Bill O\'Reilly?';
```

Although they are a clean solution for small text strings, be careful with overusing escape sequences. HTML is particularly full of quotation marks, and escaping them can get messy:

```php
$mystring = "<img src=\"foo.png\" alt=\"My picture\"
width=\"100\" height=\"200\" />";
```

In that situation, you are better off using single quotation marks to surround the text simply because it is a great deal easier on the eye!

Variable Substitution

PHP allows you to define strings using three methods: single quotation marks, double quotation marks, or heredoc notation. Heredoc isn't discussed here because it's fairly rare compared to the other two methods, but single quotation marks and double quotation marks work identically, with one minor exception—variable substitution.

Consider the following code:

```php
<?php
  $age = 25
  echo "You are ";
  echo $age;
?>
```

That is a particularly clumsy way to print a variable as part of a string. Fortunately, if you put a variable inside a string, PHP performs *variable substitution*, replacing the variable with its value. That means we can rewrite the code like so:

```php
<?php
  $age = 25
  echo "You are $age";
?>
```

The output is the same. The difference between single quotation marks and double quotation marks is that single-quoted strings do not have their variables substituted. Here's an example:

```php
<?php
  $age = 25
  echo "You are $age";
  echo 'You are $age';
?>
```

The first echo prints "You are 25", but the second one prints "You are $age".

Operators

Now that we have data values to work with, we need some operators to use, too. We have already used + to add variables together, but many others in PHP handle arithmetic, comparison, assignment, and other operators. *Operator* is just a fancy word for something that performs an operation, such as addition or subtraction. However, *operand* might be new to you. Consider this operation:

```php
$a = $b + c;
```

In this operation, = and + are operators, and $a, $b, and $c are operands. Along with +, you will also already know – (subtract), * (multiply), and / (divide), but here are some more.

Operator	What It Does
=	Assigns the right operand to the left operand.
==	Returns true if the left operand is equal to the right operand.
!=	Returns true if the left operand is not equal to the right operand.
===	Returns true if the left operand is identical to the right operand. This is not the same as ==.
!==	Returns true if the left operand is not identical to the right operand. This is not the same as !=.
<	Returns true if the left operand is smaller than the right operand.
>	Returns true if the left operand is greater than the right operand.
<=	Returns true if the left operand is equal to or smaller than the right operand.
&&	Returns true if both the left operand and the right operand are true.
¦¦	Returns true if either the left operand or the right operand is true.
++	Increments the operand by one.
—	Decrements the operand by one.
+=	Increments the left operand by the right operand.
-=	Decrements the left operand by the right operand.
.	Concatenates the left operand and the right operand (joins them together).
%	Divides the left operand by the right operand and returns the remainder.
¦	Performs a bitwise OR operation. It returns a number with bits that are set in either the left operand or the right operand.
&	Performs a bitwise AND operation. It returns a number with bits that are set both in the left operand and the right operand.

At least 10 other operators are not listed; to be fair, however, you're unlikely to use them. Even some of the ones in this list are used infrequently—bitwise AND, for example. Having said that, the bitwise OR operator is used regularly because it allows you to combine values.

Here is a code example demonstrating some of the operators:

```php
<?php
  $i = 100;
  $i++; // $i is now 101
```

```
$i—; // $i is now 100 again
$i += 10; // $i is 110
$i = $i / 2; // $i is 55
$j = $i; // both $j and $i are 55
$i = $j % 11; // $i is 0
?>
```

The last line uses modulus, which takes some people a little bit of effort to understand. The result of $i % 11 is 0 because $i is set to 55 and modulus works by dividing the left operand (55) by the right operand (11) and returning the remainder. 55 divides by 11 exactly 5 times, and so has the remainder 0.

The concatenation operator, a period, sounds scarier than it is: It just joins strings together. For example:

```
<?php
echo "Hello, " . "world!";
echo "Hello, world!" . "\n";
?>
```

There are two "special" operators in PHP that are not covered here and yet are used frequently. Before we look at them, though, it's important that you see how the comparison operators (such as <, <=, and !=) are used inside conditional statements.

Conditional Statements

In a *conditional statement* you instruct PHP to take different actions depending on the outcome of a test. For example, you might want PHP to check whether a variable is greater than 10 and, if so, print a message. This is all done with the `if` statement, which looks like this:

```
if (your condition) {
  // action to take if condition is true
} else {
  // optional action to take otherwise
}
```

The your condition part can be filled with any number of conditions you want PHP to evaluate, and this is where the comparison operators come into their own. For example:

```
if ($i > 10) {
  echo "11 or higher";
} else {
  echo "10 or lower";
}
```

PHP looks at the condition and compares $i to 10. If it is greater than 10, it replaces the whole operation with 1; otherwise, it replaces it with 0. So, if $i is 20, the result looks like this:

```
if (1) {
  echo "11 or higher";
} else {
  echo "10 or lower";
}
```

In conditional statements, any number other than 0 is considered to be equivalent to the Boolean value true, so if (1) always evaluates to true. There is a similar case for strings—if your string has any characters in, it evaluates to true, with empty strings evaluating to false. This is important because you can then use that 1 in another condition through && or || operators. For example, if you want to check whether $i is greater than 10 but less than 40, you could write this:

```
if ($i > 10 && $i < 40) {
  echo "11 or higher";
} else {
  echo "10 or lower";
}
```

If we presume that $i is set to 50, the first condition ($i, 10) is replaced with 1 and the second condition ($i < 40) is replaced with 0. Those two numbers are then used by the && operator, which requires both the left and right operands to be *true*. Whereas 1 is equivalent to true, 0 is not, so the && operand is replaced with 0 and the condition fails.

=, ==, ===, and similar operators are easily confused and often the source of programming errors. The first, a single equal sign, assigns the value of the right operand to the left operand. However, all too often you see code like this:

```
if ($i = 10) {
  echo "The variable is equal to 10!";
} else {
  echo "The variable is not equal to 10";
}
```

That is incorrect. Rather than checking whether $i is equal to 10, it assigns 10 to $i and returns true. What is needed is ==, which compares two values for equality. In PHP, this is extended so that there is also === (three equal signs), which checks whether two values are identical—more than just equal.

The difference is slight but important: If you have a variable with the string value "10" and compare it against the number value of 10, they are equal. Thus, PHP converts the type and checks the numbers. However, they are not identical. To be considered identical, the two variables must be equal (that is, have the same value) and be of the same data type (that is, both are strings, both are integers, and so on).

> **NOTE**
>
> It is common practice to put function calls in conditional statements rather than direct comparisons. For example:
>
> ```
> if (do_something()) {
> ```
>
> If the `do_something()` function returns `true` (or something equivalent to `true`, such as a nonzero number), the conditional statement evaluates to `true`.

Special Operators

The ternary operator and the execution operator work differently from those we have seen so far. The ternary operator is rarely used in PHP, thankfully, because it is really just a condensed conditional statement. Presumably it arose through someone needing to make his code occupy as little space as possible because it certainly does not make PHP code any easier to read!

The ternary operator works like this:

```
$age_description = ($age < 18) ? "child" : "adult";
```

Without explanation, that code is essentially meaningless; however, it expands into the following five lines of code:

```
if ($age < 18) {
  $age_description = "child";
} else {
  $age_description = "adult";
}
```

The ternary operator is so named because it has three operands: a condition to check (`$age < 18` in the previous code), a result if the condition is true ("`child`"), and a result if the condition is false ("`adult`"). Although we hope you never have to use the ternary operator, it is at least important to know how it works in case you stumble across it.

The other special operator is the execution operator, which is the backtick symbol, `'`. The position of the backtick key varies depending on your keyboard, but it is likely to be just to the left of the 1 key (above Tab). The execution operator executes the program inside the back ticks, returning any text the program outputs. For example:

```
<?php
  $i = 'ls -l';
  echo $i;
?>
```

That executes the `ls` program, passing in –1 (a lowercase *L*) to get the long format, and stores all its output in `$i`. You can make the command as long or as complex as you like, including piping to other programs. You can also use PHP variables inside the command.

Switching

Having multiple `if` statements in one place is ugly, slow, and prone to errors. Consider the code in Listing 25.3.

LISTING 25.3   How Multiple Conditional Statements Lead to Ugly Code

```php
<?php
  $cat_age = 3;

  if ($cat_age == 1) {
    echo "Cat age is 1";
  } else {
    if ($cat_age == 2) {
      echo "Cat age is 2";
    } else {
      if ($cat_age == 3) {
        echo "Cat age is 3";
      } else {
        if ($cat_age == 4) {
          echo "Cat age is 4";
        } else {
          echo "Cat age is unknown";
        }
      }
    }
  }
?>
```

Even though it certainly works, it is a poor solution to the problem. Much better is a `switch`/`case` block, which transforms the previous code into what's shown in Listing 25.4.

LISTING 25.4   Using a switch/case Block

```php
<?php
  $cat_age = 3;

  switch ($cat_age) {
    case 1:
      echo "Cat age is 1";
      break;
    case 2:
      echo "Cat age is 2";
      break;
    case 3:
      echo "Cat age is 3";
```

```
      break;
    case 4:
      echo "Cat age is 4";
      break;
    default:
      echo "Cat age is unknown";
  }
?>
```

Although it is only slightly shorter, it is a great deal more readable and much easier to maintain. A switch/case group is made up of a switch() statement in which you provide the variable you want to check, followed by numerous case statements. Notice the break statement at the end of each case. Without that, PHP would execute each case statement beneath the one it matches. Calling break causes PHP to exit the switch/case. Notice also that there is a default case at the end that catches everything that has no matching case.

It is important that you do not use case default: but merely default:. Also, it is the last case label, so it has no need for a break statement because PHP exits the switch/case block there anyway.

Loops

PHP has four ways you can execute a block of code multiple times: while, for, foreach, and do...while. Of the four, only do...while sees little use; the others are popular and you will certainly encounter them in other people's scripts.

The most basic loop is the while loop, which executes a block of code for as long as a given condition is true. So, we can write an infinite loop—a block of code that continues forever—with this PHP:

```
<?php
  $i = 10;
  while ($i >= 10) {
    $i += 1;
    echo $i;
  }
?>
```

The loop block checks whether $i is greater or equal to 10 and, if that condition is true, adds 1 to $i and prints it. Then it goes back to the loop condition again. Because $i starts at 10 and we only ever add numbers to it, that loop continues forever. With two small changes, we can make the loop count down from 10 to 0:

```
<?php
  $i = 10;
  while ($i >= 0) {
    $i -= 1;
```

```
    echo $i;
  }
?>
```

So, this time we check whether $i is greater than or equal to 0 and subtract 1 from it with each loop iteration. while loops are typically used when you are unsure of how many times the code needs to loop because while keeps looping until an external factor stops it.

With a for loop, you specify precise limits on its operation by giving it a declaration, a condition, and an action. That is, you specify one or more variables that should be set when the loop first runs (the *declaration*), you set the circumstances that will cause the loop to terminate (the *condition*), and you tell PHP what it should change with each loop iteration (the *action*). That last part is what really sets a for loop apart from a while loop: You usually tell PHP to change the condition variable with each iteration.

We can rewrite the script that counts down from 10 to 0 using a for loop:

```
<?php
  for($i = 10; $i >= 0; $i -= 1) {
    echo $i;
  }
?>
```

This time we do not need to specify the initial value for $i outside the loop, and neither do we need to change $i inside the loop—it is all part of the for statement. The actual amount of code is really the same, but for this purpose the for loop is arguably tidier and therefore easier to read. With the while loop, the $i variable was declared outside the loop and so was not explicitly attached to the loop.

The third loop type is foreach, which is specifically for arrays and objects, although it is rarely used for anything other than arrays. A foreach loop iterates through each element in an array (or each variable in an object), optionally providing both the key name and the value.

In its simplest form, a foreach loop looks like this:

```
<?php
  foreach($myarr as $value) {
    echo $value;
  }
?>
```

This loops through the $myarr array we created earlier, placing each value in the $value variable. We can modify that so we get the keys as well as the values from the array, like this:

```
<?php
  foreach($myarr as $key => $value) {
    echo "$key is set to $value\n";
  }
```

```
?>
```

As you can guess, this time the array keys go in $key and the array values go in $value. One important characteristic of the foreach loop is that it goes from the start of the array to the end and then stops—and by *start* we mean the first item to be added rather than the lowest index number. This script shows this behavior:

```php
<?php
  $array = array(6 => "Hello", 4 => "World",
                 2 => "Wom", 0 => "Bat");
  foreach($array as $key => $value) {
    echo "$key is set to $value\n";
  }
?>
```

If you try this script, you will see that foreach prints the array in the original order of 6, 4, 2, 0 rather than the numeric order of 0, 2, 4, 6.

The do...while loop works like the while loop, with the exception that the condition appears at the end of the code block. This small syntactical difference means a lot, though, because a do...while loop is always executed at least once. Consider this script:

```php
<?php
  $i = 10;
  do {
    $i -= 1;
    echo $i;
  } while ($i < 10);
?>
```

Without running the script, what do you think it will do? One possibility is that it will do nothing; $i is set to 10, and the condition states that the code must loop only while $i is less than 10. However, a do...while loop always executes once, so what happens is that $i is set to 10 and PHP enters the loop, decrements $i, prints it, and then checks the condition for the first time. At this point, $i is indeed less than 10, so the code loops, $i is decremented again, the condition is rechecked, $i is decremented again, and so on. This is in fact an infinite loop, and so should be avoided!

If you ever want to exit a loop before it has finished, you can use the same break statement, which we used earlier to exit a switch/case block. This becomes more interesting if you find yourself with *nested* loops—loops inside of loops. This is a common situation to be in. For example, you might want to loop through all the rows in a chessboard and, for each row, loop through each column. Calling break exits only one loop or switch/case, but you can use break 2 to exit two loops or switch/cases, or break 3 to exit three, and so on.

Including Other Files

Unless you are restricting yourself to the simplest programming ventures, you will want to share code among your scripts at some point. The most basic need for this is to have a standard header and footer for your website, with only the body content changing. However, you might also find yourself with a small set of custom functions you use frequently, and it would be an incredibly bad move to simply copy and paste the functions into each of the scripts that use them.

The most common way to include other files is with the include keyword. Save this script as include1.php:

```php
<?php
  for($i = 10; $i >= 0; $i -= 1) {
    include "echo_i.php";
  }
?>
```

Then save this script as echo_i.php:

```php
<?php
  echo $i;
?>
```

If you run include1.php, PHP loops from 10 to 0 and includes echo_i.php each time. For its part, echo_i.php just prints the value of $i, which is a crazy way of performing an otherwise simple operation, but it does demonstrate how included files share data. Note that the include keyword in include1.php is inside a PHP block, but we reopen PHP inside echo_i.php. This is important because PHP exits PHP mode for each new file, so you always have a consistent entry point.

Basic Functions

PHP has a vast number of built-in functions that enable you to manipulate strings, connect to databases, and more. There is not room here to cover even 10% of the functions; for more detailed coverage of functions, check the "Reference" section at the end of this chapter.

Strings

Several important functions are used for working with strings, and there are many more less frequently used ones for which there is not enough space here. We are going to look at the most important here, ordered by difficulty—easiest first!

The easiest function is strlen(), which takes a string as its parameter and returns the number of characters in there, like this:

```php
<?php
  $ourstring = "  The Quick Brown Box Jumped Over The Lazy Dog  ";
  echo strlen($ourstring);
?>
```

We will be using that same string in subsequent examples to save space. If you execute that script, it outputs 48 because 48 characters are in the string. Note the 2 spaces on either side of the text, which pad the 44-character phrase up to 48 characters.

We can fix that padding with the `trim()` function, which takes a string to trim and returns it with all the whitespace removed from either side. This is a commonly used function because all too often you encounter strings that have an extra new line at the end or a space at the beginning. This cleans it up perfectly.

Using `trim()`, we can turn our 48-character string into a 44-character string (the same thing, without the extra spaces), like this:

```
echo trim($ourstring);
```

Keep in mind that `trim()` returns the trimmed string, so that outputs "The Quick Brown Box Jumped Over The Lazy Dog". We can modify that so `trim()` passes its return value to `strlen()` so that the code trims it and then outputs its trimmed length:

```
echo strlen(trim($ourstring));
```

PHP always executes the innermost functions first, so the previous code takes `$ourstring`, passes it through `trim()`, uses the return value of `trim()` as the parameter for `strlen()`, and prints it.

Of course, everyone knows that boxes do not jump over dogs—the usual phrase is "the quick brown fox." Fortunately, there is a function to fix that problem: `str_replace()`. Note that it has an underscore in it; PHP is inconsistent on this matter, so you really need to memorize the function name.

The `str_replace()` function takes three parameters: the text to search for, the text to replace it with, and the string you want to work with. When working with search functions, people often talk about *needles* and *haystacks* — in this situation, the first parameter is the needle (the thing to find), and the third parameter is the haystack (what you are searching through).

So, we can fix our error and correct *box* to *fox* with this code:

```
echo str_replace("Box", "Fox", $ourstring);
```

There are two little addendums to make here. First, note that we have specified "Box" as opposed to "box" because that is how it appears in the text. The `str_replace()` function is a *case-sensitive* function, which means it does not consider "Box" to be the same as "box". If you want to do a non-case-sensitive search and replace, you can use the `stri_replace()` function, which works in the same way.

The second addendum is that, because we are actually changing only one character (*B* to *F*), we need not use a function at all. PHP enables you to read (and change) individual characters of a string by specifying the character position inside braces ({ and }). As with arrays, strings are zero based, which means in the $ourstring variable $ourstring{0} is

25

T, $ourstring{1} is *h*, $ourstring{2} is *e*, and so on. We could use this instead of str_replace(), like this:

```php
<?php
  $ourstring = "  The Quick Brown Box Jumped Over The Lazy Dog  ";
  $ourstring{18} = "F";
  echo $ourstring;
?>
```

You can extract part of a string using the substr() function, which takes a string as its first parameter, a start position as its second parameter, and an optional length as its third parameter. Optional parameters are common in PHP. If you do not provide them, PHP assumes a default value. In this case, if you specify only the first two parameters, PHP copies from the start position to the end of the string. If you specify the third parameter, PHP copies that many characters from the start.

We can write a simple script to print "Lazy Dog" by setting the start position to 38, which, remembering that PHP starts counting string positions from 0, copies from the 39th character to the end of the string:

```php
echo substr($ourstring, 38);
```

If we just want to print the word "Lazy," we need to use the optional third parameter to specify the length as 4, like this:

```php
echo substr($ourstring, 38, 4);
```

The substr() function can also be used with negative second and third parameters. If you specify just parameter one and two and provide a negative number for parameter two, substr() counts backward from the end of the string. So, rather than specifying 38 for the second parameter, we can use –10, so it takes the last 10 characters from the string. Using a negative second parameter and positive third parameter counts backward from the end string and then uses a forward length. We can print "Lazy" by counting 10 characters back from the end and then taking the next four characters forward:

```php
echo substr($ourstring, -10, 4);
```

Finally, we can use a negative third parameter, too, which also counts back from the end of the string. For example, using "-4" as the third parameter means to take everything except the last four characters. Confused yet? This code example should make it clear:

```php
echo substr($ourstring, -19, -11);
```

That counts 19 characters backward from the end of the string (which places it at the *O* in Over) and then copies everything from there until 11 characters before the end of the string. That prints "Over The". The same thing could be written using –19 and 8, or even 29 and 8—there is more than one way to do it!

Moving on, the strpos() function returns the position of a particular substring inside a string; however, it is most commonly used to answer the question, "Does this string contain a specific substring?" You need to pass it two parameters: a haystack and a needle (yes, that's a different order from str_replace()!).

In its most basic use, strpos() can find the first instance of "Box" in our phrase, like this:

```
echo strpos($ourstring, "Box");
```

This outputs 18 because that is where the *B* in Box starts. If strpos() cannot find the substring in the parent string, it returns false rather than the position. Much more helpful, though, is the ability to check whether a string contains a substring; a first attempt to check whether our string contains the word *The* might look like this:

```php
<?php
  $ourstring = "The Quick Brown Box Jumped Over The Lazy Dog";
  if (strpos($ourstring, "The")) {
    echo "Found 'The'!\n";
  } else {
    echo "'The' not found!\n";
  }
?>
```

Note that we have temporarily taken out the leading and trailing whitespace from $ourstring and we are using the return value of strpos() for our conditional statement. This reads, "If the string is found, then print a message; if not, print another message." Or does it?

Run the script, and you will see it print the "not found" message. The reason for this is that strpos() returns false if the substring is not found and otherwise returns the position where it starts. If you recall, any nonzero number equates to true in PHP, which means that 0 equates to false. With that in mind, what is the string index of the first *The* in our phrase? Because PHP's strings are zero based and we no longer have the spaces on either side of the string, the *The* is at position 0, which our conditional statement evaluates to false—hence, the problem.

The solution here is to check for identicality. We know that 0 and false are equal, but they are not identical because 0 is an integer, whereas false is a Boolean. So, we need to rewrite the conditional statement to see whether the return value from strpos() is identical to false. If it is, the substring was not found:

```php
<?php
  $ourstring = "The Quick Brown Box Jumped Over The Lazy Dog";
  if (strpos($ourstring, "The") !== false) {
    echo "Found 'The'!\n";
  } else {
```

25

```
    echo "'The' not found!\n";
  }
?>
```

Arrays

Working with arrays is no easy task, but PHP makes it easier by providing a selection of functions that can sort, shuffle, intersect, and filter them. As with other functions, there is only space here to choose a selection; this is by no means a definitive reference to PHP's array functions.

The easiest function to use is array_unique(), which takes an array as its only parameter and returns the same array with all duplicate values removed. Also in the realm of "so easy you do not need a code example" is the shuffle() function, which takes an array as its parameter and randomizes the order of its elements. Note that shuffle() does not return the randomized array; it uses your parameter as a reference and scrambles it directly. The last too-easy-to-demonstrate function is in_array(), which takes a value as its first parameter and an array as its second and returns true if the value is in the array.

With those out of the way, we can focus on the more interesting functions, two of which are array_keys() and array_values(). They both take an array as their only parameter and return a new array made up of the keys in the array or the values of the array, respectively. The array_values() function is an easy way to create a new array of the same data, just without the keys. This is often used if you have numbered your array keys, deleted several elements, and want to reorder it.

The array_keys() function creates a new array where the values are the keys from the old array, like this:

```
<?php
  $myarr = array("foo" => "red", "bar" => "blue", "baz" => "green");
  $mykeys = array_keys($myarr);
  foreach($mykeys as $key => $value) {
    echo "$key = $value\n";
  }
?>
```

That prints "0 = foo", "1 = bar", and "2 = baz".

Several functions are used specifically for array sorting, but only two get much use: asort() and ksort(), the first of which sorts the array by its values and the second of which sorts the array by its keys. Given the array $myarr from the previous example, sorting by the values would produce an array with elements in the order bar/blue, baz/green, and foo/red. Sorting by key would give the elements in the order bar/blue, baz/green, and foo/red. As with the shuffle() function, both asort() and ksort() do their work *in place*, meaning they return no value, directly altering the parameter you pass in. For interest's sake, you can also use arsort() and krsort() for reverse value sorting and reverse key sorting, respectively.

This code example reverse sorts the array by value and then prints it as before:

```php
<?php
  $myarr = array("foo" => "red", "bar" => "blue", "baz" => "green");
  arsort($myarr);
  foreach($myarr as $key => $value) {
    echo "$key = $value\n";
  }
?>
```

Previously when discussing constants, we mentioned the extract() function that converts an array into individual variables; now it is time to start using it for real. You need to provide three variables: the array you want to extract, how you want the variables prefixed, and the prefix you want used. Technically, the last two parameters are optional, but practically you should always use them to properly namespace your variables and keep them organized.

The second parameter must be one of the following:

- ▶ EXTR_OVERWRITE—If the variable exists already, overwrites it.

- ▶ EXTR_SKIP—If the variable exists already, skips it and moves on to the next variable.

- ▶ EXTR_PREFIX_SAME—If the variable exists already, uses the prefix specified in the third parameter.

- ▶ EXTR_PREFIX_ALL—Prefixes all variables with the prefix in the third parameter, regardless of whether it exists already.

- ▶ EXTR_PREFIX_INVALID—Uses a prefix only if the variable name would be invalid (for example, starting with a number).

- ▶ EXTR_IF_EXISTS—Extracts only variables that already exist. We have never seen this used.

You can also, optionally, use the bitwise OR operator, |, to add in EXTR_REFS to have extract() use references for the extracted variables. In general use, EXTR_PREFIX_ALL is preferred because it guarantees namespacing. EXTR_REFS is required only if you need to be able to change the variables and have those changes reflected in the array.

This next script uses extract() to convert $myarr into individual variables, $arr_foo, $arr_bar, and $arr_baz:

```php
<?php
  $myarr = array("foo" => "red", "bar" => "blue", "baz" => "green");
  extract($myarr, EXTR_PREFIX_ALL, 'arr');
?>
```

Note that the array keys are "foo", "bar", and "baz" and that the prefix is "arr", but that the final variables will be $arr_foo, $arr_bar, and $arr_baz. PHP inserts an underscore between the prefix and array key.

Files

As you will have learned from elsewhere in the book, the UNIX philosophy is that everything is a file. In PHP, this is also the case: A selection of basic file functions is suitable for opening and manipulating files, but those same functions can also be used for opening and manipulating network sockets. We cover both here.

Two basic read and write functions for files make performing these basic operations easy. They are file_get_contents(), which takes a filename as its only parameter and returns the file's contents as a string, and file_put_contents(), which takes a filename as its first parameter and the data to write as its second parameter.

Using these two, we can write a script that reads all the text from one file, filea.txt, and writes it to another, fileb.txt:

```php
<?php
  $text = file_get_contents("filea.txt");
  file_put_contents("fileb.txt", $text);
?>
```

Because PHP enables us to treat network sockets like files, we can also use file_get_contents() to read text from a website, like this:

```php
<?php
  $text = file_get_contents("http://www.slashdot.org");
  file_put_contents("fileb.txt", $text);
?>
```

The problem with using file_get_contents() is that it loads the whole file into memory at once; that's not practical if you have large files or even smaller files being accessed by many users. An alternative is to load the file piece by piece, which can be accomplished through the following five functions: fopen(), fclose(), fread(), fwrite(), and feof(). The *f* in those function names stands for *file*, so they open, close, read from, and write to files and sockets. The last function, feof(), returns true if the end of the file has been reached.

The fopen() function takes a bit of learning to use properly, but on the surface it looks straightforward. Its first parameter is the filename you want to open, which is easy enough. However, the second parameter is where you specify how you want to work with the file, and you should specify one of the following:

▶ r—Read only; it overwrites the file

▶ r+—Reading and writing; it overwrites the file

▶ w—Write only; it erases the existing contents and overwrites the file

▶ w+—Reading and writing; it erases the existing content and overwrites the file

- ▶ a—Write only; it appends to the file

- ▶ a+—Reading and writing; it appends to the file

- ▶ x—Write only, but only if the file does not exist

- ▶ a+—Reading and writing, but only if the file does not exist

Optionally, you can also add b (for example, a+b or rb) to switch to binary mode. This is recommended if you want your scripts and the files they write to work smoothly on other platforms.

When you call fopen(), you should store the return value. It is a resource known as a *file handle*, which the other file functions all need to do their jobs. The fread() function, for example, takes the file handle as its first parameter and the number of bytes to read as its second, returning the content in its return value. The fclose() function takes the file handle as its only parameter and frees up the file.

So, we can write a simple loop to open a file, read it piece by piece, print the pieces, and then close the handle:

```php
<?php
  $file = fopen("filea.txt", "rb");
  while (!feof($file)) {
    $content = fread($file, 1024);
    echo $content;
  }
  fclose($file);
?>
```

That only leaves the fwrite() function, which takes the file handle as its first parameter and the string to write as its second. You can also provide an integer as the third parameter, specifying the number of bytes you want to write of the string, but if you exclude this, fwrite() writes the entire string.

If you recall, you can use a as the second parameter to fopen() to append data to a file. So, we can combine that with fwrite() to have a script that adds a line of text to a file each time it is executed:

```php
<?php
  $file = fopen("filea.txt", "ab");
  fwrite($file, "Testing\n");
  fclose($file);
?>
```

To make that script a little more exciting, we can stir in a new function, filesize(), that takes a filename (not a file handle, but an actual filename string) as its only parameter and returns the file's size in bytes. Using that new function brings the script to this:

```php
<?php
```

```
  $file = fopen("filea.txt", "ab");
  fwrite($file, "The filesize was" . filesize("filea.txt") . "\n");
  fclose($file);
?>
```

Although PHP automatically cleans up file handles for you, it is still best to use `fclose()` yourself so you are always in control.

Miscellaneous

Several functions do not fall under the other categories and so are covered here. The first one is `isset()`, which takes one or more variables as its parameters and returns `true` if they have been set. It is important to note that a variable with a value set to something that would be evaluated to `false`—such as 0 or an empty string—still returns `true` from `isset()` because it does not check the value of the variable. It merely checks that it is set; hence, the name.

The `unset()` function also takes one or more variables as its parameters, simply deleting the variable and freeing up the memory. With these two, we can write a script that checks for the existence of a variable and, if it exists, deletes it (see Listing 25.5).

LISTING 25.5   Setting and Unsetting Variables

```
<?php
  $name = "Ildiko";
  if (isset($name)) {
    echo "Name was set to $name\n";
    unset($name);
  } else {
    echo "Name was not set";
  }

  if (isset($name)) {
    echo "Name was set to $name\n";
    unset($name);
  } else {
    echo "Name was not set";
  }
?>
```

That script runs the same `isset()` check twice, but it `unset()`s the variable after the first check. As such, it prints "`Name was set to Ildiko`" and then "`Name was not set`".

Perhaps the most frequently used function in PHP is `exit`, although purists will tell you that it is in fact a language construct rather than a function. `exit` terminates the processing of the script as soon as it is executed, meaning subsequent lines of code are not executed. That is really all there is to it; it barely deserves an example, but here is one just to make sure:

```php
<?php
  exit;
  echo "Exit is a language construct!\n";
?>
```

That script prints nothing because the `exit` comes before the `echo`.

One function we can guarantee you will use a lot is `var_dump()`, which dumps out information about a variable, including its value, to the screen. This is invaluable for arrays because it prints every value and, if one or more of the elements is an array, it prints all the elements from those, and so on. To use this function, just pass it a variable as its only parameter:

```php
<?php
  $drones = array("Graham", "Julian", "Nick", "Paul");
  var_dump($drones);
?>
```

The output from that script looks like this:

```
array(4) {
  [0]=>
  string(6) "Graham"
  [1]=>
  string(6) "Julian"
  [2]=>
  string(4) "Nick"
  [3]=>
  string(4) "Paul"
}
```

The `var_dump()` function sees a lot of use as a basic debugging technique because it is the easiest way to print variable data to the screen to verify it.

Finally, we briefly discuss regular expressions, with the emphasis on *briefly* because regular expression syntax is covered elsewhere in this book and the only unique thing relevant to PHP are the functions you will use to run the expressions. You have the choice of either *Perl-Compatible Regular Expressions (PCRE)* or POSIX Extended regular expressions, but there really is little to choose between them in terms of functionality offered. For this chapter, we use the PCRE expressions because, to the best of our knowledge, they see more use by other PHP programmers.

The main PCRE functions are `preg_match()`, `preg_match_all()`, `preg_replace()`, and `preg_split()`. We will start with `preg_match()` because it provides the most basic functionality by returning `true` if one string matches a regular expression. The first parameter to `preg_match()` is the regular expression you want to search for, and the second is the string to match. So, if we wanted to check whether a string had the word *Best, Test, rest, zest,* or any other word containing *est* preceded by any letter of either case, we could use this PHP code:

```php
$result = preg_match("/[A-Za-z]est/", "This is a test");
```

Because the test string matches the expression, $result is set to 1 (true). If you change the string to a nonmatching result, you get 0 as the return value.

The next function is preg_match_all(), which gives you an array of all the matches it found. However, to be most useful, it takes the array to fill with matches as a by-reference parameter and saves its return value for the number of matches that were found.

We suggest you use preg_match_all() and var_dump() to get a feel for how the function works. This example is a good place to start:

```php
<?php
  $string = "This is the best test in the west";
  $result = preg_match_all("/[A-Za-z]est/", $string, $matches);
  var_dump($matches);
?>
```

That outputs the following:

```
array(1) {
  [0]=>
  array(3) {
    [0]=>
    string(4) "best"
    [1]=>
    string(4) "test"
    [2]=>
    string(4) "west"
  }
}
```

If you notice, the $matches array is actually multidimensional in that it contains one element, which itself is an array containing all the matches to our regular expression. The reason for this is because our expression has no *subexpressions*, meaning no independent matches using parentheses. If we had subexpressions, each would have its own element in the $matches array containing its own array of matches.

Moving on, preg_replace() is used to change all substrings that match a regular expression into something else. The basic manner of using this is quite easy: You search for something with a regular expression and provide a replacement for it. However, a more useful variant is *backreferencing*, using the match as part of the replacement. For our example, we will imagine you have written a tutorial on PHP but want to process the text so each reference to a function is followed by a link to the PHP manual.

PHP manual page URLs take the form http://www.php.net/<somefunc>—for example, http://www.php.net/preg_replace. The string we need to match is a function name, which is a string of alphabetic characters, potentially also mixed with numbers and underscores and terminated with two parentheses, (). As a replacement, we will use the match we found, surrounded in HTML emphasis tags (<em></em>), and then with a link to the relevant PHP manual page. Here is how that looks in code:

```php
<?php
  $regex = "/([A-Za-z0-9_]*)\(\)/";
  $replace = "<em>$1</em> (<a href=\"http://www.php.net/$1\">manual</A>)";
  $haystack = "File_get_contents()is easier than using fopen().";
  $result = preg_replace($regex, $replace, $haystack);
  echo $result;
?>
```

The $1 is our backreference; it will be substituted with the results from the first subexpression. The way we have written the regular expression is very exact. The [A-Za-z0-9_]* part, which matches the function name, is marked as a subexpression. After that is \(\), which means the exact symbols (and), not the regular expression meanings of them, which means that $1 in the replacement will contain fopen rather than fopen(), which is how it should be. Of course, anything that is not backreferenced in the replacement is removed, so we have to put the () after the first $1 (not in the hyperlink) to repair the function name.

After all that work, the output is perfect:

```
<em>File_get_contents()</em> (<a href="http://www.php.net/
file_get_contents">manual</A>) is easier than using <em>fopen()
</em> (<a href="http://www.php.net/fopen">manual</A>).
```

Handling HTML Forms

Given that PHP's primary role is handling web pages, you might wonder why this section has been left so late in the chapter. It is because handling HTML forms is so central to PHP that it is essentially automatic.

Consider this form:

```
<form method="POST" action="thispage.php">
User ID: <input type="text" name="UserID" /><br />
Password: <input type="password" name="Password" /><br />
<input type="submit" />
</form>
```

When a visitor clicks Submit, thispage.php is called again and this time PHP has the variables available to it inside the $_REQUEST array. Given that script, if the user enters 12345 and frosties as her user ID and password, PHP provides you with $_REQUEST['UserID'] set to 12345 and $_REQUEST['Password'] set to frosties. Note that it is important that you use HTTP post unless you specifically want GET. POST enables you to send a great deal more data and stops people from tampering with your URL to try to find holes in your script.

Is that it? Well, almost. That tells you how to retrieve user data, but you should be sure to sanitize it so users do not try to sneak HTML or JavaScript into your database as something you think is innocuous. PHP gives you the strip_tags() function for this purpose. It takes a string and returns the same string with all HTML tags removed.

Databases

The ease with which PHP can be used to create dynamic, database-driven websites is for many the key reason to use it. The stock build of PHP comes with support for MySQL, PostgreSQL, SQLite, Oracle, Microsoft SQL Server, ODBC, plus several other popular databases, so you are sure to find something to work with your data.

If you want to, you can learn all the individual functions for connecting to and manipulating each database PHP supports, but a much smarter idea is to use PEAR::DB. PEAR::DB is an abstraction layer over the databases that PHP supports, which means you write your code once, and—with the smallest of changes—it will work on every database server.

PEAR is the script repository for PHP and contains numerous tools and prewritten solutions for common problems. PEAR::DB is perhaps the most popular part of the PEAR project, but it is worth checking out the PEAR site to see whether anything else catches your eye.

Introduction to PEAR::DB

To get basic use out of PEAR::DB, you need to learn how to connect to a database, run a SQL query, and work with the results. This is not a SQL tutorial, so we have assumed you are already familiar with the language. For the sake of this tutorial, we have also assumed you are working with a database called dentists and a table called patients that contains the following fields:

- ▶ **ID**—The primary key, auto-incrementing integer for storing a number unique to each patient
- ▶ **Name**—A varchar(255) field for storing a patient name
- ▶ **Age**—Integer
- ▶ **Sex**—1 for male, 2 for female
- ▶ **Occupation**—A varchar(255) field for storing a patient occupation

Also for the sake of this tutorial, we will use a database server on IP address 10.0.0.1, running MySQL, with username ubuntu and password alm65z. You will need to replace these details with your own—use localhost for connecting to the local server.

The first step to using PEAR::DB is to include the standard PEAR::DB file, DB.php. Your PHP will be configured to look inside the PEAR directory for include() files, so you do not need to provide any directory information.

PEAR::DB is object oriented, and you specify your connection details at the same time as you create the initial DB object. This is done using a URL-like system that specifies the database server type, username, password, server, and database name all in one. After you have specified the database server here, everything else is abstracted, meaning you only need to change the connection line to port your code to another database server.

This first script connects to our server and prints a status message (see Listing 25.6).

LISTING 25.6   Connecting to a Database Through PEAR::DB

```php
<?php
  include("DB.php");
  $dsn = "mysql://ubuntu:alm65z@10.0.0.1/dentists";
  $conn = DB::connect($dsn);
  if (DB::isError($conn)) {
    echo $conn->getMessage() . "\n";
  } else {
    echo "Connected successfully!\n";
  }
?>
```

You should be able to see how the connection string breaks down. It is server name first, then a username and password separated by a colon, then an @ symbol followed by the IP address to which to connect, and then a slash and the database name. Notice how the call to connect is DB::connect(), which calls PEAR::DB directly and returns a database connection object for storage in $conn. The variable name $dsn was used for the connection details because it is a common acronym standing for data source name.

If DB::connect() successfully connects to a server, it returns a database object we can use to run SQL queries. If not, we get an error returned that we can query using functions such as getMessage(). In the previous script, we print the error message if we fail to connect, but we also just print a message if we succeed. Next, we will change that so we run an SQL query if we have a connection.

Running SQL queries is done through the query() function of our database connection, passing in the SQL we want to execute. This then returns a query result that can be used to get the data. This query result can be thought of as a multidimensional array because it has many rows of data, each with many columns of attributes. This is extracted using the fetchInto() function, which loops through the query result converting one row of data into an array that it sends back as its return value. You need to pass in two parameters to fetchInto() specifying where the data should be stored and how you want it stored. Unless you have unusual needs, specifying DB_FETCHMODE_ASSOC for the second parameter is a smart move.

Listing 25.7 shows the new script.

LISTING 25.7　Running a Query Through PEAR::DB

```php
<?php
  include("DB.php");
  $dsn = "mysql://ubuntu:alm65z@10.0.0.1/dentists";
  $conn = DB::connect($dsn);
  if (DB::isError($conn)) {
    echo $conn->getMessage() . "\n";
  } else {
    echo "Connected successfully!\n";
    $result = $conn->query("SELECT ID, Name FROM patients;");
    while ($result->fetchInto($row, DB_FETCHMODE_ASSOC)) {
      extract($row, EXTR_PREFIX_ALL, 'pat');
      echo "$pat_ID is $pat_Name\n";
    }
  }
?>
```

The first half is identical to the previous script, with all the new action happening if we get a successful connection.

Going along with the saying "never leave to PHP what you can clean up yourself," the current script has problems. We do not clean up the query result, and we do not close the database connection. If this code were being used in a longer script that ran for several minutes, this would be a huge waste of resources. Fortunately, we can free up the memory associated with these two by calling `$result->free()` and `$conn->disconnect()`. If we add those two function calls to the end of the script, it will be complete.

Reference

Being as popular as it is, PHP gets a lot of coverage on the Internet. The best place to look for information, though, is the PHP online manual, at http://www.php.net. It is comprehensive, well written, and updated regularly:

▶ http://www.phpbuilder.net—A large PHP scripts and tutorials site where you can learn new techniques and also chat with other PHP developers.

▶ http://www.zend.com—The home page of a company founded by two of the key developers of PHP. Zend develops and sells proprietary software, including a powerful IDE and a code cache, to aid PHP developers.

▶ http://pear.php.net/—The home of the PEAR project contains a large collection of software you can download and try, and it has thorough documentation for it all.

▶ http://www.phparch.com/—There are quite a few good PHP magazines around, but *PHP Architect* probably leads the way. It posts some of its articles online for free, and its forums are good, too.

Quality books on PHP abound, and you are certainly spoiled for choice. For beginning developers, the best available is *PHP and MySQL Web Development* (Sams Publishing), ISBN 0-672-32672-8. For a concise, to-the-point book covering all aspects of PHP, check out *PHP in a Nutshell* (O'Reilly). Finally, for advanced developers, you can consult *Advanced PHP Programming* (Sams Publishing), ISBN 0-672-32561-6.

25

# CHAPTER 26

C/C++ Programming Tools for Ubuntu

If you're looking to learn C or C++ programming, this part of the book isn't the right place to start—unlike Perl, Python, PHP, or even C#, it takes more than a little dabbling to produce something productive with C, so this chapter is primarily focused on the tools Ubuntu offers you as a C or C++ programmer.

Whether you're looking to compile your own code or someone else's, the GNU Compiler Collection (gcc) is there to help—it understands C, C++, Fortran, Pascal, and dozens of other popular languages, which means you can try your hand at whatever interests you. Ubuntu also ships with hundreds of libraries you can link to, from the GUI toolkits behind GNOME and KDE to XML parsing and game coding. Some use C, others C++, and still others offer support for both, meaning you can choose what you're most comfortable with.

Programming in C with Linux

C is the programming language most frequently associated with Unix-like operating systems such as Linux or BSD. Since the 1970s, the bulk of the Unix operating system and its applications have been written in C. Because the C language doesn't directly rely on any specific hardware architecture, Unix was one of the first portable operating systems. In other words, the majority of the code that makes up Unix doesn't know and doesn't care which computer it is actually running on. Machine-specific features are isolated in a few modules within the Unix kernel, which makes it easy for you to modify them when you are porting to different hardware architectures.

C is a *compiled* language, which means that your C source code is first analyzed by the *preprocessor* and then translated into assembly language first and then into machine instructions that are appropriate to the target CPU. An assembler then creates a binary, or *object*, file from the machine instructions. Finally, the object file is linked to any required external software support by the *linker*. A C program is stored in a text file that ends with a .c extension and always contains at least one routine, or function, such as main(), unless the file is an *include* file (with a .h extension, also known as a *header* file) containing shared variable definitions or other data or declarations. *Functions* are the commands that perform each step of the task that the C program was written to accomplish.

> **NOTE**
>
> The Linux kernel is mostly written in C, which is why Linux works with so many different CPUs. To learn more about building the Linux kernel from source, see Chapter 32, "Kernel and Module Management."

C++ is an object-oriented extension to C. Because C++ is a superset of C, C++ compilers compile C programs correctly, and it is possible to write non–object-oriented code in C++. The reverse is not true: C compilers cannot compile C++ code.

C++ extends the capabilities of C by providing the necessary features for object-oriented design and code. C++ also provides some features, such as the capability to associate functions with data structures, that do not require the use of class-based object-oriented techniques. For these reasons, the C++ language enables existing Unix programs to migrate toward the adoption of object orientation over time.

Support for C++ programming is provided by gcc, which you run with the name g++ when you are compiling C++ code.

Using the C Programming Project Management Tools Provided with Ubuntu

Ubuntu is replete with tools that make your life as a C/C++ programmer easier. There are tools to create programs (editors), compile programs (gcc), create libraries (ar), control the source (Subversion, but a massive number of projects use the older CVS system), automate builds (make), debug programs (gdb and ddd), and determine where inefficiencies lie (gprof).

The following sections introduce some of the programming and project management tools included with Ubuntu. The disc included with this book contains many of these tools, which you can use to help automate software development projects. If you have some previous Unix experience, you will be familiar with most of these programs because they are traditional complements to a programmer's suite of software.

Building Programs with `make`

You use the `make` command to automatically build and install a C program, and for that use it is an easy tool. If you want to create your own automated builds, however, you need to learn the special syntax that `make` uses; the following sections walk you through a basic `make` setup.

Using Makefiles

The `make` command automatically builds and updates applications by using a makefile. A *makefile* is a text file that contains instructions about which options to pass on to the compiler preprocessor, the compiler, the assembler, and the linker. The makefile also specifies, among other things, which source code files have to be compiled (and the compiler command line) for a particular code module and which code modules are needed to build the program—a mechanism called *dependency checking*.

The beauty of the `make` command is its flexibility. You can use `make` with a simple makefile, or you can write complex makefiles that contain numerous macros, rules, or commands that work in a single directory or traverse your file system recursively to build programs, update your system, and even function as document management systems. The `make` command works with nearly any program, including text processing systems such as TeX.

You could use `make` to compile, build, and install a software package, using a simple command like this:

```
# make install
```

You can use the default makefile (usually called `Makefile`, with a capital *M*), or you can use `make`'s `-f` option to specify any makefile, such as `MyMakeFile`, like this:

```
# make -f MyMakeFile
```

Other options might be available, depending on the contents of your makefile.

Using Macros and Makefile Targets

Using `make` with macros can make a program portable. Macros allow users of other operating systems to easily configure a program build by specifying local values, such as the names and locations, or *pathnames*, of any required software tools. In the following example, macros define the name of the compiler (`CC`), the installer program (`INS`), where the program should be installed (`INSDIR`), where the linker should look for required libraries (`LIBDIR`), the names of required libraries (`LIBS`), a source code file (`SRC`), the intermediate object code file (`OBS`), and the name of the final program (`PROG`):

```
# a sample makefile for a skeleton program
CC= gcc
INS= install
INSDIR = /usr/local/bin
```

```
LIBDIR= -L/usr/X11R6/lib
LIBS= -lXm -lSM -lICE -lXt -lX11
SRC= skel.c
OBJS= skel.o
PROG= skel

skel:  ${OBJS}
        ${CC} -o ${PROG} ${SRC} ${LIBDIR} ${LIBS}

install: ${PROG}
        ${INS} -g root -o root ${PROG} ${INSDIR}
```

> **NOTE**
>
> The indented lines in the previous example are indented with tabs, not spaces. This is important to remember! It is difficult for a person to see the difference, but make can tell. If make reports confusing errors when you first start building programs under Linux, check your project's makefile for the use of tabs and other proper formatting.

Using the makefile from the preceding example, you can build a program like this:

```
# make
```

To build a specified component of a makefile, you can use a target definition on the command line. To build just the program, you use make with the skel target, like this:

```
# make skel
```

If you make any changes to any element of a target object, such as a source code file, make rebuilds the target automatically. This feature is part of the convenience of using make to manage a development project. To build and install a program in one step, you can specify the target of install like this:

```
# make install
```

Larger software projects might have a number of traditional targets in the makefile, such as the following:

- ▶ test—To run specific tests on the final software
- ▶ man—To process an include or a troff document with the man macros
- ▶ clean—To delete any remaining object files
- ▶ archive—To clean up, archive, and compress the entire source code tree
- ▶ bugreport—To automatically collect and then mail a copy of the build or error logs

Large applications can require hundreds of source code files. Compiling and linking these applications can be a complex and error-prone task. The make utility helps you organize the process of building the executable form of a complex application from many source files.

Using the autoconf Utility to Configure Code

The make command is only one of several programming automation utilities included with Ubuntu. There are others, such as pmake (which causes a parallel make), imake (which is a dependency-driven makefile generator that is used for building X11 clients), automake, and one of the newer tools, autoconf, which builds shell scripts that can be used to configure program source code packages.

Building many software packages for Linux that are distributed in source form requires the use of GNU's autoconf utility. This program builds an executable shell script named configure that, when executed, automatically examines and tailors a client's build from source according to software resources, or *dependencies* (such as programming tools, libraries, and associated utilities) that are installed on the target host (your Linux system).

Many Linux commands and graphical clients for X downloaded in source code form include configure scripts. To configure the source package, build the software, and then install the new program, the root user might use the script like this (after uncompressing the source and navigating into the resulting build directory):

```
$ ./configure ; make ; sudo make install
```

The autoconf program uses a file named configure.in that contains a basic *ruleset*, or set of macros. The configure.in file is created with the autoscan command. Building a properly executing configure script also requires a template for the makefile, named Makefile.in. Although creating the dependency-checking configure script can be done manually, you can easily overcome any complex dependencies by using a graphical project development tool such as KDE's KDevelop or GNOME's Glade. (See the "Graphical Development Tools" section, later in this chapter, for more information.)

Managing Software Projects with Subversion

Although make can be used to manage a software project, larger software projects require document management, source code controls, security, and revision tracking as the source code goes through a series of changes during its development. Subversion provides source code version control utilities for this kind of large software project management.

The Subversion system is used to track changes to multiple versions of files, and it can be used to backtrack or branch off versions of documents inside the scope of a project. It can also be used to prevent or resolve conflicting entries or changes made to source code files by multiple developers. Source code control with Subversion requires the use of at least the following five command options on the svn command line:

- ▶ checkout—Checks out revisions
- ▶ update—Updates your sources with changes made by other developers
- ▶ add—Adds new files to the repository

▶ delete—Eliminates files from the repository

▶ commit—Publishes changes to other repository developers

Note that some of these commands require you to use additional fields, such as the names of files. With the commit command, you should always try to pass the -m parameter (lets you provide a message describing the change) followed by some information about your changes. For example:

```
svn commit -m "This fixes bug 204982."
```

One of the most impressive features of Subversion is its ability to work offline—any local Subversion checkout automatically has a .svn directory hidden in there, which contains copies of all checked out files. Thanks to this, you can check your current files against the ones you checked out without having to contact the server—it all runs locally.

Debugging Tools

Debugging is both a science and an art. Sometimes, the simplest tool—the code listing—is the best debugging tool. At other times, however, you need to use other debugging tools. Three of these tools are splint, gprof, and gdb.

Using splint to Check Source Code

The splint command is similar to the traditional Unix lint command: It statically examines source code for possible problems, and it also has many additional features. Even if your C code meets the standards for C and compiles cleanly, it might still contain errors. splint performs many types of checks and can provide extensive error information. For example, this simple program might compile cleanly and even run:

```
$ gcc -o tux tux.c
$ ./tux
```

But the splint command might point out some serious problems with the source:

```
$ splint tux.c
Splint 3.1.1 —· 17 Feb 2004

tux.c: (in function main)
tux.c:2:19: Return value (type int) ignored: putchar(t[++j] -...
  Result returned by function call is not used. If this is intended, can cast
  result to (void) to eliminate message. (Use -retvalint to inhibit warning)
Finished checking —· 1 code warning
```

You can use the splint command's -strict option, like this, to get a more verbose report:

```
$ splint -strict tux.c
```

GCC also supports diagnostics through the use of extensive warnings (through the -Wall and -pedantic options):

```
$ gcc -Wall tux.c
tux.c:1: warning: return type defaults to 'int'
tux.c: In function 'main':
tux.c:2: warning: implicit declaration of function 'putchar'
```

Using gprof to Track Function Time

You use the gprof (profile) command to study how a program is spending its time. If a program is compiled and linked with -p as a flag, a mon.out file is created when it executes, with data on how often each function is called and how much time is spent in each function. gprof parses and displays this data. An analysis of the output generated by gprof helps you determine where performance bottlenecks occur. Using an optimizing compiler can speed up a program, but taking the time to use gprof's analysis and revising bottleneck functions significantly improves program performance.

Doing Symbolic Debugging with gdb

The gdb tool is a symbolic debugger. When a program is compiled with the -g flag, the symbol tables are retained and a symbolic debugger can be used to track program bugs. The basic technique is to invoke gdb after a *core dump* (a file containing a snapshot of the memory used by a program that has crashed) and get a stack trace. The stack trace indicates the source line where the core dump occurred and the functions that were called to reach that line. Often, this is enough to identify a problem. It isn't the limit of gdb, though.

gdb also provides an environment for debugging programs interactively. Invoking gdb with a program enables you to set breakpoints, examine the values of variables, and monitor variables. If you suspect a problem near a line of code, you can set a breakpoint at that line and run gdb. When the line is reached, execution is interrupted. You can check variable values, examine the stack trace, and observe the program's environment. You can single-step through the program to check values. You can resume execution at any point. By using breakpoints, you can discover many bugs in code.

A graphical X Window interface to gdb is called the Data Display Debugger, or ddd.

Using the GNU C Compiler

If you elected to install the development tools package when you installed Ubuntu (or perhaps later on, using synaptic), you should have the GNU C compiler (gcc). Many different options are available for the GNU C compiler, and many of them are similar to those of the C and C++ compilers that are available on other Unix systems. Look at the man page or information file for gcc for a full list of options and descriptions.

When you build a C program using gcc, the compilation process takes place in several steps:

1. First, the C preprocessor parses the file. To do so, it sequentially reads the lines, includes header files, and performs macro replacement.

2. The compiler parses the modified code to determine whether the correct syntax is used. In the process, it builds a symbol table and creates an intermediate object format. Most symbols have specific memory addresses assigned, although symbols defined in other modules, such as external variables, do not.

3. The last compilation stage, linking, ties together different files and libraries and then links the files by resolving the symbols that had not previously been resolved.

> **NOTE**
>
> Most C programs compile with a C++ compiler if you follow strict ANSI rules. For example, you can compile the standard hello.c program (everyone's first program) with the GNU C++ compiler. Typically, you name the file something like hello.cc, hello.C, hello.c++, or hello.cxx. The GNU C++ compiler accepts any of these names.

Graphical Development Tools

Ubuntu includes a number of graphical prototyping and development environments for use during X sessions. If you want to build client software for KDE or GNOME, you might find the KDevelop, Qt Designer, and Glade programs extremely helpful. You can use each of these programs to build graphical frameworks for interactive windowing clients, and you can use each of them to automatically generate the necessary skeleton of code needed to support a custom interface for your program.

Using the KDevelop Client

You can launch the KDevelop client (shown in Figure 26.1) from the application's menu, or from the command line of a terminal window, like this:

```
$ kdevelop &
```

After you press Enter, the KDevelop Setup Wizard runs, and you are taken through several short wizard dialogs that set up and ensure a stable build environment. You must then run kdevelop again (either from the command line or by clicking its menu item under the desktop panel's Programming menu). You will then see the main KDevelop window and can start your project by selecting KDevelop's Project menu and clicking the New menu item.

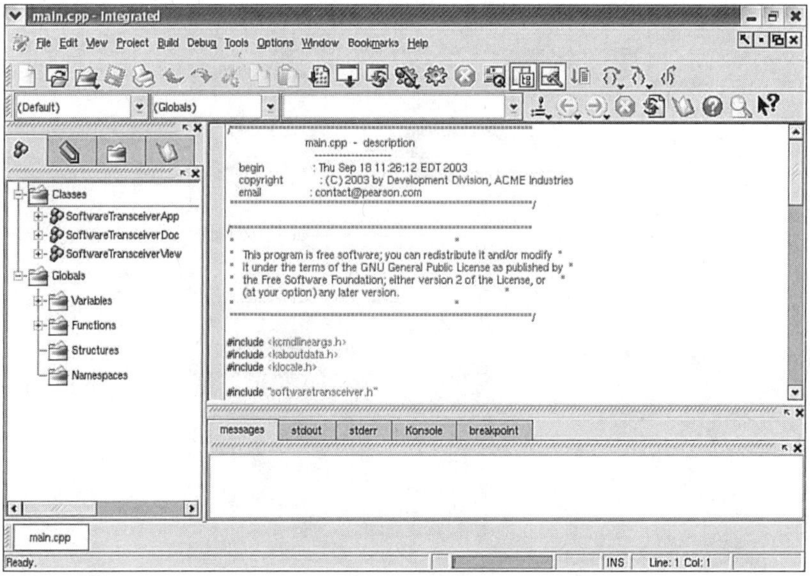

FIGURE 26.1   KDE's KDevelop is a rapid prototyping and client-building tool for use with Linux.

You can begin building your project by stepping through the wizard dialogs. When you click the Create button, KDevelop automatically generates all the files that are normally found in a KDE client source directory (including the `configure` script, which checks dependencies and builds the client's makefile). To test your client, you can either first click the Build menu's Make menu item (or press F8) or just click the Execute menu item (or press F9), and the client is built automatically. You can use KDevelop to create KDE clients, plug-ins for the `Konqueror` browser, KDE `kicker` panel applets, KDE desktop themes, Qt library–based clients, and even programs for GNOME.

The Glade Client for Developing in GNOME

If you prefer to use GNOME and its development tools, the Glade GTK+ GUI builder can help you save time and effort when building a basic skeleton for a program. You launch Glade from the desktop panel's Programming menu..

When you launch Glade, a directory named `Projects` is created in your home directory, and you see a main window, along with two floating Palette and Properties windows (see Figure 26.2, which shows a basic GNOME client with a calendar widget added to its main window). You can use Glade's File menu to save the blank project and then start building your client by clicking and adding user interface elements from the Palette window. For example, you can first click the Palette window's Gnome button and then click to create your new client's main window. A window with a menu and a toolbar appears—the basic framework for a new GNOME client!

26

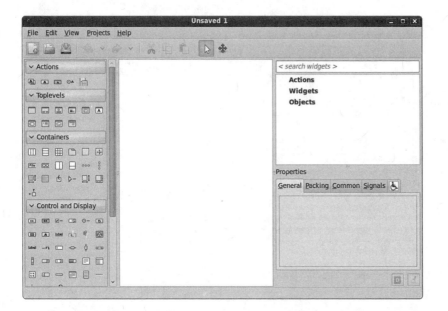

FIGURE 26.2   You can use the GNOME Glade client to build and preview a graphical interface for a custom GNOME program.

Related Ubuntu and Linux Commands

You will use many of these commands when programming in C and C++ for Linux:

- ▶ ar—The GNU archive development tool
- ▶ as—The GNU assembler
- ▶ autoconf—The GNU configuration script generator
- ▶ cervisia—A KDE client that provides a graphical interface to a CVS project
- ▶ cvs—A project revision control system
- ▶ designer—Trolltech's graphical prototyping tool for use with Qt libraries and X
- ▶ gcc—The GNU C/C++ compiler system
- ▶ gdb—The GNU interactive debugger
- ▶ glade-2—The GNOME graphical development environment for building GTK+ clients
- ▶ gprof—The GNU program profiler
- ▶ kdevelop—The KDE C/C++ graphical development environment for building KDE, GNOME, or terminal clients
- ▶ make—A GNU project management command
- ▶ patch—Larry Wall's source patching utility
- ▶ splint—The C source file checker
- ▶ svn—The Subversion revision control system

Reference

If you are interested in learning more about C and C++, you should look for the following books:

- *Sams Teach Yourself C in 21 Days*, by Peter Aitken and Bradley Jones, Sams Publishing

- *Sams Teach Yourself C++ for Linux in 21 Days*, by Jesse Liberty and David B. Horvath, Sams Publishing

- *C How to Program and C++ How to Program*, both by Harvey M. Deitel and Paul J. Deitel, Deitel Associates

- *The C Programming Language*, by Brian W. Kernighan and Dennis M. Ritchie, Prentice Hall

- *The Annotated C++ Reference Manual*, by Margaret A. Ellis and Bjarne Stroustrup, ANSI Base Document

- *Programming in ANSI C*, by Stephen G. Kochan, Sams Publishing

There are also a number of excellent websites providing more information:

- http://gcc.gnu.org/java/compile.html—More information about GCC's Java support.

- http://www.gnu.org/software/autoconf/autoconf.html—More information about the GNU Project's autoconf utility and how to build portable software projects.

- http://www.trolltech.com/products/qt/tools.html—Trolltech's page for Qt Designer and a number of programming automation tools (including translators) that you can use with Ubuntu.

- http://glade.gnome.org—Home page for the Glade GNOME developer's tool.

- http://www.kdevelop.org—Site that hosts the KDevelop Project's latest versions of the KDE graphical development environment, KDevelop.

26

CHAPTER 27

Mono

Although Microsoft intended it for Windows, Microsoft's .NET platform has grown to encompass many other operating systems. No, this isn't a rare sign of Microsoft letting customers choose which OS is best for them—instead, the spread of .NET is because of the Mono project, which is a free re-implementation of .NET available under the a GPL license.

Because of the potential for patent complications, it took most distros a long time to incorporate Mono, but it's here now and works just fine. What's more, Mono supports both C# and Visual Basic .NET, as well as the complete .NET 1.0 and 1.1 frameworks (and much of the 2.0 framework too), making it quick to learn and productive to use.

Why Use Mono?

Linux already has numerous programming languages available to it, so why bother with Mono and .NET? Here are my top five reasons:

▶ .NET is "compile once, run anywhere"; that means you can compile your code on Linux and run it on Windows, or the reverse.

▶ Mono supports C#, which is a C-like language with many improvements to help make it object-oriented and easier to use.

▶ .NET includes automatic garbage collection to remove the possibility of memory leaks.

- ▶ .NET uses comes with built-in security checks to ensure that buffer overflows and many types of exploits are a thing of the past.

- ▶ Mono uses a high-performance just-in-time compiler to optimize your code for the platform on which it's running. This lets you compile it on a 32-bit machine, then run it on a 64-bit machine and have the code dynamically re-compiled for maximum 64-bit performance.

At this point, Mono is probably starting to sound like Java, and indeed it shares several properties with it. However, Mono has the following improvements:

- ▶ The C# language corrects many of the irritations in Java, while keeping its garbage collection.

- ▶ .NET is designed to let you compile multiple languages down to the same bytecode, including C#, Visual Basic .NET, and many others. The Java VM is primarily restricted to the Java language.

- ▶ Mono even has a special project (known as "IKVM") that compiles Java source code down to .NET code that can be run on Mono.

- ▶ Mono is completely open source!

Whether you're looking to create command-line programs, graphical user interface apps, or even web pages, Mono has all the power and functionality you need.

Mono on the Command Line

Mono should already be installed on your system, however it is installed only for end users rather than for developers—you need to install a few more packages to make it usable for programming. Start up the Synaptic Package Manager and make sure the following packages are selected:

- ▶ mono-runtime

- ▶ mono-jit

- ▶ mono-gac

- ▶ mono-gmcs

- ▶ mono-common

- ▶ monodevelop

- ▶ monodoc

- ▶ monodoc-manual

- ▶ beagle

- ▶ beagle-dev

That gives you the basics to do Mono development, plus a few extra bits and pieces if you want to branch out a bit.

If you want to do some exciting things with Mono, lots of Mono-enabled libraries are available. Try going to the Search view and search for "sharp" to bring up the list of .NET-enabled libraries that you can use with Mono—the suffix is used because C# is the most popular .NET language. In this list you'll see things such as gnome-sharp2 and gtk-sharp2—we recommend you at least install the gtk-sharp2 libraries as these are used to create graphical user interfaces for Mono.

But for now, let's get you up and running with Mono on the command line. Mono is split into two distinct parts: the compiler and the interpreter. The compiler turns your source code into an executable, and is called gmcs. The interpreter actually runs your code as a working program, and is just called Mono. You should by now have installed MonoDevelop, so go the Applications menu, choose Programming, then MonoDevelop to start it up.

TIP

You don't have to use MonoDevelop to write your code, but it helps—syntax highlighting, code completion, and drag-and-drop GUI designers are just a few of its features.

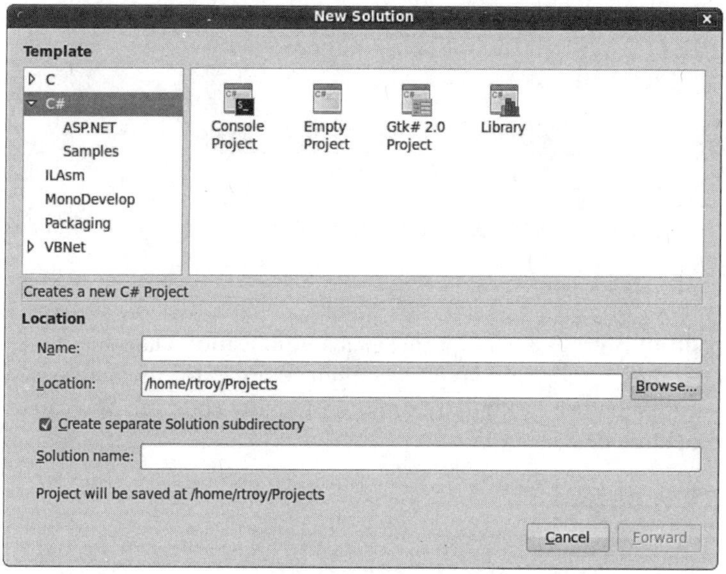

FIGURE 27.1 MonoDevelop ships with a number of templates to get you started, including one for a quick Console Project.

When MonoDevelop has loaded, go to the File menu and choose New Project. From the left of the window that appears, choose C#, then Console Project. Give it a name and choose a location to save it—all being well you should see something similar to Figure 27.1. When you're ready, click New to have MonoDevelop generate your project for you.

The default Console Project template creates a program that prints a simple message to the command line: the oh-so-traditional "Hello World!" Change it to something more insightful if you want, then press F5 to build and run the project. Just following the code view is

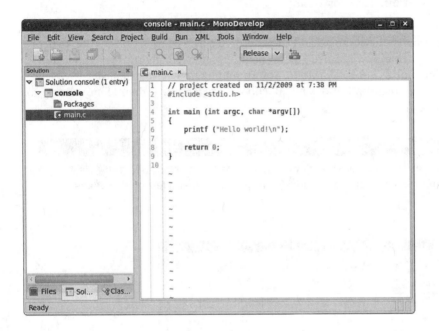

FIGURE 27.2   Your console template prints a message to the Application Output window in the bottom part of the window.

a set of tabs where debug output is printed. One of those tabs, Application Output, becomes selected when the program runs, and you'll see "Hello World!" (or the message you chose) printed there—not bad given that you haven't written any code yet! You can see how this should look in Figure 27.2.

The Structure of a C# Program

As you can guess from its name, C# draws very heavily on C and C++ for its syntax, but it borrows several ideas from Java too. C# is object-oriented, which means your program is defined as a class, which is then instantiated through the Main() method call. To be able to draw on some of the .NET framework's many libraries, you need to add using statements at the top of your files—by default there's just using System; that enables you to get access to the console to write your message.

If you've come from C or C++, you'll notice that there are no header files in C#: your class definition and its implementation are all in the same file. You might also have noticed that the Main() method accepts the parameter "string[] args", which is C#-speak for "an array of strings." C never had a native "string" data type, whereas C++ acquired it rather late in the game, and so both languages tend to use the antiquated char* data type to point to a string of characters. In C#, "string" is a data type all its own, and comes with built-in functionality such as the capability to replace substrings, the capability to trim off whitespace, and the capability to convert itself to upper- or lowercase if you want it to. Strings are also Unicode friendly out of the box in .NET, so that's one fewer thing for you to worry about.

The final thing you might have noticed—at least, if you had looked in the directory where MonoDevelop placed your compiled program (usually /path/to/your/project/bin/Debug)—is that Mono uses the Windows-like .exe file extension for its programs. because Mono aims to be 100% compatible with Microsoft .NET, which means you can take your Hello World program and run it unmodified on a Windows machine and have the same message printed out.

Printing Out the Parameters

We're going to expand your little program by having it print out all the parameters passed to it, one per line. In C# this is—rather sickeningly—just one line of code. Add this just after the existing Console.WriteLine() line in your program:

```
foreach (string arg in args) Console.WriteLine(arg);
```

The foreach keyword is a special kind of loop designed to iterate over an array of finite size. The for array exists in C#, and lets you loop a certain number of times; the while array exists too, and lets you loop continuously until you tell it to break. But the foreach loop is designed to loop over arrays that have a specific number of values, but you don't know how many values that will be. You get each value as a variable of any type you want—the preceding code says string arg in args, which means "for each array element in args, give it to me as the variable arg of type string. Of course, args is already an array of strings, so no datatype conversion will actually take place here—but it could if you wanted to convert classes or do anything of the like.

After you have each individual argument, call WriteLine() to print it out. This works whether there's one argument or one hundred arguments—or even if there are no arguments at all (in which case the loop doesn't execute at all).

Creating Your Own Variables

As you saw in the parameter list for Main() and the arg variable in your foreach loop, C# insists that each variable has a distinct data type. You can choose from quite a variety: Boolean for true/false values; string for text; int for numbers, float for floating-point numbers; and so on. If you want to be very specific, you can use int32 for a 32-bit integer (covering from –2147483648 to 2147483648) or int64 for a 64-bit integer (covering even larger numbers). But on the whole you can just use int and leave C# to work it out itself.

27

So now you can modify your program to accept two parameters, add them together as numbers, and then print the result. This gives you a chance to see variable definitions, conversion, and mathematics, all in one. Edit the `Main()` method to look like this:

```
public static void Main (string[] args)
{
    int num1 = Convert.ToInt32(args[0]);
    int num2 = Convert.ToInt32(args[1]);
    Console.WriteLine("Sum of two parameters is: " + (num1 + num2)");
}
```

As you can see, each variable needs to be declared with a type (`int`) and a name (`num1` and `num2`), so that C# knows how to handle them. Your args array contains strings, so you need to explicitly convert the strings to integers with the `Convert.ToInt32()` method. Finally, the actual addition of the two strings is done at the end of the method, while they are being printed out. Note how C# is clever enough to have `integer + integer` be added together (in the case of num + num2), whereas `string + integer` attaches the integer to the end of the string (in the case of `"Sum of two parameters is:" + the result of num1 + num2`). This isn't by accident: C# tries to convert data types cleverly, and warns you only if it can't convert a data type without losing some data. For example, if you try to treat a 64-bit integer as a 32-bit integer, it warns you because you might be throwing a lot of data away.

Adding Some Error Checking

Right now your program crashes in a nasty way if users don't provide at least two parameters. The reason for this is that we use `arg[0]` and `arg[1]` (the first and second parameters passed to your program) without even checking whether *any* parameters were passed in. This is easily solved: args is an array, and arrays can reveal their size. If the size doesn't match what you expect, you can bail out.

Add this code at the start of the `Main()` method:

```
if (args.Length != 2) {
    Console.WriteLine("You must provide exactly two parameters!");
    return;
}
```

The new piece of code in there is `return`, which is a C# keyword that forces it to exit the current method. As `Main()` is the only method being called, this has the effect of terminating the program because the user didn't supply two parameters.

Using the `Length` property of args, it is now possible for you to write your own `Main()` method that does different things, depending on how many parameters are provided. To do this properly, you need to use the `else` statement and nest multiple `if` statements like this:

```
if (args.Length == 2) {
    /// whatever...
} else if (args.Length == 3) {
    /// something else
} else if (args.Length == 4) {
    /// even more
} else {
    /// only executed if none of the others are
}
```

Building on Mono's Libraries

Ubuntu ships with several Mono-built programs, including Tomboy and Beagle. It also comes with a fair collection of .NET-enabled libraries, some of which you probably already installed earlier. The nice thing about Mono is that it lets you build on these libraries really easily: You just import them with a `using` statement, then get started.

To demonstrate how easy it is to build more complicated Mono applications, we're going to produce two: one using Beagle, the super-fast file indexer, and one using Gtk#, the GUI toolkit that's fast becoming the standard for Gnome development. Each has its own API that takes some time to master fully, but you can get started with them in minutes.

Searching with Beagle

Beagle is the de facto Linux search tool for Gnome, and is also used by several KDE-based programs. It works by scanning your computer in the background, then monitoring for file system changes so that its data always stays up to date. However, the magic is that it indexes data cleverly—if you tag your images, it reads those tags. If you have album and artist data in your MP3s, it reads that data too. It also reads your emails, your instant messenger conversations, your web browser history, and much more—and provides all this data in one place, so if you search for "firefox" you'll find the application itself, all the times you've mentioned Firefox in your emails, and so on.

In MonoDevelop, go to File, New Project, select C#, then choose Console Project. Give it the name BeagleTest, and tell MonoDevelop not to create a separate directory for the solution, and also that you don't want Gtk# support or Packaging Integration. You'll be back at the default Hello World program, but you're going to change that. First, you need to tell Mono that you want to use Beagle and Gtk# (by hand, rather than using its project wizard).

27

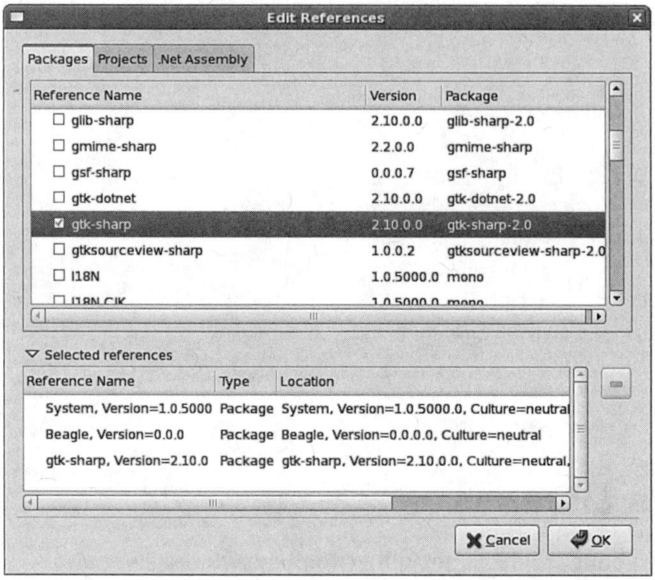

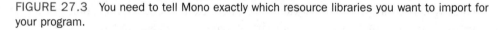

FIGURE 27.3   You need to tell Mono exactly which resource libraries you want to import for your program.

No, you're not going to create a GUI for your search, but you do want to take advantage of Gtk#'s idle loop system—we'll explain why soon.

To add references to these two libraries, right-click on the word References in the left pane (just above Resources) and select Edit References. A new window appears (shown in Figure 27.3), and from that you should make sure Beagle and gtk-sharp are selected. Now click OK, and the References group on the left should expand so that you can see you have Beagle, gtk-sharp, and System (the last one is the default reference for .NET programs).

Now it's time to write the code. At the top of the `Main.cs` file (your main code file), you need to edit the `"using"` statements to look like this:

```
using System;
using System.Collections;
using Beagle;
using Gtk;
```

The `BeagleTest` namespace and `MainClass` class aren't changing, but you do need to edit the `Main()` method so that you can run your Beagle query. Here's how it should look, with C# comments (//, as in C++) sprinkled throughout to help you understand what's going on:

```
public static void Main(string[] args)
{
    Application.Init();
```

```
    // "Query" is the main Beagle search type.
    //It does lots of magic for you - you just need to provide it with a search
term and tell it where to search
    Query q = new Query();

    // these two are callback functions.
    //What you're saying is, when a hit is returned
    // (that is, when Beagle finds something, it should
    // run your OnHitsAdded() method. That code isn't written
    // yet, but you'll get there soon.
    q.HitsAddedEvent += OnHitsAdded;
    q.FinishedEvent += OnFinished;

    // these two tell Beagle where to search
    q.AddDomain(QueryDomain.Neighborhood);
    q.AddDomain(QueryDomain.Global);

    // finally, you tell Beagle to search for the first word
    // provided to your command (args[0]), then ask it
    // to asynchronously run its search. That is, it runs
    // in the background and lets your program continue running
    q.AddText(args[0]);
    q.SendAsync();

    // tell Gtk# to run
    Application.Run();
}
```

The only thing I haven't explained in there is the Gtk# stuff, but you might already have guessed why it's needed. The problem is this: Beagle runs its search asynchronously, which means that it returns control to your program straight away. Without the Application.Run() call, the SendAsync() method is the last thing your program does, which meant that it terminates itself before Beagle actually has chance to return any data. So, Gtk# serves as an idle loop: when you call Run(), Gtk# makes sure your program carries on running until you tell it to quit, giving Beagle enough time to return its results.

Now, let's take a look at the OnHitsAdded and OnFinished methods, called whenever Beagle finds something to return and when it's finished searching, respectively:

```
static void OnHitsAdded (HitsAddedResponse response)
{
    // sometimes Beagle can return multiple hits (files)
    // in each response, so you need to go through each
    // one and print it out line by line
    foreach(Hit hit in response.Hits)
    {
```

```
        // the Uri of hits is its location, which might
        // be on the web, on your filesystem, or somewhere else
        Console.WriteLine("Hit: " + hit.Uri);
    }
}


static void OnFinished(FinishedResponse response)
{
    // the application is done, we can tell Gtk# to quit now
    Application.Quit();
}
```

When you're done, press F8 to compile your program. If you encounter any errors, you have typed something incorrectly, so check carefully against the preceding text. Now open a terminal, change to the directory where you created your project, then look inside there for the bin/Debug subdirectory. All being well, you should find the `BeagleTest.exe` file in there, which you can run like this:

```
mono BeagleTest.exe hello
```

If you get a long string of errors when you run your program, try running this command first: `export MONO_PATH=/usr/lib/beagle`. That tells Mono where to look for the Beagle library, which is probably your problem.

Creating a GUI with Gtk#

Gtk# was included with Gnome by default for the first time in Gnome 2.16, but it had been used for a couple of years prior to that and so was already mature. MonoDevelop comes with its own GUI designer called Stetic, which lets you drag and drop GUI elements onto your windows to design them.

To get started, go to File, New Project in MonoDevelop, choose C#, then Gtk# 2.0 project. Call it GtkTest, and deselect the box asking MonoDevelop to make a separate directory for the solution. You'll find that Main.cs contains a little more code this time because it needs to create and run the Gtk# application. However, the actual code to create your GUI lives in User Interface in the left pane. If you open that group, you'll see MainWindow, which, when double-clicked, brings up MonoDevelop's GUI designer.

There isn't space for me to devote much time to GUI creation, but it's very easy for you to drag and drop the different window widgets onto your form to see what properties they have. The widgets are all listed on the top right of the GUI designer, with widget properties on the bottom-right.

For now, drag a button widget onto your form. It automatically takes up all the space on your window. If you don't want this to happen, try placing one of the containers down first, then putting your button in there. For example, if you want a menu bar at the top, then a calendar, then a status bar, you ought to drop the VBox pane onto the window

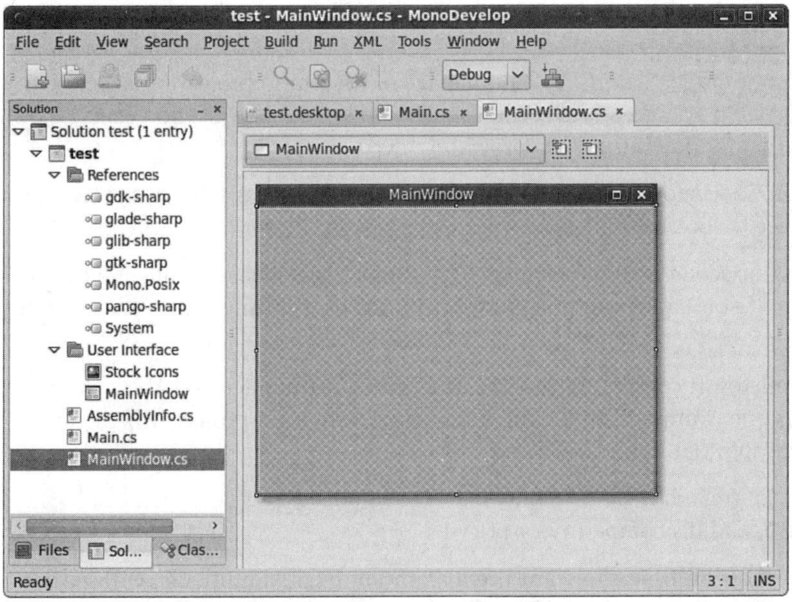

FIGURE 27.4 Using a VPane lets you space your widgets neatly on your form. Gtk# automatically handles window and widget resizing for you.

first, then drop each of those widgets into the separate parts of the VPane, as shown in Figure 27.4.

Your button will have the text "button1" by default, so click on it to select it, then look in the properties pane for Label. It might be hidden away in the Button Properties group, so you'll need to make sure that's open. Change the label to "Hello." Just at the top of the properties pane is a tab saying Properties (where you are right now), and another saying Signals. Signals are the events that happen to your widgets, such as the mouse moving over them, someone typing, or, of interest to us, when your button has been clicked. Look inside the Button Signals group for Clicked and double-click on it. MonoDevelop automatically switches you to the code view, with a pre-created method to handle button clicks.

Type this code into the method:

```
button1.Label = "World!";
```

You need to make one last change before you try compiling. MonoDevelop doesn't automatically give you variables to work with each item in your window—you need to ask for them explicitly. Beneath the code window you will see a button saying Designer—click that to get back to your GUI designer window. Now click the button you created, then click the button marked Bind to Field. This edits your code to create the button1 variable (if you click Source Code you see the variable near the top). Now press F5 to compile and run, and try clicking the button!

Reference

▶ http://www.mono-project.com/—The homepage of the Mono project is packed with information to help you get started. You can also download new Mono versions from here, if there's something you desperately need.

▶ http://www.monodevelop.com/—The MonoDevelop project has its own site, which is the best place to look for updates.

▶ http://www.icsharpcode.net/OpenSource/SD/—MonoDevelop started life as a port of SharpDevelop. If you happen to dual-boot on Windows, this might prove very useful to you.

▶ http://msdn.microsoft.com/vcsharp/—We don't print many Microsoft URLs in this book, but this one is important: It's the homepage of their C# project, which can be considered the spiritual home of C# itself.

▶ Jesse Liberty's *Programming C#* (O'Reilly, ISBN 0-596-00699-3) is compact, it's comprehensive, and it's competitively priced.

▶ If you're very short on time and want the maximum detail (admittedly, with rather limited readability), you should try *The C# Programming Language*, which was co-authored by the creator of C#, Anders Hejlsberg (Addison-Wesley, ISBN: 0-321-33443-4).

▶ For a more general book on the .NET framework and all the features it provides, you might find *.NET Framework Essentials* (O'Reilly, ISBN: 0-596-00505-9) useful.

PART VI

Ubuntu Housekeeping

IN THIS PART

CHAPTER 28

Securing Your Machines

No home computer with a connection to the Internet is 100% safe. If this information does not concern you, it should! Although there is no way to stop a serious cracker who is intent on getting into your computer or network, there are ways to make it harder for him and to warn you when he does.

In this chapter, we discuss all aspects of securing your Linux machines. You might have wondered why we did not spread this information around the book wherever it was appropriate, but the reason is simple: If you ever have a security problem with Linux, you know you can turn to this page and start reading without having to search or try to remember where you saw a tip. Everything you need is here in this one chapter, and we strongly advise you read it from start to finish.

Built-In Protection in the Kernel

A number of networking and low-level protective services are built in to the Linux kernel. These services can be enabled, disabled, or displayed using the sysctl command, or by echoing a value (usually a 1 or a 0 to turn a service on or off) to a kernel process file under the /proc directory.

Understanding Computer Attacks

There are many ways in which computer attacks can be divided, but perhaps the easiest is *internal* which are computer attacks done by someone with access to a computer on the local network, and *external*, which are attacks by someone with access to a computer through the Internet. This might sound like a trivial separation to make, but it is actually important: Unless you routinely hire talented computer hackers or allow visitors to plug computers into your network, the worst internal attack you are likely encounter is from a disgruntled employee.

Hacker Versus Cracker

In earlier days, there was a distinction made between the words *hacker* and *cracker*. A hacker was someone who used technology to innovate in new or unusual ways, whereas a cracker was someone who used technology to attack another's computers and cause harm.

This distinction was lost on the general public, so the term *hacker* has now come to mean the same as *cracker*. This book follows general usage, so a *hacker* is a malicious person using his computer to cause problems for others.

Although you should never ignore the internal threat, you should arguably be more concerned with the outside world. The big bad Internet is a security vortex. Machines connected directly to the outside world can be attacked by people across the world, and invariably are, even only a few minutes after having been connected.

This situation is not a result of malicious users lying in wait for your IP address to do something interesting. Instead, canny virus writers have created worms that exploit a vulnerability, take control of a machine, and then spread it to other machines around them. As a result, most attacks today are the result of these autohacking tools; there are only a handful of true hackers around, and, to be frank, if one of these ever actually targets you seriously, it will take a mammoth effort to repel him regardless of which operating system you run.

Autohacking scripts also come in another flavor: prewritten code that exploits a vulnerability and gives its users special privileges on the hacked machine. These scripts are rarely used by their creators; instead, they are posted online and downloaded by wannabe hackers, who then use them to attack vulnerable machines.

So, the external category is itself made up of worms, serious day job hackers, and wannabe hackers (usually called *script kiddies*). Combined they will assault your Internet-facing servers, and it is your job to make sure your boxes stay up, happily ignoring the firefight around them.

On the internal front, things are somewhat more difficult. Users who sit inside your firewall are already past your primary source of defense and, worse, they might even have physical access to your machines.

Regardless of the source of the attack, there is a five-step checklist you can follow to secure your box:

1. Assess your vulnerability. Decide which machines can be attacked, which services they are running, and who has access to them.

2. Configure the server for maximum security. Only install what you need, only run what you must, and configure a local firewall.

3. Secure physical access to the server.

4. Create worst-case-scenario policies.

5. Keep up-to-date with security news.

Each of these is covered in the following sections, and each is as important as the others.

Assessing Your Vulnerability

It is a common mistake for people to assume that switching on a firewall makes them safe. This is not the case and, in fact, has never been the case. Each system has distinct security needs, and taking the time to customize its security layout will give you maximum security and the best performance.

The following list summarizes the most common mistakes:

▶ **Installing every package**—Do you plan to use the machine as a DNS server? If not, why have BIND installed? Go through Synaptic and ensure that you have only the software you need.

▶ **Enabling unused services**—Do you want to administer the machine remotely? Do you want people to upload files? If not, turn off SSH and FTP because they just add needless attack vectors. This goes for many other services.

▶ **Disabling the local firewall on the grounds that you already have a firewall at the perimeter**—In security, depth is crucial: The more layers someone has to hack through, the higher the likelihood she will give up or get caught.

▶ **Letting your machine give out more information than it needs to**—Many machines are configured to give out software names and version numbers by default, which is just giving hackers a helping hand.

▶ **Placing your server in an unlocked room**—If so, you might as well just turn it off now and save the worry. The exception to this is if all the employees at your company are happy and trustworthy. But why take the risk?

▶ **Plugging your machine into a wireless network**—Unless you need wireless, avoid it, particularly if your machine is a server. Never plug a server into a wireless network because it is just too fraught with security problems.

After you have ruled out these, you are onto the real problem: Which attack vectors are open on your server? In Internet terms, this comes down to which services are Internet-facing and which ports they are running on.

Two tools are often used to determine your vulnerabilities: Nmap and Nessus. Nessus scans your machine, queries the services running, checks their version numbers against its list of vulnerabilities, and reports problems.

Although Nessus sounds clever, it does not work well in many modern distributions (Ubuntu included) because of the way patches are made available to software. For

28

example, if you're running Apache 2.0.52 and a bug is found that's fixed in 2.0.53, Ubuntu backports that patch to 2.0.52. This is done because the new release probably also includes new features that might break your code, so the Ubuntu team takes only what is necessary and copies it into your version. As a result, Nessus will see the version 2.0.52 and think it is vulnerable to a bug that has in fact been backported.

The better solution is to use Nmap, which scans your machine and reports on any open TCP/IP ports it finds. Any service you have installed that responds to Nmap's query is pointed out, which enables you to ensure that you have locked everything down as much as possible.

Nmap is available to install through Synaptic. Although you can use Nmap from a command line, it is easier to use with the front end—at least until you become proficient. To run the front end, select Actions, Run Application and run `nmapfe`. If you want to enable all Nmap's options, you need to switch to run `sudo nmapfe` from the console.

The best way to run Nmap is to use the SYN Stealth scan, with OS Detection and Version Probe turned on. You need to use sudo to enable the first two options (they are on by default when you use sudo), but it is well worth it. When you run Nmap (click the Scan button), it tests every port on your machine and checks whether it responds. If it does respond, Nmap queries it for version information and then prints its results onscreen.

The output lists the port numbers, service name (what usually occupies that port), and version number for every open port on your system. Hopefully, the information Nmap shows you will not be a surprise. If there is something open that you do not recognize, a hacker might have placed a backdoor on your system to allow herself easy access.

You should use the output from Nmap to help you find and eliminate unwanted services. The fewer services that are open to the outside world, the more secure you are.

Protecting Your Machine

After you have disabled all the unneeded services on your system, what remains is a core set of connections and programs that you want to keep. However, you are not finished yet: You need to clamp down your wireless network, lock your server physically, and put scanning procedures in place (such as Tripwire and promiscuous mode network monitors).

Securing a Wireless Network

Because wireless networking has some unique security issues, those issues deserve a separate discussion here.

Wireless networking, although convenient, can be very insecure by its very nature because transmitted data (even encrypted data) can be received by remote devices. Those devices could be in the same room; in the house, apartment, or building next door; or even several blocks away. Extra care must be used to protect the actual frequency used by your network. Great progress has been made in the past couple of years, but the possibility of a security breach is increased when the attacker is in the area and knows the frequency on which to listen. It should also be noted that the encryption method used by more wireless

NICs is weaker than other forms of encryption (such as SSH) and should not be considered as part of your security plan.

> **TIP**
>
> Always use OpenSSH-related tools, such as `ssh` or `sftp`, to conduct business on your wireless LAN. Passwords are not transmitted as plain text, and your sessions are encrypted. See Chapter 19, "Remote Access with SSH and Telnet," to see how to connect to remote systems using `ssh`.

The better the physical security is around your network, the more secure it will be (this applies to wired networks as well). Keep wireless transmitters (routers, switches, and so on) as close to the center of your building as possible. Note or monitor the range of transmitted signals to determine whether your network is open to mobile network sniffing—now a geek sport known as *war driving*. (Linux software is available at http://sourceforge.net/project/showfiles.php?group_id=57253.) An occasional walk around your building not only gives you a break from work, but can also give you a chance to notice any people or equipment that should not be in the area.

Keep in mind that it takes only a single rogue wireless access point hooked up to a legitimate network hub to open access to your entire system. These access points can be smaller than a pack of cigarettes, so the only way to spot them is to scan for them with another wireless device.

Passwords and Physical Security

The next step toward better security is to use secure passwords on your network and ensure that users use them as well. For somewhat more physical security, you can force the use of a password with the LILO or GRUB bootloaders, remove bootable devices such as floppy and CD-ROM drives, or configure a network-booting server for Ubuntu. This approach is not well supported or documented at the time of this writing, but you can read about one way to do this in Brieuc Jeunhomme's Network Boot and Exotic Root HOWTO, available at http://www.tldp.org/HOWTO/Network-boot-HOWTO/. You can also read more about GRUB and LILO in Chapter 32, "Kernel and Module Management."

Also, keep in mind that some studies show that as much as 90% of network break-ins are by current or former employees. If a person no longer requires access to your network, lock out access or, even better, remove the account immediately. A good security policy also dictates that any data associated with the account first be backed up and retained for a set period of time to ensure against loss of important data. If you are able, remove the terminated employee from the system before he leaves the building.

Finally, be aware of physical security. If a potential attacker can get physical access to your system, getting full access becomes trivial. Keep all servers in a locked room, and ensure that only authorized personnel are given access to clients.

28

Configuring and Using Tripwire

Tripwire is a security tool that checks the integrity of normal system binaries and reports any changes to syslog or by email. Tripwire is a good tool for ensuring that your binaries have not been replaced by Trojan horse programs. *Trojan horses* are malicious programs inadvertently installed because of identical filenames to distributed (expected) programs, and they can wreak havoc on a breached system.

Ubuntu does not include the free version of Tripwire, but it can be used to monitor your system. To set up Tripwire for the first time, go to http://www.tripwire.org, and then download and install an open-source version of the software. After installation, run the twinstall.sh script (found under /etc/tripwire) as root like so:

```
$ sudo /etc/tripwire/twinstall.sh
— — — — — — — — — — — — — — — — — — — — — — — —
The Tripwire site and local passphrases are used to
sign a variety of files, such as the configuration,
policy, and database files.

Passphrases should be at least 8 characters in length
and contain both letters and numbers.

See the Tripwire manual for more information.


— — — — — — — — — — — — — — — — — — — — — — — —
Creating key files...

(When selecting a passphrase, keep in mind that good passphrases typically
have upper and lower case letters, digits and punctuation marks, and are
at least 8 characters in length.)

Enter the site keyfile passphrase:
```

You then need to enter a password of at least eight characters (perhaps best is a string of random madness, such as 5fwkc4ln) at least twice. The script generates keys for your site (host) and then asks you to enter a password (twice) for local use. You are then asked to enter the new site password. After following the prompts, the (rather extensive) default configuration and policy files (tw.cfg and tw.pol) are encrypted. You should then back up and delete the original plain-text files installed by Ubuntu.

To then initialize Tripwire, use its — init option like so:

```
$ sudo tripwire — init
Please enter your local passphrase:
Parsing policy file: /etc/tripwire/tw.pol
Generating the database...
*** Processing Unix File System ***
```

```
....
Wrote database file: /var/lib/tripwire/shuttle2.twd
The database was successfully generated.
```

Note that not all the output is shown here. After Tripwire has created its database (which is a snapshot of your file system), it uses this baseline along with the encrypted configuration and policy settings under the /etc/tripwire directory to monitor the status of your system. You should then start Tripwire in its integrity checking mode, using a desired option. (See the tripwire manual page for details.) For example, you can have Tripwire check your system and then generate a report at the command line, like so:

```
# tripwire -m c
```

No output is shown here, but a report is displayed in this example. The output could be redirected to a file, but a report is saved as /var/lib/tripwire/report/hostname-YYYYM-MDD-HHMMSS.twr (in other words, using your host's name, the year, the month, the day, the hour, the minute, and the seconds). This report can be read using the twprint utility, like so:

```
# twprint — print-report -r \
/var/lib/tripwire/report/shuttle2-20020919-181049.twr ¦ less
```

Other options, such as emailing the report, are supported by Tripwire, which should be run as a scheduled task by your system's scheduling table, /etc/crontab, on off-hours. (It can be resource intensive on less powerful computers.) The Tripwire software package also includes a twadmin utility you can use to fine-tune or change settings or policies or to perform other administrative duties.

Devices

Do not ever advertise that you have set a NIC to promiscuous mode. Promiscuous mode (which can be set on an interface by using ifconfig's promisc option) is good for monitoring traffic across the network and can often allow you to monitor the actions of someone who might have broken into your network. The tcpdump command also sets a designated interface to promiscuous mode while the program runs; unfortunately, the ifconfig command does not report this fact while tcpdump is running!

Do not forget to use the right tool for the right job. Although a network bridge can be used to connect your network to the Internet, it would not be a good option. Bridges have almost become obsolete because they forward any packet that comes their way, which is not good when a bridge is connected to the Internet. A router enables you to filter which packets are relayed.

Viruses

In the right hands, Linux is every bit as vulnerable to viruses as Windows is. That might come as a surprise to you, particularly if you made the switch to Linux on the basis of its security record. However, the difference between Windows and Linux is that it is much easier to secure against viruses on Linux. Indeed, as long as you are smart, you need never worry about them. Here is why:

- ▶ Linux never puts the current directory in your executable path, so typing `ls` runs `/bin/ls` rather than any ls in the current directory.

- ▶ A non-root user can infect only the files he has write access to, which is usually only the files in his home directory. This is one of the most important reasons for never using sudo when you don't need to!

- ▶ Linux forces you to mark files as executable, so you can't accidentally run a file called `myfile.txt.exe`, thinking it was just a text file.

- ▶ By having more than one common web browser and email client, Linux has strength through diversity: Virus writers cannot target one platform and hit 90% of the users.

Despite saying all that, Linux is susceptible to being a carrier for viruses. If you run a mail server, your Linux box can send virus-infected mails on to Windows boxes. The Linux-based server would be fine, but the Windows client would be taken down by the virus.

In this situation, you should consider a virus scanner for your machine. You have several to choose from, both free and commercial. The most popular free suite is Clam AV (http://www.clamav.net), but Central Command, BitDefender, F-Secure, Kaspersky, McAfee, and others all compete to provide commercial solutions—look around for the best deal before you commit.

Configuring UFW (Uncomplicated firewall)

Always use a hardware-based or software-based firewall on computers connected to the Internet. Ubuntu has a firewall application installed by default named "UFW" or Uncomplicated Firewall). This tool will allow you implement selective or restrictive policies regarding access to your computer or LAN.

Start the ufw command from a console or terminal window. You must run this command as root; otherwise, you will see an error message like this:

```
$ /usr/sbin/ufw
ERROR: You need to be root to run this script.
```

Use the sudo command to run ufw like this:

```
$ sudo /usr/sbin/ufw
```

After you press Enter, you see a dialog as shown in Figure Listing 28.1.

LISTING 28.1

```
Usage: ufw COMMAND
Commands:
  enable                      enables the firewall
  disable                     disables the firewall
  default ARG                 set default policy
  logging LEVEL               set logging to LEVEL
  allow ARGS                  add allow rule
  deny ARGS                   add deny rule
  reject ARGS                 add reject rule
  limit ARGS                  add limit rule
  delete RULE                 delete RULE
  insert NUM RULE             insert RULE at NUM
  status                      show firewall status
  status numbered             show firewall status as numbered list of RULES
  status verbose               show verbose firewall status
  show ARG                    show firewall report
  version                     display version information

Application profile commands:
  app list                    list application profiles
  app info PROFILE            show information on PROFILE
  app update PROFILE          update PROFILE
  app default ARG             set default application policy
```

There is also a graphical interface that can be installed to manage ufw. From your desktop goto Applications > Ubuntu Software Center and then enter the application name of gufw and click search. Double click the "Firewall Configuration" menu item and then press the Install button. However, we'll be looking at using the command line for configuration.

By default the ufw or firewall is disabled. To enable the firewall you will run the following command, to disable replace enabled with disabled.

```
$ sudo ufw enable
```

Next, we will want to enable firewall logging. Much like the enable command we will run the following command:

```
$ sudo ufw logging on
```

To enable specific ports on the firewall you can run ufw command along with the allowed variable, for example if you want to allow port 80 (http) incoming connections to your Ubuntu server you would enter the following:

```
$ sudo ufw allow 80/tcp
```

28

To remove the firewall rule allowing port 80 connections run the following command:

```
$ sudo ufw delete allow 80
```

You can also allow incoming connections from particular IP addresses, for example if you want to let 192.168.0.1 to connect to your server you would enter the following:

```
$ sudo ufw allow from 192.168.0.1
```

To remove the firewall rule allowing the above IP address to connect you would run the following command:

```
$ sudo ufw delete allow from 192.168.0.1
```

The ufw application is relativy new and is still growing and new features are being added. However, it's a great and simple way to maintain your firewall rules.

Forming a Disaster Recovery Plan

No one likes planning for the worst, which is why two thirds of people do not have wills. It is a scary thing to have your systems hacked: One or more criminals has broken through your carefully laid blocks and caused untold damage to the machine. Your boss, if you have one, will want a full report of what happened and why, and your users will want their email when they sit down at their desks in the morning. What to do?

If you ever do get hacked, nothing will take the stress away entirely. However, if you take the time to prepare a proper response in advance, you should at least avoid premature aging. Here are some tips to get you started:

- **Do not just pull the network cable out**—This alerts the hacker that he has been detected, which rules out any opportunities for security experts to monitor for that hacker returning and actually catch him.

- **Only inform the people who need to know**—Your boss and other IT people are at the top of the list; other employees are not. Keep in mind that it could be one of the employees behind the attack, and this tips them off.

- **If the machine is not required and you do not want to trace the attack, you can safely remove it from the network**—However, do not switch it off because some backdoors are only enabled when the system is rebooted.

- **Take a copy of all the log files on the system and store them somewhere else**—These might have been tampered with, but they might contain nuggets of information.

- **Check the /etc/passwd file and look for users you do not recognize**—Change all the passwords on the system, and remove bad users.

- **Check the output of ps aux for unusual programs running**—Also check to see whether any cron jobs are set to run.

- Look in /var/www and see whether any web pages are there that should not be.

▶ Check the contents of the `.bash_history` files in the home directories of your users—Are there any recent commands for your primary user?

▶ **If you have worked with external security companies previously, call them in for a fresh audit**—Hand over all the logs you have, and explain the situation. They will be able to extract all the information from the logs that is possible.

▶ **Start collating backup tapes from previous weeks and months**—Your system might have been hacked long before you noticed, so you might need to roll back the system more than once to find out when the attack actually succeeded.

▶ **Download and install Rootkit Hunter from http://www.rootkit.nl/projects/ rootkit_hunter.html**—This searches for (and removes) the types of files that bad guys leave behind for their return.

Keep your disaster recovery plan somewhere safe; saving it as a file on the machine in question is a very bad move!

Keeping Up-to-Date on Linux Security Issues

A multitude of websites relate to security. One in particular hosts an excellent mailing list. The site is called Security Focus, and the mailing list is called BugTraq. BugTraq is well-known for its unbiased discussion of security flaws. Be warned: It receives a relatively large amount of traffic (20–100+ messages daily).

Often security holes are discussed on BugTraq before the software makers have even released the fix. The Security Focus site has other mailing lists and sections dedicated to Linux in general and is an excellent resource.

Related Ubuntu and Linux Commands

You will use these commands when managing security in your Ubuntu system:

▶ Wireshark—GNOME graphical network scanner

▶ GUFW—Ubuntu's basic graphical firewalling tool for GNOME

▶ ufw—Ubuntu's basic command-line firewalling tool

▶ ssh—The OpenSSH remote login client and preferred replacement for telnet

Reference

▶ http://www.insecure.org/nmap/—This site contains information on Nmap.

▶ http://www.securityfocus.com/—The Security Focus website.

▶ http://www.tripwire.org—Information and download links for the open-source version of Tripwire.

▶ http://www.ubuntu.com/usn—The official Ubuntu security notices list; well worth keeping an eye on!

28

CHAPTER 29

Performance Tuning

Squeezing extra performance out of your hardware might sound like a pointless task given how cheap commodity upgrades are today. To a certain degree that is true—for most of us, it is cheaper to buy a new computer than to spend hours fighting to get a 5% speed boost. But what if the speed boost were 20%? How about if it were 50%?

The amount of benefit you can get by optimizing your system varies depending on what kinds of tasks you are running, but there is something for everyone. Over the next few pages we will be looking at quick ways to optimize the Apache web server, both the KDE and Gnome desktop systems, both MySQL and PostgreSQL database servers, and more.

Before we start, you need to understand that *optimization* is not an absolute term: If we optimize a system, we have improved its performance, but it is still possible it could further be increased. We are not interested in getting 99.999% performance out of a system because optimization suffers from the law of diminishing returns—the basic changes make the biggest differences, but after that it takes increasing amounts of work to obtain decreasing speed improvements.

Hard Disk

Many Linux users love to tinker under the hood to increase the performance of their computers, and Linux gives you some great tools to do just that. Whereas Moms tell us, "Don't fix what's not broken," Dads often say, "Fix it until it breaks." In this section, you learn about many of the commands used to tune, or "tweak," your file system.

Before you undertake any "under the hood" work with Linux, however, keep a few points in mind. First, perform a benchmark on your system before you begin. Linux does not offer a well-developed benchmarking application, but availability changes rapidly. You can search online for the most up-to-date information for benchmarking applications for Linux. If you are a system administrator, you might choose to create your own bench-marking tests. Second, tweak only one thing at a time so you can tell what works, what does not work, and what breaks. Some of these tweaks might not work or might lock up your machine.

Always have a working boot disc handy and remember that you are personally assuming all risks for attempting any of these tweaks.

Using the BIOS and Kernel to Tune the Disk Drives

One method of tuning involves adjusting the settings in your BIOS. Because the BIOS is not Linux and every BIOS seems different, always read your motherboard manual for better possible settings and make certain that all the drives are detected correctly by the BIOS. Change only one setting at a time.

Linux does provide a limited means to interact with BIOS settings during the boot process (mostly overriding them). In this section, you will learn about those commands.

Other options are in the following list, and are more fully outlined in the BOOTPROMPT HOWTO and the kernel documentation. These commands can be used to force the IDE controllers and drives to be optimally configured. Of course, YMMV (Your Mileage May Vary) because these do not work for everyone.

idex=dma—This will force DMA support to be turned on for the primary IDE bus, where x=0, or the secondary bus, where x=1.

idex=autotune—This command will attempt to tune the interface for optimal performance.

hdx=ide-scsi—This command will enable SCSI emulation of an IDE drive. This is required for some CD-RW drives to work properly in write mode and it might provide some performance improvements for regular CD-R drives as well.

idebus=xx—This can be any number from 20 to 66; autodetection is attempted, but this can set it manually if dmesg says that it isn't autodetected correctly or if you have it set in the BIOS to a different value (overclocked). Most PCI controllers will be happy with 33.

pci=biosirq—Some motherboards might cause Linux to generate an error message saying that you should use this. Look in dmesg for it; if you do not see it, you don't need to use it.

These options can be entered into /etc/lilo.conf or /boot/grub/grub.conf in the same way as other options are appended.

The hdparm **Command**

The hdparm utility can be used by root to set and tune the settings for IDE hard drives. You would do this to tune the drives for optimal performance.

Once a kernel patch and associated support programs, the hdparm program is now included with Ubuntu. You should only experiment with the drives mounted read-only because some settings can damage some file systems when used improperly. The hdparm command also works with CD-ROM drives and some SCSI drives.

The general format of the command is this:

```
# hdparm command device
```

This command runs a hard disk test:

```
hdparm -tT /dev/hda
```

You will need to replace /dev/hda with the location of your hard disk. hdparm will then run two tests—cached reads and buffered disk reads. A good IDE hard disk should be getting 400-500MB/sec for the first test, and 20-30MB/sec for the second. Note your scores, then try this command:

```
hdparm -m16 -d1 -u1 -c1 /dev/hda
```

That enables various performance-enhancing settings. Now try executing the original command again—if you see an increase, then you should run this command:

```
hdparm -m16 -d1 -u1 -c1 -k1 /dev/hda
```

The extra parameter tells hdparm to write the settings to disk so they will be used each time you boot up—ensuring optimal disk performance in the future.

The man entry for hdparm is extensive and contains useful detailed information, but since the kernel configuration selected by Ubuntu already attempts to optimize the drives, it might be that little can be gained through tweaking. Because not all hardware combinations can be anticipated by Ubuntu or by Linux and performance gains are always useful, you're encouraged to try.

29

> **TIP**
>
> You can use the hdparm command to produce a disk transfer speed result with
>
> ```
> # hdparm -tT device
> ```
>
> Be aware, however, that although the resulting numbers appear quantitative, they are subject to several technical qualifications beyond the scope of what is discussed and explained in this chapter. Simply put, do not accept values generated by hdparm as absolute numbers, but only as a relative measure of performance.

File System Tuning

Never content to leave things alone, Linux provides several tools to adjust and customize the file system settings. The belief is that hardware manufacturers and distribution creators tend to select conservation settings that will work well all the time, leaving some of the potential of your system leashed—that's why you have chosen Ubuntu Unleashed to help you.

The Linux file system designers have done an excellent job of selecting default values used for file system creation and the 2.6 version of the Linux kernel now contains new code for the IDE subsystem that significantly improves I/O (input/output) transfer speeds over older versions, obviating much of the need for special tweaking of the file system and drive parameters if you use IDE disks. Although these values work well for most users, some server applications of Linux benefit from file system tuning. As always, observe and benchmark your changes.

Synchronizing the File System with sync

Because Linux uses buffers when writing to devices, the write will not occur until the buffer is full, until the kernel tells it to, or if you tell it to by using the sync command. Traditionally, the command is given twice, as in the following:

```
# sync ; sync
```

It is really overkill to do it twice. Still, it can be helpful prior to the unmounting of certain types of media with slow write speeds (such as some USB hard drives or PCMCIA storage media), but only because it delays the user from attempting to remove the media too soon, not because two syncs are better than one.

The tune2fs Command

With tune2fs, you can adjust the tunable file system parameters on an ext2 or ext3 file system. A few performance-related items of note are as follows:

To disable file system checking, the -c 0 option sets the maximal mount count to zero.

The interval between forced checks can be adjusted with the -I option.

The -m option will set the reserved blocks percentage with a lower value, freeing more space at the expense of fsck having less space to write any recovered files.

Decrease the number of superblocks to save space with the -O sparse_super option. (Modern file systems use this by default.) Always run e2fsck after you change this value.

More space can be freed with the -r option that sets the number of reserved (for root) blocks.

Note that most of these uses of tune2fs free up space on the drive at the expense of the capability of fsck to recover data. Unless you really need the space and can deal with the consequences, just accept the defaults; large drives are now relatively inexpensive.

The `e2fsck` Command

This utility checks an `ext2`/`ext3` file system. Some useful arguments taken from `man e2fsck` are as follows:

-c—Checks for bad blocks and then marks them as bad.

-f—Forces checking on a clean file system.

-v—Verbose mode.

The `badblocks` Command

Although not a performance tuning program per se, the utility `badblocks` checks an (preferably) unmounted partition for bad blocks. It is not recommended that you run this command by itself, but rather allow it to be called by `fsck`. It should only be used directly if you specify the block size accurately—don't guess or assume anything.

The options available for `badblocks` are detailed in the `man` page. They allow for very low-level manipulation of the file system that is useful for data recovery by file system experts or for file system hacking, but are beyond the scope of this chapter and the average user.

Disabling File Access Time

Whenever Linux reads a file, it changes the last access time—known as the `atime`. This is also true for your web server: If you are getting hit by 50 requests a second, your hard disk will be updating the atime 50 times a second. Do you really need to know the last time a file was accessed? If not, you can disable atime setting for a directory by typing this:

```
chattr –R +A /path/to/directory
```

The chattr command changes file system attributes, of which "don't update atime" is one. To set that attribute, use +A and specify –R so that it is recursively set. `/path/to/directory` gets changed, and so do all the files and subdirectories it contains.

Kernel

As the Linux kernel developed over time, developers sought a way to fine-tune some of the kernel parameters. Before `sysctl`, those parameters had to be changed in the kernel configuration and then the kernel had to be recompiled.

The `sysctl` command can change some parameters of a running kernel. It does this through the `/proc` file system, which is a "virtual window" into the running kernel. Although it might appear that a group of directories and files exist under `/proc`, that is only a representation of parts of the kernel. When we're the root user (or using the sudo command), we can read values from and write values to those "files," referred to as *variables*. We can display a list of the variables as shown in the following. (An annotated list is presented because roughly 250 items [or more] exist in the full list.)

```
# sysctl -A
net.ipv4.tcp_max_syn_backlog = 1024
net.ipv4.tcp_rfc1337 = 0
net.ipv4.tcp_stdurg = 0
net.ipv4.tcp_abort_on_overflow = 0
net.ipv4.tcp_tw_recycle = 0
net.ipv4.tcp_syncookies = 0
net.ipv4.tcp_fin_timeout = 60
net.ipv4.tcp_retries2 = 15
net.ipv4.tcp_retries1 = 3
net.ipv4.tcp_keepalive_intvl = 75
net.ipv4.tcp_keepalive_probes = 9
net.ipv4.tcp_keepalive_time = 7200
net.ipv4.ipfrag_time = 30
```

The items shown are networking parameters, and actually tweaking these values is beyond the scope of this book. If we wanted to change a value, however, the -w parameter is used:

```
# sysctl -w net.ipv4.tcp_retries 2=20
```

This increases the value of that particular kernel parameter.

If you find that a particular setting is useful, you can enter it into the /etc/sysctl.conf file. The format is as follows, using the earlier example:

```
net.ipv4.tcp_retries 2=20
```

Of more interest to kernel hackers than regular users, sysctl is a potentially powerful tool that continues to be developed and documented.

TIP

The kernel does a good job of balancing performance for graphical systems, so there's not a great deal you can do to tweak your desktop to run faster.

Both GNOME and KDE are "heavyweight" desktop systems: They are all-inclusive, all-singing, and all-dancing environments that do far more than browse your file system. The drawback to this is that their size makes them run slow on older systems. On the flip side, Ubuntu also comes with the Xfce desktop, which is a great deal slimmer and faster than the other two. If you find GNOME and KDE are struggling just to open a file browser, Xfce is for you.

Apache

Despite being the most popular web server on the Internet, Apache is by no means the fastest. Part of the "problem" is that Apache has been written to follow every applicable standard to the letter, so much of its development work has been geared toward standards-compliancy rather than just serving web pages quickly. That said, with a little tweaking we can convert a $1,000 Dell server into something capable of surviving the Slashdot Effect.

> **NOTE**
>
> Slashdot.org is a popular geek news website that spawned the Slashdot Effect—the result of thousands of geeks descending on an unsuspecting website simultaneously. Our $1,000 Dell server had dual-2.8GHz Xeons with 1GB of RAM and SCSI hard disks—if you have more RAM, faster chips, and a high-end network card you can kick sand in Slashdot's face.

The first target for your tuning should be the `apache2.conf` file in `/etc/apache2`, as well as the other files in `/etc/apache2`. The more modules you have loaded, the more load Apache is placing on your server—take a look through the LoadModule list and comment out (start the line with a #) the ones you do not want. Some of these modules can be uninstalled entirely through the Add or Remove Packages dialog.

As a rough guide, you will almost certainly need `mod_mime` and `mod_dir`, and probably also `mod_log_config`. The default Apache configuration in Ubuntu is quite generic, so unless you are willing to sacrifice some functionality you may also need `mod_negotiation` (a speed killer if there ever was one), and `mod_access` (a notorious problem). Both of those last two modules can and should work with little or no performance decrease, but all too often they get abused and just slow things down.

Whatever you do, when you are disabling modules you should ensure you leave either `mod_deflate` or `mod_gzip` enabled, depending on your Apache version. Your bottleneck is almost certainly going to be your bandwidth rather than your processing power, and having one of these two compressing your content will usually turn 10Kb of HTML into 3Kb for supported browsers (most of them).

Next, ensure keepalives are turned off. Yes, you read that right: turn keepalives off. This adds some latency to people viewing your site, because they cannot download multiple files through the same connection. However, in turn it reduces the number of simultaneous open connections and so allows more people to connect.

If you are serving content that does not change, you can take the extreme step of enabling MMAP support. This allows Apache to serve pages directly from RAM without bothering to check whether they have changed, which works wonders for your performance. However, the downside is that when you do change your pages you need to restart Apache. Look for the `EnableMMAP` directive—it is probably commented out and set to off, so you will need to remove the comment and set it to on.

Finally, you should do all you can to ensure that your content is static: avoid PHP if you can, avoid databases if you can, and so on. If you know you are going to get hit by a rush of visitors, use plain HTML so that Apache is limited only by your bandwidth for how fast it can serve pages.

> **TIP**
>
> Some people, when questioned about optimizing Apache, will recommend you tweak the HARD_SERVER_LIMIT in the Apache source code and recompile. While we agree that compiling your own Apache source code is a great way to get a measurable speed boost if you know what you are doing, you should only ever need to change this directive if you are hosting a huge site.
>
> The default value, 256, is enough to handle the Slashdot effect, and if you can handle that then you can handle most things.

MySQL

Tuning your MySQL server for increased performance is exceptionally easy to do, largely because you can see huge speed increases simply by getting your queries right. That said, there are various things you can tune in the server itself that help it cope with higher loads as long as your system has enough RAM.

The key is understanding its buffers—there are buffers and caches for all sorts of things, and finding out how full they are is crucial to maximizing performance. MySQL performs best when it is making full use of its buffers, which in turn places a heavy demand on system RAM. Unless you have 4GB RAM or more in your machine, you do not have enough capacity to set very high values for all your buffers—you need to pick and choose.

Measuring Key Buffer Usage

When you add indexes to your data, it enables MySQL to find data faster. However, ideally you want to have these indexes stored in RAM for maximum speed, and the variable key_buffer_size defines how much RAM MySQL can allocate for index key caching. If MySQL cannot store its indexes in RAM, you will experience serious performance problems. Fortunately, most databases have relatively small key buffer requirements, but you should measure your usage to see what work needs to be done.

To do this, log in to MySQL and type SHOW STATUS LIKE '%key_read%';. That returns all the status fields that describe the hit rate of your key buffer—you should get two rows back: Key_reads and Key_read_requests, which are the number of keys being read from disk and the number of keys being read from the key buffer. From these two numbers you can calculate the percentage of requests being filled from RAM and from disk, using this simple equation:

```
100 - ((Key_reads / Key_read_requests) &infin; 100)
```

That is, you divide Key_reads by Key_read_requests, multiply the result by 100 and then subtract the result from 100. For example, if you have Key_reads of 1000 and Key_read_requests of 100000, you divide 1000 by 100000 to get 0.01; then you multiply that by 100 to get 1.0, and subtract that from 100 to get 99. That number is the percentage of key reads being served from RAM, which means 99% of your keys are served from RAM.

Most people should be looking to get more than 95% served from RAM, although the primary exception is if you update or delete rows very often—MySQL can't cache what keeps changing. If your site is largely read only, this should be around 98%. Lower figures mean you might need to bump up the size of your key buffer.

If you are seeing problems, the next step is to check how much of your current key buffer is being used. Use the SHOW VARIABLES command and look up the value of the key_buffer_size variable. It is probably something like 8388600, which is eight million bytes, or 8MB. Now, use the SHOW STATUS command and look up the value of Key_blocks_used.

You can now determine how much of your key buffer is being used by multiplying Key_blocks_used by 1024, dividing by key_buffer_size, and multiplying by 100. For example, if Key_blocks_used is 8000, you multiply that by 1024 to get 8192000; then you divide that by your key_buffer_size (8388600) to get 0.97656, and finally multiply that by 100 to get 97.656. Thus, almost 98% of your key buffer is being used.

Now, onto the important part: You have ascertained that you are reading lots of keys from disk, and you also now know that the reason for reading from disk is almost certainly because you do not have enough RAM allocated to the key buffer. A general rule of thumb is to allocate as much RAM to the key buffer as you can, up to a maximum of 25% of system RAM—128MB on a 512MB system is about the ideal for systems that read heavily from keys. Beyond that, you will actually see drastic performance decreases because the system has to use virtual memory for the key buffer.

Open /etc/my.cnf in your text editor, and look for the line that contains key_buffer_size. If you do not have one, you need to create a new one—it should be under the line [mysqld]. When you set the new value, do not just pick some arbitrarily high number. Try doubling what is there right now (or try 16MB if there's no line already); then see how it goes. To set 16MB as the key buffer size, you would need line like this:

```
[mysqld]
set-variable = key_buffer_size=16M
datadir=/var/lib/mysql
```

Restart your MySQL server with service mysqld restart, and then go back into MySQL and run SHOW VARIABLES again to see the key_buffer_size. It should be 16773120 if you have set it to 16M. Now, because MySQL just got reset, all its values for key hits and the like will also have been reset. You need to let it run for a while so you can assess how much has changed. If you have a test system you can run, this is the time to run it.

After your database has been accessed with normal usage for a short while (if you get frequent accesses, this might be only a few minutes), recalculate how much of the key buffer is being used. If you get another high score, double the size again, restart, and retest. You should keep repeating this until you see your key buffer usage is below 50% or you find you don't have enough RAM to increase the buffer further—remember that you should never allocate more than 25% of system RAM to the key buffer.

Using the Query Cache

Newer versions of MySQL allow you to cache the results of queries so that, if new queries come in that use exactly the same SQL, the result can be served from RAM. In some ways the query cache is quite intelligent: If, for example, part of the result changes due to another query, the cached results are thrown away and recalculated next time. However, in other ways it is very simple. For example, it uses cached results only if the new query is exactly the same as a cached query, even down to the capitalization of the SQL.

The query cache works well in most scenarios. If your site has an equal mix of reading and writing, the query cache will do its best but will not be optimal. If your site is mostly reading with few writes, more queries will be cached (and for longer), thus improving overall performance.

First, you need to find out whether you have the query cache enabled. To do this, use SHOW VARIABLES and look up the value of have_query_cache. All being well, you should get YES back, meaning that the query cache is enabled. Next, look for the value of query_cache_size and query_cache_limit—the first is how much RAM in bytes is allocated to the query cache, and the second is the maximum result size that should be cached. A good starting set of values for these two is 8388608 (8MB) and 1048576 (1MB).

Next, type **SHOW STATUS LIKE 'Qcache%';** to see all the status information about the query cache. You should get output like this:

```
mysql> SHOW STATUS LIKE 'qcache%';
+-------------------------+--------+
| Variable_name           | Value  |
+-------------------------+--------+
| Qcache_free_blocks      | 1      |
| Qcache_free_memory      | 169544 |
| Qcache_hits             | 698    |
| Qcache_inserts          | 38     |
| Qcache_lowmem_prunes    | 20     |
| Qcache_not_cached       | 0      |
| Qcache_queries_in_cache | 18     |
| Qcache_total_blocks     | 57     |
+-------------------------+--------+
8 rows in set (0.00 sec)
```

From that, we can see that only 18 queries are in the cache (Qcache_queries_in_cache), we have 169544 bytes of memory free in the cache (Qcache_free_memory), 698 queries have been read from the cache (Qcache_hits), 38 queries have been inserted into the cache (Qcache_inserts), but 20 of them were removed due to lack of memory (Qcache_lowmem_prunes), giving the 18 from before. Qcache_not_cached is 0, which means 0 queries were not cached—MySQL is caching them all.

From that, we can calculate how many total queries came in—it is the sum of `Qcache_hits`, `Qcache_inserts`, and `Qcache_not_cached`, which is 736. We can also calculate how well the query cache is being used by dividing `Qcache_hits` by that number and multiplying by 100. In this case, 94.84% of all queries are being served from the query cache, which is a great number.

In our example, we can see that many queries have been trimmed because there is not enough memory in the query cache. This can be changed by editing your `/etc/my.cnf` file and adding a line like this one, somewhere in the [mysqld] section:

```
set-variable = query_cache_size=32M
```

An 8MB query cache should be enough for most people, but larger sites might want 16MB or even 32MB if you are storing a particularly large amount of data. Very few sites will have need to go beyond a 32MB query cache, but keep an eye on the `Qcache_lowmem_prunes` value to ensure you have enough RAM allocated.

Using the query cache does not incur much of a performance hit. When MySQL calculates the result of a query normally, it simply throws it away when the connection closes. With the query cache, it skips the throwing away, and so there is no extra work being done. If your site does have many updates and deletes, be sure to check whether you get any speed boost at all from the query cache.

Miscellaneous Tweaks

If you have tuned your key buffer and optimized your query cache and yet still find your site struggling, there are a handful more smaller changes you make that will add some more speed.

When reading from tables, MySQL has to open the file that stores the table data. How many files it keeps open at a time is defined by the `table_cache` setting, which is set to 64 by default. You can increase this setting if you have more than 64 tables, but you should be aware that Ubuntu does impose limits on MySQL about how many files it can have open at a time. Going beyond 256 is not recommended unless you have a particularly DB-heavy site and know exactly what you are doing.

The other thing you can tweak is the size of the read buffer, which is controlled by `read_buffer_size` and `read_buffer_rnd_size`. Both of these are allocated per connection, which means you should be very careful to have large numbers. Whatever you choose, `read_buffer_rnd_size` should be three to four times the size of `read_buffer_size`, so if `read_buffer_size` is 1MB (suitable for very large databases), `read_buffer_rnd_size` should be 4MB.

Query Optimization

The biggest speed-ups can be seen by reprogramming your SQL statements so they are more efficient. If you follow these tips, your server will thank you:

▶ Select as little data as possible. Rather than SELECT *, select only the fields you need.

▶ If you only need a few rows, use LIMIT to select the number you need.

▶ Declare fields as NOT NULL when creating tables to save space and increase speed.

▶ Provide default values for fields, and use them where you can.

▶ Be very careful with table joins because they are the easiest way to write inefficient queries.

▶ If you must use joins, be sure you join on fields that are indexed. They should also preferably be integer fields, as these are faster than strings for comparisons.

▶ Find and fix slow queries. Add log-long-format and log-slow-queries = /var/log/slow-queries.log to your /etc/my.cnf file, under [mysqld], and MySQL will tell you the queries that took a long time to complete.

▶ Use OPTIMIZE TABLE tablename to defragment tables and refresh the indexes.

Reference

▶ http://www.coker.com.au/bonnie++/—The home page of bonnie, a disk benchmarking tool. It also contains a link to RAID benchmarking utilities and Postal, a benchmarking utility for SMTP servers.

▶ http://httpd.apache.org/docs-2.0/misc/perf-tuning.html—The official Apache guide to tuning your web server.

▶ http://dev.mysql.com/doc/refman/en/5.0-optimization.html—Learn how to optimize your MySQL server direct from the source, the MySQL manual.

There is one particular MySQL optimization book that will really help you get more from your system if you run a large site, and that is High Performance MySQL by Jeremy Zawodny and Derek Balling (O'Reilly), ISBN: 0-596-00306-4.

CHAPTER 30

Command Line Masterclass

In the earlier years of Linux, people made a big fuss of the graphical environments that were available—they rushed to tell new users that you really did not need to keep going back to the command line to type things. Now Linux is more mature, people accept that the command line is still a reality, and a welcome one. While the GUI does indeed make life easier for day-to-day tasks, your options are limited by what the developers wanted you to have—you cannot bring commands together in new ways, and neither can you use any of the GUI features if, for example, your GUI is broken. It does happen!

In his book *The Art of Unix Programming**, Eric Raymond wrote a short story that perfectly illustrates the power of the command line versus the GUI. It's reprinted here with permission, for your reading pleasure:

> One evening, Master Foo and Nubi attended a gathering of programmers who had met to learn from each other. One of the programmers asked Nubi to what school he and his master belonged. Upon being told they were followers of the Great Way of Unix, the programmer grew scornful.

> "The command-line tools of Unix are crude and backward," he scoffed. "Modern, properly designed operating systems do everything through a graphical user interface."

> Master Foo said nothing, but pointed at the moon. A nearby dog began to bark at the master's hand.

> "I don't understand you!" said the programmer.

> Master Foo remained silent, and pointed at an image of the Buddha. Then he pointed at a window.

"What are you trying to tell me?" asked the programmer.

Master Foo pointed at the programmer's head. Then he pointed at a rock.

"Why can't you make yourself clear?" demanded the programmer.

Master Foo frowned thoughtfully, tapped the programmer twice on the nose, and dropped him in a nearby trash can.

As the programmer was attempting to extricate himself from the garbage, the dog wandered over and piddled on him.

At that moment, the programmer achieved enlightenment.

Whimsical as the story is, it does illustrate that there are some things that the GUI just does not do well. Enter the command line: It is a powerful and flexible operating environment on Linux, and—if you practice—can actually be quite fun, too!

In this chapter, you will learn how to master the command line so that you are able to perform common tasks through it, and also link commands together to create new command groups. We will also be looking at the two most popular Linux text editors: Vim and Emacs. The command line is also known as the shell, the console, the command prompt, and the CLI (command-line interpreter). For the purposes of this chapter these are interchangeable, although there are fine-grained differences between them!

Why Use the Shell?

Moving from the GUI to the command line is a conscious choice for most people, although it is increasingly rare that it is an either/or choice. While in X, you can press Ctrl+Alt+F1 at any time to switch to a terminal, but most people tend to run an X terminal application that allows them to have the point-and-click applications and the command-line applications side by side.

Reasons for running the shell include:

▶ You want to chain two or more commands together.

▶ You want to use a command or parameter available only on the shell.

▶ You are working on a text-only system.

▶ You have used it for a long time and feel comfortable there.

Chaining two or more commands together is what gives the shell its real power. Hundreds of commands are available and, by combining them in different ways, you get hundreds of new commands. Some of the shell commands are available through the GUI, but these commands usually have only a small subset of their parameters available, which limits what you are able to do with them.

Working from a text-only system encapsulates both working locally with a broken GUI and also connecting to a remote, text-only system. If your Linux server is experiencing problems, the last thing you want to do is load it down with a GUI connection—working in text mode is faster and more efficient.

The last use is the most common: People use the shell just because it is familiar to them, with many people even using the shell to start GUI applications just because it saves them taking their hands off the keyboard for a moment! This is not a bad thing; it provides fluency and ease with the system and is a perfectly valid way of working.

Basic Commands

It is impossible to know how many commands the average shell citizen uses, but if we had to guess, we would place it at about 25:

- ► cat—Prints the contents of a file
- ► cd—Changes directories
- ► chmod—Changes file access permissions
- ► cp—Copies files
- ► du—Prints disk usage
- ► emacs—Text editor
- ► find—Finds files by searching
- ► gcc—The C/C++/Fortran compiler
- ► grep—Searches for a string in input
- ► less—Filter for paging through output
- ► ln—Creates links between files
- ► locate—Finds files from an index
- ► ls—Lists files in the current directory
- ► make—Compiles and installs programs
- ► man—The manual page reader
- ► mkdir—Makes directories
- ► mv—Moves files
- ► ps—Lists processes
- ► rm—Deletes files and directories
- ► ssh—Connects to other machines
- ► tail—Prints the last lines of a file
- ► top—Prints resource usage
- ► vim—A text editor
- ► which—Prints the location of a command

30

▶ xargs—Executes commands from its input

Of course, many other commands are available to you that get used fairly often—diff, nmap, ping, su, uptime, who, and so on—but if you are able to understand the 25 listed here, you will have sufficient skill to concoct your own command combinations.

Note that we say *understand* the commands—not know all their possible parameters and usages. This is because several of the commands, though commonly used, are used only in any complex manner by people with specific needs. gcc and make are good examples of this: Unless you plan to become a programmer, you need not worry about these beyond just typing make and make install now and then. If you want to learn more about these two, see Chapter 26, "C/C++ Programming Tools for Ubuntu."

Similarly, both Emacs and Vim are text editors that have a text-based interface all of their own, and SSH has already been covered in detail in Chapter 15, "Remote Access with SSH and Telnet."

What remains is 20 commands, each of which has many parameters to customize what it actually does. Again, we can eliminate much of this because many of the parameters are esoteric and rarely used, and, the few times in your Linux life that you need them, you can just read the manual page!

We will be going over these commands one by one, explaining the most common ways to use them. There is one exception to this: The xargs command requires you to understand how to join commands together.

Printing the Contents of a File with cat

Many of Ubuntu's shell commands manipulate text strings, so if you want to be able to feed them the contents of files, you need to be able to output those files as text. Enter the cat command, which prints the contents of any files you pass to it.

Its most basic use is like this:

```
cat myfile.txt
```

That prints the contents of myfile.txt. For this usage there are two extra parameters that are often used: -n numbers the lines in the output, and -s ("squeeze") prints a maximum of one blank line at a time. That is, if your file has 1 line of text, 10 blank lines, 1 line of text, 10 blank lines, and so on, -s shows the first line of text, a single blank line, the next line of text, a single blank line, and so forth. When you combine -s and -n, cat numbers only the lines that are printed—the 10 blank lines shown as one will count as 1 line for numbering.

This command prints information about your CPU, stripping out multiple blank lines and numbering the output:

```
cat -sn /proc/cpuinfo
```

You can also use cat to print the contents of several files at once, like this:

```
cat -s myfile.txt myotherfile.txt
```

In that command, cat merges `myfile.txt` and `myotherfile.txt` on the output, stripping out multiple blank lines. The important thing is that cat does not distinguish between the files in the output—there are no filenames printed, and no extra breaks between the 2. This allows you to treat the 2 as 1 or, by adding more files to the command line, to treat 20 files as 1.

Changing Directories with `cd`

Changing directories is surely something that has no options, right? Not so. cd is actually more flexible than most people realize. Unlike most of the other commands here, cd is not a command in itself—it is built in to bash (or whichever shell interpreter you are using), but it is still used like a command.

The most basic usage of cd is this:

```
cd somedir
```

That looks in the current directory for the `somedir` subdirectory, then moves you into it. You can also specify an exact location for a directory, like this:

```
cd /home/paul/stuff/somedir
```

The first part of cd's magic lies in the characters (- and ~, a dash and a tilde). The first means "switch to my previous directory," and the second means "switch to my home directory." This conversation with cd shows this in action:

```
[paul@caitlin ~]$ cd /usr/local
[paul@caitlin local]$ cd bin
[paul@caitlin bin]$ cd -
/usr/local
[paul@caitlin local]$ cd ~
[paul@caitlin ~]$
```

In the first line, we change to `/usr/local` and get no output from the command. In the second line, we change to bin, which is a subdirectory of `/usr/local`. Next, cd - is used to change back to the previous directory. This time Bash prints the name of the previous directory so we know where we are. Finally, cd ~ is used to change back to our home directory, although if you want to save an extra few keystrokes, just typing cd by itself is equivalent to cd ~.

The second part of cd's magic is its capability to look for directories in predefined locations. When you specify an absolute path to a directory (that is, one starting with a /), cd always switches to that exact location. However, if you specify a relative subdirectory—for example, cd subdir—you can tell cd where you would like that to be relative to. This is accomplished with the CDPATH environment variable. If this variable is not set, cd always uses the current directory as the base; however, you can set it to any number of other directories.

This next example shows a test of this. It starts in /home/paul/empty, an empty directory, and the lines are numbered for later reference:

```
1 [paul@caitlin empty]$ pwd
2 /home/paul/empty
3 [paul@caitlin empty]$ ls
4 [paul@caitlin empty]$ mkdir local
5 [paul@caitlin empty]$ ls
6 local
7 [paul@caitlin empty]$ cd local
8 [paul@caitlin local]$ cd ..
9 [paul@caitlin empty]$ export CDPATH=/usr
10 [paul@caitlin empty]$ cd local
11 /usr/local
12 [paul@caitlin empty]$ cd -
13 /home/paul/empty
14 [paul@caitlin empty]$ export CDPATH=.:/usr
15 [paul@caitlin empty]$ cd local
16 /home/paul/empty/local
17 [paul@caitlin local]$
```

Lines 1–3 show that we are in /home/paul/empty and that it is indeed empty—ls had no output. Lines 4–6 show the local subdirectory being made, so that /home/paul/empty/local exists. Lines 7 and 8 show you can cd into /home/paul/empty/local and back out again.

In line 9, CDPATH is set to /usr. This was chosen because Ubuntu has the directory /usr/local, which means our current directory (/home/paul/empty) and our CDPATH directory (/usr) both have a local subdirectory. In line 10, while in the /home/paul/empty directory, we use cd local. This time, Bash switches us to /usr/local and even prints the new directory to ensure we know what it has done.

Lines 12 and 13 move us back to the previous directory, /home/paul/empty. In line 14, CDPATH is set to be .:/usr. The : is the directory separator, so this means Bash should look first in the current directory, ., and then in the /usr directory. In line 15 cd local is issued again, this time moving to /home/paul/empty/local. Note that Bash has still printed the new directory—it does that whenever it looks up a directory in CDPATH.

Changing File Access Permissions with chmod

Your use of chmod can be greatly extended through one simple parameter: -c. This instructs chmod to print a list of all the changes it made as part of its operation, which means we can capture the output and use it for other purposes. For example:

```
[paul@caitlin tmp]$ chmod -c 600 *
mode of '1.txt' changed to 0600 (rw——-.)
mode of '2.txt' changed to 0600 (rw——-.)
mode of '3.txt' changed to 0600 (rw——-.)
```

```
[paul@caitlin tmp]$ chmod -c 600 *
[paul@caitlin tmp]$
```

There the chmod command is issued with -c, and you can see it has output the result of the operation: Three files were changed to rw------- (read and write by user only). However, when the command is issued again, no output is returned. This is because -c prints only the changes that it made. Files that already match the permissions you are setting are left unchanged and therefore are not printed.

There are two other parameters of interest: —reference and -R. The first allows you to specify a file to use as a template for permissions rather than specifying permissions yourself. For example, if you want all files in the current directory to have the same permissions as the file /home/paul/myfile.txt, you would use this:

```
chmod —reference /home/paul/myfile.txt *
```

You can use -R to enable recursive operation, which means you can use it to chmod a directory and it will change the permissions of that directory as well as all files and subdirectories under that directory. You could use chmod -R 600 /home to change every file and directory under /home to become read/write to their owner.

Copying Files with cp

Like mv, which is covered later, cp is a command that is easily used and mastered. However, two marvelous parameters rarely see much use (which is a shame!) despite their power. These are —parents and -u, the first of which copies the full path of the file into the new directory. The second copies only if the source file is newer than the destination.

Using —parents requires a little explanation, so here is an example. You have a file, /home/paul/desktop/documents/work/notes.txt, and want to copy it to your /home/paul/backup folder. You could just do a normal cp, but that would give you /home/paul/backup/notes.txt, so how would you know where that came from later? If you use —parents, the file is copied to /home/paul/backup/desktop/documents/work/notes.txt.

The -u parameter is perfect for synchronizing two directories because it allows you to run a command like cp -Ru myfiles myotherfiles and have cp recopy only files that have changed. The -R parameter means *recursive* and allows you to copy directory contents.

Printing Disk Usage with du

The du command prints the size of each file and directory that is inside the current directory. Its most basic usage is as easy as it gets:

```
du
```

That outputs a long list of directories and how much space their files take up. You can modify that with the -a parameter, which instructs du to print the size of individual files as well as directories. Another useful parameter is -h, which makes du use human-readable sizes like 18M (18MB) rather than 17532 (the same number in bytes, unrounded). The final useful basic option is -c, which prints the total size of files.

30

So, using du we can get a printout of the size of each file in our home directory, in human-readable format, and with a summary at the end, like this:

```
du -ahc /home/paul
```

Two advanced parameters deal with filenames you want excluded from your count. The first is —exclude, which allows you to specify a pattern that should be used to exclude files. This pattern is a standard shell file matching pattern as opposed to a regular expression, which means you can use ? to match a single character or * to match 0 or many characters. You can specify multiple —exclude parameters to exclude several patterns. For example:

```
du —exclude="*.xml" —exclude="*.xsl"
```

Of course, typing numerous —exclude parameters repeatedly is a waste of time, so you can use -X to specify a file that has the list of patterns you want excluded. The file should look like this:

```
*.xml
*.xsl
```

That is, each pattern you want excluded should be on a line by itself. If that file were called xml_exclude.txt, we could use it in place of the previous example like this:

```
du -X xml_exclude.txt
```

You can make your exclusion file as long as you need, or you can just specify multiple -X parameters.

TIP

Running du in a directory where several files are hard-linked to the same inode counts the size of the file only once. If you want to count each hard link separately for some reason, use the -l parameter (lowercase *L*).

Finding Files by Searching with find

The find command is one of the darkest and least understood areas of Linux, but it is also one of the most powerful. Admittedly, the find command does not help itself by using X-style parameters. The Unix standard is -c, -s, and so on, whereas the GNU standard is —dosomething, —mooby, and so forth. X-style parameters merge the two by having words preceded by only one dash.

However, the biggest problem with find is that it has more options than most people can remember—it truly is capable of doing most things you could want. The most basic usage is this:

```
find -name "*.txt"
```

That searches the current directory and all subdirectories for files that end in .txt. The previous search finds files ending in .txt but not .TXT, .Txt, or other case variations. To search without case sensitivity, use -iname instead of -name. You can optionally specify where the search should start before the -name parameter, like this:

```
find /home -name "*.txt"
```

Another useful test is -size, which lets you specify how big the files should be to match. You can specify your size in kilobytes and optionally also use + or - to specify greater than or less than. For example:

```
find /home -name "*.txt" -size 100k
find /home -name "*.txt" -size +100k
find /home -name "*.txt" -size -100k
```

The first brings up files of exactly 100KB, the second only files larger than 100KB, and the last only files under 100KB.

Moving on, the -user option enables you to specify the user who owns the files you are looking for. So, to search for all files in /home that end with .txt, are under 100KB, and are owned by user paul, you would use this:

```
find /home -name "*.txt" -size -100k -user paul
```

You can flip any of the conditions by specifying -not before them. For example, you can add a -not before -user paul to find matching files owned by everyone *but* paul:

```
find /home -name "*.txt" -size -100k -not -user paul
```

You can add as many -not parameters as you need, even using -not -not to cancel each other out! (Yes, that is pointless.) Keep in mind, though, that -not -size -100k is essentially equivalent to -size +100k, with the exception that the former will match files of exactly 100KB whereas the latter will not.

You can use -perm to specify which permissions a file should have for it to be matched. This is tricky, so read carefully. The permissions are specified in the same way as with the chmod command: u for user, g for group, o for others, r for read, w for write, and x for execute. However, before you give the permissions, you need to specify either a plus, a minus, or a blank space. If you specify neither a plus nor a minus, the files must exactly match the mode you give. If you specify -, the files must match all the modes you specify. If you specify +, the files must match any the modes you specify. Confused yet?

The confusion can be cleared up with some examples. This next command finds all files that have permission o=r (readable for other users). Notice that if you remove the -name parameter, it is equivalent to * because all filenames are matched.

```
find /home -perm -o=r
```

30

Any files that have o=r set are returned from that query. Those files also might have u=rw and other permissions, but as long as they have o=r, they will match. This next query matches all files that have o=rw set:

```
find /home -perm -o=rw
```

However, that query does not match files that are o=r or o=w. To be matched, a file must be readable *and* writeable by other users. If you want to match readable *or* writeable (or both), you need to use +, like this:

```
find /home -perm +o=rw
```

Similarly, this next query matches files only that are readable by user, group, and others:

```
find /home -perm -ugo=r
```

Whereas this query matches files as long as they are readable by the user, or by the group, or by others, or by any combination of the three:

```
find /home -perm +ugo=r
```

If you use neither + or -, you are specifying the exact permissions to search for. For example, the next query searches for files that are readable by user, group, and others but not writeable or executable by anyone:

```
find /home -perm ugo=r
```

You can be as specific as you need to be with the permissions. For example, this query finds all files that are readable for the user, group, and others and writeable by the user:

```
find /home -perm ugo=r,u=w
```

To find files that are not readable by others, use the -not condition, like this:

```
find /home -not -perm +o=r
```

Now, on to the most advanced aspect of the find command: the -exec parameter. This enables you to execute an external program each time a match is made, passing in the name of the matched file wherever you want it. This has very specific syntax: Your command and its parameters should follow immediately after -exec, terminated by \;. You can insert the filename match at any point using {} (an opening and a closing brace side by side).

So, you can match all text files on the entire system (that is, searching recursively from / rather than from /home as in our previous examples) over 10KB, owned by paul, that are not readable by other users, and then use chmod to enable reading, like this:

```
find / -name "*.txt" -size +10k -user paul -not -perm +o=r -exec chmod o+r {} \;
```

When you type your own -exec parameters, be sure to include a space before \;. Otherwise, you might see an error such as missing argument to '-exec'.

Do you see now why some people think the find command is scary? Many people learn just enough about find to be able to use it in a very basic way, but hopefully you will see how much it can do if you give it chance.

Searches for a String in Input with grep

The grep command, like find, is an incredibly powerful search tool in the right hands. Unlike find, though, grep processes any text, whether in files, or just in standard input.

The basic usage of grep is this:

```
grep "some text" *
```

That searches all files in the current directory (but not subdirectories) for the string some text and prints matching lines along with the name of the file. To enable recursive searching in subdirectories, use the -r parameter, like this:

```
grep -r "some text" *
```

Each time a string is matched within a file, the filename and the match are printed. If a file contains multiple matches, each of the matches is printed. You can alter this behavior with the -l parameter (lowercase *L*), which forces grep to print the name of each file that contains at least one match, without printing the matching text. If a file contains more than one match, it is still printed only once. Alternatively, the -c parameter prints each filename that was searched and includes the number of matches at the end, even if there were no matches.

You have a lot of control when specifying the pattern to search for. You can, as we did previously, specify a simple string like some text, or you can invert that search by specifying the -v parameter. For example, this returns all the lines of the file myfile.txt that do not contain the word hello:

```
grep -v "hello" myfile.txt
```

You can also use regular expressions for your search term. For example, you can search myfile.txt for all references to cat, sat, or mat with this command:

```
grep "[cms]at" myfile.txt
```

Adding the -i parameter to that removes case sensitivity, matching Cat, CAT, MaT, and so on:

```
grep -i [cms]at myfile.txt
```

The output can also be controlled to some extent with the -n and —color parameters. The first tells grep to print the line number for each match, which is where it appears in the source file. The —color parameter tells grep to color the search terms in the output, which helps them stand out when among all the other text on the line. You choose which color you want using the GREP_COLOR environment variable: export GREP_COLOR=36 gives you cyan, and export GREP_COLOR=32 gives you lime green.

This next example uses these two parameters to number and color all matches to the previous command:

```
grep -in —color [cms]at myfile.txt
```

Later you will see how important grep is for piping with other commands.

Paging Through Output with less

The less command enables you to view large amounts of text in a more convenient way than the cat command. For example, your /etc/passwd file is probably more than a screen long, so if you run cat /etc/passwd, you are not able to see what the lines at the top were. Using less /etc/passwd enables you to use the cursor keys to scroll up and down the output freely. Type q to quit and return to the shell.

On the surface, less sounds like a very easy command; however, it has the infamy of being one of the few Linux commands that have a parameter for every letter of the alphabet. That is, -a does something, -b does something else, -c, -d, -e ... -x, -y, -z—they all do things, with some letters even differentiating between upper- and lowercase. Furthermore, it is only the parameter used to invoke less. After you are viewing your text, even more commands are available to you. Make no mistake—less is a complex beast to master.

Input to less can be divided into two categories: what you type before running less and what you type while running it. The former category is easy, so we shall start there.

We have already discussed how many parameters less is capable of taking, but they can be distilled down to three that are very useful: -M, -N, and +. Adding -M (this is different from -m!) enables verbose prompting in less. Rather than just printing a colon and a flashing cursor, less prints the filename, the line numbers being shown, the total number of lines, and the percentage of how far you are through the file. Adding -N (again, this is different from -n) enables line numbering.

The last option, +, allows you to pass a command to less for it to execute as it starts. To use this, you first need to know the commands available to you in less, which means we need to move onto the second category of less input: what you type while less is running.

The basic navigation keys are the up, down, left, and right cursors; Home and End (for navigating to the start and end of a file); and Page Up and Page Down. Beyond that, the most common command is /, which initiates a text search. You type what you want to search for and press Enter to have less find the first match and highlight all subsequent matches. Type / again and press Enter to have less jump to the next match. The inverse of that is ?, which searches backward for text. Type ?, enter a search string, and press Enter to go to the first previous match of that string, or just use ? and press Enter to go to the next match preceding the current position. You can use / and ? interchangeably by searching for something with / and then using ? to go backward in the same search.

Searching with / and ? is commonly used with the + command-line parameter from earlier, which passes `less` a command for execution after the file has loaded. For example, you can tell `less` to load a file and place the cursor at the first match for the search `hello`, like this:

```
less +/hello myfile.txt
```

Or, to place the cursor at the last match for the search `hello`:

```
less +?hello myfile.txt
```

Beyond the cursor keys, the controls primarily involve typing a number and then pressing a key. For example, to go to line 50 and type `50g`, or to go to the 75% point of the file and type `75p`. You can also place invisible mark points through the file by pressing `m` and then typing a single letter. Later, while in the same less session, you can press `.;` (a single quote) and then type the letter, and it will move you back to the same position. You can set up to 52 marks, named a–z and A–Z.

One clever feature of `less` is that you can, at any time, press `v` to have your file opened inside your text editor. This defaults to Vim, but you can change that by setting the `EDITOR` environment variable to something else.

If you have made it this far, you can already use less better than most users. You can, at this point, justifiably skip to the next section and consider yourself proficient with `less`. However, if you want to be a `less` guru, there are two more things to learn: how to view multiple files simultaneously and how to run shell commands.

Like most other file-based commands in Linux, `less` can take several files as its parameters. For example:

```
less -MN 1.txt 2.txt 3.txt
```

That loads all three files into `less`, starting at `1.txt`. When viewing several files, `less` usually tells you which file you are in, as well as numbering them: `1.txt (file 1 of 3)` should be at the bottom of the screen. That said, certain things will make that go away, so you should use -M anyway.

You can navigate between files by typing a colon and then pressing `n` to go to the next file or `p` to go to the previous file; these are referred to from now on as `:n` and `:p`. You can open another file for viewing by typing `:e` and providing a filename. This can be any file you have permission to read, including files outside the local directory. Use Tab to complete filenames. Files you open in this way are inserted one place after your current position, so if you are viewing file 1 of 4 and open a new file, the new file is numbered 2 of 5 and is opened for viewing straight away. To close a file and remove it from the list, use `:d`.

Viewing multiple files simultaneously has implications for searching. By default, `less` searches within only one file, but it is easy to search within all files. When you type / or ? to search, follow it with a *—you should see `EOF-ignore` followed by a search prompt. You can now type a search and it will search in the current file; if nothing is found, it looks in subsequent files until it finds a match. Repeating searches is done by pressing Esc and

30

then either n or N. The lowercase option repeats the search forward across files, and the uppercase repeats it backward.

The last thing you need to know is that you can get to a shell from less and execute commands. The simplest way to do this is just to type ! and press Enter. This launches a shell and leaves you free to type all the commands you want, as per normal. Type exit to return to less. You can also type specific commands by entering them after the exclamation mark, using the special character % for the current filename. For example, du -h % prints the size of the current file. Finally, you can use !! to repeat the previous command.

Creating Links Between Files with ln

Linux allows you to create links between files that look and work like normal files for the most part. Moreover, it allows you to make two types of links, known as *hard* links and *symbolic* links (*symlinks*). The difference between the two is crucial, although it might not be obvious at first!

Each filename on your system points to what is known as an *inode*, which is the absolute location of a file. Linux allows you to point more than one filename to a given inode, and the result is a hard link—two filenames pointing to exactly the same file. Each of these files shares the same contents and attributes. So, if you edit one, the other changes because they are both the same file.

On the other hand, a symlink—sometimes called a *soft* link—is a redirect to the real file. When a program tries to read from a symlink, it automatically is redirected to what the symlink is pointing at. The fact that symlinks are really just dumb pointers has two advantages: You can link to something that does not exist (and create it later if you want), and you can link to directories.

Both types of links have their uses. Creating a hard link is a great way to back up a file on the same disk. For example, if you delete the file in one location, it still exists untouched in the other location. Symlinks are popular because they allow a file to appear to be in a different location; you could store your website in /var/www/live and an under-construction holding page in /var/www/construction. Then you could have Apache point to a symlink /var/www/html that is redirected to either the live or construction directory depending on what you need.

> **TIP**
>
> The shred command overwrites a file's contents with random data, allowing for safe deletion. Because this directly affects a file's contents, rather than just a filename, this means that all filenames hard linked to an inode are affected.

Both types of link are created using the ln command. By default, it creates hard links, but you can create symlinks by passing it the -s parameter. The syntax is ln [-s] <something> <somewhere>, for example:

```
ln -s myfile.txt mylink
```

That creates the symlink mylink that points to `myfile.txt`. Remove the `-s` to create a hard link. You can verify that your link has been created by running `ls -l`. Your symlink should look something like this:

```
lrwxrwxrwx  1 paul paul    5 Feb 19 12:39 mylink -> myfile.txt
```

Note how the file properties start with l (lowercase *L*) for link and how `ls -l` also prints where the link is going. Symlinks are always very small in size; the previous link is 5 bytes in size. If you created a hard link, it should look like this:

```
-rw-rw-r   2 paul paul   341 Feb 19 12:39 mylink
```

This time the file has normal attributes, but the second number is 2 rather than 1. That number is how many hard links point to this file, which is why it is 2 now. The file size is also the same as that of the previous filename because it *is* the file as opposed to just being a pointer.

Symlinks are used extensively in Linux. Programs that have been superseded, such as `sh`, now point to their replacements (in this case `bash`), and library versioning is accomplished through symlinks. For example, applications that link against `zlib` load `/usr/lib/libz.so`. Internally, however, that is just a symlink that points to the actual `zlib` library: `/usr/lib/libz.so.1.2.1.2`. This enables multiple versions of libraries to be installed without applications needing to worry.

Finding Files from an Index with locate

When you use the `find` command, it searches recursively through each directory each time you request a file. This is slow, as you can imagine. Fortunately, Ubuntu ships with a cron job that creates an index of all the files on your system every night. Searching this index is extremely fast, which means that, if the file you are looking for has been around since the last index, this is the preferable way of searching.

To look for a file in your index, use the command `locate` followed by the names of the files you want to find, like this:

```
locate myfile.txt
```

On a relatively modern computer (1.5GHz or higher), `locate` should be able to return all the matching files in under a second. The trade-off for this speed is lack of flexibility. You can search for matching filenames, but, unlike `find`, you cannot search for sizes, owners, access permissions, or other attributes. The one thing you can change is case sensitivity; use the `-i` parameter to do a case-insensitive search.

Although Ubuntu rebuilds the filename index nightly, you can force a rebuild whenever you want by running the command `updatedb` with sudo. This usually takes a few minutes, but when it's done the new database is immediately available.

30

Listing Files in the Current Directory with ls

The ls command, like ln, is one of those you expect to be very straightforward. It lists files, but how many options can it possibly have? In true Linux style, the answer is many, although again you need only know a few to wield great power!

The basic usage is simply ls, which out the files and directories in the current location. You can filter that using normal wildcards, so all these are valid:

```
ls *
ls *.txt
ls my*ls *.txt *.xml
```

Any directories that match these filters are recursed into one level. That is, if you run ls my* and you have the files myfile1.txt and myfile2.txt and a directory mystuff, the matching files are printed first. Then ls prints the contents of the mystuff directory.

The most popular parameters for customizing the output of ls are

- ▶ -a—Includes hidden files.

- ▶ -h—Uses human-readable sizes.

- ▶ -l—A lowercase *L*, it enables long listing.

- ▶ -r—Reverse order.

- ▶ -R—Recursively lists directories.

- ▶ -s—Shows sizes.

- ▶ —sort—Sorts the listing.

All files that start with a period are hidden in Linux, so that includes the .gnome directory in your home directory, as well as .bash_history and the . and .. implicit directories that signify the current directory and the parent. By default, ls does not show these files, but if you run ls -a, they are shown. You can also use ls -A to show all the hidden files except . and ...

The -h parameter needs to be combined with the -s parameter, like this:

```
ls -sh *.txt
```

That outputs the size of each matching file in a human-readable format, such as 108KB or 4.5MB.

Using the -l parameter enables much more information about your files. Instead of just providing the names of the files, you get output like this:

```
drwxrwxr-x 24 paul paul  4096 Dec 24 21:33 arch
-rw-r—r—  1 paul paul 18691 Dec 24 21:34 COPYING
-rw-r—r—  1 paul paul 88167 Dec 24 21:35 CREDITS
drwxrwxr-x  2 paul paul  4096 Dec 24 21:35 crypto
```

That shows four matches and prints a lot of information about each of them. The first row shows the arch directory; you can tell it is a directory because its file attributes starts with a d. The rwxrwxr-x following that shows the access permissions, and this has special meanings because it is a directory. Read access for a directory allows users to see the directory contents, write access allows you to create files and subdirectories, and execute access allows you to cd into the directory. If a user has execute access but not read access, he will be able to cd into the directory but not list files.

Moving on, the next number on the line is 24, which also has a special meaning for directories: It is the number of subdirectories, including . and ... After that is paul paul, which is the name of the user owner and the group owner for the directory. Next is the size and modification time, and finally the directory name itself.

The next line shows the file COPYING, and most of the numbers have the same meaning, with the exception of the 1 immediately after the access permissions. For directories, this is the number of subdirectories, but for files this is the number of hard links to this file. A 1 in this column means this is the only filename pointing to this inode, so if you delete it, it is gone.

Ubuntu comes configured with a shortcut command for ls -l: ll.

The —sort parameter allows you to reorder the output from the default alphabetical sorting. You can sort by various things, although the most popular are extension (alphabetically), size (largest first), and time (newest first). To flip the sorting (making size sort by smallest first), use the -r parameter also. So, this command lists all .ogg files, sorted smallest to largest:

```
ls —sort size -r *.ogg
```

Finally, the -R parameter recurses through subdirectories. For example, typing ls /etc lists all the files and subdirectories in /etc, but ls -R /etc lists all the files in and subdirectories in /etc, all the files and subdirectories in /etc/acpi, all the files and subdirectories in /etc/acpi/actions, and so on until every subdirectory has been listed.

Reading Manual Pages with man

Time for a much-needed mental break: The man command is easy to use. Most people use only the topic argument, like this: man gcc. However, two other commands work closely with man that are very useful—whatis and apropos.

The whatis command returns a one-line description of another command, which is the same text you get at the top of that command's man page. For example:

```
[paul@caitlin ~]$ whatis ls
ls    (1) - list directory contents
```

The output there explains what ls does but also provides the man page section number for the command so you can query it further.

On the other hand, the apropos command takes a search string as its parameter and returns all man pages that match the search. For example, apropos mixer gives this list:

```
alsamixer (1) - soundcard mixer for ALSA soundcard driver
mixer (1) - command-line mixer for ALSA soundcard driver
aumix (1) - adjust audio mixer
```

So, use apropos to help you find commands and use whatis to tell you what a command does.

Making Directories with mkdir

Making directories is as easy as it sounds, although there is one parameter you should be aware of: -p. If you are in /home/paul and you want to create the directory /home/paul/audio/sound, you will get an error like this:

```
mkdir: cannot create directory 'audio/sound': No such file or directory
```

At first glance this seems wrong because mkdir cannot create the directory because it does not exist. What it actually means is that it cannot create the directory sound because the directory audio does not exist. This is where the -p parameter comes in: If you try to make a directory within another directory that does not exist, like the previous, -p creates the parent directories, too. So:

```
mkdir -p audio/sound
```

That first creates the audio directory and then creates the sound directory inside it.

Moving Files with mv

This command is one of the easiest around. There are two helpful parameters to mv: -f, which overwrites files without asking, and -u, which moves the source file only if it is newer than the destination file. That is it!

Listing Processes with ps

This is the third and last "command that should be simple, but isn't" that is discussed here. The ps command lists processes and gives you an extraordinary amount of control over its operation.

The first thing to know is that ps is typically used with what are known as BSD-style parameters. Back in the section "Finding Files by Searching with find," we discussed Unix-style, GNU-style, and X-style parameters (-c, —dosomething, and -dosomething, respectively), but BSD-style parameters are different because they use single letters without a dash.

So, the default use of ps lists all processes that you are running that are attached to the terminal. However, you can ask it to list all your processes attached to any terminal (or indeed no terminal) by adding the x parameter: ps x. You can ask it to list all processes for all users with the a parameter or combine that with x to list all processes for all users, attached to a terminal or otherwise: ps ax.

However, both of these are timid compared with the almighty u option, which enables user-oriented output. In practice, that makes a huge difference because you get important fields like the username of the owner, how much CPU time and RAM are being used, when the process was started, and more. This outputs a lot of information, so you might want to try adding the f parameter, which creates a process forest by using ASCII art to connect parent commands with their children. You can combine all the options so far with this command: ps faux (yes, with a little imagination you spell words with the parameters!).

You can control the order in which the data is returned by using the −sort parameter. This takes either a + or a - (although the + is default) followed by the field you want to sort by: command, %cpu, pid, and user are all popular options. If you use the minus sign, the results are reversed. This next command lists all processes, ordered by CPU usage descending:

```
ps aux —sort=-%cpu
```

There are many other parameters for ps, including a huge amount of options for compatibility with other Unixes. If you have the time to read the man page, you should give it a try!

Deleting Files and Directories with rm

The rm command has only one parameter of interest: −preserve-root. By now, you should know that issuing rm -rf / with sudo will destroy your Linux installation because -r means *recursive* and -f means *force* (do not prompt for confirmation before deleting). It is possible for a clumsy person to issue this command by accident—not by typing the command on purpose, but by putting a space in the wrong place. For example:

```
rm -rf /home/paul
```

That command deletes the home directory of the user paul. This is not an uncommon command; after you have removed a user and backed up her data, you will probably want to issue something similar. However, if you add an accidental space between the / and the h in "home", you get this:

```
rm -rf / home/paul
```

This time the command means "delete everything recursively from / and then delete home/paul"—quite a different result! You can stop this from happening by using the −preserve-root parameter, which stops you from catastrophe with this message:

```
rm: it is dangerous to operate recursively on '/'
rm: use —no-preserve-root to override this failsafe.
```

Of course, no one wants to keep typing −preserve-root each time they run rm, so you should add this line to the .bashrc file in your home directory:

30

```
alias rm='rm —preserve-root'
```

That alias automatically adds —preserve-root to all calls to rm in future Bash sessions.

Printing the Last Lines of a File with tail

If you want to watch a log file as it is written to, or want to monitor a user's actions as they are occurring, you need to be able to track log files as they change. In these situations you need the tail command, which prints the last few lines of a file and updates as new lines are added. This command tells tail to print the last few lines of /var/log/httpd/access_log, the Apache hit log:

```
tail /var/log/httpd/access_log
```

To get tail to remain running and update as the file changes, add the -f parameter (follow):

```
tail -f /var/log/httpd/access_log
```

You can tie the lifespan of a tail follow to the existence of a process by specifying the —pid parameter. When you do this, tail continues to follow the file you asked for until it sees that the process identified by PID is no longer running, at which point it stops tailing.

If you specify multiple files on the command line, tail follows both, printing file headers whenever the input source changes. Press Ctrl+C to terminate tail when in follow mode.

Printing Resource Usage with top

The top command is unusual in this list because the few parameters it takes are rarely, if ever, used. Instead, it has a number of commands you can use while it is running to customize the information it shows you. To get the most from these instructions, open two terminal windows. In the first, run the program yes and leave it running; in the second run sudo top.

The default sort order in top shows the most CPU-intensive tasks first. The first command there should be the yes process you just launched from the other terminal, but there should be many others also. First, we want to filter out all the other uses and focus on the user running yes. To do this, press u and enter the username you used when you ran yes. When you press Enter, top filters out processes not being run by that user.

The next step is to kill the process ID of the yes command, so you need to understand what each of the important fields means:

- ▶ PID—The process ID
- ▶ User—The owner of the process
- ▶ PR—Priority
- ▶ NI—Niceness
- ▶ Virt—Virtual image size in kilobytes

- ▶ `Res`—Resident size in kilobytes

- ▶ `Shr`—Shared memory size in kilobytes

- ▶ `S`—Status

- ▶ `%CPU`—CPU usage

- ▶ `%Mem`—Memory usage

- ▶ `Time+`—CPU time

- ▶ `Command`—The command being run

Several of them are unimportant unless you have a specific problem. The ones we are interested in are `PID`, `User`, `Niceness`, `%CPU`, `%MEM`, `Time+`, and `Command`. The `Niceness` of a process is how much time the CPU allocates to it compared to everything else on the system: 19 is the lowest, and –19 is the highest.

With the columns explained, you should be able to find the process ID of the errant `yes` command launched earlier; it is usually the first number below `PID`. Now type `k`, enter that process ID, and press Enter. You are prompted for a signal number (the manner in which you want the process killed), with 15 provided as the default. Signal 15 (also known as `SIGTERM`, for "terminate") is a polite way of asking a process to shut down, and all processes that are not wildly out of control should respond to it. Give `top` a few seconds to update itself, and hopefully the `yes` command should be gone. If not, you need to be more forceful: type `k` again, enter the PID, and press Enter. When prompted for a signal to send, enter `9` and press Enter to send `SIGKILL`, or "terminate whether you like it or not."

You can choose the fields to display by pressing `f`. A new screen appears that lists all possible fields, along with the letter you need to press to toggle their visibility. Selected fields are marked with an asterisk and have their letter, for example:

```
* A: PID      = Process Id
```

If you press the a key, the screen changes to this:

```
a: PID      = Process Id
```

When you have made your selections, press Enter to return to the normal top view with your normal column selection.

You can also press `F` to select the field you want to use for sorting. This works in the same way as the field selection screen, except that you can select only one field at a time. Again, press Enter to get back to `top` after you have made your selection, and it will be updated with the new sorting.

If you press `B`, text bolding is enabled. By default, this bolds some of the header bar as well as any programs that are currently running (as opposed to sleeping), but if you press x you can also enable bolding of the sorted column. You can use y to toggle bolding of running processes.

30

The last command to try is r, which allows you to renice—or adjust the nice value—of a process. You need to enter the PID of the process, press Enter, and enter a new nice value. Keep in mind that 19 is the lowest and –20 is the highest; anything less than 0 is considered "high" and should be used sparingly.

Printing the Location of a Command with which

The purpose of which is to tell you the exact command that would be executed if you typed it. For example, which mkdir returns /bin/mkdir, telling you that running the command mkdir runs /bin/mkdir.

Combining Commands

So far, we have only been using commands individually, and for the large part that is what you will be doing in practice. However, some of the real power of these commands lies in the ability to join them together to get exactly what you want. There are some extra little commands that we have not looked at that are often used as glue because they do one very simple thing that enables a more complex process to work.

All the commands we have looked at have printed their information to the screen, but this is often flexible. There are two ways to control where output should go: piping and output redirection. A *pipe* is a connector between one command's output and another's input. Instead of sending its output to your terminal, a command sends that output directly to another command for input. Output redirection works in a similar way to pipes but is usually used for files. We will look at pipes first and then output redirection.

Two of the commands we have looked at so far are ps and grep: the process lister and the string matcher. We can combine the two to find out which users are playing Nethack right now:

```
ps aux ¦ grep nethack
```

That creates a list of all the processes running right now and sends that list to the grep command, which filters out all lines that do not contain the word nethack. Ubuntu allows you to pipe as many commands as you can sanely string together. For example, we could add in the wc command, which counts the numbers of lines, words, and characters in its input, to count precisely how many times Nethack is being run:

```
ps aux ¦ grep nethack ¦ wc -l
```

The -1 parameter to wc (lowercase *L*) prints only the line count.

Using pipes in this way is often preferable to using the -exec parameter to find, simply because many people consider find to be a black art and so anything that uses it less frequently is better! This is where the xargs command comes in: It converts output from one command into arguments for another.

For a good example, consider this mammoth find command from earlier:

```
find / -name "*.txt" -size +10k -user paul -not -perm +o=r -exec chmod o+r {} \;
```

That searches every directory from / onward for files matching *.txt that are greater than 10KB, are owned by user paul, and do not have read permission for others. Then it executes chmod on each of the files. It is a complex command, and people who are not familiar with the workings of find might have problems understanding it. So, what we can do is break it up into two—a call to find and a call to xargs. The most conversion would look like this:

```
find / -name "*.txt" -size +10k -user paul -not -perm +o=r ¦ xargs chmod o+r
```

That has eliminated the confusing {} \; from the end of the command, but it does the same thing, and faster, too. The speed difference between the two is because using -exec with find causes it to execute chmod once for each file. However, chmod accepts many files at a time and, because we are using the same parameter each time, we should take advantage of that. The second command, using xargs, is called once with all the output from find, and so saves many command calls. The xargs command automatically places the input at the end of the line, so the previous command might look something like this:

```
xargs chmod o+r file1.txt file2.txt file3.txt
```

Not every command accepts multiple files, though, and if you specify the -l parameter, xargs executes its command once for each line in its input. If you want to check what it is doing, use the -p parameter to have xargs prompt you before executing each command.

For even more control, the -i parameter allows you to specify exactly where the matching lines should be placed in your command. This is important if you need the lines to appear before the end of the command or need it to appear more than once. Either way, using the -i parameter also enables the -l parameter so each line is sent to the command individually. This next command finds all files in /home/paul that are larger than 10,000KB in size (10MB) and copies them to /home/paul/archive:

```
find /home/paul -size +10000k ¦ xargs -i cp {} ./home/paul/archive
```

Using find with xargs is a unique case. All too often, people use pipes when parameters would do the job just as well. For example, these two commands are identical:

```
ps aux —sort=-%cpu ¦ grep -v 'whoami'
ps -N ux —sort=-%cpu
```

The former prints all users and processes and then pipes that to grep, which in turn filters out all lines that contain the output from the program whoami (our username). So, line one prints all processes being run by other uses, sorted by CPU use. Line two does not specify the a parameter to ps, which makes it list only our parameters. It then uses the -N parameter to flip that, which means it is everyone but us, without the need for grep.

The reason people use the former is often just simplicity: Many people know only a handful of parameters to each command, so they can string together two commands simply rather than write one command properly. Unless the command is to be run regularly, this is not a problem. Indeed, the first line would be better because it does not drive people to the manual to find out what ps -N does!

Multiple Terminals

It is both curious and sad that many Linux veterans have not heard of the screen command. Curious because they needlessly go to extra effort to replicate what screen takes in its stride and sad because they are missing a powerful tool that would benefit them greatly.

Picture this scene: You connect to a server via SSH and are working at the remote shell. You need to open another shell window so you can have the two running side by side; perhaps you want the output from top in one window while typing in another. What do you do? Most people would open another SSH connection, but that is both wasteful and unnecessary. screen is a *terminal multiplexer*, which is a fancy term for a program that lets you run multiple terminals inside one terminal.

The best way to learn screen is to try it yourself, so open a console, type **screen**, and then press Enter. Your display will blank momentarily and then be replaced with a console; it will look like nothing has changed. Now, let's do something with that terminal. Run top and leave it running for the time being. Hold down the Ctrl key and press a (referred to as Ctrl+a from now on); then let go of them both and press c. Your prompt will clear again, leaving you able to type. Run the uptime command.

Pop quiz: What happened to the old terminal running top? It is still running, of course. You can type Ctrl+a and then press 0 to return to it. Type Ctrl+a and then press 1 to go back to your uptime terminal. While you are viewing other terminals, the commands in the other terminals carry on running as normal so you can multitask.

Many of screen's commands are case sensitive, so the lettering used here is very specific: Ctrl+a means "press Ctrl and the a key," but Ctrl+A means "press Ctrl and Shift and the a key" so you get a capital A. Ctrl+a+A means "press Ctrl and the a key, let them go, and then press Shift and the a key."

You have seen how to create new displays and how to switch between them by number. However, you can also bring up a window list and select windows using your cursor with Ctrl+a+" (that is, press Ctrl and a together, let go, and press the double quotes key [usually Shift and the single quote key]). You will find that the screens you create have the name bash by default, which is not very descriptive. Select a window and press Ctrl+a+A. You are prompted to enter a name for the current window, and your name is used in the window list.

Once you get past window 9, it becomes impossible to switch to windows using Ctrl+a and 0–9; as soon as you type the 1 of 10, screen switches to display 1. The solution is to use either the window list or the quick change option, in which you press Ctrl+a+' (single quote), enter either the screen number or the name you gave it, then press Enter. You can also change back to the previous window by pressing Ctrl+a+Ctrl+a. If you only work within a small set of windows, you can use Ctrl+a+n and Ctrl+a+p to move to the next and previous windows, respectively. Of course, if you are changing to and from windows only to see whether something has changed, you are wasting time because screen can monitor windows for you and report if anything changes. To enable (or disable) monitoring for a window, use Ctrl+a+M; when something happens, screen flashes a message. If you miss it (the messages disappear when you type something), use Ctrl+a+m to bring up the last message.

Windows close when you kill the main program inside. Using Ctrl+a+c, this window is Bash; type **exit** to quit. Alternatively, you can use Ctrl+a+K to kill a window. When all your windows are closed, screen terminates and prints a screen is terminating message so you know you are out.

However, there are two alternatives to quitting: locking and disconnecting. The first, activated with Ctrl+a+x, locks access to your screen data until you enter your system password. The second is the most powerful feature of screen: You can exit it and do other things for a while and then reconnect later and screen will pick up where you left off. For example, you could be typing at your desk, disconnect from screen, then go home, reconnect, and carry on as if nothing had changed. What's more, all the programs you ran from screen carry on running even while screen is disconnected. It even automatically disconnects for you if someone closes your terminal window while it is in a locked state (with Ctrl+a+x).

To disconnect from screen, press Ctrl+a+d. You are returned to the prompt from which you launched screen and can carry on working, close the terminal you had opened, or even log out completely. When you want to reconnect, run the command screen -r. You can, in the meantime, just run screen and start a new session without resuming the previous one, but that is not wise if you value your sanity! You can disconnect and reconnect the same screen session as many times you want, which potentially means you need never lose your session again.

Although this has been a mere taster of screen, hopefully you can see how useful it can be.

Reference

▶ http://www.gnu.org/—The website of the GNU project, it contains manuals and downloads for lots of command-line software.

▶ http://www.linuxdevcenter.com/linux/cmd/—A wide selection of Linux commands and explanations of what they do.

▶ http://www.tuxfiles.org/linuxhelp/cli.html—Several short command-line tutorials, courtesy of tuXfiles.

▶ http://www.linuxcommand.org/—Describes itself as "your one-stop command line shop!" It contains a wealth of useful information about the console.

Books

Understanding the way UNIX works at the nuts and bolts level can be both challenging and rewarding, and there are several good books that will help guide you on your way.

Perhaps the best is *The Art of Unix Programming* by Eric Raymond (Addison-Wesley, ISBN: 0-13-142901-9), which focuses on the philosophy behind UNIX and manages to mix in much about the command line.

O'Reilly's *Unix CD Bookshelf* (ISBN: 0-596-00392-7) contains seven highly respected books in one, although it retails for more than $120 as a result! That said, it is incomparable in its depth and breadth of coverage.

CHAPTER 31

Managing Software

In this chapter, we look at the options you have to manage your software in Ubuntu. If you are used to a Windows environment where you are reliant on visiting several different vendor websites to download updates, you are in for a shock! Updating a full Ubuntu installation, including all the application software, is as easy as running the Update Manager program. You will discover just how easy it is to install and even remove various software packages.

Ubuntu provides a variety of tools for system resource management. The following sections introduce the graphical software management tools that you will use for most of your software management. (You will learn more about a collection of command-line tools in Chapter 30, "Command Line Masterclass.") This chapter also covers monitoring and managing memory and disk storage on your system.

Using Add/Remove Applications for Software Management

The Ubuntu Software Center is a graphical utility for package management in Ubuntu, it can be found in the Applications menu as Ubuntu Software Center and is actually an application named software-center. The Ubuntu Software Center allows you to easily select and install a large array of applications by using the intuitive built-in search and easy one click installation. You should see the Package Browsing screen, as shown in Figure 31.1.

Along the left side of the screen, you will see two menu options, "Get Free Software" and "Installed Software". At the top, you will have a search bar which can be used to search for packages. When you click on the Get Free Software link you will be presented with a group of 12 icons on the right side of the screen. These are the categories in which you can select to install more then 2000 applications from. Clicking the Installed Software link will present you with a listing of all the installed applications on your Ubuntu desktop.

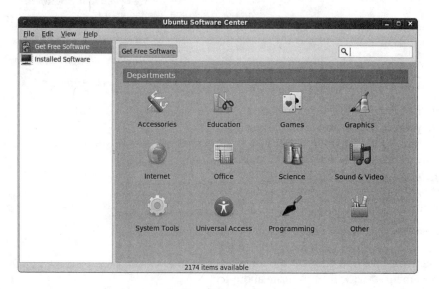

FIGURE 31.1   The initial Ubuntu Software Center screen allows you to browse through packages sorted by groups.

Installing new software via Ubuntu Software Center is as simple as finding it in the package list, double clicking and clicking the install button. Upon clicking the install button you may be asked for you password, once entered the application will be downloaded and installed. You can remove an application by finding it in Ubuntu Software Center and clicking the Remove button.

To search for a specific application in the list, type something into the Search box at the top. Note that this searches within the current category; so if you are in the Games category and search for "office," you will get no results. The best place to search is within the Get Free Software category, to make sure you search all areas.

Using Synaptic for Software Management

The Add/Remove Applications dialog works just fine for adding applications, but if you need to install something very specific—such as a library—or if you want to reconfigure your installation system, you need to use Synaptic (see Figure 31.2). You can run Synaptic by selecting it from the System, Administration, Synaptic Package Manager menu option.

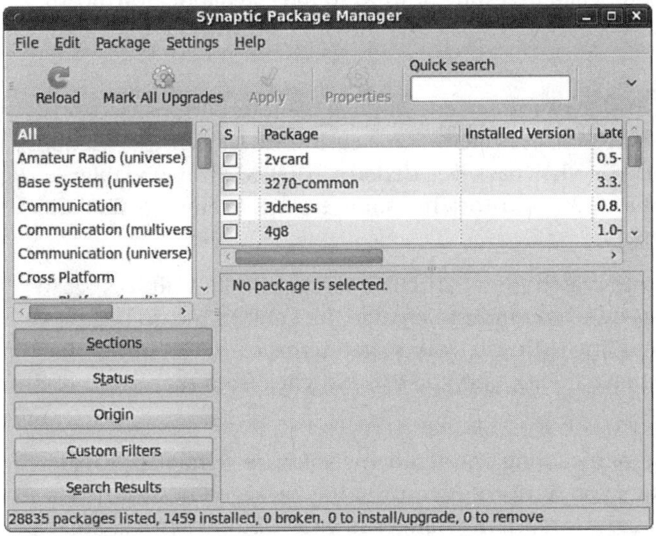

FIGURE 31.2   For more advanced software management, Synaptic is the preferred tool.

At first glance, Synaptic looks a little like the Add/Remove Applications window. Along the left are software categories (although this time there are more of them), along the top right are the package selections for that category, and on the bottom right is the Package Information window that shows information about the currently selected package. To install or remove software, click on the check box to the left of its name, and you'll see a menu appear offering the following options:

- **Unmark**—If you have marked this package for installation, upgrade, or one of the other options, this removes that mark.

- **Mark for Installation**—Add this packages to the list that will be installed.

- **Mark for Re-installation**—If you have some software already installed, but for some reason it's not working, this reinstalls it from scratch.

- **Mark for Upgrade**—If the software has updates available, this will download and install them.

▶ **Mark for Removal**—This deletes the selected package from your system, but leaves its configuration files intact so that if you ever reinstall it you do not have to reconfigure it.

▶ **Mark for Complete Removal**—This deletes the selected package from your system, but also removes any configuration files, purging everything from the system.

After you have made your changes, click the Apply button to have Synaptic download, install, upgrade, and uninstall as necessary. If you close the program without clicking Apply, your changes will be lost.

Beneath the categories on the left side of the screen, you will see four buttons: Sections, Status, Search, and Custom; with Sections selected. These customize the left list: Sections is the Categories view, Status lets you view packages that are installed or upgradable, Search stores results of your searches, and Custom has some esoteric groupings that are only really useful to advanced users.

You can press Ctrl+F at any time to search for a particular package. By default it is set to search by package name, but it is quite common to change the Look In box to be "Description and Name". As mentioned already, your search terms are saved under the Search view (the button on the bottom left), and you can just click from that list to re-search on that term.

As well as providing the method of installing and removing software, Synaptic provides the means to configure the servers you want to use for finding packages. In fact, this is where you can make one of the most important changes to your Ubuntu system: You can open it up to the Debian universe and multiverse.

Ubuntu is based on the Debian distribution, which has more than 15,000 software packages available for installation. Ubuntu uses only a small subset of that number, but makes it easy for you to enable the others. When you use Synaptic, you will see small orange Ubuntu logos next to every package; this identifies them as being officially supported by the Ubuntu developers. The other, non-Ubuntu packages you can enable will not have this logo, but they are still supported by the Debian developers.

To enable the Universe and Multiverse repositories, go to Settings, Repositories. This list shows all the servers you have configured for software installation and updates, and will include the Universe and Multiverse repositories in there. When you find them, check them and then click Close.

Synaptic shows a message box warning you that the repository listings have changed and that you need to click the Reload button (near the top left of the Synaptic window) to have it refresh the package lists. Go ahead and do that, and you should see a lot more software appear for your selection. However, notice that only a small number have the official Ubuntu "seal" attached, which means you need to be a bit more careful when installing software!

> **NOTE**
>
> Much of the software discussed in this book is only available through the Universe repository. As such, we highly recommend enabling it to get full use out of this book and your Ubuntu installation.

Staying Up-to-Date

Although you can manage your software updates through Synaptic, Ubuntu provides a dedicated tool in the form of Update Manager (launched through System, Administration, Update Manager, and shown in Figure 31.3). This tool is purposefully designed to be simple to use: when you run it, Update Manager automatically downloads the list of updates available for you and checks them all in the list it shows. If the update list was downloaded automatically not too long ago, you can force Ubuntu to refresh the list of available updates by clicking the Check button. Otherwise, all you need to do is click Install Updates and your system will be brought up-to-date. If you want a little more information about the updates, click Show Details at the bottom to see what has changed in the update.

FIGURE 31.3 If you just need to update your software to apply bug fixes and security upgrades, use Update Manager.

Ubuntu automatically checks for updates periodically and notifies you when critical updates are available. That said, there's no harm running Update Manager yourself every so often, just to make sure; it's better to be safe than sorry.

Working on the Command Line

With so much software available for install, it is no surprise that Debian-based distros have many ways to manage software installation. At their root, however, they all use Debian's world-renowned Advanced Package Tool. One poster on Slashdot once said, "Welcome to Slashdot. If you can't think of anything original, just say how much APT rocks and you'll fit right in." You see, even though many other distros have tried to equal the power of APT, nothing else even comes close.

Why is APT so cool? Well, it was the first system to properly handle dependencies in software. Other distros, such as Red Hat, used RPM files that had dependencies. For example, an RPM for the Gimp would have a dependency on Gtk, the graphical toolkit on which the Gimp is based. As a result, if you tried to install your Gimp RPM without having the Gtk RPM, your install would fail. So you grab the Gtk RPM and try again. Aha: Gtk has a dependency on three other things that you need to download. And those three other things have dependencies on 20 other things. And so on, and so on, usually until you can't actually find a working RPM for one of the dependencies, and you give up.

APT, on the other hand, was designed to automatically find and download dependencies for your packages. So if you wanted to install the Gimp, it would download the Gimp's package as well as any other software it needed to work. No more hunting around by hand, no more worrying about finding the right version, and certainly no more need to compile things by hand. APT also handles installation resuming, which means that if you lose your Internet connection part-way through an upgrade (or your battery runs out, or you have to quit, or whatever), APT will just pick up where it left off next time you rerun it.

Day-to-Day Usage

To enable you to search for packages both quickly and thoroughly, APT uses a local cache of the available packages. Try running this command:

```
sudo apt-get update
```

The apt-get update command instructs APT to contact all the servers it is configured to use and download the latest list of file updates. If your lists are outdated, it takes a minute or two for APT to download the updates. Otherwise, this command executes it in a couple of seconds.

After the latest package information has been downloaded, you are returned to the command line. You can now ask APT to automatically download any software that has been updated, using this command:

```
sudo apt-get upgrade
```

If you have a lot of software installed on your machine, there is a greater chance of things being updated. APT scans your software and compares it to the latest package information from the servers and produces a report something like this:

```
paul~$ sudo apt-get upgrade
```

31

```
Reading package lists... Done
Building dependency tree... Done
The following packages will be upgraded:
  example-content gnome-system-tools libavahi-client3 libavahi-common-data
  libavahi-common3 libavahi-glib1 ttf-opensymbol ubuntu-artwork ubuntu-minimal
  ubuntu-standard update-notifier
11 upgraded, 0 newly installed, 0 to remove and 0 not upgraded.
Need to get 27.0MB of archives.
After unpacking 147kB of additional disk space will be used.
Do you want to continue [Y/n]?
```

Each part of that report tells us something important. Starting at the top, the line "the following packages will be upgraded" gives us the exact list of packages for which updates are available. If you're installing new software or removing software, you'll see lists titled "The following packages will be installed" and "The following packages will be removed." A summary at the end shows that there's a total of 11 packages that APT will upgrade, with 0 new packages, 0 to remove, and 0 not upgraded. Because this is an upgrade rather than an installation of new software, all those new packages will only take up 147KB of additional space. Although they come to a 27MB download, they are overwriting existing files.

It's important to understand that a basic apt-get upgrade will never remove software or add new software. As a result, it is safe to use to keep your system fully patched, because it should never break things. However, occasionally you will see the "0 not upgraded" status change, which means some things cannot be upgraded. This happens when some software must be installed or removed to satisfy the dependencies of the updated package, which, as previously mentioned, apt-get upgrade will never do.

In this situation, you need to use apt-get dist-upgrade, so named because it's designed to allow users to upgrade from one version of Debian/Ubuntu to a newer version—an upgrade that inevitably involves changing just about everything on the system, removing obsolete software, and installing the latest features. This is one of the most-loved features of Debian because it allows you to move from version to version without having to download and install new CDs.

Whereas apt-get upgrade and apt-get dist-upgrade are there for upgrading packages, apt-get install is responsible for adding new software. For example, if you want to install the MySQL database server, you would run this:

```
sudo apt-get install mysql-server
```

Internally, APT would query "mysql-server" against its list of software, and find that it matches the mysql-server-5.0 package. It would then find which dependencies it needs that you don't already have installed and then give you a report like this one:

```
paul~$ sudo apt-get install mysql-server
Reading package lists... Done
Building dependency tree... Done
```

```
The following extra packages will be installed:
  libdbd-mysql-perl libdbi-perl libnet-daemon-perl libplrpc-perl
  mysql-client-5.0 mysql-server-5.0
Suggested packages:
  dbishell libcompress-zlib-perl
Recommended packages:
  mailx
The following NEW packages will be installed
  libdbd-mysql-perl libdbi-perl libnet-daemon-perl libplrpc-perl
  mysql-client-5.0 mysql-server mysql-server-5.0
0 upgraded, 7 newly installed, 0 to remove and 11 not upgraded.
Need to get 28.5MB of archives.
After unpacking 65.8MB of additional disk space will be used.
Do you want to continue [Y/n]?
```

This time you can see that APT has picked up and selected all the dependencies required to install MySQL Server 5.0, but it has also listed one recommended package and two suggested packages that it has not selected for installation. The "recommended" package is just that: The person who made the MySQL package (or its dependencies) thinks it would be a smart idea for you to also have the mailx package. If you want to add it, press N to terminate apt-get and rerun it like this:

```
apt-get install mysql-server mailx
```

The "suggested" packages are merely a lower form of recommendation. They don't add any crucial features to the software you selected for install, but it's possible that you might need them for certain, smaller things.

> **NOTE**
>
> APT maintains a package cache where it stores .deb files it has downloaded and installed. This usually lives in /var/cache/apt/archives, and can sometimes take up many hundreds of megabytes on your computer. You can have APT clean out the package cache by running apt-get clean, which deletes all the cached .deb files. Alternatively, you can run apt-get autoclean, which deletes cached .deb files that are beyond a certain age, thereby keeping newer packages.

If you try running apt-get install with packages you already have installed, APT will consider your command to be apt-get update and see whether new versions are available for download.

The last day-to-day package operation is, of course, removing things you no longer want. This is done through the apt-get remove command, as follows:

```
apt-get remove firefox
```

Removing packages can be dangerous, because APT also removes any software that relies on the packages you selected. For example, if you were to run apt-get remove libgtk2.0-0 (the main graphical toolkit for Ubuntu), you would probably find that APT insists on removing more than a hundred other things. The moral of the story is this: When you remove software, read the APT report carefully before pressing Y to continue with the uninstall.

A straight apt-get remove leaves behind the configuration files of your program so that if you ever reinstall it you do not also need to reconfigure it. If you want the configuration files removed as well as the program files, run this command instead:

```
apt-get remove —purge firefox
```

That performs a full uninstall.

> **NOTE**
>
> You can see a more extensive list of apt-get parameters by running apt-get without any parameters. The cryptic line at the bottom, "This APT has Super Cow Powers," is made even more cryptic if you run the command apt-get moo.

Finding Software

With so many packages available, it can be hard to find the exact thing you need using command-line APT. The general search tool is called apt-cache and is used like this:

```
apt-cache search kde
```

Depending on which repositories you have enabled, that will return about a thousand packages. Many of those results will not even have KDE in the package name, but will be matched because the description contains the word *KDE*.

You can filter through this information in several ways. First, you can instruct apt-cache to search only in the package names, not in their descriptions. This is done with the –n parameter, like this:

```
apt-cache -n search kde
```

Now the search has gone down from 1,006 packages to 377 packages.

Another way to limit search results is to use some basic regular expressions, such as ^, meaning "start," and $, meaning "end." For example, you might want to search for programs that are part of the main KDE suite and not libraries (usually named something like libkde), additional bits (such as xmms-kde), and things that are actually nothing to do with KDE yet still match our search (like tkdesk). This can be done by searching for packages that have a name starting with kde, as follows:

```
apt-cache -n search ^kde.
```

Perhaps the easiest way to find packages is to combine apt-cache with grep, to search within search results. For example, if you want to find all games-related packages for KDE, you could run this search:

```
apt-cache search games ¦ grep kde
```

When you've found the package you want to install, just run them through `apt-get install` as per usual. If you first want a little more information about that package, you can use `apt-cache showpkg`, like this:

```
apt-cache showpkg mysql-server-5.0
```

This shows information on "reverse depends" (which packages require, recommend, or suggest mysql-server-5.0), "dependencies" (which packages are required, recommended, or suggested to install mysql-server-5.0) and "provides" (which functions this package gives you). The "provides" list is quite powerful because it allows several different packages to provide a given resource. For example, a MySQL database-based program requires MySQL to be installed, but isn't fussy whether you install MySQL 4.1 or MySQL 5.0. In this situation, the Debian packages for MySQL 4.1 and MySQL 5.0 will both have "mysql-server-4.1" in the provides list, meaning that they offer the functionality provided by MySQL 4.1. As a result, you can install either version to satisfy the MySQL-based application.

Compiling Software from Source

Compiling applications from source is not that difficult. Most source code is available as compressed source *tarballs—that* is, `tar` files that have been compressed using `gzip` or `bzip`. The compressed files typically uncompress into a directory containing several files. It is always a good idea to compile source code as a regular user to limit any damage that broken or malicious code might inflict, so create a directory named `source` in your home directory.

From wherever you downloaded the source tarball, uncompress it into the `~/source` directory using the `-C` option to `tar`:

```
tar zxvf packagename.tgz -C  ~/source
```

```
tar zxvf packagename.tar.gz -C  ~/source
```

```
tar jxvf packagename.bz -C  ~/source
```

```
tar jxvf packagename.tar.bz2 -C  ~/source
```

If you are not certain what file compression method was used, use the `file` command to figure it out:

```
file packagename
```

Now, change directories to `~/source/packagename` and look for a file named README, INSTALL, or a similar name. Print out the file if necessary because it contains specific instructions on how to compile and install the software. Typically, the procedure to compile source code is as follows:

```
./configure
```

This runs a script to check whether all dependencies are met and the build environment is correct. If you are missing dependencies, the configure script normally tells you exactly which ones it needs. If you have the Universe and Multiverse repositories enabled in Synaptic, chances are you will find the missing software (usually libraries) in there.

When your configure script succeeds, run

```
make
```

to compile the software. And finally, run

```
sudo make install.
```

If the compile fails, check the error messages for the reason and run

```
make clean
```

before you start again. You can also run

```
sudo make uninstall
```

to remove the software if you do not like it.

Relevant Ubuntu and Linux Commands

You will use these commands while managing your Ubuntu system resources and software packages:

▶ `apt-get`—The default command-line package-management tool (see Chapter 30 for more on APT)

▶ `gnome-app-install`—The Ubuntu GUI Package Manager

▶ `synaptic`—Advanced tool for software manipulation and repository editing

▶ `update-manager`—The primary source of Ubuntu package updates

Reference

▶ http://www.debian.org/doc/manuals/project-history/ch-detailed.en.html—History of the Debian Linux package system.

▶ http://www.nongnu.org/synaptic/—Home of the Synaptic package manager.

▶ http://www.ubuntu.com/usn—The official list of Ubuntu security notices.

CHAPTER 32

Kernel and Module Management

A kernel is a complex piece of software that manages the processes and process interactions that take place within an operating system. As a user, you rarely, if ever, interact directly with it. Instead, you work with the applications that the kernel manages.

The Linux kernel is Linux. It is the result of years of cooperative (and sometimes contentious) work by numerous people around the world. There is only one common kernel source tree, but each major Linux distribution massages and patches its version slightly to add features, performance, or options. Each Linux distribution, including Ubuntu, comes with its own precompiled kernel as well as the kernel source code, providing you with absolute authority over the Linux operating system. In this chapter, we will examine the kernel and learn what it does for us and for the operating system.

In this chapter, you also learn how to obtain the kernel sources, as well as how and when to patch the kernel. The chapter leads you through an expert's tour of the kernel architecture and teaches you essential steps in kernel configuration, how to build and install modules, and how to compile drivers in Ubuntu. This chapter also teaches you important aspects of working with GRUB, the default Ubuntu boot loader. Finally, the chapter's troubleshooting information will help you understand what to do when something goes wrong with your Linux kernel installation or compilation process. As disconcerting as these problems can seem, this chapter shows you some easy fixes for many kernel problems.

Most users find that the precompiled Ubuntu kernel suits their needs. At some point, you might need to recompile the kernel to support a specific piece of hardware or add a new feature to the operating system. If you have heard horror stories about the difficulties of recompiling the Linux kernel, you can relax; this chapter gives you all the information you need to understand when recompiling is necessary and how to painlessly work through the process.

The Linux Kernel

The Linux kernel is the management part of the operating system that many people call "Linux." Although many think of the entire distribution as Linux, the only piece that can correctly be called Linux is the kernel. Ubuntu, like many Linux distributions, includes a kernel packaged with add-on software that interacts with the kernel so that the user can interface with the system in a meaningful manner.

The system utilities and user programs enable computers to become valuable tools to a user.

The First Linux Kernel

In 1991, Linus Torvalds released version .99 of the Linux kernel as the result of his desire for a powerful, UNIX-like operating system for his Intel 80386 personal computer. Linus wrote the initial code necessary to create what is now known as the Linux kernel and combined it with Richard Stallman's GNU tools. Indeed, because many of the Linux basic system tools come from the GNU Project, many people refer to the operating system as GNU/Linux. Since then, Linux has benefited as thousands of contributors add their talents and time to the Linux project. Linus still maintains the kernel, deciding on what will and will not make it into the kernel as official releases, known to many as the "vanilla" or "Linus" Linux kernel.

The Linux Source Tree

The source code for the Linux kernel is kept in a group of directories called the kernel source tree. The structure of the kernel source tree is important because the process of compiling (building) the kernel is automated; it is controlled by scripts interpreted by the make application. These scripts, known as makefiles, expect to find the pieces of the kernel code in specific places or they will not work. You will learn how to use make to compile a kernel later in this chapter.

It is not necessary for the Linux kernel source code to be installed on your system for the system to run or for you to accomplish typical tasks such as email, web browsing, or word processing. It is necessary that the kernel sources be installed, however, if you want to compile a new kernel. In the next section, we will show you how to install the kernel source files and how to set up the special symbolic link required. That link is /usr/src/linux-2.6, and it is how we will refer to the directory of the kernel source tree as we examine the contents of the kernel source tree.

The /usr/src/linux-2.6 directory contains the .config and the Makefile files among others. The .config file is the configuration of your Linux kernel as it was compiled. There is no .config file by default; you must select one from the /configs subdirectory.

There, you will find configuration files for each flavor of the kernel Ubuntu provides; simply copy the one appropriate for your system to the default directory and rename it .config.

We have already discussed the contents of the /configs subdirectory, so let us examine the other directories found under /usr/src/linux-2.6. The most useful for us is the Documentation directory. In it and its subdirectories, you will find almost all the documentation concerning every part of the kernel. The file 00-INDEX (each Documentation subdirectory also contains a 00-INDEX file as well) contains a list of the files in the main directory and a brief explanation of what they are. Many files are written solely for kernel programmers and application writers, but a few are useful to the intermediate or advanced Linux user when attempting to learn about kernel and device driver issues. Some of the more interesting and useful documents are

> devices.txt—A list of all possible Linux devices that are represented in the /dev directory, giving major and minor numbers and a short description. If you have ever gotten an error message that mentions *char-major-xxx*, this file is where that list is kept.

> ide.txt—If your system uses IDE hard drives, this file discusses how the kernel interacts with them and lists the various kernel commands that can be used to solve IDE-related hardware problems, manually set data transfer modes, and otherwise manually manage your IDE drives. Most of this management is automatic, but if you want to understand how the kernel interacts with IDE devices, this file explains it.

> initrd.txt—This file provides much more in-depth knowledge of initial ramdisks, giving details on the loopback file system used to create and mount them and explaining how the kernel interacts with them.

> kernel-parameters.txt—This file is a list of most of the arguments that you can pass at boot time to configure kernel or hardware settings, but it does not appear too useful at first glance because it is just a list. However, knowing that a parameter exists and might relate to something you are looking for can assist you in tracking down more information because now you have terms to enter into an Internet search engine such as http://www.google.com/linux.

> sysrq.txt—If you have ever wondered what that key on you keyboard marked "SysRq" was used for, this file has the answer. Briefly, it is a key combination hardwired into the kernel that can help you recover from a system lockup. Ubuntu disables this function by default for security reasons. You can re-enable it by entering the command # echo "1" > /proc/sys/kernel/sysrq and disable it by echoing a value of 0 instead of 1.

In the other directories found in Documentation, you will find similar text files that deal with the kernel modules for CD-ROM drivers, file system drivers, gameport and joystick drivers, video drivers (not graphics card drivers—those belong to X11R6 and not to the kernel), network drivers, and all the other drivers and systems found in the Linux operating system. Again, these documents are usually written for programmers, but they can provide useful information to the intermediate and advanced Linux user as well.

The directory named scripts contains many of the scripts that make uses. It really does not contain anything of interest to anyone who is not a programmer or a kernel developer (also known as a kernel hacker).

After a kernel is built, all the compiled files will wind up in the arch directory and its subdirectories. Although you can manually move them to their final location, we will show you later in this chapter how the make scripts will do it for you. In the early days of Linux, this post-compilation file relocation was all done by hand; you should be grateful for make.

> **NOTE**
>
> The make utility is a very complex program. Complete documentation on the structure of make files, as well as the arguments that it can accept, can be found at http://www. gnu.org/software/make/manual/make.html.

The remainder of the directories in /usr/src/linux-2.6 contain the source code for the kernel and the kernel drivers. When you install the kernel sources, these files are placed there automatically. When you patch kernel sources, these files are altered automatically. When you compile the kernel, these files are accessed automatically. Although you never need to touch the source code files, they can be useful. The kernel source files are nothing more than text files with special formatting, which means that we can look at them and read the programmers' comments. Sometimes, a programmer will write an application, but cannot (or often will not) write the documentation. The comments he puts in the source code are often the only documentation that exists for the code.

Small testing programs are even "hidden" in the comments of some of the code, along with comments and references to other information. Because the source code is written in a language that can be read as easily—almost—as English, a non-programmer might be able to get an idea of what the application or driver is actually doing (see Chapter 30, "C/C++ Programming Tools for Ubuntu"). This information might be of use to an intermediate to advanced Linux user when he is confronted by kernel- and driver-related problems.

> **NOTE**
>
> The interaction and control of hardware is handled by a small piece of the kernel called a *device driver*. The driver tells the computer how to interact with a modem, a SCSI card, a keyboard, a mouse, and so on in response to a user prompt. Without the device driver, the kernel does not know how to interact with the associated device.

Types of Kernels

In the early days of Linux, kernels were a single block of code containing all the instructions for the processor, the motherboard, and the other hardware. If you changed hardware, you were required to recompile the kernel code to include what you needed and discard what you did not. Including extra, unneeded code carried a penalty since the kernel became larger and occupied more memory. On older systems that had only 4MB–8MB of memory, wasting precious memory for unnecessary code was considered unacceptable. Kernel compiling was something of a "black art" as early Linux users attempted to wring the most performance from their computers. These kernels compiled as a single block of code are called *monolithic kernels*.

As the kernel code grew larger and the number of devices that could be added to a computer increased, the requirement to recompile became onerous. A new method of building the kernel was developed to make the task of compiling easier. The part of the kernel's source code that composed the code for the device drivers could be optionally compiled as a module that could be loaded and unloaded into the kernel as required. This is known as the *modular* approach to building the kernel. Now, all the kernel code could be compiled at once—with most of the code compiled into these modules. Only the required modules would be loaded; the kernel could be kept smaller, and adding hardware was much simpler.

The typical Ubuntu kernel has some drivers compiled as part of the kernel itself (called *in-line* drivers) and others compiled as modules. Only device drivers compiled in-line are available to the kernel during the boot process; modular drivers are only available after the system has been booted.

NOTE

As a common example, drivers for SCSI disk drives must be available to the kernel if you intend to boot from SCSI disks. If the kernel is not compiled with those drivers in-line, the system will not boot because it will not be able to access the disks.

A way around this problem for modular kernels is to use an initial Ram disk (`initrd`) discussed later in "Creating an Initial RAM Disk Image." The `initrd` loads a small kernel and the appropriate device driver, which then can access the device to load the actual kernel you want to run.

Some code can only be one or the other (for technical reasons unimportant to the average user), but most code can be compiled either as modular or in-line. Depending on the application, some system administrators prefer one way over the other, but with fast modern processors and abundant system memory, the performance differences are of little concern to all but the most ardent Linux hackers.

When compiling a kernel, the step in which you make the selection of modular or in-line is part of the `make config` step that we will detail later in this chapter. Unless you have a specific reason to do otherwise, we suggest that you select the modular option when given a choice. The process of managing modules is addressed in the next section because you will be managing them more frequently than you will be compiling a kernel.

Managing Modules

When using a modular kernel, special tools are required to manage the modules. Modules must be loaded and unloaded, and it would be nice if that were done as automatically as possible. We also need to be able to pass necessary parameters to modules when we load them—things such as memory addresses and interrupts. (That information varies from module to module, so you will need to look at the documentation for your modules to determine what, if any, information needs to be passed to it.) In this section, we will cover the tools provided to manage modules and then look at a few examples of using them.

Linux provides the following module management tools for our use. All these commands (and modprobe.conf) have man pages:

lsmod—This command lists the loaded modules. It is useful to pipe this through the less command because the listing is usually more than one page long.

insmod—This command loads the specified module into the running kernel. If a module name is given without a full path, the default location for the running kernel, /lib/modules/*/, will be searched. Several options are offered for this command—the most useful is -f, which forces the module to be loaded.

rmmod—This command unloads (removes) the specified module from the running kernel. More than one module at a time can be specified.

modprobe—A more sophisticated version of insmod and rmmod, it uses the dependency file created by depmod and automatically handles loading, or with the -r option, removing modules. There is no force option, however. A useful option to modprobe is –t, which causes modprobe to cycle through a set of drivers until it finds one that matches your system. If you were unsure of what module would work for your network card, you would use this command:

```
# modprobe -t net
```

The term net is used because that is the name of the directory (/lib/modules/*/kernel/net) where all the network drivers are kept. It will try each one in turn until it loads one successfully.

modinfo—This will query a module's object file and provide a list of the module name, author, license, and any other information that is there. It often is not very useful.

depmod—This program creates a dependency file for kernel modules. Some modules need to have other modules loaded first; that is, they "depend" on the other modules. (A lot of the kernel code is like this because it eliminates redundancy in the code base.) During the boot process, one of the startup files contains the command depmod -a and it is run every time you boot to re-create the file /lib/modules/*/modules.dep. If you make changes to the file /etc/modprobe.conf, run depmod -a manually. The depmod command, its list of dependencies, and the /etc/modprobe.conf file enable kernel modules to be automatically loaded as needed.

/etc/modprobe.conf—This is not a command, but a file that controls how modprobe and depmod behave; it contains kernel module variables. Although the command syntax can be quite complex, most actual needs are very simple. The most common use is to alias a module and then pass it some parameters. For example, in the following code, we alias a device name (from devices.txt) to a more descriptive word and then pass some information to an associated module. The i2c-dev device is used to read the CPU temperature and fan speed on our system. These lines for /etc/modprobe.conf were suggested for our use by the program's documentation. We added them with a text editor.

```
alias char-major-89 i2c-dev

options eeprom ignore=2,0x50,2,0x51,2,0x52
```

A partial listing of lsmod is shown here, piped through the less command, allowing us to view it a page at a time:

```
# lsmod ¦ less
Module          Size   Used by
parport_pc      19392  1
Module          Size   Used by
parport_pc      19392  1
lp              8236   0
parport         29640  2 parport_pc,lp
autofs4         10624  0
sunrpc          101064 1
```

The list is actually much longer, but here we see that the input module is being used by the joydev (joystick device) module, but the joystick module is not being used. This computer has a joystick port that was autodetected, but no joystick is connected. A scanner module is also loaded, but because the USB scanner is unplugged, the module is not being used. You would use the lsmod command to determine whether a module was loaded and what other modules were using it. If you examine the full list, you would see modules for all the devices attached to your computer.

To remove a module, joydev in this example, use

```
# rmmod joydev
```

or

```
# modprobe -r joydev
```

A look at the output of lsmod would now show that it is no longer loaded. If we removed input as well, we could then use modprobe to load both input and joydev (one depends on the other, remember) with a simple

```
# modprobe joydev
```

If Ubuntu were to balk at loading a module (because it had been compiled using a different kernel version from what we are currently running; for example, the NVIDIA graphics card module), we could force it to load like this:

```
# insmod -f nvidia
```

We would ignore the complaints (error messages) in this case if the kernel generated any.

In Chapter 10, "Multimedia Applications," we talked about loading a scanner module; in the example there, we manually loaded the scanner module and passed it the vendor ID. The scanner was not included in the lookup list because it is not supported by the GPL scanner programs; as a result, the scanner module was not automatically detected and loaded. However, the scanner will work with a closed-source application after the module is loaded. Automatic module management is nice when it works, but sometimes it is necessary to work with modules directly.

When to Recompile

Ubuntu systems use a modified version of the plain vanilla Linux kernel (a modified version is referred to as a *patched* kernel) with additional drivers and other special features compiled into it.

Ubuntu has quite an intensive testing period for all distribution kernels and regularly distributes updated versions. The supplied Ubuntu kernel is compiled with as many modules as possible to provide as much flexibility as possible. A running kernel can be further tuned with the sysctl program, which enables direct access to a running kernel and permits some kernel parameters to be changed. As a result of this extensive testing, configurability, and modularity, the precompiled Ubuntu kernel does everything most users need it to do. Most users only need to recompile the kernel to

▶ Accommodate an esoteric piece of new hardware.

▶ Conduct a system update when Ubuntu has not yet provided precompiled kernels.

▶ Experiment with the system capabilities.

Ubuntu supplies several precompiled versions of the kernel for Athlon and Pentium processors, for single- and multi-processor motherboards, and for Enterprise-class systems (higher security; uses 4GB of memory). These are all available through Synaptic, or just by grepping through the results of an apt-cache search.

Kernel Versions

The Linux kernel is in a constant state of development. As new features are added, bugs are fixed, and new technology is incorporated into the code base, it becomes necessary to provide stable releases of the kernel for use in a production environment. It is also important to have separate releases that contain the newest code for developers to test. To keep track of the kernels, version numbers are assigned to them. Programmers enjoy using sequential version numbers that have abstract meaning. Is version 8 twice as advanced as version 4 of the same application? Is version 1 of one application less developed than version 3 of another? The version numbers cannot be used for this kind of qualitative or quantitative comparison. It is entirely possible that higher version numbers can have fewer features and more bugs than older versions. The numbers exist solely to differentiate and organize sequential revisions of software.

For the latest development version of the kernel at the time of writing, for example, the kernel version number is 2.6.15-23.

The kernel version can be broken down into four sections:

- ▶ `major version`—This is the major version number, now at 2.

- ▶ `minor version`—This is the minor version number, now at 6.

- ▶ `sublevel number`—This number indicates the current iteration of the kernel; here it is number 15.

- ▶ `extraversion level`—This is the number representing a collection of patches and additions made to the kernel by the Ubuntu engineers to make the kernel work for them (and you). Each collection is numbered, and the number is indicated here in the kernel name. From our preceding example, it is 23.

Typing uname -r at the command prompt displays your current kernel version.

```
# uname -r
2.6.15-23
```

Even-numbered minor versions are stable kernels, whereas odd-numbered minor versions are development releases. Version 2.6.x is the stable production kernel, whereas version 2.5.x is the development Linux kernel. When a new version of the development kernel is started, it will be labeled 2.7.x.

For production machines, you should always use the kernels with even minor numbers. The odd minor numbers introduce new features, so you might want to use those on a test machine if you need features they provide.

Obtaining the Kernel Sources

The Linux kernel has always been freely available to anyone who wants it. If you just want to recompile the existing kernel, install the kernel sources package from the CD. To get the very latest "vanilla" version, open an FTP connection to ftp.kernel.org using your favorite FTP client and log in as anonymous. Because you are interested in the 2.6 kernel, change directories to /pub/linux/kernel/v2.6. The latest stable kernel as of this writing is 2.6.17.

NOTE

ftp.kernel.org receives more than its share of requests for download. It is considered a courtesy to use a mirror site to reduce the traffic that ftp.kernel.org bears. http://www. kernel.org/mirrors/ has a list of all mirrors around the world. Find one close to your geographic location and substitute that address for ftp.kernel.org.

A number of different entries are on the FTP archive site for each kernel version, but because you are only interested in the full kernel it is only necessary to get the full package of source code. There are two of these packages:

```
linux-2.6.17.tar.gz
linux-2.6.17.bz2
```

Although these are the same kernel packages, they are built using different compression utilities: The `.gz` extension is the `gzip` package, found on almost every Linux system available. The `.bz2` extension is the newer `bzip2` utility, which has better compression than `gzip`. Both packages have the same content, so download the one compressed with the program you use.

Once downloaded, move the package to a directory other than `/usr/src` and unpack it. If you downloaded the .gz package, the unpacking command is `tar -xzvf linux-2.6.17.tar.gz`. Otherwise, the `bzip2` unpack command is `tar -xjvf linux-2.6.17.tar.bz2`. Once unpacked, the package will create a new directory, `linux-2.6.17`. Copy it to /usr/src or move it there. Then, create a symbolic link of `linux-2.6` to `linux-2.6.17` (otherwise, some scripts will not work). Here is how to create the symbolic link:

```
# rm /usr/src/linux-2.6
# ln -s /usr/src/linux-2.6.17 /usr/src/linux-2.6
```

By creating a symbolic link to `/usr/src/linux-2.6`, it is possible to allow multiple kernel versions to be compiled and tailored for different functions: You will just change the symbolic link to the kernel directory you want to work on.

CAUTION

The correct symbolic link is critical to the operation of make. Always have the symbolic link point to the version of the kernel sources you are working with.

Patching the Kernel

It is possible to patch a kernel to the newest Linux kernel version as opposed to downloading the entire source code. This choice can be beneficial for those who are not using a high-speed broadband connection. (A typical compressed kernel source file is nearly 30MB for a download time of about 10 minutes on a 512Kb DSL connection; adjust accordingly for your connection.) Whether you are patching existing sources or downloading the full source, the end results will be identical.

Patching the kernel is not a mindless task. It requires the user to retrieve all patches from her current version to the version she wants to upgrade to. For example, if you are currently running 2.6.1 (and have those sources) and want to upgrade to 2.6.8, you must retrieve the 2.6.2 and 2.6.3 patch sets, and so on. Once downloaded, these patches must be applied in succession to upgrade to 2.6.8. This is more tedious than downloading the entire source, but useful for those who keep up with kernel hacking and want to perform incremental upgrades to keep their Linux kernel as up-to-date as possible.

To patch up to several versions in a single operation, you can use the patch-kernel script located in the kernel source directory for the kernel version you currently use. This script applies all necessary version patches to bring your kernel up to the latest version.

The format for using the patch-kernel script looks like this:

```
patch-kernel source_dir patch_dir stopversion
```

The source directory defaults to /usr/src/linux if none is given, and the patch_dir defaults to the current working directory if one is not supplied.

For example, assume that you have a 2.6.6 kernel code tree that needs to be patched to the 2.6.8 version. The 2.6.7 and 2.6.8 patch files have been downloaded from ftp.kernel.org and are placed in the /patch directory in the source tree. You issue the following command in the /usr/src/linux-2.6 directory:

```
# scripts/patch-kernel /usr/src/linux-2.6.6 /usr/src/linux-2.6.6/patch
```

Each successive patch file is applied, eventually creating a 2.6.8 code tree. If any errors occur during this operation, files named xxx# or xxx.rej are created, where xxx is the version of patch that failed. You will have to resolve these failed patches manually by examining the errors and looking at the source code and the patch. An inexperienced person will not have any success with this because you need to understand C programming and kernel programming to know what is broken and how to fix it. Because this was a stock 2.6.6 code tree, the patches were all successfully applied without errors. If you are attempting to apply a nonstandard third-party patch, the patch might likely fail.

When you have successfully patched the kernel, you are ready to begin compiling this code tree as if we started with a fresh, stock 2.6.8 kernel tree.

Using the patch Command

If you have a special, nonstandard patch to apply—such as a third-party patch for a commercial product, for example—you can use the patch command rather than the special patch-kernel script that is normally used for kernel source updates. Here are some quick steps and an alternative method of creating patched code and leaving the original code alone.

1. Create a directory in your home directory and name it something meaningful, like mylinux.

2. Copy the pristine Linux source code there with

   `cp -ravd /usr/src/linux-2.6/* ~/mylinux`

3. Copy the patch file to that same directory with

   `cp patch_filename ~/mylinux`

4. Change to the ~/mylinux directory with

   `cd ~/mylinux`

5. Apply the patch with

   patch -p1 < *patch_filename* > mypatch.log 2>&1

   (This last bit of code saves the message output to a file so that you can look at it later.)

6. If the patch applies successfully, you are done and have not endangered any of the pristine source code. In case the newly patched code does not work, you will not have to reinstall the original, pristine source code.

7. Copy your new code to `/usr/src` and make that special symbolic link described elsewhere in the chapter.

Compiling the Kernel

If you want to update the kernel from new source code you have downloaded, or you have applied a patch to add new functionality or hardware support, you will need to compile and install a new kernel to actually use that new functionality. Compiling the kernel involves translating the kernel's contents from human-readable code to binary form. Installing the kernel involves putting all the compiled files where they belong in /boot and /lib and making changes to the bootloader.

The process of compiling the kernel is almost completely automated by the make utility as is the process of installing. By providing the necessary arguments and following the steps covered next, you can recompile and install a custom kernel for your use.

Here is a checklist of steps to compile and configure the kernel:

1. Verify a working bootdisk for the old kernel to be able to reboot your system in case something goes wrong with the new kernel.

CAUTION

Before making any changes to your current, working kernel, make sure that you have a backup copy on a floppy disk. This will allow you to boot into your system with a known working kernel in case something goes wrong during configuration. The command to do this is as follows:

```
# mkbootdisk —device /dev/fd0 'uname -r'
```

This assumes that your floppy drive is /dev/fd0. (Here is a good shell script tip: the ′ character tells the shell to execute what is within ′ first and then returns that output as part of the input of the mkbootdisk command.) On this machine, the result is

```
# mkbootdisk —device /dev/fd0 2.6.7-1
```

This command will not be echoed to your screen, but it is what the system will execute.

---

2. Apply all patches, if any, so that you have the features you desire. See the previous section for details.

3. Back up the .config file, if it exists, so that you can recover from the inevitable mistake. Use the following cp command:

```
# cp .config .config.bak
```

NOTE

If you are recompiling the Ubuntu default kernel, the `/usr/src/linux-2.6/configs` directory contains several versions of configuration files for different purposes.

Ubuntu provides a full set of `.config` files in the subdirectory configs, all named for the type of system they were compiled for. For example, `kernel-2.6.7-i686-smp.config` is a configuration file for a multiprocessor Pentium-class computer. If you want to use one of these default configurations as the basis for a custom kernel, simply copy the appropriate file to `/usr/src/linux-2.6` and rename it `.config`.

---

4. Run the `make mrproper` directive to prepare the kernel source tree, cleaning out any old files or binaries.

5. Restore the `.config` file that the command `make mrproper` deleted, and edit the Makefile to change the EXTRAVERSION number.

NOTE

If you want to keep any current version of the kernel that was compiled with the same code tree, manually edit the Makefile with your favorite text editor and add some unique string to the EXTRAVERSION variable.

You can use any description you prefer, however.

---

6. Modify the kernel configuration file using `make config`, `make menuconfig`, or `make xconfig`—we recommend the latter.

7. Run make dep to create the code dependencies used later in the compilation process.

TIP

If you have a multi-processor machine, you can use both processors to speed the make process by inserting −j*x* after the make command, where as a rule of thumb, *x* is one more than the number of processors you have. You might try a larger number and even try this on a single processor machine (we have used -j8 successfully on an SMP machine); it will only load up your CPU. For example,

```
# make -j3 bzImage
```

All the make processes except make dep will work well with this method of parallel compiling.

8. Run `make clean` to prepare the sources for the actual compilation of the kernel.

9. Run `make bzImage` to create a binary image of the kernel.

NOTE

Several choices of directives exist, although the most common ones are as follows:

zImage—This directive compiles the kernel, creating an uncompressed file called zImage.

bzImage—This directive creates a compressed kernel image necessary for some systems that require the kernel image to be under a certain size for the BIOS to be able to parse them; otherwise, the new kernel will not boot. It is the most commonly used choice. However, the Ubuntu kernel compiled with bzImage is still too large to fit on a floppy, so a smaller version with some modules and features removed is used for the boot floppies. Ubuntu recommends that you boot from the rescue CD-ROM.

bzDisk—This directive does the same thing as bzImage, but it copies the new kernel image to a floppy disk for testing purposes. This is helpful for testing new kernels without writing kernel files to your hard drive. Make sure that you have a floppy disk in the drive because you will not be prompted for one.

10. Run `make modules` to compile any modules your new kernel needs.

11. Run `make modules_install` to install the modules in /lib/modules and create dependency files.

12. Run `make install` to automatically copy the kernel to /boot, create any other files it needs, and modify the bootloader to boot the new kernel by default.

13. Using your favorite text editor, verify the changes made to /etc/lilo.conf or /boot/grub/grub.conf; fix if necessary and rerun /sbin/lilo if needed.

14. Reboot and test the new kernel.

15. Repeat the process if necessary, choosing a Configuration Interface.

Over time, the process for configuring the Linux kernel has changed. Originally, you configured the kernel by responding to a series of prompts for each configuration parameter (this is the make config utility described shortly). Although you can still configure Linux this way, most users find this type of configuration confusing and inconvenient; moving back through the prompts to correct errors, for instance, is impossible.

The make config utility is a command-line tool. The utility presents a question regarding kernel configuration options. The user responds with a Y, N, M, or ?. (It is not case sensitive.) Choosing M configures the option to be compiled as a module. A response of ? displays context help for that specific options, if available. (If you choose ? and no help is available, you can turn to the vast Internet resources to find information.) We recommend that you avoid the make config utility, shown in Figure 32.1.

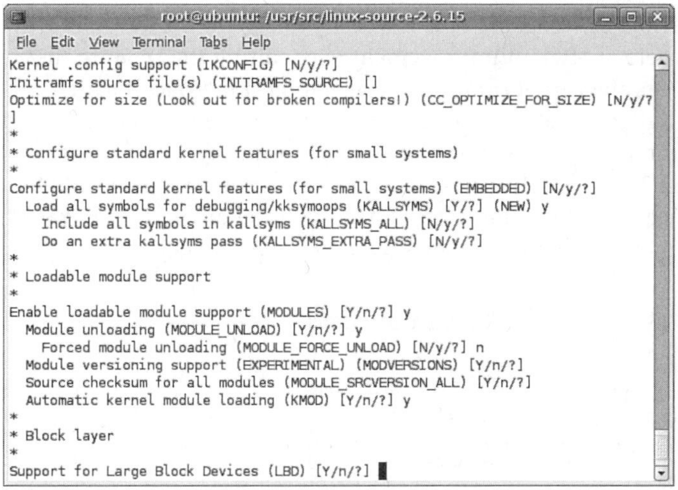

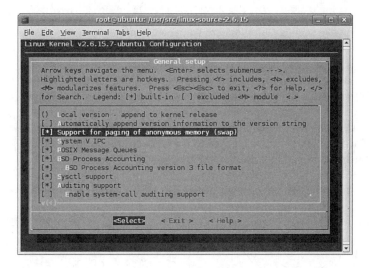

FIGURE 32.1   The make config utility in all its Spartan glory.

If you prefer to use a command-line interface, you can use make menuconfig to configure the Linux kernel. menuconfig provides a graphical wrapper around a text interface. Although it is not as raw as make config, menuconfig is not a fancy graphical interface either; you cannot use a mouse, but must navigate through it using keyboard commands. The same information presented in make config is presented by make menuconfig, but as you can see in Figure 32.2, it looks a little nicer. Now, at least, you can move back and forth in the selection process in case you change your mind or have made a mistake.

FIGURE 32.2   The make menuconfig utility, a small improvement over make config.

In make menuconfig, you use the arrow keys to move the selector up and down and the spacebar to toggle a selection. The Tab key moves the focus at the bottom of the screen to either Select, Exit, or Help.

If a graphical desktop is not available, menuconfig is the best you can do. However, both menuconfig and xconfig (see below) offer an improvement over editing the .config file directly. If you want to configure the kernel through a true graphical interface—with mouse support and clickable buttons—make xconfig is the best configuration utility option. To use this utility, you must have the X Window System running. The application xconfig is really nothing but a Tcl/Tk graphics *widget set* providing borders, menus, dialog boxes, and the like. Its interface is used to wrap around data files that are parsed at execution time. Figure 32.3 shows the main menu of xconfig for the 2.6.7 kernel.

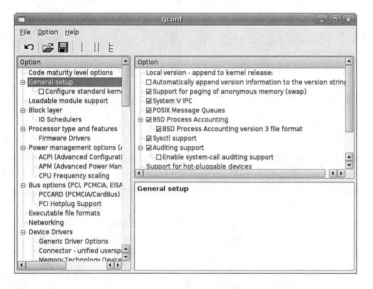

FIGURE 32.3   The much nicer make xconfig GUI interface. We recommend that you use this interface if you are able.

After loading this utility, you use it by clicking on each of the buttons that list the configuration options. Each button you click opens another window that has the detail configuration options for that subsection. Three buttons are at the bottom of each window: Main Menu, Next, and Prev(ious). Clicking the Main Menu button closes the current window and displays the main window. Clicking Next takes you to the next configuration section. When configuring a kernel from scratch, click the button labeled Code Maturity Level Options, and then continue to click the Next button in each subsection window to proceed through all the kernel configuration choices. When you have selected all options, the main menu is again displayed. The buttons on the lower right of the main menu are for saving and loading configurations. Their functions are self-explanatory. If you just want to have a look, go exploring! Nothing will be changed if you elect not to save it.

If you are upgrading kernels from a previous release, it is not necessary to go though the entire configuration from scratch. Instead, you can use the directive make oldconfig; it uses the same text interface that make config uses, and it is noninteractive. It will just prompt for changes for any new code.

Using xconfig to Configure the Kernel

For simplicity's sake, during this brisk walk-through, we will assume that you are using make xconfig. Prior to this point, we also assume that you will have completed the first five steps in our kernel compilation checklist shown previously.

As you learned in the preceding section, you configure the kernel using make xconfig by making choices in several configuration subsection windows. Each subsection window contains specific kernel options. With hundreds of choices, the kernel is daunting to configure. We cannot really offer you detailed descriptions of which options to choose because your configuration will not match your own system and setup.

Table 32.1 provides a brief description of each subsection's options so that you can get an idea of what you might encounter. We recommend that you copy your kernel's .config file to /usr/src/linux-2.6 and run make xconfig from there. Explore all the options. As long as you do not save the file, absolutely nothing will be changed on your system.

TABLE 32.1   Kernel Subsections for Configuration

Name	Description
Code maturity level options	Enables development code to be compiled into the kernel even if it has been marked as obsolete or as testing code only. This option should only be used by kernel developers or testers because of the possible unusable state of the code during development.
General setup	This section contains several different options covering how the kernel talks to the BIOS, whether it should support PCI or PCMCIA, whether it should use APM or ACPI, and what kind of Linux binary formats will be supported. Contains several options for supporting kernel structures necessary to run binaries compiled for other systems directly without recompiling the program.
Loadable module support	Determines whether the kernel enables drivers and other nonessential code to be compiled as loadable modules that can be loaded and unloaded at runtime. This option keeps the basic kernel small so that it can run and respond more quickly; in that regard, choosing this option is generally a good idea.

TABLE 32.1   Kernel Subsections for Configuration

Name	Description
Processor type and features	Several options dealing with the architecture that will be running the kernel.
Power management options	Options dealing with ACPI and APM power management features.
Bus options	Configuration options for the PCMCIA bus found in laptops and PCI hotplug devices.
Memory Technology Devices	Options for supporting flash memory devices, such as (MTD) EEPROMS. Generally, these devices are used in embedded systems.
Parallel port support	Several options for configuring how the kernel will support parallel port communications.
Plug-and-play configuration	Options for supporting Plug and Play PCI, ISA, and plug-and-play BIOS support. Generally, it is a good idea to support plug-and-play for PCI and ISA devices.
Block devices	Section dealing with devices that communicate with the kernel in blocks of characters instead of streams. This includes IDE and ATAPI devices connected via parallel ports, as well as enabling network devices to communicate as block devices.
ATA/IDE/MFM/RLL support	Large collection of options to configure the kernel to communicate using different types of data communication protocols to talk to mass storage devices, such as hard drives. Note that this section does not cover SCSI.
SCSI device support	Options for configuring the kernel to support Small Computer Systems Interface. This subsection covers drivers for specific cards, chipsets, and tunable parameters for the SCSI protocol.
Old CD-ROM drivers	Configuration options to support obscure, older CD-ROM devices that do not conform to the SCSI or IDE standards. These are typically older CD-ROM drivers that are usually a proprietary type of SCSI (not SCSI, not IDE).
Multi-device support	Options for enabling the kernel to support RAID devices in (RAID and LVM) software emulation and the different levels of RAID. Also contains options for support of a logical volume manager.
Fusion MPT device support	Configures support for LSI's Logic Fusion Message Passing Technology. This technology is for high performance SCSI and local area network interfaces.
IEEE1394 (firewire) support	Experimental support for Firewire devices.

TABLE 32.1   Kernel Subsections for Configuration

Name	Description
I2O device support	Options for supporting the Intelligent Input/Output architecture. This architecture enables the hardware driver to be split from the operating system driver, thus enabling a multitude of hardware devices to be compatible with an operating system in one implementation.
Networking support	Several options for the configuration of networking in the kernel. The options are for the types of supported protocols and configurable options of those protocols.
Amateur radio support	Options for configuring support of devices that support the AX25 protocol.
IrDA (infrared) support	Options for configuring support of the infrared Data Association suite of protocols and devices that use these protocols.
Bluetooth support	Support for the Bluetooth wireless protocol. Includes options to support the Bluetooth protocols and hardware devices.
ISDN subsystem	Options to support Integrated Services Digital Networks protocols and devices. ISDN is a method of connection to a large area network digitally over conditioned telephone lines, largely found to connect users to ISPs.
Telephony support	Support for devices that enable the use of regular telephone lines to support VoIP applications. This section does not handle the configuration of modems.
Input device support	Options for configuring Universal Serial Bus (USB) Human Interface Devices (HID). These include keyboards, mice, and joysticks.
Character devices	Configuration options for devices that communicate to the server in sequential characters. This is a large subsection containing the drivers for several motherboard chipsets.
Multimedia devices	Drivers for hardware implementations of video and sound devices such as video capture boards, TV cards, and AM/FM radio adapter cards.
Graphics support	Configures VGA text console, video mode selection, and support for frame buffer cards.
Sound	Large subsection to configure supported sound card drivers and chipset support for the kernel.
USB support	Universal Serial Bus configuration options. Includes configuration for USB devices, as well as vendor-specific versions of USB.
File system	Configuration options for supported file system types.
Additional device driver support	A section for third-party patches.

32

TABLE 32.1   Kernel Subsections for Configuration

Name	Description
Profiling support	Profiling kernel behavior to aid in debugging and development.
Kernel hacking	This section determines whether the kernel will contain advanced debugging options. Most users will not want to include this option in their production kernels because it increases the kernel size and slows performance by adding extra routines.
Security options	Determines whether NSA Security Enhanced Linux (SELinux) is enabled.
Cryptographic options	Support for cryptography hardware (Ubuntu patches not found in the "vanilla" kernel sources).
Library routines	Contains zlib compression support.

After you select all the options you want, you can save the configuration file and continue with step 7 in the kernel compiling checklist shown earlier.

Creating an Initial RAM Disk Image

If you require special device drivers to be loaded in order to mount the root file system (for SCSI drives, network cards, or exotic file systems, for example), you must create an initial RAM disk image named /boot/initrd.img. For most users, it is not necessary to create this file, but if you are not certain, it really does not hurt. To create an initrd.img file, use the shell script /sbin/mkinitrd.

The format for the command is the following:

```
/sbin/mkinitrd file_name kernel_version
```

where file_name is the name of the image file you want created.

mkinitrd looks at /etc/fstab, /etc/modprobe.conf, and /etc/ raidtab to obtain the information it needs to determine which modules should be loaded during boot. For our system, we use

```
# mkinitrd initrd-2.6.7-1.img 2.6.7-1
```

When Something Goes Wrong

Several things might go wrong during a kernel compile and installation, and several clues will point to the true problem. You will see error messages printed to the screen, and some error messages will be printed to the file /var/log/messages, which can be examined with a text editor. If you have followed our directions for patching the kernel, you will need to examine a special error log as well. Do not worry about errors because many problems are easily fixed with some research on your part. Some errors may be unfixable, however, depending on your skill level and the availability of technical information.

Errors During Compile

Although it is rare that the kernel will not compile, there is always a chance that something has slipped though the regression testing. Let's take a look at an example of a problem that might crop up during the compile.

It is possible that the kernel compile will crash and not complete successfully, especially if you attempt to use experimental patches, add untested features, or build newer and perhaps unstable modules on an older system.

At this juncture, you have two options:

- ► Fix the errors and recompile.

- ► Remove the offending module or option and wait for the errors to be fixed by the kernel team.

Most users will be unable to fix some errors because of the complexity of the kernel code, although you should not rule out this option. It is possible that someone else discovered the same error during testing of the kernel and developed a patch for the problem: check the Linux kernel mailing list archive. If the problem is not mentioned there, a search on Google might turn up something.

The second option, removing the code, is the easiest and is what most people do in cases in which the offending code is not required. In the case of the NTFS module failing, it is almost expected because NTFS support is still considered experimental and subject to errors. This is primarily because the code for the file system is reverse-engineered instead of implemented via documented standards. Read-only support has gotten better in recent kernels; write support is still experimental.

Finally, should you want to take on the task of trying to fix the problem yourself, this is a great opportunity to get involved with the Linux kernel and make a contribution that could help many others.

If you are knowledgeable about coding and kernel matters, you might want to look in the MAINTAINERS file in the /usr/src/linux-2.6/ directory of the kernel source and find the maintainer of the code. The recommended course of action is to contact the maintainer and see if he is aware of the problems you are having. If nothing has been documented for the specific error, submitting the error to the kernel mailing list is an option. The guidelines for doing this are in the README file in the base directory of the kernel source under the section "If Something Goes Wrong."

Runtime Errors, Boot Loader Problems, and Kernel Oops

Runtime errors occur as the kernel is loading. Error messages are displayed on the screen or written to the /var/log/messages file. Bootloader problems display messages to the screen; no log file is produced. *Kernel oops* are errors in a running kernel, and error messages are written to the /var/log/messages file.

Excellent documentation on the Internet exists for troubleshooting just about every type of error that LILO, GRUB, or the kernel could give during boot. The best way to find this documentation is to go to your favorite search engine and type in the keywords of the error you received. You will need to adjust the keywords you use as you focus your search.

In this category, the most common problems deal with LILO configuration issues. Diagnosis and solutions to these problems can be found in the LILO mini-HOWTO found on the Linux Documentation project's website at http://www.ibiblio.org/pub/Linux/docs/HOWTO/other-formats/html_single/LILO.html.

If you have GRUB problems, the GRUB manual is online at http://www.gnu.org/software/grub/manual/.

TIP

For best results, go to http://www.google.com/linux to find all things Linux on the Internet. Google has specifically created a Linux area of its database, which should allow faster access to information on Linux than any other search engine.

The Usenet newsgroup postings are searchable at http://www.google.com/grphp.

Mail list discussions can be searched in the Mailing list ARChives (MARC) at http://marc.theaimsgroup.com/.

Relevant Ubuntu and Linux Commands

You will use the following commands when managing the kernel and its modules in Ubuntu:

▶ gcc—The GNU compiler system

▶ make—GNU project and file management command

▶ mkbootdisk—Ubuntu's boot disk creation tool

▶ sysctl—The interface to manipulating kernel variables at runtime

▶ mkinitrd—Create a RAM-disk file system for bootloading support

Reference

▶ http://www.kernel.org/—Linux Kernel Archives. The source of all development discussion for the Linux kernel.

▶ http://www.kerneltraffic.org/kernel-traffic/index.html—Linux Kernel Traffic. Summarized version and commentary of the Linux Kernel mailing list produced weekly.

▶ http://www.gnu.org/—Free Software Foundation. Source of manuals and software for programs used throughout the kernel compilation process. Tools such as make and gcc have their official documentation here.

▶ http://slashdot.org/article.pl?sid=01/08/22/1453228&mode=thread—The famous AC Patches from Alan Cox, for whom they are named.

▶ http://www.digitalhermit.com/linux/Kernel-Build-HOWTO.html—The Linux Kernel Rebuild Guide; configuration, compilation, and troubleshooting.

▶ http://www.ibiblio.org/pub/Linux/docs/HOWTO/other-formats/html_single/ KernelAnalysis-HOWTO.html—KernelAnalysis HOWTO. Describes the mysterious inner workings of the kernel.

▶ http://www.tldp.org/HOWTO/Module-HOWTO/—Kernel Module HOWTO. Includes a good discussion about unresolved symbols.

▶ http://www.ibiblio.org/pub/Linux/docs/HOWTO/other-formats/html_single/ Modules.html—The Linux Kernel Modules Installation HOWTO; an older document discussing recompiling kernel modules.

▶ http://www.tldp.org/—The Linux Documentation Project. The Mecca of all Linux documentation. Excellent source of HOWTO documentation, as well as FAQs and online books, all about Linux.

▶ http://www.minix.org/—The unofficial minix website. It contains a selection of links to information about minix and a link to the actual homepage. Although minix is still copyrighted, the owner has granted unlimited rights to everyone. See for yourself the OS used to develop Linux.

▶ http://jungla.dit.upm.es/~jmseyas/linux/kernel/hackers-docs.html—Web page with links to Linux kernel documentation, books, hacker tomes, and other helpful information for budding and experienced Linux kernel and kernel module developers. This list will also be found in the file /usr/src/linux-2.6/Documentation/kernel-docs.txt if you install the Ubuntu kernel sources.

PART VII

Appendixes

IN THIS PART

APPENDIX A

Ubuntu Under the Hood

As with any new thing, it's worthwhile finding out a bit about its history. Ubuntu is no different, and in this appendix you'll learn a little more about where Linux (and Ubuntu) came from.

What Is Linux?

Linux is the core, or kernel, of a free operating system first developed and released to the world by Linus Benedict Torvalds in 1991. Torvalds, then a graduate student at the University of Helsinki, Finland, is now a Fellow at the Linux Foundation (http://www.linux-foundation.org/). He is an engineer and previously worked for the CPU design and fabrication company Transmeta, Inc. Fortunately for all Linux users, Torvalds chose to distribute Linux under a free software license named the GNU General Public License (GPL).

> **NOTE**
>
> The free online resource Wikipedia has a great biography of Linus Torvalds that examines his life and notable achievements. You can find it at http://en.wikipedia.org/wiki/Linux_Torvalds. Or you can head on over to http://groups.google.com/group/comp.os.minix/msg/b813d52cbc5a044b?hl=en to read a copy of Linus's first post about Linux to the world.

The GNU GPL is the brainchild of Richard M. Stallman, the founder of the Free Software Foundation. Stallman, the famous author of the Emacs editing environment and GCC compiler system, crafted the GPL to ensure that software that used the GPL for licensing would always be free and available in source-code form. The GPL is the guiding document for Linux and its ownership, distribution, and copyright. Torvalds holds the rights to the Linux trademark, but thanks to a combination of his generosity, the Internet, thousands of programmers around the world, GNU software, and the GNU GPL, Linux will remain forever free and unencumbered by licensing or royalty issues.

Distribution Version and Kernel Numbering Schema

There is a specific numbering system for Linux kernels, kernel development, and Ubuntu's kernel versions. Note that these numbers bear no relation to the version number of your Ubuntu Linux distribution. Ubuntu distribution version numbers are assigned by the Ubuntu developers, whereas most of the Linux kernel version numbers are assigned by Linus Torvalds and his legion of kernel developers.

To see the date your Linux kernel was compiled, use the uname command with its -v command-line option. To see the version of your Linux kernel, use the -r option. The numbers, such as 2.6.24-5, represent the major version (2), minor version (6), and patch level (24). The final number (5) is the developer patch level and is assigned by the Ubuntu developers.

Even minor numbers are considered "stable" and generally fit for use in production environments, whereas odd minor numbers (such as a Linux 2.7 source tree, not yet in existence) represent versions of the Linux kernel under development and testing. You will find only stable versions of the Linux kernel included with this book. You can choose to download and install a beta (test) version of the kernel, but this is not recommended for a system destined for everyday use. Most often, beta kernels are installed to provide support and testing of new hardware or operating system features.

Linux, pronounced "lih-nucks," is free software. Combining the Linux kernel with GNU software tools—drivers, utilities, user interfaces, and other software such as the X.Org Foundation's X Window System—creates a Linux distribution. There are many different Linux distributions from different vendors, but many derive from or closely mimic the Debian Linux distribution, on which Ubuntu is founded.

NOTE

To see just how many distributions are based on Debian Linux, go to http://www.linux. org/, click Distributions, and search for "Debian-based." At the time of writing, 52 distributions owe their existence to Debian.

Why Use Linux?

Millions of clever computer users have been putting Linux to work for more than 14 years. Over the past year, many individuals, small office/home office (SOHO) users, businesses and corporations, colleges, nonprofits, and government agencies (local, state, and federal) in a number of countries have incorporated Linux with great success. And, today, Linux is being incorporated into many information service/information technology (IS/IT) environments as part of improvements in efficiency, security, and cost savings. Using Linux is a good idea for a number of reasons, including the following:

▶ **Linux provides an excellent return on investment (ROI)**—There is little or no cost on a per-seat basis. Unlike commercial operating systems, Linux has no royalty or licensing fees, and a single Linux distribution on CD-ROM or network shared folder can form the basis of an enterprise-wide software distribution, replete with applications and productivity software. Custom corporate CD-ROMs can be easily crafted or network shares can be created to provide specific installs on enterprise-wide hardware. This feature alone can save hundreds of thousands, if not millions, of dollars in IS/IT costs—all without the threat of a software audit from the commercial software monopoly or the need for licensing accounting and controls of base operating system installations.

▶ **Linux can be put to work on the desktop**—Linux, in conjunction with its supporting graphical networking protocol and interface (the X Window System), has worked well as a consumer UNIX-like desktop operating system since the mid-1990s. The fact that UNIX is ready for the consumer desktop is now confirmed with the introduction, adoption, and rapid maturation of Apple Computer BSD UNIX—based on Mac OS X—supported, according to Apple, by more than 3,000 Mac OS X-specific programs that are known as native applications. This book's disc contains more than 800 software packages, including Internet connection utilities, games, a full office suite, many different fonts, and hundreds of graphics applications.

▶ **Linux can be put to work as a server platform**—Linux is fast, secure, stable, scalable, and robust. The latest versions of the Linux kernel easily support multiple-processor computers, large amounts of system memory (up to 64GB RAM), individual file sizes in excess of hundreds of gigabytes, a choice of modern journaling file systems, hundreds of process monitoring and control utilities, and the (theoretical) capability to simultaneously support more than four billion users. IBM, Oracle, and other major database vendors all have versions of their enterprise software available for Linux.

▶ **Linux has a low entry and deployment cost barrier**—Maintenance costs can also be reduced because Linux works well on a variety of PCs, including legacy hardware, such as some Intel-based 486 and early Pentium CPUs. Although the best program performance will be realized with newer hardware, because clients can be recompiled and optimized for Pentium-class CPUs, base installs can even be performed on lower-end computers or embedded devices with only 8MB of RAM. This feature provides for a much wider user base; extends the life of older working hardware; and can help save money for home, small business, and corporate users.

▶ **Linux appeals to a wide audience in the hardware and software industry—** Versions of Linux exist for nearly every CPU. Embedded-systems developers now turn to Linux when crafting custom solutions using ARM, MIPS, and other low-power processors. Linux is the first full operating system available for Intel's Itanium CPU, as well as the AMD64 group of CPUs; ports have also been available for HP/Compaq's Alpha and Sun Microsystems SPARC CPUs for some time. PowerPC users regularly use the PPC port of Linux on IBM and Apple hardware.

▶ **Linux provides a royalty-free development platform for cross-platform development—** Because of the open-source development model and availability of free, high-quality development tools, Linux provides a low-cost entry point to budding developers and tech industry start-ups.

▶ **Big-player support in the computer hardware industry from such titans as IBM now lends credibility to Linux as a viable platform—** IBM has enabled Linux on the company's entire line of computers, from low-end laptops through "Big Iron" mainframes. New corporate customers are lining up and using Linux as part of enterprise-level computing solutions. It has been used on some of the world's fastest computers, including IBM's Blue Gene/L. HP also certifies Linux across a large portion of its hardware offering.

Look forward to even more support as usage spreads worldwide throughout all levels of business in search of lower costs, better performance, and stable and secure implementations.

What Is Ubuntu?

Ubuntu is an operating system based on the Linux kernel; created, improved, refined, and distributed by the Ubuntu Community at http://www/ubuntu.com/. Ubuntu, sponsored by Canonical Software, is an open-source project supported by a worldwide community of software developers.

Roots of Ubuntu

Ubuntu is one of the newer Linux distributions currently available today, having released its first version in October 2004. It quickly gained a reputation for ease of installation and use, combined with the slightly wacky code names given to each release. However, Ubuntu itself is based on Debian, which is a much older distribution steeped in respect from the wider Linux community. Ubuntu describes Debian as being the rock on which it is founded, and this is a good way to describe the relationship between the two. It is also worth noting that Debian garnered a reputation for infrequent releases. The move from Debian 3.0 to 3.1 took almost three years, during which time many other Linux distros had moved far ahead of Debian.

Sponsored by Canonical Software and with the formidable resources of Mark Shuttleworth, Ubuntu got off to a great start with version 4.10, the Warty Warthog. From the start, Ubuntu specified clear goals: to provide a distribution that was easy to install and use, that did not overly confuse the user, and that came on a single CD (something increasingly rare these days when a distro can occupy four or five CDs). Releasing every six months, Ubuntu made rapid progress into the Linux community and is now one of the most popular Linux distros across the world.

Ubuntu Versions

As mentioned earlier, Ubuntu has chosen some peculiar code names for their releases since the first launch in October 2004. Doing away with the typical version numbering found elsewhere, Ubuntu decided to take the month and year of release and reverse them. Hence, the first release in October 2004 became 4.10, followed quickly by 5.04 (April 2005), 5.10, 6.06LTS, 6.10, 7.04, and 7.10.

The version covered in this book was released in October 2009, and thus bears the version number 9.10. What's even more special about some releases is that they also carries the LTS (Long Term Support) label, meaning that Canonical will support LTS versions for three years on the desktop and a total of five years for the server version after its release.

The code names during development are even better: 4.10 was christened the Warty Warthog in recognition that it was a first release, warts and all. The second release, 5.04, was dubbed the Hoary Hedgehog. Things got slightly better with 5.10, code-named the Breezy Badger. 6.06 was announced as the Dapper Drake and was the first Ubuntu distribution to carry the LTS badge. Beyond Dapper, there was the Edgy Eft (6.10) followed by the Feisty Fawn (7.04), and more, up to what was known during development as the karmic koala (9.10), which is what this book covers.

Ubuntu for Business

Linux has matured over the years, and features considered essential for use in enterprise-level environments, such as CPU architecture support, file systems, and memory handling, have been added and improved. The addition of virtual memory (the capability to swap portions of RAM to disk) was one of the first necessary ingredients, along with a copyright-free implementation of the TCP/IP stack (mainly due to BSD UNIX being tied up in legal entanglements at the time). Other features quickly followed, such as support for a variety of network protocols.

Ubuntu includes a Linux kernel that can use multiple processors, which allows you to use Ubuntu in more advanced computing environments with greater demands on CPU power. This kernel will support at least 16 CPUs; in reality, however, small business servers typically use only dual-CPU workstations or servers. However, Ubuntu can run Linux on more powerful hardware.

Ubuntu will automatically support your multiple-CPU Intel-based motherboard, and you will be able to take advantage of the benefits of symmetric multiprocessors (SMPs) for software development and other operations. The Linux kernels included with Ubuntu can use system RAM sizes up to 64GB, allow individual file sizes in excess of 2GB, and host the demands of—theoretically—billions of users.

Businesses that depend on high-availability, large-scale systems can also be served by Ubuntu, along with the specialist commercial support on offer from hundreds of support partners across the world.

However, Ubuntu can be used in many of these environments by customers with widely disparate computing needs. Some of the applications for Ubuntu include desktop support; small file, print, or mail servers; intranet web servers; and security firewalls deployed at strategic points inside and outside company LANs.

Commercial customers will also benefit from Debian's alliances with several top-tier system builders, including Hewlett-Packard.

Debian itself is also available for multiple architectures, and until recently was developed in tandem on 11 different architectures, from x86 to the older Motorola 680x0 chips (as found in the Commodore Amiga), along with several other architectures.

Small business owners can earn great rewards by stepping off the software licensing and upgrade treadmill and adopting a Linux-based solution. Using Ubuntu not only avoids the need for licensing accounting and the threat of software audits, but also provides viable alternatives to many types of commercial productivity software.

Using Ubuntu in a small business setting makes a lot of sense for other reasons, too, such as not having to invest in cutting-edge hardware to set up a productive shop. Ubuntu easily supports older, or *legacy*, hardware, and savings are compounded over time by avoiding unnecessary hardware upgrades. Additional savings will be realized because software and upgrades are free. New versions of applications can be downloaded and installed at little or no cost, and office suite software is free.

Ubuntu is easy to install on a network and plays well with others, meaning it works well in a mixed-computing situation with other operating systems such as Windows, Mac OS X, and, of course, UNIX. A simple Ubuntu server can be put to work as an initial partial solution or made to mimic file, mail, or print servers of other operating systems. Clerical staff should quickly adapt to using familiar Internet and productivity tools, while your business gets the additional benefits of stability, security, and a virus-free computing platform.

By carefully allocating monies spent on server hardware, a productive and efficient multi-user system can be built for much less than the cost of comparable commercial software. Combine these benefits with support for laptops, PDAs, and remote access, and you will find that Ubuntu supports the creation and use of an inexpensive yet efficient work environment.

Ubuntu in Your Home

Ubuntu installs a special set of preselected software packages onto your hard drive; these are suitable for small office/home office (SOHO) users. This option provides a wealth of productivity tools for document management, printing, communication, and personal productivity.

The standard installation requires nearly 2GB of hard drive space but should easily fit onto smaller hard drives in older Pentium-class PCs. The install also contains administrative tools, additional authoring and publishing clients, a variety of editors, a GNOME-based X11 desktop, support for sound, graphics editing programs, and graphical and text-based Internet tools.

64-Bit Ubuntu

Advances in computing saw the introduction of 64-bit x86-compatible CPUs from AMD in the spring of 2003. Intel's EM64T extensions for x86, which largely mirror the advances made by AMD, have further increased the availability of commodity x86-64 hardware.

Ubuntu fully supports AMD64 and Intel EM64T processors, and you are encouraged to use the 64-bit version of Ubuntu to get the maximum from these advanced processors.

As far as the Intel Itanium architecture goes, unfortunately Ubuntu does not currently support ia64. However, you may want to investigate Debian, which is available for the ia64 platform.

Ubuntu on the PPC Platform

As well as being available on the popular x86 and x86-64 architectures, Ubuntu is compatible with the Power architecture developed by both IBM and Freescale. PowerPC, or PPC, uses a RISC processor that in some cases outperforms a similar Intel-based processor. Until recently, Apple produced all of its computers with PowerPC processors at the core. However, issues with supply and the delay in moving to a 3Ghz+ G5 chip forced Apple to look to Intel to provide the chips. However, both IBM and Freescale are heavily supporting the Power architecture, and companies such as Mercury and Genesi continue to provide workstations based around the Power chipset.

Getting the Most from Ubuntu and Linux Documentation

Nearly all commercial Linux distributions include shrink-wrapped manuals and documentation covering installation and configuration. You will not find official documentation included on the DVD provided with this book. However, you can read or get copies of assorted manuals or topic discussions online at http://www.ubuntu.com/. There you will find the links to various Ubuntu documentation projects.

Documentation for Ubuntu (and many Linux software packages) is distributed and available in a variety of formats. Some guides are available in Portable Document Format (PDF) and can be read using Adobe's Acrobat Reader for Linux or the `evince` client. Guides are also available as bundled HTML files for reading with a web browser such as links, KDE's Konqueror, GNOME's Epiphany, or Firefox. Along with these guides, Ubuntu provides various tips, frequently asked questions (FAQs), and HOWTO documents.

You will find traditional Linux software package documentation, such as manual pages, under the `/usr/share/man` directory, with documentation for each installed software package under `/usr/share/doc`.

Linux manual pages are compressed text files containing succinct information about how to use a program. Each manual page generally provides a short summary of a command's use, a synopsis of command-line options, an explanation of the command's purpose, potential caveats or bugs, the name of the author, and a list of related configuration files and programs.

For example, you can learn how to read manual pages by using the `man` command to display its own manual page, as follows:

```
$ man man
```

After you press Enter, a page of text appears on the screen or in your window on the desktop. You can then scroll through the information using your keyboard's cursor keys, read, and then press the Q key to quit reading.

Many of the software packages also include separate documents known as HOWTOs that contain information regarding specific subjects or software.

If the HOWTO documents are simple text files in compressed form (with filenames ending in `.gz`), you can easily read the document by using the `zless` command, which is a text pager that enables you to scroll back and forth through documents. (Use the `less` command to read plain-text files.) You can start the command by using `less`, followed by the complete directory specification and name of the file, or *pathname*, like this:

```
$ less /usr/share/doc/httpd-2.0.50/README
```

To read a compressed version of this file, use the `zless` command in the same way:

```
$ zless /usr/share/doc/attr-2.4.1/CHANGES.gz
```

After you press Enter, you can scroll through the document using your cursor keys. Press the Q key to quit.

If the HOWTO document is in HTML format, you can simply read the information using a web browser, such as Firefox. Or if you are reading from a console, you can use the links or lynx text-only web browsers, like this:

```
$ links /usr/share/doc/stunnel-4.0.5/stunnel.html
```

The links browser offers drop-down menus, accessed by clicking at the top of the screen. You can also press the Q key to quit.

If the documentation is in PostScript format (with filenames ending in .ps), you can use the gv client to read or view the document like this:

```
$ gv /usr/share/doc/iproute-2.4.7/ip-crefs.ps
```

Finally, if you want to read a document in Portable Document Format (with a filename ending in .pdf), use the evince client, as follows:

```
$ evince /usr/share/doc/xfig/xfig-howto.pdf
```

> **NOTE**
>
> This book was developed and written using the standard Ubuntu CD. You can use the disc included with this book for your install or download your own copy, available as ISO9660 images (with filenames ending in .iso), and burn it onto a 700MB CD-R or a DVD. You can also order prepressed CDs directly from Ubuntu at http://shipit. ubuntu.com.
>
> Along with the full distribution, you will get access to the complete source code to the Linux kernel and source for all software in the distribution—more than 55 million lines of C and nearly 5 million lines of C++ code. Browse to http://www.ubuntu.com/download/ to get started.

Ubuntu Developers and Documentation

If you are interested in helping with Ubuntu, you can assist in the effort by testing beta releases (known as preview releases, and usually named after the animal chosen for the release name), writing documentation, and contributing software for the core or contributed software repositories. You should have some experience in installing Linux distributions, a desire to help with translation of documentation into different languages, or be able to use various software project management systems, such as CVS.

Mailing lists are also available as an outlet or forum for discussions about Ubuntu. The lists are categorized. For example, general users of Ubuntu discuss issues on the ubuntu-users mailing list. Beta testers and developers via the ubuntu-devel, and documentation contributors via the ubuntu-doc mailing list. You can subscribe to mailing lists by selecting the ones you are interested in at http://lists.ubuntu.com/mailman/listinfo/. Be warned; some of the mailing lists have in excess of 200 to 300 emails per day!

Reference

- ▶ http://www-1.ibm.com/linux/—Information from IBM regarding its efforts and offerings of Linux hardware, software, and services.

- ▶ http://www.dwheeler.com/sloc—David A. Wheeler's amazing white paper covering the current state of GNU/Linux, its size, worth, components, and market penetration.

▶ http://www.ubuntu.com/—Home page for Ubuntu, sponsored by Canonical Software, and your starting point for learning more about Ubuntu.

▶ http://help.ubuntu.com/—Web page with links to current Ubuntu documentation and release notes.

▶ http://www.tldp.org/—The definitive starting point for the latest updates to generic Linux FAQs, guides, and HOWTO documents.

▶ http://www.ciac.org/ciac/—The U.S. Department of Energy's Computer Incident Advisory website, with details of security problems and fixes pertaining not only to Ubuntu, but many other operating systems. This site is useful for federal software contractors, developers, and system administrators.

▶ http://www.justlinux.com/—One site to which new Linux users can browse to learn more about Linux.

▶ http://www.linuxquestions.org/—A popular site that allows users to communicate and support each other with questions and problems spanning the entire Linux world.

APPENDIX B

Installation Resources

Installing a new operating system is always a major event, especially if you have never had to install an OS before. This is especially true if you are used to running Microsoft Windows XP or Vista that was pre-installed for you on your computer. In many cases "recovery" discs are supplied that contain a mirror image of how your system was the day it rolled off the production line, so in reality you are not actually installing Windows, just copying some files. This appendix is all about helping you prepare for installing Ubuntu, taking you through some of the considerations that you perhaps do not realize are important to think about.

It wasn't all that long ago that Linux had a reputation as being pretty difficult to install. You had to know every conceivable fact and specification about all the components of your computer to ensure that the installation went smoothly. Now, however, Ubuntu does most of the hard work for you, having much improved hardware detection and auto-configuration. This is definitely a good thing, and vastly reduces the time needed to install Ubuntu. Perhaps the most useful feature of Ubuntu is that it comes as a Live CD, which gives you a fully functional operating system on a CD. If you have ever been concerned about whether your system is compatible with Linux then take one of these Live CDs for a spin to help you make your decision.

This chapter will help guide you toward an installation of Ubuntu that closely matches your requirements. We start off with a look at some of the things you should take in to account when considering moving to Linux, including what your aims and objectives are for using Ubuntu. We also take a look at the hardware requirements of Ubuntu, along with information on how to check whether your hardware is compatible with Ubuntu. Finally, you will get a general overview of what installing Ubuntu looks like as well as how to avoid pitfalls with partitioning your hard drive. By the end of this chapter you should recognize just how flexible Ubuntu really is, both in the software it provides and also by the many ways in which you can install it.

Planning Your Ubuntu Deployment

The first thing you need to decide is why you are installing Ubuntu. By working out the 'end use scenario' for the proposed installation, you then can begin to make choices and decisions about hardware specifications as well as software options. Before planning the specific steps of an installation, you need to make decisions about the type of deployment you want to undertake. For example, if you were going to use Ubuntu for 3D graphics work, then you would need to factor in the amount of space needed to store the sometimes intricate 3D models and graphics, as well as the graphics card needed for rendering, not to mention the amount of system memory and processor speed. On the flip side, if all you are doing is providing an elderly relative with a quick and easy way to access the Internet, then RAM, hard drive storage, and processor speed are less likely to be important rather than a decent monitor, keyboard and mouse. You learn more about these issues in the sections that follow. These sections also include a table you can use as a pre-deployment planning checklist and some final advice for planning the installation.

Business Considerations

Making a choice of operating system for business can often be a thorny issue. Certainly there is a monopoly already in place from Microsoft, and there are a lot of users who have only ever used Microsoft products. This alone is a powerful argument to go down the Microsoft path, but there are other ways to implement Ubuntu in business. Your company may have been the target of a virus attack, or perhaps you have had to deal with one too many spyware and adware outbreaks on users desktops. Making the switch to Linux can eradicate many of these problems, increasing the uptime of users and reducing the security risk. The important thing is to work closely with the business to ensure that whatever is delivered is in line with the business requirements. If you consider that Linux is still in a minority, you need to think about how other companies will be able to work with you. Staff training and overall cost of change needs to be closely monitored at all times to ensure a smooth delivery. However, don't expect it to be perfect; anyone who has worked on a project knows that unexpected problems can and will occur, and you need to be as prepared as possible to deal with them.

Bear in mind that what works for your company may not work for another, so when swapping stories over a beer with other long-suffering sysadmins, think about how their successes can be adapted to your enterprise, but also pay close attention to things that went wrong. Even better, get one of their business users to present to your users and management to demonstrate the impact that moving to Linux has had. It's surprising how much good a relationship with other companies can do for your own IT infrastucture.

NOTE

As an example of inter-company relationships, most of the large law firms in London have their own soccer teams that regularly meet to do battle on the soccer pitch. They also meet to discuss IT issues and swap ideas between each other, which benefits all of them. Why not set up a local corporate Linux User Group in your area? You don't have to make it a sports-related meeting; just make it clear that you want to share ideas and best practice.

Of course if you are happy with the move to Linux then you can ease the change by downloading versions of OpenOffice.org, Firefox, and Thunderbird for your existing platform so users can test them out before the migration.

Sometimes it is not always the visible changes that make the most difference. You should give careful thought to the potential deployment of Linux into such areas as web servers and file and print servers. You can extend the life of existing hardware long beyond their useful "Windows" life by deploying them as print or web servers. Thankfully, Linux and open source software is pervasive enough to provide plenty of flexibility should you decide to test the water before diving in. Nowadays, popular open source applications such as OpenOffice.org are available for both Windows and Mac platforms, allowing you to try the software before deciding to switch. Also consider the ability to change back-end systems across to Linux-based alternatives. There are many Linux equivalents to Microsoft Exchange, for example, that can handle email and calendaring. Other popular servers ripe for moving across to Linux include file and print servers, web servers, and firewalls.

Don't think that you have to switch everything over in one go. Thankfully Linux plays well in a mixed environment (including Mac OS X and Windows XP), so you can quite safely plan a step-by-step migration that allows you to implement each phase one at a time. Moving servers across to new operating systems should be done on a server-by-server basis. Luckily Linux can easily coexist in a multi-operating system environment, being compatible with Mac OS X, Windows, and UNIX.

We have collated some of the questions that need to be asked when considering a move to Ubuntu in Table B.1, titled "Deploying Ubuntu." As mentioned earlier you need to identify the need that is going to be satisfied by moving to Ubuntu. Any project needs to meet a specific objective to be considered a success, so having this clear right at the start is essential. Another area of consideration is the impact to the existing computing environment. How will users cope with moving onto Linux— are they dyed-in-the-wool Windows users who will resist any move to a different platform? Do you have the full support of management, something that is critical for projects of all sizes? By making successful changes behind the scenes, management can quickly be won over by the flexibility and choice of open source.

TABLE B.1   Deploying Ubuntu

Consideration	Description
Applicability	How is Ubuntu going to be used?
Boot Management	Will remote booting be required?
Connectivity	Will the system be used in an internal network, or connected to the Internet? Is there a requirement for wireless connectivity? What about bandwidth?
Context	How does this install fit in with academic, business, or corporate needs?
Consensus	Are managers and potential users on board with the project?
Comparison	Is this install part of platform comparison or benchmarking?
Development Platform	Will development tools be used?
Embedded Device	Is it an embedded device project?
Hardware	Are there any special hardware or device interfacing requirements?
Finance	How much is in the budget? Will cost comparison be required?
Marketing	Will a product or service be offered as a result?
Networking	What type of networking will be required?
Objective	Is there a specific objective of the install?
Pilot Project	Is this a pilot or test install?
Power Management	Any special power or energy requirements?
Public Relations	Does the public need to know?
Quality of Service	Is high availability or data integrity an issue?
Roadmap	What other steps might precede or follow the install?
Reporting	Are follow-up reports required?
Security	What level or type of security will be required?
Server	Is this a server installation?
Site Considerations	Does the location provide needed temperature and security, or does it even matter?
Software	Are any special device drivers needed for success?
Storage	Are there size or integrity needs? Has a backup plan been devised?
Timeline	Are there time constraints or deadlines to the install?
Training	Will special training be required for users or administrators?
Users	How many and what type of users are expected?
Workstation	Is this a workstation or personal desktop install? Is the workstation portable?

One of the key buzzwords to have come out of the dot com era is *Total Cost of Ownership*, and it is one that is fiercely debated when people talk about Linux. Those against Linux argue that although the software is free; the real cost comes in the amount of retraining and support necessary to move users to a new operating system. This can be circumvented by implementing Linux in situations where the end users are not directly affected, such as that web server that you have been planning to retire or the file and print server that needs more drive space. What is also often unseen is the increased availability that Linux-based systems offer companies. Quite simply they very rarely go down, unlike their Windows counterparts. Stability counts for a lot in this modern world of e-commerce where even a few minutes can cost thousands of dollars in lost orders and new customers. Talking about stability, one of the great things about Linux is that it does not necessarily need the latest hardware to function effectively—I have a router at home that is based on an old 486 machine that I bought sometime in 1994 coupled with a minimalist Linux distro! Think how many computers are needlessly disposed of that could be used as print servers or Internet gateways. The savings generated by sensibly recycling existing hardware are very tempting, and easily obtainable if you choose the Linux route.

In all of this, you need to be very clear what the objectives are. Specify exactly what you want to achieve from the project, what the Linux implementation will deliver, and how it will be used to replace any existing machines. What is the Linux machine replacing and what resources will be needed to maintain and support it? If you are rolling out to end users, what specific applications will they be using that you will have to provide support for?

Research is definitely a must before you embark on any project. It is also sensible to set up a test environment so that you can examine the performance of the new machine under set conditions to ensure that it functions in the way that you require. It is crucial that you spend a decent amount of time on testing because doing so will pay off in the long run with fewer bugs to fix and more positive user feedback and end user experience.

System Considerations

Ubuntu is flexible enough to cope with a wide range of computing needs, but with any switch of operating system you need to be aware of some of the issues that switching might cause. Some of them are listed in Table B.1. For example, how you choose to use Ubuntu could affect your choice of computer hardware, might affect your network configuration, and could dictate software policy issues (such as access, security, and allowable protocols).

Linux-based operating systems can be used to provide many different services. For example, one server might be boot management for a thin-client network in which work-stations boot to a desktop by drawing a kernel and remotely mounted file systems over a network. This mechanism is not supported out of the box, so some effort can be expended if such a system is required. Other services more easily implemented (literally in an hour or less) could be centralized server environments for file serving, web hosting for a company intranet, or bridging of networks and routing services.

Linux supports nearly every network protocol, which enables it to be used to good effect even in mixed operating system environments. The security features of the Linux kernel and companion security software also make Linux a good choice when security is a top priority. Although no operating system or software package is perfect, the benefit of open source of the kernel and other software for Linux allows peer review of pertinent code and rapid implemen-tation of any necessary fixes. Even with the secure features of Linux, some effort will have to be made in designing and implementing gateways, firewalls, or secure network routers.

Ubuntu can serve as a development platform for applications, e-commerce sites, new operating systems, foreign hardware systems, or design of new network devices using Linux as an embedded operating system. Setting up workstations, required servers, source code control systems, and industrial security will require additional effort.

Hardware compatibility can be an issue to consider when setting up a Linux server or building a Linux-based network. Fortunately, most of the larger server manufacturers such as IBM, HP, and even Dell realize that Linux-based operating systems (like other open source operating systems such as BSD) are increasingly popular, support open standards, and offer technologies that can help rapid introduction of products into the market (through third-party developer communities).

Ubuntu can help ease system administration issues during migration. The latest suite of Ubuntu's configuration utilities provides intuitive and easy-to-use graphical interfaces for system administration of many common services, such as networking, printing, and Windows-based file sharing. Ubuntu can also be used to support a legacy application environment, such as DOS, if required.

User Considerations

Humans are creatures of habit. It can be hard to transition a workforce, customer base, or other community to a new environment. The Ubuntu desktop, however, provides a friendly and familiar interface with menus and icons that new users can readily learn and put to work.

Part of the migration process can involve addressing user concerns, especially if Linux will take over the desktop. Ubuntu can be deployed in stages to make the migration process a bit easier, but the issue of user training must be addressed early on. This is especially true if users will be required to develop new skills or be aware of any caveats when using Linux (such as deleting all files in one's home directory). Although Ubuntu can be configured to provide a "turn-key" desktop in which only several graphical applications (such as a web browser, organizer, or word processor) can be used, some users will want and need to learn more about Linux.

A Predeployment Planning Checklist

Table B.1 provides a minimal checklist you can use to help plan a deployment.

Do not forget to address follow-up issues on your migration roadmap. You should pay attention to how satisfied or how well new users, especially those new to Linux, are adapting if a new desktop is used. However, if Ubuntu is deployed in a mixed environment, many users might not even know (or need to know) that Linux is being used!

Planning the Installation

There are many factors in favor of using Ubuntu as a computing solution. Ubuntu can fill many different roles on various tiers and hardware platforms because of the huge variety of software on offer.

Addressing software concerns beforehand can help quell any worries or fears felt by new users. Some key factors for a successful installation include

▶ **Preparation**—Thoroughly discuss the migration or deployment, along with benefits, such as greater stability and availability of service.

▶ **Pre-configuration**—If possible, give users a voice in software choices or categories and poll for comments regarding concerns.

▶ **Correct installation**—Ensure that the installed systems are working properly, including access permissions, password systems, or other user-related issues and interaction with the deployment.

▶ **The right hardware to do the job**—Make sure that users have the hardware they need for their work, and that computers match the tasks required. For example, developers will have workstation requirements vastly different from administrative personnel.

Hardware Requirements

Ubuntu can be installed on and will run on a wide variety of Intel-based hardware. This does not include pre-Pentium legacy platforms, but many older PCs, workstations, rack-mounted systems, and multiprocessor servers are supported. Small-, medium-, and even large-scale deployments of specially tuned Linux distributions are available through a number of companies such as IBM, which offers hardware, software, and service solutions.

> **TIP**
>
> It is always a good idea to explore your hardware options extensively before jumping on board with a specific vendor. You can buy computer hardware with a Linux distribution preinstalled. At the time of this writing, Dell Computer offered systems complete with Ubuntu (such as desktop PCs and laptops) through http://www.dell.com/ubuntu/. IBM also offers Linux on its product line, and more information can be found through http://www.ibm.com/linux/. To find HP and preinstalled Linux systems, browse to http://www.hp.com/linux/.

The type of deployment you choose also determines the hardware required for a successful deployment of Linux—and post-deployment satisfaction. The range of Linux hardware requirements and compatible hardware types is quite wide, especially when you consider that Linux can be used with mainframe computers as well as embedded devices.

Meeting the Minimum Ubuntu Hardware Requirements

The Ubuntu Project publishes general minimum hardware requirements for installing and using its base distribution in a file named RELEASE NOTES on the first CD-ROM or DVD, or available at http://www.ubuntu.com/products/whatisubuntu/desktopedition. For the current release, your PC should at least have a Pentium III CPU, 4GB hard drive space, and

256MB RAM for using (and installing) Ubuntu without a graphical interface. For obvious reasons, a faster CPU, larger capacity hard drive, and more RAM are desired. Servers and development workstations require more storage and RAM.

Using Legacy Hardware

If you have an older PC based on an Intel 486 CPU with only 32MB RAM and a 500MB hard drive (which can be hard to find nowadays), you can install other Linux distributions such as Debian from The Debian Project at http://www.debian.org/.

Installing Ubuntu on legacy hardware will be easier if you choose to use more recent Pentium-class PCs such as Pentium 4, but even older Pentium PCs can be used and purchased at a fraction of their original cost. Such PCs can easily handle many mundane but useful tasks. Some of the tasks suitable for older hardware include

- ▶ Acting as a firewall, router, or gateway
- ▶ Audio jukebox and music file storage server
- ▶ Handling email
- ▶ Hosting a remote printer and providing remote printing services
- ▶ Network font server
- ▶ Providing FTP server access
- ▶ Remote logging capture
- ▶ Secondary network-attached backup server
- ▶ Serving as an Intranet (internal LAN) web server
- ▶ Unattended dial-up gateway, voice mailbox, or fax machine
- ▶ Use as a "thin client" workstation for basic desktop tasks

Older PCs can handle any task that does not require a CPU with a lot of horsepower. To get the most out of your hardware, do not install any more software than required (a good idea in any case, especially if you are building a server). To get a little performance boost, add as much RAM as economically and practically feasible. If you cannot do this, cut down on memory usage by turning off unwanted or unneeded services. You can also recompile a custom Linux kernel to save a bit more memory and increase performance.

Planning for Hard Drive Storage for Your Ubuntu Installation

Making room for Ubuntu requires you to decide on how to use existing hard drive space. You might decide to replace existing hard drives entirely, for example, or you might decide to use only one operating system on your computer, making partitioning unnecessary. A full install from this book's DVD will require at least 7GB hard drive space just for the software, so if you plan to install everything, a 10GB hard drive could be ideal for a workstation. Note that depending on how you plan to use Linux, a smaller capacity disk can be used, or a disk capacity many times the size of your system will be required.

Checking Hardware Compatibility

Ubuntu software for Intel-based PCs is compiled for the minimum x86 platform supported by the Linux kernel.

> **NOTE**
>
> The compatibility information in this chapter relates to Ubuntu. Other distributions might have different storage and CPU requirements. Also bear in mind that Ubuntu is available for 32 bit x86 and 64 bit EM64T architectures. Consult the release notes to get a detailed specification for these versions.

Specific issues regarding Linux hardware compatibility can be researched online at a number of sites. The community offers a hardware compatibility database at http://www.ubuntuhcl.org/pub/.

Other sites, such as the Linux-USB device overview at http://www.qbik.ch/usb/devices/, offer an interactive browsing of supported devices, and printer compatibility can be researched at LinuxPrinting.org at http://linuxprinting.org/. Some hardware categories to consider in your research include

- **Controller cards**—Such as SCSI, IDE, SATA, FireWire
- **CPUs**—Intel, AMD, Power, 64 Bit and Multi-Core
- **Input devices**—Keyboards
- **Modems**—External, PCMCIA, PCI, and controllerless workarounds
- **Network cards**—ISA, PCI, USB, and others
- **Pointing devices**—Mice, tablets, and possibly touchscreens
- **Printers**—Various printer models
- **RAM**—Issues regarding types of system memory
- **Sound cards**—Issues regarding support
- **Specific motherboard models**—Compatibility or other issues
- **Specific PCs, servers, and laptop models**—Compatibility reports, vendor certification
- **Storage devices**—Removables, fixed, and others
- **Video cards**—Console issues (X compatibility depends on the version of X or vendor-based X distribution used)

If you have a particular laptop or PC model, you should also check with its manufacturer for Linux support issues. Some manufacturers such as HP now offer a Linux operating system pre-installed, or have an in-house Linux hardware certification program. Laptop users will definitely want to browse to Linux on Laptops at http://linux-laptop.net/.

> **TIP**
>
> There is a company called EmperorLinux in the US that supplies laptops from prominent manufacturers with Linux pre-installed complete with support. They have been in business for a few years now, and ensure 100% compatibility with the laptops that they sell. Check out their selection at http://www.emperorlinux.com.

If you cannot find compatibility answers in various online databases, continue your research by reading the Linux Hardware HOWTO at http://www.tldp.org/HOWTO/Hardware-HOWTO/. At that address, you will find loads of general information and links to additional sources of information.

Keep in mind that when PC hardware is unsupported under Linux, it is generally because the manufacturer cannot or will not release technical specifications or because no one has taken the time and effort to develop a driver. If you hit a roadblock with a particular piece of hardware, check the hardware manufacturer's support web pages, or Google's Linux pages at http://www.google.com/linux. You can then type in a specific search request and hopefully find answers to how to make the hardware work with Linux. This is also a good way to research answers to questions about software issues.

Preparing for Potential Hardware Problems

Ubuntu will work "out-of-the-box" with nearly every Intel- or PowerPC-based desktop, server and laptop; drivers for thousands of different types of hardware peripherals are included. But you can sometimes run into problems if Linux does not recognize a hardware item, if Ubuntu does not correctly initialize the hardware, or if an initialized item is incorrectly configured. For these reasons, some hardware items are prone to creating problems during an install. In the sections that follow, you learn some important pointers for avoiding these problems or resolving those that do occur.

Controllerless Modems

As you read earlier, most Linux hardware-related installation problems stem from a lack of technical specifications from the manufacturer, thwarting efforts of open source developers to create a driver. In the recent past, one hardware item that triggered both types of difficulties was the controllerless modem, also colloquially known as a *WinModem*. The good news is that modem chipset manufacturers have been more forthcoming with driver details. Some original equipment manufacturers, such as IBM, have made a concerted effort to provide Linux support. Support for the ACP Mwave modem, used in ThinkPad 600/Es and 770s, is included in the Linux kernel. Drivers have been developed for many of the controllerless modem chipsets that formally did not work with Linux.

If a driver is not available for your controllerless modem, you have a few options. You can download the driver's source code and build the driver yourself. Alternatively, you can download a binary-only software package and install the driver.

Some controllerless modems might also need to be initialized and configured using a separate utility program. The modem, if supported, should work normally after installing and configuring the driver.

You can research Linux support for controllerless modems by browsing to http://www.linmodems.org/.

USB Devices

Ubuntu supports hundreds of different Universal Serial Bus devices. USB is a design specification and a protocol used to enable a host computer to talk to attached peripherals. Because of lack of manufacturer and device ID information or lack of technical specifications regarding certain chipsets, some devices might not work with Ubuntu. USB 1.1 devices are designed to support data transfer speeds between 1.5 and 12Mbps.

Common USB devices include cameras, keyboards, mice, modems, network interfaces, printers, scanners, storage devices, video (such as webcams), and hubs (to chain additional devices).

Although some enlightened manufacturers are aware of opportunities in the Linux marketplace, most still do not support Linux. It pays to determine Linux support before you buy any USB device; again, research Linux USB support and its current state of development by browsing to http://www.qbik.ch/usb/devices/.

The newer USB 2.0 specification enables devices (such as hard and CD drives) to use speeds up to 480Mbps. Ubuntu supports USB 2.0 with the ehci-hcd kernel module. This driver, in development since early 2001, enables the use of many forms of newer USB 2.0 devices as long as you have a supported USB controller. Check out the current state of Linux USB 2.0 support by browsing to http://www.linux-usb.org/usb2.html.

Motherboard-Based Hardware

Small form factor PCs, thin clients, notebooks, and embedded devices are part of a growing trend in the PC industry. Manufacturers are cramming more functionality into fewer chips to simplify design and lower power requirements. Today, many computers come with built-in video graphics, audio chipsets, and network interfaces, along with a host of peripheral support.

Common modern (1996-onward) PC motherboard form factors are designed according to industry-assigned specifications (usually from Intel), and are ATX (12–9.6 inches); MicroATX (9.6–9.6 inches); and FlexATX (9–7.5 inches). One of the newest and even smaller motherboard forms is from VIA Technologies, Inc.—the mini-ITX (approximately 6.5–6.5 inches), which has an embedded CPU. CPUs commonly used in all these motherboards will vary, and have different socketing requirements based on chipset pins: Socket 478 for K7-type CPUs (from AMD); Socket 939 for some Athlon and Sempron processors, Socket AM2 for newer Athlon 64 and AMD FX processors, Socket 370 for Pentium IIIs and Celerons from Intel, or C3s from VIA; Socket 478 for Intel's Pentium 4s (early versions of which used a 423-pin socket) and socket LGA775 for newer Core 2 and Pentium D processors. Older socket types are Socket A, Socket 7 (and Super 7), Slot 1, and Slot B.

Fortunately, nearly all controllers, bridges, and other chipsets are supported by Linux. Although flaky or unsupported built-in hardware can (usually) be sidestepped by installing a comparable PCI card component, cutting-edge notebook users are at the most risk for compatibility problems because internal components are not user-replaceable. Potential pitfalls can be avoided through careful research (vote with your money for Linux-compatible hardware), or by choosing PC motherboards with a minimum of built-in features, and then using PCI (Peripheral Component Interconnect), AGP (Accelerated Graphics Port), or PCI Express cards known to work.

CPU, Symmetric Multiprocessing, and Memory Problems

Ubuntu supports all Pentium class x86-compatible CPUs. Code is included in the Linux kernel to recognize the CPU type when booting, and to then implement any required fixes to overcome architecture bugs (such as the now-infamous divide-by-zero error). After you install Ubuntu, you can also rebuild the Linux kernel to specifically support and take advantage of the host PC's CPU. You might not realize extreme improvements in computational speed, but you'll be assured that Linux is crafted for your CPU's architecture, which can help stability and reliability. Some of the x86-based CPUs with specific supporting code for Linux include those from Advanced Micro Devices, Transmeta, and VIA Technologies.

Ubuntu's Linux kernel also should automatically recognize and use the amount of installed RAM. The Linux kernel should also recognize and map out any memory holes in system memory (perhaps used for video graphics).

If you are installing Ubuntu on a working, stable PC, you should not have any problems related to the system's memory. If you are putting together a new system, you need to avoid combining or configuring the system in ways that will interfere with its capability to process data. Some issues to be aware of are

▶ Do not expect similar CPU performance across product lines from different manufacturers, such as AMD or VIA. Some CPU models offer better floating point or integer math operations, which are important for a number of CPU-intensive tasks (such as graphics, audio, and video rendering or conversion). If you need better performance, try to find a faster CPU compatible with your motherboard, or switch to a CPU with better Floating Point Unit (FPU) performance.

▶ Overclocking can cause problems with overheating, memory access, and other hardware performance, and it is not a good idea for any Linux system. Overclocking is a popular geek pastime and a great way to get a bit of performance boost out of slower CPUs by altering voltage settings and/or clock timings via the BIOS. You can try to push your CPU to higher speeds, but this approach is not recommended if your aim is system stability. The Linux kernel will report the recognized CPU speed on booting (which you can view using the dmesg command).

- Along the same lines, CPU and motherboard overheating will cause problems. Proper attachment of the CPU's heatsink using a quality thermal paste (never use thermal tape), along with one or more fans providing adequate airflow lessens the chance of hardware damage and system failure.

- You can run into problems if you switch the type of CPU installed in your computer, and especially if your PC's BIOS does not automatically recognize or configure for newly installed mainboard hardware and components. In some instances, a system reinstall is warranted, but BIOS issues should be resolved first.

- Not all CPUs support symmetric multiprocessing, or SMP. Ubuntu readily supports use of two or more CPUs.. You can avoid problems by reading the Linux SMP HOWTO (available through http://www.tldp.org/). Note that some CPUs, such as the current crop of VIA C3s, might not be used for SMP. Also, SMP motherboards require that all CPUs be identical. This means that you need two identical CPUs to take advantage of SMP.

- Faulty or bad memory causes Linux kernel panics or Signal 11 errors (segmentation faults), causing a system crash or a program to abort execution. Linux is quite sensitive to faulty hardware, but runs with great stability in a correctly configured system with good hardware. Problems can arise from incorrect BIOS settings, especially if video memory must occupy and use a portion of system RAM. Always install quality (and appropriate) memory in your PC to avoid problems.

Preparing and Using a Hardware Inventory

Buying a turn-key Linux solution is one way to avoid hardware problems, and many vendors are standing by, ready to prescribe solutions. However, managing deployments aimed at using existing hardware requires some information collection.

If you are a small business or individual user, you are well advised to prepare detailed checklists of existing hardware before attempting a migration to Linux. Not only do you benefit from the collected information, but you might also be able to sidestep or antici-pate problems before, during, or after installation. Problems are most likely to occur with newer hardware, cutting-edge hardware such as new motherboard chipsets and video cards, or extraneous hardware such as operating system–specific scanners, printers, or wireless devices.

Table B.2 provides a comprehensive checklist you can use to take inventory of target hard-ware, such as the computer and any peripherals. Veteran Linux users can take the collected information to build custom systems by adding known hardware or substituting cheaper but equivalent hardware.

Use the checklist in Table B.2 as a general guideline for recording your computer's hard-ware and other capabilities. You can get quite a bit of information through hardware manuals or other documentation included with your PC, video, sound, or network inter-face card. Don't worry if you cannot fill out the entire checklist; Ubuntu will most likely recognize and automatically configure your PC's hardware during installation. Much of this information can be displayed by the `dmesg` command after booting. However, some of these details, such as your video card's graphics chipset and installed video RAM, can come in handy if you need to perform troubleshooting. You can also use the list as a post-installation check-off sheet to see how well Ubuntu works with your system.

Preparing for the Install Process

The basic steps in installing Ubuntu are to plan, install, and configure. You have to decide how to boot to an install and how much room to devote to Linux. Then perform the install (a sample step-by-step installation is discussed in Chapter 1, "Installing Ubuntu") and afterward, configure your system to host new users and specific software services. Much of the initial work is done during the install process because the installer, Anaconda, walks you through partitioning, configuring the desktop, and configuration of any recognized network adapter.

TABLE B.2   System and Peripheral Inventory Checklist

Item	Errata
Audio Devices	Microphone:
	Line out:
	Line in:
BIOS	Type:
	Revision:
	ACPI:
	APM:
CD-ROM Drive	Brand:
	Type:
CD-RW Drive	Brand:
	Type:
	CDR Write Speed:
	CD Re-Write Speed:
	CD-ROM Read Speed:
DVD Drive	Brand:
	Type:
DVD+/-RW Drive	Brand:
	Type:
	Dual layer?:
Digital Camera	Brand:
	Model:

TABLE B.2   System and Peripheral Inventory Checklist   Continued

Item	Errata
	Interface:
CPU	Brand:
	Socket Type:
	Speed:
FireWire (IEEE 1394)	Chipset:
	Device(s):
IrDA Port	Device number:
	Port IRQ:
Keyboard	Brand:
	Type:
Laptop	Brand:
	Model:
	Hibernation partition:
Legacy Ports	Parallel type:
	Parallel IRQ:
	RS-232 number(s):
	RS-232 IRQ(s):
Mice	Brand:
	Type:
Modem	Brand:
	Type:
Motherboard	Brand:
	Type:
	Chipset:
Monitor(s)	Brand:
	Model:
	Horizontal freq:
	Vertical freq:
	Max. Resolution:
Network Card	Wireless:
	Brand:
	Type:
	Speed:
PCI Bus	Version:
	Model:
	Type:

TABLE B.2   System and Peripheral Inventory Checklist   Continued

Item	Errata
PCMCIA	Controller:
	Cardbus:
	Brand:
	Type:
Printer(s)	Brand:
	Model:
System RAM	Amount:
	Type:
	Speed:
S-Video Port	X Support:
Scanner	Brand:
	Model:
	Interface type:
Sound Card	Chipset:
	Type:
	I/O Addr:
	IRQ:
	DMA:
	MPU Addr:
Storage Device(s)	Removable:
	Size:
	Brand:
	Model:
	Controller(s):
Storage Device Controller	Type:
Tablet	Brand:
	Model:
	Interface:
Universal Serial Bus	Controller:
	BIOS MPS Setting:
	BIOS Plug-n-Play Setting:
	Device(s):
Video Device(s)	Brand:
	Model:

TABLE B.2   System and Peripheral Inventory Checklist   Continued

Item	Errata
	Xinerama:
	Chipset:
	VRAM:

There are many different ways to install Ubuntu, and selecting an installation method might depend on the equipment on hand, existing bandwidth, or equipment limitations. Here are some of the most commonly used installation methods:

▶ **CD-ROM/DVD**—Using a compatible CD-ROM or DVD drive attached to the computer (laptop users with an external CD-ROM drive will need PCMCIA support from a driver disk image included under the first CD-ROM's images directory).

▶ **Network File System (NFS)**—You can install Ubuntu from a remotely mounted hard drive containing the Ubuntu software. To perform this installation, you must have an installed and supported network interface card, along with a boot floppy with network support. (You learn how to make boot floppies later in this section of the chapter.)

▶ **File Transfer Protocol (FTP)**—As with an NFS install, installation via FTP requires that the Ubuntu software be available on a public FTP server. You also need an installed and supported network interface card, along with a boot floppy with network support.

▶ **Installation via the Internet**—If you have the bandwidth, it might be possible to install Ubuntu via the Internet; however, this method might not be as reliable as using a Local Area Network (LAN) because of availability and current use of servers on mirror sites.

▶ **A hard drive partition**—By copying the .iso images to a hard drive partition, you can then boot to an install.

▶ **Pre-installed media**—It is also possible to install Linux on another hard drive and then transfer the hard drive to your computer. This is handy, especially if your site uses removable hard drives or other media.

After booting and choosing to use either a graphical or text-based install interface, the installation procedure is nearly the same for each type of install. Chapter 1 walks you through a typical installation.

Preparing to Install from a CD-ROM

Installing Ubuntu can be as simple as inserting the first CD/DVD into your computer's CD drive and rebooting the computer. But if you choose this method, you should first make sure that your system's BIOS is set to boot from CD-ROM.

Entering the BIOS to make this change is usually accomplished by depressing a particular key, such as Del or F2, immediately after turning on the computer. After entering the BIOS, navigate to the BIOS Boot menu, perhaps such as that shown in Figure B.1.

```
                         PhoenixBIOS Setup Utility
      Main      Advanced      Security      Power      Boot      Exit

                                                  Item Specific Help
         CD-ROM Drive
        +Removable Devices
        +Hard Drive                              Keys used to view or
         Network boot from AMD Am79C970A         configure devices:
                                                 <Enter> expands or
                                                 collapses devices with
                                                 a + or -
                                                 <Ctrl+Enter> expands
                                                 all
                                                 <Shift + 1> enables or
                                                 disables a device.
                                                 <+> and <-> moves the
                                                 device up or down.
                                                 <n> May move removable
                                                 device between Hard
                                                 Disk or Removable Disk
                                                 <d> Remove a device
                                                 that is not installed.

      F1   Help   ↑↓  Select Item   -/+   Change Values    F9   Setup Defaults
      Esc  Exit   ↔   Select Menu   Enter Select ▶ Sub-Menu F10  Save and Exit
```

FIGURE B.1   To boot to an install using your Ubuntu CD-ROM or DVD, set your BIOS to have your computer boot using its CD drive.

Partitioning Before and During Installation

Partitioning your hard drive for Linux can be done before or during installation.

If you plan to prepare your partitions before installing Linux, you will need to use commercial partitioning software. Some of the popular commercial software utilities you can use to create Linux partitions are Symantec's PartitionMagic or VCOM Products' Partition Commander. Alternatively, it might be possible to prepare partitions before installing Ubuntu by using the free FIPS.EXE command.

If you want to partition a hard drive using an existing Linux system, you can attach the hard drive to a spare IDE channel, and then use the Linux fdisk or GNU parted partitioning utilities. Both utilities offer a way to interactively partition and prepare storage media. Linux recognizes IDE hard drives using a device name such as /dev/sda (for the master device on IDE channel 0), /dev/sdb (for the slave device on IDE channel 0), /dev/sdc (for the master device on IDE channel 1), and /dev/sdd (for the slave device on IDE channel 1). With more modern computers that use the SATA interface, Linux will refer to drives as /dev/sda (for the master device on channel 0), /dev/sdb (for the slave device on channel 0), and so on.

If a new hard drive is properly attached to your PC and you then boot Linux, you can see whether the kernel recognizes the device by viewing the output of the dmesg command. You can then use fdisk with the device name to begin partitioning like so:

```
# fdisk /dev/sdb
```

Note that you will need root permission, and in this example, the new drive is attached as a slave on IDE channel 0. Do not change partitioning on your root device, or you will bork your system! The fdisk command is interactive, and you can press M to get help when using the utility. You can use parted in much the same way if you specify the i, or interactive option on the command line like so:

```
# parted -i /dev/sdb
```

To get help when using parted interactively, press ? or type **help followed by a command keyword. The parted** command has other helpful features, such as the capability to copy a file system directly from one partition to another.

Finally, you can prepare partitions ahead of installation by booting your system using a live Linux distribution (such as the LNX Bootable Business Card, available at http://www. lnx-bbc.org/) and then using a native Linux utility such as fdisk to partition your drive.

TIP

You can use the Ubuntu CD or the DVD to perform other tasks aside from installing Linux. The CD-ROM/DVD features a rescue mode and can also be used to partition and prepare a hard drive for Linux using fdisk as described earlier.

NOTE

It is possible to create a dual-boot configuration, which allows the choice of booting Ubuntu and another operating system, such as Windows XP. To configure your system for dual-booting, you must first install Windows and then install Linux. Note that many Windows system-restore CD-ROMs wipe out all data on your hard drive, including Linux. During installation of Ubuntu, you automatically install the GRUB Linux bootloader in the primary drive's Master Boot Record, or MBR. When properly configured, GRUB allows your system to reboot to Windows or Linux. Browse to http://www.gnu.org/software/grub/manual/ to read the GRUB manual online.

CAUTION

Before you begin partitioning your drive, get your safety nets in order. First, back up all critical data! Any changes to your system's hard drive or operating system put your existing data at risk. To prevent the loss of time and resources that inevitably follow data loss, do full backups before you make any changes to your system. Create a bootdisk during the install (you will be asked before the install finishes) so that you will be able to at least boot Linux if something goes wrong.

Choosing a Partitioning Scheme

As with deployment and installation of Linux, partitioning your hard drive to accept Ubuntu requires some forethought, especially if the target computer is going to be used other than as a home PC on which to learn Linux. If Linux is to be the only resident operating system, you can have the installer automatically create and use a partition scheme according to the type of installation you select during the install. If you plan to have a dual-boot system in which you can boot Linux or another operating system, you have to manually partition your hard drive before and possibly during the install.

The simplest and most basic partitioning scheme for a Linux system requires a Linux native root partition and a swap partition. On a single-drive system with 12GB storage and 512MB RAM, the scheme might look like this:

```
Hard Drive Partition    Mount Point    Size
/dev/hda1               /              10.74GB
/dev/hda2               swap           1GB
```

On a system running Windows, the scheme might look like this:

```
Hard Drive Partition    Mount Point    Size
/dev/hda1               /media/dos      4GB
/dev/hda2               /              7.74GB
/dev/hda3               swap           1GB
```

> **CAUTION**
>
> Notebook users should be careful when partitioning. Some notebooks use a special partition equal to the size of install RAM in order to perform suspend-to-disk or other hibernation operations. Always examine your computer's initial partitioning scheme if configuring a dual-boot system, and leave the special partition alone! One way around this problem is to use a software suspend approach as outlined at www.suspend2.net/.

Hosting Parts of the Linux File System on Separate Partitions

Your choice of specific partitioning scheme will depend on how Ubuntu will be used. On a system being designed for expansion, greater capacity, or the capability to host additional software or users, you can use separate partitions to host various parts of the Linux file system. Some candidates for these separate partitions include

▶ /home—Users will store hundreds and hundreds of megabytes of data under their directories. This is important data, perhaps even more so than the system itself. Using a separate partition (on a different volume) to store this user data helps make the data easier to find and it segregates user and system data. You must decide ahead of time how much storage to allocate to users. For a single workstation, you should reserve several gigabytes of storage.

▶ /opt—As the home directory for additional software packages, this directory can have its own partition or remote file system. Ubuntu does not populate this directory, but it might be used by other software packages you install later. One gigabyte of storage should be adequate, depending on applications to be installed.

▶ /tmp—This directory can be used as temporary storage by users, especially if disk quotas are enforced; as such, it could be placed on its own partition. This directory can be as small as 100MB.

▶ /usr—This directory holds nearly all the software on a Ubuntu system and can become quite large if additional software is added, especially on a workstation configuration. Using a separate partition can make sense. A full install requires at least 6GB for this directory or more if additional software is added.

▶ /var—Placing this directory (or perhaps some of its subdirectories) on a separate partition can be a good idea, especially because security logs, mail, and print spooling take place under this tree. You should reserve at least one gigabyte of storage for /var, especially if using Ubuntu as a print server (as spooled documents will reside under /var/spool).

TIP

As a general rule, it is a good idea to segregate user and system data. Although a Linux system can be quickly restored, user data has a much greater value and can be much more difficult to replace. Segregating data can make the job of backing up and restoring much easier. If you ever have a problem accessing your partition, we recommend that you get the excellent Knoppix distribution that boots and runs entirely from CD. This will enable you to access your partitions and make any necessary repairs.

Reference

▶ http://www.yale.edu/pclt/BOOT/DEFAULT.HTM—A basic primer to partitioning that is operating system nonspecific.

▶ http://www-1.ibm.com/linux/—Home page for Linux at IBM, with links to products, services, and downloads.

▶ http://www-124.ibm.com/developerworks/opensource/linux390/—Home page for IBM S/390 Linux solutions.

▶ http://www.dell.com/linux/—Dell Computer's Linux information pages.

▶ http://hardware.redhat.com/hcl/—Entry point to Red Hat's hardware compatibility database.

▶ http://www.linux1394.org/—Home page for the Linux FireWire project, with information regarding the status of drivers and devices for this port.

▶ http://www.linux-usb.org/—Home page for the Linux USB project, with lists of supported devices and links to drivers.

▶ http://elks.sourceforge.net/—Home page for Linux for x286 and below CPUs, ELKS Linux.

▶ http://www.lnx-bbc.org/—Home page for the Bootable Business Card, a 50MB compressed Linux distribution that offers hundreds of networking clients, a live X session, web browsing, PDA backup, wireless networking, rescue sessions, and file recovery.

▶ http://www.coyotelinux.com/—Home page for several compact Linux distributions offering firewalling and VPN services. The floppy-based distribution works quite well on older PCs and does not require a hard drive.

▶ http://www.freesco.org/—Home page for a floppy-based Linux router solution that works on 386 PCs, requires only 6MB RAM, and provides bridging, firewalling, IP masquerading, DNS, DHCP, web, telnet, print, time, and remote access functions.

▶ http://www.bitwizard.nl/sig11/—A detailed overview of some root causes of Linux Signal 11 errors.

▶ http://www.gnu.org/software/parted/parted.html#introduction—Home page for the GNU parted utility.

▶ http://www.linux.org/vendors/systems.html—One place to check for a vendor near you selling Linux preinstalled on a PC, laptop, server, or hard drive.

Ubuntu and Linux Internet Resources

Ubuntu enjoys a wealth of Internet support in the form of websites with technical information, specific program documentation, targeted whitepapers, bug fixes, user experiences, third-party commercial technical support, and even free versions of specialized, fine-tuned clone distributions.

This appendix lists many of the supporting websites, FTP repositories, Usenet newsgroups, and electronic mailing lists that you can use to get more information and help with your copy of Ubuntu.

If You Need Help 24/7

If you are a small business, corporate, or enterprise-level Ubuntu user, don't forget that you can always turn to the source, Canonical, or third-party companies who supply Ubuntu support for commercial technical support on a 24/7 onsite basis, by phone, by electronic mail, or even on a per-incident basis. Canonical Software offers a spectrum of support options for its software products. You can read more about support options from the Ubuntu website: http://www.ubuntu.com/support/paid.

The appendix is divided into the following sections:

▶ Websites with Linux information arranged by category

▶ Usenet newsgroups pertaining to Linux

▶ Mailing lists providing Linux user and developer discussions

► Internet Relay Chat groups for Linux information

This appendix also lists websites that might be of general interest when using Ubuntu or specific components such as Xorg. Every effort has been made to ensure the accuracy of the URLs, but keep in mind that the Internet is always in flux!

Keep Up-to-Date

Keeping informed about bug fixes, security updates, and other errata is critical to the success and health of a Ubuntu system. To keep abreast of the most important developments when using Ubuntu, be sure to register with the Ubuntu Announcements mailing list. From there, you will learn which updates have been issued and what has been fixed as a result. Go to https://lists.ubuntu.com/mailman/listinfo/ubuntu-security-announce to register for this mailing list. You should also keep an eye out for Update Manager notifications in order to keep up with bug fixes, new software packages, and security updates.

Websites and Search Engines

Literally thousands of websites exist with information about Linux and Ubuntu. The key to getting the answers you need right away involves using the best search engines and techniques. Knowing how to search can mean the difference between frustration and success when troubleshooting problems. This section provides some Internet search tips and lists Ubuntu- and Linux-related sites sorted by various topics. The lists are not comprehensive, but have been checked and were available at the time of this writing.

Web Search Tips

Troubleshooting problems with Linux by searching the Web can be an efficient and productive way to get answers to vexing problems. One of the most basic rules for conducting productive searches is to use specific search terms to find specific answers. For example, if you simply search for "Ubuntu Linux," you will end up with too many links and too much information. If you search for "Ubuntu sound," however, you are more likely to find the information you need. If you've received an error message, use it; otherwise, use the Linux kernel diagnostic message as your search criterion.

Other effective techniques include the following:

► Using symbols in the search string, such as the plus sign (+) to force matches of web pages containing both strings (if such features are supported by the search engine used by web search site)

► Searching within returned results

► Sorting results (usually by date to get the latest information)

► Searching for related information

► Stemming searches; for example, specifying returns for not only "link" but also "linking" and "linked"

Invest some time and experiment with your favorite search engine's features—the result will be more productive searches. In addition to sharpening your search skills, also take the time to choose the best search engine for your needs.

Google Is Your Friend

Some of the fastest and most comprehensive search engines on the Web are powered by Linux, so it makes sense to use the best available resources. Out of the myriad number of websites with search engines, http://google.com stands out from the crowd, with millions of users per month. The site uses advanced hardware and software to bring speed and efficiency to your searches. If you are looking for specific Linux answers, take advantage of Google's Linux page at http://google.com/linux.

Why is Google (named after a math number) so powerful? You can get a quick overview from the Google folks at http://www.google.com/technology/. Part of its success is because of great algorithms, good programming, and simple interface design; but most users really seem to appreciate Google's uncanny capability to provide links to what you are looking for in the first page of a search return. Google's early success was also assured because the site ran its search engine on clusters of thousands of PCs running a version of Red Hat Linux! It is also rumored that an Ubuntu-based distribution is in use on desktops at Google, with the claimed moniker of Goobuntu.

Google has the largest database size of any search engine on the Web, with more than eight billion web pages searched and indexed. The database size is important because empty search results are useless to online users, and the capability to return hits on esoteric subjects can make the difference between success and failure or satisfaction and frustration. Some of Google's features include a GoogleScout link to return similar pages on the results page, the capability to see the exact version of a web page as returned to a search engine (known as a *cached* feature), advanced searches, and more recently, a link to an active Usenet news feed!

To get a better idea of what Google can offer you, browse to http://www.google.com/options/. You will find links to many different services and tools covering specialized searches, databases, information links, translators, and other helpful browsing tools.

Ubuntu Package Listings

You can quickly and easily view a list of the installed packages on your Ubuntu system, along with a short description of each package, by using `synaptic`.

`synaptic` also shows you descriptions of each package so you can decide whether to have it installed. For more information on `synaptic`, refer to Chapter 31, "Managing Software."

Certification

Linux certification courses are part of the rapidly growing information technology training industry. Hundreds of different vendors now offer courses about and testing of Linux skill sets. However, because Linux is open-source software, there are no formal rules or mandates concerning what knowledge or level of expertise is required for certification. If you are interested in certification and want to pursue a career or obtain employment with a company using Linux, you really should seek training. You can find a good list of companies that can provide training at http://www.ubuntu.com/training/, split down by geographical region.

Commercial Support

Commercial support for Ubuntu is an essential ingredient to the success of Linux in the corporate and business community. Although hundreds, if not thousands, of consultants well versed in Linux and UNIX are available on call for a fee, here is a short list of the best-known Linux support providers:

▶ http://www.ubuntu.com/support/paid—Go straight to the source for a range of support options. You can get help on Ubuntu direct from Canonical software, or from a local support provider.

▶ http://www.hp.com/linux—HP offer a comprehensive package of Linux services and hardware that cover almost everything that you would want to do, including consultancy, business solutions, and hardware specification and implementation.

▶ http://www.ibm.com/linux/—Linux services offered by IBM include e-business solutions, open-source consulting, database migration, clustering, servers, and support.

In addition to service-oriented support companies, nearly every commercial distributor of Linux has some form of easily purchased commercial support. There are various ways in which to take advantage of support services (such as remote management, onsite consulting, device driver development, and so on), but needs will vary according to customer circumstances and installations.

The Benefits of Joining a Linux User Group

Join a local *Linux Users Group (LUG)*! Joining and participating in a local LUG has many benefits. You will be able to get help, trade information, and learn many new and wonderful things about Linux. Most LUGs do not have membership dues, and many often sponsor regular lectures and discussions from leading Linux, GNU, and open-source experts. For one great place to start, browse to http://www.tux.org/luglist.html.

Documentation

Nearly all Linux distributions include thousands of pages of documentation in the form of manual pages, HOWTO documents (in various formats, such as text and HTML), mini-HOWTO documents, or software package documentation (usually found under the

/usr/share/doc/ directory). However, the definitive site for reading the latest versions of these documents is the Linux Documentation Project, found at http://www.tldp.org.

Linux Guides

If you are looking for more extensive and detailed information concerning a Linux subject, try reading one of the many Linux guides. These guides, available for a number of subjects, dwell on technical topics in more detail and at a more leisurely pace than a HOWTO. You can find copies of

- ▶ "Advanced Bash-Scripting Guide," by Mendel Cooper; a guide to shell scripting using bash

- ▶ "LDP Author Guide," by Mark F. Komarinski; how to write LDP documentation

- ▶ "Linux Administration Made Easy," by Steve Frampton

- ▶ "Linux Consultants Guide," by Joshua Drake; a worldwide listing of commercial Linux consultants

- ▶ "Linux from Scratch," by Gerard Beekmans; creating a Linux distribution from software

- ▶ "Linux Kernel Module Programming Guide," by Peter J Salzman, Michael Burian, and Ori Pomerantz; a good guide to building 2.4 and 2.6 series modules

- ▶ "Securing and Optimizing Linux," by Gerhard Mourani

- ▶ Linux certification

- ▶ "The Linux Network Administrator's Guide, Second Edition," by Olaf Kirch and Terry Dawson; a comprehensive Net admin guide

Ubuntu

- ▶ http://www.ubuntu.com—Home page for Ubuntu, Canonical's community-based free Linux distribution. Ubuntu is the main release of this Linux distribution and includes thousands of software packages that form the core of an up-to-date, cutting-edge Linux-based desktop. You can also find links to the other *buntus, such as Kubuntu, Xubuntu, and edubuntu.

- ▶ http://www.ubuntuforums.org—A good place to go if you need specific Ubuntu support.

Mini-CD Linux Distributions

Mini-CD Linux distributions are used for many different purposes. Some distributions are used to boot to a read-only firewall configuration; others are used to provide as complete a rescue environment as possible; whereas others are used to either install or help jumpstart an install of a full distribution. Mini-CDs are available in a wide variety of sizes, such as 3"

CD-Rs (or CD-RW) with sizes ranging from 185MB to 210MB. You can also download an
.iso image and create a Linux bootable business card, typically fitting on a 40MB or 50MB
credit-card–size CD-R. (Consider using a mini–CD-RW, especially if you want to upgrade
your distribution often.) Here are some links to these distributions:

▶ http://www.lnx-bbc.com—Home page for the Linux BBC, a 40MB image hosting a
  rather complete live Linux session with X, a web browser, and a host of networking
  tools.

▶ http://crux.nu/—Home page of the CRUX i686–optimized Linux distribution.

▶ http://www.smoothwall.org—The 69MB SmoothWall distribution is used to install a
  web-administered firewall, router, or gateway with SSH, HTTP, and other services.

Various Intel-Based Linux Distributions

Choosing a Linux *distribution (distro)* for an Intel-based PC is generally a matter of personal
preference or need. Many Linux users prefer Red Hat's distro because of its excellent
support, commercial support options, and widespread use around the world. However,
many different Linux distributions are available for download. One of the best places to
start looking for a new distro or new version of your favorite distro is http://www.
distrowatch.com:

▶ http://www.xandros.net—Home of the original and improved version of Corel's
  Debian-based Linux

▶ http://www.debian.org—The Debian Linux distribution, consisting only of software
  distributed under the GNU GPL license. Ubuntu, itself, is based upon Debian.

▶ http://www.slackware.com—Home page for download of the newest version of one
  of the oldest Linux distributions, Slackware

▶ http://www.opensuse.org—Home page for SUSE Linux, also available for the
  PowerPC and x86_64 platforms

▶ http://www.mepis.org—An increasingly popular distribution based on Debian

▶ http://www.mandrivalinux.com—A Pentium-optimized, RPM-based distribution,
  originally based on Red Hat's Linux distribution

PowerPC-Based Linux Distributions

▶ http://penguinppc.org/—Home page for the PowerPC GNU/Linux distribution

▶ http://www.opensuse.org—SUSE PPC Linux

▶ http://www.yellowdoglinux.com—Home page for Terra Soft Solutions's Yellow Dog
  Linux for the PowerPC, which is based on Fedora

Linux on Laptops and PDAs

One of the definitive sites for getting information about running Linux on your laptop is Kenneth Harker's Linux Laptop site. Although not as actively updated as in the past, this site (http://www.linux-laptop.net) still contains the world's largest collection of Linux and laptop information, with links to user experiences and details concerning specific laptop models.

Another site to check is Werner Heuser's Tuxmobil-Mobile UNIX website at http://www.tuxmobil.org. You will find links to information such as IrDA, Linux PDAs, and cell phones. Linux Zaurus PDA users can browse to http://www.openzaurus.org to download a complete open-source replacement operating system for the Zaurus 5000 and 5500 models.

The X Window System

Although much technical information is available on the Internet regarding the X Window System, finding answers to specific questions when troubleshooting can prove problematic. If you are having a problem using X, first try to determine whether the problem is software or hardware related. When searching or asking for help (such as on Usenet's `comp.os.linux.x` newsgroup, which you can access through Google's Groups link; see the next section for other helpful Linux newsgroups), try to be as specific as possible. Some critical factors or information needed to adequately assess a problem include the Linux distribution in use; the kernel version used; the version of X used; the brand, name, and model of your video card; the names, brands, and models of your monitor and other related hardware.

This section lists just some of the basic resources for Linux X users. Definitive technical information regarding X is available from http://www.X.org:

- ▶ http://www.rahul.net/kenton/index.shtml—Ken Lee's X and Motif website with numerous links to tutorial, development, and other information about X

- ▶ http://www.x.org—Home page for X.org, the X server used in Ubuntu

- ▶ http://www.xig.com/—Home page for a commercial version of X for Linux (along with other software products)

Usenet Newsgroups

Linux-related Usenet newsgroups are another good source of information if you're having trouble using Linux. If your ISP does not offer a comprehensive selection of Linux newsgroups, you can browse to http://groups.google.com/.

The primary Linux and Linux-related newsgroups are as follows:

- ▶ `alt.os.linux.dial-up`—Using PPP for dial-up

- ▶ `alt.os.linux.mandriva`—All about Mandriva Linux

- ▶ `alt.os.linux.slackware`—Using Slackware Linux
- ▶ `alt.os.linux.ubuntu`—Using Ubuntu Linux
- ▶ `comp.os.linux.advocacy`—Heated discussions about Linux and other related issues
- ▶ `comp.os.linux.alpha`—Using Linux on the Alpha CPU
- ▶ `comp.os.linux.announce`—General Linux announcements
- ▶ `comp.os.linux.answers`—Releases of new Linux FAQs and other information
- ▶ `comp.os.linux.development.apps`—Using Linux development tools
- ▶ `comp.os.linux.development.system`—Building the Linux kernel
- ▶ `comp.os.linux.embedded`—Linux embedded device development
- ▶ `comp.os.linux.hardware`—Configuring Linux for various hardware devices
- ▶ `comp.os.linux.m68k`—Linux on Motorola's 68K-family CPUs
- ▶ `comp.os.linux.misc`—Miscellaneous Linux topics
- ▶ `comp.os.linux.networking`—Networking and Linux
- ▶ `comp.os.linux.portable`—Using Linux on laptops
- ▶ `comp.os.linux.powerpc`—Using PPC Linux
- ▶ `comp.os.linux.security`—Linux security issues
- ▶ `comp.os.linux.setup`—Linux installation topics
- ▶ `comp.os.linux.x`—Linux and the X Window System
- ▶ `comp.windows.x.apps`—Using X-based clients
- ▶ `comp.windows.x.i386unix`—X for Unix PCs
- ▶ `comp.windows.x.intrinsics`—X Toolkit library topics
- ▶ `comp.windows.x.kde`—Using KDE and X discussions
- ▶ `comp.windows.x.motif`—All about Motif programming
- ▶ `comp.windows.x`—Discussions about X
- ▶ `linux.admin.*`—Two newsgroups for Linux administrators
- ▶ `linux.debian.*`—30 newsgroups about Debian
- ▶ `linux.dev.*`—25 or more Linux development newsgroups
- ▶ `linux.help`—Get help with Linux
- ▶ `linux.kernel`—The Linux kernel

Mailing Lists

Mailing lists are interactive or digest-form electronic discussions about nearly any topic. To use a mailing list, you must generally send an email request to be subscribed to the list, and then verify the subscription with a return message from the master list mailer. After subscribing to an interactive form of list, each message sent to the list will appear in your email inbox. However, many lists provide a digest form of subscription in which a single- or half-day's traffic is condensed in a single message. The digest form is generally preferred unless you have set up electronic mail filtering.

The main Ubuntu mailing lists are detailed here, but there are quite a few Linux-related lists. You can search for nearly all online mailing lists by using a typical mailing list search web page, such as the one at http://www.lsoft.com/lists/list_q.html.

GNOME and KDE Mailing Lists

GNOME users and developers should know that more than two dozen mailing lists are available through http://mail.gnome.org/. KDE users will also benefit by perusing the KDE-related mailing lists at http://www.kde.org/mailinglists.html.

Ubuntu Project Mailing Lists

The Ubuntu Project is always expanding, as many new users continue to find Ubuntu for the first time. You will find many other knowledgeable users with answers to your questions by participating in one of Ubuntu's mailing lists. The lists are focused on using, testing, and developing and participating in Ubuntu's development:

- ▶ http://lists.ubuntu.com/mailman/listinfo/ubuntu-security-announce—Security announcements from the Ubuntu developers

- ▶ http://lists.ubuntu.com/mailman/listinfo/ubuntu-announce—Announcements concerning Ubuntu

- ▶ http://lists.ubuntu.com/mailman/listinfo/ubuntu-users—Discussions among users of Ubuntu releases

- ▶ http://lists.ubuntu.com/mailman/listinfo/ubuntu-devel—Queries and reports from developers and testers of Ubuntu test releases

Internet Relay Chat

Internet Relay Chat (IRC) is a popular form and forum of communication for many Linux developers and users because it allows an interactive, real-time exchange of information and ideas. To use IRC, you must have an IRC client and the address of a network and server hosting the desired chat channel for your discussions.

You can use the `irc.freenode.net` IRC server, or one listed at http://www.freenode.net/ to chat with other Ubuntu users. Some current channels are as follows:

▶ #Ubuntu—General chat about Ubuntu

▶ #edubuntu—General chat about EdUbuntu

▶ #xubuntu—General chat about Xubuntu

▶ #kubuntu—General chat about Kubuntu

For more channels to look at head on over to https://help.ubuntu.com/community/ InternetRelayChat for an exhaustive list of "official" channels.

However, Google can help you find other channels to explore. Simply enter in the distro name and IRC into the search options to retrieve information on any IRC channels relevant to your requirements. To get help with getting started with IRC, browse to http://www.irchelp.org/. Some of the channels of interest might be

▶ #linux—General discussions about Linux

▶ #linuxhelp—A help chat discussion for new users

Most IRC networks provide one or more Linux channels, although some providers require signup and registration before you can access any chat channel.

Index

Symbols and Numerics

How can we make this index more useful? Email us at indexes@samspublishing.com

How can we make this index more useful? Email us at indexes@samspublishing.com

How can we make this index more useful? Email us at indexes@samspublishing.com

E

How can we make this index more useful? Email us at indexes@samspublishing.com

How can we make this index more useful? Email us at indexes@samspublishing.com

How can we make this index more useful? Email us at indexes@samspublishing.com

USB (Universal Serial Bus)

    printers, troubleshooting, 403–404

    scanners, 166

    troubleshooting, 747

use function (Perl), 552

Usenet

    newsgroups websites, 766

    posts to (Perl coding example), 555–556

user accounts, 81

    Fetchmail, configuring in, 481–483

    MySQL, adding to, 512

User configuration directive (Apache Server), 417–418

user information

    FTP servers, displaying, 464–465

    wu-ftpd servers, configuring, 452–455

user information directives (ftpaccess configuration file)

    displaying adminsitrator email address, 455

    displaying files, 453–455

    displaying prelogin banners, 452

    last modification date notifications, 455–456

user jobs

    /var/spool/cron directories, 246

    running, 245

user variables (shell scripts), 258

useradd command, 105

UserDir configuration directive (Apache Server), 419

users

    FTP users, 442–444

    granting, 224–229

UTP (Unshielded Twisted Pair) cable, 337

V

values function, Perl hashes, 541

van Rossum, Guido, 561

var dump() function, 605–606

variable substitution (PHP), 587

variables

    class object variables in Python, 574

    interactive interpreter (Python), handling in, 562

    Mono, creating, 629–630

    Perl variables

        arrays, 540–541

        hashes, 540–540

        special variables, 541

    PHP variables, 580

        arrays, 582–583

        resources, 582

        types of, 581

        variable substitution, 587

    shell scripts

        built-in, 258–263

        built-in, viewing, 263

        environment, 258

        storing strings in, 259

            unexpanded variables, 265–266

        user, 258

        values, accessing, 259

    values, assigning, 258

Vaults of Parnassus website, 577

vi command, 286

vi text editor, 557

video cards, X Window System updates, 61

VideoLAN HOWTO, 182

viewing

    batch job numbers, 244

    built-in variables, 263

vim, 96

virtual file systems, 87

virtual hosts, Apache Web server

    address-based hosts, 432

How can we make this index more useful? Email us at indexes@samspublishing.com

Related Linux and Open Source Titles

What's on the DVD

The book's DVD includes the binary version of Ubuntu 9.10 i386—the equivalent of at least four CDs.

DESKTOPS

- X.Org 7.4
- GNOME 2.28.1

ACCESSIBILITY

- GNOME On-screen keyboard
- Screen reader and magnifier

ACCESSORIES

- 7zip
- Ark
- Calculator
- Character Map
- Dictionary
- GVim Text Editor
- KAlarm
- KArchiver
- KCalc
- KNotes
- KPilot
- Mousepad
- Scribes Text Editor
- SpeedCrunch
- Terminal
- Text Editor
- Tomboy Notes
- Xarchiver
- Xfburn

EDUCATION

- Kalzium
- Kanagram
- KBruch
- KHangMan
- Kig
- KLettres
- KmPlot
- KStars
- KTouch
- KTurtle
- LabPlot

GAMES

- Abe's Amazing Adventure
- Atomix

GAMES, (continued)

- Chess
- Chromium
- Four-in-a-row
- FreeCol
- Freeciv
- Gnu Backgammon
- KAtomic
- KBattleship
- KBlackBox
- KBounce
- KFourInLine
- KGoldrunner
- KJumpingCube
- KMahjongg
- KMines
- Kolf
- Konquest
- KReversi
- KSirtK
- KBlocks
- KSnake
- KSpaceDuel
- KSudoku
- KTron
- Lincity
- Mahjongg
- Mines
- Potato Guy
- Robots
- SameGame
- Shisen-Sho
- Sudoku
- TuxMath
- TuxTyping
- Zatacka

GRAPHICS

- Dia
- digiKam
- Document Viewer
- FontForge
- F-Spot Photo Manager
- GIMP Image Editor
- GNU Paint

GRAPHICS (continued)

- GQview
- gThumb Image Viewer
- Gwenview
- Image Viewer
- Inkscape Vector Graphics Editor
- KFax
- KPhotoAlbum
- Krita
- KSnapshot
- OpenOffice.org Drawing
- Scribus
- XaoS
- XSane Image Scanner

INTERNET

- Akregator
- Balsa
- BitTorrent
- Ekiga Softphone
- Epiphany Web Browser
- Firefox Web Browser
- gFTP
- kasablanca
- KMail
- KNetworkManager
- KNetDockApp
- Konversation
- Kopete
- KPPP
- KRDC
- Krfb
- KTorrent
- Network Manager
- OBEXTool
- Pan Newsreader
- Pidgin Internet Messenger
- SWScanner
- Vuze

OFFICE

- AbiWord Word Processor
- Evolution Mail and Calendar
- Gnumeric Spreadsheet
- KAddressBook

OFFICE (continued)

- Karbon14
- KChart
- Kexi
- KFormula
- Kivio
- KOffice Workspace
- Kontact
- KOrganizer
- KPlato
- KPresenter
- KSpread
- OpenOffice.org Database
- OpenOffice.org Formula
- OpenOffice.org Presentation
- OpenOffice.org Spreadsheet
- OpenOffice.org Word Processor

PROGRAMMING

- Bug Report Tool
- Devhelp
- Emacs 22 (X11)
- Glade Interface Designer
- IDLE
- KImageMapEditor
- KLinkStatus
- Kommander Editor
- KXSLDbg
- MIT/GNU Scheme
- MonoDevelop
- Python
- Qt3/Qt4
- Quanta Plus
- Screem HTML/XML Editor

SOUND & VIDEO

- Amarok
- CD Player
- GNU Denemo
- JuK
- K3b
- Kaffeine
- Kino
- Kmidimon
- KMix
- KsCD
- Movie Player

SOUND & VIDEO (continued)

- Serpentine Audio CD Creator
- Sound Recorder
- VolumeControl
- XawTV

SYSTEM TOOLS

- Adept Manager
- Cluster Management
- Configuration Editor
- GDebi Package Installer
- Gnome Partition Editor
- Keep
- Kickstart
- Konsole
- KPackage
- KSystemLog
- Language Support
- Synaptic Package Manager
- Ubuntu Device Database
- Update Manager
- VirtualBox OSE

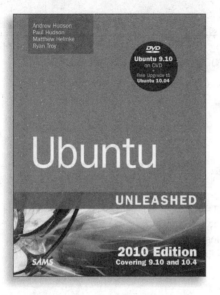

FREE Online Edition

Your purchase of **Ubuntu Unleashed 2010 Edition** includes access to a free online edition for 45 days through the Safari Books Online subscription service. Nearly every Sams book is available online through Safari Books Online, along with more than 5,000 other technical books and videos from publishers such as Cisco Press, Exam Cram, IBM Press, O'Reilly, Prentice Hall, Que, and Addison-Wesley Professional.

SAFARI BOOKS ONLINE allows you to search for a specific answer, cut and paste code, download chapters, and stay current with emerging technologies.

Activate your FREE Online Edition at www.informit.com/safarifree

> **STEP 1:** Enter the coupon code: DUZNJFH.

> **STEP 2:** New Safari users, complete the brief registration form.
> Safari subscribers, just log in.

If you have difficulty registering on Safari or accessing the online edition, please e-mail customer-service@safaribooksonline.com